Election records from 1872 to 1970 for the offices of president, governor, senator, and representative in Congress are published here in a usable form for the first time. *Party Strength in the United States* is the only convenient source of this important voting information. Paul T. David began this study by calculating the percentage divisions of the vote among Democratic, Republican, and other candidate parties. Using this as a basis, he was able to devise a new and more accurate method of measuring political party strength and of discerning and predicting voting trends over a period of time.

With this comprehensive election information finally collected it has been possible for the first time to plot election trends. These trends make up almost two hundred pages of graphic material in which states are analyzed individually, nationally, regionally, and in special groups according to their long-term partisan affiliations. There are also two diagrams for each state—one Democratic and the other Republican—to show each party's share of the vote since 1872.

To measure party strength accurately, clearly, and easily over a period of time, the author devised a system of index numbers. One index combines the data for all four offices; another combines the data for offices other than president; and the third combines data for sena-

tors and representatives in Congress. These indexes allow maximum comparability of election results and measurement of long-term trends in party strength at the polls for each state.

This compilation of numerical data and its accompanying text is an indispensable reference work for anyone interested in elections in the United States. It represents an important advance in the techniques of assembling election data and projecting their contemporary meaning. *Party Strength in the United States* will significantly revise and clarify American election history.

Paul T. David is Professor of Government and Foreign Affairs at the University of Virginia. He is a co-author of *The Presidential Election and Transition, 1960–1961, The Politics of National Party Conventions,* and *Presidential Nominating Politics in 1952.*

PARTY STRENGTH IN THE UNITED STATES
1872–1970

Party Strength
in the United States
1872–1970

Paul T. David

University Press of Virginia

Charlottesville

The University Press of Virginia

Copyright © 1972 by the Rector and Visitors
of the University of Virginia

First published 1972

ISBN: 0-8139-0396-3
Library of Congress Catalog Card Number: 77-183897
Printed in the United States of America

To Bernice Harrison David
Born December 28, 1871
Who has lived through the century
covered by this volume

Contents

Tables and Figures in Part I

Tables

Figures

Preface

THE research that resulted in the present book began initially as a modest attempt to put together two or three tables for use in a quite different book that has not yet been written. The difficulties encountered in constructing those simple tables suggested serious inadequacies in the existing resources for putting together any long-term view of the data on voting for major offices other than president. Indications that other reseachers were afflicted by similar difficulties led to the present effort to provide statistically rational index numbers of party strength. Simple, descriptive, factual information of this kind can operate as a powerful input in the political system when it is basic, comprehensive, and reliable—and especially when it is put forward in areas where the previous state of the art, statistically speaking, has been primitive.

Serious work began in the summer of 1968 and was assisted greatly by the cooperation of the Historical Archives of the Inter-University Consortium for Political Research (ICPR) of Ann Arbor, Michigan, which furnished a printout of their complete file of election returns at congressional district and statewide levels for the major offices under study. A year later, ICPR was able to supply counterpart data for all states on electronic tape and on a much more fully edited basis. Meanwhile, the technical problems of index number construction in using election data had been studied at length. The decision had been reached to convert all of the series to a biennial basis as a first step in the calculations. Results on this basis were presented and discussed at the annual meeting of the American Political Science Association in 1969, and the reaction seemed favorable.

The following year was devoted largely to the solution of the problems of party identity and party identification that arise in using the ICPR data. The working paper which formed the basis for the Appendix in this book was prepared, circulated, and discussed, leading to many adjustments in the data as supplied by the ICPR in adapting them for present purposes.

The present study would not have been possible without the cooperation of the ICPR and the accessibility of its comprehensive file of historical election data. It should be understood, however, that the present data differ at many points from the counterpart data as available from ICPR. The ICPR is in no way responsible for those differences or for the further processing that is involved in converting election percentages into index numbers.

At the time this research was initiated, the author was on a research leave financed by a Ford Foundation Faculty Award, which thus provided the initial financing for the project. Other financial assistance was derived in modest amounts from several sources: University of Virginia Institutional NSF Subgrants Nos. 4225–8133, 4250–9133, and 4243–0133; a series of University Computing Grants from the Computer Science Center of the University of Virginia to finance the use of its facilities; and awards from the University of Virginia Committee on Summer Grants.

Student research assistants who participated at one time or another included Robert S. Bozarth, Donald W. Chamberlayne, Francis W. Johnstone, Judith B. Lasky, and Robert P. Steed. The aid of Gary L. Greenhalgh was especially important in the work leading up to the 1969 APSA paper, and he has continued to be helpful after moving on to other assignments. Joseph L. Kayne merits special recognition both for the duration and the intensity of his participation in the project. He was responsible for reviewing the entire data file, state by state and year by year, while questions of party identity and completeness of the data were under examination. He carried out the data adjustments described in the Appendix, maintained liaison with the Computer Science Center during the computation work, and was generally helpful as the material and the manuscript assumed its present form. The programmers at the Computer Science Center who successively provided essential services were Linda Wright and C. Lynne Huxsaw.

Colleagues at Virginia and elsewhere have been involved repeatedly in consultations as the project moved through successive phases. My indebtedness is especially great to Walter Dean Burnham, who probably knows more than anyone else about the matters discussed in the Appendix; to Jerome E. Clubb, both for information and for counseling that was wise and impartial; to Bertram M. Gross, Richard M. Scammon, and James L. Sundquist for their early and favorable interest in the project; and to James N. Holtz, Richard I. Hofferbert, Gudmund R. Iversen, and Rutledge Vining for help on technical matters.

As noted, most of the data underlying this project came initially from the ICPR; but much data from other sources has been used in supplementing and cross-checking at points of interest, for reasons noted in the text. For the underlying data for 1970, I am especially indebted to the Republican National Committee, which for its own purposes had compiled and produced the official returns for all states for the offices under study at an earlier date in 1971 than any other publishing agency.

In view of the total amount of data handled in this project and the number of points where idiosyncrasies in the data have required special programming, it would indeed be remarkable if all errors had been avoided. The help of users who discover error is earnestly solicited, as are suggestions for improving the methodology as well as the data. The basic material at the point of origin is undoubtedly much better for some states than others; where the original material is poor in quality, some improvement may still be possible through local efforts in the states concerned, and would be actively welcomed, not only by the present author but undoubtedly also by the archival authorities at Ann Arbor.

All of this is said in the expectation that means will be found to maintain the index number data files reflected in this book. Eventually they may be extended back to a point earlier than 1872, and can be readily updated for future elections as they occur. The extent to which the file can be made available on electronic tape depends on financial and administrative arrangements that will require further development, but active efforts will be made to assure the availability of the data on some appropriate basis in machine-readable form for those interested.

Finally, in view of the number of other persons and agencies that have been involved in this project, the usual caveats are especially necessary. The author accepts full responsibility for all errors and shortcomings in this work, and looks forward with interest to finding out more about them.

Paul T. David

Charlottesville, Virginia
October, 1971

PART I

The Study of Party Strength

Chapter 1

Introduction

THIS is a book of numbers, helped along by diagrams. It seeks to fill some important gaps in the basic data readily available for the study of American election history. In doing so, it repeats presidential election data that have long been familiar and adds counterpart data for governors, senators, and representatives in Congress.

The data that are presented here begin in all cases with the percentages of the vote won by Democratic, Republican, and other candidates and parties. These are the all-purpose numbers used most frequently by election analysts—regardless of whether the analyst happens to be a campaign manager plotting strategy, a statehouse reporter in the thick of events, or a scholar who is studying history or political science.

The period covered begins in 1872, the year of the second presidential election after the end of the Civil War. Reconstruction was not yet over, but the normal procedures of partisan politics were becoming reestablished throughout the South. Election reporting improved rapidly in the following years.

The critical election years of 1896 and 1932 fall within the century of elections here under review. In both cases the elections before and after are included in enough fullness of facilitate the study of election trends leading up to and following after those critical years. If a party realignment comparable to those of 1896 and 1932 is currently in progress or impending, as some analysts—most notably, Walter Dean Burnham (1970)—tend to suspect, the data of the present volume may be useful for study in that connection.[1] This could be especially the case for studies of the great variance from state to state in the impact of both historical and contemporary trends.

In assembling the data presented in this book, the primary objective from the first has been a set of index numbers that can be used as measures over time of party strength at the polls. The making of index numbers is a technical business, and one that comes late to the present set of opportunities. For generations, the presidential vote has been quoted as the principal measure of the party vote at county, state, and national levels. The idea that the voting for several offices should somehow be combined when assessing party strength is not new, but it has not often been given expression in time series covering more than a few election

---

[1] See Bibliographical Note and References for further details on the works cited throughout this volume.

years. The formulas used for the purpose in the present work are original with this study, and have been extended much farther back into history than in any similar effort. The technical problems involved are discussed in chapter 2.

Three alternative sets of biennial index numbers have been produced: Composite A, which combines the data for all four offices studied; Composite B, which combines the data for the three offices other than president; and Composite C, which combines the data for senators and representatives in Congress. The alternative merits and utility of the three composite indexes are discussed in chapter 3.

The percentage divisions of the vote in the elections for the several offices were developed originally as a computation step in the direction of the desired index numbers. Since they have not previously been published in anything like the present historical depth, it was concluded that they did indeed merit publication —both as a fuller explanation of what underlies the index numbers and as a set of numbers of great interest and usefulness in their own right. They appear in Part II, along with the other basic data for individual states. Quite possibly some scholars, suspicious of any contraption as artificial as a genuine index number, will find the percentage divisions useful where, for them, the index numbers are not.

The graphic material of the present book includes two diagrams for each state, one Democratic and one Republican. Much other material, although only a small part of the total, is presented graphically. Any time series lends itself well to graphic presentation, and generally takes on a new life of its own when it can be perceived visually and as a whole.

The numerical data and charts of Part II, arranged alphabetically by states, comprise the major portion of the book and are its principal reason for publication. The text with which the book begins has three functions. One is to present, explain, and illustrate the procedures by which the data were brought to their present position. A second is to present aspects of the data that merit special attention, including several kinds of multistate analyses. A third is to take note of some obvious revisions in the conventional wisdom, especially in regard to the study of party realignment, that might be brought on by the data assembled in their present form for the first time. The first of these functions is performed mainly by chapters 1 to 3 and the Appendix; the others are the basis for the presence of chapters 4 to 6.

No attempt has been made to exploit the many possibilities of the data for further research involving the use of collateral data. That will be a task for many scholars who may seek to trace the relationships between party strength, interparty competition, and such other social and economic factors as industrialization, urbanization, education, income levels, and so on. The research on state politics and state policy that has been going on for the last ten years suggests both the need for the present data and the speed with which they may be seized for comparative analyses in a variety of contexts. Meanwhile, the data presented here have great potential interest as the source of a clarified view of some salient features of American election history. The object of this study is to fulfill that promise as completely and concisely as possible.

The previous work that is most relevant to the present enterprise has been concerned mainly with the classification of states in terms of their one-party vs. two-party characteristics, and with the development of measures of interparty competition, frequently known as "IPC." Every measure of interparty competition—several are currently in use—involves some concept of party strength and its measurement. Combined measures are frequently used, built for example on the election returns for governor on the one hand and on the number of seats held by each party in the state legislature on the other.

Austin Ranney and Willmoore Kendall can be credited with having done more than anyone else to initiate studies in this field. In work first published in 1954, they utilized election data from all states for president, governor, and senator in developing a classification of state party systems in five categories ranging from one-party Democratic to one-party Republican. Election data for the period 1914–54 were combined and summarized as averages for the entire period covered. Differences over time—temporal differences—were disregarded and in fact suppressed. Differences among states—spatial differences within the larger system—were emphasized within a somewhat static view of the system as a whole.

In the years following, several other scholars struggled with the complexities of measuring interparty competition. Some of the more noteworthy contributions included those of Joseph A. Schlesinger (1955), Robert T. Golembiewski (1958), Richard E. Dawson and James A. Robinson (1963), and Richard I. Hofferbert (1964). The approaches sponsored by these authors all had utility for the purposes intended, but in most cases their methodology was ill-adapted for handling any measurement of change over time.

Austin Ranney returned to the subject in 1965 in his contribution to the well-known work on state politics edited by Herbert Jacob and Kenneth N. Vines. For this purpose, Ranney developed an "index of competitiveness," in which four figures were averaged: "(1) the average per cent of the popular vote won by Democratic gubernatorial candidates; (2) the average per cent of the seats in the state senate held by Democrats; (3) the average per cent of the seats in the state house of representatives held by Democrats; and (4) the per cent of all terms for governor, senate, house in which the Democrats held control" (p. 64). In this formula, Ranney combined the approaches of several other scholars, whom he cited, and his formula was in turn influential in the work of other scholars making comparative state analyses, many of whom simply used his published results. Potentially, his formula was applicable to the data for any period of four years or more, but the period actually used was that from 1946 to 1963, which was considered representative of conditions after World War II. Again the data were averaged for the entire time period.

Two years later, David G. Pfeiffer published an article on interparty competition, in which he was directly concerned with system change and system stability. His work was an exceptionally good critique of the previous literature, and he was able to specify five goals that had been sought by various scholars: measurement of variance in party competition among levels of elective office (Schlesinger); measurement of variance in party competition among states (Ranney and Kendall); measurement of variance in party competition from one election year to another

(Louis Bean and Pfeiffer himself); measurement of trends toward or away from two-party competition (Pfeiffer); and, finally, measures useful in estimating the stability of a party system (Pfeiffer).

All these goals could more readily be achieved with better measures of party strength from which to begin. This was the special concern of Edward F. Cox in an article published in 1960 and in other work published later. Cox computed "Party Strength Percentages" (PSP) for each state for biennial election years, using all of the available election returns for president, senator, and representative in Congress, and combining them to derive average percentages of the Democratic, Republican, and "other" vote. He gave equal weight to whatever elections occurred in his office categories in any given election year, simply adding the votes together before computing the percentages. This had the effect of giving full weight to the presidential vote in presidential years and no weight to the presidential vote in off years. His computed percentages of Democratic party strength in Texas thus came out at around 73 percent for presidential years and 87 percent for nonpresidential years in a biennial series for the elections from 1946 to 1958 (Cox 1960, p. 1036).

Aside from Cox's own later work, this was the only biennial series involving multioffice averages that has so far reached print. It had the effect of showing that if indicators of party strength are to be published biennially on some multioffice basis, something must be done about the irregularities in the data that result from the irregularities of the election calendar as it applies to the different offices.

Pfeiffer faced this same problem and seems to have followed procedures much the same as those used by Cox, but since he did not publish his data as a time series, the biennial fluctuations in his averages were not revealed for examination. In his methodology, they were largely irrelevant, since, like Ranney, he was mainly interested in averaging the data for an entire base period, in this case 1940-64. The same comment can be made for most, if not all, students of state politics who have used measures of interparty competition in various forms of multifactor analysis in recent years.

It can thus be said that the field has been remarkably lacking in efforts to construct time series that in turn could be combined as index numbers of party strength at the polls, using methods that could be defended as meeting normal standards for good practice in statistics. Several factors have undoubtedly inhibited such efforts. One has already been referred to, the difficulties arising because the President is elected for a term of four years, governors for terms either of two or four years, senators for terms of six years, and representatives in Congress for terms of two years. Methods for overcoming these difficulties are discussed in chapter 2. A second factor is the limited extent to which the basic election data have been published systematically and in historical depth for offices other than the Presidency. Historical compilations assembled with the care that Edgar E. Robinson (1935) and Walter Dean Burnham (1955) devoted to the presidential vote simply do not exist on a nationwide scale for offices as important as governor, senator, and representative in Congress. Third is the unsatisfactory condition of the data as found in existing archives and scattered reference works, especially as the student moves back in time and as he moves away from the election returns for the more visible offices to those for the less visible ones.

Many of these limitations are being systematically removed as work continues in the Historical Archives of the Inter-University Consortium for Political Research (ICPR). For some years, the Consortium has been assembling all available records, county and state, official and unofficial, on the voting from 1828 onward for the four offices studied here. The present work has been made possible by the availability of the data bank currently maintained by the ICPR, with all of its richness of historical detail. At the same time, much of the work involved in preparing this volume was brought on by that very wealth of detail in reporting electoral contests, especially the variety of party names and other designations under which candidates have sought election.

In the early years of popular elections, what is presently known as the Democratic party had existed for some time before the present name was adopted by national convention action in 1840. It had been known after 1824 as the Democratic-Republican party, and still earlier simply as the Republican party. The present Republican party, not organized until the 1850s, achieved a stable nomenclature somewhat more rapidly, but not until after the Civil War. Party fusions, party splits, independent candidacies, and the creation of indigenous third parties continued to be frequent in state and local elections throughout the nineteenth century. They have become less frequent in recent decades, but opportunities are still provided for independent candidates and for the creation of new political parties under new names. The recently renewed use of these opportunities on a wide scale as in the years leading up to 1896 and 1932, is one of the principal aspects of the contemporary scene that merits analysis.

Balloting procedures have a direct relation to the amount of confusion in party nomenclature. In the earliest years, much voting occurred simply by show of hands in public meetings. The candidates who were elected became a matter of public record, but the party affiliations of the candidates, including those who lost, were not initially a matter of much official recognition. When printed ballots came into use, they were provided at first by the parties and the candidates, who naturally set up the designations on the ballots as they and their printers saw fit. The result was much variation in party names that was merely casual or related to the sloganeering requirements of a particular election campaign. The Australian ballot was adopted in most states before 1900, with public control of ballot printing as a consequence, but ample opportunity has continued for differences in practice from state to state in the designations by which political parties are known.

The resulting problem for the statistician is indicated by the fact that over 1,050 different code numbers for party designations have been used by the Historical Archives of the ICPR in preparing their data for electronic processing. "Democrat" or "Democratic," unqualified, was given the code number 100; "Democratic-Republican," with its earlier appearance, the code number 13; "Republican" the code number 200. The Liberal Republicans of 1872 were coded as 208, the Gold Democrats of 1896 as 508, the Progressives of 1912 as 370, and so on. All of the well-known party names are in the code list, along with hundreds of local and little-known designations, many of which are merely variations on some better known terminology.

The preservation of all of this variation was necessary for accuracy of identification in further study, and it undoubtedly has value for the historian tracing local election history. When facing variant coding, however, how does one decide which are the "real" Democrats and which are the "real" Republicans? Even when the two major parties are present under codes 100 and 200, some combination of circumstances may suggest doubt about whether one or the other has been properly represented.

Students who have worked only with presidential data have had available the compilations prepared for earlier times by Robinson and Burnham, and more recently by Richard M. Scammon and other authorities for the period since 1936. Robinson, Burnham, and Scammon have all had to deal with party identity and party identification in putting their data together. Generally they have been able to follow the rule that any vote for the recognized candidate of a major party for president is a vote for that party, regardless of the labeling under which he may have appeared on the ballot in particular states. With this basic rule as a help, variances in ballot nomenclature in presidential voting have usually been suppressed in editing the data for national publication. Most students using the national volumes have had little occasion to become familiar with the complications in some states and some elections with which the editors have had to deal.

These complications recur, however, in the presidential data as provided by the Historical Archives; and they appear even more frequently in the data as provided for other offices. It has therefore been necessary to identify the main categories of situations that bring on problematical outcomes, and to develop a set of rules for dealing with such situations as reflected in the data. These rules are presented and discussed in the Appendix. They relate primarily to the data from 1872 onward; similar rules might be applicable for earlier periods of party history, but further study would be necessary before that claim could be sustained.

The application of the rules has brought on a series of data adjustments, and the adjusted data are in turn the basis for the percentage divisions and index numbers reported in Part II.[2] Inevitably the adjusted data differ in many instances from the data as initally supplied by the Historical Archives, which should be absolved of any responsibility for the figures in the form in which they are produced here.

[2]Those who wish to work further with the data for individual states as supplied by the Historical Archives can secure information from the author on the specific data adjustments for each state. In most cases the adjustments can easily be traced from the rules as specified and discussed in the Appendix, but correspondence would be welcomed on any problems that are encountered in using the adjusted data in further research.

Chapter 2

The Construction of Index Numbers
of Party Strength

INDEX numbers reflecting change over time are produced by combining two or more statistical time series. A time series, in turn, consists of any set of data showing the variation in magnitude of any item at successive and usually equal time intervals. The combining operation is what distinguishes a time series consisting of index numbers from a simple time series. Ordinarily a time series is held not to constitute a set of index numbers unless some process of averaging has entered into the calculation.

Before the averaging can begin, however, it is necessary to solve problems of comparability. The data to be averaged must be arrayed on some basis that brings them into alignment with each other.

Biennial Time Series as a First Step

As previously noted, the first difficulty encountered in the present undertaking is the fact that the election calendar for president, governor, senator, and representative in Congress produces data at differing intervals. Yet a sufficient number of these offices of high visibility are up for election biennially to justify considerable efforts to create a biennial time series for each office on a comparable basis. Since no other solution is available, it seems clear that the process of interpolation must be resorted to. It is, after all, one of the oldest and most necessary expedients when working with data that have to be taken as found in the operations of the system they reflect.

The simplest case is that of representative in Congress. For that office, the elections are indeed biennial, are usually contested, and occur typically in a standard pattern of nonoverlapping districts that never cross state lines. The data can thus be readily accumulated to form the basis for a biennial time series of the statewide percentages of each major category of the vote in each state, Democratic, Republican, and "other."

In the case of presidential elections, mid-term percentages can be created to make the series biennial by averaging the percentages from the previous and following presidential election. This method is not available for the most recent mid-term year until the next regular election has occured but can be used for the remainder of any historical series. The mid-term figure so calculated is an artificial figure, but it is presumably the best available approximation of what would have occurred in a presidential election if one had been held. In any graphic presentation in which the points are connected between the actual election years, the curve will pass through the point specified as it passes through the mid-term year. Reputable political scientists have been publishing charts of presidential election data on this basis for a very long time without apparent qualms.

For states in which the governor has a four-year term, either identical with the presidential term or staggered against it, a similar procedure can be followed. A biennial series comparable to the presidential series can thereby be produced. This would seem to be the best way by which the four-year term states can be placed on a parity with the two-year term states for statistical purposes in using data from gubernatorial elections.

Senators present the most complicated case, since each state has two senators and ordinarily a Senate seat is up in each state in two biennial elections out of three. Senators may also die or retire within the six year term and elections for short terms result. The most appropriate formula for reducing the senatorial data to a biennial basis for an individual state would thus seem to be as follows. Use the actual popular vote figures in computing the percentages for any biennial year in which a senator is elected. If two Senate seats are up in the same year, combine the figures for the popular vote and then determine the percentages for the year. If neither seat is up, average the percentages from the previous and following senatorial election.

By these various means, a biennial time series offering counterpart numbers can be created for each party's percentage of the vote for each office in each state. In most of these biennial series, except that for the House of Representatives, some of the numbers will be artificial in the sense that they have been computed in an effort to approximate a reality that never existed. Any such series should be used with caution, especially if for any reason it is used alone. Usually a series containing such artificial numbers should not be used in isolation from other data. The object of the construction, typically, is to produce data in a form that allows combination or correlation with other data. In the present instance, the biennial time series for president, senator, and for many governors is merely a construct to be used with similar constructs in the further processes of averaging that will result in what can be identified as an index number or set of index numbers.

Composite Index Numbers for Several Offices

Index numbers originated in the study of price changes and are still best known in connection with the recurring publication of changes in the official indexes of consumer prices and wholesale prices. Their use for such purposes was well established by the end of the nineteenth century, but was severely tested during the rapid price changes of World War I, when deficiencies and alleged deficiencies in the existing methods of index number construction became highly controverisal both among scholars and in the political arena. The result was a massive technical literature in which the most enduring contributions were those of Wesley C. Mitchell (1921) and Irving Fisher (1923) (Mudgett, 1951).

The basic data under study here involve two principal kinds of opportunities for combining processes that will yield index numbers. One is the opportunity to combine data from the elections for two or more offices; the other is the opportunity to combine data from two or more states. The multi-state opportunities may also involve incidentally the combining of office data.

The averaging process in any of these combinations involves two main technical questions: Whether to use the geometric mean or the arithmetic mean in calculating the averages, and whether to aggregate the data without weighting—in effect giving equal weight to each office and each state—or alternatively what system of weights to use in each case.

The geometric mean was an element in Fisher's Ideal Formula and has had some use in part because of the influence of his work. It repeatedly involves calculations in which it is necessary to find the nth root of the product of N numbers, a laborious process in the days of hand calculations. It is especially useful in averaging ratios and rates of change, a recurring problem in index number construction; but for most data, the difference in results by comparison with the arithmetic mean is usually trivial. For the present data, involving percentages that are under 100 and that usually fluctuate around 50, the geometric average seems unnecessary. The arithmetic average has been used throughout.

The weighting problem is less easily settled and in practice is probably much more important, as it usually has been in index number construction. For the office composites, the basic question is whether to give equal weight to each office—president, governor, senator, representative—when the data for two or more of these offices are combined. At the state level, this would mean that intermittent voting for the two senators is given the same weight as voting for the single governor, and also the same weight as voting for the president and for members of the House of Representatives. At the national level, it would mean that voting for the president is given the same weight as voting for members of each house of Congress and for the governors—and no more.

The power of the president in the enactment of legislation has been computed as relating to that of each house of Congress in the ratio of 2:5:5 (Shapley and Shubik 1954, p. 789). But the President has many powers beyond that of approving or disapproving proposed legislation after it is ready for signature, and the whole business becomes largely incommensurable. Similarly, many governors seem more important than anyone else to the internal politics of their own states, yet the governors seem weak in most of the arenas of national policy. Most governors would happily accept a "promotion" to a seat in the Senate. Discussion of this kind brings one back to an ancient statistical rule: when the data seem comparable in importance and there is no means of precisely determining their relative importance, equal treatment is indicated. Accordingly, in producing the composite indexes of office data, no weighting by offices has entered into the formulas.

Multistate and National Index Numbers

A different answer or set of answers seems indicated in combining data from all or several of the states, in view of the great differences in state size. One answer, in fact, would be to go back to the basic voting data and aggregate the popular vote in each case for whatever group of states is intended before computing the partisan percentage divisions. This is what was done in one well-known study of fluctuations in the partisan vote for members of the House of Representatives since the Civil War (Stokes and Iversen 1966, p. 183). It has often been done for the presidential vote, as in the study just cited and in previous work by the present author (David, Goldman, and Bain 1960, pp. 43, 444).

With the data already organized for each state, however, convenience and comparability suggest the flexible use of the state data already in percentage form in further derivations for multistate purposes. Substantive considerations give at least minor support for doing so. Each state is a separate unit in the electoral college vote for president, in electing governors and senators, and in electing members of the House of Representatives. Turnout levels have varied widely among the states, and such variations have persisted over long periods of time. Yet the political importance of a state is unaffected by turnout levels, since it is determined primarily by the state's population and by the institutional features of its membership in the federal union.

A system of weights is accordingly needed that can be used conveniently for all purposes when combining the state data in multistate groupings. Three alternatives suggest themselves, each of which would require adjustment for the changing population results of each decennial census: each state's proportion of the total national population; each state's number of votes in the electoral college; and each state's number of seats in the House of Representatives.

The choice makes almost no difference in the results except as it affects the smallest states. The population basis of weighting tends to underweight the small states by comparison with their importance in the electoral college and in voting for the Senate. Conversely, the electoral college basis overweights the small states for all purposes other than those just noted. Since every state has at least one seat in the House of Representatives, weighting on the basis of House seats gives more importance to the smallest states than would the direct use of population. In other respects, the number of House seats can be taken as a conveniently rounded-off version of population. It seems to be the best available compromise, and has accordingly been used in this study.

Actually, the mix of states in any multistate grouping is likely to be such that any one of the three systems of weighting could be used with no difference in outcomes large enough to be visible by the time the data had been placed in graphic form on a chart. Certainly this is true for the national, regional, and other multistate groupings that are used for the purposes of the present volume.

Metropolitan Area Index Numbers

No data are presented in this volume for units smaller than a state. In principle, however, the techniques used here for index number construction can be applied to any territorial unit for which the data can be accumulated. The Historical Archives of the ICPR is currently able to supply processed, machine-readable election data on the four offices studied for every county in the United States.

The county-level data may well prove of greatest interest in the thriving field of metropolitan area studies. The possibilities have been tested in at least one study involving the Standard Metropolitan Statistical Area of Detroit, which includes three counties (David 1969). Noteworthy differences among the three counties in trends in party strength were readily apparent. Consolidated data for metropolitan areas would probably hold great interest in comparative studies of the larger metropolitan areas, north and south.

Index Numbers of Party Competition

Percentage divisions and index numbers of party strength can be used as indicators of the extent to which an individual election or a set of elections is the subject of active competition. As noted in chapter 1, a number of scholars have simply taken their measures of party strength and read them as indexes of competition. Usually assuming that only the two major political parties and their candidates were significant in American elections, they worked accordingly with divisions of the two-party vote, and could thus assume that the percentage of the two-party vote gained by one party was the converse of that of the other. On this basis, the more the vote of the larger major party fell toward the 50 percent line dividing victory and defeat, the more competitive the outcome.

An advance in the arithmetical form of the measure occurred when several scholars began subtracting the majority party score from its potential limit of 100.0 per cent. If the winning party achieved all of the vote, the index of competition became 0.0, while if the winning party had only a close 50.1 percent of the vote, the index of competition could rise to 49.9, as pointed out, for example by Thomas R. Dye (1966, p. 55).

The idea that indexes of party competition could well be converted to a scale ranging from 0.00 to 1.00 soon followed. It was presented by Douglas S. Gatlin in 1968, without citation to any previous use but without any claim of originality. Gatlin commented that he had found twenty-two different methods of measuring interparty competition in the literature (p. 217). He computed his own scale by doubling the majority party percentage of the two-party vote and subtracting it from 2.000. On this basis, to use his example (p. 235), a majority party score of .504 becomes an index of .992. Identical results can be obtained by other arithmetical procedures, such as subtracting .504 from 1.000 and doubling the difference, or taking the corresponding minority major party score of .496 and doubling it, or taking the difference between majority and minority major party scores, .008, and subtracting it from 1.000.

The Gatlin scale seems plausible, but the question arises of how distances along the scale can be interpreted. What kind of reality is competition, and how is it divisible? If a system is fully competitive when leading competitors are persistently of nearly equal strength, when, for example, is the system "half competitive"?

Competition is essentially a relationship among those who compete. In most American elections, the competition exists primarily between two leading competitors, usually but not always the candidates of the two major political parties.

Hence, for American conditions, the most important competitive relationship would seem to be that between the winning candidate and the runner-up, or, when the results for several offices are combined as averages, the relationship between the winning party and the party that is the runner-up.

Probably this relationship can best be measured by looking at what the runner-up would have to do to win, which generally seems to mean looking at the differences between the runner-up's percentage and the 50 percent mark he would have to pass in order to win. This suggests that an index of competitiveness could best be computed by finding the runner-up's percentage of one-half of the total vote for winner and runner-up (David 1972). On this basis, for example, if the runner-up's proportion of the vote is 45:55 or 45 percent, the percentage of one-half the total becomes 90.0, which in turn can be read as the index of competition. Other ratios and corresponding indexes of competition are as follows:

50:50	100.0
35:65	70.0
25:75	50.0
10:90	20.0
0:100	0.0

Actually, the index of party competition so computed is identical with the Gatlin scale, thus illustrating a fifth method of computing that scale; only the rationale seems new. Any of the computation methods available for the Gatlin scale can be used, including the simple doubling of the runner-up's percentage of the vote for the two leading parties.

Students working with the index numbers of party strength as offered in the present volume may frequently find need to convert them into some more direct measure of party competition. The method identified here is recommended; but since very few of the figures in this volume are presented on a two-party basis and the percentaging has been done on the basis of the total vote, it will be necessary to add the percentages for winner and runner-up before computing the runner-up's percentage of the resulting total, which can in turn be doubled to produce the index of competition on a scale of 100. This method is used in some of the analyses of chapters 4 and 5.

Chapter 3

Which Composite Index is Best?
For What?

THE composite index numbers of the present volume—Composites A, B, and C—have been tabulated for each state from 1872 to 1970 and can be found in Part II. They were produced in the hope that they would be useful both for system description and for the further analysis of system change. This chapter is concerned with the respective merits of the three composites as a general purpose measure of party strength.

When the voting for two or more of the offices tends consistently to track together, presumably it reflects mainly the influence of partisan preference, which in turn may change over time, for reasons which may be temporary or enduring. Conversely, when the voting for two or more of these partisan offices of high visibility tends to diverge, it has to be assumed that influences other than those with a general effect on party preference must be at work. Presumably these are mainly the factors that influence attitudes toward the individual candidates as distinguished from attitudes toward their respective political parties. Such factors could in turn be expected to be most important for the offices of highest visibility, for which voters can become most aware of the personalities, attitudes, and group identifications of the candidates and are most able to give these factors separate attention. The separability of the elements that enter into the voter's decision has been much emphasized in recent survey research, most notably in *The American Voter* (Campbell, Converse, Miller, and Stokes 1960).

The extent to which the various offices track together affects the choice of which composite index is best for general purposes; but it also merits study in connection with the usefulness of the index numbers for any purpose. It is always desirable to know how much variation has been suppressed by the averaging processes that are inherent in constructing any set of index numbers. For each state this can be ascertained to a considerable extent simply by inspection of the underlying data, but more precise measures are needed. This chapter presents such measures in terms of averages for all states; data for the individual states are arrayed in chapter 4.

The Extent of Variation among Office Data

In some states and some elections, the party vote for different offices may be nearly identical; more often it is not. Voters have always engaged in split-ticket voting to some extent, or have voted for the top of the ticket without bothering with a choice among candidates for other offices, or have turned out in smaller numbers and different partisan proportions in different elections. Split-ticket voting, roll-off, and drop-off, as they are called, have been increasing in recent decades, with progressively divergent voting results for offices that are up for election at the same time or in elections adjacent in time.

With the present data, six pairs of offices can be used in making comparisons of the differences in the party vote as found for each pair of offices: President and Governor, President and Senator, President and Representatives (statewide), Governor and Senator, Governor and Representatives (statewide), Senator and Representatives (statewide). The comparisons can be made most conveniently by using the biennial series as a source of counterpart data from each state for each of the four offices. The results of assembling and averaging the data on this basis for the periods indicated are presented in table 3.1.

Table 3.1. *Average differences between party office percentages*

Time Period	P–G	P–S	P–R	G–S	G–R	S–R	Pair averages
Democratic							
1872–1894	6.5	0.0	6.3	0.0	5.3	0.0	6.0
1896–1930	8.5	—	7.9	—	6.0	—	7.5
1914–1930	—	10.6	—	7.0	—	6.4	8.0
1932–1970	11.1	10.9	10.4	7.4	6.3	6.6	8.8
Republican							
1872–1894	6.0	0.0	4.9	0.0	5.1	0.0	5.3
1896–1930	7.5	—	6.8	—	5.6	—	6.6
1914–1930	—	9.0	—	6.1	—	6.3	7.1
1932–1970	9.5	9.3	8.6	7.5	6.4	6.4	8.0

NOTE: The symbols used as column heads indicate the various pairing combinations for president, governor, senator, and representative in Congress: P–G, president and governor; P–S, president and senator; P–R, president and representatives (statewide); G–S, governor and senator; G–R, governor and representatives (statewide); S–R, senator and representatives (statewide). The computations are based on the biennial series for each office in each state.

Senators first became subject to popular election on a nation-wide basis in the election of 1914. Data involving Senate elections are accordingly not available for the period 1872–1894 or for the first half of the period from 1896 to 1930. The time periods otherwise used in the table—1872–1894, 1896–1930, and 1932–1970—reflect simply the total span of a hundred years, divided by the critical elections of 1896 and 1932, each of which is included in the period that followed. The rationale for using these time periods was briefly indicated in chapter 1, and they are used where relevant throughout the present volume. They are not of equal length; the first includes twelve biennial election years, the second eighteen, and the third twenty.

The data of Table 3.1 show patterns of noteworthy consistency. Average differences are greater—that is, there is more split-ticket voting or the equivalent—in the pairings involving the presidency than for any of the other pairs of offices. This is true for both parties and for all three time periods studied, with only one exception, the close relationship between Republican voting for president and representatives in Congress prior to 1896. The smallest differences conversely, are found consistently (and with the same exception) between the voting for governors and representatives in Congress, followed by the senator-representative and governor-senator relationships in that order. In every case—six pairs of offices for each of the two parties—the values increase from one time period to the next, indicating the persistence with which split-ticket voting has been slowly increasing for a hundred years.

All of the data of Table 3.1 are based on simple averages, that is, the differences in the percentages of the relevant biennial series for each state were first averaged for the relevant time periods; and the fifty-state averages were then produced without any weighting for size of state or for the length of time the state had been in the data. The results undoubtedly overweight the small states, but a more complex calculation did not seem necessary.

More significantly, the process of arithmetic averaging gives heavy weight to the deviant states where especially wide differences are found in the voting for the several offices. If the states are ranked on the basis of an average of the pair differences for 1932–1970, as in table 4.2 in chapter 4, it appears that 34 states are below average in the differences in Democratic voting, while 33 are similarly below average on the Republican side. Statisticians may well ask why the median was not used in table 3.1 instead of the arithmetic mean; it apparently would have produced figures for 1932–1970 lower by around 1.5 percentage points than those shown. However, the six office pairings would produce six different rank orderings for use in determining a median for each, states vary considerably in rank for the different pairings, and the arithmetic mean continues to have the virtue that it does produce averages that are affected by all of the data in the set.

The Implications of Choice

Table 3.1 confirms what election statisticians have known for a long time: the vote for president varies more widely from that for other noteworthy offices than the voting for those offices varies among them. This has two major implications: that the vote for president is the least reliable of the four offices votes as a measure of party strength, and that in combining office votes to produce a general measure of party strength, the voting for president is the voting that should most clearly be omitted.

Composite B, combining the data for governor, senator, and representative in Congress, emerges as the best general measure of party strength. With data from two offices that are always voted on statewide and from a third than can be cumulated on a statewide basis, Composite B has the broad base of three distinct sets of office data to support it. For most states most of the time, it will do a good job of smoothing variations in the data that arise from personality and special issue factors in the election of governors and senators, thus producing a good indicator of party strength as it shifts through time.

Composite C, combining the data for senators and representatives for the period since 1914, has institutional value as a combined measure of voting for both houses of Congress. It may have special usefulness for students of Congress. For other purposes, it seems less useful than Composite B, which it closely parallels for most states.

A different two-office composite, one combining the data for governors and representatives, would seemingly be the best available two-office composite as a measure of party strength, simply because those two offices track together most closely in the data, as shown in Table 3.1. As it happens, this is the basis on which Composite B has had to be composed for the period prior to 1914, since the Senate data were not available nationwide before that year.

Composite A, the four-office composite, was originally developed because of the seeming advantages of a set of indexes as broadly based as possible. It uses data for all of the major offices on which voting occurs in all states. It may still have appeal for many scholars because of its broad base and despite the conclusions previously drawn from the data of table 3.1. It may prove especially useful for the states where the presidential data track closely with the other data most of the time, as seems to be the case for half or more of the states.

There is little danger that the presidential data will be downgraded in importance because of the conclusions reached here. The presidential vote will continue to have its unique importance, and one of the principal virtues of Composite B is that it provides an independent reading for comparison with the presidential vote. The two are shown together in most of the diagrams presented in this volume.

Chapter 4

The Finite Variety of the Fifty States

THERE are at least two kinds of variation among the states of which the analyst needs to be strongly aware while using the data of the present volume. One kind consists of the differences plainly visible in the data themselves, of which there are mainly three of continuing importance: the differences among states and over time in the closeness of the election results for the several offices, the differences in levels of identification with one political party or the other, and the corresponding differences in levels of party competition. The other kind of variation includes all of the other aspects that give each state its special identity. Not all of these aspects can be measured or even specified, but several of them deserve note for their potential consequences in the interpretation of the data.

The existing fifty states include the original thirteen, another twenty-four that had been admitted before 1872, and thirteen more that came in after 1872. Members of the latter group are reflected in the data of this volume only after their respective dates of admission, as follows:

Colorado, 1876	Utah, 1896
North Dakota, 1889	Oklahoma, 1907
South Dakota, 1889	New Mexico, 1912
Montana, 1889	Arizona, 1912
Washington, 1889	Alaska, 1959
Idaho, 1890	Hawaii, 1959
Wyoming, 1890	

The oldest states might be suspected of having political systems more mature, simply because they are older, just as the newest states might be suspected of having political systems more advanced. Differences of this kind may indeed exist, and presumably might be related to the structure and competitiveness of party systems, but their relationships to the data of the present volume are not strikingly visible. The persisting effects of the Civil War are much more apparent in the patterns of regional partisanship that are identified later in this chapter and studied further in chapter 5.

State population is highly important for almost all purposes, and it is also a factor on which the states have changed steadily in relation to each other during the hundred-year period studied. Since the data of this book begin with election returns that have already been percentaged, the impressions of state size that are latent in any collection of raw vote totals have been suppressed. Relative state size is reflected, however, in the number of seats in the House of Representatives that is allocated to each state at any given time, and as noted in chapter 2, the averaging of data for regional and other groupings of states presented in this book has gen-

Table 4.1. *Apportionment of seats in the House of Representatives, 1872–1972*

State	1872–1880	1882–1890	1892–1900	1902–1910	1912–1930	1932–1940	1942–1950	1952–1960	1962–1970	1972–
Alabama	8	8	9	9	9	9	9	9	8	7
Alaska								1	1	1
Arizona					1	1	2	2	3	4
Arkansas	4	5	6	7	7	7	7	6	4	4
California	4	6	7	8	11	20	23	30	38	43
Colorado	1	1	2	3	4	4	4	4	4	5
Connecticut	4	4	4	5	5	6	6	6	6	6
Delaware	1	1	1	1	1	1	1	1	1	1
Florida	2	2	2	3	4	5	6	8	12	15
Georgia	9	10	11	11	12	10	10	10	10	10
Hawaii								1	2	2
Idaho		1	1	1	2	2	2	2	2	2
Illinois	19	20	25	25	27	27	26	25	24	24
Indiana	13	13	13	13	13	12	11	11	11	11
Iowa	9	11	11	11	11	9	8	8	7	6
Kansas	3	7	8	8	8	7	6	6	5	5
Kentucky	10	11	11	11	11	9	9	8	7	7
Louisiana	6	6	6	7	8	8	8	8	8	8
Maine	5	4	4	4	4	3	3	3	2	2
Maryland	6	6	6	6	6	6	6	7	8	8
Massachusetts	11	12	13	14	16	15	14	14	12	12
Michigan	9	11	12	12	13	17	17	18	19	19
Minnesota	3	5	7	9	10	9	9	9	8	8
Mississippi	6	7	7	8	8	7	7	6	5	5
Missouri	13	14	15	16	16	13	13	11	10	10
Montana		1	1	2	2	2	2	2	2	2
Nebraska	1	3	6	6	6	5	4	4	3	3
Nevada	1	1	1	1	1	1	1	1	1	1
New Hampshire	3	2	2	2	2	2	2	2	2	2
New Jersey	7	7	8	10	12	14	14	14	15	15
New Mexico					1	1	2	2	2	2
New York	33	34	34	37	43	45	45	43	41	39
North Carolina	8	9	9	10	10	11	12	12	11	11
North Dakota		1	1	2	3	2	2	2	2	1
Ohio	20	21	21	21	22	24	23	23	24	23
Oklahoma				5	8	9	8	6	6	6
Oregon	1	1	2	2	3	3	4	4	4	4
Pennsylvania	27	28	30	32	36	34	33	30	27	25
Rhode Island	2	2	2	2	3	2	2	2	2	2
South Carolina	5	7	7	7	7	6	6	6	6	6

Table 4.1 *(cont.)*

South Dakota		2	2	2	3	2	2	2	2	2
Tennessee	10	10	10	10	10	9	10	9	9	8
Texas	6	11	13	16	18	21	21	22	23	24
Utah			1	1	2	2	2	2	2	2
Vermont	3	2	2	2	2	1	1	1	1	1
Virginia	9	10	10	10	10	9	9	10	10	10
Washington		1	2	3	5	6	6	7	7	7
West Virginia	3	4	4	5	6	6	6	6	5	4
Wisconsin	8	9	10	11	11	10	10	10	10	9
Wyoming		1	1	1	1	1	1	1	1	1
Totals	293	332	360	392	434	435	435	437	435	435

NOTE: The column totals include all states represented at the end of a decade; for dates of admission, see text.

erally involved the use of each state's number of seats in the House—a number that is typically subject to change after each decennial census, although no change was made after the census of 1920.

Table 4.1 shows the number of seats for each state in the House from 1872 to the present; it can be read as an indicator of relative state size at any time. It also reflects the extent to which the population of each state was growing at rates above or below the national average, since the consequences of divergent growth rates affected the decennial reapportionments of seats in the House of Representatives.

The states are arranged alphabetically in table 4.1, as they are in Part II. This seems to be necessary for convenient reference in view of the extent to which the conventional practice of alphabetical listings has become established. However, it obscures almost totally the salient features of similarity and difference that leap from the page when the data for neighboring states are placed in close juxtaposition. In previous work, I have often preferred geographical arrangements of the states, beginning with Maine and ending with Hawaii, moving generally west and south from one contiguous state to another as nearly as possible (David, Moos, and Goldman 1954; David, Goldman, and Bain 1960). The practice is recommended for many of the purposes for which the data of the present volume might be used on a multistate basis, and is used for some of the analyses of chapter 5. The political culture of this country has noteworthy regional and subregional aspects that become most apparent when comparisons can readily be made within appropriate groupings of contiguous states (Sharkansky 1970, and references cited therein).

Ranges and Distributions of Office Variation

Differences in the closeness of office election results were discussed in chapter 3 on the basis of long-term averages for all states, but something more is needed to indicate the ranges and distributions of such differences. A beginning can be found in table 4.2, in which a ranking of the states is provided for each party for the period

*Table 4.2. States ranked according to average differences among
paired office percentages, 1932–1970*

Voting for Democratic Candidates		Voting for Republican Candidates	
Rank	Average Difference	Rank	Average Difference
1. Indiana	3.2	1. Indiana	3.0
2. Missouri	3.7	2. Missouri	3.5
3. Illinois	3.8	3. Connecticut	3.9
4. Delaware	4.0	4. Illinois	4.0
5. Pennsylvania	4.2	5. West Virginia	4.2
6. West Virginia	4.2	6. Pennsylvania	4.5
7. Connecticut	4.8	7. Delaware	4.5
8. New Hampshire	4.9	8. New Mexico	4.7
9. New Mexico	4.9	9. New York	4.8
10. South Dakota	5.3	10. New Hampshire	5.2
11. New Jersey	5.5	11. South Dakota	5.5
12. Iowa	5.5	12. North Carolina	5.6
13. Michigan	5.7	13. Iowa	5.7
14. Wyoming	5.7	14. New Jersey	5.7
15. Kansas	5.8	15. Wyoming	6.0
16. Kentucky	6.0	16. Kansas	6.1
17. Ohio	6.1	17. Wisconsin	6.1
18. New York	6.2	18. Kentucky	6.2
19. Idaho	6.3	19. Michigan	6.2
20. Maryland	6.5	20. Minnesota	6.4
21. Utah	6.5	21. Nebraska	6.4
22. Rhode Island	6.7	22. Maryland	6.4
23. North Carolina	6.8	23. Ohio	6.6
24. Arizona	6.9	24. Arizona	6.6
25. Washington	7.2	25. Idaho	6.7
26. Colorado	7.3	26. Rhode Island	6.8
27. Maine	7.4	27. Nevada	6.9
28. Nebraska	7.5	28. Utah	7.0
29. Vermont	7.5	29. Washington	7.3
30. Nevada	7.8	30. Oklahoma	7.4
31. Oklahoma	7.8	31. Maine	7.6
32. Montana	7.9	32. Vermont	7.8
33. Massachusetts	8.2	33. Montana	7.9
34. Alaska	8.4	34. Colorado	8.2
35. Oregon	9.1	35. South Carolina	8.4
36. Wisconsin	10.2	36. Massachusetts	8.5
37. Tennessee	11.0	37. Alaska	9.3
38. North Dakota	11.2	38. Oregon	9.6
39. Virginia	11.8	39. North Dakota	10.6
40. Minnesota	12.5	40. Mississippi	10.9
41. California	13.2	41. California	12.3
42. Hawaii	13.5	42. Alabama	12.4
43. Texas	14.9	43. Georgia	13.2

Table 4.2 (*cont.*)

44. Florida	15.9	44. Tennessee	13.5
45. Georgia	16.1	45. Texas	13.5
46. Alabama	17.9	46. Hawaii	13.6
47. Arkansas	18.1	47. Louisiana	13.7
48. South Carolina	18.7	48. Florida	14.5
49. Louisiana	19.7	49. Arkansas	15.8
50. Mississippi	20.8	50. Virginia	18.9

1932–1970 on the basis of averages of the differences in the office pairings previously discussed in chapter 3.

Table 4.3 moreover, also illustrates the range of variation among office pairings

Table 4.3. Average differences between office percentages, selected states, 1932–1970

Rank (from table 4.2)	P–G	P–S	P–R	G–S	G–R	S–R	Average of pairings
Democratic							
1. Indiana	2.9	4.5	3.2	3.1	2.7	2.5	3.2
13. Michigan	7.6	6.2	4.7	7.0	4.4	4.2	5.7
Median*	8.2	7.9	6.3	7.5	5.5	8.2	7.3
38. N. Dakota	9.9	13.0	13.5	11.1	11.5	7.7	11.2
50. Mississippi	34.7	32.8	38.1	7.8	4.7	6.6	20.8
Republican							
1. Indiana	2.4	3.7	3.4	3.1	2.9	2.6	3.0
13. Iowa	6.1	5.6	5.8	6.5	4.0	5.9	5.7
Median†	8.9	6.5	5.4	8.9	6.6	4.6	6.8
38. Oregon	11.8	12.3	8.8	9.8	9.2	5.4	9.6
50. Virginia	18.8	30.9	13.8	20.8	10.0	19.0	18.9

NOTE: The six column heads that indicate office pairings include symbols for all of the pair combinations for president, governor, senator, and representative; see table 3.1.

*The numbers are averages of the data for the twenty-fifth state, Washington, and the twenty-sixth state, Colorado.

†The numbers are averages of the data for the twenty-fifth state, Idaho, and the twenty-sixth state, Rhode Island.

by giving the details at quartile points along the range. The progressions in the various columns of table 4.3 are not entirely consistent; they reflect the idiosyncrasies of the particular states that were identified for each party. The general pattern, however, is clear enough. It confirms that presidential voting tracks closely with voting for other prominent offices in many states, most notably in states like Indiana, with its long-term development of a highly competitive partisan politics. Conversely, presidential voting tends to depart most widely from other voting in the states with the highest scores for variance of all kinds. These are predominantly the one-party states of the South, and, to a lesser extent, the states from

Wisconsin westward in which the Progressive movement took place early in this century.

The kinds of differences that can occur in the patterns of variation in voting for the several offices are illustrated in figures 4.1 and 4.2. The diagrams for Michigan in figure 4.1 show patterns that might be considered somewhat typical for a northern state that was predominantly rural and agricultural until after World War I and that has since become heavily urban and industrial. In the rank ordering of table 4.2, Michigan ranks thirteenth on the Democratic side and nineteenth on the Republican. When the Democratic party was at its weakest in Michigan, between 1900 and 1930, the widest variations in election results occurred. From 1932 to 1960, the Democratic vote in Michigan for the three major offices other than president was quite consistent; since 1960 it has split widely. The Republican diagram for Michigan shows more consistency in Republican voting than Democratic throughout the hundred years it covers, but it also shows the break-up in patterns since 1960.

The Virginia diagrams of figure 4.2 show clearly how much the voting patterns of a southern state can vary from those found elsewhere. The presidential vote, vagrant as it is, is nonetheless the most consistent of the four categories of office voting—presumably because there was always an alternative major party candidate for president. The frequency with which the Republican vote for governor or senator drops to the zero line in the Republican diagram is simply a reflection of the frequency with which that party failed to produce a candidate for one office or the other. The result in most cases was a larger amount of voting for independent or third-party candidates than might otherwise have occurred, reflected in the fact that the Republican vote is shown at the zero percentage line much more often than the Democratic percentage reached 100.

Similar diagrams could be prepared for every state from the data of Part II, and would merit close attention by students with a special interest in the politics of a particular state. Diagrams in which the presidential vote is plotted against Composite B can be found in Part II. In general, however, the student can arrive at some anticipation of what the diagrams would look like if plotted on a four-office basis by checking the rank order of states of interest in table 4.2.

Clearly, Composite B cannot be interpreted in the same way both for states with low office differences and for those with high office differences. In the first case, any of the composites will serve as a convenient summary of data already closely grouped. In the second, a composite index strikes an average among readings widely divergent; it may be especially needed for that very reason, but its attributes as a summary are open to question, and there may be a constant need to recur to the underlying data when in search of a fuller understanding.

Finally, it should be noted that the data of tables 4.2 and 4.3 support the merits of Composite B as the best general purpose index of party strength—or, at least, of voting identification with a partisan label as locally understood. Composite B would also seem to be the most useful basis for computing an index of party competition, for determining the partisan identification of major groupings of states, and for studying those shifts in party identification that are generally referred to as party realignment.

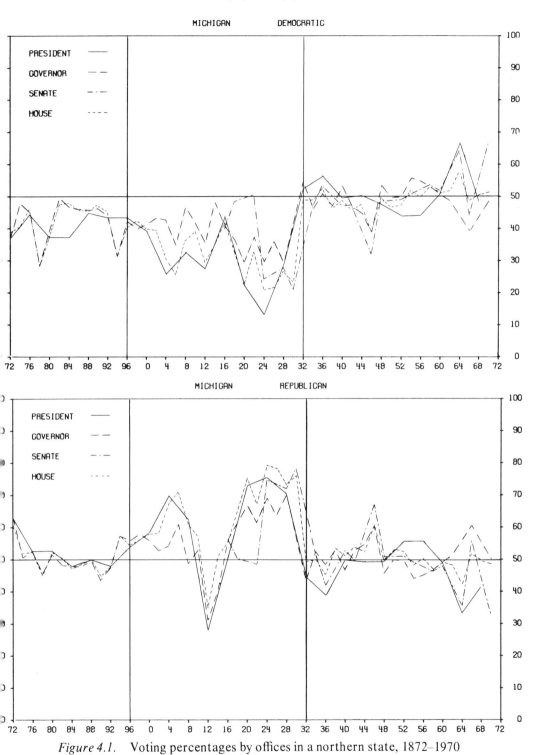

Figure 4.1. Voting percentages by offices in a northern state, 1872–1970

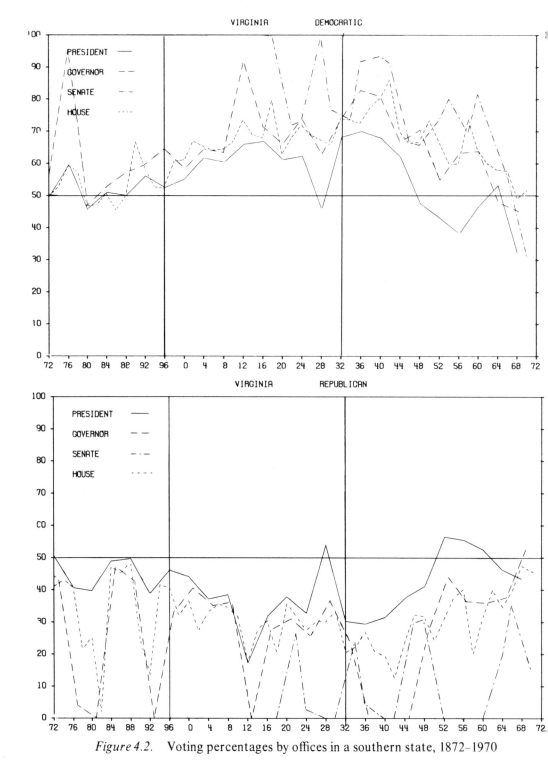

Figure 4.2. Voting percentages by offices in a southern state, 1872–1970

Regional Categories and Their Differences

Some presentation of the data in regional terms is necessary, in order to provide a level of presentation between the individual states and the nation as a whole, and in order to do so on the basis of regional territories that have an established identity. For this purpose, the Northeast, the Middle West, the South, and the West are the regions that are used. The Northeast is defined as the twelve-state region from Maine to West Virginia; the Middle West as the twelve-state region from Ohio to Kansas, Nebraska, and the Dakotas. The South is defined on a thirteen-state basis that includes Kentucky and Oklahoma as well as the eleven Confederate states; it ranges from Virginia to Texas. The West includes the thirteen mountain and Pacific states, including the two newest states, Alaska and Hawaii. (For brief discussions of the historical and geographical bases of regional identity in the case of these large regions, see the opening chapters of the four regional volumes edited by David, Moos, and Goldman 1954.) The basic data for each of these regions are presented after the individual state data in Part II. Diagrams in which the presidential vote for each major party can be read against the Composite B percentages are provided herewith in figures 4.3 to 4.6.

The diagrams for the Northeast in figure 4.3 illustrate a number of points that are peculiar to the region and others that will recur as similar diagrams for other regions and for individual states are examined. Somewhat distinctive of the region is the nearly competitive level of Democratic strength that prevailed from 1876 to 1892, collapsed sharply between 1892 and 1896, and then remained more or less at the 1896 level until 1928. Thereafter the data for 1930, 1932, and 1934 reflect the New Deal realignment in voting patterns as it affected the Northeast. After 1936 Democratic strength slipped noticeably, as shown by Composite B, but did not return to the level of the early 1900s. Presidential voting became increasingly erratic in relation to other voting, but the major parties were competitive for the region as a whole after 1936.

In looking at figure 4.3 for the Northeast, it should also be noted that the Democratic and Republican diagrams are by no means completely the mirror images of each other. The differences arise in the vote for "Other" candidates and parties, which can be found for the Northeast in figure 4.7. In 1912, the Republicans were much more affected than the Democrats by third-party voting. In 1924, the reverse was true, while in 1968 and 1970 the results were especially mixed.

At first glance, the diagrams for the Middle West in figure 4.4 may seem almost the same as those for the Northeast in 4.3, but there are differences meriting some comment. Most noticeably, the profile is flatter for both parties. The party realignment of 1896 is almost invisible in these diagrams, presumably because of countervailing tendencies by which some portions of the region moved in directions opposite to those taken by others. A long-term secular decline in Democratic strength from 1876 to 1928 is visible, followed by the sharp realignment upward between 1928 and 1932. After 1936, the reassertion of Republican strength came sooner and was more persistent than in the Northeast.

The diagrams for the South in figure 4.5 hold special interest, since no other region has been so homogeneous in the oddities of its political behavior. The continuing growth of Democratic party dominance in nonpresidential voting from

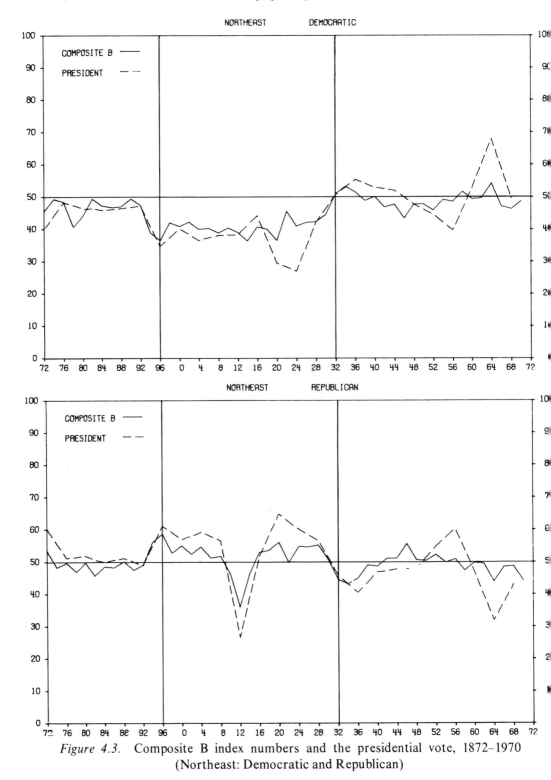

Figure 4.3. Composite B index numbers and the presidential vote, 1872–1970 (Northeast: Democratic and Republican)

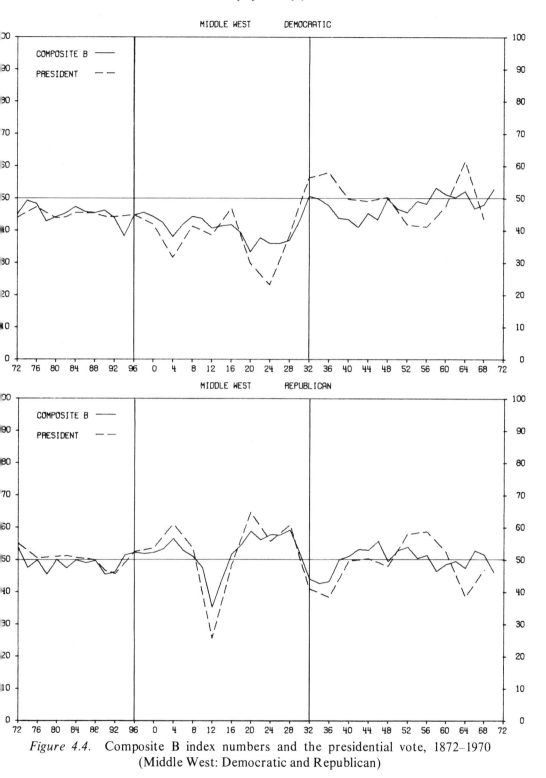

Figure 4.4. Composite B index numbers and the presidential vote, 1872–1970
(Middle West: Democratic and Republican)

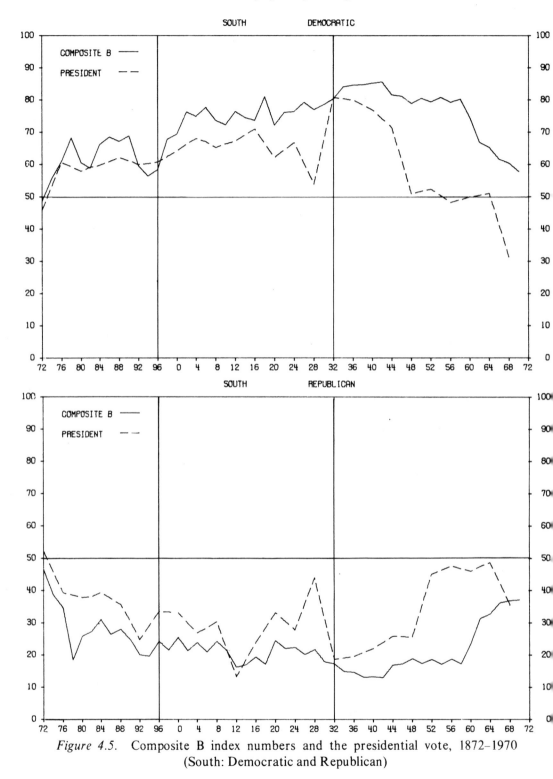

Figure 4.5. Composite B index numbers and the presidential vote, 1872–1970 (South: Democratic and Republican)

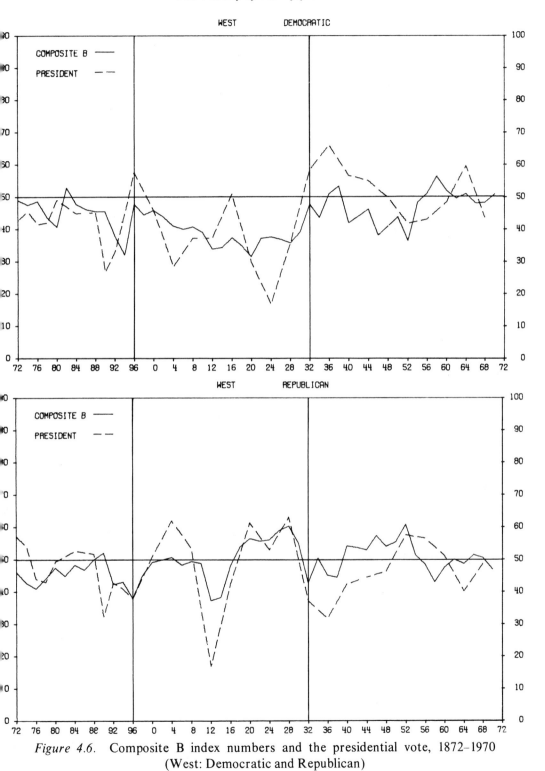

Figure 4.6. Composite B index numbers and the presidential vote, 1872–1970 (West: Democratic and Republican)

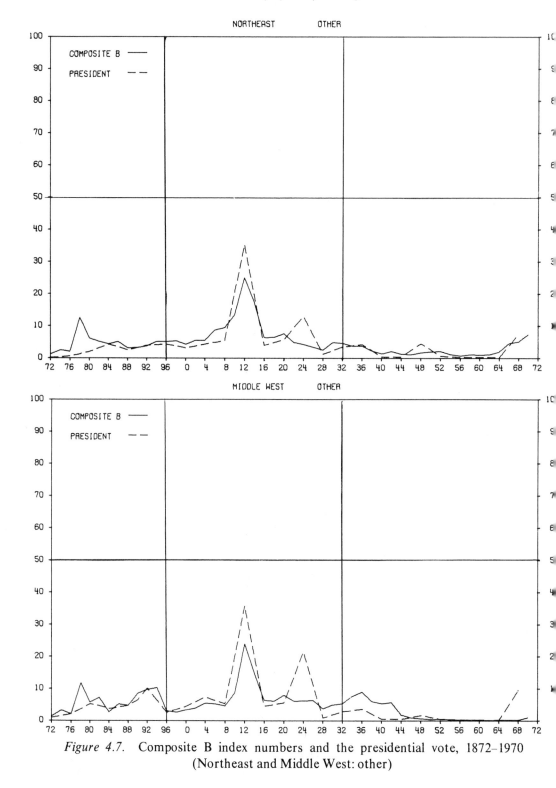

Figure 4.7. Composite B index numbers and the presidential vote, 1872–1970 (Northeast and Middle West: other)

1872 to World War II is evident. In presidential voting, the four elections of Franklin D. Roosevelt stand out as a twelve-year interruption in a long-term tendency to separate presidential voting from nonpresidential voting throughout the region, a tendency that continued at least until 1958. For most of a century, and also until 1958, the Republican party was less than half competitive in non-presidential voting; so far as the South was concerned, the two-party system was a misnomer. These matters are discussed further in later chapters.

The diagrams for the West in figure 4.6 reflect its special character. As non-South, it has much in common with the Northeast and the Middle West; the diagrams for all three regions are similar in terms of their central tendencies. But historically the western voting patterns have been much more erratic, with wider swings in both the presidential voting and the Composite B indexes and with less relationship between them. On the other hand, the erratic voting behavior that is so apparent since 1960 in the curves for the Northeast and the Middle West seems merely normal in the diagrams for the West.

Other differences among the four regions are apparent in the diagrams reporting graphically the "other" vote in figures 4.7 and 4.8. Again the Northeast and the Middle West have much in common, along with differences that can be found in close comparative study. The South and the West are revealed as the most important areas of third-party activity in earlier times, especially as the party realignment of 1896 approached. Since 1944, the South has been by far the most important locale of third-party activity in presidential elections; and it has had a noticeable amount of continuing activity by independent and third-party candidates for other offices.

Partisanship, 1896–1930, as a Defining Criterion

The period from 1896 to 1930 began with the critical election of 1896; the following period was initiated by the critical election of 1932. Both elections have long been recognized by historians as turning points in American political history, each involving a massive realignment in popular voting habits in some states and regions. The well-known article on the subject by V. O. Key, Jr., "A Theory of Critical Elections" (1955), has been followed by a series of studies identifying the unique characteristics of the intervening period (Chambers and Burnham 1967, pp. 14, 298–301; Burnham 1970, and other works cited in his first chapter).

The party system was more distinctly sectional between 1896 and 1930 than at any other time in American history; and by the same token more states were dominated by one-party politics than at any other time. As Burnham has put the matter,

The alignment system which was set up during the 1890's marks the point at which American party development began clearly to diverge from developmental patterns in other industrial societies. This system was unique among the five [historical party systems] under discussion: it was structured not around competition between the parties, but around the elimination of such competition both on the national level and in a large majority of the states. (Chambers and Burnham 1967, p. 300)

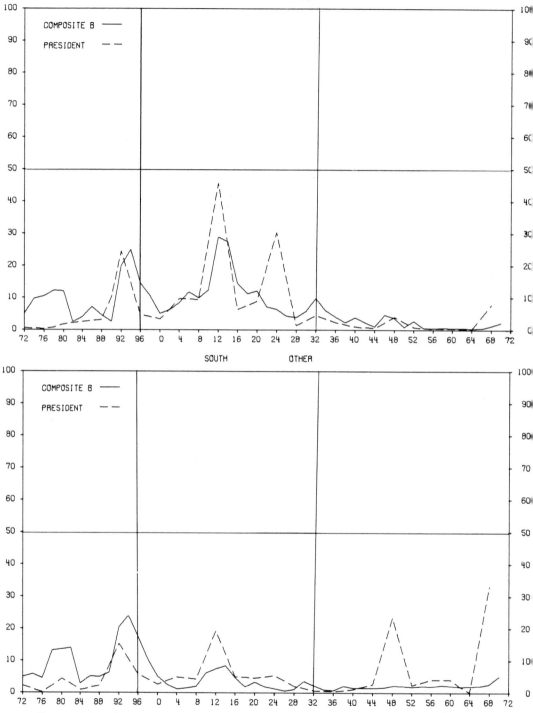

Figure 4.8. Composite B index numbers and the presidential vote, 1872–1970 (South and West: other)

Major questions of historical analysis revolve around such topics as why it was that the system moved so definitely in a non-competitive direction during the years centering on 1896, as well as around what happened and why it happened during the years centering on 1932. A full examination of those questions would go well beyond the scope of this book; but they do suggest the importance of partisanship during the period from 1896 to 1930 as a defining criterion. If one wishes, for example, to trace the political evolution of the states that were predominantly Republican during the period of greatest sectionalism, it is first of all necessary to identify which states comprise the group. It would seem that the Composite B data of the present volume might provide a better basis for that kind of an exercise than has previously been available (cf. David, Goldman, and Bain 1960, pp. 399, 514).

Tables 4.4, 4.5, and 4.6 identify three groups of states on the basis of the techniques worked out for this volume: (1) the eighteen states that were predominantly Republican during the period 1896–1930, (2) the twelve states that were predominantly Democratic during the same period, and (3) the intermediate group of eighteen states that were characterized by active party competition even during the period 1896–1930.

Table 4.4 States predominantly Republican from 1896 to 1930

State	Average no. of representatives in Congress	Average % of two-party vote Rep	Dem.	Index of competition for the period
Vermont	2.0	71.9	28.1	56.2
Minnesota	9.2	65.5	34.5	69.0
Wisconsin	10.8	65.4	34.6	69.2
Pennsylvania	33.9	64.0	36.0	72.0
South Dakota	2.6	63.6	36.4	72.8
Michigan	12.6	62.8	37.2	74.4
North Dakota	2.4	62.4	37.6	75.2
California	9.5	61.8	38.2	76.4
Iowa	11.0	61.0	39.0	78.0
Washington	3.9	60.2	39.8	79.6
Maine	4.0	58.8	41.2	82.4
Kansas	8.0	57.2	42.8	85.6
Massachusetts	14.9	57.0	43.0	86.0
Idaho	1.6	56.8	43.2	86.4
New Hampshire	2.0	56.7	43.3	86.6
Connecticut	4.8	56.5	43.5	87.0
Oregon	2.6	56.4	43.6	87.2
Illinois	25.6	55.8	44.2	88.4
Total	161.4			
Averages*		60.7	39.3	78.6

NOTE: States have been ranked from least to most competitive on the basis of voting for governors, senators, and representatives in Congress. The presidential vote is excluded.

*In computing the averages, the percentages for each state were weighted by its number of representatives in Congress.

Table 4.5. States predominantly Democratic from 1896 to 1930

State	Average no. of representatives in Congress	Average % of two-party vote		Index of competition for the period
		Dem.	Rep.	
South Carolina	7.0	98.4	1.6	3.2
Mississippi	7.8	95.9	4.1*	8.2*
Georgia	11.6	92.5	7.5*	15.0*
Louisiana	7.4	87.7	12.3*	24.6*
Florida	3.4	84.1	15.9	31.8
Texas	17.2	84.1	15.9	31.8
Alabama	9.6	84.0	16.0	32.0
Arkansas	6.8	77.8	22.2	44.4
Virginia	10.0	72.7	27.3	54.6
North Carolina	9.8	60.1	39.9	79.8
Tennessee	10.0	59.7	40.3	80.6
Arizona	1.0	59.4	40.6	81.2
Total	101.6			
Averages†		81.8	18.2	36.4

NOTE: States have been ranked from least to most competitive on the basis of voting for governors, senators, and representatives in Congress. The presidential vote is excluded.

*In these states the vote for independent and third-party candidates exceeded the Republican vote during the period, and it is accordingly the average percentage of the vote for such candidates that appears here and is used in computing the index of competition.

†In computing the averages, the percentages for each state were weighted by its number of representatives in Congress at each date.

The Republican states are defined as those in which the average of the Republican percentage of the two-party vote for the three offices other than president exceeded 55 percent for the period; the index numbers provided by Composite B were used as the basis for the calculation. Correspondingly, the Republican states can also be defined as those in which the index of competition was less than 90 percent for the average of the period, with the Republican party in the dominant position. Counterpart definitions are used to identify the predominantly Democratic states; and the competitive states are those occupying an intermediate position, with an index of competition of 90 percent or higher.

These categories are the basis for the discussions of the following chapter, but a number of the characteristics displayed in the tables are immediately deserving of note. First, the composition of the Democratic group as defined by the preceding criteria is striking. It consisted of the eleven Confederate states plus Arizona. Not one of the border states was in the group, whereas Arizona, which qualified with a score not much different from that of Tennessee and North Carolina, had not entered the Union until 1912. New Mexico, which separates Arizona from Texas and which also entered the Union in 1912, is rated as the most competitive state of all in table 4.6, with an index of competition for the period of 99.2.

Second, the size and composition of the group of states rated as competitive may hold surprises for some readers. It was not the largest of the three categories of

Table 4.6. States characterized by active party competition from 1896 to 1930

State	Average no. of representatives in Congress	Average % of two-party vote Rep.	Dem.	Index of competition for the period
Wyoming	1.0	54.9	45.1	90.2
Rhode Island	2.6	54.7	45.3	90.6
Utah	1.6	53.1	46.9	93.8
New Jersey	10.8	53.0	47.0	94.0
Ohio	21.6	52.4	47.6	95.2
West Virginia	5.4	52.0	48.0	96.0
Delaware	1.0	51.5	48.5	97.0
New York	39.8	51.5	48.5	97.0
Nebraska	6.0	51.2	48.8	97.6
Indiana	13.0	51.0	49.0	98.0
New Mexico	1.0	49.6	50.4	99.2
Missouri	15.8	48.5	51.5	97.0
Maryland	6.0	48.3	51.7	96.6
Kentucky	11.0	48.1	51.9	96.2
Colorado	3.4	47.2	52.8	94.4
Montana	1.6	46.4	53.6	92.8
Nevada	1.0	45.4	54.6	90.8
Oklahoma	7.5	45.1	54.9	90.2
Total	150.1			
Averages*		50.8	49.2	98.4

NOTE: States have been ranked on the basis of the two-party divisions in voting for governors, senators, and representatives in Congress. The presidential vote is excluded.

*In computing the averages, the percentages for each state were weighted by its number of representatives in Congress at each date.

states, either in terms of population or of seats in the House of Representatives, but it was not much smaller than the group rated as predominantly Republican. It included most of the border states, as might be expected, as well as New York, New Jersey, and Indiana. More surprising was the inclusion of Ohio, the home state of so many Republican presidents, with a score suggesting that Ohio was not much less competitive than New York during the period of concern.

Third, any defensible shifting of the points used to define the competitive group would produce some immediate shifting of states from Republican to competitive, but would have no effect on the size and composition of the Democratic group. As previously noted, states have been classified as competitive if the average split in the two-party vote fell within the ten-point 45 to 55 percent range, using Composite B data as the basis for the calculation. The choice of the 45 to 55 range is arbitrary but it follows a rule of thumb that has become widely established in practical political analysis. A seat in Congress is generally considered vulnerable, for example, if it has been won by less than 55 percent, while seats won by more than 55 percent are normally classified as "safe"—and especially so if they have been won regularly or on average by more than that amount (Cox 1960, p. 1069).

Alternative cut-points that might be considered would include the twelve-point 44 to 56 percentage range (Pfeiffer 1967, p. 462), which would shift Illinois from Republican to competitive for the 1896–1930 period; 43.5 to 56.5, which would shift Oregon, with Connecticut right on the line; and 42.5 to 57.5, which would shift Connecticut, New Hampshire, Idaho, Massachusetts, and Kansas from Republican to competitive, with Maine just over the line. It seems unlikely that any political historian would be happy with any of these changes, and they all seem undesirable to the present writer. Conversely, it seems unlikely that any proposal to narrow the range to less than ten percentage points would meet with approval from anyone. Hence, arbitrary as the 45 to 55 range may be, there is not much basis for preferring any other choice.

Fourth, the predominantly Republican group of states as so determined, while larger than the Democratic, was much less solidly of one party. Even in Vermont, the most Republican state, the Democratic party was polling an average of 28 percent of the two-party vote, with an index of competition of 56.2. In four southern states, conversely, the Republican party virtually disappeared, while in four others it polled less than a quarter of the two-party vote. The eight southern states with an index of competition below 50 percent could be considered the real "one-party" states of the period; the other predominantly Democratic states and all of those identified as Republican could be placed in what has sometimes been called the "one-and-one-half-party" category.

Fifth and finally, the limited but normal predominance of the Republican party in the nation as a whole during the period is confirmed by the data in a variety of ways. The predominantly Republican group of states was substantially larger than the Democratic; and within the competitive group, the states "leaning" Republican, where Republicans normally held more than 50 percent of the two-party vote, greatly outnumbered the states leaning Democratic in terms of their weight in the political system as a whole. It can be calculated from other sources that the Republicans had a normal majority of over thirty seats in the House of Representatives for the period 1896–1930 as a whole (David, Goldman, and Bain, 1960 p. 512), despite the number of Democrats who were regularly elected from the competitive states and from enclaves within Republican states. A similar or greater predominance was characteristic of the Republican party during most of the period in voting for other offices such as governor, senator, and president.

Chapter 5

A Brief Review of Long-Term
Partisan Groupings

FOR more than a century, the most enduring effects in American domestic politics have been those produced or left unsolved by the Civil War. Initially in the aftermath of the war, the Republican party appeared supreme, confirming its victory in 1868 and 1872 by the election and reelection of Ulysses S. Grant. By 1876 the Democratic party was reviving strongly in the North and awaiting only the end of Reconstruction for pre-eminence in the South. Thereafter for twenty years the two parties continued strong on opposite sides of the Potomac and Ohio Rivers while dissident agrarian movements grew strongly west of the Mississippi, and occasionally reached threatening proportions in the South.

In the climax of 1896, the Republican party won the election with a considerable reorganization of its power base; and the Democratic party lost much of its previous following in the states from Maine to Oregon while strengthening its position in the south. The period thereafter was one of Republican predominance, but that dominance was almost always under internal attack and was shattered in 1912 by dissidence within the party itself. Since the progressive elements within the Republican party usually lost and the Democrats remained primarily agrarian, many of the ills of a growing industrial society were left unattended. All were accentuated by the financial collapse of 1929 and the depression that followed.

Herbert Hoover was overtaken by fate in 1932 in the person of Franklin D. Roosevelt, but the realignment of political forces was not completed until 1936, when the Democratic party consolidated elements of its coalition that have remained together most of the time since 1932 and that were again visible in 1970. Yet the breakup of that coalition has been recurrently announced from 1948 onward, and change has been occurring, most visibly in the presidential election returns from the South since 1948. Whereas in 1936, the defeated Republican candidate for president carried only Maine and Vermont, in 1964 he carried only South Carolina, Georgia, Alabama, Mississippi, Louisiana, and Arizona—a reversal of the regional centers of extreme Democratic presidential weakness that was about as drastic as could be imagined. In 1968, no southern state was carried by the Democratic presidential candidate except Texas, and what was happening to the Democratic presidential vote was surfacing widely in the party's pursuit of other offices throughout the South.

The full story of this hundred years of politics obviously cannot be told here; readers who need the story in greater detail are referred to other works, espe-

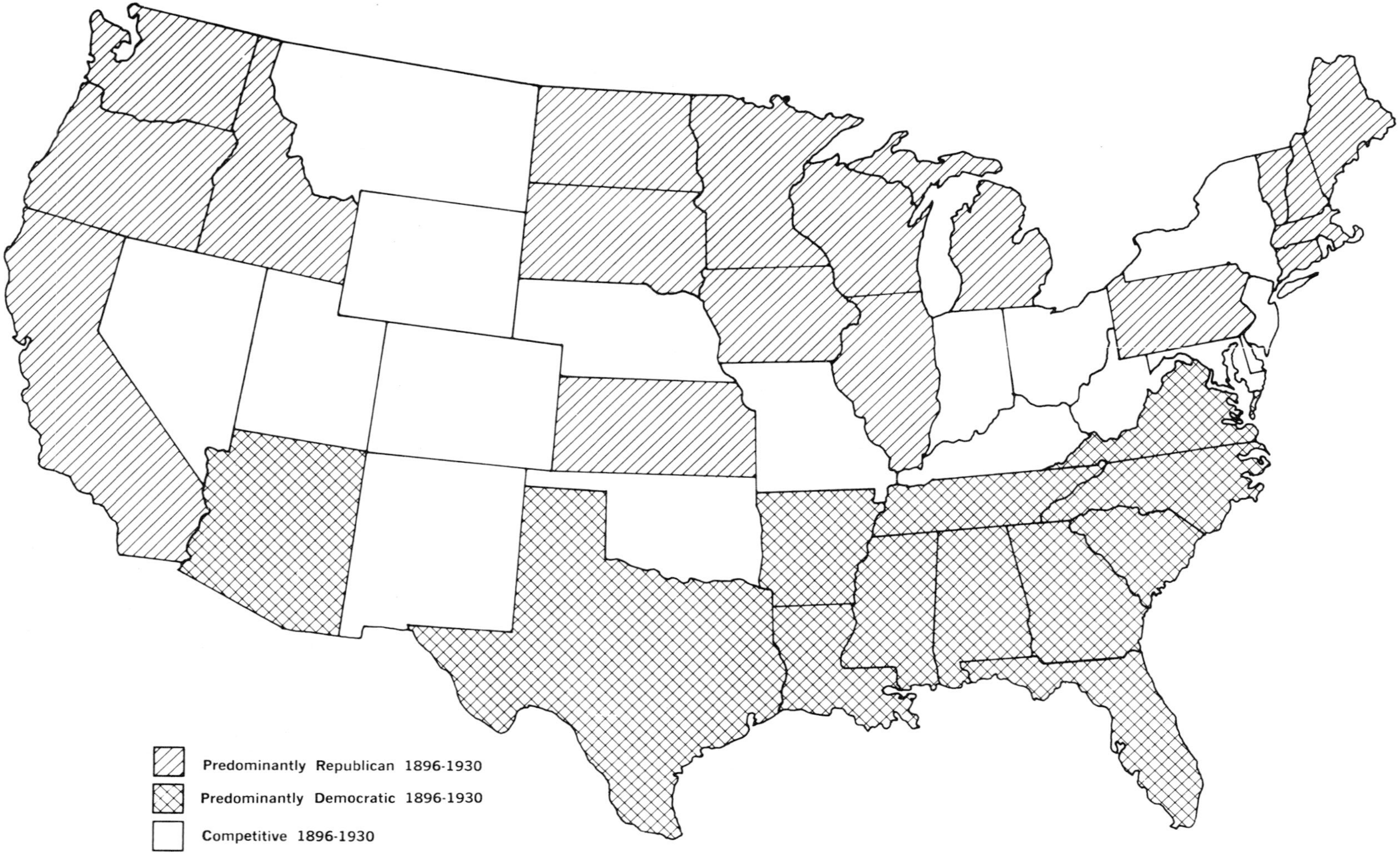

Figure 5.1. Partisanship in the United States, 1896–1930

Predominantly Republican 1896-1930

Predominantly Democratic 1896-1930

Competitive 1896-1930

cially the historical chapter of V. O. Key's well-known textbook (1964, pp. 166–98); David, Goldman, and Bain (1960, pp. 37–45, 443–47); Chambers and Burnham (1967, esp. pp. 295–304); and the recent books by Ladd and Burnham, both published in 1970.

The contributions to the understanding of history that can be made by the present study are limited, but they are nonetheless highly specific. Some of them will be new to all but a handful of specialists. Much insight can be gained by any reader who works his way through Part II with enough time for a thoughtful consideration of the diagrams for each state; the interested reader can well begin by looking first at the half dozen states he knows best. But in order to summarize this mass of data in terms that are both comprehensive and comprehensible, it seems desirable to exploit to the maximum the possibilities inherent in the three partisan groupings of states that were specified in chapter 4. These groups of states are identified on the map of figure 5.1. The present chapter has the function of tracing their partisan evolution during the successive periods of 1872–1894, 1896–1930, and 1932–1970.

The Formerly Republican North

Eighteen states have been identified as comprising the once-Republican North. As indicated by figure 5.1, they include all of the New England states except Rhode Island; Pennsylvania, still a powerful state but relatively much more so in earlier times; Michigan, Illinois, and most of the states of the Middle West to the west of them; and a far western group consisting of Idaho and the three Pacific Coast states.

A concise overview of the partisan history of this group of states is provided by the diagrams of figure 5.2 and the statistics of table 5.1. Between 1872 and 1896, the group as a whole could be rated as competitive with the Republican party averaging about 51 percent of the vote for governors and representatives in Congress, the Democratic 43, and the other parties and candidates about 6. After 1896 and until 1930, the Democratic party was not within striking distance of victory in terms of the group averages except in 1912. These were the states that were solidly Republican on any statewide basis for most of the period from 1896 to 1930, except as they divided within themselves.

In 1932 and 1936, the group as a whole went Democratic in the elections for president and the Republican party showed weakness in the elections for other offices. By 1938, the Republican party had regained its customary position of dominance in most of the group for elections for the offices other than president, and retained it until 1954. Since then, the record has been extremely mixed in terms of group averages, as figure 5.2 clearly shows.

The differing positions of the individual states within the group emerge from the data of table 5.1 and can be pursued further by looking at the details of the data and the diagrams for individual states in Part II. No state in the group could be considered predominantly Democratic in the period before 1896, but eight

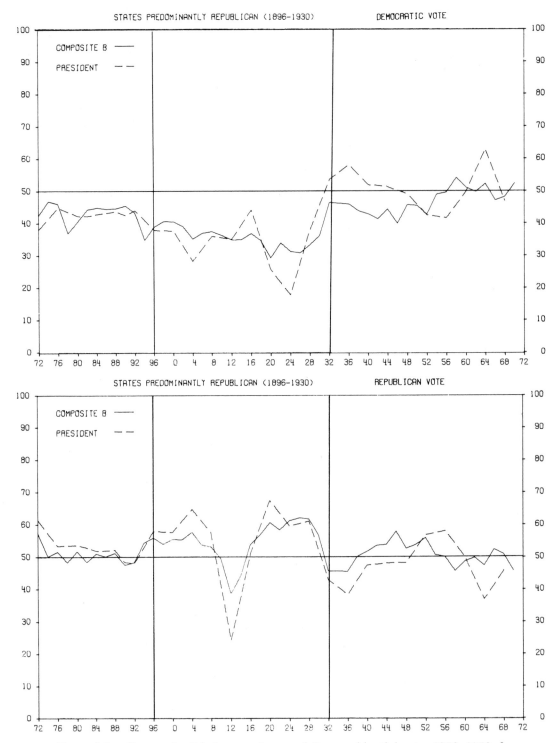

Figure 5.2. Composite B index numbers and the presidential vote, 1872–1970, for states predominantly Republican, 1896–1930

Table 5.1. Indexes of competition, 1872-1970, for states predominantly Republican from 1896 to 1930

State*	Index of competition, based on Composite B			Partisan category, each period†		
	1872–1894	1896–1930	1932–1970	1872–1894	1896–1930	1932–1970
Maine	82.8	82.4	90.0	R	R	R
New Hampshire	96.8	86.6	89.6	Comp.	R	R
Vermont	59.8	56.2	76.0	R	R	R
Massachusetts	86.8	86.0	96.8	R	R	Comp.
Connecticut	99.8	87.0	97.6	Comp.	R	Comp.
Pennsylvania	95.2	72.0	97.2	Comp.	R	Comp.
Illinois	96.6	88.4	98.2	Comp.	R	Comp.
Michigan	91.0	74.4	98.6	Comp.	R	Comp.
Wisconsin	96.2	69.2	93.2	Comp.	R	Comp.
Minnesota	85.4	69.0	90.6	R	R	Comp.
Iowa	87.8	78.0	95.2	R	R	Comp.
North Dakota	68.2	75.2	79.8	R	R	R
South Dakota	50.6	72.8	88.2	R	R	R
Kansas	70.4	85.6	89.8	R	R	R
Idaho	84.2	86.4	98.0	R	R	Comp.
Washington	86.8	79.6	90.6	R	R	Comp.
Oregon	95.6	87.2	88.2	Comp.	R	R
California	97.2	76.4	87.6	Comp.	R	R
Average index of competition‡	91.6	78.6	96.4			

*States are arranged according to a geographic sequence.

†Based on the defining criteria used for tables 4.4, 4.5, and 4.6; see chapter 4. States are rated competitive when the index of competition exceeds 90.0.

‡Calculated from the Composite B data for the group, which incorporated weights for each state based on its number of seats in the House of Representatives at each date.

members of the group could be rated at that time as competitive: New Hampshire, Connecticut, Pennsylvania, Illinois, Michigan, Wisconsin, Oregon, and California. All of these changed sufficiently after 1896 to be rated as predominantly Republican on the basis of the criteria discussed in chapter 4; the shift in the direction of Republicanism was especially noteworthy in the cases of Pennsylvania, Michigan, and California, in all of which the Democratic portion of the two-party vote dropped well below 40 percent on average.

For the period 1932 to 1970, all of the eighteen states became markedly less Republican and at least somewhat more competitive than they had been during the previous period. Not one shifted so far that it could be rated as predominantly Democratic on average for the period as a whole, but ten shifted to the "Competitive" column. Several of these states became intensely competitive and have remained so, mostly notably Massachusetts, Connecticut, Pennsylvania, Illinois, and Michigan.

Averages for a period as long as 1932 to 1970 can conceal much that occurs within the interval, hence the need for further inspection of the record of individual states. Maine and Vermont have been moving erratically but recurrently in the Democratic direction for the last twenty years, as have North and South Dakota. Oregon and California have become closely competitive states since 1954, with the shift in California helped along by changes in the election laws to clarify partisan identification of the candidates on primary ballots, and later by the abolition of cross-filing in the party primaries (Key 1964, pp. 392–93). Presumably there was a considerable increase in Democratic and independent strength in California before the election law changes could be achieved; both involved active campaigns and statewide referenda. But once in effect, the election law changes consolidated a revolution in the politics of what is now the largest state.

The Solid South (and Arizona)

The states identified previously as predominantly Democratic during the period from 1896 to 1930 were twelve in number: the eleven Confederate states and Arizona, as noted in chapter 4. All twelve are reflected in the diagrams of figure 5.3 and in the data of table 5.2. Arizona does not come into the figures until 1912 and did not achieve much weight in the group until after 1940. Among the other eleven states, at least nine were strongly Democratic by 1896, with North Carolina and Tennessee somewhat less so. North Carolina could even be rated as competitive for the earlier period. All became quite solidly Democratic during the period from 1896 to 1930, although again this was somewhat less true for North Carolina and Tennessee than for the others. All remained predominantly Democratic on average in the most recent period from 1932 to 1970.

There was nonetheless a wide range of differences among the states throughout most of the present century, as table 5.2 suggests; but before exploring those differences further, something should be said about major characteristics of the group as revealed by the diagrams of figure 5.3. The diagrams provide a summary of much that has been highly important, not only for the South, but for the nation as a whole.

First of all there is the recurring wide divergence between the voting for president and the voting for other offices—tendencies that begin in the present data as far back as 1878 and 1880, and which became especially important on the Democratic side after 1948 and on the Republican after 1952. The Wallace movement closed the gap for the Republicans in 1968, while widening it for the Democrats, but the future of these relationships clearly remains in doubt.

A second major feature is the Composite B record of voting behavior during and after the realignments of 1896 and 1932. Between 1876 and 1896, the Republican party had lost ground heavily; for twenty years the ruling Democratic party was threatened as seriously by third party movements and independent candidates as by the surviving Republicans. After 1896, Democratic strength moved up sharply and more or less continuously for a generation—a movement much stronger and more continuous than the counterpart movement toward the Republican party in the predominantly Republican states of the time. After 1896, moreover, third

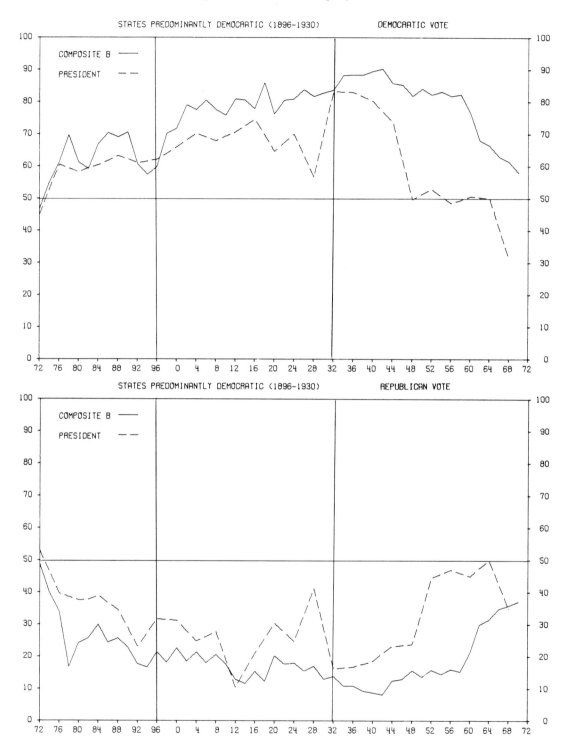

Figure 5.3. Composite B index numbers and the presidential vote, 1872–1970, for states predominantly Democratic, 1896–1930

Table 5.2. Indexes of competition, 1872–1970, for states predominantly
Democratic from 1896 to 1930

State*	Index of competition, based on Composite B			Partisan category, each period†		
	1872–1894	1896–1930	1932–1970	1872–1894	1896–1930	1932–1970
Virginia	67.0	54.6	49.6	D	D	D
North Carolina	90.4	79.8	67.4	Comp.	D	D
Tennessee	86.0	80.6	61.4	D	D	D
South Carolina	49.4	3.2	18.6	D	D	D
Georgia	31.6	15.0	13.0	D	D	D
Florida	78.4	31.8	47.2	D	D	D
Alabama	49.4	32.0	28.8	D	D	D
Mississippi	49.0	8.2	8.4	D	D	D
Arkansas	53.2	44.4	27.0	D	D	D
Louisiana	71.4	24.6	12.8	D	D	D
Texas	45.8	31.8	37.0	D	D	D
Arizona		81.2	82.6		D	D
Average index of competition‡	60.8	36.4	37.6			

*States are arranged according to a geographic sequence.

†Based on the defining criteria used for Tables 4.4, 4.5, and 4.6; see chapter 4. States are rated competitive when the index of competition exceeds 90.0.

‡Calculated from the Composite B data for the group, which incorporated weights for each state based on its number of seats in the House of Representatives at each date.

party movements were much less important in the South in developing candidates for offices other than president, unlike the recurring dissidencies that afflicted Republican candidates for these offices in other parts of the country, especially in the western states, as shown in figures 4.7 and 4.8.

Increasingly the major battles were fought inside the Democratic primaries, with the general elections serving merely to ratify what had already been decided, if indeed there was any contest in the general election. The Composite B averages portrayed in figure 5.3 are much affected by the many instances when the Republican party offered no candidate. In many of these cases, there was no independent candidate willing to take the trouble or to incur the risks involved in filing (Key 1949). The election returns then reported 100 percent of the vote for the Democratic candidate and nothing for anyone else; and these were the figures that went into the averages in such cases.

After 1896, the North and the South went in opposite partisan directions; but after 1932, both shifted in the direction of what was identified locally as the Democratic party. In the North, this could be considered in many respects a modernizing realignment; it brought on increasingly competitive conditions throughout a wide range of northern state party systems. In the South, the effect for nearly thirty years was the opposite of what would ordinarily be considered a modernization of politics. After 1932, the South became more heavily one-party in its orientation than it had been even between 1896 and 1930. The

Republican party reached its lowest point in 1942 and achieved only a modest recovery up to 1958 in the voting for offices other than president.

A third major feature of the diagrams is the change in voting for major offices other than president that set in after 1958 and has continued persistently throughout most of the region since that date. The Republican vote for these major offices has doubled since 1958, while the Democratic vote has declined from above the 80 percent level to below 60 percent. Republican candidates have been increasingly successful in winning southern state elections for governor, senator, and representative in Congress (Sundquist 1968, pp. 526–34).

The impact of these developments has been highly variable from state to state and in many instances they are too recent to have much effect on the averages of state voting behavior in table 5.2 for the entire period 1932–1970. Even as period averages, however, these figures show noteworthy differences between what is sometimes called the peripheral South—Virginia, North Carolina, Tennessee, Florida, and Texas—and the so-called Deep South of South Carolina, Georgia, Alabama, Mississippi, and Louisiana. Arkansas, omitted from these listings, occupies a somewhat ambiguous intermediate position; for some purposes it seems to be Deep South, for others peripheral.

The five states just called peripheral have all been marked by trends in recent years that have greatly narrowed the gap between Republican and Democratic voting levels for major offices other than president. These trends were most advanced and the gap was narrowest in the recent elections of Tennessee and Florida, with North Carolina and Virginia not far behind. Texas politics has moved a long way from where it was between 1934 and 1944, as shown by the chart for the state in Part II, but was still showing a twenty-point spread in the major party averages on Composite B in 1970.

Among the states identified as Deep South, South Carolina has produced the most startling illustration of the speed with which changes can occur when old patterns finally break. Between 1962 and 1970, South Carolina shifted from almost totally one-party Democratic to a situation in which the Republican party has become effectively competitive for a number of major offices, including especially the Senate seat held by Senator Strom Thurmond. Georgia also has been noteworthy for the persistence with which it has moved in the Republican direction since 1960, with the Republican candidate for governor polling a plurality in the election of 1966 only to lose in a final decision in the Georgia legislature.

Alamama, Mississippi, and Louisiana have been especially erratic in their partisan behavior in recent years. All were carried heavily by Senator Barry M. Goldwater for president in 1964 and had brief upsurges of voting for Republican candidates for other offices in 1964 and 1966. Since then the political life of all three states has been carried on mainly within what is considered locally the regular Democratic party in each of the three states, while voting was heavy for Governor George C. Wallace as a third-party candidate for president in 1968. Since then the three states have continued as the principal stronghold of the Wallace movement.

Before leaving the predominantly Democratic states of 1896–1930, something more should be said about Arizona. Since 1940 it has been one of the fastest growing states. It will have four seats in the House of Representatives after the elections of 1972—as many as Arkansas, which once had seven, or West Virginia, which once had six, or Oregon, which has never had more than four. Arizona has differed from most of the states of the old South in its relatively modest differences between the vote for president and the voting for other major offices, as shown by the chart for the state in Part II, and it began moving in the Republican direction at an earlier date and with more persistence than most of the southern states. It has been competitive since 1952, with strong Republican majorities in several recent elections for major offices. More than most states previously Democratic, it seems likely either to remain competitive or to become predominantly Republican.

The Competitive Middle

The states in which a closely competitive partisan politics existed between 1896 and 1930 have in effect been defined residually. They are the eighteen states that were neither predominantly Republican nor predominantly Democratic during that period. They were identified in chapter 4, are exhibited on the map of figure 5.1, and are further described collectively in terms of their long term voting trends in figure 5.4 and table 5.3.

There is no special reason why the group of states defined as competitive, 1896–1930, should have some further bond of cohesion, and there is not much in their appearance on the map to suggest it. No doubt New York and New Jersey have much in common beyond the boundary that separates them, as presumably do Ohio and Indiana. Delaware, Maryland, West Virginia, Kentucky, Missouri, and Oklahoma make up a band of contiguous states and can all be defined in some sense as border states, which gives them much in common but not necessarily a common identity. In some ways the six mountain states in the group—New Mexico, Colorado, Wyoming, Montana, Utah, Nevada—have had most in common by way of regional identity. They were important as silver mining states when silver was important in politics; and they all continue to have an intense interest in the politics of the management of the public lands.

Whatever the reason, a competitive politics has been characteristic of most of the eighteen-state group for an entire century. For all three time periods studied, the group average on the index of competition is above 95.0 The most conspicuous feature of the diagrams of figure 5.4 is the lack of conspicuous features—at least by comparison with most of the other diagrams in this book. The Republican split in 1912 is of course visible, along with Democratic weakness in presidential voting in 1920–28 and again in 1952–56, with the equally remarkable aberrations in presidential voting in both parties in 1964. But the Composite B data stay close to the mid-line, with relatively little impact from the party realignment of 1896, while the nonpresidential consequences of the realignment of 1932 had disappeared by 1940. The Composite B impact of third-party movements was generally inconsequential, except in 1912 and 1914.

Not all of the states in the group could be classified as competitive in all three

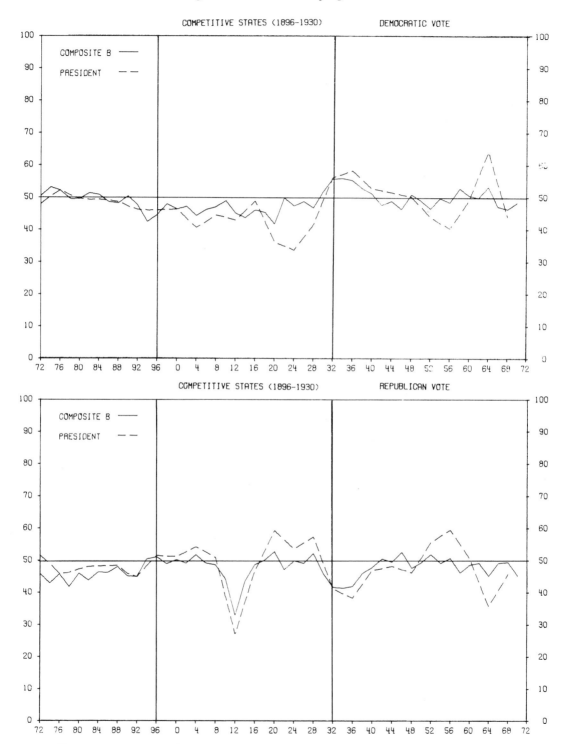

Figure 5.4. Composite B index numbers and the presidential vote, 1872–1970, for competitive states, 1896–1930

Table 5.3.   Indexes of competition, 1872–1970, for states characterized by active party competition from 1896 to 1930

State*	Index of competition, based on Composite B			Partisan category, each period†		
	1872–1894	1896–1930	1932–1970	1872–1894	1896–1930	1932–1970
Rhode Island	82.4	90.6	79.2	R	Comp.	D
New York	99.2	97.0	99.6	Comp.	Comp.	Comp.
New Jersey	98.8	94.0	98.4	Comp.	Comp.	Comp.
Delaware	77.4	97.0	97.8	D	Comp.	Comp.
Maryland	90.6	96.6	89.8	Comp.	Comp.	D
West Virginia	88.8	96.0	89.2	D	Comp.	D
Ohio	98.0	95.2	97.2	Comp.	Comp.	Comp.
Indiana	99.8	98.0	99.6	Comp.	Comp.	Comp.
Kentucky	81.0	96.2	90.4	D	Comp.	Comp.
Missouri	86.2	97.0	87.6	D	Comp.	D
Nebraska	80.6	97.6	84.6	R	Comp.	R
Oklahoma		90.2	82.6		Comp.	D
Montana	98.8	92.8	92.2	Comp.	Comp.	Comp.
Wyoming	91.0	90.2	97.6	Comp.	Comp.	Comp.
Colorado	89.0	94.4	98.2	R	Comp.	Comp.
New Mexico		99.2	90.6		Comp.	Comp.
Utah		93.8	95.4		Comp.	Comp.
Nevada	96.6	90.8	85.2	Comp.	Comp.	D
Average index of competition†	95.8	98.4	97.2			

*States are arranged according to a geographic sequence.

†Based on the definining criteria used for tables 4.4, 4.5, and 4.6; see chapter 4. States are rated competitive when the index of competition exceeds 90.0.

‡Calculated from the Composite B data for the group, which incorporated weights for each state based on its number of seats in the House of Representatives at each date.

time periods, at table 5.3 makes clear, but most of the larger states in the group could be so classified, most notably New York, New Jersey, Ohio, and Indiana. Missouri, relatively much more important from 1900 to 1930 than it has been since, went from predominantly Democratic to competitive and back to predominantly Democratic. Kentucky, also more important before 1930 than since, went through a similar pattern of shifting while still qualifying as competitive in recent times.

Rhode Island, geographically small, heavily urban, and a center of ethnic politics, displays one of the most interesting sets of diagrams in Part II. For a century it has been moving erratically but persistently from Republican to Democratic. More clearly than any other state in the group, it has moved from one partisan affiliation to the other by means of a century-long secular trend. Nebraska, by contrast, once strongly Republican, became highly competitive while William Jennings Bryan was in his prime, and then reverted more strongly than ever to Republicanism after 1940.

The diagrams for New York and Ohio in Part II merit inspection, if only because of the size and importance of both states. New York is presented in a dual form (with the first form used in the eighteen-state averages), for the reasons explained in the Appendix and in the introduction to Part II; the influence of dual nominations in New York politics, in which two political parties are allowed to nominate the same candidate, can be traced in the differences in the two sets of diagrams and in the data on which they are based. Dual nominations add as much complexity as the cross-filing that California abolished in 1959; hopefully New York will eventually remove this aberration in its political system, which confuses the politics of the state as much as it does the statistical outcomes.

The diagrams for New York and Ohio show more fluctuation than the eighteen-state diagrams of figure 5.4, but have in common their generally flat profile for an entire century. The data for both states could doubtless be subjected successfully to the mathematical procedures by which Stokes and Iversen demonstrated (1966) the existence of long-term forces that tend to restore competition within the national party system whenever the system has previously moved strongly in the direction of one-party dominance. On the face of things as revealed in the various charts of this volume, it would seem that those forces must have been present most strongly in the larger states of the present group, as well as in some of those identified previously as predominantly Republican between 1896 and 1930.

If the preservation of a two-party system in the nation at large has been a virtue, as most Americans might suppose, presumably much of the credit must go to the states just discussed. Their special characteristic was the extent to which they reflected within their own internal politics the forces at work in the whole nation—and did so in a balanced fashion that preserved an effective system of competitive politics both for themselves and for the nation.

Data for the Study of Party Realignment

Recently there has been an intensification of interest in the study of party realignment and more generally in the future of the party system. Several works have appeared that address themselves largely to a popular audience, but are nonetheless based on extensive efforts at data collection and research—most noticeably the volumes by Phillips (1969), Lubell (1970), and Scammon and Wattenberg (1970). Meanwhile, there has also been a renewal and intensification of the tradition of scholarly research on party realignment that mainly dates from the initial work by V. O. Key, Jr., was continued in the conceptual clarification produced in the two major volumes by Campbell, Converse, Miller, and Stokes (1960, 1966) and in the contributions by Gerald Pomper (1968), and is exemplified most recently in Burnham's study, *Critical Elections* (1970), and in continuing, related research (Flanigan and Zingale 1971).

Some of this work uses survey research on voter attitudes in an attempt to speculate about the presence or absence of a genuine party realignment in recent times, or its prospects in the near future (cf. Converse 1966). Hence, it should be remarked that in the party realignments of 1896 and 1932, there was no contemporary survey research to produce data on changes in voters' party identification that could be compared with their actual changes in voting. Quite possibly it was the actual voting that changed first, with changes in sentiments of party identification coming along later if at all. This would seem especially the case for those voters who switched parties in their presidential voting, but were slower to change in voting for governors, senators, and representatives in Congress—and slower still to change in voting for alternatives in the elections for state legislatures, county boards, and other local offices.

The hypothesis has not been fully explored, but it has long been the view of the present writer that when a party realignment occurs, generally it works down from the top—from presidential voting to voting for other offices of high visibility and clear partisan identification, and only later to the lower offices where election nevertheless occurs on a partisan basis (David 1955, p. 196; Key 1956, p. 205). Problems of the supply of candidates for such offices in a party long out of power probably have at least as much to do with the mechanics of this process as the internal psychological mechanisms of the voter. Presumably the typical voter is nonetheless most likely to go against his previous partisan predispositions in connection with candidates who come on strongly in campaigns of high visibility, and least likely to do so in the opposite case.

It is also true that much of the previous study of party realignment has been limited to analyses of voting in presidential elections. This was not the case for the work by V. O. Key or for the recent research by Burnham, in which six northern states are studied intensively for the period 1891–1957, using the vote for "all statewide elective offices" (1970, pp. 20–24), and there are other exceptions. But the continued use of the presidential vote in discussions of party realignment, as in the recent paper by Flanigan and Zingale (1971), does sharpen an issue for which the present volume has relevance: When does a realignment in presidential voting constitute a party realignment? The present writer would reply, only when it is confirmed by an accompanying parallel realignment in the voting for other offices of high partisan visibility.

In chapter 3 it was argued that the Composite B index numbers are probably the best available general measure of party strength. It is an obvious corollary that the Composite B index numbers are probably the best available indicator to use in studying party realignment as it occurs in actual voting.

The methods used in the previous tables are simple and deal with the individual states only in terms of averages over considerable periods of time. The sophisticated statistical methods that have been developed by Burnham and others could be applied to the underlying data in order to identify more precisely the turning points of party realignment in particular states. This is one of the many purposes for which the data of Part II may prove useful but which also go beyond the scope of the present volume. Something more can be done, however, with the simple analyses that have already been produced in tables 5.1, 5.2, and 5.3.

In table 5.4 the states that shifted from one partisan category to another between historical periods are brought together from the previous tables. The top of the table reflects shifts in direction from Democratic toward Republican—from Democratic to Competitive or from Competitive to Republican or all the way

Table 5.4. States shifting in partisan category, 1872–1970

Nature of the shift	Realignment of 1896: 1872–1894 vs. 1896–1930	Realignment of 1932: 1896–1930 vs. 1932–1970
Democratic to Competitive	Delaware West Virginia Kentucky Missouri	none
Competitive to Republican	New Hampshire Connecticut Pennsylvania Illinois Michigan Wisconsin Oregon California	Nebraska
Democratic to Republican	none	none
Republican to Competitive	Rhode Island Nebraska Colorado	Massachusetts Connecticut Pennsylvania Illinois Michigan Wisconsin Minnesota Iowa Idaho Washington
Competitive to Democratic	North Carolina	Rhode Island Maryland West Virginia Missouri Oklahoma Nevada
Republican to Democratic	none	none

NOTE: Recapitulated from tables 5.1, 5.2, and 5.3.

from Democratic to Republican; the bottom of the table reflects the opposite trends.

Table 5.4 supports at least four conclusions of the kind that V. O. Key once characterized as standing out like a red barn on a snow-covered landscape. First and most obvious, is the extent to which the realignment of 1896 moved the country in the direction of the Republican party, while conversely that of 1932 moved the country in the direction of the Democratic. Second is the extent to which the realignment in each case was concentrated in a group of states, including several large states, that moved in the first instance from competitive to

Republican and in the second from Republican to competitive. Third is the very small number of states that moved sufficiently contrary to trend in either instance to become visible in the underpopulated cells of the table. Fourth, no single state was found in either realignment that moved all the way from an alignment predominantly of one party to one predominantly of the other.

A final point, not so obvious from table 5.4, is the fact that all of the eleven Confederate states except North Carolina are completely missing from the table. The other ten were already predominantly Democratic before 1896; after that year they merely became more so, as they did again for a while after 1932. The implications that can be drawn from table 5.4 are applicable primarily for the non-South; the special characteristics of the eleven-state Confederate South as a political region are again emphasized by its almost complete absence from this set of data.

Chapter 6

Where Are the Trends Going?

MUCH of this book shows patterns that are intriguing for what they suggest about the future of the American party system. Accordingly, some summary of the data from this point of view and some speculation about it may be in order. For the most part the numbers and the diagrams will have to speak for themselves, but the messages they give forth are certainly susceptible of more than one interpretation.

National Indexes and Their Limited Meaning

One possibility for the use of the data is to assemble them on a consolidated national basis and consider what trends if any are revealed. Figure 6.1 produces the consolidation in the form of diagrams similar to those previously used for states, regions, and multistate partisan groupings. The related sets of numbers for each of the four offices and for the three composite index numbers can be found at the end of Part II.

Figure 6.1, when examined closely, suggests a somewhat revisionist view of a rather considerable amount of American political history. In part this revisionism is well merited, but also in part it reflects the substitution of one set of statistical distortions for another.

A truly shocking aspect of the diagrams of figure 6.1 is the extent to which the Composite B line for the *Democrats* follows the 50 percent line from 1876 to 1928, while conversely the Composite B line for the *Republicans* runs along most of the time on a plateau that gradually rises from around the 42 percent level in the 1880's to around the 46 percent level in the 1920s—all during a time when the Republican party was supposed to be dominant in the country at large. These relationships will become somewhat more credible to the inquiring reader who looks carefully at the counterpart diagrams for the four major regions and for the three groupings of the states on the basis of their partisanship between 1896 and 1930—and then considers what would be produced by averaging either set of diagrams, giving each group of states its due weight.

The poor Republican and excellent Democratic showing of figure 6.1, in other words, is the result of combining the very heavy Democratic majorities of the South with the much more narrow Republican majorities elsewhere. The Republican predominance from 1896 to 1930 that is referred to at the end of chapter 4

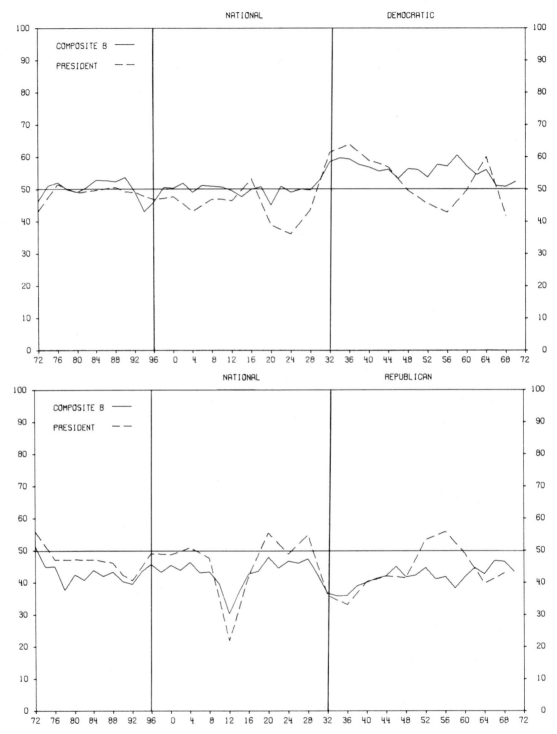

Figure 6.1 Composite B index numbers and the presidential vote, 1872–1970 (national: Democratic and Republican)

was indeed a fact for some purposes, but it consisted primarily of an ability to win elections, often by rather slim margins, both in the states rated as competitive and in those rated as Republican. Together these groups of states held noteworthy majorities in the electoral college, in the Senate, and in the House of Representatives. As shown in tables 4.4, 4.5, and 4.6, the competitive and Republican groups together averaged over three hundred seats in the House against the South's slightly more than one hundred during the period; but the average Republican majority in the House of Representatives, as noted previously, was not much more than thirty seats—adequate but not overwhelming.

For the most recent period, from 1932 to 1970, the Democratic strength and Republican weakness revealed by figure 6.1 may be less surprising. Even here, however, the diagrams tend to exaggerate these characteristics, especially for the years before 1958, because of the lopsided Democratic majorities in a dozen states that are put into the averages against modest Democratic majorities or even minority positions in a much larger number of states.

Quite a different picture would emerge for the entire century from 1872 to 1970 if popular vote totals were aggregated nationwide for the voting in either presidential or congressional elections, as in the diagram produced by Stokes and Iversen (1966, p. 183). In their diagram, a different set of distortions is operative: the Democratic vote in the South is given much less weight than its political importance might suggest because of the low levels of turnout that were characteristic of the region until recently. No defense of low turnout is intended here; quite possibly states with low turnout should be subject to some kind of penalty. Nonetheless, under the political arrangements of the American Constitution, states of similar population are entitled to similar weight in the political system as a whole, and they can receive it whether turnout rates are high or low—facts that must be kept in mind in any interpretation of nationwide popular voting statistics. (Compare the discussion of how popular vote converts into votes in the electoral college or in Congress, David 1961, pp. 322–23.)

The most important conclusion to be drawn from this discussion is that limited credence should be given to any national averages as reflections of conditions throughout the entire United States—as long as the country shows as little political homogeneity as it has during most of the period since the Civil War. The political realignment of 1932 was one kind of realignment in the non-South; it was an entirely different kind in the South, if indeed it deserves to be called a realignment at all in that region. The genuine realignment in the South seems to have begun in the presidential voting of 1948 and has become progressively visible in the voting for other offices since 1958. Eventually the heterogeneity of regions within the United States may become less pronounced; meanwhile, the regional divergences should not be forgotten in any use of the national data.

The same logic suggests that the trend lines of figure 6.1, such as they are, are almost useless in any effort to predict the future, except as they suggest the probable continuation of a two-party system in the country at large despite its present vicissitudes. If any forecasting is to be undertaken from the present data, it seems necessary to place much more emphasis on the data for individual states and regions, where a greater clarity of view may be somewhat possible.

A Recapitulation of State and Regional Trends

A considerable amount of data for individual states and regions was discussed in chapters 4 and 5. It does not easily lend itself to summary on any precisely statistical basis, and especially for the period since World War II. Within the mass of detail, however, some distinctions can be made between the South and non-South, between some categories of states within each, and between large states and small.

The significant trends that have been operating in the South since 1958 were noted in chapters 4 and 5 and are especially apparent in the diagrams of figures 4.5 and 5.3. The South as a whole has been visibly moving toward much lower levels of one-party dominance in its elections for governors, senators and representatives in Congress. Virginia, North Carolina, Tennessee, and Florida have become substantially competitive in terms of state averages in their elections for these offices. South Carolina, Georgia, and Texas have moved sharply in that direction, as apparently Arkansas had also for a time. Alabama, Mississippi, and Louisiana remain in a condition of great internal turmoil, and the old order has clearly been shaken to its foundations.

Similar changes in the states that were once predominantly Republican took place at earlier dates. Massachusetts, Connecticut, Pennsylvania, Michigan, and Illinois all shifted from predominantly Republican to competitive in statewide politics either before, during, or shortly after the election of 1932; having shifted, they have remained competitive. More recently they have been joined by California and Oregon, while Maine, Vermont, and the Dakotas have been moving toward a competitive status.

Among the considerable group of states that were competitive even between 1896 and 1930, few have shifted to a condition in which either political party could be considered strongly dominant. Nebraska is the leading case of a shift in the Republican direction, while Rhode Island, West Virginia, Missouri, and Nevada have shifted to become more Democratic.

New York, Ohio, and the other big states with long-term records of competitive politics have retained that position, while almost all of the other states that could currently be considered big, including Texas, have been moving in the direction of a much more actively competitive partisan politics. Missouri seems to be the only state of its own size or larger that could be considered an exception. The smaller states have a more variable record and may be more susceptible to a long-term secular drift in the direction of one party or the other, as illustrated by the trend toward the Democratic party in Rhode Island and toward the Republican in Arizona. In a small state, there may be less room for the operation of the forces that presumably exist to restore competition in the larger system as a whole and in the larger states, if Stokes and Iversen (1966) are correct in their well-known thesis.

Realignment to Competition or to Other Party Dominance?

Despite what has just been said, much discussion of party realignment seems to assume or imply that if a party realignment occurs, it involves necessarily a shift from a situation in which one political party is dominant to a situation in which the other political party is dominant (Converse 1966, p. 213). Samuel Lubell, for example, has long been known for his enunciation in 1952 of a "sun-and-moon" theory of American politics, in which during every important political era, one of the major political parties occupies the position of the sun and the other the moon. This theory assumes that the Republicans were dominant from the Civil War until 1932 and the Democrats from 1932 onward, and goes on to conclude that at some future time another reversal may occur by which the Republicans will regain dominance.

The present writer does not share this reading of the past, nor does the data of the present study sustain it. Even after 1896, the Republican party was never as solidly dominant as it seemed to be for a generation in the minds of some observers. Conversely, the Democratic party has never been as dominant as some more recent analysts have seemed at times to believe. The spectacular Democratic victories in presidential elections from 1932 to 1944 were not matched in elections for other offices after 1936. Of the six presidential elections since the death of Franklin D. Roosevelt, decisive popular majorities were polled in only three: 1952, 1956, and 1964. All were dominated by personality and issue factors extraneous to the long term flow of the party system. In the other three, 1948, 1960, and 1968, each of which was a sharp test of national party strength in support of clearly partisan candidates, the outcomes were very close. In presidential voting, at least, neither party has been dominant since World War II; and the apparent dominance of the Democratic party in Congress has been based upon an uneasy alliance between unlike elements that has been increasingly difficult to maintain (Bailey 1970; Turner and Schnier 1970).

Those difficulties were much in the mind of the present author when writing a series of hypotheses on party realignment some years ago. One of these was as follows:

> The party system within a state is likely to be in a condition of unstable equilibrium when the party alignment in the state is grossly out of accord with the national party alignment; conversely, party realignment on a national basis is unlikely to reach a position of stable equilibrium as long as powerful state party systems are out of accord with the national party alignment. (David 1955, p. 191)

These situations of "unstable equilibrium" have brought on political crises of one kind or another in every southern state since the end of World War II. The clear trend lines of figure 5.3 are the obvious consequence, and they bring on a reformulation of the question posed in the title of this section: If party realignment reaches some kind of climax in the South, will the region go Republican on a permanent basis or merely become and remain competitive? This is a genuine question, actively under debate among analysts who share a vigorous interest in southern politics. The question itself is not answered by the trend lines of the chart; if they go on indefinitely without interruption or reversal, the South will indeed become predominantly Republican, as Kevin Phillips has predicted (1970, pp. 286–89). But how long can the present trends continue without interruption?

If an answer to this question can be found in any solid set of data, it would seem that it will have to be found in the experience of the states that were once predominantly Republican. As a guide, their experience leaves much to be desired. The formerly Republican states were not as solidly Republican as the Solid South was solidly Democratic. Moreover, even if a competitive status should be the eventual outcome, the sociological processes by which a state or region moves from Democratic to competitive are not necessarily the mirror image of the processes by which other states have moved at an earlier time from Republican to competitive.

To the extent that the formerly Republican states do provide a guide, the first and most important point to observe is that they did *not* become predominantly Democratic when they realigned; they merely became competitive, and they did so initially only for the elective offices of greatest visibility. Furthermore, the states that were first and most clearly to become competitive were the ones that were larger, more industrial, more urban, more heterogeneous, and more capable of generating a situation in which average income levels were relatively high and rising—all factors that have often been mentioned as associated with active party competition or conducive to it (Gatlin 1968, pp. 219–34). The states that were less able to meet these specifications, such as Maine and Vermont and the Dakotas, lingered on in their one-partyism much longer; but when they did begin to shift, they shifted in the direction of greater party competition, with not much of any tendency so far to reverse completely their previous partisan affiliation.

The likelihood of a similar pattern in the South during the next ten to twenty years would seem obvious; and that likelihood is reinforced by two other sets of considerations. One is the persistence of traditionalism in voting preferences, emphasized so much in the conclusions drawn by the analysts of the Survey Research Center (Converse 1966). Many southern voters who are traditional Democrats will presumably continue for a long time to vote for candidates of their own sort, also labeled Democratic, in the elections for state legislatures, rural county boards, and the various minor elective offices that abound in the counties. This means that in the most conservative areas, those that might otherwise seem most likely to go completely Republican in voting for offices of note, the label of the Democratic party will stay alive and the machinery will be active.

The other set of considerations is the one that Stokes and Iversen identified (1966), although without spelling out its implications for state politics: the tendency in any reasonably large-scale political system, once it has become competitive, for the forces of competition to assert themselves in the restoration of a competitive equilibrium when the previous equilibrium has been violently disturbed in a one-party direction. Currently both California and New York are larger and in some respects considerably more complex than was the entire United States in 1840. If the Stokes-Iversen theory has merit, it would seem that it should eventually be as applicable to the large states of the present day, including those of the South, as it was to the entire country at an earlier period.

Furthermore, the data reviewed in chapter 5 would suggest that the theory has indeed been applicable for quite a long time in the older group of large, competitive states—the states that seem most likely to provide the model for the other states that are becoming larger, more complex and more diversified. If this is true, the total system must inevitably become more competitive; and the nationalizing tendencies that E. E. Schattschneider was writing about in 1960 (pp. 78–96) as a consequence of competition may indeed be appearing.

It should be understood that this final chapter is not an attempt to deal with all of the major issues that would be involved in a more general consideration of the future of the party system. This highly specialized volume is not the appropriate place to deal with such questions as the effect of a larger infiltration of amateurs into politics (Wilson 1962), or of a more issue-oriented politics at the national level (David 1971), or of challenges to the primacy of the political parties in their competition with other forms of political activity (Sorauf 1968), or of what Walter Dean Burnham has referred to as "The Onward March of Party Decomposition" (1970, p. 91). Such issues cannot be more than mentioned as a concession to the importance of alternative aspects when the attempt is made to put the party future in reasonable perspective.

Levels of interparty competition nonetheless have a most pervasive relationship to other issues in the institutional evolution of the party system. Previously I have suggested that there are underlying relationships among the levels of competition, cohesion, and centralization within party systems, and between all three and the success of modernizing tendencies within old party systems (David, Goldman, and Bain 1960, pp. 46–48, 506–08; David 1963). Most scholars undoubtedly think that at present, the rather limited centralization that once existed within the American national party system is breaking down and that such cohesion as was formerly visible is disappearing. To this, it can only be replied that if the intensification of partisan competition is genuine, then new forms of cohesion may be emerging in places where they did not previously exist. Some more appropriate forms of centralization or nationalization may in turn emerge to replace what is evidently in decay.

Clearly this view can be held at the moment only as an act of faith, but there is nothing in this book to impair the writer's faith in a healthy future for the American party system, and much to support it.

Appendix

Bibliographical Note and References

Party Identity, Party Identification, and the Use of Historical Election Data

AS noted in chapter 2, many problems of party identity arise when using the historical election data as available from the Historical Archives of the Inter-University Consortium for Political Research (ICPR). The rules for adjusting the data that have been developed in organizing the time series for this volume are presented herewith.

Rules for Adjusting the Data

1. Treat the Liberal Republican vote of 1972 for president, governor, and representative in Congress as the Democratic vote in all of the elections where it appeared and where Democratic party candidates were not otherwise present.

2. Credit the Democratic party with all votes cast for William Jennings Bryan in 1896, including any cast for Bryan as the candidate of the Populist party, of Democratic-Populist fusions, or of the Silver Republicans. Also treat votes under these labels for other offices in 1896 as Democratic where Democratic party candidates were not otherwise present.

3. In cases where a combined name indicates a party fusion, with one of the major parties included in the designation and not otherwise present, treat the vote as the major party vote of that party.

4. Similarly, in cases where the ballot designation is simply "Fusion" or some equivalent term, and one (but only one) of the major parties is not otherwise present, treat the Fusion vote as the vote of the missing major party.

5. Treat the Anti-Tammany vote or the vote for any fusion involving Anti-Tammany as Republican in cases where the Republican party is not otherwise present.

6. In party splits producing candidates from ambiguously coordinate factions of a dominant party, credit the winner's vote to the party and credit the loser's vote to the "other" column, unless there is reason for assigning it to the minority major party, with that party not otherwise present. (Cases meeting these specifications usually predate the establishment of regular primary elections held under public authority.)

7. In party splits producing slates of presidential electors and other candidates from ambiguously coordinate factions of a minority major party, with all such candidates suffering defeat, combine the votes of the factions as the vote of the minority major party.

8. In cases where a major party is missing from the ballot and some designation occurs that appears to be a variant form or euphemism for it, credit the vote to the missing major party in the absence of specific evidence to the contrary and having regard for apparent continuities in the form and distribution of the total vote.

9. Where a candidate is identified as Independent Democrat or Independent Republican on the ballot and the corresponding major party is not otherwise present, credit the vote to the missing major party. Votes for independent candidates running in opposition to the regular candidate of the same party should be treated as "other," as should all votes for candidates running on a plain independent label.

10. In the California data, treat the vote for any Democratic-Republican candidate as Democratic and the vote for any Republican-Democratic candidate as Republican.

11. In the New York data, where a major party candidate is also the candidate of a minor party and receives votes as such, organize the data for use both on a combined basis as the vote for major party candidates, and on a noncombined basis reflecting the parties as separate entities, with the minor party vote in the "other" column. Prefer the combined basis in preparing multistate combinations of data that include New York.

12. In cases other than those previously specified or closely analogous to them, credit the Democratic and Republican parties only with the votes cast for candidates running under their designation, and assign other votes, including write-in votes, to the "other" column.

Data Reflecting Party Fusions

Major parties have participated rather conspicuously in fusions with "third" parties in some instances, much less so in others. At the national level, the leading cases are those involving the Democratic party in 1872 and 1896, but both major parties have occasionally been involved in fusions with third parties at state and local levels. The first five of the rules previously specified all arise from situations involving fusions of one kind or another.

Liberal Republicans and Democrats of 1872 (Rule 1)

The Democratic party in effect entered into a fusion with the Liberal Republicans who refused to participate in the renomination of President Ulysses S. Grant in 1872. The Liberal Republican ticket, headed by Horace Greeley, was adopted by the Democrats as their own (Wilfred E. Binkley 1958, pp. 297–300; Richard C. Bain 1960, pp. 93–96). The ticket was carried on the ballot only under the Liberal Republican designation in several northern states and in a few cases elsewhere. Under its rules, the ICPR reports the Liberal Republican vote for Bryan separately under code number 208,[1] but for present purposes the entire vote for the

---

[1] Hereafter these code numbers are given in parentheses where relevant.

ticket is credited to the state and national totals of the Democratic party, as it has been by W. Dean Burnham and other compilers of historical statistics.

The same process by which the Democrats ceded their ballot rights for the presidential ticket to the Liberal Republicans in some instances seems also to have operated for other offices in the same states in 1872. The Democratic party was missing from the election returns for such offices as governor and representative in most of these states, and Liberal Republican candidates apparently received the vote that previously would have been Democratic.

Democrats and Populists in 1896 (Rule 2)

The People's Party, or the Populists (340), held its first national party convention in 1892 and also reached its zenith in that year, winning twenty-two electoral votes. In 1896, the Democrats, by nominating William Jennings Bryan and adopting the platform he favored, took over the Populist program with such success that the party virtually disappeared. It was on the ballot with its own presidential candidate in Colorado, but disappeared completely from the presidential balloting in most states, while remaining on the ballot with Bryan as its candidate in a few states. Under the circumstances, the vote for Bryan was cast and counted almost entirely as a Democratic vote. But where the combined Democrat and Populist label (346) did appear in support of the Bryan ticket, as in Illinois, or where both parties were on the ballot with Bryan as their candidate, the vote is treated as Democratic for present purposes.

The year 1896 was one of fissions and fusions in both major parties as the result of the Bryan nomination and the repudiation of the Cleveland Administration by the Democratic party. The Gold Democrats (508) held a convention and nominated candidates of their own, becoming a third party with some variation in local labels. The Silver Republicans (1160) also met, but endorsed the Democratic ticket, thus in effect entering into a fusion with the Democratic party. The Silver Republican designation appeared on the ballot in various instances in 1896, but it did not operate as a separate third party to any noteworthy extent. Where it did so, its votes have been credited to the "other" category.

Combined Name Fusions (Rule 3)

Combined name designations involving one major party label or the other have appeared intermittently throughout party history. Frequently they reflect an obvious effort by the major party to assimilate either a dissident faction of the other major party or the supporters of a rapidly rising indigenous third party—sometimes both. The combined Democrats and Populists of Illinois in 1896 have already been mentioned; the same year produced the Democratic, People's, and Silver Republican party (980) in Oregon, and a miscellany of similar designations elsewhere, especially in the balloting for governor and representative.

Combined name fusions have persisted in some states for long periods, as in North Dakota in the 1920s, where the Republican and Non-Partisan party (214) was regularly opposed by the Democrat and Independent (1246). In Minnesota, the Democratic-Farmer-Labor party (DFL) (809) has persisted since 1944 and has been the Democratic party of that state for all intents and purposes, as it still is. Other examples of combined name fusions, incomplete but somewhat representative, are as follows:

> Maine, 1880, Democrat and Greenback (324)
> New York, 1888, Tammany Democrat and Union Labor (1180)
> Colorado, 1894, Populist and Democrat (343)
> Montana, 1904, Democrat, Labor, People's (972)
> Nevada, 1904, Democrat and Silver (959)
> New Jersey, 1912, Republican and Progressive (591)
> Oregon, 1912, Republican and Progressive (591)
> Utah, 1914, Democrat and Progressive (594)

Under ICPR usage, every combined name fusion that involves a different combination of words is given its own separate party code; no distinction is made between situations in which the major party was separately present on the ballot in its own right and those where it was not. But when the major party is not otherwise present in an election, any combined name fusion that includes the major party designation seems likely to pick up most of the vote that would otherwise be cast for the major party. Such cases are therefore treated as part of the major party vote for present purposes.

Fusion Tickets (Rule 4)

Candidates designated simply as "Fusion" appear in the data for various elections and have been given party code 843 by ICPR. Most of these cases occurred between 1880 and 1900 in states of the northern tier that were strongly Republican. The Democratic party was absent in these elections, and the Fusion party seems to have been a substitute that was comparable to the combined name fusion parties just reviewed. Presumably all of these votes should be credited to the Democratic party, as has been done in this volume; if counterpart cases are found in elections where the Democratic party is present and the Republican party is absent, presumably the votes in such cases should be credited to the Republican party.

Anti-Tammany Tickets (Rule 5)

Data for the New York City congressional districts during the latter part of the nineteenth century show frequent examples of Anti-Tammany (1080), Republican and Anti-Tammany (1084), and similar tickets, most of which were fusions in opposition to the Democratic Tammany machine. In some of these cases, the Republican party was also separately present under its own name, but usually it was not, since Republican strength was likely to be an essential element in any worthwhile fusion against Tammany. Where the Republican party was not present by name, it has been credited with the vote of the Anti-Tammany fusions.

Miscellaneous Apparent Fusion Tickets

Still other tickets have appeared under variant names that suggest fusions operating as a substitute for a missing major party. Cases where the vote for such candidates has been credited to a major party include, for example, the Coalition party of North Carolina in 1872 (967), treated as Democratic.

Data Reflecting Party Splits

Every split in a major party that produces alternative candidates for the same office or offices is reflected in some splitting of the vote that might otherwise be attributed to the party. Generally, as in the classic Republican presidential case of 1912, some group of regulars retains control of the party apparatus, a regular nomination is recognized as such, and the departing faction, as in the case of the Progressives of 1912, adopts an alternative third-party designation under which to run its candidates. Frequently these third-party designations differ somewhat from state to state, but they are easily recognized as third parties and have ordinarily been treated as such, and there is no apparent reason why they should not be so treated in standard reporting.

Several other cases similar to the Progressives of 1912 are well known and readily identified. They include the Gold Democrats of 1896, the Progressives of 1924, and the States Rights Democrats who supported Thurmond and Wright in 1948. They also include the Wallace movement of 1968 and its various ballot labels if it is considered the result of a split in the Democratic party. Alternatively, the Wallace movement can be considered an indigenous protest drawing voters from both of the major parties. Either theory is tenable for some states, but in either case the Wallace candidacy clearly produced third-party voting and must be treated accordingly.

The party splits that have created real difficulties for the data analyst are for the most party historically less significant and also more local than cases of the kind just noted. At least two kinds of case, found in the data with some frequency, can be distinguished.

Coordinate Factions of a Dominant Party (Rule 6)

Coordinate factionalism within a dominant party occurs when both factions arising from a split maintain serious claims to party regularity, both use the regular party name or some variation of it, both poll substantial fractions of the total vote, and the situation generally is so ambiguous that an outside observer can consider the claims of one faction about as good as those of the other. Such ambiguity was especially prevalent when both factions could print their own ballots, as often occurred during the nineteenth century, with each claiming the regular party designation or some distinguishing variation as they saw fit.

In all such cases of coordinate factionalism within a dominant party, there is much to be said for the retrospective recognition of the claims of whichever faction polled the larger vote—especially if it won the election, since victory frequently was followed by control of the party machinery and by the demise of the other faction in subsequent elections.

The converse of according recognition as the party to the faction that polled the larger vote is the denial of such recognition of the faction or factions that polled the lesser vote. Uusually this means putting the lesser vote into the "other" column, although in rare instances there may be a case for crediting the minority major party with the vote instead if it is not otherwise present. Some examples of cases that meet many of these specifications, all from the data files of the ICPR, along with examples of what has been done to solve the problems of data adjustment for present purposes, are as follows.

Arkansas, 1872, representative at large. Under the Republican Reconstruction government in power at the time, the contest was between a Minstrel Republican (coded as 1390) and a Brindle Tail Republican (coded as 1391). The latter won by a close margin and was seated in Congress as a Republican. Solution: Credit the winner's vote to the Republican party, and credit the loser's vote to the Democratic party, in view of the extent of the coincidence between the vote for the Minstrel Republican and the vote for a Liberal Republican in the gubernatorial race.

West Virginia, 1872, Second C.D. (Congressional District). The seven candidates included three Republicans (200) and one Democrat; one of the Republicans won with over 80 per cent of the vote. Solution: Credit the winner's vote to the Republican party, treat the vote for all losers except the Democrat as "other" party votes.

Tennessee, 1896, Sixth C.D. The contest was between a Gold Democrat (508) and a Democrat (Silver) (510), who was presumably aligned with the silver platform of the national party in 1896 and who won. Solution: Credit the winner's vote to the Democratic party, treat the loser's vote as "other" party vote.

Delaware, 1896, representative at large. The contest involved five candidates, including a Democrat (100) who won, and both a Higgins Republican (1168) and an Addicks Republican (1169), of whom the latter polled the larger vote. Solution: Credit the vote for the Addicks Republican to the Republican party, treat the vote for the Higgins Republican as part of the "other" vote.

Massachusetts, 1902, Ninth C.D. The four candidates included a Democratic Citizens (1203), who won and was seated in Congress as a Democrat; a Democratic National (1215); a Republican (200); and a Socialist (380). Solution: Credit the vote of the winner to the Democratic party and the vote of the losers, except the Republican, to "other" parties.

Wisconsin, 1930, Seventh C.D. The vote reportedly was divided between two Republicans (200) and a Prohibitionist (361). Solution: Credit the winner's vote to the Republican party and the remainder to "other" parties.

Coordinate Factions of a Minority Major Party (Rule 7)

Splits within a minority major party that has little or no chance to win locally take on a different character from those just reviewed. Frequently these have been contests that were intended primarily to maintain a basis for recognition by national party authorities in connection with seating at the national party conventions and the control of federal patronage in the event of national victory. Factions divided on this basis have usually supported the same presidential nominee after the outcome was known, and have seldom devoted much campaign effort to candidates for other offices even when they made such nominations. Where they do appear separately in the election returns either for president or for other offices, it would seem that their voting totals might as well be combined to reflect the available voting strength of the minority major party at the time. When such a party begins to approach the possibility of victory, the factions tend to consolidate behind single candidacies; but as long as victory in local elections is remote, there is little incentive to do so. Some examples of the cases and solutions follow.

Tennessee, 1880, governor. The candidates included a Republican (200), who won, and both a Straight Credit Democrat (1117) and a Low Tax Democrat (1118). Solution: Credit the Democratic party with the total of the votes for the two variant Democratic candidates for Governor.

Kansas, 1894, governor. The candidates included a Republican (200), who won, and both a Democratic-People's (1013) and a Stalwart Democratic (1167) candidate. Solution: Combine the votes of the two variant Democrats and credit the Democratic party.

South Carolina, 1896, president and other offices. The Democratic party was dominant and carried the state for its candidates. Both the Lily White (1121) and the Black and Tan (1179) Republicans ran slates supporting McKinley, with candidates for governor and other offices. Solution: Combine the votes for the two Republican factions as the total vote for the party in all cases.

Mississippi, 1932, 1936, 1944, president and other offices. The Democratic party was dominant and carried the state for its candidates. Both the Lily White (1121) and the Black and Tan (1179) Republicans ran slates of electors for the same presidential candidates along with alternative candidates for various other offices. Solution: Combine the votes for the two factions and credit the total to the Republican party.

South Carolina, 1936, president. The Democratic party was dominant. Two Republican factions, Republican-Farm Labor (1191) and Tolbert Republican (1192), ran slates for Alfred M. Landon. Solution: Combine the votes and credit the Republican party.

Data Reflecting Variant Nomenclature (Rule 8)

Examples of variant party nomenclature have already been liberally provided. What is considered here, however, is a situation in which there is mainly a desire to escape adverse consequences from the use of the regular party name—or alternatively a desire to use a name with greater local appeal.

During the Reconstruction period, examples occurred in Virginia, North Carolina, and perhaps elsewhere in the South, where the Republican party was sometimes on the ballot as the Radical party (404)—the party of the Radical Republicans in Congress—and the Democratic party appeared conversely as the Conservative party (112). Other euphemisms were used for the Democratic party in the South during Republican control under Reconstruction, and in the North for a considerable period for opposite reasons, as in the northern cases already noted where the Liberal Republicans were on the ballot and the Democrats were not. Other such cases included the Reform party (575) that replaced the Democrats in Wisconsin in 1874 and the Anti-Monopoly party (955) that replaced the Democrats in Iowa in the same year.

Later, when Reconstruction was over and the Republican party was struggling to survive in the South, some shifts in name occurred that were apparently attempts to arrive at an acceptable name for the opposition party in southern states that were solidifying in the direction of a one-party Democratic alignment. The North Carolina Liberals (402) of 1882 seems to be such a case.

In all of these cases where the drift of the party vote was relatively consistent and it was mainly the nomenclature that was changing, the changes in designations on the ballot have been disregarded and votes attributed to the major parties in accordance with the apparent line of descent in voter attachments. Frequently the essential clues are provided by the seating results in the House of Representatives, where products of variant nomenclature were nonetheless usually seated as Republicans or Democrats.

One of the clearest of these cases occurred in Michigan during the elections of 1896 and 1898, where the Democratic party (100) became the Democratic Party of the United States (521) in most congressional districts. In New York City, in the 1880s and 1890s, the strength of the Tammany Hall organization was such that it frequently printed its ballots as those of the "Tammany Democratic Party" (115), or simply "Tammany" (1081). Since the affiliation of Tammany with state and national Democrats was seldom in doubt, despite a long history of factional infighting, any designation that reflected the main Tammany effort has been treated as Democratic. In New York State from 1906 to 1912, candidates appeared in several congressional districts under the label of the Veteran Victory party (828), with the Democratic party unrepresented as such. The Veteran Victory candidates who won were seated in Congress as Democrats; the entire vote for that label has accordingly been treated as Democratic.

California produced two odd cases in 1938. The Democratic party was not successful in nominating a candidate for Senator under the prevailing system of cross-filing, whereupon a Labor-Gumption-Justice (1109) candidate (Sheridan Downey) secured a place on the ballot, won the election, and was seated in the Senate as a Democrat. In the 4th congressional district, where again there was no Democratic candidate, a Light Wines & Beer (549) candidate was elected and seated as a Democrat. In both cases the vote has been attributed to the Democratic party. Other similar cases undoubtedly exist in the California data, but since such candidates usually lost, there was usually no official determination on seating to guide a decision on classification.

In Alabama in 1964, the presidential contest took place between Unpledged Democratic electors, coded 1397 by ICPR, and the Republican ticket, which won. Despite the irregularities, the vote for the Unpledged Democrats has been credited to the Democratic party.

"Independent" Candidates (Rule 9)

Candidates have occasionally appeared on ballots as "Independent Democrat" or "Independent Republican," in some cases with regular candidates of the same party also on the ballot, in others not. In such cases, where the regular party was missing, the vote for an Independent Democrat or Independent Republican has been counted for present purposes as the regular party vote, since in effect the voters of the party had nowhere else to go as the result of the failure of regular procedures to produce a nominee.

Votes for independent candidates running in opposition to the regular candidate of the same party are naturally counted as "other." This is also the case for candidates running on a plain Independent (328) label, although they have often been a substitute for a regular party nominee in situations where the party organization was unable to nominate. In most states in recent decades, with public administration of ballot printing and voting machines, independent candidates have not been permitted to indicate a party affiliation and the plain Independent label (328) has been all that was available.

Cross-Filing and Dual Nominations

Cross-filing occurs when the same candidate seeks the nomination of two political parties for the same office; dual nomination occurs when a candidate is successful in securing both nominations. Dual nominations were rare as long as nominations were made by party caucuses, committees, or conventions, except where the nomination reflected a definite act of fusion. When nominations by direct primary were provided by law, as occurred in most states early in the present century, it was usually provided that a candidate could seek and accept only the nomination of his own political party. Exceptions have occurred in only a few states, of which California and New York have been much the most important.

California Dual Nominations (Rule 10)

From 1913 to 1959, California permitted candidates for governor, senator, representative, and various other offices to file for the nominations of more than one political party, including the possibility of filing for the nominations of both major parties. During most of this period, the party affiliations of the candidates running in the primaries were omitted from the ballots. Voters could vote only in the primary of the party in which they were registered. Candidates in the primaries were required to have a party affiliation by registration, and were not permitted to run in the primary of another party unless running in their own. Furthermore, a victory in the primary of the other party did not count unless the candidate won the primary in his own party. If he did win both primaries, however, with the votes counted separately, he then was placed on the general election ballot as the candidate of both parties. A Republican winning both primaries was designated as a "Republican-Democrat," while a Democrat winning both primaries was designated as a "Democrat-Republican."

Under this system, cross-filing by leading candidates was common for most of the offices for which it was available. Dual nominations, in turn, were a frequent but far from invariable result. They were relatively uncommon in the contests for governor and senator, where the partisan affiliations of the candidates were likely to be well known and influential, but Governor Earl Warren won both major party nominations in two of his three successful races for Governor of California. Successful cross-filing resulting in dual nominations was much more common in congressional elections, where the system was especially beneficial to incumbent representatives. The results are apparent in the historical data collected by ICPR and present one of the major sets of problematical data for present purposes. Following its usual practice for candidates with variant designations, ICPR refrains from crediting the votes to either major party in the case of the California Democrat-Republicans and Republican-Democrats.

The solution that has been adopted for dealing with these data proceeds on the assumption that the party that has lost out in a dual nomination has no candidate, and accordingly credits all of the vote for a dual nominee to the party with which he is affiliated. This means that all votes for Democratic-Republicans (13) are counted as votes for the Democratic party, and all votes for Republican-Democrats (749) are counted as votes for the Republican party, except as noted in the earlier discussion of California in connection with variant nomenclature.

The results are not fully satisfactory as indicators of party strength either for particular elections or in combined index numbers, but are clearly more realistic than any results obtained by consigning the entire vote for the dual nominees to the "other" column. In general, there was a considerable amount of offsetting by which the 100 percent Republican votes in some congressional elections were offset by 100 percent Democratic votes in other congressional elections in the same year. In 1946, for example, in the twenty-three congressional districts then existing in the state, the two major parties were separately represented by nominees of their own in thirteen districts, by Democratic-Republicans only in six districts, and by Republican-Democrats only in four. In 1948, both were represented separately in eleven districts, with Democratic-Republicans only in three and Republican-Democrats only in nine. The system as a whole undoubtedly gave the Republican party some advantage during most of the period in which it was in effect, although Democrats who were incumbent or otherwise well known were also assisted.

The statistical solution that has been followed does no more violence to reality than the statistical results of the many elections in one-party congressional districts in other states where the minority major party has refrained from fielding a candidate although it probably could have polled from 10 to 30 percent of the vote with a respectable candidate. The statistical results of all such elections inevitably tend to make a dominant party seem more monolithic than it actually is.

New York Dual Nominations (Rule 11)

Traditionally the major political parties have been rather evenly balanced in New York state politics, and have been effectively competitive over longer periods of time than in most other states. The most unusual aspect of New York politics, however, has been the continuing effectiveness of third parties that have maintained a separate existence while working closely with one major political party or the other, or both. This process has been facilitated in recent decades by election law provisions that are unusual if not unique, under which, when a minor party endorses a candidate of one of the major parties instead of running a candidate of its own, it is still given a separate position on the ballot or on the voting machine. Such an endorsement amounts to a dual nomination; both parties are on the ballot for the office, but with the same candidate, and the voter can vote for either party label while voting for the same candidate.

The American Labor Party (522), formed in 1936 with trade union sponsorship, participated actively in the reelection of President Franklin D. Roosevelt in 1936, 1940, and 1944, providing his margin of victory within the state in the latter two years. In 1944, a split in the ALP brought on the formation of the Liberal Party (402) of New York, which also supported Roosevelt and provided votes equivalent to his margin of victory in the state that year. In 1948, the Liberal Party endorsed the nomination of President Harry S. Truman, while the American Labor Party endorsed that of Henry A. Wallace. In 1952, the Liberal Party endorsed Adlai Stevenson for President, but ran its own candidate for Senator, bringing on the defeat of the Democratic senatorial candidate. Since 1952, the record has continued to be mixed, with the Liberal Party growing weaker as insurgent movements of the left developed inside the Democratic party. It is nonetheless still a factor; in 1970, for example, it joined the Democratic party in nominating Arthur J. Goldberg for Governor. Meanwhile, the Conservative Party (112) of New York has been formed, mainly as a vehicle for outraged conservatives of previous Republican affiliation, and has recently shown strength, especially in statewide elections for governor and senator.

The basic ambiguity of this situation seems to reside in the fact that New York state third parties have been allowed to enter into temporary fusions on a one-time, one-office basis while still retaining their own separate identity for balloting and election law purposes. For some years, the Liberal Party divided its favors, endorsing Democratic nominees for some offices, Republican nominees for others, and running candidates of its own in still other cases. Yet it generally supported the Democratic party in national politics, and from an out-of-state point of view was essentially a part of the Democratic party in national affairs.

For present purposes, there seems no single way of handling the New York state data which can be regarded unqualifiedly as most appropriate. The New York third parties have had a definite and continuing separate identity even when they joined in nominating major party candidates. Hence it seems necessary to present the New York statistics in a double format that is not required for any other state: one presentation in which the major parties are credited with all of the votes cast for their candidates for the offices under study, and a second presentation in which the minor party contribution to the vote of any major party nominee is included, with its other votes, in the "other" party column. In national and other multistate indexes of party strength, the data contained in the first or candidate presentation are used; the second presentation may be useful in special studies of New York state politics.

Other Dual Nominations

The ICPR data for Massachusetts provide scattered instances from 1926 to 1964 in which the candidates in individual congressional district races are identified as

Democratic-Republican (13) nominees, with no opposition from either of the major parties. All of these candidates were elected, were thereupon seated in Congress as Democrats, and have been so treated for present purposes. No cases of major party dual nominations have been found in other states in the data under study for the period since 1872.

Recognized Third Parties

Well-known third parties recur in the data, not only in presidential elections but also in the statewide and congressional district elections. The vote for any candidate running on such labels as those following has been placed in the "other" column for present purposes:

Greenback (320)	Socialist Labor (505)
Populist (340)	Progressive (370)
Prohibition (361)	Industrial Labor (881)
National Prohibition (531)	Union (553)
Socialist (380)	American Independent Party (1404)
Communist (543)	Freedom and Peace (1411)

The Critical Differences for Classifying Purposes

The cases reviewed throughout this appendix indicate that if the major parties are credited only with the part of the vote that they receive as coded by ICPR, their voting strength will be overstated in a few instances but understated in most of the cases studied. On the other hand, a third party that represents a revolt from one of the major parties or some general dissatisfaction with the system deserves full recognition as such. No third party can be formed except by attracting voters away from the major parties or by pulling them out of the mass of nonvoters and new voters. In any effort to achieve a full statement of the vote that can appropriately be credited to one major party or the other, it is equally important to avoid any impairment of the "other" vote that is appropriately credited to third parties and independent candidates. Accordingly, the practice throughout has been conservative in adjusting the data as found by ICPR. The precedents created by the work of other scholars who have dealt with similar problems in handling presidential data have generally been followed, and frequently have been extended to similar cases in the data for other elections.

Throughout, the implicit test could be phrased as follows: Faced with the candidates and party labels available to him, what would a regular party voter of each major party do if he were trying to be as regular as the situation permitted? If the labeling is regular and contesting candidates are available for both major parties, there is no need to go behind the data as reported by ICPR. When one or the other major party is missing, however, or is present only under a variant label that has been given a variant coding, then the situation must be examined.

Surrounding circumstances—contextual elements—that have been examined for clues involve many different types of data. Perhaps most important is the presence or absence of national party splits and third party movements of some strength, and their known regional variations. The presidential voting aspects of these movements have been much dwelt upon by party historians; generally there was some spillover, restricted by candidate availability, into state and local elections for governor, senator, and representative. Some consistency in handling the presidential and other votes in similar circumstances seems obviously desirable.

Seating at a national party convention is one sign of the legitimacy of a state party as a federated unit of the national party. This is obviously relevant to such cases as that of the Democratic-Farmer-Labor party in Minnesota, which has been given national party recognition as the Democratic party of that state since its consolidation in 1944.

Actions by state government authorities in according or withholding party recognition are relevant but must always be used with caution when they have occurred in a controversial situation—which is when they are most likely to be of interest. In the long history of seating contests at national party conventions, the prejudicial character of much action by state government officials in recognizing one party faction rather than another has been repeatedly documented. (David, Goldman, and Bain 1960, pp. 258–67.)

More useful is the record of party designations in seating the winners in the House of Representatives and (after 1913) the Senate, and the corresponding data on the announced party affiliations of governors on taking office. When the winner under a deviant designation maintains it even after he has won, his third-party character and that of the voters who were with him seems evident. Conversely, the seating of the winner as a major party affiliate is a retrospective clarification that deserves weight in determining the identity of the voters who supported him—if that identity is otherwise unclear.

One way to establish the antecedents of any political party is to trace back through previous elections the bodies of voters who supported it after its identity was fully recognized. Where continuities can be found, the question then arises of when the eventual party left the inchoate mass of prehistory and achieved a continuing identity, although perhaps under a name or various names later changed and consolidated. This question has been studied for all of the major national political parties that have so far existed in the United States, with somewhat varying answers by different scholars. Presumably full answers would require detailed study, at the state and local level, of a kind beyond possibility in the present effort; and that is one reason why this effort has been limited to the period since 1872. Both of the existing major parties had been formed before 1872, and in most states their identity was not subject to much doubt after the post-Civil War period of readjustment had been completed.

The work reported here is based almost entirely on the examination of summary data at the statewide and congressional district level, with collateral information from the standard sources used by most students of party history. No attempt has been made to trace the continuities of party history by detailed study of county level election data for any individual state; and not much use has been made of the specialized literature for individual states except in the cases of New York and California, where the work is certainly much less than complete.

77

It can be hoped that further research will be undertaken by other scholars as they become familiar with the problems and reach conclusions on their significance. As in most work with time series when they are first created, it is necessary to work initially with provisional solutions. If the series themselves prove valuable, the probability is that they will eventually become the subject of a considerable amount of perfecting labor; but first their usefulness must be assured. In the present case, much of the perfecting labor may have to come from scholars who have access to local data sources and who can find their incentives and their motivation in the local need to know more of each state's own history.

Bibliographical Note and References

THE consolidated listing in this appendix includes all authors and works referred to in the present volume, arranged alphabetically by author and chronologically under each author, with appropriate bibliographical detail. Where page numbers are needed to identify specific passages cited, they have been included in the text along with the references to the authors.

Works by other scholars that are most relevant to this enterprise as a whole were briefly noted in chapter 1 and to some extent elsewhere. The articles by Pfeiffer (1967) and by Fenton and Chamberlayne (1969) are especially useful for their bibliographical content. Only a few works have been cited in connection with methodological questions; the statistical concepts underlying this volume are for the most part quite simple and are adequately explained in any standard textbook on statistics, as for example in the paperback by Boris Parl, 1967.

Bailey, S. K. *Congress in the Seventies.* New York: St. Martin's Press, 1970.

Bain, Richard C. *Convention Decisions and Voting Records.* Washington, D.C.: The Brookings Institution, 1960.

Binkley, Wilfred E. *American Political Parties.* 3d ed. New York: A. A. Knopf, 1958.

Burnham, Walter Dean. *Presidential Ballots 1836–1892.* Baltimore: The Johns Hopkins Press, 1955.

————. *Critical Elections and the Mainsprings of American Politics.* New York: W. W. Norton & Co., 1970.

Campbell, Angus, P. E. Converse, W. E. Miller, and D. E. Stokes. *The American Voter.* New York: John Wiley and Sons, 1960.

————. *Elections and the Political Order.* New York: John Wiley and Sons, 1966.

Chambers, W. N., and Walter Dean Burnham, eds. *The American Party Systems: Stages of Political Development.* New York: Oxford University Press, 1967.

Converse, P. E. "On the Possibility of Major Political Realignment in the South." In Angus Campbell et al., *Elections and the Political Order.*

Cox, Edward F. "The Measurement of Party Strength." *Western Political Quarterly,* 13 (1960): 1022–42.

————. *Voting in Postwar Federal Elections: A Statistical Analysis of Party Strengths since 1945.* Dayton, Ohio: University Publications, Wright State University, 1968.

David, Paul T. "Comparative State Politics and the Problem of Party Realignment." In S. K. Bailey et al., *Research Frontiers in Politics and Government.* Washington, D.C.: The Brookings Institution, 1955.

———. "The Changing Political Parties." in Marian Irish, ed., *Continuing Crisis in American Politics*. Englewood Cliffs, N.J.: Prentice-Hall, 1963.

———. "Index Numbers of Party Strength in the American Electorate: National, State, and Local." Annual meeting paper, 1969, American Political Science Association. Published for the Association by University Microfilms, Ann Arbor, Michigan. Supplemented by P. T. David. *Charts of Index Numbers of Party Strength*. Charlottesville, Va.: Woodrow Wilson Department of Government and Foreign Affairs, University of Virginia, 1969. Xeroxed.

———. "Party Platforms as National Plans." *Public Administration Review*, 31 (May/June 1971): 303–15.

———. "How Can an Index of Party Competition Best Be Derived?" *Journal of Politics*, 1972, forthcoming.

David, Paul T., et al. *The Presidential Election and Transition 1960–1961*. Washington, D.C.: The Brookings Institution, 1961.

David, Paul T., R. M. Goldman, and R. C. Bain, *The Politics of National Party Conventions*. Washington, D.C.: The Brookings Institution, 1960.

David, Paul T., Malcolm Moos, and R. M. Goldman, *Presidential Nominating Politics in 1952*. 5 vols. Baltimore: The Johns Hopkins Press, 1954.

Dawson, Richard E., and James A. Robinson. "Inter-Party Competition, Economic Variables, and Welfare Policies in the American States." *Journal of Politics*, 25 (1963) 265–289.

Dye, Thomas R. *Politics, Economics, and the Public*. Chicago: Rand, McNally & Co., 1966.

Fenton, J. H., and D. W. Chamberlayne. "The Literature Dealing with the Relationships between Political Processes, Socioeconomic Conditions and Public Policies in the American States: A Bibliographical Essay." *Polity*, 1 (1968/69) 388–404.

Fisher, Irving. *The Making of Index Numbers*. New York: Houghton, Mifflin Co., 1923.

Flanigan, W. H., and N. H. Zingale. "Measurement of Electoral Stability and Change, 1832 to 1968." Annual meeting paper, 1971, American Political Science Association.

Gatlin, Douglas S. "Toward a Functionalist Theory of Political Parties: Inter-Party Competition in North Carolina." In W. J. Crotty, ed., *Approaches to the Study of Party Organization*. Boston: Allyn & Bacon, 1968.

Golembiewski, Robert T. "A Taxonomic Approach to State Political Party Strength." *Western Political Quarterly*, 11 (1958), 494–513.

Hofferbert, Richard I. "Classification of American State Party Systems." *Journal of Politics*, 26 (1964), 550–67.

Key, V. O., Jr. *Southern Politics*. New York: Alfred A. Knopf, 1949.

———. "A Theory of Critical Elections." *Journal of Politics*, 17 (1955): 3–18.

———. *American State Politics*. New York: Alfred A. Knopf, 1956.

———. *Politics, Parties, and Pressure Groups*. 5th ed. New York: Thomas Y. Crowell, 1964.

Ladd, E. C., Jr. *American Political Parties*. New York: W. W. Norton, 1970.

Lubell, Samuel. *The Future of American Politics*. New York: Harper, 1952.

———. *The Hidden Crisis in American Politics*. New York: W. W. Norton & Co., 1970.

Mitchell, Wesley C. *Index Numbers of Wholesale Prices in the United States and Foreign Countries*. Bulletin No. 284, U.S. Bureau of Labor Statistics. Washington, D.C.: Government Printing Office, 1921.

References

Mudgett, B. D. *Index Numbers*. New York: John Wiley & Sons, 1951.

Parl, Boris. *Basic Statistics*. Garden City, N.Y.: Doubleday & Co., 1967.

Pfeiffer, David G. "The Measurement of Inter-Party Competition and Systemic Stability." *American Political Science Review,* 61 (1967): 457-67.

Phillips, Kevin B. *The Emerging Republican Majority*. Garden City, N.Y.: Doubleday & Co., 1970.

Pomper, G. M. *Elections in America*. New York: Dodd, Mead & Co., 1968.

Ranney, Austin. "Parties in State Politics." In H. Jacobs and K. N. Vines, eds., *Politics in the American States*. Boston: Little, Brown, & Co., 1965.

Ranney, Austin, and Willmoore Kendall. "The American Party System." *American Political Science Review*, 48 (1954): 477-85. Also in revised form in chapter 7 of *Democracy and the American Party System*, by the same authors. New York: Harcourt, Brace & Co., 1956.

Robinson, Edgar E. *The Presidential Vote 1896-1932*. Stanford, Calif.: Stanford University Press, 1935.

Scammon, Richard M., and B. J. Wattenberg. *The Real Majority*. New York: Coward-McCann, 1970.

Scammon, Richard M., ed. *America Votes*. Published biennially since 1956. New York: Macmillan, Vols. 1, 2; Pittsburgh, University of Pittsburgh Press, Vols. 3-6; Washington, D.C., Governmental Affairs Institute, Vols. 7, 8.

Schattschneider, E. E. *The Semi-Sovereign People*. New York: Holt, Rinehart and Winston, 1960.

Schlesinger, Joseph A. "A Two-Dimensional Scheme for Classifying the States According to Degree of Inter-Party Competition." *American Political Science Review*, 49 (1955): 1120-28.

Shapley, L.S., and Martin Shubik. "A Method for Evaluating the Distribution of Power in a Committee System." *American Political Science Review*, 48 (1954): 787-92.

Sharkansky, Ira. *Regionalism in American Politics*. Indianapolis: Bobbs-Merrill, 1970.

Sorauf, F. J. *Party Politics in America*. Boston: Little, Brown, and Co., 1968.

Stokes, D. E. and G. R. Iversen. "On the Existence of Forces Restoring Party Competition." In A. Campbell et al., *Elections and the Political Order*. Reprinted from *Public Opinion Quarterly*, 26 (1962).

Sundquist, J. L. *Politics and Policy*. Washington, D.C.: The Brookings Institution, 1968.

Turner, Julius and E. V. Schneier, Jr. *Party and Constituency: Pressures on Congress*. Rev. ed. Baltimore: The Johns Hopkins Press, 1970.

Wilson, J. Q. *The Amateur Democrat*. Chicago: University of Chicago Press, 1962.

PART II

Basic Data and State Diagrams

Introductory Note

THE material that follows is arranged so far as possible according to a standard. pattern. Data for individual states are given first, with the states in alphabetical order and with four pages for each state.[1] The first of these pages reports the percentages of the actual vote won by Democratic, Republican, and other candidates and parties in the election years for president, governor, and, beginning in 1914, the two Senate seats allocated to each state. Popular elections for the Class I Senate seats were first held on a nationwide basis in 1916, for Class II in 1918, and for Class III in 1914. Governors have usually been elected in the even-numbered years for terms of either two or four years, as shown, but where governors have been elected in odd-numbered years for a term of four years, as in New Jersey and Virginia in recent decades, the results have been carried forward into the next even-numbered year. Similar adjustments were made in the cases, mainly in the nineteenth century, of governors on three year terms when the election fell in an odd-numbered year.

The second page for each state presents the data for each office in biennial form. For the offices of president, governor, and senator, this involves the processes of averaging and interpolation that are explained in chapter 2. For the regular elections for the House of Representatives, which have always occurred biennially, the raw vote totals have been cumulated for the several districts on a statewide basis, and the percentage figures that appear on the second page for each state have been computed from the statewide voting totals. In the rather unusual instances when a state has elected at large in a single year more than one representative in Congress, the results have been averaged. In other occasional instances where most of the elections have occurred in districts but one or two seats have been filled by elections at large, the results have been figured into the statewide averages on a basis that gives the elections at large no more than their proportionate weight in the state's outcome as a whole. Election data resulting from special elections to fill vacancies in the House have been disregarded.

Some special computation problems arose in the case of Arkansas, which in recent decades has often omitted uncontested candidates from the general election ballot. In these cases, it is not possible to add the popular vote figures on a statewide basis that includes all congressional districts. The percentage figures for the districts were therefore averaged to obtain the statewide percentages, crediting the

---

[1]The data for Alaska and Hawaii fill only two pages.

party of each uncontested winner with 100 percent of the vote for the district concerned. In similar cases where no popular vote was reported for a winning, uncontested candidate for the Senate, his party was put into the tables with 100 percent of the vote in order to complete the series.

The third page for each state presents the data for the three composite index numbers, as explained in chapter 2: Composite A, an average of the biennial data for all four offices; Composite B, an average for the three offices other than president; and Composite C, an average of the data for Senate and House elections. For the years prior to 1914, the Composite C data are the same as the House data, the Composite B data reflect averages of the data for governors and representatives only, and the Composite A averages similarly omit any Senate election data.

The fourth page for each state presents diagrams, one Democratic and one Republican, for the Composite B averages and for the percentage data for presidential elections, permitting ready visual comparison of the two series for each party. All of these diagrams were produced by a computer plotter from the data previously noted. Frequently the Democratic and Republican diagrams are mirror images of each other in whole or in part. They differ primarily because of the varying impact of the voting for third-party and independent candidates, which usually affects one major party much more than the other. Since the Composite B data for the "other" vote have not been plotted for the individual states, readers studying the diagrams with care should take special note of the figures for the "other" vote under Composite B on the facing page.

Special handling of the 1970 data has been necessary wherever further elections must be awaited before a biennial figure for 1970 can be calculated by interpolation. This applies throughout on the biennial data for the presidential series, for states with four-year governors who were not up for election in 1970, and for the approximately one-third of the states in which there was no Senate election in 1970. The Composite A series is omitted completely for 1970, and the other composites have been calculated on a preliminary basis from incomplete data in some instances, as will be apparent. Composite B is omitted when there were no data for governor in 1970.

The data for California presented special problems for the period when cross-filing was permissible; see Rule 10 and the related portion of the text in the Appendix.

The data for New York are presented in a dual form, the first of which, identified as "Candidate," cumulates all of the votes for major party candidates, including minor-party voting for major-party candidates; the second, identified as "Party," credits the major parties only with votes cast under their own labels, and puts third-party voting for major party candidates in the "other" column. See Rule 11 and the related portion of the text in the Appendix. In all presentations in this volume involving multistate averages where New York is included, the "Candidate" set of data has been used.

Following the data for individual states, the next section of Part II presents data for each of four regions in the following order: Northeast, Middle West, South, West. For each region, the first page of data reports the biennial series for each of the four offices, paralleling the similar data for each state and computed from those data by use of weights for each state equal to its number of seats in the House of

Representatives; see chapter 4 for the area definition of each region, and table 4.1 for seats in the House. The second page of data for each region presents Composites A, B, and C. Related graphic material for the several regions can be found in chapter 4.

Next after the regional data is a set of statistical data for three groups of states that are defined in the third section of chapter 4 and discussed further in chapter 5: (1) states that were predominantly Republican between 1896 and 1930, (2) states that were predominantly Democratic during the same period, and (3) states that were competitive during the period. For each of these groups, the material includes one page of biennial averages for the four offices, again using the weights previously referred to, and one page of composite averages. The related major party diagrams can be found in chapter 5.

Finally, the biennial office data and the composites are presented for the nation as a whole at the end of Part II; the related major party diagrams can be found in chapter 6.

ALABAMA

YEAR	PRESIDENT			GOVERNOR			SENATE CLASS II			SENATE CLASS III		
	DEM.	REP.	OTHER	DEM.	REP.	OTHER	DEM.	REP.	OTHER	DEM.	REP.	OTHER
1872	46.8	53.2	0.0	47.5	52.5	0.0						
1874				53.3	46.7	0.0						
1876	60.0	40.0	0.0	63.4	36.6	0.0						
1878				100.0	0.0	0.0						
1880	60.0	37.1	2.9	76.1	0.0	23.9						
1882				68.7	31.3	0.0						
1884	60.4	38.7	0.9	99.7	0.0	0.3						
1886				79.4	20.1	0.4						
1888	67.0	32.7	0.3	77.6	22.2	0.2						
1890				76.1	23.1	0.8						
1892	59.4	3.9	36.6	52.2	0.0	47.8						
1894				57.1	0.0	42.9						
1896	54.2	28.6	17.2	59.0	0.0	41.0						
1898				67.0	0.0	33.0						
1900	60.8	34.8	4.4	71.0	17.4	11.6						
1902				73.7	26.3	0.0						
1904	73.4	20.7	6.0									
1906				85.5	13.9	0.6						
1908	70.7	24.3	4.9									
1910				78.7	19.4	1.9						
1912	69.9	8.3	21.8							90.3	6.7	3.0
1914				78.7	15.1	6.2						
1916	76.0	22.0	2.0									
1918				80.2	0.0	19.8	100.0	0.0	0.0			
1920	66.7	31.9	1.4				71.4	27.4	1.2	68.0	31.2	0.9
1922				77.6	21.3	1.2						
1924	69.7	25.0	5.3				75.2	24.8	0.0			
1926				81.2	18.8	0.0				80.9	19.1	0.0
1928	51.3	48.5	0.2									
1930				61.8	0.0	38.2	59.7	0.0	40.3			
1932	84.7	14.1	1.1							86.2	13.8	0.0
1934				86.9	12.7	0.4						
1936	86.4	12.8	0.8				87.0	12.2	0.7			
1938				87.4	12.5	0.2				86.4	13.6	0.0
1940	85.2	14.3	0.4				100.0	0.0	0.0			
1942				89.0	10.5	0.5						
1944	81.3	18.2	0.5				100.0	0.0	0.0	81.8	16.9	1.3
1946				88.7	11.3	0.0						
1948	44.4	10.6	45.0				84.0	16.0	0.0			
1950				91.1	8.9	0.0				76.5	0.0	23.5
1952	64.6	35.0	0.4				82.5	17.5	0.0			
1954				73.4	26.6	0.0						
1956	56.4	39.5	4.1							100.0	0.0	0.0
1958				88.4	11.2	0.3						
1960	56.8	42.1	1.1				70.2	29.8	0.0			
1962				96.3	0.0	3.7				50.9	49.1	0.0
1964	30.5	69.5	0.0				60.1	39.0	0.9			
1966				63.4	31.0	5.6						
1968	18.8	14.0	67.2							70.0	22.0	8.0
1970				74.5	0.0	25.5						

88

ALABAMA

YEAR	PRESIDENT			GOVERNOR			SENATE			HOUSE OF REPRESENTATIVES		
	DEM.	REP.	OTHER	DEM.	REP.	OTHER	DEM.	REP.	OTHER	DEM.	REP.	OTHER
1872	46.8	53.2	0.0	47.5	52.5	0.0				48.6	51.4	0.0
1874	53.4	46.6	0.0	53.3	46.7	0.0				52.1	47.9	0.0
1876	60.0	40.0	0.0	63.4	36.6	0.0				60.6	23.6	15.8
1878	60.0	38.6	1.5	100.0	0.0	0.0				62.0	7.4	30.6
1880	60.0	37.1	2.9	76.1	0.0	23.9				57.4	25.8	16.8
1882	60.2	37.9	1.9	68.7	31.3	0.0				63.6	20.0	16.5
1884	60.4	38.7	0.9	99.7	0.0	0.3				66.1	32.7	1.2
1886	63.7	35.7	0.6	79.4	20.1	0.4				71.8	25.3	3.0
1888	67.0	32.7	0.3	77.6	22.2	0.2				68.1	31.3	0.6
1890	63.2	18.3	18.5	76.1	23.1	0.8				69.4	6.2	24.4
1892	59.4	4.0	36.7	52.2	0.0	47.8				58.8	5.1	36.2
1894	56.8	16.3	26.9	57.1	0.0	42.9				57.5	12.1	30.4
1896	54.2	28.6	17.2	59.0	0.0	41.0				56.2	20.0	23.9
1898	57.5	31.7	10.8	67.0	0.0	33.0				73.0	24.9	2.1
1900	60.8	34.8	4.4	71.0	17.5	11.6				74.1	25.6	0.3
1902	67.1	27.7	5.2	73.7	26.3	0.0				74.4	25.6	0.0
1904	73.4	20.7	6.0	79.6	20.1	0.3				80.6	19.0	0.4
1906	72.1	22.5	5.5	85.5	13.9	0.6				90.9	9.1	0.0
1908	70.8	24.3	5.0	82.1	16.7	1.2				80.7	12.3	7.0
1910	70.3	16.3	13.4	78.7	19.5	1.9				84.5	15.4	0.1
1912	69.9	8.3	21.8	78.7	17.3	4.0				85.8	8.6	5.5
1914	72.9	15.1	11.9	78.7	15.1	6.2	90.3	6.7	3.0	81.2	14.9	3.8
1916	76.0	22.0	2.0	79.5	7.6	13.0	95.2	3.4	1.5	80.3	19.1	0.6
1918	71.4	27.0	1.7	80.2	0.0	19.8	100.0	0.0	0.0	85.8	14.2	0.0
1920	66.7	31.9	1.4	78.9	10.6	10.5	69.7	29.3	1.1	71.9	27.7	0.4
1922	68.2	28.5	3.3	77.6	21.3	1.2	72.4	27.1	0.5	81.1	0.0	18.9
1924	69.7	25.0	5.3	79.4	20.0	0.6	75.2	24.8	0.0	79.3	20.7	0.0
1926	60.5	36.8	2.7	81.2	18.8	0.0	80.9	19.1	0.0	84.4	15.6	0.0
1928	51.3	48.5	0.2	71.5	9.4	19.1	70.3	9.6	20.1	82.3	17.8	0.0
1930	68.0	31.3	0.7	61.8	0.0	38.2	59.7	0.0	40.3	83.4	10.1	6.5
1932	84.7	14.1	1.1	74.4	6.3	19.3	86.3	13.8	0.0	89.6	9.8	0.6
1934	85.6	13.5	1.0	86.9	12.7	0.4	86.6	13.0	0.4	90.4	6.2	3.4
1936	86.4	12.8	0.8	87.1	12.6	0.3	87.0	12.2	0.7	93.5	6.3	0.2
1938	85.8	13.6	0.6	87.4	12.5	0.2	86.4	13.6	0.0	92.2	7.7	0.0
1940	85.2	14.3	0.4	88.2	11.5	0.4	93.2	6.8	0.0	94.4	5.5	0.1
1942	83.3	16.3	0.5	89.0	10.5	0.5	100.0	0.0	0.0	99.4	0.6	0.0
1944	81.3	18.2	0.5	88.8	10.9	0.3	81.8	17.0	1.3	90.2	9.8	0.0
1946	62.9	14.4	22.8	88.7	11.3	0.0	100.0	0.0	0.0	92.1	7.9	0.0
1948	44.4	10.6	45.0	89.9	10.1	0.0	84.0	16.0	0.0	93.1	6.9	0.0
1950	54.5	22.8	22.7	91.1	8.9	0.0	76.5	0.0	23.5	99.4	0.6	0.0
1952	64.6	35.0	0.4	82.2	17.8	0.0	79.5	8.8	11.7	94.6	5.5	0.0
1954	60.5	37.3	2.3	73.4	26.6	0.0	82.5	17.5	0.0	96.0	4.0	0.0
1956	56.4	39.5	4.1	80.9	18.9	0.2	100.0	0.0	0.0	86.3	13.7	0.0
1958	56.6	40.8	2.6	88.4	11.2	0.3	85.1	14.9	0.0	97.5	2.6	0.0
1960	56.8	42.1	1.1	92.4	5.6	2.0	70.2	29.8	0.0	89.0	11.0	0.0
1962	43.7	55.8	0.5	96.3	0.0	3.7	50.9	49.1	0.0	83.3	15.5	1.2
1964	30.6	69.5	0.0	79.8	15.5	4.7	55.5	44.1	0.5	48.3	51.4	0.3
1966	24.7	41.7	33.6	63.4	31.0	5.6	60.1	39.0	0.9	60.9	39.1	0.0
1968	18.8	14.0	67.2	68.9	15.5	15.6	70.0	22.1	8.0	60.4	26.9	12.7
1970				74.5	0.0	25.5				64.0	25.5	10.5

YEAR	COMPOSITE A (P+G+S+H/4)			COMPOSITE B (G+S+H/3)			COMPOSITE C (S+H/2)		
	DEM.	REP.	OTHER	DEM.	REP.	OTHER	DEM.	REP.	OTHER
1872	47.7	52.4	0.0	48.1	51.9	0.0	48.6	51.4	0.0
1874	52.9	47.1	0.0	52.7	47.3	0.0	52.1	47.9	0.0
1876	61.3	33.4	5.3	62.0	30.1	7.9	60.6	23.6	15.8
1878	74.0	15.3	10.7	81.0	3.7	15.3	62.0	7.4	30.6
1880	64.5	21.0	14.5	66.7	12.9	20.3	57.4	25.8	16.8
1882	64.2	29.7	6.1	66.1	25.6	8.2	63.6	20.0	16.5
1884	75.4	23.8	0.8	82.9	16.4	0.7	66.1	32.7	1.2
1886	71.6	27.0	1.3	75.6	22.7	1.7	71.8	25.3	3.0
1888	70.9	28.7	0.4	72.9	26.8	0.4	68.1	31.3	0.6
1890	69.6	15.9	14.6	72.7	14.7	12.6	69.4	6.2	24.4
1892	56.8	3.0	40.2	55.5	2.5	42.0	58.8	5.1	36.2
1894	57.1	9.5	33.4	57.3	6.1	36.7	57.5	12.1	30.4
1896	56.4	16.2	27.4	57.6	10.0	32.4	56.2	20.0	23.9
1898	65.8	18.9	15.3	70.0	12.4	17.6	73.0	24.9	2.1
1900	68.6	26.0	5.4	72.5	21.5	5.9	74.1	25.6	0.3
1902	71.7	26.5	1.7	74.1	25.9	0.0	74.4	25.6	0.0
1904	77.8	19.9	2.2	80.1	19.6	0.4	80.6	19.0	0.4
1906	82.8	15.2	2.0	88.2	11.5	0.3	90.9	9.1	0.0
1908	77.9	17.8	4.4	81.4	14.5	4.1	80.7	12.3	7.0
1910	77.8	17.1	5.1	81.6	17.4	1.0	84.5	15.4	0.1
1912	78.1	11.4	10.5	82.3	13.0	4.8	85.8	8.6	5.5
1914	80.8	13.0	6.2	83.4	12.3	4.3	85.8	10.8	3.4
1916	82.7	13.0	4.3	85.0	10.0	5.0	87.7	11.2	1.1
1918	84.3	10.3	5.4	88.7	4.7	6.6	92.9	7.1	0.0
1920	71.8	24.9	3.3	73.5	22.5	4.0	70.8	28.5	0.7
1922	74.8	19.2	6.0	77.0	16.1	6.9	76.8	13.5	9.7
1924	75.9	22.6	1.5	78.0	21.9	0.2	77.2	22.8	0.0
1926	76.7	22.6	0.7	82.2	17.8	0.0	82.6	17.4	0.0
1928	68.9	21.3	9.9	74.7	12.2	13.1	76.3	13.7	10.1
1930	68.2	10.4	21.4	68.3	3.4	28.3	71.5	5.1	23.4
1932	83.7	11.0	5.3	83.4	10.0	6.6	87.9	11.8	0.3
1934	87.4	11.3	1.3	88.0	10.6	1.4	88.5	9.6	1.9
1936	88.5	11.0	0.5	89.2	10.4	0.4	90.3	9.3	0.5
1938	87.9	11.9	0.2	88.7	11.3	0.1	89.3	10.7	0.0
1940	90.2	9.5	0.2	91.9	7.9	0.2	93.8	6.2	0.1
1942	92.9	6.8	0.3	96.1	3.7	0.2	99.7	0.3	0.0
1944	85.5	14.0	0.5	86.9	12.6	0.5	86.0	13.4	0.6
1946	85.9	8.4	5.7	93.6	6.4	0.0	96.1	3.9	0.0
1948	77.9	10.9	11.3	89.0	11.0	0.0	88.6	11.4	0.0
1950	80.4	8.1	11.5	89.0	3.2	7.8	88.0	0.3	11.7
1952	80.2	16.8	3.0	85.4	10.7	3.9	87.0	7.1	5.9
1954	78.1	21.4	0.6	83.9	16.1	0.0	89.2	10.8	0.0
1956	80.9	18.0	1.1	89.1	10.9	0.1	93.2	6.9	0.0
1958	81.9	17.4	0.7	90.3	9.6	0.1	91.3	8.7	0.0
1960	77.1	22.1	0.8	83.9	15.5	0.7	79.6	20.4	0.0
1962	68.5	30.1	1.4	76.8	21.6	1.7	67.1	32.3	0.6
1964	53.5	45.1	1.4	61.2	37.0	1.8	51.9	47.7	0.4
1966	52.2	37.7	10.0	61.4	36.4	2.2	60.5	39.1	0.5
1968	54.5	19.6	25.9	66.4	21.5	12.1	65.2	24.5	10.3
1970				69.3	12.7	18.0	64.0	25.5	10.5

90

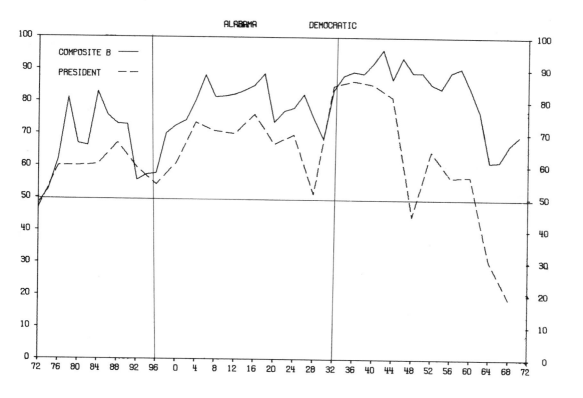

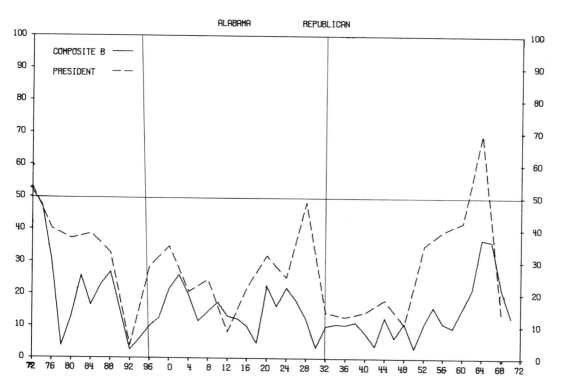

ALASKA

YEAR	PRESIDENT			GOVERNOR			SENATE CLASS II			SENATE CLASS III		
	DEM.	REP.	OTHER	DEM.	REP.	OTHER	DEM.	REP.	OTHER	DEM.	REP.	OTHER
1956												
1958				59.6	39.4	1.0	83.8	14.9	1.2	52.6	47.4	0.0
1960	49.1	50.9	0.0				63.4	36.6	0.0			
1962				52.3	47.7	0.0				58.1	41.9	0.0
1964	65.9	34.1	0.0									
1966				48.4	50.0	1.6	75.5	24.5	0.0			
1968	42.6	45.3	12.1							45.1	37.4	17.4
1970				52.4	46.1	1.5	40.4	59.6	0.0			

ALASKA

YEAR	PRESIDENT			GOVERNOR			SENATE			HOUSE OF REPRESENTATIVES		
	DEM.	REP.	OTHER	DEM.	REP.	OTHER	DEM.	REP.	OTHER	DEM.	REP.	OTHER
1956												
1958				59.6	39.4	1.0	68.1	31.3	0.6	57.5	42.6	0.0
1960	49.1	50.9	0.0	55.9	43.6	0.5	63.4	36.6	0.0	56.8	43.2	0.0
1962	57.5	42.5	0.0	52.3	47.7	0.0	58.1	41.9	0.0	54.5	45.5	0.0
1964	65.9	34.1	0.0	50.3	48.9	0.8	66.8	33.2	0.0	51.5	48.5	0.0
1966	54.3	39.7	6.0	48.4	50.0	1.6	75.5	24.5	0.0	48.4	51.7	0.0
1968	42.7	45.3	12.1	50.4	48.1	1.6	45.1	37.4	17.4	45.8	54.2	0.0
1970				52.4	46.1	1.5	40.4	59.6	0.0	55.1	44.9	0.0

ALASKA

YEAR	COMPOSITE A (P+G+S+H/4)			COMPOSITE B (G+S+H/3)			COMPOSITE C (S+H/2)		
	DEM.	REP.	OTHER	DEM.	REP.	OTHER	DEM.	REP.	OTHER
1956									
1958				61.7	37.8	0.5	62.8	36.9	0.3
1960	56.3	43.6	0.1	58.7	41.1	0.2	60.1	39.9	0.0
1962	55.6	44.4	0.0	55.0	45.0	0.0	56.3	43.7	0.0
1964	58.7	41.2	0.2	56.2	43.5	0.3	59.2	40.8	0.0
1966	56.6	41.5	1.9	57.4	42.0	0.6	62.0	38.1	0.0
1968	46.0	46.3	7.8	47.1	46.6	6.3	45.5	45.8	8.7
1970				49.3	50.2	0.5	47.8	52.3	0.0

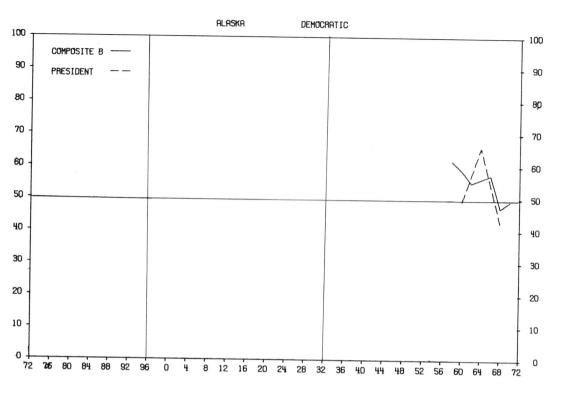

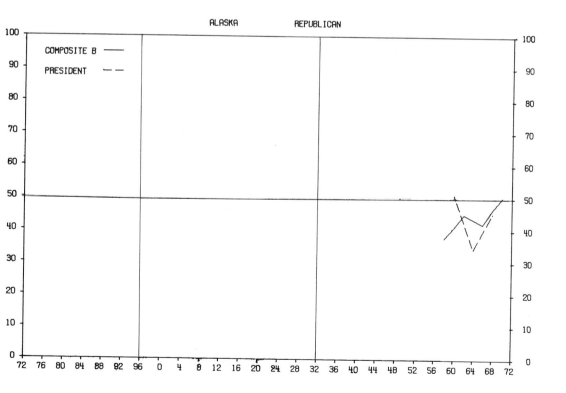

93

ARIZONA

YEAR	PRESIDENT			GOVERNOR			SENATE CLASS I			SENATE CLASS III		
	DEM.	REP.	OTHER	DEM.	REP.	OTHER	DEM.	REP.	OTHER	DEM.	REP.	OTHER
1872												
1874												
1876												
1878												
1880												
1882												
1884												
1886												
1888												
1890												
1892												
1894												
1896												
1898												
1900												
1902												
1904												
1906												
1908												
1910												
1912	43.6	12.6	43.8	51.6	42.5	6.0						
1914				49.5	34.5	16.0				53.2	18.9	27.8
1916	57.2	35.4	7.5	47.9	48.0	4.1	55.4	39.4	5.2			
1918				49.2	49.9	0.9						
1920	44.4	55.6	0.0	45.9	54.1	0.0				44.8	55.2	0.0
1922				54.9	45.1	0.0	65.0	35.0	0.0			
1924	35.5	41.3	23.3	50.5	49.5	0.0						
1926				50.3	49.7	0.0				58.3	41.7	0.0
1928	42.2	57.6	0.2	48.2	51.7	0.1	54.2	45.8	0.0			
1930				51.4	48.6	0.0						
1932	67.0	30.5	2.4	63.2	35.4	1.3				66.7	32.1	1.3
1934				59.7	38.2	2.2	72.0	25.6	2.3			
1936	69.8	26.9	3.2	70.7	29.1	0.2						
1938				68.6	27.3	4.1				76.5	23.5	0.0
1940	63.5	36.0	0.5	65.5	33.8	0.7	71.6	28.0	0.4			
1942				72.5	26.9	0.6						
1944	58.8	40.9	0.3	77.9	21.2	0.9				69.4	30.6	0.0
1946				60.1	39.9	0.0	69.2	30.1	0.7			
1948	53.8	43.8	2.4	59.2	40.1	0.8						
1950				49.2	50.8	0.0				62.8	37.2	0.0
1952	41.7	58.3	0.0	39.8	60.2	0.0	48.7	51.3	0.0			
1954				52.5	47.5	0.0						
1956	38.9	61.0	0.1	59.5	40.5	0.0				61.4	38.6	0.0
1958				44.9	55.1	0.0	43.9	56.1	0.0			
1960	44.4	55.5	0.1	40.7	59.3	0.0						
1962				45.2	54.8	0.0				54.9	45.1	0.0
1964	49.5	50.4	0.1	53.2	46.8	0.0	48.6	51.4	0.0			
1966				46.2	53.8	0.0						
1968	35.0	54.8	10.2	42.2	57.8	0.0				42.8	57.2	0.0
1970				49.1	50.9	0.0	44.0	56.0	0.0			

94

YEAR	PRESIDENT			GOVERNOR			SENATE			HOUSE OF REPRESENTATIVES		
	DEM.	REP.	OTHER	DEM.	REP.	OTHER	DEM.	REP.	OTHER	DEM.	REP.	OTHER
1872												
1874												
1876												
1878												
1880												
1882												
1884												
1886												
1888												
1890												
1892												
1894												
1896												
1898												
1900												
1902												
1904												
1906												
1908												
1910												
1912	43.6	12.6	43.8	51.6	42.5	6.0				51.1	25.8	23.1
1914	50.4	24.0	25.6	49.5	34.5	16.0	53.2	19.0	27.8	74.6	17.0	8.5
1916	57.2	35.4	7.5	47.9	48.0	4.1	55.4	39.4	5.2	65.7	28.5	5.9
1918	50.8	45.5	3.7	49.3	49.9	0.9	50.1	47.3	2.6	60.4	37.9	1.7
1920	44.4	55.6	0.0	45.9	54.2	0.0	44.8	55.2	0.0	57.8	42.2	0.0
1922	39.9	48.4	11.6	54.9	45.1	0.0	65.0	35.0	0.0	71.9	28.2	0.0
1924	35.5	41.3	23.3	50.5	49.5	0.0	61.7	38.3	0.0	82.4	17.6	0.0
1926	38.9	49.4	11.7	50.3	49.8	0.0	58.3	41.7	0.0	64.1	35.9	0.0
1928	42.2	57.6	0.2	48.2	51.7	0.1	54.3	45.8	0.0	61.6	38.5	0.0
1930	54.6	44.1	1.3	51.4	48.6	0.0	60.5	38.9	0.6	100.0	0.0	0.0
1932	67.0	30.5	2.4	63.2	35.4	1.4	66.7	32.1	1.3	70.8	27.9	1.3
1934	68.4	28.7	2.8	59.7	38.2	2.2	72.0	25.6	2.3	68.6	29.5	1.9
1936	69.9	26.9	3.2	70.7	29.1	0.2	74.3	24.6	1.2	77.6	18.7	3.7
1938	66.7	31.5	1.9	68.6	27.3	4.1	76.5	23.5	0.0	80.3	19.7	0.0
1940	63.5	36.0	0.5	65.5	33.8	0.7	71.6	28.0	0.4	71.1	28.9	0.0
1942	61.2	38.5	0.4	72.5	26.9	0.6	70.5	29.3	0.2	73.0	26.8	0.2
1944	58.8	40.9	0.3	77.9	21.2	0.9	69.4	30.6	0.0	69.8	30.0	0.2
1946	56.3	42.4	1.3	60.1	39.9	0.0	69.2	30.1	0.7	66.5	33.2	0.4
1948	53.8	43.8	2.4	59.2	40.1	0.8	66.0	33.7	0.3	60.8	37.7	1.5
1950	47.7	51.1	1.2	49.2	50.8	0.0	62.8	37.2	0.0	65.0	35.0	0.0
1952	41.7	58.4	0.0	39.8	60.2	0.0	48.7	51.3	0.0	51.5	48.5	0.0
1954	40.3	59.7	0.1	52.5	47.5	0.0	55.0	45.0	0.0	54.3	45.7	0.0
1956	38.9	61.0	0.1	59.6	40.5	0.0	61.4	38.6	0.0	52.4	47.6	0.0
1958	41.6	58.3	0.1	44.9	55.1	0.0	43.9	56.1	0.0	50.3	49.8	0.0
1960	44.4	55.5	0.1	40.7	59.3	0.0	49.4	50.6	0.0	47.6	52.4	0.0
1962	46.9	53.0	0.1	45.2	54.8	0.0	54.9	45.1	0.0	48.6	51.4	0.0
1964	49.5	50.5	0.1	53.2	46.8	0.0	48.6	51.4	0.0	50.1	49.9	0.0
1966	42.2	52.6	5.2	46.2	53.8	0.0	45.7	54.3	0.0	43.9	56.1	0.0
1968	35.0	54.8	10.2	42.2	57.8	0.0	42.8	57.2	0.0	43.8	56.2	0.0
1970				49.1	50.9	0.0	44.0	56.0	0.0	45.3	54.3	0.3

YEAR	COMPOSITE A (P+G+S+H/4)			COMPOSITE B (G+S+H/3)			COMPOSITE C (S+H/2)		
	DEM.	REP.	OTHER	DEM.	REP.	OTHER	DEM.	REP.	OTHER
1872									
1874									
1876									
1878									
1880									
1882									
1884									
1886									
1888									
1890									
1892									
1894									
1896									
1898									
1900									
1902									
1904									
1906									
1908									
1910									
1912	48.7	27.0	24.3	51.3	34.2	14.5	51.1	25.8	23.1
1914	56.9	23.6	19.5	59.1	23.5	17.4	63.9	18.0	18.1
1916	56.5	37.8	5.7	56.3	38.6	5.1	60.5	33.9	5.5
1918	52.6	45.1	2.2	53.3	45.0	1.7	55.3	42.6	2.2
1920	48.2	51.8	0.0	49.5	50.5	0.0	51.3	48.7	0.0
1922	57.9	39.2	2.9	63.9	36.1	0.0	68.4	31.6	0.0
1924	57.5	36.7	5.8	64.9	35.1	0.0	72.0	28.0	0.0
1926	52.9	44.2	2.9	57.6	42.4	0.0	61.2	38.8	0.0
1928	51.6	48.4	0.1	54.7	45.3	0.0	57.9	42.1	0.0
1930	66.6	32.9	0.5	70.6	29.2	0.2	80.2	19.5	0.3
1932	66.9	31.5	1.6	66.9	31.8	1.3	68.7	30.0	1.3
1934	67.2	30.5	2.3	66.8	31.1	2.2	70.3	27.5	2.1
1936	73.1	24.8	2.1	74.2	24.1	1.7	75.9	21.6	2.4
1938	73.0	25.5	1.5	75.1	23.5	1.4	78.4	21.6	0.0
1940	67.9	31.7	0.4	69.4	30.2	0.4	71.4	28.4	0.2
1942	69.3	30.4	0.4	72.0	27.7	0.4	71.7	28.1	0.2
1944	69.0	30.7	0.4	72.4	27.3	0.4	69.6	30.3	0.1
1946	63.0	36.4	0.6	65.3	34.4	0.4	67.8	31.6	0.5
1948	59.9	38.8	1.2	62.0	37.2	0.9	63.4	35.7	0.9
1950	56.2	43.5	0.3	59.0	41.0	0.0	63.9	36.1	0.0
1952	45.4	54.6	0.0	46.7	53.3	0.0	50.1	49.9	0.0
1954	50.5	49.5	0.0	54.0	46.0	0.0	54.7	45.3	0.0
1956	53.1	46.9	0.0	57.8	42.2	0.0	56.9	43.1	0.0
1958	45.2	54.8	0.0	46.4	53.7	0.0	47.1	52.9	0.0
1960	45.5	54.5	0.0	45.9	54.1	0.0	48.5	51.5	0.0
1962	48.9	51.1	0.0	49.6	50.4	0.0	51.8	48.2	0.0
1964	50.3	49.6	0.0	50.6	49.4	0.0	49.3	50.7	0.0
1966	44.5	54.2	1.3	45.3	54.7	0.0	44.8	55.2	0.0
1968	40.9	56.5	2.6	42.9	57.1	0.0	43.3	56.7	0.0
1970				46.1	53.8	0.1	44.7	55.2	0.2

96

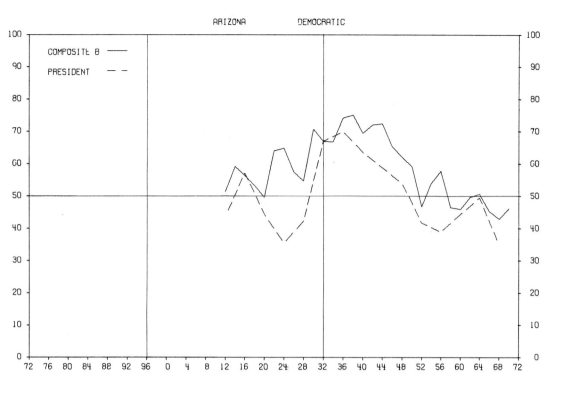

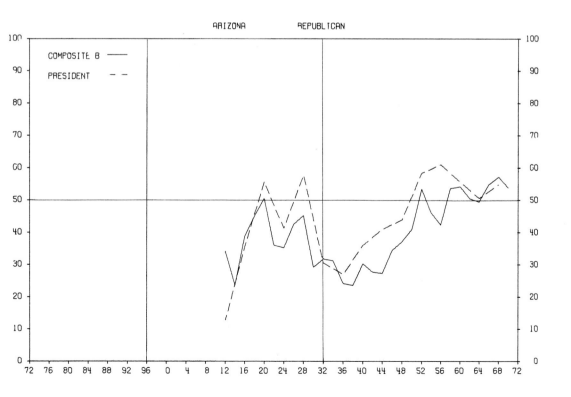

97

YEAR	PRESIDENT			GOVERNOR			SENATE CLASS II			SENATE CLASS III		
	DEM.	REP.	OTHER	DEM.	REP.	OTHER	DEM.	REP.	OTHER	DEM.	REP.	OTHER
1872	47.8	52.2	0.0	48.0	51.6	0.4						
1874				100.0	0.0	0.0						
1876	59.9	39.9	0.2	65.6	34.1	0.3						
1878				100.0	0.0	0.0						
1880	56.1	38.7	5.2	72.8	0.0	27.2						
1882				59.6	33.5	6.9						
1884	57.8	40.7	1.5	64.6	35.4	0.0						
1886				55.3	33.0	11.7						
1888	54.8	38.0	7.2	54.1	0.0	45.9						
1890				55.5	44.5	0.0						
1892	59.3	31.8	8.9	57.7	21.5	20.8						
1894				59.1	20.6	20.3						
1896	73.7	25.1	1.2	64.3	25.3	10.5						
1898				67.3	24.6	8.1						
1900	63.5	35.0	1.5	66.7	30.6	2.7						
1902				64.6	24.4	11.0						
1904	55.4	40.2	4.4	61.0	36.4	2.6						
1906				69.1	27.3	3.6						
1908	57.3	37.3	5.4	68.1	27.7	4.3						
1910				67.4	26.5	6.1						
1912	55.0	20.5	24.5	64.7	27.4	7.9						
1914				67.5	21.9	10.6						
1916	66.0	28.7	5.3	69.4	25.0	5.5				69.3	30.7	0.0
1918				93.4	0.0	6.6	100.0	0.0	0.0			
1920	58.5	38.7	2.8	65.0	24.4	10.6				65.9	34.1	0.0
1922				78.1	21.9	0.0						
1924	61.2	29.3	9.5	79.8	20.2	0.0	73.5	26.5	0.0			
1926				76.4	23.6	0.0				82.8	17.2	0.0
1928	60.3	39.3	0.4	77.3	22.7	0.0						
1930				81.2	18.8	0.0	100.0	0.0	0.0			
1932	86.3	12.7	1.1	90.4	8.9	0.7				89.5	10.5	0.0
1934				89.2	9.4	1.3						
1936	81.8	17.9	0.3	84.9	14.7	0.4	81.8	16.4	1.8			
1938				86.3	4.9	8.8	39.3	0.0	60.7	89.6	10.4	0.0
1940	78.4	21.0	0.5	91.4	8.2	0.4						
1942				100.0	0.0	0.0	100.0	0.0	0.0			
1944	70.0	29.8	0.2	86.0	14.0	0.0				85.1	14.9	0.0
1946				84.1	15.9	0.0						
1948	61.7	21.0	17.3	89.2	10.8	0.0	93.3	0.0	6.7			
1950				84.1	15.9	0.0				100.0	0.0	0.0
1952	55.9	43.8	0.3	87.4	12.6	0.0						
1954				62.1	37.9	0.0	100.0	0.0	0.0			
1956	52.5	45.8	1.7	80.6	19.4	0.0				83.0	17.0	0.0
1958				82.5	17.5	0.0						
1960	50.6	43.2	6.2	69.2	30.8	0.0	100.0	0.0	0.0			
1962				73.3	26.7	0.0				68.7	31.3	0.0
1964	56.1	43.4	0.5	57.0	43.0	0.0						
1966				45.6	54.4	0.0	100.0	0.0	0.0			
1968	30.3	31.0	38.7	47.6	52.4	0.0				59.1	40.9	0.0
1970				61.7	32.4	5.9						

YEAR	PRESIDENT			GOVERNOR			SENATE			HOUSE OF REPRESENTATIVES		
	DEM.	REP.	OTHER	DEM.	REP.	OTHER	DEM.	REP.	OTHER	DEM.	REP.	OTHER
1872	47.8	52.2	0.0	48.0	51.6	0.4				51.7	47.9	0.3
1874	53.9	46.0	0.1	100.0	0.0	0.0				64.2	35.8	0.0
1876	59.9	39.9	0.2	65.6	34.1	0.3				58.1	30.8	11.2
1878	58.0	39.3	2.7	100.0	0.0	0.0				63.4	0.0	36.6
1880	56.1	38.7	5.2	72.8	0.0	27.2				52.5	38.4	9.1
1882	57.0	39.7	3.3	59.6	33.5	6.9				66.6	16.1	17.3
1884	57.8	40.7	1.5	64.6	35.5	0.0				58.1	41.9	0.0
1886	56.3	39.4	4.3	55.3	33.0	11.7				66.1	15.4	18.5
1888	54.8	38.0	7.2	54.1	0.0	45.9				57.2	21.3	21.5
1890	57.1	34.9	8.0	55.5	44.5	0.0				61.9	6.6	31.5
1892	59.3	31.8	8.9	57.7	21.5	20.8				68.7	6.9	24.4
1894	66.5	28.4	5.1	59.1	20.6	20.3				71.7	19.8	8.5
1896	73.7	25.1	1.2	64.3	25.3	10.5				72.4	27.6	0.0
1898	68.6	30.1	1.4	67.4	24.6	8.1				89.9	9.8	0.3
1900	63.5	35.0	1.5	66.7	30.6	2.7				66.4	33.6	0.0
1902	59.4	37.6	3.0	64.6	24.4	11.0				83.3	16.7	0.0
1904	55.4	40.2	4.4	61.0	36.4	2.6				70.4	29.5	0.1
1906	56.4	38.8	4.9	69.1	27.3	3.6				75.4	24.5	0.1
1908	57.3	37.3	5.4	68.1	27.7	4.3				68.6	31.4	0.0
1910	56.2	28.9	15.0	67.4	26.5	6.1				72.9	27.1	0.0
1912	55.0	20.5	24.5	64.7	27.4	7.9				77.2	22.8	0.0
1914	60.5	24.6	14.9	67.5	21.9	10.6				86.5	9.5	4.1
1916	66.0	28.7	5.3	69.5	25.0	5.5	69.3	30.7	0.0	82.9	17.1	0.0
1918	62.2	33.7	4.0	93.4	0.0	6.6	100.0	0.0	0.0	100.0	0.0	0.0
1920	58.5	38.7	2.8	65.0	24.4	10.6	65.9	34.1	0.0	67.4	32.6	0.0
1922	59.9	34.0	6.1	78.1	21.9	0.0	69.7	30.3	0.0	87.7	0.0	12.3
1924	61.2	29.3	9.5	79.8	20.2	0.0	73.5	26.5	0.0	72.9	27.1	0.0
1926	60.8	34.3	4.9	76.5	23.6	0.0	82.8	17.2	0.0	85.8	14.2	0.0
1928	60.3	39.3	0.4	77.3	22.7	0.0	91.4	8.6	0.0	78.3	21.6	0.1
1930	73.3	26.0	0.7	81.2	18.8	0.0	100.0	0.0	0.0	100.0	0.0	0.0
1932	86.3	12.7	1.1	90.4	8.9	0.7	89.5	10.5	0.0	97.7	2.3	0.0
1934	84.0	15.3	0.7	89.2	9.4	1.4	85.7	13.4	0.9	93.3	6.8	0.0
1936	81.8	17.9	0.3	84.9	14.7	0.4	81.8	16.4	1.8	92.3	7.7	0.0
1938	80.1	19.4	0.4	86.3	4.9	8.8	67.2	5.8	27.1	100.0	0.0	0.0
1940	78.4	21.0	0.6	91.4	8.2	0.4	83.6	2.9	13.5	95.9	4.1	0.0
1942	74.2	25.4	0.4	100.0	0.0	0.0	100.0	0.0	0.0	100.0	0.0	0.0
1944	70.0	29.8	0.2	86.0	14.0	0.0	85.1	14.9	0.0	92.4	7.6	0.0
1946	65.8	25.4	8.7	84.1	15.9	0.0	89.2	7.5	3.4	94.7	1.9	3.4
1948	61.7	21.0	17.3	89.2	10.9	0.0	93.3	0.0	6.7	91.3	8.7	0.0
1950	58.8	32.4	8.8	84.1	15.9	0.0	100.0	0.0	0.0	100.0	0.0	0.0
1952	55.9	43.8	0.3	87.4	12.6	0.0	100.0	0.0	0.0	85.3	14.3	0.3
1954	54.2	44.8	1.0	62.1	37.9	0.0	100.0	0.0	0.0	100.0	0.0	0.0
1956	52.5	45.8	1.7	80.7	19.4	0.0	83.0	17.0	0.0	87.3	12.7	0.0
1958	51.5	44.5	4.0	82.5	17.5	0.0	91.5	8.5	0.0	97.1	2.9	0.0
1960	50.6	43.2	6.2	69.2	30.8	0.0	100.0	0.0	0.0	91.5	0.0	8.5
1962	53.3	43.3	3.4	73.3	26.7	0.0	68.7	31.3	0.0	86.7	13.3	0.0
1964	56.1	43.4	0.5	57.0	43.0	0.0	84.4	15.6	0.0	88.6	11.4	0.0
1966	43.2	37.2	19.6	45.6	54.4	0.0	100.0	0.0	0.0	78.0	22.0	0.0
1968	30.3	31.0	38.7	47.6	52.4	0.0	59.2	40.9	0.0	75.5	24.5	0.0
1970				61.7	32.4	5.9				83.2	16.8	0.0

YEAR	COMPOSITE A (P+G+S+H/4)			COMPOSITE B (G+S+H/3)			COMPOSITE C (S+H/2)		
	DEM.	REP.	OTHER	DEM.	REP.	OTHER	DEM.	REP.	OTHER
1872	49.2	50.6	0.2	49.9	49.8	0.4	51.7	47.9	0.3
1874	72.7	27.3	0.0	82.1	17.9	0.0	64.2	35.8	0.0
1876	61.2	34.9	3.9	61.8	32.5	5.7	58.1	30.8	11.2
1878	73.8	13.1	13.1	81.7	0.0	18.3	63.4	0.0	36.6
1880	60.5	25.7	13.8	62.6	19.2	18.2	52.5	38.4	9.1
1882	61.1	29.8	9.2	63.1	24.8	12.1	66.6	16.1	17.3
1884	60.2	39.4	0.5	61.3	38.7	0.0	58.1	41.9	0.0
1886	59.2	29.3	11.5	60.7	24.2	15.1	66.1	15.4	18.5
1888	55.4	19.8	24.9	55.6	10.6	33.7	57.2	21.3	21.5
1890	58.2	28.7	13.2	58.7	25.6	15.7	61.9	6.6	31.5
1892	61.9	20.1	18.0	63.2	14.2	22.6	68.7	6.9	24.4
1894	65.8	23.0	11.3	65.4	20.2	14.4	71.7	19.8	8.5
1896	70.1	26.0	3.9	68.3	26.4	5.2	72.4	27.6	0.0
1898	75.3	21.5	3.2	78.6	17.2	4.2	89.9	9.8	0.3
1900	65.5	33.1	1.4	66.5	32.1	1.4	66.4	33.6	0.0
1902	69.1	26.3	4.7	73.9	20.6	5.5	83.3	16.7	0.0
1904	62.2	35.4	2.4	65.7	33.0	1.4	70.4	29.5	0.1
1906	67.0	30.2	2.8	72.3	25.9	1.8	75.4	24.5	0.1
1908	64.7	32.1	3.2	68.3	29.6	2.1	68.6	31.4	0.0
1910	65.5	27.5	7.0	70.2	26.8	3.1	72.9	27.1	0.0
1912	65.7	23.5	10.8	71.0	25.1	3.9	77.2	22.8	0.0
1914	71.5	18.7	9.9	77.0	15.7	7.3	86.5	9.5	4.1
1916	71.9	25.4	2.7	73.9	24.3	1.9	76.1	23.9	0.0
1918	88.9	8.4	2.7	97.8	0.0	2.2	100.0	0.0	0.0
1920	64.2	32.4	3.4	66.1	30.3	3.5	66.7	33.3	0.0
1922	73.8	21.5	4.6	78.5	17.4	4.1	78.7	15.1	6.2
1924	71.9	25.8	2.4	75.4	24.6	0.0	73.2	26.8	0.0
1926	76.4	22.3	1.2	81.7	18.4	0.0	84.3	15.7	0.0
1928	76.8	23.1	0.1	82.3	17.7	0.0	84.8	15.1	0.1
1930	88.6	11.2	0.2	93.7	6.3	0.0	100.0	0.0	0.0
1932	91.0	8.6	0.4	92.5	7.2	0.2	93.6	6.4	0.0
1934	88.0	11.2	0.7	89.4	9.9	0.8	89.5	10.1	0.5
1936	85.2	14.2	0.6	86.3	12.9	0.7	87.1	12.0	0.9
1938	83.4	7.5	9.1	84.5	3.6	12.0	83.6	2.9	13.5
1940	87.3	9.1	3.6	90.3	5.1	4.7	89.7	3.5	6.8
1942	93.6	6.4	0.1	100.0	0.0	0.0	100.0	0.0	0.0
1944	83.4	16.6	0.1	87.8	12.2	0.0	88.8	11.3	0.0
1946	83.5	12.7	3.9	89.3	8.4	2.3	91.9	4.7	3.4
1948	83.9	10.1	6.0	91.3	6.5	2.2	92.3	4.4	3.4
1950	85.7	12.1	2.2	94.7	5.3	0.0	100.0	0.0	0.0
1952	82.2	17.7	0.2	90.9	9.0	0.1	92.7	7.2	0.2
1954	79.1	20.7	0.3	87.4	12.6	0.0	100.0	0.0	0.0
1956	75.8	23.7	0.4	83.6	16.4	0.0	85.1	14.9	0.0
1958	80.7	18.3	1.0	90.4	9.6	0.0	94.3	5.7	0.0
1960	77.8	18.5	3.7	86.9	10.3	2.8	95.8	0.0	4.2
1962	70.5	28.7	1.8	76.2	23.8	0.0	77.7	22.3	0.0
1964	71.5	28.4	0.1	76.7	23.3	0.0	86.5	13.5	0.0
1966	66.7	28.4	4.9	74.5	25.5	0.0	89.0	11.0	0.0
1968	53.1	37.2	9.7	60.7	39.3	0.0	67.3	22.7	0.0
1970				72.5	24.6	2.9	83.2	16.8	0.0

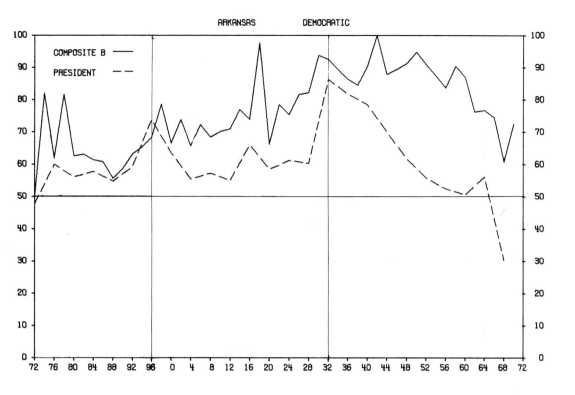

ARKANSAS   DEMOCRATIC

COMPOSITE B ——
PRESIDENT   – –

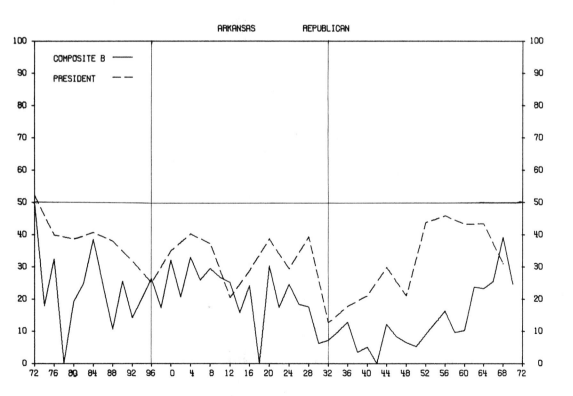

ARKANSAS   REPUBLICAN

COMPOSITE B ——
PRESIDENT   – –

101

CALIFORNIA

YEAR	PRESIDENT			GOVERNOR			SENATE CLASS I			SENATE CLASS III		
	DEM.	REP.	OTHER	DEM.	REP.	OTHER	DEM.	REP.	OTHER	DEM.	REP.	OTHER
1872	43.6	56.4	0.0	47.9	52.1	0.0						
1874												
1876	49.1	50.9	0.0	50.0	25.5	24.5						
1878												
1880	49.0	48.9	2.1	29.7	42.4	27.8						
1882				55.1	40.8	4.1						
1884	45.3	52.0	2.7									
1886				43.4	43.1	13.5						
1888	46.8	49.7	3.5									
1890				46.4	49.6	4.0						
1892	43.8	43.8	12.4									
1894				39.3	38.9	21.7						
1896	41.2	49.1	9.6									
1898				45.0	51.7	3.3						
1900	41.3	54.5	4.2									
1902				47.2	48.1	4.7						
1904	26.9	61.9	11.2									
1906				37.7	40.4	22.0						
1908	33.0	55.5	11.6									
1910				40.1	45.9	13.9						
1912	41.8	0.6	57.6									
1914				12.5	29.4	58.1				31.6	28.7	39.7
1916	46.6	46.3	7.1				29.5	61.1	9.4			
1918				0.0	56.3	43.7						
1920	24.3	66.2	9.5							40.7	49.0	10.3
1922				36.0	59.7	4.3	23.8	62.2	14.1			
1924	8.2	57.2	34.6									
1926				24.7	71.2	4.1				36.9	63.1	0.0
1928	34.2	63.9	1.9				18.2	74.1	7.7			
1930				24.1	72.2	3.7						
1932	58.4	37.4	4.1							43.4	30.8	25.8
1934				37.8	48.9	13.4	0.0	94.5	5.5			
1936	67.0	31.7	1.3									
1938				52.5	44.2	3.3				54.4	44.7	0.9
1940	57.4	41.3	1.2				0.0	82.5	17.5			
1942				41.8	57.1	1.2						
1944	56.5	43.0	0.5							52.3	47.7	0.0
1946				0.0	91.6	8.4	36.3	44.5	19.2			
1948	47.6	47.1	5.3									
1950				35.1	64.8	0.0				40.8	59.2	0.0
1952	42.7	56.3	0.9				0.0	87.7	12.3			
1954				43.2	56.8	0.0				45.5	53.2	1.3
1956	44.3	55.4	0.3							45.6	54.0	0.4
1958				59.7	40.2	0.1	57.0	42.9	0.1			
1960	49.6	50.1	0.3									
1962				51.9	46.8	1.3				43.4	56.3	0.3
1964	59.1	40.8	0.1				48.5	51.5	0.0			
1966				42.3	57.6	0.2						
1968	44.7	47.8	7.4							51.8	46.9	1.3
1970				45.1	52.8	2.0	53.9	44.3	1.8			

102

YEAR	PRESIDENT			GOVERNOR			SENATE			HOUSE OF REPRESENTATIVES		
	DEM.	REP.	OTHER	DEM.	REP.	OTHER	DEM.	REP.	OTHER	DEM.	REP.	OTHER
1872	43.6	56.4	0.0	47.9	52.1	0.0				48.5	51.1	0.4
1874	46.4	53.6	0.0	49.0	38.8	12.3				48.2	47.3	4.5
1876	49.1	50.9	0.0	50.0	25.5	24.5				47.9	43.5	8.6
1878	49.0	49.9	1.1	39.9	34.0	26.2				43.8	45.9	10.4
1880	49.0	48.9	2.1	29.8	42.4	27.8				39.7	48.2	12.2
1882	47.2	50.4	2.4	55.1	40.8	4.1				53.3	44.5	2.3
1884	45.3	52.0	2.7	49.3	41.9	8.8				46.5	52.0	1.5
1886	46.1	50.8	3.1	43.4	43.1	13.5				47.2	48.4	4.4
1888	46.8	49.7	3.5	44.9	46.3	8.8				46.6	50.8	2.6
1890	45.3	46.7	8.0	46.4	49.6	4.0				45.6	50.8	3.6
1892	43.8	43.8	12.4	42.9	44.2	12.9				44.8	42.0	13.2
1894	42.5	46.5	11.0	39.3	38.9	21.7				33.2	41.0	25.8
1896	41.2	49.2	9.6	42.2	45.3	12.5				46.7	46.4	7.0
1898	41.3	51.8	6.9	45.0	51.7	3.3				46.9	51.0	2.1
1900	41.3	54.5	4.2	46.1	49.9	4.0				41.2	53.9	4.9
1902	34.1	58.2	7.7	47.2	48.1	4.7				43.4	52.4	4.3
1904	26.9	61.9	11.2	42.5	44.2	13.3				34.3	56.8	8.9
1906	30.0	58.7	11.4	37.7	40.4	22.0				35.8	55.3	8.9
1908	33.0	55.5	11.6	38.9	43.2	17.9				36.3	54.5	9.3
1910	37.4	28.0	34.6	40.1	45.9	13.9				30.8	56.2	13.0
1912	41.8	0.6	57.6	26.3	37.6	36.0				31.6	46.1	22.3
1914	44.2	23.4	32.4	12.5	29.4	58.1	31.6	28.7	39.7	25.7	44.4	29.9
1916	46.6	46.3	7.1	6.3	42.8	50.9	29.5	61.1	9.4	32.1	49.1	18.9
1918	35.5	56.3	8.3	0.0	56.3	43.7	35.1	55.0	9.9	34.6	56.6	8.8
1920	24.3	66.2	9.5	18.0	58.0	24.0	40.7	49.0	10.3	19.8	68.5	11.7
1922	16.3	61.7	22.0	36.0	59.7	4.3	23.8	62.2	14.1	19.8	76.2	4.1
1924	8.2	57.2	34.6	30.3	65.5	4.2	30.3	62.6	7.1	32.1	59.0	9.0
1926	21.2	60.5	18.2	24.7	71.2	4.1	36.9	63.1	0.0	17.7	78.8	3.5
1928	34.2	63.9	1.9	24.4	71.7	3.9	18.2	74.1	7.7	11.5	85.0	3.5
1930	46.3	50.7	3.0	24.1	72.2	3.7	30.8	52.5	16.7	11.9	85.5	2.7
1932	58.4	37.4	4.1	30.9	60.5	8.6	43.4	30.8	25.8	45.3	46.6	8.1
1934	62.7	34.6	2.7	37.8	48.9	13.4	0.0	94.5	5.5	46.0	50.6	3.5
1936	67.0	31.7	1.3	45.1	46.5	8.4	27.2	69.6	3.2	53.5	43.1	3.5
1938	62.2	36.5	1.3	52.5	44.2	3.4	54.4	44.7	0.9	46.2	46.5	7.3
1940	57.4	41.3	1.2	47.1	50.6	2.3	0.0	82.5	17.5	42.7	53.1	4.1
1942	57.0	42.2	0.9	41.8	57.1	1.2	26.1	65.1	8.8	47.7	49.2	3.1
1944	56.5	43.0	0.6	20.9	74.4	4.8	52.3	47.7	0.0	50.5	49.2	0.3
1946	52.0	45.1	2.9	0.0	91.6	8.4	36.3	44.5	19.2	47.4	51.5	1.1
1948	47.6	47.1	5.3	17.6	78.3	4.2	38.6	51.9	9.6	37.9	55.5	6.7
1950	45.2	51.7	3.1	35.1	64.9	0.0	40.8	59.2	0.0	44.1	52.2	3.7
1952	42.7	56.3	0.9	39.2	60.8	0.0	0.0	87.7	12.3	44.5	52.2	3.3
1954	43.5	55.9	0.6	43.2	56.8	0.0	45.5	53.2	1.3	51.4	48.5	0.1
1956	44.3	55.4	0.3	51.5	48.5	0.1	45.6	54.0	0.4	52.4	47.6	0.0
1958	46.9	52.7	0.3	59.8	40.2	0.1	57.0	42.9	0.1	60.0	40.0	0.0
1960	49.6	50.1	0.4	55.8	43.5	0.7	50.2	49.6	0.2	53.9	46.1	0.0
1962	54.3	45.5	0.2	51.9	46.8	1.3	43.4	56.3	0.3	51.9	48.1	0.0
1964	59.1	40.8	0.1	47.1	52.2	0.7	48.5	51.5	0.0	52.9	47.1	0.0
1966	51.9	44.3	3.8	42.3	57.6	0.2	50.1	49.2	0.7	46.8	53.2	0.1
1968	44.7	47.8	7.4	43.7	55.2	1.1	51.8	46.9	1.3	44.1	54.4	1.5
1970				45.1	52.8	2.0	53.9	44.3	1.8	47.8	49.0	3.2

103

CALIFORNIA

YEAR	COMPOSITE A (P+G+S+H/4)			COMPOSITE B (G+S+H/3)			COMPOSITE C (S+H/2)		
	DEM.	REP.	OTHER	DEM.	REP.	OTHER	DEM.	REP.	OTHER
1872	46.7	53.2	0.1	48.2	51.6	0.2	48.5	51.1	0.4
1874	47.8	46.6	5.6	48.6	43.0	8.4	48.2	47.3	4.5
1876	49.0	40.0	11.0	49.0	34.5	16.5	47.9	43.5	8.6
1878	44.2	43.2	12.5	41.8	39.9	18.3	43.8	45.9	10.4
1880	39.5	46.5	14.0	34.7	45.3	20.0	39.7	48.2	12.2
1882	51.8	45.2	3.0	54.2	42.6	3.2	53.3	44.5	2.3
1884	47.0	48.6	4.4	47.9	47.0	5.2	46.5	52.0	1.5
1886	45.6	47.4	7.0	45.3	45.7	8.9	47.2	48.4	4.4
1888	46.1	48.9	4.9	45.8	48.6	5.7	46.6	50.8	2.6
1890	45.8	49.0	5.2	46.0	50.2	3.8	45.6	50.8	3.6
1892	43.8	43.4	12.8	43.8	43.1	13.0	44.8	42.0	13.2
1894	38.4	42.1	19.5	36.3	40.0	23.8	33.2	41.0	25.8
1896	43.4	46.9	9.7	44.4	45.8	9.7	46.7	46.4	7.0
1898	44.4	51.5	4.1	46.0	51.4	2.7	46.9	51.0	2.1
1900	42.9	52.8	4.3	43.7	51.9	4.4	41.2	53.9	4.9
1902	41.6	52.9	5.6	45.3	50.2	4.5	43.4	52.4	4.3
1904	34.6	54.3	11.2	38.4	50.5	11.1	34.3	56.8	8.9
1906	34.5	51.4	14.1	36.8	47.8	15.4	35.8	55.3	8.9
1908	36.1	51.0	12.9	37.6	48.8	13.6	36.3	54.5	9.3
1910	36.1	43.4	20.5	35.5	51.1	13.5	30.8	56.2	13.0
1912	33.2	28.1	38.7	29.0	41.9	29.2	31.6	46.1	22.3
1914	28.5	31.5	40.0	23.3	34.2	42.6	28.7	36.6	34.8
1916	28.6	49.8	21.6	22.6	51.0	26.4	30.8	55.1	14.1
1918	26.3	56.1	17.7	23.2	56.0	20.8	34.9	55.8	9.3
1920	25.7	60.4	13.9	26.2	58.5	15.4	30.2	58.8	11.0
1922	23.9	64.9	11.1	26.5	66.0	7.5	21.8	69.2	9.1
1924	25.2	61.1	13.7	30.9	62.3	6.7	31.2	60.8	8.0
1926	25.1	68.4	6.5	26.4	71.1	2.5	27.3	71.0	1.7
1928	22.1	73.7	4.2	18.0	76.9	5.0	14.9	79.6	5.6
1930	28.3	65.2	6.5	22.3	70.0	7.7	21.3	69.0	9.7
1932	44.5	43.8	11.7	39.9	46.0	14.2	44.3	38.7	16.9
1934	36.6	57.1	6.3	27.9	64.7	7.4	23.0	72.6	4.5
1936	48.2	47.7	4.1	41.9	53.1	5.0	40.3	56.3	3.3
1938	53.8	43.0	3.2	51.0	45.1	3.9	50.3	45.6	4.1
1940	36.8	56.9	6.3	29.9	62.1	8.0	21.4	67.8	10.8
1942	43.1	53.4	3.5	38.5	57.1	4.3	36.9	57.2	5.9
1944	45.0	53.6	1.4	41.2	57.1	1.7	51.4	48.5	0.2
1946	33.9	58.2	7.9	27.9	62.5	9.6	41.8	48.0	10.2
1948	35.4	58.2	6.5	31.3	61.9	6.8	38.2	53.7	8.2
1950	41.3	57.0	1.7	40.0	58.8	1.2	42.4	55.7	1.9
1952	31.6	64.3	4.1	27.9	66.9	5.2	22.3	69.9	7.8
1954	45.9	53.6	0.5	46.7	52.8	0.5	48.5	50.8	0.7
1956	48.4	51.4	0.2	49.8	50.0	0.2	49.0	50.8	0.2
1958	55.9	44.0	0.1	58.9	41.0	0.1	58.5	41.5	0.0
1960	52.4	47.3	0.3	53.3	46.4	0.3	52.1	47.9	0.1
1962	50.4	49.2	0.5	49.1	50.4	0.5	47.7	52.2	0.2
1964	51.9	47.9	0.2	49.5	50.3	0.3	50.7	49.3	0.0
1966	47.8	51.1	1.2	46.4	53.3	0.3	48.5	51.2	0.4
1968	46.1	51.1	2.8	46.6	52.2	1.3	48.0	50.6	1.4
1970				48.9	48.7	2.4	50.8	46.7	2.5

104

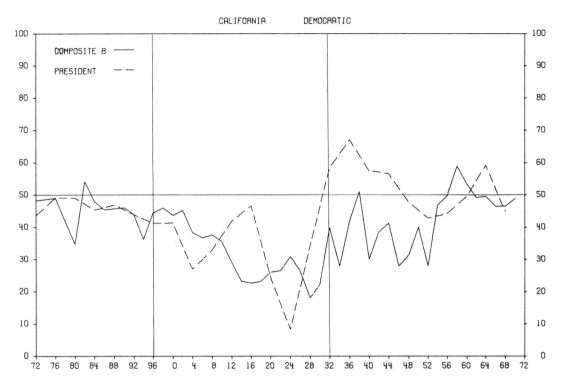

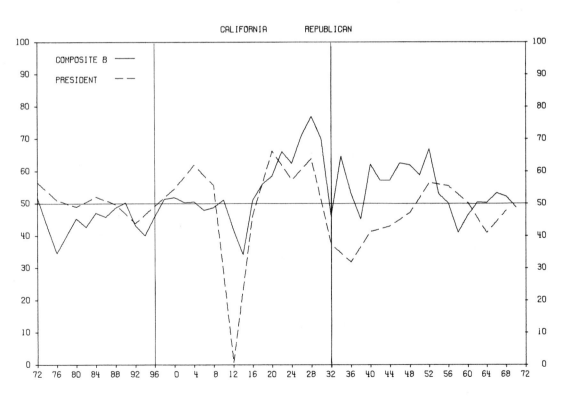

105

YEAR	PRESIDENT			GOVERNOR			SENATE CLASS II			SENATE CLASS III		
	DEM.	REP.	OTHER	DEM.	REP.	OTHER	DEM.	REP.	OTHER	DEM.	REP.	OTHER
1872												
1874												
1876				48.5	51.5	0.0						
1878				40.3	50.0	9.7						
1880	46.0	51.3	2.7	44.1	53.3	2.6						
1882				51.1	46.9	2.0						
1884	41.7	54.2	4.1	46.1	50.7	3.2						
1886				49.7	45.6	4.8						
1888	40.8	55.2	3.9	42.6	53.8	3.5						
1890				42.4	50.1	7.5						
1892	0.0	41.1	58.9	9.6	41.8	48.6						
1894				4.6	52.0	43.4						
1896	83.7	13.9	2.5	46.2	12.7	41.1						
1898				62.8	34.1	3.0						
1900	55.5	42.0	2.5	53.8	43.5	2.7						
1902				43.2	46.9	9.8						
1904	41.1	55.3	3.7	50.6	46.8	2.6						
1906				36.6	45.6	17.8						
1908	48.0	46.9	5.1	49.4	45.2	5.4						
1910				54.0	46.0	0.0						
1912	42.8	22.0	35.2	42.9	23.7	33.4	47.3	26.8	25.9	44.9	26.8	28.2
1914				34.2	48.7	17.2				40.3	39.0	20.7
1916	60.8	34.7	4.5	53.3	41.3	5.4						
1918				46.5	51.1	2.4	47.9	49.5	2.6			
1920	35.9	59.4	4.7	37.1	59.5	3.3				39.3	54.5	6.2
1922				49.6	48.3	2.1						
1924	23.0	59.4	17.6	44.0	51.9	4.0	43.9	50.2	5.9	43.7	50.2	6.2
1926				59.8	38.1	2.1				46.4	50.3	3.3
1928	34.0	64.8	1.1	61.9	37.1	1.0						
1930				60.4	38.1	1.5	55.8	42.7	1.5			
1932	54.9	41.3	3.8	57.2	40.8	2.0	48.5	48.8	2.7	51.9	45.5	2.6
1934				58.1	39.9	2.0						
1936	60.3	37.1	2.5	54.6	43.6	1.8	63.5	35.2	1.3			
1938				43.7	55.8	0.5				58.2	40.2	1.6
1940	48.4	50.9	0.7	45.0	54.4	0.7						
1942				43.4	56.2	0.4	50.2	49.2	0.6	42.1	56.1	1.7
1944	46.4	53.2	0.4	45.0	54.4	0.7				43.6	56.4	0.0
1946				52.1	47.9	0.0						
1948	51.9	46.5	1.6	66.3	33.7	0.0	66.8	32.4	0.8			
1950				47.2	52.4	0.3				46.7	53.3	0.0
1952	39.0	60.3	0.8	42.4	57.1	0.5						
1954				53.6	46.4	0.0	48.7	51.3	0.0			
1956	39.8	59.5	0.7	51.3	48.7	0.0				50.2	49.8	0.0
1958				58.4	41.6	0.0						
1960	44.9	54.6	0.5				46.0	53.5	0.5			
1962				42.6	56.7	0.7				45.6	53.6	0.8
1964	61.3	38.2	0.5									
1966				43.5	54.0	2.5	41.9	58.0	0.1			
1968	41.3	50.5	8.2							41.4	58.6	0.0
1970				45.2	52.5	2.3						

COLORADO

YEAR	PRESIDENT			GOVERNOR			SENATE			HOUSE OF REPRESENTATIVES		
	DEM.	REP.	OTHER	DEM.	REP.	OTHER	DEM.	REP.	OTHER	DEM.	REP.	OTHER
1872												
1874												
1876				48.5	51.5	0.0				48.1	51.9	0.0
1878				40.3	50.0	9.7				41.9	49.9	8.1
1880	46.0	51.3	2.7	44.1	53.3	2.6				46.0	50.8	3.2
1882	43.9	52.8	3.4	51.1	46.9	2.0				47.8	50.2	2.0
1884	41.7	54.3	4.1	46.1	50.7	3.2				43.1	53.2	3.8
1886	41.3	54.7	4.0	49.7	45.6	4.8				46.2	47.6	6.2
1888	40.8	55.2	3.9	42.6	53.8	3.5				41.0	55.0	4.0
1890	20.4	48.2	31.4	42.4	50.1	7.5				41.3	51.3	7.5
1892	0.0	41.1	58.9	9.6	41.8	48.6				36.6	40.2	23.3
1894	41.8	27.5	30.7	4.6	52.0	43.4				27.8	50.5	21.8
1896	83.7	13.9	2.5	46.2	12.7	41.1				84.6	13.4	2.0
1898	69.6	27.9	2.5	62.8	34.1	3.0				66.1	32.0	2.0
1900	55.6	42.0	2.5	53.8	43.5	2.7				55.7	42.7	1.6
1902	48.3	48.6	3.1	43.2	46.9	9.8				46.3	46.4	7.3
1904	41.1	55.3	3.7	50.6	46.8	2.6				45.8	50.9	3.3
1906	44.5	51.1	4.4	36.6	45.6	17.8				39.4	52.1	8.5
1908	48.0	46.9	5.1	49.4	45.2	5.4				48.8	46.9	4.3
1910	45.4	34.4	20.2	54.0	46.0	0.0				46.5	44.3	9.2
1912	42.8	22.0	35.2	42.9	23.7	33.4				44.4	24.8	30.9
1914	51.8	28.3	19.9	34.2	48.7	17.2	40.3	39.0	20.7	49.0	41.4	9.7
1916	60.8	34.7	4.5	53.3	41.3	5.5	44.1	44.2	11.6	50.2	43.6	6.3
1918	48.3	47.1	4.6	46.5	51.1	2.4	47.9	49.5	2.6	43.6	52.4	4.0
1920	35.9	59.4	4.7	37.1	59.6	3.4	39.3	54.5	6.2	39.5	60.5	0.0
1922	29.5	59.4	11.1	49.6	48.3	2.1	41.6	52.4	6.1	48.1	51.6	0.4
1924	23.0	59.4	17.6	44.0	51.9	4.0	43.8	50.2	6.0	43.6	53.1	3.3
1926	28.5	62.1	9.4	59.8	38.1	2.1	46.4	50.3	3.3	44.8	54.4	0.9
1928	34.0	64.8	1.1	61.9	37.1	1.0	51.1	46.5	2.4	40.0	59.8	0.3
1930	44.5	53.1	2.5	60.4	38.1	1.5	55.9	42.7	1.5	46.5	53.2	0.4
1932	54.9	41.3	3.8	57.2	40.8	2.0	50.2	47.1	2.7	54.7	44.7	0.6
1934	57.6	39.2	3.2	58.1	39.9	2.0	56.8	41.2	2.0	60.0	35.4	4.6
1936	60.3	37.1	2.5	54.6	43.7	1.8	63.5	35.3	1.3	61.9	37.1	1.1
1938	54.4	44.0	1.6	43.7	55.8	0.5	58.2	40.2	1.6	59.0	40.5	0.5
1940	48.4	50.9	0.7	45.0	54.4	0.7	52.2	46.4	1.4	54.5	45.2	0.3
1942	47.4	52.1	0.6	43.4	56.2	0.4	46.2	52.6	1.2	41.4	58.2	0.4
1944	46.4	53.2	0.4	45.0	54.4	0.7	43.6	56.4	0.0	42.6	57.0	0.4
1946	49.1	49.9	1.0	52.1	47.9	0.0	55.2	44.4	0.4	43.9	55.6	0.6
1948	51.9	46.5	1.6	66.3	33.7	0.0	66.8	32.4	0.9	54.8	45.2	0.0
1950	45.4	53.4	1.2	47.2	52.4	0.3	46.8	53.3	0.0	48.4	51.0	0.6
1952	39.0	60.3	0.8	42.4	57.1	0.5	47.7	52.3	0.0	44.5	55.3	0.2
1954	39.4	59.9	0.7	53.6	46.4	0.0	48.7	51.3	0.0	49.9	50.0	0.1
1956	39.8	59.5	0.7	51.3	48.7	0.0	50.2	49.8	0.0	52.8	47.2	0.0
1958	42.4	57.1	0.6	58.4	41.6	0.0	48.1	51.7	0.2	58.0	41.8	0.2
1960	44.9	54.6	0.5	50.5	49.1	0.3	46.0	53.5	0.5	51.8	48.2	0.0
1962	53.1	46.4	0.5	42.6	56.7	0.7	45.6	53.6	0.9	47.4	52.7	0.0
1964	61.3	38.2	0.5	43.1	55.4	1.6	43.8	55.8	0.5	58.1	41.8	0.2
1966	51.3	44.3	4.4	43.5	54.0	2.5	41.9	58.0	0.1	53.1	46.6	0.4
1968	41.3	50.5	8.2	44.4	53.3	2.4	41.5	58.6	0.0	46.4	50.3	3.3
1970				45.2	52.5	2.3				48.7	49.9	1.5

YEAR	COMPOSITE A (P+G+S+H/4)			COMPOSITE B (G+S+H/3)			COMPOSITE C (S+H/2)		
	DEM.	REP.	OTHER	DEM.	REP.	OTHER	DEM.	REP.	OTHER
1872									
1874									
1876				48.3	51.7	0.0	48.1	51.9	0.0
1878				41.1	50.0	8.9	41.9	49.9	8.1
1880	45.4	51.8	2.8	45.0	52.1	2.9	46.0	50.8	3.2
1882	47.6	50.0	2.5	49.4	48.5	2.0	47.8	50.2	2.0
1884	43.6	52.7	3.7	44.6	52.0	3.5	43.1	53.2	3.8
1886	45.7	49.3	5.0	47.9	46.6	5.5	46.2	47.6	6.2
1888	41.5	54.7	3.8	41.8	54.4	3.8	41.0	55.0	4.0
1890	34.7	49.9	15.5	41.8	50.7	7.5	41.3	51.3	7.5
1892	15.4	41.0	43.6	23.1	41.0	35.9	36.6	40.2	23.3
1894	24.7	43.3	32.0	16.2	51.2	32.6	27.8	50.5	21.8
1896	71.5	13.3	15.2	65.4	13.0	21.5	84.6	13.4	2.0
1898	66.2	31.3	2.5	64.5	33.1	2.5	66.1	32.0	2.0
1900	55.0	42.7	2.3	54.7	43.1	2.1	55.7	42.7	1.6
1902	45.9	47.3	6.7	44.8	46.7	8.6	46.3	46.4	7.3
1904	45.9	51.0	3.2	48.2	48.8	2.9	45.8	50.9	3.3
1906	40.2	49.6	10.2	38.0	48.9	13.2	39.4	52.1	8.5
1908	48.7	46.3	5.0	49.1	46.0	4.9	48.8	46.9	4.3
1910	48.6	41.6	9.8	50.2	45.2	4.6	46.5	44.3	9.2
1912	43.4	23.5	33.2	43.6	24.3	32.1	44.4	24.8	30.9
1914	43.8	39.3	16.9	41.1	43.0	15.9	44.6	40.2	15.2
1916	52.1	41.0	7.0	49.2	43.0	7.8	47.2	43.9	9.0
1918	46.6	50.0	3.4	46.0	51.0	3.0	45.8	50.9	3.3
1920	38.0	58.5	3.6	38.7	58.2	3.2	39.4	57.5	3.1
1922	42.2	52.9	4.9	46.4	50.7	2.9	44.8	52.0	3.2
1924	38.6	53.7	7.7	43.8	51.7	4.5	43.7	51.6	4.7
1926	44.9	51.2	3.9	50.3	47.6	2.1	45.6	52.3	2.1
1928	46.8	52.0	1.2	51.0	47.8	1.2	45.6	53.1	1.3
1930	51.8	46.7	1.5	54.2	44.6	1.1	51.2	47.9	0.9
1932	54.3	43.5	2.3	54.1	44.2	1.8	52.5	45.9	1.7
1934	58.2	38.9	2.9	58.3	38.8	2.8	58.4	38.3	3.3
1936	60.1	38.3	1.7	60.0	38.7	1.4	62.7	36.2	1.2
1938	53.8	45.1	1.1	53.6	45.5	0.9	58.6	40.3	1.1
1940	50.0	49.2	0.8	50.6	48.7	0.8	53.4	45.8	0.8
1942	44.6	54.8	0.6	43.7	55.7	0.6	43.8	55.4	0.8
1944	44.4	55.3	0.4	43.7	55.9	0.4	43.1	56.7	0.2
1946	50.1	49.4	0.5	50.4	49.3	0.3	49.5	50.0	0.5
1948	59.9	39.4	0.6	62.6	37.1	0.3	60.8	38.8	0.4
1950	47.0	52.5	0.5	47.5	52.2	0.3	47.6	52.1	0.3
1952	43.4	56.2	0.4	44.9	54.9	0.2	46.1	53.8	0.1
1954	47.9	51.9	0.2	50.7	49.3	0.0	49.3	50.7	0.0
1956	48.6	51.3	0.2	51.5	48.5	0.0	51.5	48.5	0.0
1958	51.7	48.0	0.3	54.9	45.0	0.2	53.1	46.7	0.2
1960	48.3	51.4	0.3	49.5	50.3	0.3	48.9	50.9	0.2
1962	47.2	52.3	0.5	45.2	54.3	0.5	46.5	53.1	0.4
1964	51.6	47.8	0.7	48.3	51.0	0.7	50.9	48.8	0.3
1966	47.4	50.8	1.8	46.2	52.9	1.0	47.5	52.3	0.2
1968	43.4	53.2	3.5	44.1	54.0	1.9	43.9	54.4	1.6
1970				47.0	51.2	1.9	48.7	49.9	1.5

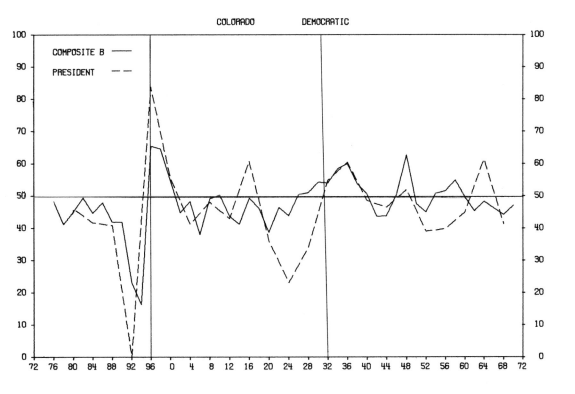

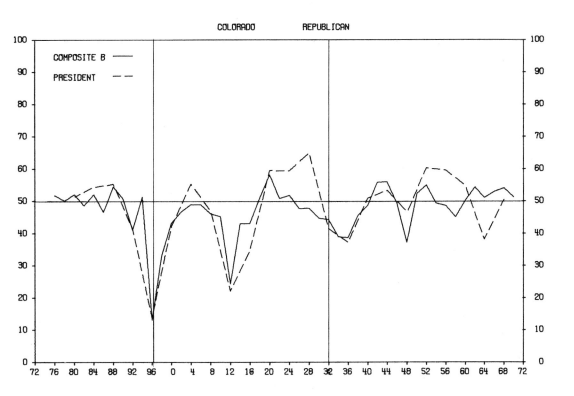

109

CONNECTICUT

YEAR	PRESIDENT			GOVERNOR			SENATE CLASS I			SENATE CLASS III		
	DEM.	REP.	OTHER	DEM.	REP.	OTHER	DEM.	REP.	OTHER	DEM.	REP.	OTHER
1872	47.6	52.4	0.0	47.9	50.0	2.1						
1874				52.9	45.6	1.5						
1876	50.7	48.3	1.0	51.9	46.1	1.9						
1878				44.3	46.7	9.0						
1880	48.5	50.5	1.0	48.4	50.5	1.0						
1882				51.0	47.4	1.5						
1884	48.9	48.0	3.0	49.3	48.1	2.5						
1886				47.7	46.2	6.1						
1888	48.7	48.4	2.9	48.9	47.9	3.2						
1890				50.0	47.3	2.7						
1892	50.1	46.8	3.1	50.3	46.6	3.1						
1894				42.8	54.2	3.0						
1896	32.5	63.2	4.2	32.5	62.5	5.0						
1898				42.9	54.2	2.9						
1900	41.1	56.9	2.0	45.1	53.0	1.9						
1902				43.4	53.4	3.2						
1904	38.1	58.1	3.7	41.5	54.9	3.6						
1906				42.0	54.8	3.1						
1908	35.9	59.4	4.7	43.5	51.9	4.6						
1910				46.5	44.2	9.3						
1912	39.2	35.9	25.0	41.1	35.5	23.4						
1914				40.8	50.4	8.8				42.1	49.8	8.2
1916	46.7	49.8	3.5	45.3	51.1	3.6	46.2	50.2	3.6			
1918				45.9	50.7	3.4						
1920	33.0	62.7	4.3	32.8	63.0	4.2				36.1	59.4	4.5
1922				45.7	52.4	1.9	45.5	52.3	2.2			
1924	27.5	61.5	10.9	31.9	66.2	1.9						
1926				35.4	63.6	1.1				35.6	63.3	1.0
1928	45.6	53.6	0.8	45.6	53.6	0.8	45.6	53.9	0.5			
1930				49.9	48.6	1.4						
1932	47.4	48.5	4.1	49.0	47.1	3.9				48.5	47.7	3.8
1934				46.7	45.2	8.1	51.7	48.3	0.0			
1936	55.3	40.3	4.3	55.3	41.1	3.6						
1938				36.0	35.9	28.1				39.8	42.9	17.3
1940	53.4	46.2	0.4	49.5	47.7	2.8	53.2	45.6	1.2			
1942				44.4	48.9	6.7						
1944	52.3	46.9	0.8	47.4	50.5	2.2				52.0	47.3	0.7
1946				40.4	54.4	5.2	40.8	55.9	3.3			
1948	47.9	49.5	2.5	49.3	49.0	1.7						
1950				47.7	49.7	2.6	49.2	49.1	1.8	51.7	46.6	1.7
1952	43.9	55.7	0.4				44.4	52.5	3.2	48.5	51.2	0.3
1954				49.5	49.2	1.3						
1956	36.3	63.7	0.0							43.0	54.8	2.1
1958				62.3	37.0	0.7	57.5	42.5	0.0			
1960	53.7	46.3	0.0									
1962				53.2	46.8	0.0				51.3	48.7	0.0
1964	67.8	32.1	0.1				64.6	35.3	0.0			
1966				55.7	44.3	0.0						
1968	49.5	44.3	6.2							54.3	45.7	0.0
1970				46.2	53.8	0.0	33.8	41.7	24.5			

110

YEAR	PRESIDENT			GOVERNOR			SENATE			HOUSE OF REPRESENTATIVES		
	DEM.	REP.	OTHER	DEM.	REP.	OTHER	DEM.	REP.	OTHER	DEM.	REP.	OTHER
1872	47.6	52.4	0.0	47.9	50.0	2.1				49.7	50.4	0.0
1874	49.2	50.4	0.5	52.9	45.6	1.5				48.9	51.1	0.0
1876	50.7	48.3	1.0	51.9	46.1	1.9				50.9	47.9	1.2
1878	49.6	49.4	1.0	44.3	46.7	9.0				46.9	49.6	3.6
1880	48.5	50.5	1.0	48.4	50.5	1.1				48.2	51.1	0.7
1882	48.7	49.3	2.0	51.0	47.4	1.5				50.3	48.3	1.4
1884	49.0	48.0	3.0	49.3	48.1	2.6				48.6	49.0	2.4
1886	48.8	48.2	3.0	47.7	46.2	6.1				47.6	46.5	5.9
1888	48.7	48.4	2.9	48.9	47.9	3.2				48.4	48.9	2.7
1890	49.4	47.6	3.0	50.0	47.3	2.7				50.3	47.2	2.4
1892	50.1	46.8	3.1	50.3	46.6	3.1				50.0	46.9	3.1
1894	41.3	55.0	3.7	42.8	54.2	3.0				41.8	55.2	3.0
1896	32.5	63.2	4.2	32.5	62.5	5.0				32.4	62.8	4.8
1898	36.8	60.1	3.1	42.9	54.2	2.9				42.4	54.8	2.8
1900	41.1	56.9	2.0	45.1	53.0	1.9				41.4	56.7	1.9
1902	39.6	57.5	2.9	43.4	53.4	3.2				43.4	53.5	3.1
1904	38.2	58.1	3.7	41.5	54.9	3.6				38.9	57.5	3.6
1906	37.0	58.8	4.2	42.1	54.8	3.1				41.7	55.2	3.1
1908	35.9	59.4	4.7	43.5	51.9	4.6				37.1	58.5	4.3
1910	37.6	47.7	14.8	46.5	44.3	9.3				45.0	47.2	7.8
1912	39.2	35.9	25.0	41.1	35.5	23.4				40.2	37.0	22.9
1914	42.9	42.8	14.3	40.8	50.4	8.8	42.1	49.8	8.2	43.1	49.1	7.9
1916	46.7	49.8	3.5	45.3	51.1	3.6	46.2	50.2	3.6	46.3	50.1	3.6
1918	39.8	56.3	3.9	45.9	50.7	3.5	41.2	54.8	4.1	46.9	49.7	3.4
1920	33.0	62.7	4.3	32.8	63.0	4.2	36.1	59.4	4.5	33.6	62.7	3.7
1922	30.3	62.1	7.6	45.7	52.4	1.9	45.5	52.3	2.2	45.7	52.6	1.7
1924	27.5	61.5	10.9	31.9	66.2	1.9	40.6	57.8	1.6	32.2	65.7	2.2
1926	36.6	57.6	5.9	35.4	63.6	1.1	35.6	63.3	1.1	35.4	63.7	0.9
1928	45.6	53.6	0.8	45.6	53.6	0.8	45.6	53.9	0.6	45.4	54.0	0.6
1930	46.5	51.1	2.4	49.9	48.6	1.4	47.0	50.8	2.2	48.7	50.5	0.8
1932	47.4	48.5	4.1	49.0	47.1	3.9	48.5	47.7	3.8	48.0	48.4	3.6
1934	51.4	44.4	4.2	46.7	45.2	8.1	51.8	48.3	0.0	49.6	47.0	3.4
1936	55.3	40.4	4.3	55.3	41.1	3.6	45.8	45.6	8.7	54.3	41.1	4.6
1938	54.4	43.3	2.4	36.0	35.9	28.1	39.8	42.9	17.3	39.9	43.4	16.7
1940	53.4	46.2	0.4	49.5	47.7	2.8	53.2	45.6	1.2	52.4	46.6	1.0
1942	52.9	46.6	0.6	44.4	48.9	6.7	52.6	46.4	1.0	45.9	50.2	4.0
1944	52.3	46.9	0.8	47.4	50.5	2.2	52.0	47.3	0.7	51.1	48.4	0.5
1946	50.1	48.2	1.7	40.4	54.4	5.2	40.8	55.9	3.3	41.3	55.6	3.1
1948	47.9	49.6	2.5	49.3	49.0	1.7	45.6	51.9	2.5	49.1	49.3	1.5
1950	45.9	52.6	1.5	47.7	49.7	2.6	50.4	47.8	1.7	49.2	49.0	1.8
1952	43.9	55.7	0.4	48.6	49.4	2.0	46.4	51.8	1.7	45.5	54.3	0.2
1954	40.1	59.7	0.2	49.5	49.2	1.3	44.8	53.3	1.9	49.0	50.8	0.3
1956	36.3	63.7	0.0	55.9	43.1	1.0	43.1	54.8	2.1	38.9	61.0	0.1
1958	45.0	55.0	0.0	62.3	37.0	0.7	57.5	42.5	0.0	54.8	45.2	0.0
1960	53.7	46.3	0.0	57.8	41.9	0.4	54.4	45.6	0.0	53.7	46.3	0.1
1962	60.8	39.2	0.1	53.2	46.8	0.0	51.3	48.8	0.0	53.3	46.6	0.1
1964	67.8	32.1	0.1	54.4	45.5	0.0	64.6	35.3	0.0	62.3	37.7	0.0
1966	58.6	38.2	3.2	55.7	44.3	0.0	59.5	40.5	0.0	54.1	44.2	1.7
1968	49.5	44.3	6.2	51.0	49.0	0.0	54.3	45.7	0.0	51.8	47.2	0.9
1970				46.2	53.8	0.0	33.8	41.7	24.5	49.7	49.0	1.3

111

CONNECTICUT

YEAR	COMPOSITE A (P+G+S+H/4)			COMPOSITE B (G+S+H/3)			COMPOSITE C (S+H/2)		
	DEM.	REP.	OTHER	DEM.	REP.	OTHER	DEM.	REP.	OTHER
1872	48.4	50.9	0.7	48.8	50.2	1.1	49.7	50.4	0.0
1874	50.3	49.0	0.7	50.9	48.4	0.7	48.9	51.1	0.0
1876	51.2	47.5	1.4	51.4	47.0	1.6	50.9	47.9	1.2
1878	46.9	48.6	4.5	45.6	48.1	6.3	46.9	49.6	3.6
1880	48.4	50.7	0.9	48.3	50.8	0.9	48.2	51.1	0.7
1882	50.0	48.3	1.6	50.7	47.9	1.5	50.3	48.3	1.4
1884	49.0	48.4	2.7	49.0	48.6	2.5	48.6	49.0	2.4
1886	48.0	47.0	5.0	47.7	46.4	6.0	47.6	46.5	5.9
1888	48.6	48.4	2.9	48.6	48.4	3.0	48.4	48.9	2.7
1890	49.9	47.4	2.7	50.2	47.3	2.6	50.3	47.2	2.4
1892	50.1	46.8	3.1	50.1	46.8	3.1	50.0	46.9	3.1
1894	42.0	54.8	3.2	42.3	54.7	3.0	41.8	55.2	3.0
1896	32.5	62.9	4.7	32.5	62.7	4.9	32.4	62.8	4.8
1898	40.7	56.3	2.9	42.7	54.5	2.8	42.4	54.8	2.8
1900	42.5	55.5	2.0	43.2	54.8	1.9	41.4	56.7	1.9
1902	42.2	54.8	3.0	43.4	53.5	3.1	43.4	53.5	3.1
1904	39.5	56.8	3.6	40.2	56.2	3.6	38.9	57.5	3.6
1906	40.3	56.3	3.5	41.9	55.0	3.1	41.7	55.2	3.1
1908	38.9	56.6	4.5	40.3	55.2	4.5	37.1	58.5	4.3
1910	43.0	46.4	10.6	45.7	45.7	8.6	45.0	47.2	7.8
1912	40.2	36.1	23.7	40.7	36.2	23.1	40.2	37.0	22.9
1914	42.2	48.0	9.8	42.0	49.7	8.3	42.6	49.4	8.0
1916	46.1	50.3	3.6	45.9	50.5	3.6	46.2	50.2	3.6
1918	43.5	52.9	3.7	44.7	51.7	3.6	44.1	52.2	3.7
1920	33.9	62.0	4.2	34.2	61.7	4.1	34.9	61.0	4.1
1922	41.8	54.9	3.4	45.6	52.4	2.0	45.6	52.5	2.0
1924	33.0	62.8	4.2	34.9	63.2	1.9	36.4	61.7	1.9
1926	35.7	62.1	2.2	35.5	63.5	1.0	35.5	63.5	1.0
1928	45.6	53.8	0.7	45.6	53.8	0.7	45.5	53.9	0.6
1930	48.0	50.3	1.7	48.5	50.0	1.5	47.8	50.7	1.5
1932	48.2	48.0	3.8	48.5	47.8	3.8	48.2	48.1	3.7
1934	49.9	46.2	3.9	49.4	46.8	3.8	50.7	47.6	1.7
1936	52.7	42.0	5.3	51.8	42.6	5.6	50.1	43.3	6.6
1938	42.5	41.4	16.1	38.6	40.8	20.7	39.8	43.2	17.0
1940	52.1	46.5	1.3	51.7	46.6	1.7	52.8	46.1	1.1
1942	48.9	48.0	3.1	47.6	48.5	3.9	49.2	48.3	2.5
1944	50.7	48.3	1.0	50.2	48.7	1.1	51.5	47.8	0.6
1946	43.2	53.5	3.3	40.9	55.3	3.9	41.1	55.8	3.2
1948	48.0	49.9	2.1	48.0	50.1	1.9	47.4	50.6	2.0
1950	48.3	49.8	1.9	49.1	48.8	2.0	49.8	48.4	1.8
1952	46.1	52.8	1.1	46.8	51.9	1.3	46.0	53.1	1.0
1954	45.8	53.2	0.9	47.7	51.1	1.2	46.9	52.1	1.1
1956	43.5	55.7	0.8	46.0	53.0	1.1	41.0	57.9	1.1
1958	54.9	44.9	0.2	58.2	41.6	0.2	56.2	43.9	0.0
1960	54.9	45.0	0.1	55.3	44.6	0.2	54.0	45.9	0.1
1962	54.6	45.3	0.0	52.6	47.4	0.0	52.3	47.7	0.0
1964	62.3	37.7	0.0	60.5	39.5	0.0	63.5	36.5	0.0
1966	57.0	41.8	1.2	56.4	43.0	0.6	56.8	42.4	0.9
1968	51.6	46.6	1.8	52.4	47.3	0.3	53.1	46.5	0.5
1970				43.2	48.2	8.6	41.7	45.4	12.9

112

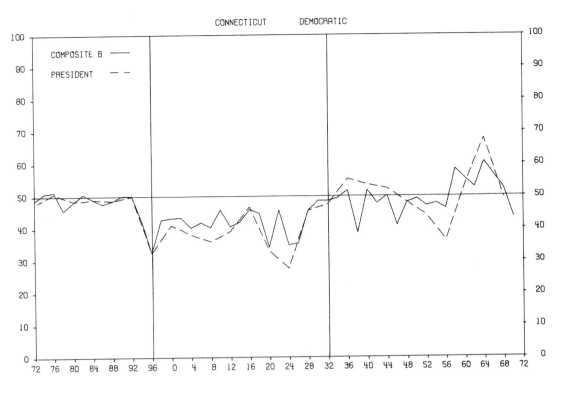

CONNECTICUT   DEMOCRATIC

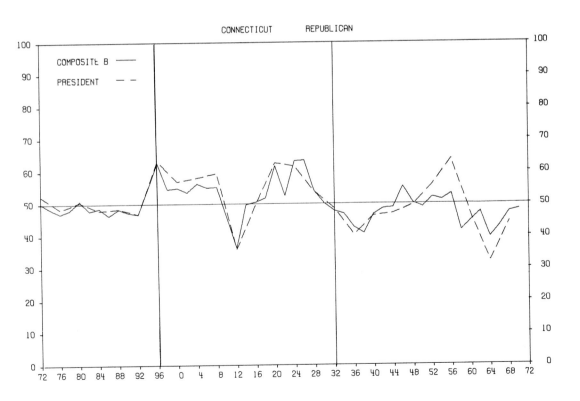

CONNECTICUT   REPUBLICAN

113

DELAWARE

YEAR	PRESIDENT			GOVERNOR			SENATE CLASS I			SENATE CLASS II		
	DEM.	REP.	OTHER	DEM.	REP.	OTHER	DEM.	REP.	OTHER	DEM.	REP.	OTHER
1872	46.8	51.0	2.2									
1874				52.6	47.4	0.0						
1876	55.4	44.6	0.0									
1878				79.1	0.0	20.9						
1880	51.5	48.0	0.4									
1882				53.1	46.9	0.0						
1884	56.6	43.2	0.2									
1886				63.6	0.6	35.7						
1888	55.1	43.5	1.3									
1890				50.4	48.9	0.7						
1892	49.9	48.5	1.5									
1894				47.7	50.8	1.5						
1896	43.1	53.2	3.7	44.2	31.4	24.4						
1898												
1900	44.9	53.7	1.4	44.9	53.6	1.5						
1902												
1904	44.1	54.1	1.8	45.1	51.4	3.5						
1906												
1908	45.9	52.1	2.0	47.6	52.0	0.5						
1910												
1912	46.5	32.9	20.7	44.3	47.0	8.7						
1914												
1916	47.8	50.2	2.0	47.0	52.1	1.0	49.7	44.8	5.6			
1918										47.8	51.2	1.0
1920	42.1	55.7	2.2	43.7	55.2	1.1						
1922							49.7	49.5	0.8			
1924	36.8	57.7	5.5	39.2	59.6	1.2						
1926										40.6	59.4	0.0
1928	33.8	65.8	0.4	39.1	60.9	0.0	39.1	60.9	0.0			
1930										45.2	54.6	0.1
1932	48.1	50.6	1.3	44.9	54.2	0.9						
1934							46.2	53.3	0.6			
1936	54.6	42.3	3.0	51.6	41.6	6.8						
1938										53.0	41.4	5.6
1940	54.7	45.1	0.2	45.4	52.4	2.2	50.6	47.3	2.1			
1942										44.9	54.2	0.9
1944	54.4	45.3	0.4	49.2	50.5	0.3						
1946							44.8	55.2	0.0			
1948	48.8	50.0	1.2	53.7	46.3	0.0						
1950										50.9	48.3	0.9
1952	47.9	51.8	0.4	47.9	52.1	0.0	45.5	54.5	0.0			
1954										56.9	43.1	0.0
1956	44.6	55.1	0.3	48.0	52.0	0.0						
1958							46.7	53.3	0.0			
1960	50.6	49.0	0.4	51.7	48.3	0.0						
1962										49.3	50.7	0.0
1964	60.9	38.8	0.3	51.4	48.6	0.0	48.3	51.7	0.0			
1966										40.9	59.1	0.0
1968	41.6	45.1	13.3	49.5	50.5	0.0						
1970							40.1	58.8	1.1			

YEAR	PRESIDENT			GOVERNOR			SENATE			HOUSE OF REPRESENTATIVES		
	DEM.	REP.	OTHER	DEM.	REP.	OTHER	DEM.	REP.	OTHER	DEM.	REP.	OTHER
1872	46.8	51.0	2.2	54.1	45.9	0.0				49.2	50.8	0.0
1874	51.1	47.8	1.1	52.6	47.4	0.0				53.3	46.7	0.0
1876	55.5	44.6	0.0	65.8	23.7	10.5				55.4	44.6	0.0
1878	53.5	46.3	0.2	79.1	0.0	20.9				78.1	0.0	21.9
1880	51.5	48.0	0.4	66.1	23.5	10.5				51.1	48.9	0.0
1882	54.0	45.6	0.3	53.1	46.9	0.0				53.0	46.9	0.1
1884	56.6	43.2	0.3	58.4	23.8	17.9				56.7	43.2	0.1
1886	55.9	43.4	0.8	63.6	0.6	35.8				62.2	0.0	37.8
1888	55.2	43.5	1.3	57.0	24.8	18.2				55.2	43.5	1.3
1890	52.5	46.0	1.5	50.4	48.9	0.7				50.6	48.7	0.7
1892	49.9	48.6	1.6	49.1	49.9	1.1				49.9	48.6	1.5
1894	46.5	50.9	2.6	47.7	50.8	1.5				47.6	50.7	1.7
1896	43.1	53.2	3.7	44.2	31.4	24.4				44.0	31.8	24.2
1898	44.0	53.4	2.6	44.6	42.5	13.0				45.5	53.1	1.4
1900	44.9	53.7	1.4	44.9	53.6	1.5				45.5	53.1	1.4
1902	44.5	53.9	1.6	45.0	52.5	2.5				42.9	21.0	36.1
1904	44.1	54.1	1.8	45.1	51.4	3.5				44.6	53.7	1.7
1906	45.0	53.1	1.9	46.3	51.7	2.0				44.8	52.8	2.4
1908	45.9	52.1	2.0	47.6	52.0	0.5				46.9	50.7	2.4
1910	46.2	42.5	11.3	45.9	49.5	4.6				46.1	50.9	3.0
1912	46.5	32.9	20.7	44.3	47.0	8.7				46.2	34.4	19.5
1914	47.1	41.5	11.3	45.6	49.5	4.9				45.2	50.1	4.6
1916	47.8	50.2	2.0	47.0	52.1	1.0	49.7	44.8	5.6	47.6	47.3	5.1
1918	44.9	53.0	2.1	45.3	53.7	1.0	47.8	51.2	1.0	47.6	51.4	1.0
1920	42.1	55.7	2.2	43.7	55.2	1.1	48.8	50.3	0.9	43.0	55.7	1.3
1922	39.4	56.7	3.9	41.4	57.4	1.1	49.7	49.5	0.8	53.9	44.9	1.3
1924	36.8	57.7	5.5	39.2	59.6	1.2	40.6	59.4	0.0	40.9	58.6	0.6
1926	35.3	61.8	2.9	39.1	60.3	0.6	39.8	60.2	0.0	43.1	56.9	0.0
1928	33.8	65.8	0.4	39.1	60.9	0.0	39.1	61.0	0.0	36.4	63.6	0.0
1930	41.0	58.2	0.9	42.0	57.6	0.5	45.2	54.6	0.1	44.4	55.4	0.2
1932	48.1	50.6	1.3	44.9	54.2	0.9	45.7	54.0	0.4	46.1	43.6	10.3
1934	51.4	46.4	2.2	48.2	47.9	3.9	46.2	53.3	0.6	46.5	53.1	0.5
1936	54.6	42.3	3.1	51.6	41.6	6.8	53.0	41.4	5.6	51.7	44.0	4.4
1938	54.7	43.7	1.6	48.5	47.0	4.5	51.8	44.4	3.9	43.3	55.9	0.9
1940	54.7	45.1	0.2	45.4	52.4	2.2	50.6	47.3	2.1	50.6	47.8	1.6
1942	54.6	45.2	0.3	47.3	51.5	1.2	44.9	54.2	0.9	45.8	53.6	0.7
1944	54.4	45.3	0.4	49.2	50.5	0.3	44.9	54.7	0.5	50.3	49.3	0.3
1946	51.6	47.7	0.8	51.4	48.4	0.2	44.9	55.2	0.0	43.6	56.4	0.0
1948	48.8	50.0	1.2	53.7	46.3	0.0	50.9	48.3	0.9	49.0	50.6	0.4
1950	48.3	50.9	0.8	50.8	49.2	0.0	48.2	51.4	0.4	43.4	56.7	0.0
1952	47.9	51.8	0.4	47.9	52.1	0.0	45.5	54.5	0.0	48.1	51.9	0.0
1954	46.3	53.4	0.3	48.0	52.0	0.0	56.9	43.1	0.0	54.9	45.1	0.0
1956	44.6	55.1	0.3	48.1	52.0	0.0	51.8	48.2	0.0	48.0	52.0	0.0
1958	47.6	52.1	0.3	49.9	50.1	0.0	46.7	53.3	0.0	50.2	49.8	0.0
1960	50.6	49.0	0.4	51.7	48.3	0.0	49.3	50.7	0.0	50.5	49.5	0.0
1962	55.8	43.9	0.3	51.5	48.5	0.0	48.8	51.2	0.0	52.9	46.9	0.2
1964	61.0	38.8	0.3	51.4	48.7	0.0	48.3	51.7	0.0	56.6	43.4	0.0
1966	51.3	42.0	6.8	50.4	49.6	0.0	40.9	59.1	0.0	44.2	55.8	0.0
1968	41.6	45.1	13.3	49.5	50.5	0.0	40.5	59.0	0.5	41.3	58.7	0.0
1970							40.1	58.8	1.1	44.6	53.7	1.7

115

YEAR	COMPOSITE A (P+G+S+H/4)			COMPOSITE B (G+S+H/3)			COMPOSITE C (S+H/2)		
	DEM.	REP.	OTHER	DEM.	REP.	OTHER	DEM.	REP.	OTHER
1872	50.0	49.2	0.8	51.7	48.3	0.0	49.2	50.8	0.0
1874	52.3	47.3	0.4	53.0	47.0	0.0	53.3	46.7	0.0
1876	58.9	37.6	3.5	60.6	34.1	5.2	55.4	44.6	0.0
1878	70.2	15.4	14.3	78.6	0.0	21.4	78.1	0.0	21.9
1880	56.2	40.1	3.6	58.6	36.2	5.2	51.1	48.9	0.0
1882	53.4	46.5	0.2	53.1	46.9	0.1	53.0	46.9	0.1
1884	57.2	36.7	6.1	57.5	33.5	9.0	56.7	43.2	0.1
1886	60.6	14.7	24.8	62.9	0.3	36.8	62.2	0.0	37.8
1888	55.8	37.3	7.0	56.1	34.2	9.8	55.2	43.5	1.3
1890	51.2	47.9	1.0	50.5	48.8	0.7	50.6	48.7	0.7
1892	49.6	49.0	1.4	49.5	49.2	1.3	49.9	48.6	1.5
1894	47.3	50.8	1.9	47.7	50.8	1.6	47.6	50.7	1.7
1896	43.8	38.8	17.4	44.1	31.6	24.3	44.0	31.8	24.2
1898	44.7	49.7	5.6	45.0	47.8	7.2	45.5	53.1	1.4
1900	45.1	53.4	1.5	45.2	53.3	1.5	45.5	53.1	1.4
1902	44.2	42.5	13.4	44.0	36.8	19.3	42.9	21.0	36.1
1904	44.6	53.0	2.3	44.9	52.5	2.6	44.6	53.7	1.7
1906	45.4	52.5	2.1	45.6	52.3	2.2	44.8	52.8	2.4
1908	46.8	51.6	1.6	47.2	51.3	1.5	46.9	50.7	2.4
1910	46.1	47.6	6.3	46.0	50.2	3.8	46.1	50.9	3.0
1912	45.7	38.1	16.3	45.2	40.7	14.1	46.2	34.4	19.5
1914	46.0	47.1	6.9	45.4	49.8	4.7	45.2	50.1	4.6
1916	48.0	48.6	3.4	48.1	48.0	3.9	48.7	46.0	5.3
1918	46.4	52.3	1.3	46.9	52.1	1.0	47.7	51.3	1.0
1920	44.4	54.2	1.4	45.1	53.8	1.1	45.9	53.0	1.1
1922	46.1	52.1	1.8	48.3	50.6	1.1	51.8	47.2	1.0
1924	39.4	58.8	1.8	40.2	59.2	0.6	40.7	59.0	0.3
1926	39.3	59.8	0.9	40.7	59.1	0.2	41.5	58.6	0.0
1928	37.1	62.8	0.1	38.2	61.8	0.0	37.7	62.3	0.0
1930	43.2	56.5	0.4	43.9	55.9	0.3	44.8	55.0	0.1
1932	46.2	50.6	3.2	45.6	50.6	3.9	45.9	48.8	5.3
1934	48.1	50.2	1.8	47.0	51.4	1.6	46.3	53.2	0.5
1936	52.7	42.3	5.0	52.1	42.3	5.6	52.3	42.7	5.0
1938	49.6	47.7	2.7	47.9	49.1	3.1	47.5	50.1	2.4
1940	50.3	48.1	1.5	48.9	49.2	2.0	50.6	47.5	1.8
1942	48.1	51.1	0.8	46.0	53.1	0.9	45.4	53.9	0.8
1944	49.7	49.9	0.4	48.1	51.5	0.4	47.6	52.0	0.4
1946	47.9	51.9	0.2	46.6	53.3	0.1	44.2	55.8	0.0
1948	50.6	48.8	0.6	51.2	48.4	0.4	49.9	49.4	0.6
1950	47.7	52.0	0.3	47.4	52.4	0.1	45.8	54.0	0.2
1952	47.3	52.6	0.1	47.2	52.8	0.0	46.8	53.2	0.0
1954	51.5	48.4	0.1	53.3	46.7	0.0	55.9	44.1	0.0
1956	48.1	51.8	0.1	49.3	50.7	0.0	49.9	50.1	0.0
1958	48.6	51.3	0.1	49.0	51.1	0.0	48.5	51.5	0.0
1960	50.5	49.4	0.1	50.5	49.5	0.0	49.9	50.1	0.0
1962	52.3	47.6	0.1	51.1	48.9	0.1	50.9	49.1	0.1
1964	54.3	45.6	0.1	52.1	47.9	0.0	52.4	47.6	0.0
1966	46.7	51.6	1.7	45.2	54.8	0.0	42.6	57.5	0.0
1968	43.2	53.3	3.5	43.8	56.1	0.2	40.9	58.8	0.3
1970							42.3	56.3	1.4

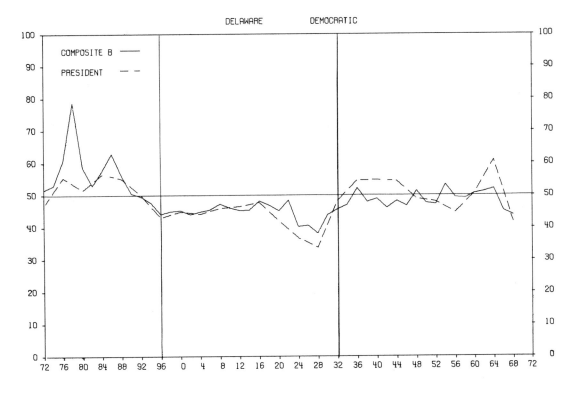

DELAWARE   DEMOCRATIC

COMPOSITE B ———
PRESIDENT   — —

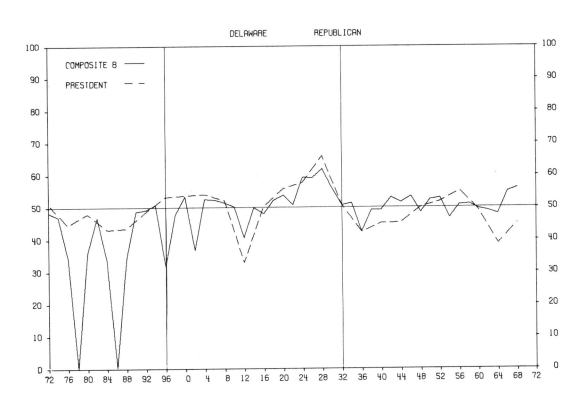

DELAWARE   REPUBLICAN

COMPOSITE B ———
PRESIDENT   — —

YEAR	PRESIDENT			GOVERNOR			SENATE CLASS I			SENATE CLASS III		
	DEM.	REP.	OTHER	DEM.	REP.	OTHER	DEM.	REP.	OTHER	DEM.	REP.	OTHER
1872 1874	46.5	53.5	0.0	47.6	52.4	0.0						
1876 1878	49.6	50.4	0.0	50.0	50.0	0.0						
1880 1882	54.2	45.8	0.0	54.9	45.1	0.0						
1884 1886	53.0	46.7	0.3	53.5	46.5	0.0						
1888 1890	59.5	39.9	0.6	60.4	39.6	0.0						
1892 1894	85.0	0.0	15.0	78.7	0.0	21.3						
1896 1898	66.0	24.3	9.7	66.5	20.3	13.2						
1900 1902	71.3	18.6	10.1	82.0	18.0	0.0						
1904 1906	68.3	21.5	10.2	79.2	17.4	3.5						
1908 1910	63.0	21.6	15.4	78.8	15.4	5.8						
1912 1914	69.5	8.4	22.1	80.2	5.5	14.3				99.5	0.0	0.5
1916 1918	69.3	18.1	12.6	84.3	12.5	3.2	82.9	12.5	4.7			
1920 1922	47.1	19.7	33.2	77.9	17.9	4.2	88.0	11.7	0.3	74.3	20.9	4.8
1924 1926	56.9	28.1	15.1	82.8	17.2	0.0				77.9	9.4	12.8
1928 1930	39.9	57.1	3.1	61.0	39.0	0.0	68.5	31.5	0.0			
1932 1934	74.9	25.1	0.0	66.6	33.4	0.0	100.0	0.0	0.0	99.8	0.0	0.2
1936 1938	76.1	23.9	0.0	80.9	19.1	0.0				89.5 82.4	10.5 17.6	0.0 0.0
1940 1942	74.0	26.0	0.0	100.0	0.0	0.0	100.0	0.0	0.0			
1944 1946	70.3	29.7	0.0	78.9	21.1	0.0	78.6	21.4	0.0	71.3	28.7	0.0
1948 1950	48.8	33.6	17.5	83.4	16.6	0.0				76.2	23.7	0.1
1952 1954	45.0	55.0	0.0	74.8 80.5	25.2 19.5	0.0 0.0	99.8	0.0	0.2			
1956 1958	42.7	57.2	0.1	73.7	26.3	0.0	71.2	28.8	0.0	100.0	0.0	0.0
1960 1962	48.5	51.5	0.0	59.8	40.2	0.0				70.0	30.0	0.0
1964 1966	51.1	48.9	0.0	56.1 44.9	41.3 55.1	2.6 0.0	63.9	36.0	0.0			
1968 1970	30.9	40.5	28.5	56.9	43.1	0.0	53.9	46.1	0.0	44.1	55.9	0.0

118

YEAR	PRESIDENT			GOVERNOR			SENATE			HOUSE OF REPRESENTATIVES		
	DEM.	REP.	OTHER	DEM.	REP.	OTHER	DEM.	REP.	OTHER	DEM.	REP.	OTHER
1872	46.5	53.5	0.0	47.6	52.4	0.0				23.7	52.5	23.8
1874	48.0	52.0	0.0	48.8	51.2	0.0				48.5	51.5	0.0
1876	49.6	50.4	0.0	50.0	50.0	0.0				49.5	50.5	0.0
1878	51.9	48.1	0.0	52.5	47.5	0.0				54.2	45.9	0.0
1880	54.2	45.8	0.0	54.9	45.1	0.0				54.9	45.1	0.0
1882	53.6	46.3	0.2	54.2	45.8	0.0				50.4	42.2	7.4
1884	53.0	46.7	0.3	53.5	46.5	0.0				53.3	46.4	0.4
1886	56.2	43.3	0.5	57.0	43.1	0.0				58.8	40.8	0.4
1888	59.5	39.9	0.6	60.4	39.6	0.0				59.2	40.8	0.0
1890	72.3	20.0	7.8	69.5	19.8	10.7				65.3	34.7	0.0
1892	85.0	0.0	15.0	78.7	0.0	21.3				86.5	0.0	13.5
1894	75.5	12.2	12.3	72.6	10.2	17.2				82.7	0.0	17.3
1896	66.1	24.3	9.7	66.6	20.3	13.2				69.0	22.1	8.9
1898	68.7	21.4	9.9	74.3	19.2	6.6				77.8	22.2	0.0
1900	71.3	18.6	10.1	82.0	18.0	0.0				83.4	16.6	0.0
1902	69.8	20.0	10.2	80.6	17.7	1.7				100.0	0.0	0.0
1904	68.3	21.5	10.2	79.2	17.4	3.5				78.1	18.4	3.5
1906	65.7	21.5	12.8	79.0	16.4	4.6				89.0	0.0	11.0
1908	63.0	21.6	15.4	78.8	15.4	5.8				76.9	16.0	7.1
1910	66.3	15.0	18.7	79.5	10.5	10.0				82.5	3.7	13.8
1912	69.5	8.4	22.1	80.2	5.5	14.3				79.3	6.1	14.6
1914	69.4	13.3	17.3	82.3	9.0	8.8	99.5	0.0	0.5	99.5	0.0	0.5
1916	69.3	18.1	12.6	84.3	12.5	3.2	82.9	12.5	4.7	77.9	16.3	5.8
1918	58.2	18.9	22.9	81.1	15.2	3.7	78.6	16.7	4.7	100.0	0.0	0.0
1920	47.1	19.7	33.2	77.9	17.9	4.2	74.3	21.0	4.8	78.9	17.1	4.1
1922	52.0	23.9	24.1	80.4	17.6	2.1	88.0	11.7	0.3	87.5	12.4	0.0
1924	56.9	28.1	15.1	82.8	17.2	0.0	82.9	10.5	6.6	74.7	22.3	3.1
1926	48.4	42.6	9.1	71.9	28.1	0.0	77.9	9.4	12.8	76.5	16.9	6.6
1928	39.9	57.1	3.1	61.0	39.0	0.0	68.5	31.5	0.0	68.1	31.9	0.0
1930	57.4	41.1	1.5	63.8	36.2	0.0	84.2	15.7	0.1	87.6	12.3	0.1
1932	74.9	25.1	0.0	66.6	33.4	0.0	99.8	0.0	0.2	82.6	17.3	0.1
1934	75.5	24.5	0.0	73.8	26.2	0.0	100.0	0.0	0.0	100.0	0.0	0.0
1936	76.1	23.9	0.0	80.9	19.1	0.0	89.5	10.5	0.0	81.9	18.1	0.0
1938	75.1	24.9	0.0	90.5	9.5	0.0	82.5	17.6	0.0	95.6	4.4	0.0
1940	74.0	26.0	0.0	100.0	0.0	0.0	100.0	0.0	0.0	86.2	13.8	0.0
1942	72.2	27.8	0.0	89.5	10.5	0.0	85.6	14.4	0.0	93.6	6.4	0.0
1944	70.3	29.7	0.0	78.9	21.1	0.0	71.3	28.7	0.0	84.7	15.3	0.0
1946	59.6	31.7	8.8	81.2	18.9	0.0	78.7	21.4	0.0	80.9	19.1	0.0
1948	48.8	33.6	17.6	83.4	16.6	0.0	77.4	22.5	0.0	84.1	15.9	0.0
1950	46.9	44.3	8.8	79.1	20.9	0.0	76.2	23.7	0.1	90.4	9.6	0.0
1952	45.0	55.0	0.0	74.8	25.2	0.0	99.8	0.0	0.2	74.2	25.8	0.0
1954	43.8	56.1	0.1	80.5	19.5	0.0	99.9	0.0	0.1	78.2	21.8	0.0
1956	42.7	57.2	0.1	73.7	26.3	0.0	100.0	0.0	0.0	62.6	37.4	0.0
1958	45.6	54.4	0.1	66.8	33.2	0.0	71.2	28.8	0.0	71.8	28.2	0.0
1960	48.5	51.5	0.0	59.9	40.2	0.0	70.6	29.4	0.0	69.0	31.0	0.0
1962	49.8	50.2	0.0	58.0	40.7	1.3	70.0	30.0	0.0	62.6	37.4	0.0
1964	51.2	48.9	0.0	56.1	41.3	2.6	63.9	36.0	0.0	70.1	29.7	0.2
1966	41.0	44.7	14.3	44.9	55.1	0.0	54.0	46.0	0.0	64.6	35.0	0.4
1968	30.9	40.5	28.5	50.9	49.1	0.0	44.1	55.9	0.0	57.2	42.8	0.0
1970				56.9	43.1	0.0	53.9	46.1	0.0	54.5	45.5	0.0

FLORIDA

YEAR	COMPOSITE A (P+G+S+H/4)			COMPOSITE B (G+S+H/3)			COMPOSITE C (S+H/2)		
	DEM.	REP.	OTHER	DEM.	REP.	OTHER	DEM.	REP.	OTHER
1872	39.3	52.8	7.9	35.7	52.4	11.9	23.7	52.5	23.8
1874	48.5	51.5	0.0	48.7	51.3	0.0	48.5	51.5	0.0
1876	49.7	50.3	0.0	49.8	50.2	0.0	49.5	50.5	0.0
1878	52.8	47.2	0.0	53.3	46.7	0.0	54.2	45.9	0.0
1880	54.7	45.3	0.0	54.9	45.1	0.0	54.9	45.1	0.0
1882	52.7	44.7	2.5	52.3	44.0	3.7	50.4	42.2	7.4
1884	53.3	46.5	0.2	53.4	46.4	0.2	53.3	46.4	0.4
1886	57.3	42.4	0.3	57.9	41.9	0.2	58.8	40.8	0.4
1888	59.7	40.1	0.2	59.8	40.2	0.0	59.2	40.8	0.0
1890	69.0	24.8	6.2	67.4	27.3	5.3	65.3	34.7	0.0
1892	83.4	0.0	16.6	82.6	0.0	17.4	86.5	0.0	13.5
1894	76.9	7.4	15.6	77.6	5.1	17.3	82.7	0.0	17.3
1896	67.2	22.3	10.6	67.8	21.2	11.0	69.0	22.1	8.9
1898	73.6	20.9	5.5	76.0	20.7	3.3	77.8	22.2	0.0
1900	78.9	17.7	3.4	82.7	17.3	0.0	83.4	16.6	0.0
1902	83.5	12.6	4.0	90.3	8.9	0.9	100.0	0.0	0.0
1904	75.2	19.1	5.7	78.6	17.9	3.5	78.1	18.4	3.5
1906	77.9	12.6	9.5	84.0	8.2	7.8	89.0	0.0	11.0
1908	72.9	17.7	9.4	77.9	15.7	6.4	76.9	16.0	7.1
1910	76.1	9.7	14.2	81.0	7.1	11.9	82.5	3.7	13.8
1912	76.3	6.7	17.0	79.7	5.8	14.4	79.3	6.1	14.6
1914	87.7	5.6	6.8	93.8	3.0	3.3	99.5	0.0	0.5
1916	78.6	14.8	6.6	81.7	13.8	4.6	80.4	14.4	5.3
1918	79.5	12.7	7.8	86.6	10.6	2.8	89.3	8.4	2.4
1920	69.5	18.9	11.6	77.0	18.7	4.3	76.6	19.0	4.4
1922	77.0	16.4	6.6	85.3	13.9	0.8	87.8	12.1	0.2
1924	74.3	19.5	6.2	80.1	16.7	3.2	78.8	16.4	4.8
1926	68.7	24.2	7.1	75.4	18.1	6.5	77.2	13.1	9.7
1928	59.4	39.9	0.8	65.9	34.1	0.0	68.3	31.7	0.0
1930	73.2	26.3	0.4	78.5	21.4	0.1	85.9	14.0	0.1
1932	81.0	18.9	0.1	83.0	16.9	0.1	91.2	8.6	0.2
1934	87.3	12.7	0.0	91.3	8.7	0.0	100.0	0.0	0.0
1936	82.1	17.9	0.0	84.1	15.9	0.0	85.7	14.3	0.0
1938	85.9	14.1	0.0	89.5	10.5	0.0	89.0	11.0	0.0
1940	90.1	9.9	0.0	95.4	4.6	0.0	93.1	6.9	0.0
1942	85.2	14.8	0.0	89.6	10.4	0.0	89.6	10.4	0.0
1944	76.3	23.7	0.0	78.3	21.7	0.0	78.0	22.0	0.0
1946	75.1	22.7	2.2	80.2	19.8	0.0	79.8	20.2	0.0
1948	73.4	22.2	4.4	81.6	18.4	0.0	80.8	19.2	0.0
1950	73.2	24.6	2.2	81.9	18.1	0.0	83.3	16.6	0.0
1952	73.5	26.5	0.1	82.9	17.0	0.1	87.0	12.9	0.1
1954	75.6	24.4	0.0	86.2	13.8	0.0	89.1	10.9	0.1
1956	69.7	30.2	0.0	78.8	21.2	0.0	81.3	18.7	0.0
1958	63.8	36.1	0.0	69.9	30.1	0.0	71.5	28.5	0.0
1960	62.0	38.0	0.0	66.5	33.5	0.0	69.8	30.2	0.0
1962	60.1	39.6	0.3	63.5	36.0	0.5	66.3	33.7	0.0
1964	60.3	39.0	0.7	63.4	35.7	1.0	67.0	32.9	0.1
1966	51.1	45.2	3.7	54.5	45.4	0.1	59.3	40.5	0.2
1968	45.8	47.1	7.1	50.7	49.3	0.0	50.6	49.4	0.0
1970				55.1	44.9	0.0	54.2	45.8	0.0

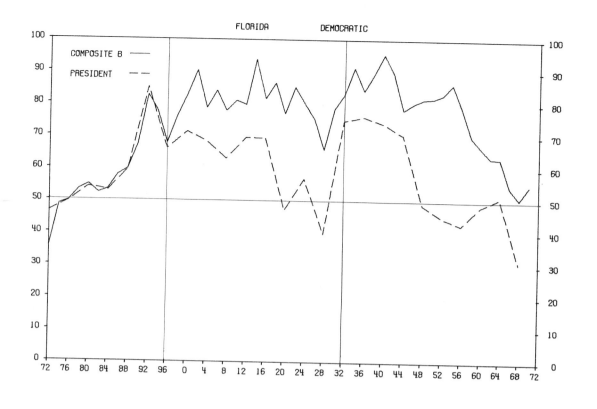

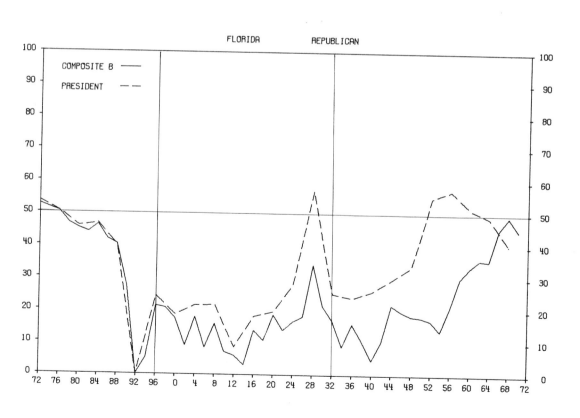

121

GEORGIA

YEAR	PRESIDENT			GOVERNOR			SENATE CLASS II			SENATE CLASS III		
	DEM.	REP.	OTHER	DEM.	REP.	OTHER	DEM.	REP.	OTHER	DEM.	REP.	OTHER
1872	55.0	45.0	0.0	69.2	30.8	0.0						
1874												
1876	72.0	28.0	0.0	76.2	23.8	0.0						
1878												
1880	65.4	34.6	0.0	64.9	0.0	35.1						
1882				70.6	0.0	29.4						
1884	65.9	33.8	0.2	100.0	0.0	0.0						
1886				99.2	0.0	0.8						
1888	70.3	28.3	1.4	100.0	0.0	0.0						
1890				100.0	0.0	0.0						
1892	58.0	21.7	20.3	66.7	0.0	33.3						
1894				55.6	0.0	44.4						
1896	57.5	36.6	5.9	58.9	0.0	41.1						
1898				69.7	0.0	30.3						
1900	66.9	28.2	4.9	78.6	0.0	21.4						
1902				93.6	0.0	6.4						
1904	63.7	18.3	18.0	100.0	0.0	0.0						
1906				99.9	0.0	0.1						
1908	54.6	31.2	14.2	90.5	0.0	9.5						
1910				50.0	0.0	50.0						
1912	76.6	4.3	19.1	100.0	0.0	0.0						
1914				100.0	0.0	0.0	68.8	0.0	31.2	68.4	0.0	31.6
1916	79.5	7.0	13.5	100.0	0.0	0.0						
1918				100.0	0.0	0.0	88.4	11.6	0.0			
1920	70.9	28.7	0.4	100.0	0.0	0.0				94.9	0.0	5.1
1922				100.0	0.0	0.0				100.0	0.0	0.0
1924	74.1	18.2	7.6	100.0	0.0	0.0				100.0	0.0	0.0
1926				100.0	0.0	0.0				100.0	0.0	0.0
1928	56.6	27.7	15.7	100.0	0.0	0.0						
1930				100.0	0.0	0.0	100.0	0.0	0.0			
1932	91.6	7.8	0.6	100.0	0.0	0.0	100.0	0.0	0.0	92.8	7.2	0.0
1934				100.0	0.0	0.0						
1936	87.1	12.6	0.3	99.7	0.0	0.3	100.0	0.0	0.0			
1938				94.3	0.0	5.7				95.1	0.0	4.9
1940	84.8	7.7	7.5	91.8	0.0	8.2						
1942				96.3	0.0	3.7	96.9	0.0	3.1			
1944	81.7	17.2	1.0							100.0	0.0	0.0
1946				98.5	0.0	1.5						
1948	60.8	18.3	20.9	97.5	0.0	2.5	99.9	0.0	0.1			
1950				98.4	0.0	1.6				100.0	0.0	0.0
1952	69.7	30.3	0.0									
1954				100.0	0.0	0.0	100.0	0.0	0.0			
1956	66.4	33.3	0.3							100.0	0.0	0.0
1958				100.0	0.0	0.0						
1960	62.5	37.4	0.0				99.9	0.0	0.1			
1962				99.9	0.0	0.1				100.0	0.0	0.0
1964	45.8	54.1	0.0				100.0	0.0	0.0			
1966				47.4	47.7	4.8						
1968	26.7	30.4	42.8							77.5	22.5	0.0
1970				59.3	40.7	0.0						

GEORGIA

YEAR	PRESIDENT			GOVERNOR			SENATE			HOUSE OF REPRESENTATIVES		
	DEM.	REP.	OTHER	DEM.	REP.	OTHER	DEM.	REP.	OTHER	DEM.	REP.	OTHER
1872	55.0	45.0	0.0	69.2	30.8	0.0				56.0	43.1	0.9
1874	63.5	36.5	0.0	72.7	27.3	0.0				67.8	25.5	6.8
1876	72.0	28.0	0.0	76.2	23.8	0.0				71.4	28.6	0.0
1878	68.7	31.3	0.0	70.6	11.9	17.5				55.8	2.9	41.3
1880	65.4	34.6	0.0	64.9	0.0	35.1				62.3	17.0	20.7
1882	65.7	34.2	0.1	70.6	0.0	29.4				70.1	18.4	11.5
1884	65.9	33.8	0.2	100.0	0.0	0.0				60.4	34.3	5.3
1886	68.1	31.1	0.8	99.2	0.0	0.8				92.4	0.1	7.4
1888	70.3	28.3	1.4	100.0	0.0	0.0				73.9	18.1	8.0
1890	64.2	25.0	10.8	100.0	0.0	0.0				80.5	15.7	3.8
1892	58.0	21.7	20.3	66.7	0.0	33.3				63.5	32.3	4.2
1894	57.8	29.1	13.1	55.6	0.0	44.4				61.5	0.0	38.5
1896	57.5	36.6	5.9	58.9	0.0	41.1				58.6	19.1	22.3
1898	62.2	32.4	5.4	69.8	0.0	30.3				81.4	10.4	8.3
1900	66.9	28.2	4.9	78.6	0.0	21.4				78.9	11.0	10.1
1902	65.3	23.3	11.4	93.6	0.0	6.4				99.0	0.0	1.0
1904	63.7	18.3	18.0	100.0	0.0	0.0				85.0	13.5	1.5
1906	59.2	24.8	16.1	99.9	0.0	0.1				98.7	1.3	0.0
1908	54.6	31.2	14.2	90.5	0.0	9.5				99.5	0.5	0.0
1910	65.6	17.7	16.6	50.0	0.0	50.0				77.9	4.1	18.0
1912	76.6	4.3	19.1	100.0	0.0	0.0				99.7	0.3	0.0
1914	78.1	5.7	16.3	100.0	0.0	0.0	68.6	0.0	31.4	99.2	0.0	0.8
1916	79.5	7.0	13.5	100.0	0.0	0.0	78.5	5.8	15.7	94.3	0.0	5.7
1918	75.2	17.9	6.9	100.0	0.0	0.0	88.4	11.6	0.0	95.3	4.7	0.0
1920	70.9	28.7	0.4	100.0	0.0	0.0	94.9	0.0	5.1	88.4	11.6	0.0
1922	72.5	23.5	4.0	100.0	0.0	0.0	100.0	0.0	0.0	97.9	1.3	0.8
1924	74.1	18.2	7.6	100.0	0.0	0.0	100.0	0.0	0.0	97.8	0.0	2.2
1926	65.4	23.0	11.7	100.0	0.0	0.0	100.0	0.0	0.0	99.2	0.0	0.8
1928	56.6	27.7	15.7	100.0	0.0	0.0	100.0	0.0	0.0	100.0	0.0	0.0
1930	74.1	17.7	8.2	100.0	0.0	0.0	100.0	0.0	0.0	96.6	0.0	3.4
1932	91.6	7.8	0.6	100.0	0.0	0.0	96.3	3.7	0.0	94.8	3.5	1.8
1934	89.4	10.2	0.5	100.0	0.0	0.0	98.2	1.9	0.0	99.5	0.5	0.0
1936	87.1	12.6	0.3	99.7	0.0	0.3	100.0	0.0	0.0	94.3	5.7	0.0
1938	86.0	10.1	3.9	94.3	0.0	5.7	95.1	0.0	4.9	98.8	0.0	1.2
1940	84.8	7.7	7.5	91.8	0.0	8.2	96.0	0.0	4.0	95.7	3.7	0.6
1942	83.3	12.4	4.3	96.3	0.0	3.7	96.9	0.0	3.1	94.3	0.0	5.7
1944	81.7	17.2	1.0	97.4	0.0	2.6	100.0	0.0	0.0	98.9	0.0	1.1
1946	71.3	17.8	11.0	98.5	0.0	1.5	99.9	0.0	0.1	100.0	0.0	0.0
1948	60.8	18.3	20.9	97.5	0.0	2.5	99.9	0.0	0.1	99.9	0.0	0.1
1950	65.2	24.3	10.5	98.4	0.0	1.6	100.0	0.0	0.0	100.0	0.0	0.0
1952	69.7	30.3	0.0	99.2	0.0	0.8	100.0	0.0	0.0	100.0	0.0	0.0
1954	68.0	31.8	0.2	100.0	0.0	0.0	100.0	0.0	0.0	90.1	8.5	1.5
1956	66.4	33.3	0.3	100.0	0.0	0.0	100.0	0.0	0.0	88.1	10.0	1.9
1958	64.5	35.4	0.2	100.0	0.0	0.1	100.0	0.0	0.1	100.0	0.0	0.0
1960	62.5	37.4	0.0	100.0	0.0	0.1	99.9	0.0	0.1	95.7	4.3	0.1
1962	54.2	45.8	0.0	100.0	0.0	0.1	100.0	0.0	0.0	81.7	17.9	0.4
1964	45.9	54.1	0.0	73.7	23.9	2.4	100.0	0.0	0.0	67.3	29.7	3.0
1966	36.3	42.3	21.4	47.4	47.8	4.8	100.0	0.0	0.1	65.6	34.3	0.1
1968	26.8	30.4	42.9	53.4	44.2	2.4	77.5	22.5	0.0	79.4	20.6	0.0
1970				59.4	40.7	0.0				74.4	25.6	0.0

123

YEAR	COMPOSITE A (P+G+S+H/4)			COMPOSITE B (G+S+H/3)			COMPOSITE C (S+H/2)		
	DEM.	REP.	OTHER	DEM.	REP.	OTHER	DEM.	REP.	OTHER
1872	60.1	39.6	0.3	62.6	36.9	0.5	56.0	43.1	0.9
1874	68.0	29.7	2.3	70.3	26.4	3.4	67.8	25.5	6.8
1876	73.2	26.8	0.0	73.8	26.2	0.0	71.4	28.6	0.0
1878	65.0	15.4	19.6	63.2	7.4	29.4	55.8	2.9	41.3
1880	64.2	17.2	18.6	63.6	8.5	27.9	62.3	17.0	20.7
1882	68.8	17.5	13.7	70.3	9.2	20.5	70.1	18.4	11.5
1884	75.4	22.7	1.8	80.2	17.2	2.6	60.4	34.3	5.3
1886	86.6	10.4	3.0	95.8	0.1	4.1	92.4	0.1	7.4
1888	81.4	15.5	3.1	87.0	9.1	4.0	73.9	18.1	8.0
1890	81.6	13.6	4.9	90.3	7.8	1.9	80.5	15.7	3.8
1892	62.8	18.0	19.3	65.1	16.2	18.7	63.5	32.3	4.2
1894	58.3	9.7	32.0	58.5	0.0	41.5	61.5	0.0	38.5
1896	58.3	18.5	23.1	58.8	9.5	31.7	58.6	19.1	22.3
1898	71.1	14.3	14.6	75.6	5.2	19.3	81.4	10.4	8.3
1900	74.8	13.1	12.2	78.8	5.5	15.8	78.9	11.0	10.1
1902	86.0	7.8	6.3	96.3	0.0	3.7	99.0	0.0	1.0
1904	82.9	10.6	6.5	92.5	6.8	0.8	85.0	13.5	1.5
1906	85.9	8.7	5.4	99.3	0.6	0.1	98.7	1.3	0.0
1908	81.6	10.6	7.9	95.0	0.2	4.7	99.5	0.5	0.0
1910	64.5	7.3	28.2	63.9	2.1	34.0	77.9	4.1	18.0
1912	92.1	1.5	6.4	99.9	0.2	0.0	99.7	0.3	0.0
1914	86.5	1.4	12.1	89.3	0.0	10.7	83.9	0.0	16.1
1916	88.1	3.2	8.7	90.9	1.9	7.1	86.4	2.9	10.7
1918	89.7	8.6	1.7	94.6	5.5	0.0	91.8	8.2	0.0
1920	88.6	10.1	1.4	94.4	3.9	1.7	91.7	5.8	2.6
1922	92.6	6.2	1.2	99.3	0.4	0.3	99.0	0.6	0.4
1924	93.0	4.6	2.5	99.3	0.0	0.7	98.9	0.0	1.1
1926	91.1	5.7	3.1	99.7	0.0	0.3	99.6	0.0	0.4
1928	89.1	6.9	3.9	100.0	0.0	0.0	100.0	0.0	0.0
1930	92.7	4.4	2.9	98.9	0.0	1.1	98.3	0.0	1.7
1932	95.7	3.7	0.6	97.0	2.4	0.6	95.5	3.6	0.9
1934	96.8	3.1	0.1	99.2	0.8	0.0	98.9	1.2	0.0
1936	95.3	4.6	0.2	98.0	1.9	0.1	97.2	2.9	0.0
1938	93.5	2.5	3.9	96.1	0.0	3.9	97.0	0.0	3.0
1940	92.1	2.8	5.1	94.5	1.2	4.3	95.9	1.8	2.3
1942	92.7	3.1	4.2	95.9	0.0	4.2	95.6	0.0	4.4
1944	94.5	4.3	1.2	98.8	0.0	1.2	99.5	0.0	0.5
1946	92.4	4.4	3.1	99.5	0.0	0.5	100.0	0.0	0.1
1948	89.5	4.6	5.9	99.1	0.0	0.9	99.9	0.0	0.1
1950	90.9	6.1	3.0	99.5	0.0	0.5	100.0	0.0	0.0
1952	92.2	7.6	0.2	99.7	0.0	0.3	100.0	0.0	0.0
1954	89.5	10.1	0.4	96.7	2.8	0.5	95.0	4.2	0.7
1956	88.6	10.8	0.6	96.0	3.3	0.6	94.0	5.0	0.9
1958	91.1	8.8	0.1	100.0	0.0	0.0	100.0	0.0	0.0
1960	89.5	10.4	0.1	98.5	1.4	0.1	97.8	2.1	0.1
1962	84.0	15.9	0.1	93.9	6.0	0.2	90.9	8.9	0.2
1964	71.7	26.9	1.4	80.3	17.9	1.8	83.7	14.8	1.5
1966	62.3	31.1	6.6	71.0	27.4	1.7	82.8	17.2	0.1
1968	59.3	29.4	11.3	70.1	29.1	0.8	78.5	21.5	0.0
1970				66.9	33.1	0.0	74.4	25.6	0.0

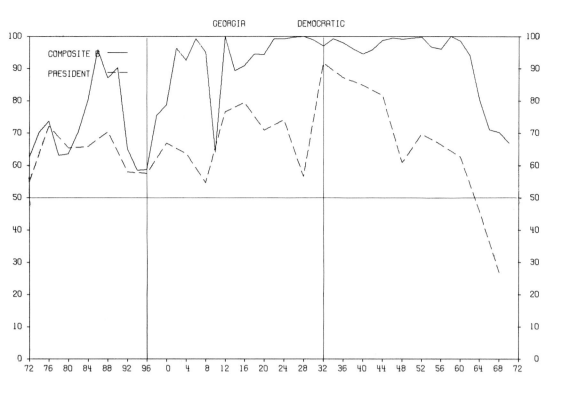

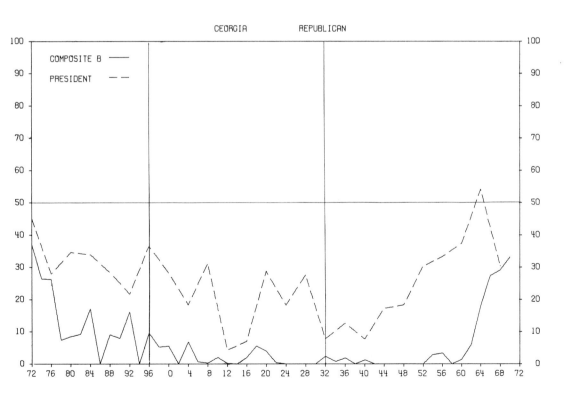

HAWAII

YEAR	PRESIDENT			GOVERNOR			SENATE CLASS I			SENATE CLASS III		
	DEM.	REP.	OTHER	DEM.	REP.	OTHER	DEM.	REP.	OTHER	DEM.	REP.	OTHER
1960	50.0	50.0	0.0	48.7	51.1	0.2	47.1	52.9	0.0	51.1	48.3	0.6
1962				58.3	41.7	0.0				69.4	30.6	0.0
1964	78.8	21.2	0.0				46.4	53.0	0.6			
1966				51.1	48.9	0.0						
1968	59.8	38.7	1.5							83.4	15.0	1.6
1970				51.4	48.6	0.0	48.4	51.6	0.0			

HAWAII

YEAR	PRESIDENT			GOVERNOR			SENATE			HOUSE OF REPRESENTATIVES		
	DEM.	REP.	OTHER	DEM.	REP.	OTHER	DEM.	REP.	OTHER	DEM.	REP.	OTHER
1960	50.0	50.0	0.0	48.7	51.1	0.2	49.1	50.6	0.3	71.5	28.3	0.3
1962	64.4	35.6	0.0	58.3	41.7	0.0	69.4	30.6	0.0	67.9	32.2	0.0
1964	78.8	21.2	0.0	54.7	45.3	0.0	46.4	53.0	0.6	62.9	37.1	0.0
1966	69.3	30.0	0.7	51.1	48.9	0.0	64.9	34.0	1.1	68.4	31.6	0.0
1968	59.8	38.7	1.5	51.2	48.8	0.0	83.4	15.0	1.6	71.8	27.2	1.0
1970				51.4	48.6	0.0	48.4	51.6	0.0	84.7	15.3	0.0

HAWAII

YEAR	COMPOSITE A (P+G+S+H/4)			COMPOSITE B (G+S+H/3)			COMPOSITE C (S+H/2)		
	DEM.	REP.	OTHER	DEM.	REP.	OTHER	DEM.	REP.	OTHER
1960	54.8	45.0	0.2	56.4	43.3	0.3	60.3	39.4	0.3
1962	65.0	35.0	0.0	65.2	34.8	0.0	68.6	31.4	0.0
1964	60.7	39.2	0.2	54.7	45.1	0.2	54.6	45.1	0.3
1966	63.4	36.1	0.5	61.5	38.2	0.4	66.6	32.8	0.6
1968	66.6	32.4	1.0	68.8	30.3	0.9	77.6	21.1	1.3
1970				61.5	38.5	0.0	66.6	33.4	0.0

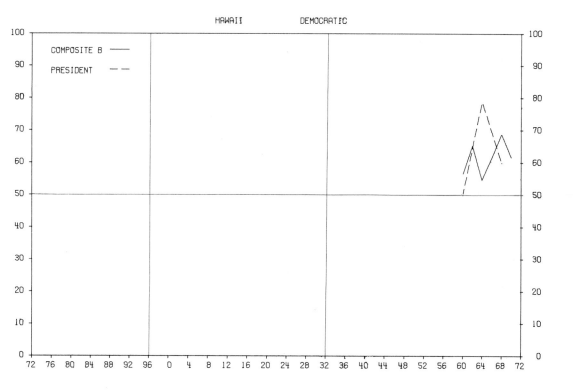

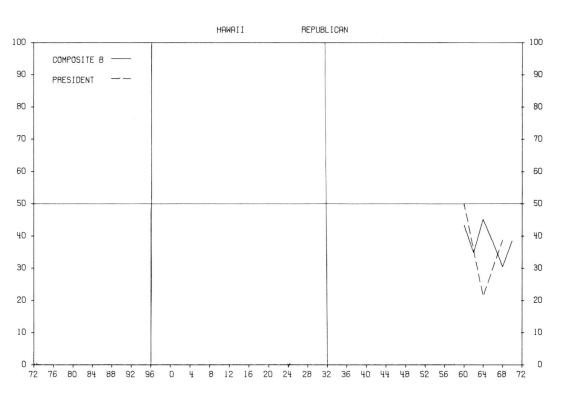

127

IDAHO

YEAR	PRESIDENT			GOVERNOR			SENATE CLASS II			SENATE CLASS III		
	DEM.	REP.	OTHER	DEM.	REP.	OTHER	DEM.	REP.	OTHER	DEM.	REP.	OTHER
1872												
1874												
1876												
1878												
1880												
1882												
1884												
1886												
1888												
1890				43.6	56.4	0.0						
1892	54.2	44.3	1.5	33.7	40.7	25.5						
1894				28.7	41.5	29.8						
1896	78.1	21.3	0.6	76.8	22.4	0.8						
1898				48.8	34.7	16.5						
1900	50.8	46.9	2.2	52.0	48.0	0.0						
1902				43.2	52.9	3.9						
1904	25.5	65.8	8.7	34.0	58.7	7.2						
1906				40.1	52.2	7.7						
1908	37.2	54.1	8.7	41.6	49.6	8.8						
1910				47.4	46.4	6.2						
1912	32.1	31.0	36.9	32.2	33.2	34.5						
1914				44.1	37.4	18.5				38.1	43.9	18.0
1916	52.0	41.1	6.8	47.5	47.1	5.4						
1918				40.1	59.9	0.0	32.8	67.2	0.0	50.5	49.5	0.0
1920	34.3	65.6	0.1	26.9	53.0	20.1				45.9	54.1	0.0
1922				28.8	39.5	31.7						
1924	16.1	48.1	35.8	16.8	43.9	39.3	20.1	79.5	0.4			
1926				20.6	51.0	28.4				25.0	45.4	29.6
1928	34.9	64.2	0.9	41.6	57.8	0.6				36.7	62.6	0.7
1930				56.0	44.0	0.0	27.6	72.4	0.0			
1932	58.7	38.2	3.0	61.7	36.4	1.8				55.7	42.3	2.1
1934				54.6	44.3	1.2						
1936	63.0	33.2	3.8	57.2	41.5	1.3	36.6	63.4	0.0			
1938				41.9	57.3	0.8				54.7	44.9	0.5
1940	54.4	45.3	0.3	50.5	49.5	0.0	47.1	52.9	0.0			
1942				49.8	50.2	0.0	48.5	51.5	0.0			
1944	51.6	48.1	0.4	52.6	47.4	0.0				51.1	48.9	0.0
1946				43.6	56.4	0.0	41.4	58.6	0.0			
1948	50.0	47.3	2.8				50.0	48.5	1.6			
1950				47.4	52.6	0.0	48.1	51.9	0.0	38.3	61.7	0.0
1952	34.4	65.4	0.2									
1954				45.8	54.2	0.0	37.2	62.8	0.0			
1956	38.8	61.2	0.1							56.2	38.7	5.1
1958				49.0	51.0	0.0						
1960	46.2	53.8	0.0				47.7	52.3	0.0			
1962				45.4	54.6	0.0	49.1	50.9	0.0	54.7	45.3	0.0
1964	50.9	49.1	0.0									
1966				37.1	41.4	21.5	44.6	55.4	0.0			
1968	30.7	56.8	12.5							60.3	39.7	0.0
1970				52.2	47.8	0.0						

YEAR	PRESIDENT			GOVERNOR			SENATE			HOUSE OF REPRESENTATIVES		
	DEM.	REP.	OTHER	DEM.	REP.	OTHER	DEM.	REP.	OTHER	DEM.	REP.	OTHER
1872												
1874												
1876												
1878												
1880												
1882												
1884												
1886												
1888												
1890				43.7	56.4	0.0				44.0	56.0	0.0
1892	54.2	44.3	1.5	33.7	40.7	25.6				31.1	44.1	24.7
1894	66.1	32.8	1.0	28.7	41.5	29.8				24.4	43.4	32.3
1896	78.1	21.3	0.6	76.8	22.4	0.8				46.6	21.4	32.0
1898	64.5	34.1	1.4	48.8	34.7	16.5				0.0	33.4	66.6
1900	50.9	46.9	2.3	52.0	48.0	0.0				51.1	48.9	0.0
1902	38.2	56.4	5.5	43.2	52.9	3.9				41.7	54.3	4.0
1904	25.5	65.8	8.7	34.0	58.7	7.3				28.6	63.7	7.7
1906	31.3	60.0	8.7	40.1	52.2	7.7				33.1	58.6	8.3
1908	37.2	54.1	8.8	41.6	49.6	8.8				39.2	52.0	8.8
1910	34.6	42.6	22.8	47.4	46.4	6.2				38.0	55.4	6.5
1912	32.1	31.0	36.9	32.2	33.2	34.5				31.0	49.9	19.1
1914	42.1	36.1	21.9	44.1	37.4	18.5	38.1	43.9	18.0	38.3	44.5	17.2
1916	52.0	41.1	6.8	47.5	47.1	5.4	39.9	51.1	9.0	43.3	50.4	6.3
1918	43.2	53.4	3.4	40.1	60.0	0.0	41.7	58.3	0.0	36.8	63.2	0.0
1920	34.3	65.6	0.1	26.9	53.0	20.1	45.9	54.1	0.0	32.3	61.4	6.3
1922	25.3	56.8	17.9	28.8	39.5	31.7	33.0	66.8	0.2	27.8	47.4	24.9
1924	16.2	48.1	35.8	16.8	43.9	39.3	20.1	79.5	0.4	24.9	57.5	17.6
1926	25.5	56.1	18.3	20.6	51.1	28.4	25.0	45.4	29.6	18.2	62.9	18.8
1928	34.9	64.2	0.9	41.6	57.8	0.6	36.7	62.6	0.7	33.1	66.2	0.7
1930	46.8	51.2	2.0	56.0	44.0	0.0	27.6	72.4	0.0	36.1	63.9	0.0
1932	58.7	38.2	3.0	61.7	36.4	1.8	55.7	42.3	2.1	55.0	43.0	2.1
1934	60.8	35.7	3.5	54.6	44.3	1.2	46.2	52.8	1.0	61.1	38.7	0.3
1936	63.0	33.2	3.9	57.2	41.5	1.4	36.6	63.4	0.0	64.7	35.3	0.0
1938	58.7	39.2	2.1	41.9	57.3	0.8	54.7	44.9	0.5	53.5	46.5	0.0
1940	54.4	45.3	0.3	50.5	49.5	0.0	47.1	53.0	0.0	53.5	46.5	0.0
1942	53.0	46.7	0.4	49.9	50.2	0.0	48.5	51.5	0.0	48.8	51.2	0.0
1944	51.6	48.1	0.4	52.6	47.4	0.0	51.1	48.9	0.0	51.5	48.5	0.0
1946	50.8	47.7	1.6	43.6	56.4	0.0	41.4	58.6	0.0	43.5	56.5	0.0
1948	50.0	47.3	2.8	45.5	54.5	0.0	50.0	48.5	1.6	49.9	48.6	1.5
1950	42.2	56.3	1.5	47.4	52.6	0.0	43.2	56.8	0.0	45.6	54.4	0.0
1952	34.4	65.4	0.2	46.6	53.4	0.0	40.2	59.8	0.0	40.6	59.4	0.0
1954	36.6	63.3	0.1	45.8	54.2	0.0	37.2	62.8	0.0	45.5	54.5	0.0
1956	38.8	61.2	0.1	47.4	52.6	0.0	56.2	38.7	5.1	46.4	53.7	0.0
1958	42.5	57.5	0.0	49.0	51.0	0.0	52.0	45.5	2.5	52.0	48.0	0.0
1960	46.2	53.8	0.0	47.2	52.8	0.0	47.7	52.3	0.0	54.8	45.2	0.0
1962	48.6	51.4	0.0	45.4	54.6	0.0	51.9	48.1	0.0	52.9	47.1	0.0
1964	50.9	49.1	0.0	41.2	48.0	10.7	48.3	51.7	0.0	49.3	50.7	0.0
1966	40.8	52.9	6.3	37.1	41.4	21.5	44.6	55.4	0.0	39.8	60.2	0.0
1968	30.7	56.8	12.6	44.7	44.6	10.7	60.3	39.7	0.0	42.0	56.4	1.6
1970				52.2	47.8	0.0				37.4	61.4	1.2

129

YEAR	COMPOSITE A (P+G+S+H/4)			COMPOSITE B (G+S+H/3)			COMPOSITE C (S+H/2)		
	DEM.	REP.	OTHER	DEM.	REP.	OTHER	DEM.	REP.	OTHER
1872									
1874									
1876									
1878									
1880									
1882									
1884									
1886									
1888									
1890				43.8	56.2	0.0	44.0	56.0	0.0
1892	39.7	43.1	17.3	32.4	42.4	25.1	31.1	44.1	24.7
1894	39.7	39.2	21.0	26.5	42.4	31.0	24.4	43.4	32.3
1896	67.2	21.7	11.1	61.7	21.9	16.4	46.6	21.4	32.0
1898	37.8	34.1	28.2	24.4	34.1	41.5	0.0	33.4	66.6
1900	51.3	48.0	0.8	51.5	48.5	0.0	51.1	48.9	0.0
1902	41.0	54.5	4.5	42.5	53.6	4.0	41.7	54.3	4.0
1904	29.4	62.7	7.9	31.3	61.2	7.5	28.6	63.7	7.7
1906	34.8	56.9	8.3	36.6	55.4	8.0	33.1	58.6	8.3
1908	39.3	51.9	8.8	40.4	50.8	8.8	39.2	52.0	8.8
1910	40.0	48.1	11.9	42.7	50.9	6.4	38.0	55.4	6.5
1912	31.8	38.1	30.2	31.6	41.6	26.8	31.0	49.9	19.1
1914	40.7	40.5	18.9	40.2	41.9	17.9	38.2	44.2	17.6
1916	45.7	47.4	6.9	43.6	49.5	6.9	41.6	50.8	7.7
1918	40.4	58.7	0.9	39.5	60.5	0.0	39.2	60.8	0.0
1920	34.9	58.5	6.6	35.1	56.2	8.8	39.1	57.8	3.1
1922	28.7	52.6	18.7	29.9	51.2	18.9	30.4	57.1	12.5
1924	19.5	57.2	23.3	20.6	60.3	19.1	22.5	68.5	9.0
1926	22.3	53.9	23.8	21.3	53.1	25.6	21.6	54.2	24.2
1928	36.6	62.7	0.7	37.1	62.2	0.7	34.9	64.4	0.7
1930	41.6	57.9	0.5	39.9	60.1	0.0	31.8	68.2	0.0
1932	57.8	40.0	2.3	57.5	40.6	2.0	55.3	42.6	2.1
1934	55.7	42.9	1.5	53.9	45.2	0.8	53.6	45.7	0.7
1936	55.4	43.3	1.3	52.9	46.7	0.5	50.7	49.3	0.0
1938	52.2	47.0	0.8	50.0	49.6	0.4	54.1	45.7	0.2
1940	51.3	48.6	0.1	50.3	49.7	0.0	50.3	49.7	0.0
1942	50.0	49.9	0.1	49.0	51.0	0.0	48.6	51.4	0.0
1944	51.7	48.2	0.1	51.8	48.3	0.0	51.3	48.7	0.0
1946	44.8	54.8	0.4	42.9	57.2	0.0	42.5	57.5	0.0
1948	48.8	49.7	1.5	48.5	50.5	1.0	49.9	48.5	1.5
1950	44.6	55.0	0.4	45.4	54.6	0.0	44.4	55.6	0.0
1952	40.5	59.5	0.0	42.5	57.5	0.0	40.4	59.6	0.0
1954	41.3	58.7	0.0	42.8	57.2	0.0	41.3	58.7	0.0
1956	47.2	51.5	1.3	50.0	48.3	1.7	51.3	46.2	2.5
1958	48.9	50.5	0.6	51.0	48.2	0.8	52.0	46.8	1.3
1960	49.0	51.0	0.0	49.9	50.1	0.0	51.3	48.7	0.0
1962	49.7	50.3	0.0	50.1	49.9	0.0	52.4	47.6	0.0
1964	47.4	49.9	2.7	46.3	50.2	3.6	48.8	51.2	0.0
1966	40.6	52.5	6.9	40.5	52.3	7.2	42.2	57.8	0.0
1968	44.4	49.4	6.2	49.0	46.9	4.1	51.2	48.1	0.8
1970				44.8	54.6	0.6	37.4	61.4	1.2

130

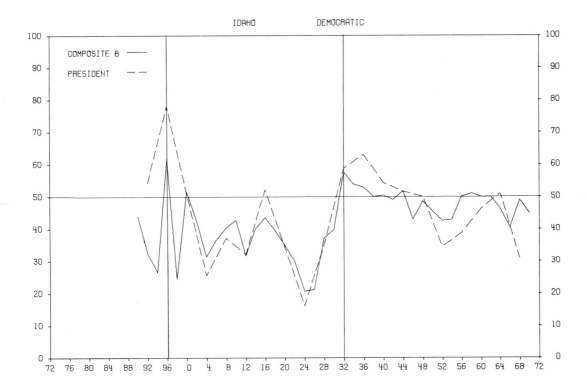

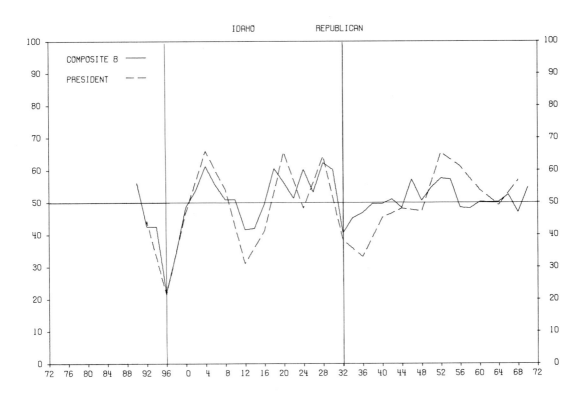

131

YEAR	PRESIDENT			GOVERNOR			SENATE CLASS II			SENATE CLASS III		
	DEM.	REP.	OTHER	DEM.	REP.	OTHER	DEM.	REP.	OTHER	DEM.	REP.	OTHER
1872 1874	43.7	56.3	0.0	45.1	54.4	0.5						
1876 1878	46.6	50.2	3.2	49.4	50.6	0.1						
1880 1882	44.6	51.1	4.3	44.5	50.4	5.1						
1884 1886	46.4	50.2	3.4	47.5	49.6	2.9						
1888 1890	46.6	49.5	3.9	47.5	49.1	3.4						
1892 1894	48.8	45.7	5.5	48.7	46.1	5.1						
1896 1898	42.6	55.7	1.8	43.7	54.1	2.2						
1900 1902	44.4	52.8	2.7	46.1	51.5	2.5						
1904 1906	30.4	58.8	10.8	31.2	59.1	9.7						
1908 1910	39.0	54.5	6.4	45.6	47.6	6.7						
1912 1914	35.3	22.1	42.5	38.1	27.4	34.5				36.8	38.5	24.8
1916 1918	43.3	52.6	4.1	42.1	52.7	5.2	44.9	50.5	4.6			
1920 1922	25.5	67.8	6.7	34.6	58.9	6.5				26.8	66.8	6.4
1924 1926	23.4	58.8	17.8	42.4	56.7	0.9	35.4	63.5	1.1	43.1	46.9	10.0
1928 1930	42.2	57.0	0.8	42.7	56.8	0.6	64.0	30.7	5.2	44.9	54.5	0.6
1932 1934	55.2	42.0	2.7	57.6	40.7	1.7				52.2	46.0	1.7
1936 1938	57.7	39.7	2.6	53.1	43.2	3.6	56.5	40.7	2.8	51.3	48.3	0.3
1940 1942	51.0	48.5	0.5	46.7	52.9	0.3	49.6 46.4	50.1 53.2	0.4 0.3			
1944 1946	51.5	48.0	0.4	48.9	50.8	0.3				52.6	47.1	0.3
1948 1950	50.1	49.2	0.7	57.1	42.6	0.3	55.1	44.6	0.3	45.8	53.9	0.4
1952 1954	44.9	54.8	0.2	47.3	52.5	0.2	53.6	46.4	0.0			
1956 1958	40.3	59.5	0.2	49.5	50.3	0.2				45.7	54.1	0.2
1960 1962	50.0	49.8	0.2	55.5	44.3	0.2	54.6	45.2	0.2	47.1	52.9	0.0
1964 1966	59.5	40.5	0.0	51.9	48.1	0.0	43.9	54.9	1.2			
1968 1970	44.2	47.1	8.8	48.4	51.2	0.4				46.6 57.4	53.0 42.2	0.4 0.4

ILLINOIS

YEAR	PRESIDENT			GOVERNOR			SENATE			HOUSE OF REPRESENTATIVES		
	DEM.	REP.	OTHER	DEM.	REP.	OTHER	DEM.	REP.	OTHER	DEM.	REP.	OTHER
1872	43.7	56.3	0.0	45.1	54.4	0.5				44.6	55.2	0.2
1874	45.2	53.2	1.6	47.2	52.5	0.3				49.5	46.2	4.3
1876	46.7	50.2	3.2	49.4	50.6	0.1				48.5	48.7	2.8
1878	45.6	50.7	3.8	46.9	50.5	2.6				37.7	47.1	15.2
1880	44.6	51.1	4.3	44.5	50.4	5.1				45.0	51.3	3.7
1882	45.5	50.6	3.9	46.0	50.0	4.0				46.6	44.4	8.9
1884	46.4	50.2	3.4	47.5	49.6	2.9				47.5	49.1	3.4
1886	46.5	49.9	3.6	47.5	49.4	3.1				42.9	49.0	8.1
1888	46.6	49.5	3.9	47.5	49.2	3.4				46.6	49.9	3.5
1890	47.7	47.6	4.7	48.1	47.6	4.3				50.6	46.1	3.3
1892	48.8	45.7	5.5	48.7	46.1	5.1				48.8	45.8	5.4
1894	45.7	50.7	3.6	46.2	50.1	3.7				36.7	52.6	10.6
1896	42.6	55.7	1.8	43.7	54.1	2.2				42.7	55.6	1.7
1898	43.5	54.3	2.2	44.9	52.8	2.4				44.7	53.0	2.2
1900	44.4	52.8	2.7	46.1	51.5	2.5				44.9	52.9	2.2
1902	37.4	55.8	6.8	38.6	55.3	6.1				45.8	49.9	4.3
1904	30.4	58.8	10.8	31.2	59.1	9.7				32.4	57.5	10.1
1906	34.7	56.7	8.6	38.4	53.4	8.2				37.8	52.8	9.4
1908	39.0	54.5	6.5	45.6	47.6	6.7				40.1	53.8	6.0
1910	37.2	38.3	24.5	41.9	37.5	20.6				46.2	46.3	7.5
1912	35.3	22.1	42.5	38.1	27.4	34.5				37.2	29.2	33.7
1914	39.3	37.3	23.3	40.1	40.0	19.9	36.8	38.5	24.8	40.4	42.4	17.2
1916	43.3	52.6	4.1	42.1	52.7	5.2	40.8	44.5	14.7	41.5	53.6	4.9
1918	34.4	60.2	5.4	38.4	55.8	5.9	44.9	50.5	4.6	39.9	55.8	4.3
1920	25.5	67.8	6.7	34.6	58.9	6.5	26.8	66.8	6.4	28.1	66.0	5.9
1922	24.4	63.3	12.2	38.5	57.8	3.7	31.1	65.2	3.7	41.2	55.0	3.8
1924	23.4	58.8	17.8	42.4	56.7	0.9	35.4	63.5	1.1	31.1	67.5	1.4
1926	32.8	57.9	9.3	42.5	56.7	0.7	43.1	46.9	10.0	39.7	60.0	0.4
1928	42.2	57.0	0.8	42.7	56.8	0.6	44.9	54.5	0.6	41.0	58.5	0.5
1930	48.7	49.5	1.8	50.1	48.7	1.1	64.0	30.7	5.3	51.2	48.3	0.5
1932	55.2	42.0	2.7	57.6	40.7	1.7	52.2	46.0	1.8	53.7	44.6	1.7
1934	56.5	40.9	2.7	55.4	42.0	2.7	54.4	43.4	2.3	55.6	43.5	0.9
1936	57.7	39.7	2.6	53.1	43.2	3.6	56.5	40.7	2.8	55.2	42.8	2.0
1938	54.4	44.1	1.5	49.9	48.1	2.0	51.3	48.3	0.3	51.3	48.5	0.2
1940	51.0	48.5	0.5	46.7	52.9	0.3	49.6	50.1	0.4	48.7	51.1	0.2
1942	51.3	48.3	0.5	47.8	51.8	0.3	46.4	53.2	0.4	47.0	52.8	0.2
1944	51.5	48.1	0.4	48.9	50.8	0.3	52.6	47.1	0.3	51.1	48.7	0.2
1946	50.8	48.6	0.6	53.0	46.7	0.3	53.8	45.8	0.3	44.0	55.8	0.2
1948	50.1	49.2	0.7	57.1	42.6	0.3	55.1	44.6	0.3	52.0	47.4	0.6
1950	47.5	52.0	0.5	52.2	47.5	0.3	45.8	53.9	0.4	46.1	53.9	0.0
1952	44.9	54.8	0.2	47.3	52.5	0.2	49.7	50.2	0.2	46.1	54.0	0.0
1954	42.6	57.2	0.2	48.4	51.4	0.2	53.6	46.4	0.0	50.2	49.8	0.0
1956	40.3	59.5	0.2	49.5	50.3	0.2	45.7	54.1	0.2	46.4	53.6	0.0
1958	45.1	54.7	0.2	52.5	47.3	0.2	50.2	49.7	0.2	54.3	45.5	0.2
1960	50.0	49.8	0.2	55.5	44.3	0.2	54.6	45.2	0.2	50.7	49.3	0.0
1962	54.7	45.2	0.1	53.7	46.2	0.1	47.1	52.9	0.0	49.7	50.2	0.1
1964	59.5	40.5	0.0	51.9	48.1	0.0	45.5	53.9	0.6	54.5	45.5	0.0
1966	51.8	43.8	4.4	50.2	49.6	0.2	43.9	55.0	1.2	45.7	54.3	0.0
1968	44.2	47.1	8.8	48.4	51.2	0.4	46.6	53.0	0.4	46.4	53.6	0.0
1970							57.4	42.2	0.4	51.9	48.1	0.0

133

ILLINOIS

YEAR	COMPOSITE A (P+G+S+H/4)			COMPOSITE B (G+S+H/3)			COMPOSITE C (S+H/2)		
	DEM.	REP.	OTHER	DEM.	REP.	OTHER	DEM.	REP.	OTHER
1872	44.5	55.3	0.2	44.9	54.8	0.3	44.6	55.2	0.2
1874	47.3	50.6	2.1	48.4	49.3	2.3	49.5	46.2	4.3
1876	48.2	49.8	2.0	48.9	49.7	1.4	48.5	48.7	2.8
1878	43.4	49.4	7.2	42.3	48.8	8.9	37.7	47.1	15.2
1880	44.7	50.9	4.4	44.8	50.8	4.4	45.0	51.3	3.7
1882	46.0	48.4	5.6	46.3	47.2	6.5	46.6	44.4	8.9
1884	47.1	49.6	3.2	47.5	49.4	3.2	47.5	49.1	3.4
1886	45.6	49.4	5.0	45.2	49.2	5.6	42.9	49.0	8.1
1888	46.9	49.5	3.6	47.0	49.5	3.4	46.6	49.9	3.5
1890	48.8	47.1	4.1	49.4	46.9	3.8	50.6	46.1	3.3
1892	48.8	45.9	5.3	48.8	46.0	5.3	48.8	45.8	5.4
1894	42.9	51.1	6.0	41.5	51.4	7.2	36.7	52.6	10.6
1896	43.0	55.1	1.9	43.2	54.8	2.0	42.7	55.6	1.7
1898	44.4	53.4	2.3	44.8	52.9	2.3	44.7	53.0	2.2
1900	45.1	52.4	2.5	45.5	52.2	2.3	44.9	52.9	2.2
1902	40.6	53.7	5.7	42.2	52.6	5.2	45.8	49.9	4.3
1904	31.4	58.4	10.2	31.8	58.3	9.9	32.4	57.5	10.1
1906	37.0	54.3	8.7	38.1	53.1	8.8	37.8	52.8	9.4
1908	41.6	52.0	6.4	42.9	50.7	6.4	40.1	53.8	6.0
1910	41.8	40.7	17.5	44.0	41.9	14.1	46.2	46.3	7.5
1912	36.9	26.2	36.9	37.7	28.3	34.1	37.2	29.2	33.7
1914	39.1	39.6	21.3	39.1	40.3	20.6	38.6	40.4	21.0
1916	41.9	50.8	7.2	41.5	50.2	8.3	41.2	49.0	9.8
1918	39.4	55.6	5.0	41.1	54.0	4.9	42.4	53.2	4.4
1920	28.8	64.9	6.4	29.8	63.9	6.3	27.4	66.4	6.1
1922	33.8	60.3	5.9	37.0	59.3	3.7	36.2	60.1	3.8
1924	33.1	61.7	5.3	36.3	62.6	1.1	33.3	65.5	1.2
1926	39.5	55.4	5.1	41.8	54.5	3.7	41.4	53.4	5.2
1928	42.7	56.7	0.6	42.9	56.6	0.5	43.0	56.5	0.5
1930	53.5	44.3	2.2	55.1	42.6	2.3	57.6	39.5	2.9
1932	54.7	43.3	2.0	54.5	43.8	1.7	53.0	45.3	1.7
1934	55.5	42.4	2.1	55.1	43.0	1.9	55.0	43.4	1.6
1936	55.6	41.6	2.8	54.9	42.2	2.8	55.8	41.7	2.4
1938	51.7	47.3	1.0	50.9	48.3	0.8	51.3	48.4	0.3
1940	49.0	50.7	0.4	48.3	51.4	0.3	49.1	50.6	0.3
1942	48.1	51.6	0.3	47.1	52.6	0.3	46.7	53.0	0.3
1944	51.0	48.6	0.3	50.9	48.8	0.3	51.9	47.9	0.3
1946	50.4	49.2	0.4	50.3	49.4	0.3	48.9	50.8	0.3
1948	53.6	46.0	0.5	54.7	44.9	0.4	53.5	46.0	0.5
1950	47.9	51.8	0.3	48.0	51.8	0.2	45.9	53.9	0.2
1952	47.0	52.9	0.2	47.7	52.2	0.1	47.9	52.1	0.1
1954	48.7	51.2	0.1	50.7	49.2	0.1	51.9	48.1	0.0
1956	45.5	54.4	0.1	47.2	52.7	0.1	46.1	53.9	0.1
1958	50.5	49.3	0.2	52.3	47.5	0.2	52.2	47.6	0.2
1960	52.7	47.1	0.2	53.6	46.3	0.1	52.7	47.2	0.1
1962	51.3	48.6	0.1	50.2	49.8	0.1	48.4	51.6	0.0
1964	52.9	47.0	0.1	50.6	49.2	0.2	50.0	49.7	0.3
1966	47.9	50.7	1.4	46.6	53.0	0.5	44.8	54.6	0.6
1968	46.4	51.2	2.4	47.1	52.6	0.3	46.5	53.3	0.2
1970							54.6	45.2	0.2

134

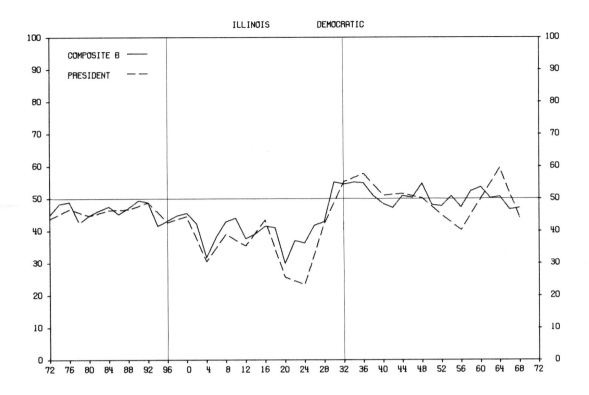

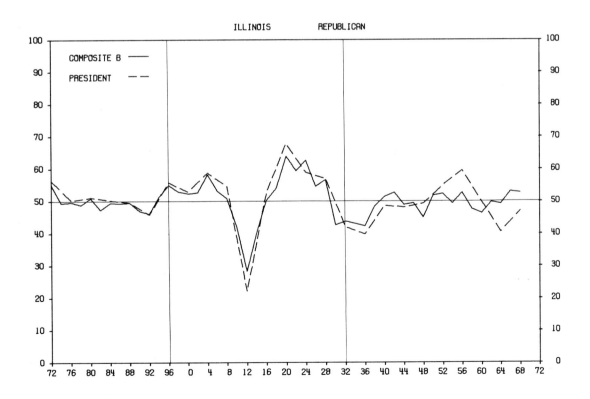

135

YEAR	PRESIDENT			GOVERNOR			SENATE CLASS I			SENATE CLASS III		
	DEM.	REP.	OTHER	DEM.	REP.	OTHER	DEM.	REP.	OTHER	DEM.	REP.	OTHER
1872 1874	46.8	53.2	0.0	50.1	49.8	0.1						
1876 1878	49.5	48.3	2.2	49.1	47.9	3.0						
1880 1882	47.9	49.3	2.8	47.7	49.2	3.2						
1884 1886	49.8	48.5	1.7	49.5	48.0	2.5						
1888 1890	48.6	49.0	2.4	48.6	49.0	2.4						
1892 1894	47.5	46.2	6.4	47.5	46.2	6.3						
1896 1898	48.0	50.8	1.2	46.8	50.9	2.3						
1900 1902	46.6	50.6	2.8	46.7	50.5	2.8						
1904 1906	40.2	54.0	5.8	41.0	53.5	5.5						
1908 1910	46.9	48.4	4.7	48.9	46.9	4.2						
1912 1914	43.1	23.1	33.8	42.9	22.1	35.0				42.1	35.1	22.8
1916 1918	46.5	47.4	6.1	46.0	47.8	6.2	46.1	47.8	6.1	46.3	47.7	6.0
1920 1922	40.5	55.1	4.4	41.2	54.6	4.2	50.9	47.8	1.3	41.1	54.6	4.3
1924 1926	38.7	55.3	6.1	46.3	52.9	0.8	48.4	50.6	1.0	49.0	50.0	1.0
1928 1930	39.6	59.7	0.7	48.1	51.2	0.7	44.1	55.3	0.6			
1932 1934	54.7	42.9	2.4	55.0	42.7	2.2	51.5	47.5	1.1	55.6	42.3	2.2
1936 1938	56.6	41.9	1.5	55.4	44.3	0.3				49.8	49.5	0.6
1940 1942	49.0	50.5	0.5	49.9	49.7	0.4	49.1	50.5	0.4			
1944 1946	46.7	52.4	0.9	48.2	51.0	0.8	47.1 43.4	52.1 54.9	0.8 1.7	48.9	50.2	0.9
1948 1950	48.8	49.6	1.6	53.6	45.1	1.3				46.4	52.8	0.8
1952 1954	41.0	58.1	0.9	43.6	55.7	0.7	46.8	52.4	0.7			
1956 1958	39.7	59.9	0.4	44.0	55.6	0.4	56.5	42.4	1.1	44.4	55.2	0.4
1960 1962	44.6	55.0	0.4	50.4	49.3	0.3				50.3	49.7	0.0
1964 1966	56.0	43.6	0.5	56.2	43.5	0.3	54.3	45.3	0.3			
1968 1970	38.0	50.3	11.7	47.1	52.7	0.1	50.1	49.9	0.0	51.7	48.1	0.2

YEAR	PRESIDENT			GOVERNOR			SENATE			HOUSE OF REPRESENTATIVES		
	DEM.	REP.	OTHER	DEM.	REP.	OTHER	DEM.	REP.	OTHER	DEM.	REP.	OTHER
1872	46.8	53.2	0.0	50.1	49.8	0.1				33.3	50.1	16.7
1874	48.2	50.7	1.1	49.6	48.9	1.6				50.7	46.7	2.7
1876	49.5	48.3	2.2	49.1	47.9	3.1				48.9	47.6	3.5
1878	48.7	48.8	2.5	48.4	48.5	3.1				47.7	44.4	8.0
1880	47.9	49.3	2.8	47.7	49.2	3.2				47.9	48.9	3.2
1882	48.9	48.9	2.2	48.6	48.6	2.8				50.3	47.2	2.6
1884	49.8	48.5	1.7	49.5	48.0	2.5				50.5	48.4	1.1
1886	49.2	48.8	2.0	49.1	48.5	2.4				47.3	48.3	4.5
1888	48.6	49.1	2.4	48.6	49.0	2.4				48.5	49.4	2.1
1890	48.0	47.6	4.4	48.0	47.6	4.3				50.5	45.7	3.7
1892	47.5	46.2	6.4	47.5	46.2	6.3				47.2	46.1	6.7
1894	47.7	48.5	3.8	47.1	48.6	4.3				42.7	50.9	6.4
1896	48.0	50.8	1.2	46.8	50.9	2.3				48.2	50.9	0.9
1898	47.3	50.7	2.0	46.8	50.7	2.5				48.3	50.1	1.7
1900	46.6	50.6	2.8	46.7	50.5	2.8				47.6	50.5	1.9
1902	43.4	52.3	4.3	43.8	52.0	4.2				45.9	50.5	3.6
1904	40.2	54.0	5.8	41.0	53.5	5.5				43.0	52.6	4.4
1906	43.6	51.2	5.3	45.0	50.2	4.9				47.4	48.5	4.1
1908	46.9	48.4	4.7	49.0	46.9	4.2				49.4	47.0	3.7
1910	45.0	35.8	19.3	46.0	34.5	19.6				50.2	44.7	5.1
1912	43.1	23.1	33.8	43.0	22.1	35.0				45.5	26.0	28.5
1914	44.8	35.3	20.0	44.5	35.0	20.6	42.1	35.1	22.8	43.8	37.0	19.3
1916	46.5	47.4	6.1	46.0	47.8	6.2	46.2	47.7	6.1	45.6	48.5	5.9
1918	43.5	51.3	5.2	43.6	51.2	5.2	43.7	51.1	5.2	44.3	54.1	1.6
1920	40.5	55.1	4.4	41.2	54.6	4.2	41.2	54.6	4.3	41.2	55.6	3.2
1922	39.6	55.2	5.2	43.8	53.8	2.5	50.9	47.8	1.3	48.4	50.5	1.1
1924	38.7	55.3	6.1	46.3	52.9	0.8	49.8	49.1	1.2	43.7	55.4	1.0
1926	39.1	57.5	3.4	47.2	52.1	0.7	48.7	50.3	1.0	46.8	53.2	0.0
1928	39.6	59.7	0.7	48.1	51.3	0.7	44.1	55.3	0.6	45.4	54.5	0.2
1930	47.1	51.3	1.6	51.6	47.0	1.4	49.8	48.8	1.4	52.8	47.1	0.1
1932	54.7	42.9	2.4	55.0	42.8	2.2	55.6	42.3	2.2	55.0	44.2	0.9
1934	55.7	42.4	1.9	55.2	43.5	1.3	51.5	47.5	1.1	52.2	47.2	0.7
1936	56.6	41.9	1.5	55.4	44.3	0.3	50.7	48.5	0.9	55.9	43.4	0.7
1938	52.8	46.2	1.0	52.6	47.0	0.4	49.8	49.5	0.7	49.2	50.8	0.0
1940	49.0	50.5	0.5	49.9	49.7	0.4	49.1	50.5	0.4	49.1	50.9	0.0
1942	47.9	51.4	0.7	49.1	50.3	0.6	48.6	50.8	0.6	44.5	55.5	0.0
1944	46.7	52.4	0.9	48.2	51.0	0.9	48.0	51.2	0.8	46.5	52.9	0.7
1946	47.8	51.0	1.3	50.9	48.1	1.1	43.4	54.9	1.7	44.2	54.5	1.4
1948	48.8	49.6	1.7	53.6	45.1	1.3	44.9	53.9	1.3	51.2	47.9	0.9
1950	44.9	53.8	1.3	48.6	50.4	1.0	46.4	52.8	0.8	45.8	53.6	0.6
1952	41.0	58.1	0.9	43.6	55.7	0.7	46.8	52.4	0.7	42.9	56.5	0.6
1954	40.4	59.0	0.7	43.8	55.7	0.6	45.6	53.8	0.6	47.1	52.5	0.4
1956	39.7	59.9	0.4	44.0	55.6	0.4	44.4	55.2	0.4	44.1	55.7	0.2
1958	42.2	57.5	0.4	47.2	52.5	0.4	56.5	42.4	1.1	53.6	46.4	0.1
1960	44.6	55.0	0.4	50.4	49.3	0.3	53.4	46.1	0.6	48.7	51.3	0.1
1962	50.3	49.3	0.4	53.3	46.4	0.3	50.3	49.7	0.0	49.1	50.9	0.0
1964	56.0	43.6	0.5	56.2	43.5	0.3	54.3	45.3	0.3	52.8	47.2	0.0
1966	47.0	46.9	6.1	51.7	48.1	0.2	53.0	46.7	0.3	46.5	53.5	0.1
1968	38.0	50.3	11.7	47.1	52.7	0.2	51.7	48.2	0.2	46.3	53.7	0.0
1970							50.1	49.9	0.0	50.9	49.1	0.0

INDIANA

YEAR	COMPOSITE A (P+G+S+H/4)			COMPOSITE B (G+S+H/3)			COMPOSITE C (S+H/2)		
	DEM.	REP.	OTHER	DEM.	REP.	OTHER	DEM.	REP.	OTHER
1872	43.4	51.0	5.6	41.7	50.0	8.4	33.3	50.1	16.7
1874	49.5	48.8	1.8	50.1	47.8	2.1	50.7	46.7	2.7
1876	49.2	47.9	2.9	49.0	47.8	3.3	48.9	47.6	3.5
1878	48.3	47.2	4.5	48.0	46.4	5.5	47.7	44.4	8.0
1880	47.8	49.1	3.1	47.8	49.0	3.2	47.9	48.9	3.2
1882	49.3	48.2	2.5	49.4	47.9	2.7	50.3	47.2	2.6
1884	50.0	48.3	1.7	50.0	48.2	1.8	50.5	48.4	1.1
1886	48.5	48.5	3.0	48.2	48.4	3.4	47.3	48.3	4.5
1888	48.6	49.1	2.3	48.6	49.2	2.2	48.5	49.4	2.1
1890	48.9	47.0	4.2	49.3	46.7	4.0	50.5	45.7	3.7
1892	47.4	46.2	6.5	47.3	46.2	6.5	47.2	46.1	6.7
1894	45.9	49.3	4.8	44.9	49.7	5.4	42.7	50.9	6.4
1896	47.6	50.9	1.5	47.5	50.9	1.6	48.2	50.9	0.9
1898	47.4	50.5	2.1	47.5	50.4	2.1	48.3	50.1	1.7
1900	47.0	50.5	2.5	47.2	50.5	2.4	47.6	50.5	1.9
1902	44.4	51.6	4.0	44.9	51.3	3.9	45.9	50.5	3.6
1904	41.4	53.4	5.2	42.0	53.1	5.0	43.0	52.6	4.4
1906	45.3	50.0	4.8	46.2	49.4	4.5	47.4	48.5	4.1
1908	48.4	47.4	4.2	49.2	46.9	3.9	49.4	47.0	3.7
1910	47.1	38.3	14.7	48.1	39.6	12.4	50.2	44.7	5.1
1912	43.8	23.7	32.4	44.2	24.1	31.7	45.5	26.0	28.5
1914	43.8	35.6	20.6	43.5	35.7	20.9	43.0	36.0	21.0
1916	46.1	47.9	6.1	45.9	48.0	6.1	45.9	48.1	6.0
1918	43.8	51.9	4.3	43.9	52.1	4.0	44.0	52.6	3.4
1920	41.0	55.0	4.0	41.2	54.9	3.9	41.2	55.1	3.8
1922	45.7	51.8	2.5	47.7	50.7	1.6	49.7	49.2	1.2
1924	44.6	53.2	2.3	46.6	52.4	1.0	46.7	52.2	1.1
1926	45.5	53.3	1.3	47.6	51.9	0.6	47.7	51.8	0.5
1928	44.3	55.2	0.5	45.9	53.7	0.5	44.7	54.9	0.4
1930	50.3	48.6	1.1	51.4	47.6	1.0	51.3	48.0	0.7
1932	55.1	43.0	1.9	55.2	43.1	1.8	55.3	43.2	1.5
1934	53.6	45.2	1.2	52.9	46.1	1.0	51.8	47.3	0.9
1936	54.6	44.5	0.8	54.0	45.4	0.6	53.3	46.0	0.8
1938	51.1	48.4	0.5	50.6	49.1	0.3	49.5	50.2	0.3
1940	49.3	50.4	0.3	49.4	50.4	0.3	49.1	50.7	0.2
1942	47.5	52.0	0.5	47.4	52.2	0.4	46.6	53.1	0.3
1944	47.4	51.8	0.8	47.6	51.7	0.8	47.2	52.0	0.7
1946	46.5	52.1	1.4	46.1	52.5	1.4	43.8	54.7	1.6
1948	49.6	49.1	1.3	49.9	49.0	1.2	48.1	50.9	1.1
1950	46.4	52.7	0.9	46.9	52.3	0.8	46.1	53.2	0.7
1952	43.6	55.7	0.7	44.4	54.9	0.7	44.9	54.5	0.7
1954	44.2	55.3	0.5	45.5	54.0	0.5	46.4	53.2	0.5
1956	43.0	56.6	0.4	44.1	55.5	0.4	44.2	55.5	0.3
1958	49.8	49.7	0.5	52.4	47.1	0.5	55.0	44.4	0.6
1960	49.3	50.4	0.3	50.8	48.9	0.3	51.0	48.7	0.3
1962	50.7	49.1	0.2	50.9	49.0	0.1	49.7	50.3	0.0
1964	54.8	44.9	0.3	54.4	45.3	0.2	53.6	46.2	0.2
1966	49.5	48.8	1.7	50.4	49.4	0.2	49.7	50.1	0.2
1968	45.8	51.2	3.0	48.4	51.5	0.1	49.0	50.9	0.1
1970							50.5	49.5	0.0

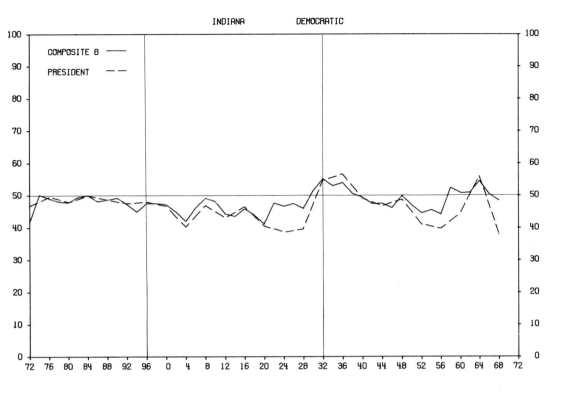

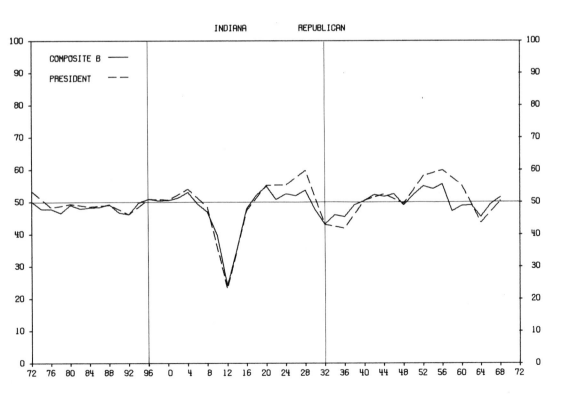

139

YEAR	PRESIDENT			GOVERNOR			SENATE CLASS II			SENATE CLASS III		
	DEM.	REP.	OTHER	DEM.	REP.	OTHER	DEM.	REP.	OTHER	DEM.	REP.	OTHE
1872	32.9	60.8	6.3	38.4	61.6	0.0						
1874				43.2	56.0	0.9						
1876	38.2	58.4	3.4	42.6	57.0	0.4						
1878				32.3	49.4	18.3						
1880	32.8	56.9	10.3	29.3	53.9	16.8						
1882				31.2	56.7	12.1						
1884	47.0	52.3	0.7	42.8	50.1	7.1						
1886				48.7	50.8	0.5						
1888	44.4	52.3	3.3	45.4	50.1	4.4						
1890				49.9	48.1	2.0						
1892	44.3	49.6	6.1	49.4	47.4	3.2						
1894				42.0	49.7	8.3						
1896	42.9	55.5	1.6	37.2	52.0	10.8						
1898				44.5	51.3	4.3						
1900	39.5	58.0	2.5	42.3	55.3	2.4						
1902				36.8	58.1	5.1						
1904	30.7	63.4	5.9	38.2	57.1	4.6						
1906				45.3	50.2	4.5						
1908	40.6	55.6	3.8	41.8	54.6	3.6						
1910				45.4	49.8	4.8						
1912	37.6	24.3	38.0	39.6	39.9	20.5						
1914				42.9	49.3	7.7				39.2	48.2	12.6
1916	42.9	54.2	2.9	36.4	61.0	2.6						
1918				46.9	50.6	2.5	34.6	65.4	0.0			
1920	25.5	70.9	3.6	38.6	58.7	2.7				37.4	61.4	1.2
1922				29.5	70.5	0.0	36.9	63.1	0.0			
1924	16.4	55.0	28.6	27.3	72.7	0.0	50.0	50.0	0.0			
1926				28.4	71.3	0.3				27.3	72.6	0.1
1928	37.6	61.8	0.7	37.2	62.8	0.0						
1930				33.6	65.7	0.7	43.0	56.3	0.7			
1932	57.7	40.0	2.3	52.8	47.2	0.0				54.9	40.7	4.4
1934				54.3	45.7	0.0						
1936	54.4	42.7	2.9	48.7	48.4	2.9	50.5	47.1	2.4	51.9	46.6	1.6
1938				45.7	52.7	1.6				49.7	49.4	0.8
1940	47.6	52.0	0.4	47.1	52.7	0.2						
1942				37.0	62.7	0.3	41.7	58.0	0.3			
1944	47.5	52.0	0.5	43.6	56.0	0.4				48.4	51.3	0.3
1946				42.1	57.4	0.5						
1948	50.3	47.6	2.1	43.7	55.7	0.7	57.8	41.6	0.6			
1950				40.5	59.1	0.4				44.7	54.8	0.5
1952	35.6	63.8	0.7	47.8	51.9	0.3						
1954				48.3	51.4	0.3	47.5	52.2	0.3			
1956	40.7	59.1	0.3	51.2	48.8	0.0				46.1	53.9	0.0
1958				54.1	45.9	0.0						
1960	43.2	56.7	0.1	47.9	52.1	0.0	48.1	51.9	0.0			
1962				52.6	47.4	0.0				46.6	53.4	0.0
1964	61.9	37.9	0.2	68.0	31.3	0.7						
1966				55.3	44.2	0.5	37.8	60.9	1.3			
1968	40.8	53.0	6.2	45.9	54.1	0.1				50.2	49.7	0.1
1970				46.6	51.0	2.4						

140

YEAR	PRESIDENT			GOVERNOR			SENATE			HOUSE OF REPRESENTATIVES		
	DEM.	REP.	OTHER	DEM.	REP.	OTHER	DEM.	REP.	OTHER	DEM.	REP.	OTHER
1872	32.9	60.8	6.3	38.4	61.6	0.0				38.5	61.4	0.1
1874	35.6	59.6	4.8	43.2	56.0	0.9				43.0	56.7	0.2
1876	38.2	58.4	3.4	42.6	57.0	0.4				40.5	57.6	2.0
1878	35.5	57.7	6.9	32.3	49.4	18.3				29.1	50.6	20.3
1880	32.8	56.9	10.3	29.3	53.9	16.8				37.0	56.7	6.3
1882	39.9	54.6	5.5	31.2	56.7	12.1				39.9	49.0	11.1
1884	47.0	52.3	0.7	42.8	50.1	7.1				47.6	52.4	0.1
1886	45.7	52.3	2.0	48.7	50.8	0.5				42.3	49.8	7.9
1888	44.5	52.3	3.3	45.4	50.1	4.4				45.8	52.6	1.6
1890	44.4	50.9	4.7	49.9	48.1	2.0				50.1	47.7	2.2
1892	44.3	49.6	6.1	49.4	47.5	3.2				45.7	49.7	4.6
1894	43.6	52.5	3.9	42.0	49.7	8.3				40.1	55.0	4.9
1896	42.9	55.5	1.6	37.2	52.0	10.8				43.8	55.7	0.6
1898	41.2	56.8	2.1	44.5	51.3	4.3				42.3	55.6	2.1
1900	39.5	58.0	2.5	42.3	55.3	2.4				40.5	58.0	1.5
1902	35.1	60.7	4.2	36.8	58.1	5.1				40.4	56.7	3.0
1904	30.7	63.4	5.9	38.2	57.1	4.6				33.9	61.9	4.2
1906	35.6	59.5	4.9	45.4	50.2	4.5				41.6	55.2	3.2
1908	40.6	55.6	3.8	41.8	54.6	3.6				42.6	54.7	2.7
1910	39.1	40.0	20.9	45.4	49.8	4.8				42.0	55.3	2.7
1912	37.6	24.3	38.0	39.6	39.9	20.5				42.6	43.0	14.5
1914	40.3	39.3	20.5	42.9	49.3	7.8	39.2	48.2	12.7	39.9	52.1	8.0
1916	42.9	54.3	2.9	36.4	61.0	2.6	36.9	56.8	6.3	39.0	59.0	2.0
1918	34.2	62.6	3.3	46.9	50.6	2.5	34.6	65.4	0.0	35.0	64.0	1.0
1920	25.5	70.9	3.6	38.7	58.7	2.7	37.4	61.4	1.2	12.4	84.4	3.2
1922	20.9	63.0	16.1	29.5	70.5	0.0	36.9	63.1	0.0	38.6	61.0	0.4
1924	16.4	55.0	28.6	27.3	72.7	0.0	50.0	50.0	0.0	31.3	68.7	0.0
1926	27.0	58.4	14.6	28.4	71.3	0.3	27.3	72.6	0.1	30.6	69.1	0.3
1928	37.6	61.8	0.7	37.2	62.8	0.0	35.2	64.5	0.4	29.0	71.0	0.0
1930	47.6	50.9	1.5	33.6	65.7	0.7	43.0	56.3	0.7	39.2	60.7	0.2
1932	57.7	40.0	2.3	52.8	47.2	0.0	54.9	40.8	4.4	53.0	47.0	0.0
1934	56.0	41.3	2.6	54.3	45.7	0.0	53.0	43.8	3.2	53.5	46.5	0.0
1936	54.4	42.7	2.9	48.7	48.4	2.9	51.2	46.9	2.0	49.7	48.9	1.4
1938	51.0	47.4	1.6	45.7	52.7	1.6	49.7	49.4	0.9	43.9	55.6	0.5
1940	47.6	52.0	0.4	47.1	52.7	0.2	45.7	53.7	0.6	45.2	54.7	0.0
1942	47.6	52.0	0.4	37.0	62.8	0.3	41.7	58.0	0.3	38.0	61.8	0.3
1944	47.5	52.0	0.5	43.6	56.0	0.4	48.4	51.3	0.3	43.2	56.8	0.0
1946	48.9	49.8	1.3	42.1	57.4	0.5	53.1	46.4	0.5	38.5	61.6	0.0
1948	50.3	47.6	2.1	43.7	55.7	0.7	57.8	41.6	0.6	45.2	54.5	0.4
1950	43.0	55.7	1.4	40.5	59.1	0.4	44.7	54.8	0.5	38.7	61.0	0.3
1952	35.6	63.8	0.7	47.8	51.9	0.3	46.1	53.5	0.4	33.1	66.7	0.2
1954	38.1	61.4	0.5	48.4	51.4	0.3	47.5	52.2	0.3	41.5	58.5	0.0
1956	40.7	59.1	0.3	51.2	48.8	0.0	46.1	53.9	0.0	45.6	54.4	0.0
1958	41.9	57.9	0.2	54.1	45.9	0.0	47.1	52.9	0.0	50.3	49.7	0.0
1960	43.2	56.7	0.1	47.9	52.1	0.0	48.1	51.9	0.0	45.9	54.1	0.0
1962	52.6	47.3	0.1	52.6	47.4	0.0	46.6	53.4	0.0	46.1	53.9	0.0
1964	61.9	37.9	0.2	68.1	31.3	0.7	42.2	57.2	0.6	54.6	45.3	0.2
1966	51.4	45.5	3.2	55.3	44.2	0.5	37.8	60.9	1.3	47.5	52.2	0.3
1968	40.8	53.0	6.2	45.9	54.1	0.1	50.3	49.7	0.1	45.8	54.3	0.0
1970				46.6	51.0	2.4				49.7	49.8	0.5

YEAR	COMPOSITE A (P+G+S+H/4)			COMPOSITE B (G+S+H/3)			COMPOSITE C (S+H/2)		
	DEM.	REP.	OTHER	DEM.	REP.	OTHER	DEM.	REP.	OTHER
1872	36.6	61.3	2.1	38.5	61.5	0.1	38.5	61.4	0.1
1874	40.6	57.4	2.0	43.1	56.4	0.6	43.0	56.7	0.2
1876	40.4	57.7	1.9	41.5	57.3	1.2	40.5	57.6	2.0
1878	32.3	52.6	15.2	30.7	50.0	19.3	29.1	50.6	20.3
1880	33.0	55.9	11.2	33.1	55.3	11.6	37.0	56.7	6.3
1882	37.0	53.4	9.6	35.6	52.9	11.6	39.9	49.0	11.1
1884	45.8	51.6	2.6	45.2	51.3	3.6	47.6	52.4	0.1
1886	45.6	51.0	3.5	45.5	50.3	4.2	42.3	49.8	7.9
1888	45.2	51.7	3.1	45.6	51.4	3.0	45.8	52.6	1.6
1890	48.1	48.9	3.0	50.0	47.9	2.1	50.1	47.7	2.2
1892	46.5	48.9	4.6	47.6	48.6	3.9	45.7	49.7	4.6
1894	41.9	52.4	5.7	41.1	52.4	6.6	40.1	55.0	4.9
1896	41.3	54.4	4.3	40.5	53.8	5.7	43.8	55.7	0.6
1898	42.7	54.5	2.8	43.4	53.4	3.2	42.3	55.6	2.1
1900	40.8	57.1	2.2	41.4	56.6	2.0	40.5	58.0	1.5
1902	37.4	58.5	4.1	38.6	57.4	4.1	40.4	56.7	3.0
1904	34.3	60.8	4.9	36.1	59.5	4.4	33.9	61.9	4.2
1906	40.9	55.0	4.2	43.5	52.7	3.8	41.6	55.2	3.2
1908	41.7	55.0	3.4	42.2	54.6	3.1	42.6	54.7	2.7
1910	42.2	48.4	9.5	43.7	52.6	3.7	42.0	55.3	2.7
1912	39.9	35.8	24.3	41.1	41.5	17.5	42.6	43.0	14.5
1914	40.6	47.2	12.2	40.7	49.9	9.5	39.5	50.2	10.3
1916	38.8	57.8	3.5	37.4	58.9	3.7	37.9	57.9	4.2
1918	37.7	60.6	1.7	38.8	60.0	1.2	34.8	64.7	0.5
1920	28.5	68.9	2.7	29.5	68.2	2.4	24.9	72.9	2.2
1922	31.5	64.4	4.1	35.0	64.9	0.2	37.7	62.1	0.2
1924	31.2	61.6	7.1	36.2	63.8	0.0	40.6	59.4	0.0
1926	28.3	67.9	3.8	28.8	71.0	0.2	29.0	70.8	0.2
1928	34.7	65.0	0.3	33.8	66.1	0.1	32.1	67.7	0.2
1930	40.9	58.4	0.8	38.6	60.9	0.5	41.1	58.5	0.4
1932	54.6	43.7	1.7	53.5	45.0	1.5	53.9	43.9	2.2
1934	54.2	44.3	1.5	53.6	45.3	1.1	53.2	45.2	1.6
1936	51.0	46.7	2.3	49.8	48.1	2.1	50.4	47.9	1.7
1938	47.6	51.3	1.1	46.5	52.6	1.0	46.8	52.5	0.7
1940	46.4	53.3	0.3	46.0	53.7	0.3	45.5	54.2	0.3
1942	41.1	58.6	0.3	38.9	60.8	0.3	39.9	59.9	0.3
1944	45.7	54.0	0.3	45.1	54.7	0.3	45.8	54.0	0.2
1946	45.7	53.8	0.6	44.6	55.1	0.3	45.8	54.0	0.3
1948	49.2	49.8	0.9	48.9	50.6	0.6	51.5	48.0	0.5
1950	41.7	57.7	0.6	41.3	58.3	0.4	41.7	57.9	0.4
1952	40.7	59.0	0.4	42.3	57.4	0.3	39.6	60.1	0.3
1954	43.9	55.9	0.3	45.8	54.0	0.2	44.5	55.4	0.1
1956	45.9	54.0	0.1	47.6	52.4	0.0	45.8	54.2	0.0
1958	48.4	51.6	0.0	50.5	49.5	0.0	48.7	51.3	0.0
1960	46.3	53.7	0.0	47.3	52.7	0.0	47.0	53.0	0.0
1962	49.5	50.5	0.0	48.4	51.6	0.0	46.4	53.6	0.0
1964	56.7	42.9	0.4	54.9	44.6	0.5	48.4	51.2	0.4
1966	48.0	50.7	1.3	46.9	52.4	0.7	42.7	56.6	0.8
1968	45.7	52.8	1.6	47.3	52.7	0.1	48.0	52.0	0.0
1970				48.2	50.4	1.4	49.7	49.8	0.5

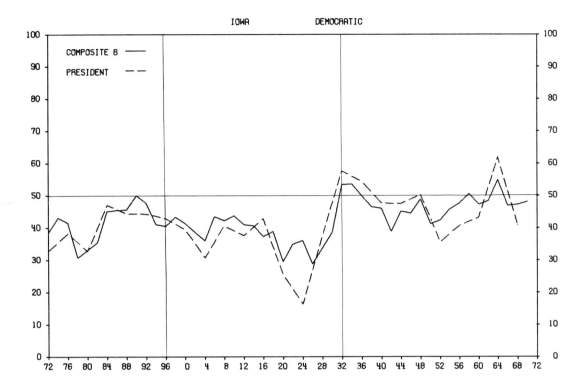

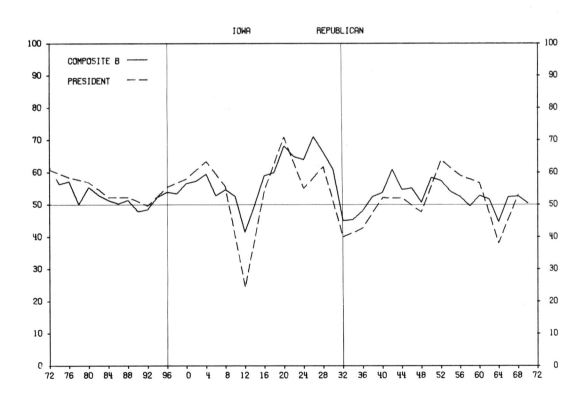

143

YEAR	PRESIDENT			GOVERNOR			SENATE CLASS II			SENATE CLASS III		
	DEM.	REP.	OTHER	DEM.	REP.	OTHER	DEM.	REP.	OTHER	DEM.	REP.	OTHER
1872	32.8	66.5	0.7	34.2	65.8	0.0						
1874				40.8	56.4	2.8						
1876	30.5	63.1	6.4	37.9	56.8	5.3						
1878				26.9	53.5	19.6						
1880	29.7	60.4	9.8	32.0	57.9	10.1						
1882				46.4	41.9	11.7						
1884	33.9	58.1	8.0	40.8	55.3	3.8						
1886				42.3	54.7	3.0						
1888	31.0	55.2	13.8	32.5	54.7	12.8						
1890				24.2	39.0	36.7						
1892	50.3	48.3	1.4	0.0	48.7	51.3						
1894				39.4	49.5	11.1						
1896	37.7	47.5	14.9	50.5	48.3	1.2						
1898				46.5	51.8	1.6						
1900	17.0	52.6	30.4	47.0	51.9	1.1						
1902				40.8	55.5	3.8						
1904	26.2	64.9	8.9	36.3	57.9	5.8						
1906				47.6	48.2	4.2						
1908	42.9	52.5	4.7	43.3	52.5	4.2						
1910				44.8	49.8	5.4						
1912	39.3	20.5	40.2	46.6	46.5	6.9						
1914				30.6	39.7	29.7				34.8	35.5	29.7
1916	49.9	44.1	6.0	33.0	60.8	6.2						
1918				30.7	66.4	2.9	33.7	63.7	2.6			
1920	32.5	64.7	2.7	39.3	58.4	2.3				33.4	64.0	2.6
1922				50.9	47.4	1.7						
1924	23.6	61.5	14.9	27.7	49.0	23.3	25.2	70.1	4.7			
1926				35.3	63.3	1.4				34.7	63.6	1.7
1928	27.1	72.0	0.9	33.2	65.6	1.2						
1930				35.0	34.9	30.1	38.9	61.1	0.0	50.0	47.9	2.0
1932	53.6	44.1	2.3	34.1	34.8	31.1				45.7	42.0	12.3
1934				45.6	53.5	0.9						
1936	53.7	46.0	0.4	51.1	48.5	0.4	48.4	51.0	0.6			
1938				45.1	52.1	2.8				43.8	56.2	0.0
1940	42.4	56.9	0.7	49.6	49.6	0.8						
1942				41.8	56.7	1.6	40.3	57.1	2.6			
1944	39.2	60.2	0.6	32.8	65.7	1.4				40.7	57.8	1.5
1946				44.0	53.5	2.5						
1948	44.6	53.6	1.8	40.4	57.0	2.6	42.7	54.9	2.4			
1950				44.5	53.8	1.7				44.3	54.7	1.0
1952	30.5	68.8	0.7	41.7	56.3	2.0						
1954				46.0	53.0	1.1	41.8	56.3	1.8			
1956	34.2	65.4	0.4	55.5	42.1	2.4				40.5	57.9	1.6
1958				56.5	42.5	1.0						
1960	39.1	60.4	0.4	43.6	55.4	0.9	43.8	54.6	1.6			
1962				45.6	53.4	1.0	42.5	56.2	1.3	35.9	62.4	1.6
1964	54.1	45.1	0.9	47.1	50.9	2.1						
1966				54.8	43.9	1.2	45.2	52.1	2.7			
1968	34.7	54.8	10.4	51.9	47.6	0.5				38.7	60.1	1.3
1970				54.3	44.7	1.0						

YEAR	PRESIDENT			GOVERNOR			SENATE			HOUSE OF REPRESENTATIVES		
	DEM.	REP.	OTHER	DEM.	REP.	OTHER	DEM.	REP.	OTHER	DEM.	REP.	OTHER
1872	32.8	66.5	0.7	34.2	65.8	0.0				33.6	66.4	0.0
1874	31.7	64.8	3.6	40.8	56.4	2.8				12.9	56.1	31.1
1876	30.5	63.1	6.4	37.9	56.8	5.3				12.9	62.9	24.3
1878	30.1	61.8	8.1	26.9	53.5	19.6				26.4	54.2	19.4
1880	29.7	60.4	9.8	32.0	57.9	10.2				19.8	60.0	20.2
1882	31.8	59.3	8.9	46.4	41.9	11.7				31.4	58.6	10.0
1884	33.9	58.1	8.0	40.8	55.3	3.8				37.2	59.8	3.0
1886	32.5	56.7	10.9	42.3	54.7	3.0				40.3	55.0	4.7
1888	31.0	55.2	13.8	32.5	54.7	12.8				31.6	55.6	12.8
1890	40.7	51.7	7.6	24.2	39.1	36.7				9.3	42.2	48.5
1892	50.3	48.3	1.4	0.0	48.7	51.3				41.7	48.5	9.8
1894	44.0	47.9	8.1	39.4	49.5	11.1				14.1	50.7	35.2
1896	37.7	47.5	14.9	50.5	48.3	1.2				48.5	48.5	3.0
1898	27.4	50.0	22.6	46.6	51.8	1.6				44.3	52.6	3.1
1900	17.0	52.6	30.4	47.0	51.9	1.1				44.8	52.5	2.7
1902	21.6	58.7	19.7	40.8	55.5	3.8				41.5	56.3	2.2
1904	26.2	64.9	8.9	36.3	57.9	5.8				35.1	60.1	4.8
1906	34.5	58.7	6.8	47.6	48.2	4.2				41.8	54.1	4.1
1908	42.9	52.5	4.7	43.3	52.5	4.2				43.3	52.5	4.3
1910	41.1	36.5	22.4	44.8	49.8	5.5				39.4	55.2	5.4
1912	39.3	20.5	40.2	46.6	46.5	6.9				46.8	45.4	7.8
1914	44.6	32.3	23.1	30.6	39.7	29.7	34.8	35.5	29.7	40.5	38.9	20.6
1916	50.0	44.1	6.0	33.1	60.8	6.2	34.3	49.6	16.1	46.0	46.0	8.0
1918	41.2	54.4	4.4	30.7	66.4	2.9	33.7	63.7	2.6	40.1	57.0	3.0
1920	32.5	64.8	2.7	39.3	58.4	2.3	33.4	64.0	2.6	36.5	61.8	1.8
1922	28.1	63.1	8.8	50.9	47.4	1.7	29.3	67.1	3.7	44.5	54.2	1.2
1924	23.6	61.5	14.9	27.7	49.0	23.3	25.2	70.1	4.7	44.2	54.8	1.0
1926	25.3	66.8	7.9	35.3	63.3	1.4	34.7	63.6	1.7	40.8	59.1	0.0
1928	27.1	72.0	0.9	33.2	65.6	1.2	39.6	59.1	1.3	36.8	63.3	0.0
1930	40.3	58.1	1.6	35.0	34.9	30.1	44.4	54.6	1.0	42.9	57.1	0.0
1932	53.6	44.1	2.3	34.1	34.8	31.1	45.7	42.0	12.3	49.7	48.7	1.6
1934	53.6	45.0	1.3	45.6	53.5	0.9	47.0	46.5	6.4	48.6	50.2	1.3
1936	53.7	46.0	0.4	51.1	48.5	0.4	48.4	51.0	0.6	47.2	51.5	1.3
1938	48.0	51.4	0.6	45.1	52.1	2.8	43.8	56.2	0.0	41.0	59.0	0.0
1940	42.4	56.9	0.7	49.6	49.6	0.8	42.0	56.7	1.3	42.3	57.7	0.0
1942	40.8	58.6	0.7	41.8	56.7	1.6	40.3	57.1	2.6	39.4	60.6	0.0
1944	39.2	60.3	0.6	32.8	65.7	1.4	40.7	57.8	1.5	37.0	63.0	0.0
1946	41.9	56.9	1.2	44.0	53.5	2.5	41.7	56.4	1.9	40.2	59.2	0.6
1948	44.6	53.6	1.8	40.4	57.0	2.6	42.7	54.9	2.4	42.5	57.5	0.0
1950	37.6	61.2	1.3	44.5	53.8	1.8	44.3	54.7	1.0	41.2	58.8	0.0
1952	30.5	68.8	0.7	41.7	56.3	2.0	43.1	55.5	1.4	40.6	59.4	0.0
1954	32.4	67.1	0.5	46.0	53.0	1.1	41.8	56.3	1.8	43.5	56.5	0.0
1956	34.2	65.4	0.4	55.5	42.1	2.4	40.5	57.9	1.6	46.8	53.0	0.2
1958	36.7	63.0	0.4	56.5	42.5	1.0	42.1	56.3	1.6	50.1	49.4	0.5
1960	39.1	60.5	0.5	43.6	55.5	1.0	43.8	54.6	1.6	45.8	54.2	0.0
1962	46.6	52.8	0.7	45.6	53.4	1.0	39.2	59.3	1.5	39.9	60.1	0.0
1964	54.1	45.1	0.9	47.1	50.9	2.1	42.2	55.7	2.1	44.5	55.5	0.0
1966	44.4	50.0	5.6	54.8	43.9	1.2	45.2	52.2	2.7	36.6	63.1	0.4
1968	34.7	54.8	10.4	51.9	47.6	0.5	38.7	60.1	1.3	37.9	62.1	0.0
1970				54.3	44.7	1.0				42.2	56.6	1.2

KANSAS

YEAR	COMPOSITE A (P+G+S+H/4)			COMPOSITE B (G+S+H/3)			COMPOSITE C (S+H/2)		
	DEM.	REP.	OTHER	DEM.	REP.	OTHER	DEM.	REP.	OTHER
1872	33.5	66.2	0.3	33.9	66.1	0.0	33.6	66.4	0.0
1874	28.5	59.1	12.5	26.8	56.3	16.9	12.9	56.1	31.1
1876	27.1	60.9	12.0	25.4	59.8	14.8	12.9	62.9	24.3
1878	27.8	56.5	15.7	26.6	53.9	19.5	26.4	54.2	19.4
1880	27.2	59.5	13.4	25.9	59.0	15.2	19.8	60.0	20.2
1882	36.5	53.3	10.2	38.9	50.3	10.8	31.4	58.6	10.0
1884	37.3	57.7	4.9	39.0	57.5	3.4	37.2	59.8	3.0
1886	38.4	55.5	6.2	41.3	54.9	3.8	40.3	55.0	4.7
1888	31.7	55.2	13.1	32.1	55.1	12.8	31.6	55.6	12.8
1890	24.7	44.3	30.9	16.8	40.6	42.6	9.3	42.2	48.5
1892	30.7	48.5	20.8	20.9	48.6	30.5	41.7	48.5	9.8
1894	32.5	49.4	18.1	26.8	50.1	23.1	14.1	50.7	35.2
1896	45.6	48.1	6.4	49.5	48.4	2.1	48.5	48.5	3.0
1898	39.4	51.5	9.1	45.4	52.2	2.4	44.3	52.6	3.1
1900	36.3	52.3	11.4	45.9	52.2	1.9	44.8	52.5	2.7
1902	34.6	56.8	8.5	41.2	55.9	3.0	41.5	56.3	2.2
1904	32.5	61.0	6.5	35.7	59.0	5.3	35.1	60.1	4.8
1906	41.3	53.7	5.0	44.7	51.2	4.1	41.8	54.1	4.1
1908	43.2	52.5	4.4	43.3	52.5	4.2	43.3	52.5	4.3
1910	41.8	47.1	11.1	42.1	52.5	5.4	39.4	55.2	5.4
1912	44.2	37.5	18.3	46.7	46.0	7.4	46.8	45.4	7.8
1914	37.6	36.6	25.8	35.3	38.0	26.7	37.6	37.2	25.2
1916	40.8	50.1	9.1	37.8	52.1	10.1	40.1	47.8	12.0
1918	36.4	60.4	3.2	34.8	62.3	2.8	36.9	60.3	2.8
1920	35.4	62.2	2.4	36.4	61.4	2.2	34.9	62.9	2.2
1922	38.2	58.0	3.9	41.6	56.2	2.2	36.9	60.7	2.4
1924	30.2	58.9	11.0	32.4	58.0	9.6	34.7	62.5	2.8
1926	34.1	63.2	2.8	37.0	62.0	1.0	37.8	61.4	0.9
1928	34.1	65.0	0.9	36.5	62.7	0.9	38.2	61.2	0.7
1930	40.6	51.2	8.2	40.7	48.9	10.4	43.6	55.9	0.5
1932	45.8	42.4	11.8	43.2	41.9	15.0	47.7	45.4	7.0
1934	48.7	48.8	2.5	47.1	50.1	2.9	47.8	48.4	3.9
1936	50.1	49.3	0.7	48.9	50.3	0.8	47.8	51.3	0.9
1938	44.5	54.7	0.9	43.3	55.8	1.0	42.4	57.6	0.0
1940	44.1	55.2	0.7	44.7	54.7	0.7	42.2	57.2	0.7
1942	40.6	58.2	1.2	40.5	58.1	1.4	39.9	58.8	1.3
1944	37.4	61.7	0.9	36.8	62.2	1.0	38.8	60.4	0.8
1946	42.0	56.5	1.5	42.0	56.4	1.7	41.0	57.8	1.2
1948	42.6	55.8	1.7	41.9	56.5	1.6	42.6	56.2	1.2
1950	41.9	57.1	1.0	43.3	55.8	0.9	42.7	56.8	0.5
1952	39.0	60.0	1.0	41.8	57.1	1.1	41.8	57.5	0.7
1954	40.9	58.2	0.9	43.8	55.3	1.0	42.7	56.4	0.9
1956	44.2	54.6	1.1	47.6	51.0	1.4	43.6	55.5	0.9
1958	46.3	52.8	0.9	49.6	49.4	1.0	46.1	52.9	1.0
1960	43.1	56.2	0.8	44.4	54.8	0.9	44.8	54.4	0.8
1962	42.8	56.4	0.8	41.6	57.6	0.8	39.6	59.7	0.7
1964	47.0	51.8	1.2	44.6	54.0	1.4	43.4	55.6	1.0
1966	45.3	52.3	2.5	45.5	53.0	1.4	40.9	57.6	1.5
1968	40.8	56.2	3.1	42.8	56.6	0.6	38.3	61.1	0.6
1970				48.3	50.7	1.1	42.2	56.6	1.2

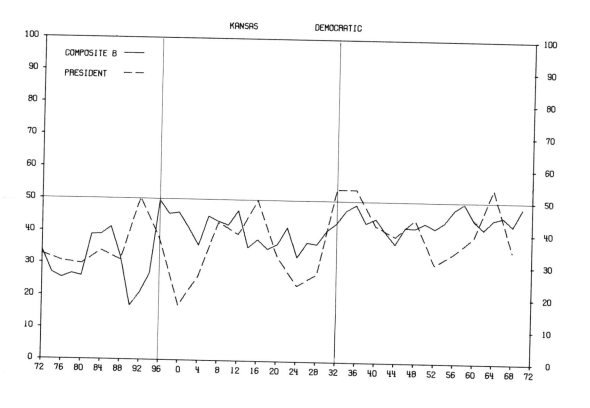

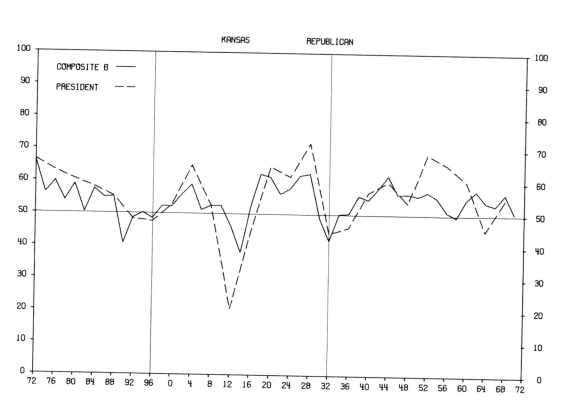

147

KENTUCKY

YEAR	PRESIDENT			GOVERNOR			SENATE CLASS II			SENATE CLASS III		
	DEM.	REP.	OTHER	DEM.	REP.	OTHER	DEM.	REP.	OTHER	DEM.	REP.	OTHER
1872	52.3	46.4	1.2	58.6	41.4	0.0						
1874												
1876	61.4	37.4	1.2	58.3	41.7	0.0						
1878												
1880	55.7	39.9	4.4	55.4	36.2	8.4						
1882												
1884	55.3	42.9	1.7	60.0	40.0	0.0						
1886												
1888	53.3	45.0	1.7	50.7	44.8	4.5						
1890												
1892	51.5	39.7	8.8	49.9	40.1	10.0						
1894												
1896	48.9	48.9	2.2	45.8	48.3	5.9						
1898												
1900	50.2	48.5	1.3	48.8	48.6	2.6						
1902												
1904	49.8	47.1	3.1	52.1	46.2	1.7						
1906												
1908	49.7	48.0	2.2	46.9	51.2	2.0						
1910												
1912	48.5	25.5	26.0	53.7	46.3	0.0				52.9	41.5	5.6
1914												
1916	51.9	46.5	1.6	49.1	49.0	2.0	50.8	49.2	0.0			
1918												
1920	49.8	49.2	1.1	45.3	53.8	0.9				49.7	50.3	0.0
1922												
1924	46.1	48.8	5.1	53.3	45.8	0.9	48.4	51.6	0.0	51.8	48.2	0.0
1926												
1928	40.5	59.3	0.2	47.9	52.1	0.0	52.1	47.9	0.0			
1930												
1932	59.1	40.2	0.8	54.3	45.4	0.3				59.1	40.5	0.3
1934												
1936	58.5	39.9	1.6	54.5	45.1	0.4	58.8	39.8	1.4	62.0	38.0	0.0
1938												
1940	57.4	42.3	0.3	56.5	43.5	0.0	58.3	41.7	0.0			
1942							55.3	44.7	0.0			
1944	54.5	45.2	0.3	48.9	50.5	0.6				54.8	44.9	0.3
1946							46.5	53.3	0.3			
1948	56.7	41.5	1.8	57.2	42.5	0.3	51.4	48.3	0.3			
1950										54.2	45.1	0.7
1952	49.9	49.8	0.2	54.6	45.4	0.0	48.5	51.5	0.0			
1954							54.5	45.5	0.0			
1956	45.2	54.3	0.5	58.0	41.4	0.5	46.8	53.2	0.0	49.7	50.3	0.0
1958												
1960	46.4	53.6	0.0	60.6	39.4	0.0	40.8	59.2	0.0			
1962										47.2	52.8	0.0
1964	64.0	35.7	0.3	50.7	49.3	0.0						
1966							35.5	64.5	0.0			
1968	37.6	43.8	18.6	48.0	51.2	0.8				47.6	51.4	1.0
1970												

148

KENTUCKY

YEAR	PRESIDENT			GOVERNOR			SENATE			HOUSE OF REPRESENTATIVES		
	DEM.	REP.	OTHER	DEM.	REP.	OTHER	DEM.	REP.	OTHER	DEM.	REP.	OTHER
1872	52.3	46.4	1.2	58.6	41.4	0.0				64.7	16.8	18.5
1874	56.9	41.9	1.2	58.5	41.5	0.0				61.3	18.9	19.8
1876	61.4	37.4	1.2	58.3	41.7	0.0				59.6	37.1	3.3
1878	58.6	38.7	2.8	56.9	38.9	4.2				58.6	24.2	17.2
1880	55.7	39.9	4.4	55.4	36.2	8.4				57.6	38.1	4.3
1882	55.5	41.4	3.1	57.7	38.1	4.2				53.5	40.7	5.8
1884	55.3	42.9	1.8	60.0	40.0	0.0				58.4	38.4	3.2
1886	54.3	44.0	1.7	55.3	42.4	2.3				53.3	39.9	6.9
1888	53.3	45.0	1.7	50.7	44.8	4.5				53.7	45.1	1.2
1890	52.4	42.4	5.3	50.3	42.5	7.3				60.9	38.0	1.1
1892	51.5	39.7	8.8	49.9	40.1	10.0				54.2	37.9	7.8
1894	50.2	44.3	5.5	47.8	44.2	8.0				47.2	45.0	7.8
1896	48.9	48.9	2.2	45.8	48.3	5.9				46.9	48.0	5.1
1898	49.5	48.7	1.8	47.3	48.5	4.3				50.0	50.0	0.0
1900	50.2	48.5	1.3	48.8	48.6	2.6				50.3	49.4	0.3
1902	50.0	47.8	2.2	50.4	47.4	2.2				54.0	42.8	3.2
1904	49.8	47.1	3.1	52.1	46.2	1.7				51.2	47.6	1.3
1906	49.8	47.6	2.6	49.5	48.7	1.8				54.0	43.0	3.0
1908	49.7	48.0	2.2	46.9	51.2	2.0				50.8	48.1	1.1
1910	49.1	36.8	14.1	50.3	48.8	1.0				53.4	44.8	1.8
1912	48.5	25.5	26.0	53.7	46.3	0.0				52.6	21.7	25.7
1914	50.2	36.0	13.8	51.4	47.7	1.0	52.9	41.5	5.6	53.6	38.2	8.2
1916	51.9	46.5	1.6	49.1	49.0	2.0	51.8	45.4	2.8	52.0	46.8	1.2
1918	50.9	47.8	1.3	47.2	51.4	1.4	50.8	49.2	0.0	52.2	47.8	0.0
1920	49.8	49.2	1.1	45.3	53.8	0.9	49.7	50.3	0.0	50.7	48.0	1.3
1922	48.0	49.0	3.1	49.3	49.8	0.9	49.1	50.9	0.0	55.5	39.0	5.5
1924	46.1	48.8	5.1	53.3	45.8	0.9	48.4	51.6	0.0	56.1	41.6	2.3
1926	43.3	54.0	2.6	50.6	49.0	0.5	51.8	48.2	0.0	52.3	47.7	0.0
1928	40.5	59.3	0.2	47.9	52.1	0.0	52.0	48.0	0.0	43.9	56.1	0.0
1930	49.8	49.7	0.5	51.1	48.8	0.1	52.1	47.9	0.0	54.4	44.6	1.1
1932	59.1	40.2	0.8	54.3	45.4	0.3	59.2	40.5	0.3	59.3	40.4	0.3
1934	58.8	40.0	1.2	54.4	45.3	0.4	59.0	40.2	0.9	54.2	43.9	1.9
1936	58.5	39.9	1.6	54.5	45.1	0.4	58.8	39.8	1.4	58.8	40.2	1.0
1938	58.0	41.1	0.9	55.5	44.3	0.2	62.0	38.0	0.0	59.1	40.9	0.0
1940	57.4	42.3	0.3	56.5	43.5	0.0	58.3	41.7	0.0	62.5	37.5	0.0
1942	56.0	43.8	0.3	52.7	47.0	0.3	55.3	44.7	0.0	62.7	36.0	1.3
1944	54.5	45.2	0.3	48.9	50.5	0.6	54.8	44.9	0.3	54.5	45.2	0.3
1946	55.6	43.4	1.1	53.1	46.5	0.4	46.5	53.3	0.3	51.3	48.6	0.1
1948	56.7	41.5	1.8	57.2	42.5	0.3	51.4	48.3	0.3	61.2	38.3	0.6
1950	53.3	45.7	1.0	55.9	43.9	0.1	54.2	45.1	0.7	63.0	37.0	0.0
1952	49.9	49.8	0.2	54.6	45.4	0.0	48.5	51.5	0.0	52.1	47.8	0.1
1954	47.6	52.1	0.4	56.3	43.4	0.3	54.5	45.5	0.0	64.6	35.3	0.1
1956	45.2	54.3	0.5	58.0	41.5	0.5	48.2	51.8	0.0	52.3	47.7	0.0
1958	45.8	53.9	0.2	59.3	40.5	0.3	44.5	55.5	0.0	65.1	34.6	0.3
1960	46.4	53.6	0.0	60.6	39.4	0.0	40.8	59.2	0.0	59.1	40.9	0.0
1962	55.2	44.6	0.2	55.7	44.4	0.0	47.2	52.8	0.0	59.0	40.9	0.1
1964	64.0	35.7	0.3	50.7	49.3	0.0	41.4	58.6	0.0	64.8	35.3	0.0
1966	50.8	39.7	9.4	49.4	50.2	0.4	35.5	64.5	0.0	52.8	47.2	0.0
1968	37.7	43.8	18.6	48.0	51.2	0.8	47.6	51.4	1.0	51.0	48.7	0.4
1970										52.3	47.0	0.7

KENTUCKY

YEAR	COMPOSITE A (P+G+S+H/4)			COMPOSITE B (G+S+H/3)			COMPOSITE C (S+H/2)		
	DEM.	REP.	OTHER	DEM.	REP.	OTHER	DEM.	REP.	OTHER
1872	58.5	34.9	6.6	61.6	29.1	9.2	64.7	16.8	18.5
1874	58.9	34.1	7.0	59.9	30.2	9.9	61.3	18.9	19.8
1876	59.8	38.7	1.5	59.0	39.4	1.7	59.6	37.1	3.3
1878	58.0	33.9	8.1	57.7	31.6	10.7	58.6	24.2	17.2
1880	56.3	38.1	5.7	56.5	37.1	6.3	57.6	38.1	4.3
1882	55.6	40.1	4.4	55.6	39.4	5.0	53.5	40.7	5.8
1884	57.9	40.5	1.7	59.2	39.2	1.6	58.4	38.4	3.2
1886	54.3	42.1	3.6	54.3	41.1	4.6	53.3	39.9	6.9
1888	52.6	44.9	2.5	52.2	44.9	2.9	53.7	45.1	1.2
1890	54.5	41.0	4.5	55.6	40.2	4.2	60.9	38.0	1.1
1892	51.9	39.3	8.9	52.0	39.0	8.9	54.2	37.9	7.8
1894	48.4	44.5	7.1	47.5	44.6	7.9	47.2	45.0	7.8
1896	47.2	48.4	4.4	46.3	48.2	5.5	46.9	48.0	5.1
1898	48.9	49.1	2.0	48.6	49.2	2.1	50.0	50.0	0.0
1900	49.8	48.8	1.4	49.5	49.0	1.5	50.3	49.4	0.3
1902	51.5	46.0	2.5	52.2	45.1	2.7	54.0	42.8	3.2
1904	51.0	47.0	2.0	51.6	46.9	1.5	51.2	47.6	1.3
1906	51.1	46.4	2.5	51.8	45.8	2.4	54.0	43.0	3.0
1908	49.1	49.1	1.8	48.8	49.6	1.5	50.8	48.1	1.1
1910	50.9	43.4	5.6	51.8	46.8	1.4	53.4	44.8	1.8
1912	51.6	31.2	17.2	53.1	34.0	12.8	52.6	21.7	25.7
1914	52.0	40.9	7.1	52.6	42.5	4.9	53.3	39.9	6.9
1916	51.2	46.9	1.9	51.0	47.1	2.0	51.9	46.1	2.0
1918	50.3	49.1	0.7	50.1	49.5	0.5	51.5	48.5	0.0
1920	48.9	50.3	0.8	48.6	50.7	0.7	50.2	49.1	0.7
1922	50.5	47.2	2.4	51.3	46.6	2.1	52.3	45.0	2.8
1924	51.0	46.9	2.1	52.6	46.3	1.1	52.3	46.6	1.2
1926	49.5	49.7	0.8	51.6	48.3	0.2	52.1	47.9	0.0
1928	46.1	53.9	0.0	47.9	52.1	0.0	48.0	52.0	0.0
1930	51.8	47.7	0.4	52.5	47.1	0.4	53.2	46.2	0.6
1932	57.9	41.6	0.4	57.6	42.1	0.3	59.2	40.4	0.3
1934	56.6	42.4	1.1	55.9	43.1	1.0	56.6	42.0	1.4
1936	57.6	41.3	1.1	57.4	41.7	0.9	58.8	40.0	1.2
1938	58.6	41.1	0.3	58.9	41.1	0.1	60.6	39.4	0.0
1940	58.7	41.3	0.1	59.1	40.9	0.0	60.4	39.6	0.0
1942	56.7	42.9	0.5	56.9	42.6	0.5	59.0	40.3	0.7
1944	53.2	46.5	0.4	52.8	46.9	0.4	54.7	45.1	0.3
1946	51.6	47.9	0.5	50.3	49.5	0.3	48.9	50.9	0.2
1948	56.6	42.6	0.7	56.6	43.0	0.4	56.3	43.3	0.4
1950	56.6	42.9	0.5	57.7	42.0	0.3	58.6	41.1	0.4
1952	51.3	48.7	0.1	51.7	48.3	0.0	50.3	49.7	0.0
1954	55.7	44.1	0.2	58.5	41.4	0.1	59.5	40.4	0.0
1956	50.9	48.8	0.3	52.8	47.0	0.2	50.2	49.8	0.0
1958	53.7	46.1	0.2	56.3	43.5	0.2	54.8	45.0	0.2
1960	51.7	48.3	0.0	53.5	46.5	0.0	49.9	50.1	0.0
1962	54.3	45.7	0.1	54.0	46.0	0.1	53.1	46.8	0.1
1964	55.2	44.7	0.1	52.3	47.7	0.0	53.1	46.9	0.0
1966	47.1	50.4	2.5	45.9	54.0	0.1	44.1	55.9	0.0
1968	46.1	48.8	5.2	48.9	50.4	0.7	49.3	50.0	0.7
1970							52.3	47.0	0.7

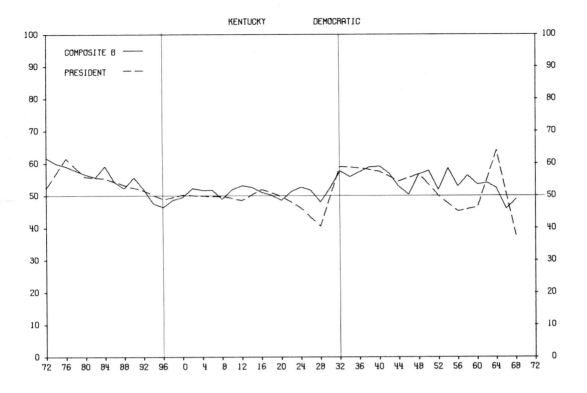

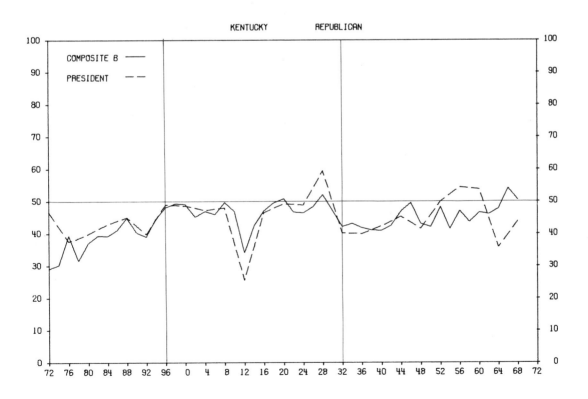

151

LOUISIANA

YEAR	PRESIDENT			GOVERNOR			SENATE CLASS II			SENATE CLASS III		
	DEM.	REP.	OTHER	DEM.	REP.	OTHER	DEM.	REP.	OTHER	DEM.	REP.	OTHER
1872 1874	22.4	51.6	26.1	48.1	51.8	0.0						
1876 1878	50.3	49.7	0.0	50.7	49.3	0.0						
1880 1882	62.7	37.3	0.4	64.6	35.4	0.0						
1884 1886	57.2	42.4	0.4	67.1	32.9	0.0						
1888 1890	73.4	26.5	0.2	72.5	27.5	0.0						
1892 1894	76.5	23.5	0.0	26.4	16.6	57.0						
1896 1898	76.4	18.1	5.5	56.9	43.0	0.1						
1900 1902	79.0	21.0	0.0	78.3	3.2	18.5						
1904 1906	88.5	9.7	1.8	89.0	11.0	0.0						
1908 1910	84.6	11.9	3.4	87.1	11.1	1.8						
1912 1914	76.8	4.8	18.4	89.5	8.8	1.7						
1916 1918	85.9	7.0	7.1	62.5	0.0	37.5	100.0	0.0	0.0	100.0	0.0	0.0
1920 1922	69.2	30.5	0.3							100.0	0.0	0.0
1924 1926	76.4	20.2	3.3	97.9	2.1	0.0	100.0	0.0	0.0	100.0	0.0	0.0
1928 1930	76.3	23.7	0.0	96.1	3.9	0.0	100.0	0.0	0.0			
1932 1934	92.8	7.0	0.2	99.9	0.0	0.1				100.0	0.0	0.0
1936 1938	88.8	11.1	0.0	100.0	0.0	0.0	100.0	0.0	0.0	99.8	0.0	0.2
1940 1942	85.9	14.1	0.0	99.4	0.6	0.0	100.0	0.0	0.0			
1944 1946	80.6	19.4	0.0	100.0	0.0	0.0				100.0	0.0	0.0
1948 1950	32.7	17.5	49.8	100.0	0.0	0.0	100.0	0.0	0.0	74.9 87.7	25.1 12.3	0.0 0.0
1952 1954	52.9	47.1	0.0	96.0	4.0	0.0	100.0	0.0	0.0			
1956 1958	39.5	53.3	7.2	100.0	0.0	0.0				100.0	0.0	0.0
1960 1962	50.4	28.6	21.0	80.5	17.0	2.5	79.8	20.2	0.0	75.6	24.4	0.0
1964 1966	43.2	56.8	0.0	60.7	38.5	0.8	100.0	0.0	0.0			
1968 1970	28.2	23.5	48.3	100.0	0.0	0.0				100.0	0.0	0.0

152

YEAR	PRESIDENT			GOVERNOR			SENATE			HOUSE OF REPRESENTATIVES		
	DEM.	REP.	OTHER	DEM.	REP.	OTHER	DEM.	REP.	OTHER	DEM.	REP.	OTHER
1872	22.4	51.6	26.1	48.1	51.8	0.0				43.3	54.9	1.8
1874	36.3	50.7	13.0	49.4	50.6	0.0				47.9	51.2	0.9
1876	50.3	49.7	0.0	50.8	49.3	0.0				52.5	47.5	0.0
1878	56.3	43.5	0.2	57.7	42.4	0.0				66.9	18.7	14.4
1880	62.3	37.3	0.4	64.6	35.4	0.0				64.9	35.1	0.0
1882	59.7	39.8	0.4	65.8	34.2	0.0				62.7	29.4	7.9
1884	57.2	42.4	0.4	67.1	32.9	0.0				57.3	33.4	9.4
1886	65.3	34.4	0.3	69.8	30.2	0.0				74.5	24.6	0.9
1888	73.4	26.5	0.2	72.5	27.6	0.0				76.1	23.6	0.2
1890	75.0	25.0	0.1	49.4	22.1	28.5				80.5	17.3	2.1
1892	76.5	23.5	0.0	26.4	16.6	57.0				74.8	18.3	7.0
1894	76.5	20.8	2.8	41.7	29.8	28.5				68.1	19.7	12.2
1896	76.4	18.1	5.5	56.9	43.0	0.1				66.3	6.4	27.3
1898	77.7	19.6	2.8	67.6	23.1	9.3				83.3	11.8	5.0
1900	79.0	21.0	0.0	78.3	3.2	18.5				78.3	21.6	0.0
1902	83.8	15.3	0.9	83.7	7.1	9.3				84.6	15.4	0.0
1904	88.5	9.7	1.9	89.0	11.0	0.0				90.3	8.8	0.9
1906	86.6	10.8	2.7	88.1	11.0	0.9				87.8	10.6	1.6
1908	84.6	11.9	3.5	87.1	11.1	1.8				90.3	7.6	2.2
1910	80.7	8.4	10.9	88.3	9.9	1.8				90.6	7.6	1.8
1912	76.8	4.8	18.4	89.5	8.8	1.7				95.7	0.0	4.3
1914	81.4	5.9	12.7	76.0	4.4	19.6				79.4	0.0	20.7
1916	85.9	7.0	7.1	62.5	0.0	37.5				90.9	0.4	8.7
1918	77.6	18.7	3.7	80.2	1.1	18.7	100.0	0.0	0.0	100.0	0.0	0.0
1920	69.2	30.5	0.3	80.2	1.1	18.7	100.0	0.0	0.0	100.0	0.0	0.0
1922	72.8	25.4	1.8	80.2	1.1	18.7	100.0	0.0	0.0	99.9	0.0	0.1
1924	76.4	20.2	3.3	97.9	2.1	0.0	100.0	0.0	0.0	100.0	0.0	0.0
1926	76.4	22.0	1.7	97.0	3.0	0.0	100.0	0.0	0.0	98.4	1.6	0.0
1928	76.3	23.7	0.0	96.1	3.9	0.0	100.0	0.0	0.0	91.3	8.8	0.0
1930	84.5	15.4	0.1	98.0	1.9	0.0	100.0	0.0	0.0	98.3	1.7	0.0
1932	92.8	7.0	0.2	100.0	0.0	0.1	100.0	0.0	0.0	100.0	0.0	0.0
1934	90.8	9.1	0.1	100.0	0.0	0.0	100.0	0.0	0.0	100.0	0.0	0.0
1936	88.8	11.1	0.0	100.0	0.0	0.0	100.0	0.0	0.0	100.0	0.0	0.0
1938	87.4	12.6	0.0	99.7	0.3	0.0	99.8	0.0	0.2	100.0	0.0	0.0
1940	85.9	14.1	0.0	99.4	0.6	0.0	99.9	0.0	0.1	95.7	4.3	0.0
1942	83.2	16.7	0.0	99.7	0.3	0.0	100.0	0.0	0.0	100.0	0.0	0.0
1944	80.6	19.4	0.0	100.0	0.0	0.0	100.0	0.0	0.0	100.0	0.0	0.0
1946	56.7	18.4	24.9	100.0	0.0	0.0	93.1	6.9	0.0	94.7	5.3	0.0
1948	32.8	17.5	49.8	100.0	0.0	0.0	86.1	13.9	0.0	95.8	4.2	0.0
1950	42.8	32.3	24.9	98.0	2.0	0.0	87.7	12.3	0.0	100.0	0.0	0.0
1952	52.9	47.1	0.0	96.0	4.0	0.0	93.9	6.1	0.0	91.3	8.7	0.0
1954	46.2	50.2	3.6	98.0	2.0	0.0	100.0	0.0	0.0	96.2	3.8	0.0
1956	39.5	53.3	7.2	100.0	0.0	0.0	100.0	0.0	0.0	85.2	14.8	0.0
1958	45.0	40.9	14.1	90.3	8.5	1.2	89.9	10.1	0.0	97.7	2.3	0.0
1960	50.4	28.6	21.0	80.5	17.0	2.5	79.8	20.2	0.0	84.9	15.1	0.0
1962	46.8	42.7	10.5	70.6	27.8	1.6	75.6	24.4	0.0	87.8	12.3	0.0
1964	43.2	56.8	0.0	60.7	38.5	0.8	87.8	12.2	0.0	71.5	28.5	0.0
1966	35.7	40.1	24.2	80.4	19.3	0.4	100.0	0.0	0.0	81.8	18.2	0.0
1968	28.2	23.5	48.3	100.0	0.0	0.0	100.0	0.0	0.0	81.3	18.7	0.0
1970										95.3	2.8	1.9

LOUISIANA

YEAR	COMPOSITE A (P+G+S+H/4)			COMPOSITE B (G+S+H/3)			COMPOSITE C (S+H/2)		
	DEM.	REP.	OTHER	DEM.	REP.	OTHER	DEM.	REP.	OTHER
1872	37.9	52.8	9.3	45.7	53.4	0.9	43.3	54.9	1.8
1874	44.6	50.8	4.7	48.7	50.9	0.5	47.9	51.2	0.9
1876	51.2	48.8	0.0	51.6	48.4	0.0	52.5	47.5	0.0
1878	60.3	34.9	4.9	62.3	30.5	7.2	66.9	18.7	14.4
1880	63.9	36.0	0.1	64.7	35.3	0.0	64.9	35.1	0.0
1882	62.8	34.5	2.8	64.3	31.8	4.0	62.7	29.4	7.9
1884	60.5	36.2	3.3	62.2	33.1	4.7	57.3	33.4	9.4
1886	69.9	29.7	0.4	72.1	27.4	0.5	74.5	24.6	0.9
1888	74.0	25.9	0.1	74.3	25.6	0.1	76.1	23.6	0.2
1890	68.3	21.5	10.2	65.0	19.7	15.3	80.5	17.3	2.1
1892	59.2	19.5	21.3	50.6	17.5	32.0	74.8	18.3	7.0
1894	62.1	23.5	14.5	54.9	24.8	20.4	68.1	19.7	12.2
1896	66.5	22.5	11.0	61.6	24.7	13.7	66.3	6.4	27.3
1898	76.2	18.1	5.7	75.5	17.4	7.1	83.3	11.8	5.0
1900	78.6	15.3	6.2	78.3	12.4	9.3	78.3	21.6	0.0
1902	84.0	12.6	3.4	84.1	11.2	4.6	84.6	15.4	0.0
1904	89.3	9.8	0.9	89.7	9.9	0.5	90.3	8.8	0.9
1906	87.5	10.8	1.7	87.9	10.8	1.3	87.8	10.6	1.6
1908	87.4	10.2	2.5	88.7	9.3	2.0	90.3	7.6	2.2
1910	86.5	8.6	4.8	89.5	8.8	1.8	90.6	7.6	1.8
1912	87.3	4.5	8.1	92.6	4.4	3.0	95.7	0.0	4.3
1914	78.9	3.4	17.7	77.7	2.2	20.1	79.4	0.0	20.7
1916	79.8	2.5	17.8	76.7	0.2	23.1	90.9	0.4	8.7
1918	89.4	5.0	5.6	93.4	0.4	6.3	100.0	0.0	0.0
1920	87.4	7.9	4.8	93.4	0.4	6.3	100.0	0.0	0.0
1922	88.2	6.6	5.2	93.4	0.4	6.3	100.0	0.0	0.1
1924	93.6	5.6	0.8	99.3	0.7	0.0	100.0	0.0	0.0
1926	92.9	6.6	0.4	98.5	1.5	0.0	99.2	0.8	0.0
1928	90.9	9.1	0.0	95.8	4.2	0.0	95.6	4.4	0.0
1930	95.2	4.7	0.0	98.8	1.2	0.0	99.2	0.8	0.0
1932	98.2	1.8	0.1	100.0	0.0	0.0	100.0	0.0	0.0
1934	97.7	2.3	0.0	100.0	0.0	0.0	100.0	0.0	0.0
1936	97.2	2.8	0.0	100.0	0.0	0.0	100.0	0.0	0.0
1938	96.7	3.2	0.1	99.8	0.1	0.1	99.9	0.0	0.1
1940	95.2	4.8	0.0	98.3	1.7	0.0	97.8	2.2	0.0
1942	95.7	4.3	0.0	99.9	0.1	0.0	100.0	0.0	0.0
1944	95.1	4.9	0.0	100.0	0.0	0.0	100.0	0.0	0.0
1946	86.1	7.7	6.2	95.9	4.1	0.0	93.9	6.1	0.0
1948	78.7	8.9	12.5	94.0	6.0	0.0	91.0	9.0	0.0
1950	82.1	11.6	6.2	95.2	4.8	0.0	93.9	6.1	0.0
1952	83.5	16.5	0.0	93.7	6.3	0.0	92.6	7.4	0.0
1954	85.1	14.0	0.9	98.1	1.9	0.0	98.1	1.9	0.0
1956	81.2	17.0	1.8	95.1	4.9	0.0	92.6	7.4	0.0
1958	80.7	15.5	3.8	92.6	7.0	0.4	93.8	6.2	0.0
1960	73.9	20.2	5.9	81.7	17.5	0.8	82.3	17.7	0.0
1962	70.2	26.8	3.0	78.0	21.5	0.5	81.7	18.3	0.0
1964	65.8	34.0	0.2	73.3	26.4	0.3	79.7	20.4	0.0
1966	74.5	19.4	6.1	87.4	12.5	0.1	90.9	9.1	0.0
1968	77.4	10.5	12.1	93.8	6.2	0.0	90.7	9.4	0.0
1970							95.3	2.8	1.9

154

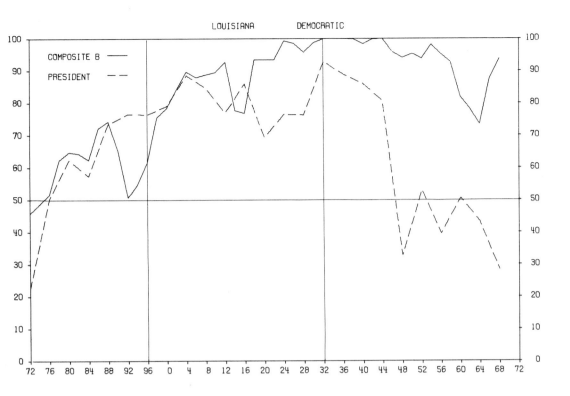

LOUISIANA   DEMOCRATIC

COMPOSITE B ———
PRESIDENT   — —

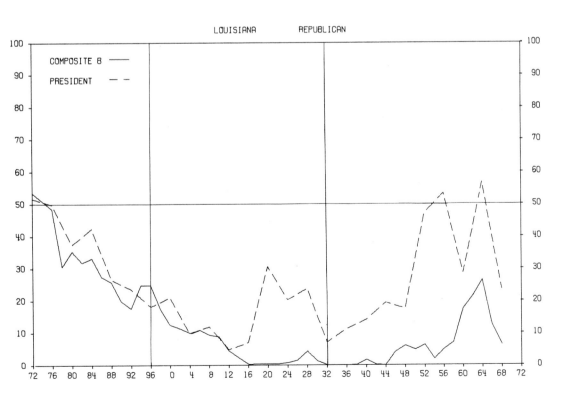

LOUISIANA   REPUBLICAN

COMPOSITE B ———
PRESIDENT   — —

155

YEAR	PRESIDENT			GOVERNOR			SENATE CLASS I			SENATE CLASS II		
	DEM.	REP.	OTHER	DEM.	REP.	OTHER	DEM.	REP.	OTHER	DEM.	REP.	OTHER
1872	32.1	67.9	0.0	43.5	56.5	0.0						
1874				42.5	54.6	2.9						
1876	42.6	56.6	0.7	46.0	53.8	0.2						
1878				31.2	48.3	20.5						
1880	45.3	51.5	3.2	33.3	49.6	17.1						
1882				46.2	52.4	1.5						
1884	40.0	55.3	4.7	41.5	55.4	3.1						
1886				43.1	53.7	3.1						
1888	39.4	57.5	3.2	42.2	54.6	3.2						
1890				39.8	56.4	3.8						
1892	41.3	54.0	4.7	42.5	52.1	5.4						
1894				28.2	64.3	7.5						
1896	27.2	67.9	4.9	27.8	66.9	5.3						
1898				33.2	62.9	3.9						
1900	34.8	61.9	3.3	34.0	62.3	3.7						
1902				34.7	59.5	5.8						
1904	28.5	67.4	4.1	38.1	58.5	3.3						
1906				46.0	52.0	2.0						
1908	33.3	63.0	3.7	46.5	51.5	2.0						
1910				52.0	45.9	2.1						
1912	39.4	20.5	40.1	47.7	50.0	2.3						
1914				43.8	41.6	14.6						
1916	47.0	51.0	2.0	44.9	54.0	1.1	46.0	52.8	1.2	45.5	54.3	0.2
1918				47.7	52.3	0.0				44.4	55.6	0.0
1920	33.3	65.5	1.2	34.1	65.9	0.0						
1922				42.0	58.0	0.0	42.5	57.5	0.0			
1924	21.8	72.0	6.1	42.8	57.2	0.0				39.6	60.4	0.0
1926				44.5	55.5	0.0						
1928	31.0	68.6	0.4	30.7	69.3	0.0	30.4	69.6	0.0	28.2	71.8	0.0
1930				44.9	55.1	0.0				39.1	60.9	0.0
1932	43.2	55.8	1.0	50.3	49.3	0.5						
1934				54.0	45.9	0.1	49.7	50.1	0.2			
1936	41.6	55.6	2.9	42.1	56.0	1.9				49.3	50.7	0.0
1938				47.0	52.9	0.1						
1940	48.8	51.1	0.1	36.1	63.8	0.1	41.3	58.6	0.1			
1942				33.2	66.8	0.0				33.3	66.7	0.0
1944	47.4	52.4	0.1	29.7	70.3	0.0						
1946				38.7	61.3	0.0	36.5	63.5	0.0			
1948	42.4	56.9	0.7	34.4	65.6	0.0				28.7	71.3	0.0
1950				39.1	60.5	0.4						
1952	33.8	66.2	0.0	33.4	52.1	14.5	37.3	62.7	0.0			
1954				54.5	45.5	0.0				41.4	58.6	0.0
1956	29.1	70.9	0.0	59.2	40.8	0.0						
1958				52.0	48.0	0.0	60.8	39.2	0.0			
1960	43.0	57.0	0.0	47.3	52.7	0.0				38.4	61.6	0.0
1962				49.9	50.1	0.0						
1964	68.8	31.2	0.0				66.6	33.4	0.0			
1966				53.1	46.9	0.0				41.1	58.9	0.0
1968	55.3	43.1	1.6									
1970				50.1	49.9	0.0	61.7	38.3	0.0			

156

MAINE

YEAR	PRESIDENT			GOVERNOR			SENATE			HOUSE OF REPRESENTATIVES		
	DEM.	REP.	OTHER	DEM.	REP.	OTHER	DEM.	REP.	OTHER	DEM.	REP.	OTHER
1872	32.1	67.9	0.0	43.5	56.5	0.0				42.8	57.0	0.1
1874	37.4	62.3	0.4	42.5	54.6	2.9				43.4	56.3	0.3
1876	42.7	56.6	0.7	46.0	53.8	0.2				44.6	55.0	0.5
1878	44.0	54.1	2.0	31.2	48.3	20.5				16.7	45.2	38.1
1880	45.3	51.5	3.2	33.3	49.6	17.1				49.5	50.1	0.4
1882	42.6	53.4	4.0	46.2	52.4	1.5				11.5	52.8	35.7
1884	40.0	55.3	4.7	41.5	55.4	3.1				42.1	55.0	2.9
1886	39.7	56.4	3.9	43.1	53.7	3.1				40.9	53.6	5.5
1888	39.4	57.5	3.2	42.2	54.6	3.2				42.1	55.0	2.9
1890	40.3	55.8	3.9	39.8	56.4	3.8				40.3	56.5	3.1
1892	41.3	54.1	4.7	42.5	52.1	5.4				42.4	51.4	6.2
1894	34.2	61.0	4.8	28.2	64.3	7.5				28.3	64.3	7.4
1896	27.2	67.9	4.9	27.8	66.9	5.3				27.7	67.6	4.7
1898	31.0	64.9	4.1	33.2	62.9	3.9				33.8	63.4	2.8
1900	34.8	61.9	3.3	34.0	62.3	3.7				34.5	62.0	3.5
1902	31.7	64.7	3.7	34.7	59.5	5.8				36.0	61.1	2.9
1904	28.5	67.4	4.1	38.1	58.5	3.4				39.0	59.3	1.7
1906	30.9	65.2	3.9	46.0	52.0	2.0				46.0	52.3	1.7
1908	33.3	63.0	3.7	46.5	51.6	2.0				45.2	52.8	2.0
1910	36.4	41.7	21.9	52.0	45.9	2.1				50.2	48.0	1.8
1912	39.4	20.5	40.1	47.7	50.0	2.3				47.2	50.7	2.1
1914	43.2	35.7	21.1	43.8	41.6	14.6				43.0	42.8	14.2
1916	47.0	51.0	2.0	44.9	54.0	1.1	45.7	53.6	0.7	45.4	53.6	1.1
1918	40.1	58.2	1.6	47.7	52.3	0.0	44.4	55.6	0.0	44.1	55.9	0.0
1920	33.3	65.5	1.2	34.1	65.9	0.0	43.5	56.5	0.0	33.3	66.7	0.0
1922	27.6	68.8	3.7	42.0	58.0	0.0	42.5	57.5	0.0	42.4	57.6	0.0
1924	21.8	72.0	6.1	42.8	57.2	0.0	39.6	60.4	0.0	39.8	60.3	0.0
1926	26.4	70.3	3.3	44.5	55.5	0.0	34.6	65.4	0.0	38.3	61.7	0.0
1928	31.0	68.6	0.4	30.7	69.3	0.0	29.6	70.4	0.0	29.8	70.2	0.0
1930	37.1	62.2	0.7	44.9	55.1	0.0	39.1	60.9	0.0	38.6	61.4	0.0
1932	43.2	55.8	1.0	50.3	49.3	0.5	44.4	55.5	0.1	50.3	49.3	0.4
1934	42.4	55.7	1.9	54.0	45.9	0.1	49.7	50.1	0.2	51.0	49.0	0.0
1936	41.6	55.6	2.9	42.1	56.0	1.9	49.3	50.8	0.0	39.6	56.6	3.8
1938	45.2	53.3	1.5	47.0	52.9	0.1	45.3	54.7	0.1	39.9	59.1	1.1
1940	48.8	51.1	0.1	36.1	63.8	0.1	41.3	58.6	0.1	35.4	64.6	0.0
1942	48.1	51.8	0.1	33.2	66.8	0.0	33.3	66.7	0.0	30.4	69.6	0.0
1944	47.5	52.4	0.1	29.7	70.3	0.0	34.9	65.1	0.0	29.3	70.7	0.0
1946	44.9	54.7	0.4	38.7	61.3	0.0	36.5	63.6	0.0	36.7	63.4	0.0
1948	42.4	56.9	0.7	34.4	65.6	0.0	28.7	71.3	0.0	33.7	66.3	0.0
1950	38.1	61.5	0.4	39.1	60.5	0.4	33.0	67.0	0.0	42.4	57.6	0.0
1952	33.8	66.2	0.0	33.4	52.1	14.5	37.3	62.7	0.0	32.9	67.1	0.0
1954	31.5	68.5	0.0	54.5	45.5	0.0	41.4	58.6	0.0	45.0	55.0	0.0
1956	29.1	70.9	0.0	59.2	40.8	0.0	51.1	48.9	0.0	48.6	51.4	0.0
1958	36.0	64.0	0.0	52.0	48.0	0.0	60.8	39.2	0.0	53.2	46.8	0.0
1960	43.0	57.1	0.0	47.3	52.7	0.0	38.4	61.7	0.0	43.5	56.5	0.0
1962	55.9	44.1	0.0	49.9	50.1	0.0	52.5	47.5	0.0	44.6	55.4	0.0
1964	68.8	31.2	0.0	51.5	48.5	0.0	66.6	33.4	0.0	55.8	44.2	0.0
1966	62.1	37.1	0.8	53.1	46.9	0.0	41.1	59.0	0.0	53.5	44.3	2.3
1968	55.3	43.1	1.6	51.6	48.4	0.0	51.4	48.6	0.0	56.2	43.8	0.0
1970				50.1	49.9	0.0	61.7	38.3	0.0	61.5	38.5	0.0

157

MAINE

YEAR	COMPOSITE A (P+G+S+H/4)			COMPOSITE B (G+S+H/3)			COMPOSITE C (S+H/2)		
	DEM.	REP.	OTHER	DEM.	REP.	OTHER	DEM.	REP.	OTHER
1872	39.5	60.5	0.1	43.2	56.8	0.1	42.8	57.0	0.1
1874	41.1	57.7	1.2	43.0	55.5	1.6	43.4	56.3	0.3
1876	44.4	55.1	0.5	45.3	54.4	0.4	44.6	55.0	0.5
1878	30.6	49.2	20.2	24.0	46.8	29.3	16.7	45.2	38.1
1880	42.7	50.4	6.9	41.4	49.9	8.8	49.5	50.1	0.4
1882	33.5	52.8	13.7	28.9	52.6	18.6	11.5	52.8	35.7
1884	41.2	55.3	3.6	41.8	55.2	3.0	42.1	55.0	2.9
1886	41.2	54.6	4.2	42.0	53.7	4.3	40.9	53.6	5.5
1888	41.2	55.7	3.1	42.1	54.8	3.1	42.1	55.0	2.9
1890	40.2	56.2	3.6	40.1	56.5	3.5	40.3	56.5	3.1
1892	42.1	52.5	5.4	42.5	51.8	5.8	42.4	51.4	6.2
1894	30.2	63.2	6.6	28.2	64.3	7.4	28.3	64.3	7.4
1896	27.6	67.4	5.0	27.8	67.2	5.0	27.7	67.6	4.7
1898	32.7	63.7	3.6	33.5	63.1	3.4	33.8	63.4	2.8
1900	34.4	62.1	3.5	34.2	62.2	3.6	34.5	62.0	3.5
1902	34.1	61.7	4.1	35.4	60.3	4.4	36.0	61.1	2.9
1904	35.2	61.7	3.0	38.6	58.9	2.5	39.0	59.3	1.7
1906	41.0	56.5	2.6	46.0	52.1	1.9	46.0	52.3	1.7
1908	41.7	55.8	2.6	45.8	52.2	2.0	45.2	52.8	2.0
1910	46.2	45.2	8.6	51.1	47.0	2.0	50.2	48.0	1.8
1912	44.8	40.4	14.8	47.5	50.3	2.2	47.2	50.7	2.1
1914	43.4	40.0	16.6	43.4	42.2	14.4	43.0	42.8	14.2
1916	45.7	53.0	1.2	45.3	53.7	1.0	45.6	53.6	0.9
1918	44.1	55.5	0.4	45.4	54.6	0.0	44.3	55.7	0.0
1920	36.0	63.7	0.3	37.0	63.1	0.0	38.4	61.6	0.0
1922	38.6	60.5	0.9	42.3	57.7	0.0	42.4	57.6	0.0
1924	36.0	62.5	1.5	40.7	59.3	0.0	39.7	60.3	0.0
1926	36.0	63.2	0.8	39.1	60.9	0.0	36.5	63.5	0.0
1928	30.3	69.6	0.1	30.0	70.0	0.0	29.7	70.3	0.0
1930	39.9	59.9	0.2	40.9	59.1	0.0	38.9	61.2	0.0
1932	47.0	52.5	0.5	48.3	51.4	0.3	47.4	52.4	0.2
1934	49.3	50.2	0.5	51.6	48.4	0.1	50.4	49.6	0.1
1936	43.1	54.7	2.1	43.6	54.5	1.9	44.4	53.7	1.9
1938	44.3	55.0	0.7	44.0	55.5	0.4	42.6	56.9	0.6
1940	40.4	59.5	0.1	37.6	62.3	0.1	38.3	61.6	0.1
1942	36.3	63.7	0.0	32.3	67.7	0.0	31.9	68.1	0.0
1944	35.3	64.6	0.0	31.3	68.7	0.0	32.1	67.9	0.0
1946	39.2	60.7	0.1	37.3	62.7	0.0	36.6	63.5	0.0
1948	34.8	65.0	0.2	32.3	67.7	0.0	31.2	68.8	0.0
1950	38.1	61.7	0.2	38.2	61.7	0.2	37.7	62.3	0.0
1952	34.4	62.0	3.6	34.5	60.7	4.8	35.1	64.9	0.0
1954	43.1	56.9	0.0	47.0	53.1	0.0	43.2	56.8	0.0
1956	47.0	53.0	0.0	52.9	47.1	0.0	49.8	50.2	0.0
1958	50.5	49.5	0.0	55.3	44.7	0.0	57.0	43.0	0.0
1960	43.0	57.0	0.0	43.1	56.9	0.0	40.9	59.1	0.0
1962	50.7	49.3	0.0	49.0	51.0	0.0	48.5	51.5	0.0
1964	60.7	39.3	0.0	58.0	42.0	0.0	61.2	38.8	0.0
1966	52.4	46.8	0.8	49.2	50.0	0.8	47.3	51.6	1.1
1968	53.6	46.0	0.4	53.1	46.9	0.0	53.8	46.2	0.0
1970				57.8	42.2	0.0	61.6	38.4	0.0

158

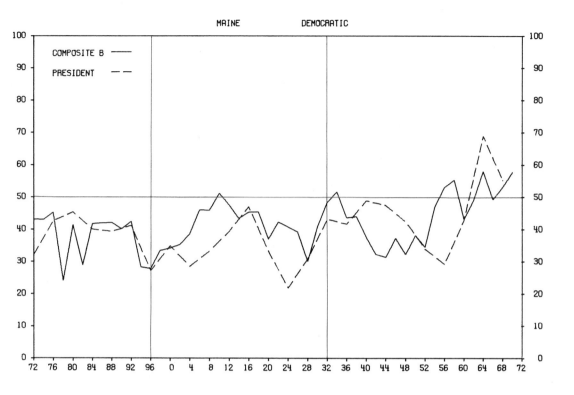

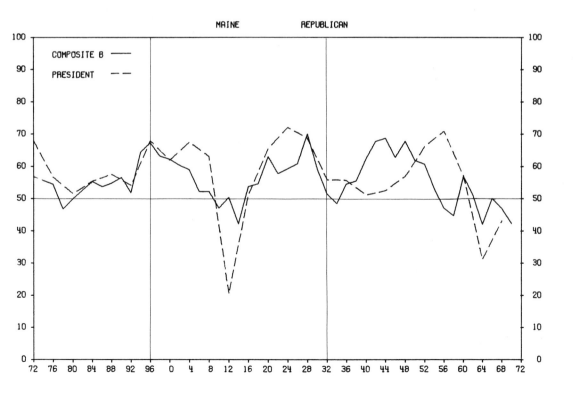

159

MARYLAND

YEAR	PRESIDENT			GOVERNOR			SENATE CLASS I			SENATE CLASS III		
	DEM.	REP.	OTHER	DEM.	REP.	OTHER	DEM.	REP.	OTHER	DEM.	REP.	OTHER
1872	50.3	49.7	0.0	55.7	44.3	0.0						
1874												
1876	56.0	44.0	0.0	54.1	45.9	0.0						
1878												
1880	54.4	45.6	0.0	56.9	43.1	0.0						
1882												
1884	52.1	46.1	1.8	53.5	46.5	0.0						
1886												
1888	50.3	47.4	2.3	52.1	45.6	2.3						
1890												
1892	53.4	43.5	3.1	56.5	40.8	2.7						
1894												
1896	41.6	54.7	3.7	44.2	52.0	3.8						
1898												
1900	46.2	51.5	2.3	51.1	46.3	2.6						
1902												
1904	48.8	48.8	2.4	52.0	46.0	2.0						
1906												
1908	48.6	48.8	2.6	50.7	46.8	2.5						
1910												
1912	48.6	23.7	27.7	47.9	49.3	2.9						
1914										51.0	43.9	5.1
1916	52.8	44.8	2.4	49.6	48.2	2.2	47.6	49.3	3.1			
1918												
1920	42.2	55.1	2.7	49.1	49.0	2.0				43.3	47.3	9.5
1922							52.6	45.6	1.8			
1924	41.3	45.3	13.4	56.0	43.3	0.8						
1926				57.9	41.4	0.7				57.6	41.3	1.1
1928	42.3	57.1	0.6				45.2	54.0	0.7			
1930				56.0	42.8	1.3						
1932	61.5	36.0	2.5							66.2	31.2	2.6
1934				48.3	49.5	2.2	56.1	42.0	2.0			
1936	62.3	37.0	0.6									
1938				54.6	42.9	2.5				68.3	29.3	2.4
1940	58.3	40.8	0.9				64.7	33.5	1.8			
1942				52.6	47.4	0.0						
1944	52.0	48.0	0.0							61.7	38.3	0.0
1946				54.7	45.3	0.0	50.2	49.8	0.0			
1948	47.8	49.2	3.0									
1950				42.7	57.3	0.0				46.0	53.0	1.0
1952	43.8	55.4	0.8				47.5	52.5	0.0			
1954				45.5	54.5	0.0						
1956	40.0	60.0	0.0							47.0	53.0	0.0
1958				63.6	36.4	0.0	49.0	51.0	0.0			
1960	53.6	46.4	0.0									
1962				55.6	44.4	0.0				62.0	38.0	0.0
1964	65.5	34.5	0.0				62.8	37.2	0.0			
1966				40.6	49.5	9.9						
1968	43.6	41.9	14.5							39.1	47.8	13.1
1970				65.7	32.3	2.0	48.1	50.7	1.1			

160

YEAR	PRESIDENT			GOVERNOR			SENATE			HOUSE OF REPRESENTATIVES		
	DEM.	REP.	OTHER	DEM.	REP.	OTHER	DEM.	REP.	OTHER	DEM.	REP.	OTHER
1872	50.3	49.7	0.0	55.7	44.3	0.0				50.3	49.7	0.0
1874	53.2	46.8	0.0	54.9	45.1	0.0				55.8	44.2	0.0
1876	56.1	44.0	0.0	54.1	45.9	0.0				55.3	44.7	0.0
1878	55.2	44.8	0.0	55.5	44.5	0.0				56.8	34.1	9.0
1880	54.4	45.6	0.0	56.9	43.1	0.0				53.0	46.7	0.3
1882	53.2	45.8	0.9	55.2	44.8	0.0				51.4	47.4	1.2
1884	52.1	46.1	1.8	53.5	46.6	0.0				52.5	46.9	0.7
1886	51.2	46.8	2.1	52.8	46.1	1.2				55.9	35.3	8.7
1888	50.3	47.4	2.3	52.1	45.6	2.3				50.5	47.5	2.0
1890	51.9	45.4	2.7	54.3	43.2	2.5				55.2	42.7	2.2
1892	53.4	43.5	3.1	56.5	40.8	2.7				53.8	43.3	2.9
1894	47.5	49.1	3.4	50.4	46.4	3.2				46.7	48.0	5.3
1896	41.6	54.7	3.7	44.2	52.0	3.8				43.1	54.4	2.5
1898	43.9	53.1	3.0	47.7	49.2	3.2				46.6	49.4	4.0
1900	46.2	51.5	2.3	51.1	46.3	2.6				46.6	51.4	2.0
1902	47.5	50.2	2.3	51.6	46.1	2.3				46.4	50.7	2.8
1904	48.8	48.8	2.4	52.0	46.0	2.0				47.7	50.0	2.4
1906	48.7	48.8	2.5	51.3	46.4	2.3				46.4	49.8	3.8
1908	48.6	48.9	2.6	50.7	46.8	2.5				50.3	47.4	2.3
1910	48.6	36.3	15.2	49.3	48.0	2.7				49.7	46.6	3.7
1912	48.6	23.7	27.7	47.9	49.3	2.9				59.7	34.7	5.6
1914	50.7	34.2	15.1	48.7	48.8	2.5	51.0	43.9	5.1	51.4	44.1	4.6
1916	52.8	44.8	2.4	49.6	48.2	2.2	47.6	49.3	3.1	48.6	47.0	4.4
1918	47.5	50.0	2.6	49.3	48.6	2.1	45.4	48.3	6.3	50.9	47.5	1.6
1920	42.2	55.1	2.7	49.1	49.0	2.0	43.3	47.3	9.5	43.1	49.9	7.0
1922	41.7	50.2	8.1	52.5	46.1	1.4	52.6	45.6	1.8	49.8	47.8	2.4
1924	41.3	45.3	13.4	56.0	43.3	0.8	55.1	43.5	1.4	50.8	47.9	1.3
1926	41.8	51.2	7.0	57.9	41.4	0.7	57.6	41.3	1.1	59.9	39.4	0.8
1928	42.3	57.1	0.6	56.9	42.1	1.0	45.2	54.1	0.7	48.8	50.7	0.5
1930	51.9	46.6	1.5	56.0	42.8	1.3	55.7	42.6	1.7	59.1	40.7	0.2
1932	61.5	36.0	2.5	52.1	46.2	1.7	66.2	31.2	2.6	66.1	33.2	0.7
1934	61.9	36.5	1.5	48.3	49.5	2.2	56.1	42.0	2.0	58.6	39.6	1.7
1936	62.4	37.0	0.6	51.5	46.2	2.3	62.2	35.6	2.2	59.2	39.6	1.2
1938	60.3	38.9	0.8	54.6	42.9	2.5	68.3	29.3	2.4	59.7	39.5	0.8
1940	58.3	40.8	0.9	53.6	45.2	1.3	64.7	33.5	1.8	60.9	39.1	0.0
1942	55.1	44.4	0.5	52.6	47.5	0.0	63.2	35.9	0.9	56.3	43.8	0.0
1944	52.0	48.0	0.0	53.6	46.4	0.0	61.7	38.3	0.0	56.4	43.6	0.0
1946	49.9	48.6	1.5	54.7	45.3	0.0	50.2	49.8	0.0	52.3	47.8	0.0
1948	47.8	49.2	3.0	48.7	51.3	0.0	48.1	51.4	0.5	54.5	43.2	2.3
1950	45.8	52.3	1.9	42.7	57.3	0.0	46.0	53.0	1.0	49.5	49.9	0.6
1952	43.8	55.4	0.8	44.1	55.9	0.0	47.5	52.5	0.0	48.2	51.8	0.0
1954	41.9	57.7	0.4	45.5	54.5	0.0	47.2	52.8	0.0	53.6	46.2	0.2
1956	40.0	60.0	0.0	54.6	45.5	0.0	47.0	53.0	0.0	51.3	48.7	0.0
1958	46.8	53.2	0.0	63.6	36.5	0.0	49.0	51.0	0.0	65.1	34.9	0.0
1960	53.6	46.4	0.0	59.6	40.4	0.0	55.5	44.5	0.0	59.4	40.6	0.0
1962	59.5	40.5	0.0	55.6	44.4	0.0	62.0	38.0	0.0	55.9	44.1	0.0
1964	65.5	34.5	0.0	48.1	46.9	4.9	62.8	37.2	0.0	66.1	33.9	0.0
1966	54.5	38.2	7.2	40.6	49.5	9.9	50.9	42.5	6.6	56.1	43.9	0.0
1968	43.6	41.9	14.5	53.2	40.9	5.9	39.1	47.8	13.1	52.6	47.5	0.0
1970				65.7	32.3	2.0	48.1	50.7	1.2	51.1	48.6	0.3

MARYLAND

YEAR	COMPOSITE A (P+G+S+H/4)			COMPOSITE B (G+S+H/3)			COMPOSITE C (S+H/2)		
	DEM.	REP.	OTHER	DEM.	REP.	OTHER	DEM.	REP.	OTHER
1872	52.1	47.9	0.0	53.0	47.0	0.0	50.3	49.7	0.0
1874	54.6	45.4	0.0	55.4	44.6	0.0	55.8	44.2	0.0
1876	55.2	44.8	0.0	54.7	45.3	0.0	55.3	44.7	0.0
1878	55.9	41.1	3.0	56.2	39.3	4.5	56.8	34.1	9.0
1880	54.8	45.1	0.1	55.0	44.9	0.1	53.0	46.7	0.3
1882	53.3	46.0	0.7	53.3	46.1	0.6	51.4	47.4	1.2
1884	52.7	46.5	0.8	53.0	46.7	0.3	52.5	46.9	0.7
1886	53.3	42.7	4.0	54.4	40.7	5.0	55.9	35.3	8.7
1888	51.0	46.8	2.2	51.3	46.6	2.2	50.5	47.5	2.0
1890	53.8	43.8	2.5	54.7	42.9	2.4	55.2	42.7	2.2
1892	54.6	42.6	2.9	55.2	42.1	2.8	53.8	43.3	2.9
1894	48.2	47.8	4.0	48.6	47.2	4.2	46.7	48.0	5.3
1896	43.0	53.7	3.3	43.6	53.2	3.2	43.1	54.4	2.5
1898	46.1	50.6	3.4	47.1	49.3	3.6	46.6	49.4	4.0
1900	48.0	49.7	2.3	48.9	48.8	2.3	46.6	51.4	2.0
1902	48.5	49.0	2.5	49.0	48.4	2.6	46.4	50.7	2.8
1904	49.5	48.3	2.3	49.8	48.0	2.2	47.7	50.0	2.4
1906	48.8	48.4	2.8	48.9	48.1	3.0	46.4	49.8	3.8
1908	49.9	47.7	2.5	50.5	47.1	2.4	50.3	47.4	2.3
1910	49.2	43.6	7.2	49.5	47.3	3.2	49.7	46.6	3.7
1912	52.1	35.9	12.1	53.8	42.0	4.2	59.7	34.7	5.6
1914	50.4	42.7	6.8	50.4	45.6	4.1	51.2	44.0	4.8
1916	49.6	47.3	3.0	48.6	48.2	3.2	48.1	48.2	3.7
1918	48.3	48.6	3.1	48.6	48.2	3.3	48.2	47.9	3.9
1920	44.4	50.3	5.3	45.1	48.7	6.2	43.2	48.6	8.3
1922	49.2	47.4	3.4	51.7	46.5	1.8	51.2	46.7	2.1
1924	50.8	45.0	4.2	54.0	44.9	1.2	53.0	45.7	1.4
1926	54.3	43.3	2.4	58.5	40.7	0.8	58.7	40.3	0.9
1928	48.3	51.0	0.7	50.3	48.9	0.7	47.0	52.4	0.6
1930	55.7	43.2	1.2	56.9	42.1	1.0	57.4	41.7	0.9
1932	61.5	36.6	1.9	61.5	36.8	1.7	66.2	32.2	1.7
1934	56.3	41.9	1.9	54.4	43.7	2.0	57.4	40.8	1.9
1936	58.8	39.6	1.6	57.6	40.5	1.9	60.7	37.6	1.7
1938	60.7	37.7	1.6	60.9	37.2	1.9	64.0	34.4	1.6
1940	59.4	39.6	1.0	59.8	39.2	1.0	62.8	36.3	0.9
1942	56.8	42.9	0.3	57.4	42.4	0.3	59.7	39.8	0.4
1944	55.9	44.1	0.0	57.3	42.7	0.0	59.1	40.9	0.0
1946	51.8	47.9	0.4	52.4	47.6	0.0	51.2	48.8	0.0
1948	49.8	48.8	1.4	50.4	48.6	0.9	51.3	47.3	1.4
1950	46.0	53.1	0.9	46.1	53.4	0.5	47.8	51.5	0.8
1952	45.9	53.9	0.2	46.6	53.4	0.0	47.8	52.2	0.0
1954	47.1	52.8	0.2	48.8	51.2	0.1	50.4	49.5	0.1
1956	48.2	51.8	0.0	51.0	49.1	0.0	49.2	50.9	0.0
1958	56.1	43.9	0.0	59.2	40.8	0.0	57.1	42.9	0.0
1960	57.0	43.0	0.0	58.2	41.8	0.0	57.5	42.6	0.0
1962	58.3	41.7	0.0	57.9	42.1	0.0	59.0	41.0	0.0
1964	60.6	38.2	1.2	59.0	39.4	1.7	64.4	35.6	0.0
1966	50.6	43.5	5.9	49.2	45.3	5.5	53.5	43.2	3.3
1968	47.1	44.5	8.4	48.3	45.4	6.3	45.8	47.6	6.6
1970				55.0	43.9	1.1	49.6	49.7	0.7

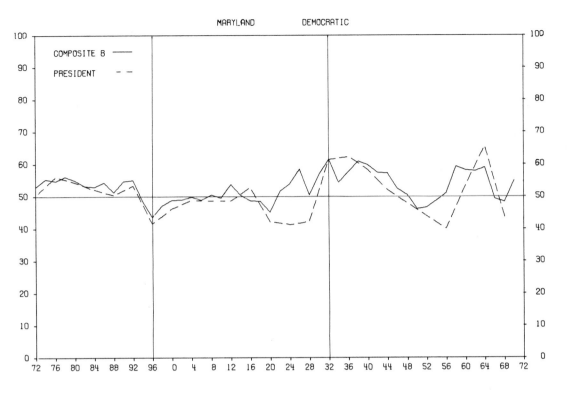

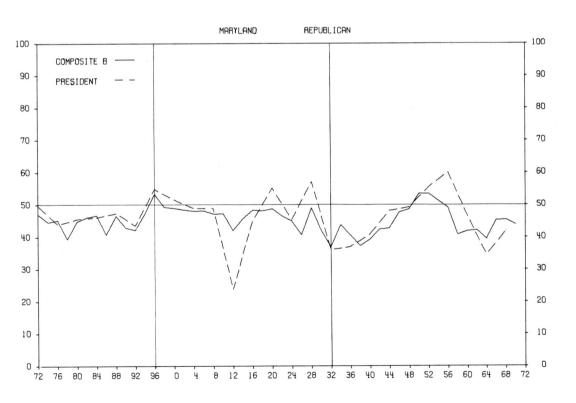

163

YEAR	PRESIDENT			GOVERNOR			SENATE CLASS I			SENATE CLASS II		
	DEM.	REP.	OTHER	DEM.	REP.	OTHER	DEM.	REP.	OTHER	DEM.	REP.	OTHER
1872	30.7	69.3	0.0	30.8	69.1	0.1						
1874				48.9	50.7	0.3						
1876	41.9	57.8	0.3	43.1	51.5	5.5						
1878				18.9	51.3	29.8						
1880	39.6	58.5	1.9	23.1	54.7	22.2						
1882				45.5	52.3	2.2						
1884	40.3	48.4	11.3	42.5	51.8	5.7						
1886				44.8	51.7	3.4						
1888	44.0	53.4	2.5	44.5	52.0	3.5						
1890				47.6	47.2	5.2						
1892	45.2	51.9	2.9	49.1	47.8	3.1						
1894				40.1	54.5	5.4						
1896	22.5	69.5	8.0	27.8	62.3	9.8						
1898				31.9	60.6	7.5						
1900	37.8	57.6	4.6	34.1	57.9	7.9						
1902				37.8	52.8	9.3						
1904	37.2	57.9	4.8	47.1	47.1	5.9						
1906				35.5	51.2	13.3						
1908	34.0	58.2	7.7	29.3	51.0	19.7						
1910				46.9	46.2	6.9						
1912	35.5	32.0	32.5	40.0	38.3	21.8						
1914				42.8	34.3	22.9						
1916	46.6	50.5	2.8	44.7	49.8	5.6	45.3	51.7	3.0			
1918				41.2	54.4	4.4				49.7	45.1	5.3
1920	27.8	68.5	3.6	32.6	64.9	2.5						
1922				45.4	52.2	2.3	46.7	47.6	5.7			
1924	24.9	62.3	12.9	42.2	56.0	1.8				48.6	50.3	1.1
1926				40.2	58.8	1.0	52.0	46.5	1.5			
1928	50.2	49.2	0.6	48.8	50.1	1.1	53.6	45.5	0.9			
1930				49.5	48.2	2.3				54.0	44.7	1.3
1932	50.6	46.6	2.7	52.8	45.0	2.2						
1934				49.7	42.3	8.0	59.4	37.4	3.2			
1936	51.2	41.8	7.0	47.6	46.1	6.3				41.0	48.5	10.4
1938				45.0	53.3	1.7						
1940	53.1	46.4	0.5	49.5	49.7	0.8	55.6	42.8	1.5			
1942				45.0	54.1	0.9				46.6	52.4	1.0
1944	52.8	47.0	0.2	53.6	45.9	0.4				34.9	64.3	0.8
1946				45.3	54.1	0.6	39.7	59.5	0.7			
1948	54.7	43.2	2.2	59.0	40.5	0.5				46.4	52.9	0.6
1950				56.3	43.1	0.6						
1952	45.5	54.2	0.3	49.3	49.9	0.8	51.3	48.3	0.3			
1954				47.8	51.8	0.4				49.0	50.5	0.4
1956	40.4	59.3	0.3	52.8	46.9	0.4						
1958				56.2	43.1	0.7	73.2	26.2	0.6			
1960	60.2	39.6	0.2	46.8	52.5	0.7				43.5	56.2	0.4
1962				49.9	49.7	0.4	55.4	41.9	2.7			
1964	76.2	23.4	0.4	49.3	50.3	0.4	74.3	25.4	0.3			
1966				36.9	62.6	0.5				38.7	60.7	0.6
1968	63.0	32.9	4.1									
1970				42.8	56.7	0.5	62.1	37.0	0.9			

MASSACHUSETTS

YEAR	PRESIDENT			GOVERNOR			SENATE			HOUSE OF REPRESENTATIVES		
	DEM.	REP.	OTHER	DEM.	REP.	OTHER	DEM.	REP.	OTHER	DEM.	REP.	OTHER
1872	30.7	69.3	0.0	30.8	69.1	0.1				31.6	68.0	0.4
1874	36.3	63.5	0.2	48.9	50.7	0.3				49.7	48.0	2.2
1876	41.9	57.8	0.3	43.1	51.5	5.5				43.2	55.8	1.0
1878	40.8	58.1	1.1	18.9	51.3	29.8				32.1	53.7	14.2
1880	39.6	58.5	1.9	23.1	54.7	22.2				39.8	58.5	1.7
1882	40.0	53.4	6.6	45.5	52.3	2.2				46.7	50.8	2.6
1884	40.3	48.4	11.3	42.5	51.8	5.7				36.1	54.3	9.6
1886	42.2	50.9	6.9	44.8	51.7	3.4				46.9	48.9	4.2
1888	44.0	53.4	2.6	44.5	52.0	3.5				45.2	52.5	2.3
1890	44.6	52.6	2.7	47.6	47.2	5.2				49.0	46.3	4.8
1892	45.2	51.9	2.9	49.1	47.8	3.1				44.3	50.2	5.5
1894	33.9	60.7	5.5	40.1	54.5	5.4				34.8	57.5	7.7
1896	22.5	69.5	8.0	27.8	62.3	9.8				32.2	65.8	2.0
1898	30.2	63.6	6.3	31.9	60.6	7.5				39.6	56.4	4.1
1900	37.9	57.6	4.6	34.1	57.9	8.0				38.6	56.7	4.7
1902	37.5	57.8	4.7	37.8	52.8	9.4				38.5	49.2	12.3
1904	37.2	57.9	4.8	47.1	47.1	5.9				37.0	57.2	5.9
1906	35.6	58.1	6.3	35.5	51.2	13.3				38.2	56.7	5.1
1908	34.0	58.2	7.8	29.3	51.0	19.7				35.0	59.0	6.0
1910	34.8	45.1	20.1	46.9	46.2	6.9				47.8	47.7	4.6
1912	35.5	32.0	32.5	40.0	38.3	21.8				40.2	38.2	21.6
1914	41.1	41.3	17.7	42.8	34.3	22.9				42.3	49.8	8.0
1916	46.6	50.5	2.9	44.7	49.8	5.6	45.3	51.7	3.0	39.2	55.8	5.0
1918	37.2	59.5	3.2	41.2	54.4	4.4	49.7	45.1	5.3	38.2	59.3	2.5
1920	27.8	68.6	3.6	32.6	64.9	2.5	48.2	46.3	5.5	31.2	66.0	2.9
1922	26.4	65.4	8.3	45.4	52.2	2.3	46.8	47.6	5.7	42.1	57.7	0.2
1924	24.9	62.3	12.9	42.2	56.0	1.8	48.6	50.3	1.1	38.6	60.2	1.2
1926	37.6	55.7	6.7	40.3	58.8	1.0	52.0	46.5	1.5	45.9	54.1	0.0
1928	50.2	49.2	0.6	48.8	50.1	1.1	53.6	45.5	0.9	43.3	56.4	0.4
1930	50.4	47.9	1.7	49.5	48.2	2.3	54.0	44.7	1.3	45.0	53.5	1.5
1932	50.6	46.6	2.7	52.8	45.0	2.2	56.7	41.0	2.3	47.8	51.3	1.0
1934	50.9	44.2	4.9	49.7	42.3	8.1	59.4	37.4	3.2	52.8	46.3	0.9
1936	51.2	41.8	7.0	47.6	46.1	6.3	41.0	48.5	10.5	45.8	49.6	4.7
1938	52.2	44.1	3.8	45.0	53.3	1.7	48.3	45.7	6.0	46.1	53.8	0.1
1940	53.1	46.4	0.5	49.5	49.7	0.8	55.6	42.8	1.5	47.3	52.4	0.2
1942	53.0	46.7	0.4	45.0	54.1	0.9	46.6	52.4	1.0	46.1	53.8	0.2
1944	52.8	47.0	0.2	53.6	45.9	0.4	34.9	64.3	0.8	47.0	53.0	0.0
1946	53.7	45.1	1.2	45.3	54.1	0.6	39.7	59.6	0.7	46.1	53.4	0.6
1948	54.7	43.2	2.2	59.0	40.5	0.5	46.4	53.0	0.6	50.2	49.8	0.0
1950	50.1	48.7	1.3	56.3	43.1	0.6	48.9	50.7	0.5	49.5	50.0	0.4
1952	45.5	54.2	0.3	49.3	49.9	0.8	51.4	48.4	0.3	46.5	52.9	0.6
1954	42.9	56.8	0.3	47.8	51.8	0.4	49.0	50.5	0.4	53.2	46.8	0.0
1956	40.4	59.3	0.3	52.8	46.9	0.4	61.1	38.4	0.5	48.6	51.4	0.0
1958	50.3	49.4	0.3	56.2	43.1	0.7	73.2	26.2	0.6	57.5	42.5	0.0
1960	60.2	39.6	0.2	46.8	52.5	0.7	43.5	56.2	0.4	61.0	39.0	0.0
1962	68.2	31.5	0.3	49.9	49.7	0.4	55.4	41.9	2.7	58.2	41.0	0.8
1964	76.2	23.4	0.4	49.3	50.3	0.4	74.3	25.4	0.3	68.9	30.7	0.4
1966	69.6	28.2	2.2	36.9	62.6	0.5	38.7	60.7	0.6	60.6	39.4	0.0
1968	63.0	32.9	4.1	39.8	59.6	0.5	50.4	48.8	0.7	50.2	47.2	2.6
1970				42.8	56.7	0.5	62.1	37.0	0.9	56.6	39.9	3.5

YEAR	COMPOSITE A (P+G+S+H/4)			COMPOSITE B (G+S+H/3)			COMPOSITE C (S+H/2)		
	DEM.	REP.	OTHER	DEM.	REP.	OTHER	DEM.	REP.	OTHER
1872	31.0	68.8	0.2	31.2	68.6	0.2	31.6	68.0	0.4
1874	45.0	54.1	0.9	49.3	49.4	1.3	49.7	48.0	2.2
1876	42.7	55.0	2.3	43.1	53.6	3.2	43.2	55.8	1.0
1878	30.6	54.4	15.0	25.5	52.5	22.0	32.1	53.7	14.2
1880	34.2	57.2	8.6	31.4	56.6	12.0	39.8	58.5	1.7
1882	44.1	52.2	3.8	46.1	51.5	2.4	46.7	50.8	2.6
1884	39.6	51.5	8.9	39.3	53.1	7.7	36.1	54.3	9.6
1886	44.6	50.5	4.9	45.9	50.3	3.8	46.9	48.9	4.2
1888	44.6	52.7	2.8	44.8	52.3	2.9	45.2	52.5	2.3
1890	47.1	48.7	4.2	48.3	46.7	5.0	49.0	46.3	4.8
1892	46.2	50.0	3.9	46.7	49.0	4.3	44.3	50.2	5.5
1894	36.3	57.6	6.2	37.5	56.0	6.5	34.8	57.5	7.7
1896	27.5	65.9	6.6	30.0	64.1	5.9	32.2	65.8	2.0
1898	33.9	60.2	5.9	35.7	58.5	5.8	39.6	56.4	4.1
1900	36.9	57.4	5.7	36.4	57.3	6.3	38.6	56.7	4.7
1902	38.0	53.3	8.8	38.2	51.0	10.8	38.5	49.2	12.3
1904	40.4	54.1	5.5	42.0	52.1	5.9	37.0	57.2	5.9
1906	36.4	55.3	8.2	36.8	54.0	9.2	38.2	56.7	5.1
1908	32.8	56.1	11.2	32.1	55.0	12.9	35.0	59.0	6.0
1910	43.1	46.3	10.5	47.3	46.9	5.8	47.8	47.7	4.6
1912	38.6	36.2	25.3	40.1	38.3	21.7	40.2	38.2	21.6
1914	42.1	41.8	16.2	42.6	42.0	15.4	42.3	49.8	8.0
1916	43.9	51.9	4.1	43.1	52.4	4.5	42.3	53.7	4.0
1918	41.6	54.6	3.9	43.0	52.9	4.1	43.9	52.2	3.9
1920	34.9	61.4	3.6	37.3	59.1	3.6	39.7	56.2	4.2
1922	40.2	55.7	4.1	44.8	52.5	2.7	44.4	52.7	2.9
1924	38.6	57.2	4.3	43.1	55.5	1.4	43.6	55.2	1.2
1926	43.9	53.8	2.3	46.1	53.1	0.8	49.0	50.3	0.7
1928	49.0	50.3	0.7	48.6	50.7	0.8	48.5	50.9	0.6
1930	49.7	48.6	1.7	49.5	48.8	1.7	49.5	49.1	1.4
1932	52.0	46.0	2.0	52.4	45.8	1.8	52.2	46.1	1.6
1934	53.2	42.6	4.3	54.0	42.0	4.1	56.1	41.8	2.1
1936	46.4	46.5	7.1	44.8	48.1	7.1	43.4	49.1	7.6
1938	47.9	49.2	2.9	46.5	50.9	2.6	47.2	49.8	3.0
1940	51.4	47.8	0.8	50.8	48.3	0.9	51.5	47.6	0.9
1942	47.7	51.7	0.6	45.9	53.4	0.7	46.4	53.1	0.6
1944	47.1	52.6	0.4	45.2	54.4	0.4	40.9	58.7	0.4
1946	46.2	53.0	0.8	43.7	55.7	0.6	42.9	56.5	0.7
1948	52.6	46.6	0.8	51.9	47.8	0.4	48.3	51.4	0.3
1950	51.2	48.1	0.7	51.6	47.9	0.5	49.2	50.3	0.5
1952	48.2	51.3	0.5	49.1	50.4	0.6	48.9	50.6	0.5
1954	48.2	51.5	0.3	50.0	49.7	0.3	51.1	48.7	0.2
1956	50.7	49.0	0.3	54.2	45.6	0.3	54.8	44.9	0.3
1958	59.3	40.3	0.4	62.3	37.3	0.5	65.3	34.4	0.3
1960	52.9	46.8	0.3	50.4	49.2	0.4	52.2	47.6	0.2
1962	58.0	41.0	1.0	54.5	44.2	1.3	56.8	41.4	1.7
1964	67.2	32.5	0.4	64.2	35.5	0.4	71.6	28.1	0.3
1966	51.5	47.7	0.8	45.4	54.2	0.4	49.7	50.0	0.3
1968	50.9	47.1	2.0	46.8	51.9	1.3	50.3	48.0	1.7
1970				53.9	44.5	1.6	59.4	38.4	2.2

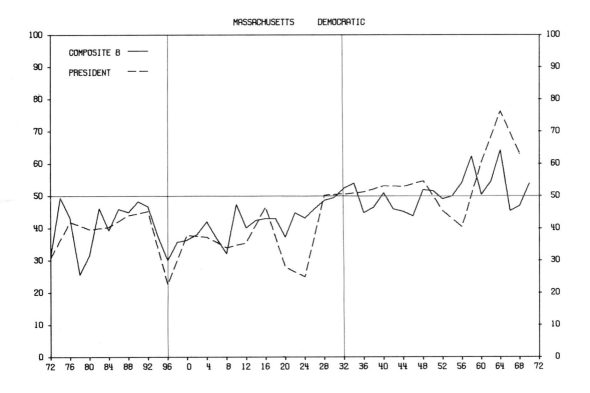

MASSACHUSETTS   DEMOCRATIC

COMPOSITE B ———
PRESIDENT   — —

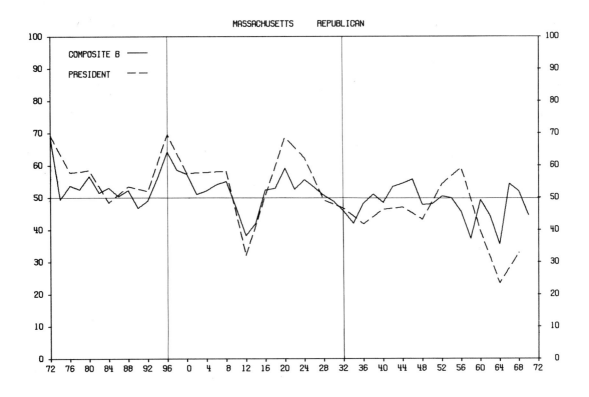

MASSACHUSETTS   REPUBLICAN

COMPOSITE B ———
PRESIDENT   — —

MICHIGAN

YEAR	PRESIDENT			GOVERNOR			SENATE CLASS I			SENATE CLASS II		
	DEM.	REP.	OTHER	DEM.	REP.	OTHER	DEM.	REP.	OTHER	DEM.	REP.	OTHER
1872	36.8	62.6	0.6	37.0	63.0	0.0						
1874				47.8	50.5	1.8						
1876	44.5	52.4	3.1	44.9	52.3	2.9						
1878				28.2	45.4	26.4						
1880	37.3	52.5	10.2	39.4	51.3	9.3						
1882				49.5	48.0	2.5						
1884	37.2	47.8	15.0	46.7	47.7	5.7						
1886				45.7	47.7	6.6						
1888	44.9	49.7	5.4	45.6	49.2	5.2						
1890				46.2	43.3	10.5						
1892	43.3	47.7	9.0	43.8	47.2	9.0						
1894				31.4	56.9	11.7						
1896	43.5	53.8	2.8	42.1	55.6	2.3						
1898				39.9	57.8	2.3						
1900	38.9	58.1	3.0	41.3	55.7	3.0						
1902				43.3	52.5	4.2						
1904	25.8	69.5	4.7	42.6	54.1	3.3						
1906				34.8	60.9	4.3						
1908	32.4	61.9	5.6	46.6	48.4	5.0						
1910				41.6	52.8	5.5						
1912	27.4	27.6	45.0	35.3	31.0	33.7						
1914				48.1	40.0	11.8						
1916	43.9	52.2	3.9	40.6	55.8	3.6	39.9	56.3	3.8			
1918				36.4	61.4	2.2				48.5	50.2	1.3
1920	22.3	72.8	4.9	29.3	66.4	4.2						
1922				37.4	61.2	1.5	50.6	48.3	1.1			
1924	13.1	75.4	11.5	29.6	68.8	1.6				24.2	74.6	1.1
1926				36.0	63.3	0.6						
1928	28.9	70.4	0.7	29.4	69.9	0.6	27.6	71.8	0.6	27.8	72.0	0.2
1930				42.0	56.9	1.1				20.9	78.1	0.9
1932	52.4	44.4	3.2	54.9	43.1	2.0						
1934				45.8	52.4	1.8	47.0	51.3	1.7			
1936	56.3	38.8	4.9	51.0	48.2	0.8				53.3	41.8	4.9
1938				47.0	52.8	0.3						
1940	49.5	49.9	0.6	53.1	46.6	0.4	47.0	52.6	0.4			
1942				46.7	52.6	0.7				47.2	49.6	3.3
1944	50.2	49.2	0.6	44.8	54.7	0.5						
1946				38.7	60.3	1.0	32.0	67.1	0.9			
1948	47.6	49.2	3.2	53.4	45.7	0.9				48.5	50.7	0.8
1950				49.8	49.7	0.5						
1952	44.0	55.4	0.6	50.0	49.7	0.4	49.0	50.6	0.3	48.7	51.2	0.0
1954				55.6	44.0	0.3				50.8	48.9	0.3
1956	44.1	55.6	0.2	54.7	45.1	0.2						
1958				53.0	46.6	0.4	53.6	46.1	0.3			
1960	50.9	48.8	0.3	50.5	49.2	0.3				51.7	48.0	0.3
1962				48.4	51.4	0.2						
1964	66.7	33.1	0.2	43.7	55.9	0.4	64.4	35.3	0.3			
1966				39.1	60.5	0.3				43.8	56.0	0.3
1968	48.2	41.5	10.4									
1970				48.7	50.4	0.9	66.8	32.9	0.3			

MICHIGAN

YEAR	PRESIDENT			GOVERNOR			SENATE			HOUSE OF REPRESENTATIVES		
	DEM.	REP.	OTHER	DEM.	REP.	OTHER	DEM.	REP.	OTHER	DEM.	REP.	OTHER
1872	36.8	62.6	0.6	37.0	63.0	0.0				38.6	60.9	0.5
1874	40.6	57.5	1.8	47.8	50.5	1.8				40.6	51.9	7.5
1876	44.5	52.4	3.1	44.9	52.3	2.9				46.4	52.3	1.3
1878	40.9	52.5	6.7	28.2	45.4	26.4				27.6	45.0	27.4
1880	37.3	52.5	10.2	39.4	51.3	9.3				37.2	52.2	10.6
1882	37.2	50.1	12.6	49.5	48.0	2.5				47.4	50.4	2.2
1884	37.2	47.8	15.0	46.7	47.7	5.7				48.0	47.4	4.6
1886	41.0	48.8	10.2	45.7	47.7	6.6				45.8	48.4	5.8
1888	44.9	49.7	5.4	45.6	49.2	5.2				45.4	50.0	4.6
1890	44.1	48.7	7.2	46.2	43.3	10.5				47.3	44.8	7.9
1892	43.4	47.7	9.0	43.8	47.2	9.0				45.2	47.8	7.0
1894	43.4	50.7	5.9	31.4	56.9	11.7				31.7	57.4	10.9
1896	43.5	53.8	2.8	42.1	55.6	2.3				40.5	54.5	5.0
1898	41.2	55.9	2.9	39.9	57.8	2.3				42.5	55.9	1.6
1900	38.9	58.1	3.0	41.3	55.8	3.0				40.0	57.8	2.2
1902	32.3	63.8	3.9	43.3	52.5	4.2				39.6	58.1	2.2
1904	25.8	69.5	4.7	42.6	54.1	3.3				30.7	66.8	2.5
1906	29.1	65.7	5.2	34.8	60.9	4.3				25.5	71.0	3.5
1908	32.5	61.9	5.6	46.6	48.4	5.0				36.3	60.9	2.8
1910	29.9	44.8	25.3	41.6	52.9	5.5				39.1	56.7	4.1
1912	27.4	27.6	45.0	35.4	31.0	33.7				29.4	35.0	35.7
1914	35.7	39.9	24.4	48.2	40.0	11.8				34.8	50.8	14.3
1916	43.9	52.2	3.9	40.6	55.8	3.6	39.9	56.3	3.8	42.1	55.3	2.7
1918	33.1	62.5	4.4	36.4	61.4	2.2	48.5	50.2	1.4	33.4	65.2	1.4
1920	22.3	72.8	4.9	29.3	66.4	4.2	49.5	49.3	1.2	22.6	75.4	2.0
1922	17.7	74.1	8.2	37.4	61.2	1.5	50.6	48.4	1.1	32.7	67.0	0.3
1924	13.1	75.4	11.5	29.6	68.8	1.6	24.2	74.6	1.1	20.8	79.1	0.1
1926	21.0	72.9	6.1	36.0	63.4	0.6	26.0	73.3	0.8	21.8	78.1	0.1
1928	28.9	70.4	0.7	29.4	69.9	0.6	27.7	71.9	0.4	26.7	73.1	0.2
1930	40.6	57.4	2.0	42.0	56.9	1.1	20.9	78.2	0.9	23.0	76.2	0.8
1932	52.4	44.4	3.2	54.9	43.1	2.0	34.0	64.7	1.3	48.8	49.1	2.1
1934	54.4	41.6	4.1	45.8	52.4	1.8	47.0	51.3	1.7	48.7	49.9	1.4
1936	56.3	38.8	4.9	51.0	48.2	0.8	53.3	41.8	4.9	52.3	45.1	2.6
1938	52.9	44.3	2.8	47.0	52.8	0.3	50.1	47.2	2.6	46.2	53.7	0.2
1940	49.5	49.9	0.6	53.1	46.6	0.4	47.0	52.7	0.4	48.8	51.0	0.2
1942	49.9	49.5	0.6	46.7	52.6	0.7	47.2	49.6	3.3	45.7	53.8	0.5
1944	50.2	49.2	0.6	44.8	54.7	0.6	39.6	58.3	2.1	47.5	52.1	0.4
1946	48.9	49.2	1.9	38.7	60.3	1.0	32.0	67.1	0.9	38.6	60.8	0.6
1948	47.6	49.2	3.2	53.4	45.7	0.9	48.5	50.7	0.8	49.5	49.6	0.8
1950	45.8	52.3	1.9	49.8	49.7	0.5	48.7	50.8	0.5	46.5	53.0	0.5
1952	44.0	55.4	0.6	50.0	49.7	0.4	48.9	50.9	0.2	47.3	52.4	0.3
1954	44.1	55.5	0.4	55.6	44.1	0.3	50.8	48.9	0.3	51.6	48.2	0.2
1956	44.2	55.6	0.2	54.7	45.1	0.2	52.2	47.5	0.3	49.8	50.1	0.1
1958	47.5	52.2	0.3	53.0	46.6	0.4	53.6	46.1	0.3	53.0	46.8	0.2
1960	50.9	48.8	0.3	50.5	49.2	0.3	51.7	48.0	0.3	51.0	48.8	0.2
1962	58.8	41.0	0.3	48.5	51.4	0.2	58.1	41.7	0.3	51.7	48.2	0.1
1964	66.7	33.1	0.2	43.7	55.9	0.4	64.4	35.3	0.3	57.8	42.1	0.1
1966	57.4	37.3	5.3	39.1	60.5	0.3	43.8	56.0	0.3	48.6	51.4	0.0
1968	48.2	41.5	10.4	43.9	55.5	0.6	55.3	44.4	0.3	50.4	49.5	0.1
1970				48.7	50.4	0.9	66.8	32.9	0.3	51.3	48.5	0.3

169

YEAR	COMPOSITE A (P+G+S+H/4)			COMPOSITE B (G+S+H/3)			COMPOSITE C (S+H/2)		
	DEM.	REP.	OTHER	DEM.	REP.	OTHER	DEM.	REP.	OTHER
1872	37.5	62.2	0.4	37.8	61.9	0.2	38.6	60.9	0.5
1874	43.0	53.3	3.7	44.2	51.2	4.6	40.6	51.9	7.5
1876	45.3	52.3	2.4	45.6	52.3	2.1	46.4	52.3	1.3
1878	32.2	47.6	20.2	27.9	45.2	26.9	27.6	45.0	27.4
1880	38.0	52.0	10.1	38.3	51.7	10.0	37.2	52.2	10.6
1882	44.7	49.5	5.8	48.5	49.2	2.3	47.4	50.4	2.2
1884	43.9	47.6	8.5	47.3	47.5	5.2	48.0	47.4	4.6
1886	44.2	48.3	7.5	45.8	48.0	6.2	45.8	48.4	5.8
1888	45.3	49.6	5.1	45.5	49.6	4.9	45.4	50.0	4.6
1890	45.9	45.6	8.5	46.7	44.1	9.2	47.3	44.8	7.9
1892	44.1	47.6	8.3	44.5	47.5	8.0	45.2	47.8	7.0
1894	35.5	55.0	9.5	31.6	57.1	11.3	31.7	57.4	10.9
1896	42.0	54.6	3.4	41.3	55.1	3.6	40.5	54.5	5.0
1898	41.2	56.5	2.3	41.2	56.8	1.9	42.5	55.9	1.6
1900	40.1	57.2	2.7	40.7	56.8	2.6	40.0	57.8	2.2
1902	38.4	58.2	3.4	41.5	55.3	3.2	39.6	58.1	2.2
1904	33.0	63.5	3.5	36.7	60.5	2.9	30.7	66.8	2.5
1906	29.8	65.9	4.3	30.1	65.9	3.9	25.5	71.0	3.5
1908	38.4	57.1	4.5	41.4	54.7	3.9	36.3	60.9	2.8
1910	36.9	51.5	11.7	40.4	54.8	4.8	39.1	56.7	4.1
1912	30.7	31.2	38.1	32.4	33.0	34.7	29.4	35.0	35.7
1914	39.6	43.6	16.9	41.5	45.4	13.1	34.8	50.8	14.3
1916	41.6	54.9	3.5	40.8	55.8	3.4	41.0	55.8	3.3
1918	37.8	59.8	2.3	39.4	58.9	1.6	40.9	57.7	1.4
1920	30.9	66.0	3.1	33.8	63.7	2.5	36.1	62.3	1.6
1922	34.6	62.7	2.8	40.2	58.8	0.9	41.6	57.7	0.7
1924	21.9	74.5	3.6	24.9	74.2	0.9	22.5	76.9	0.6
1926	26.2	71.9	1.9	27.9	71.6	0.5	23.9	75.7	0.4
1928	28.2	71.3	0.5	27.9	71.7	0.4	27.2	72.5	0.3
1930	31.7	67.2	1.2	28.7	70.4	0.9	22.0	77.2	0.9
1932	47.5	50.3	2.2	45.9	52.3	1.8	41.4	56.9	1.7
1934	49.0	48.8	2.2	47.2	51.2	1.6	47.9	50.6	1.5
1936	53.2	43.5	3.3	52.2	45.0	2.8	52.8	43.5	3.8
1938	49.0	49.5	1.5	47.8	51.2	1.0	48.1	50.5	1.4
1940	49.6	50.0	0.4	49.6	50.1	0.3	47.9	51.8	0.3
1942	47.4	51.4	1.3	46.5	52.0	1.5	46.4	51.7	1.9
1944	45.5	53.6	0.9	44.0	55.0	1.0	43.6	55.2	1.2
1946	39.5	59.3	1.1	36.4	62.7	0.9	35.3	63.9	0.8
1948	49.8	48.8	1.4	50.5	48.7	0.9	49.0	50.2	0.8
1950	47.7	51.5	0.9	48.3	51.2	0.5	47.6	51.9	0.5
1952	47.5	52.1	0.4	48.7	51.0	0.3	48.1	51.7	0.2
1954	50.5	49.2	0.3	52.7	47.1	0.3	51.2	48.6	0.3
1956	50.2	49.6	0.2	52.2	47.6	0.2	51.0	48.8	0.2
1958	51.8	47.9	0.3	53.2	46.5	0.3	53.3	46.5	0.3
1960	51.0	48.7	0.3	51.1	48.7	0.3	51.4	48.4	0.2
1962	54.3	45.5	0.2	52.8	47.1	0.2	54.9	44.9	0.2
1964	58.2	41.6	0.2	55.3	44.5	0.3	61.1	38.7	0.2
1966	47.2	51.3	1.5	43.8	56.0	0.2	46.2	53.7	0.1
1968	49.4	47.7	2.8	49.9	49.8	0.3	52.8	47.0	0.2
1970				55.6	43.9	0.5	59.1	40.7	0.3

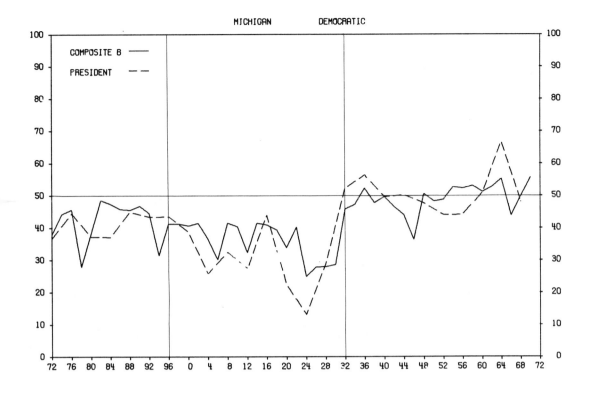

MICHIGAN   DEMOCRATIC

COMPOSITE B ——
PRESIDENT ——

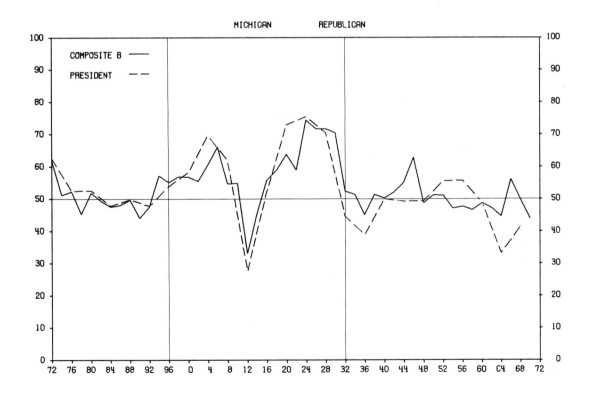

MICHIGAN   REPUBLICAN

COMPOSITE B ——
PRESIDENT ——

171

YEAR	PRESIDENT			GOVERNOR			SENATE CLASS I			SENATE CLASS II		
	DEM.	REP.	OTHER	DEM.	REP.	OTHER	DEM.	REP.	OTHER	DEM.	REP.	OTHER
1872	38.5	61.4	0.2									
1874				46.4	53.6	0.0						
1876	39.3	58.8	1.9	42.8	57.2	0.0						
1878				40.7	59.3	0.0						
1880	35.4	62.3	2.4	39.3	54.0	6.7						
1882				36.4	63.6	0.0						
1884	36.9	58.8	4.4	44.6	55.4	0.0						
1886				47.4	48.5	4.1						
1888	39.7	54.1	6.2	42.1	51.3	6.6						
1890				35.6	36.6	27.8						
1892	26.8	32.7	40.6	37.0	42.7	20.4						
1894				18.1	49.9	32.0						
1896	40.9	56.6	2.5	48.1	49.2	2.7						
1898				52.3	44.3	3.5						
1900	35.7	60.2	4.1	48.0	48.7	3.4						
1902				36.7	57.5	5.8						
1904	18.8	74.0	7.2	48.7	46.1	5.2						
1906				60.9	34.8	4.3						
1908	33.1	59.3	7.6	52.2	43.8	4.0						
1910				35.2	55.7	9.0						
1912	31.8	19.2	48.9	31.3	40.7	28.0						
1914				45.5	41.9	12.6						
1916	46.2	46.3	7.4	23.8	62.9	13.2	30.8	48.6	20.6			
1918				20.8	45.0	34.2				0.0	60.1	39.9
1920	19.4	70.6	10.0	10.4	53.1	36.6						
1922				11.7	45.2	43.1	17.9	35.0	47.1			
1924	6.8	51.2	42.0	5.9	48.7	45.4				6.4	46.5	47.1
1926				5.4	56.5	38.1						
1928	40.8	57.8	1.4	21.4	55.0	23.6	0.0	33.7	66.3			
1930				3.7	36.3	60.0				36.1	37.6	26.3
1932	59.9	36.3	3.8	16.4	32.3	51.2						
1934				16.8	37.7	45.4	29.2	19.8	51.0			
1936	61.8	31.0	7.1	0.0	38.6	61.4				0.0	39.9	60.1
1938				5.8	59.9	34.3						
1940	51.5	47.7	0.9	11.1	52.0	36.8	20.6	53.0	26.4			
1942				9.5	51.6	38.9				13.6	51.2	35.2
1944	52.4	46.9	0.7	38.3	61.1	0.6						
1946				39.7	59.0	1.3	39.8	58.9	1.3			
1948	57.2	39.9	2.9	45.1	53.1	1.8				59.9	39.7	0.4
1950				38.3	60.7	1.0						
1952	44.1	55.3	0.6	44.0	55.3	0.7	42.5	56.6	0.8			
1954				52.7	46.8	0.5				56.4	42.1	1.5
1956	46.1	53.7	0.2	51.4	48.2	0.4						
1958				56.8	42.3	0.9	52.9	46.6	0.5			
1960	50.6	49.2	0.3	49.1	50.6	0.4				57.5	42.2	0.3
1962				49.7	49.7	0.6						
1964	63.8	36.0	0.2				60.3	39.3	0.4			
1966				46.9	52.6	0.5				53.9	45.2	0.8
1968	54.0	41.5	4.5									
1970				54.0	45.5	0.4	57.8	41.6	0.6			

YEAR	PRESIDENT			GOVERNOR			SENATE			HOUSE OF REPRESENTATIVES		
	DEM.	REP.	OTHER	DEM.	REP.	OTHER	DEM.	REP.	OTHER	DEM.	REP.	OTHER
1872	38.5	61.4	0.2	46.4	52.0	1.6				38.6	61.4	0.0
1874	38.9	60.1	1.1	46.4	53.6	0.0				47.0	53.0	0.0
1876	39.3	58.8	1.9	42.8	57.2	0.0				42.0	55.7	2.3
1878	37.3	60.5	2.1	40.7	59.3	0.0				45.9	54.1	0.0
1880	35.4	62.3	2.4	39.3	54.0	6.7				38.2	56.6	5.2
1882	36.1	60.5	3.4	36.4	63.6	0.0				32.0	52.0	16.1
1884	36.9	58.8	4.4	44.6	55.4	0.0				40.9	57.4	1.7
1886	38.3	56.5	5.3	47.4	48.5	4.1				37.9	58.5	3.6
1888	39.7	54.2	6.2	42.1	51.3	6.6				41.3	53.3	5.5
1890	33.2	43.4	23.4	35.6	36.6	27.8				36.9	41.7	21.4
1892	26.8	32.7	40.6	37.0	42.7	20.4				37.1	44.5	18.4
1894	33.8	44.6	21.5	18.1	49.9	32.0				25.6	52.2	22.3
1896	40.9	56.6	2.5	48.1	49.2	2.7				43.3	55.4	1.3
1898	38.3	58.4	3.3	52.3	44.3	3.5				41.2	54.8	4.0
1900	35.7	60.2	4.1	48.0	48.7	3.4				40.2	56.7	3.0
1902	27.3	67.1	5.6	36.7	57.5	5.8				34.5	60.0	5.6
1904	18.8	74.0	7.2	48.7	46.1	5.2				25.7	72.5	1.7
1906	26.0	66.6	7.4	60.9	34.8	4.3				25.7	67.8	6.5
1908	33.1	59.3	7.6	52.2	43.8	4.0				28.2	62.9	8.9
1910	32.5	39.3	28.2	35.2	55.7	9.0				25.4	67.9	6.6
1912	31.8	19.3	48.9	31.3	40.7	28.0				24.7	56.5	18.9
1914	39.1	32.8	28.2	45.5	41.9	12.6	34.0	55.7	10.3	27.0	56.2	16.7
1916	46.3	46.4	7.4	23.8	62.9	13.2	30.8	48.6	20.6	24.8	55.1	20.1
1918	32.8	58.5	8.7	20.8	45.1	34.2	0.0	60.1	39.9	24.8	65.1	10.2
1920	19.4	70.6	10.0	10.4	53.1	36.6	9.0	47.6	43.5	14.0	59.9	26.1
1922	13.1	60.9	26.0	11.7	45.2	43.1	17.9	35.0	47.1	23.0	60.5	16.6
1924	6.8	51.2	42.0	5.9	48.7	45.4	6.4	46.5	47.1	6.6	52.0	41.5
1926	23.8	54.5	21.7	5.4	56.5	38.1	3.2	40.1	56.7	5.7	58.7	35.6
1928	40.8	57.8	1.4	21.4	55.0	23.6	0.0	33.7	66.3	18.0	54.1	28.0
1930	50.4	47.0	2.6	3.7	36.4	60.0	36.1	37.6	26.3	8.6	54.3	37.0
1932	59.9	36.3	3.8	16.4	32.3	51.2	32.7	28.7	38.6	25.0	35.7	39.3
1934	60.9	33.7	5.5	16.8	37.7	45.5	29.2	19.8	51.0	25.7	32.5	41.8
1936	61.8	31.0	7.1	0.0	38.6	61.5	0.0	39.9	60.1	17.5	38.5	44.0
1938	56.7	39.3	4.0	5.8	59.9	34.3	10.3	46.4	43.3	17.8	50.2	32.1
1940	51.5	47.7	0.9	11.1	52.1	36.8	20.6	53.0	26.5	21.8	53.1	25.1
1942	52.0	47.3	0.8	9.5	51.6	38.9	13.6	51.2	35.2	20.6	59.4	20.1
1944	52.4	46.9	0.7	38.3	61.1	0.6	26.7	55.1	18.2	40.8	58.9	0.3
1946	54.8	43.4	1.8	39.7	59.0	1.3	39.8	58.9	1.3	40.9	58.8	0.3
1948	57.2	39.9	2.9	45.1	53.2	1.8	59.9	39.7	0.4	49.8	50.2	0.0
1950	50.6	47.6	1.8	38.3	60.8	1.0	51.2	48.1	0.6	46.5	52.9	0.6
1952	44.1	55.3	0.6	44.0	55.3	0.7	42.5	56.6	0.9	46.0	54.0	0.0
1954	45.1	54.5	0.4	52.7	46.8	0.5	56.4	42.1	1.5	53.0	47.0	0.0
1956	46.1	53.7	0.2	51.4	48.2	0.4	54.6	44.4	1.0	51.3	48.7	0.0
1958	48.3	51.4	0.3	56.8	42.3	0.9	52.9	46.6	0.5	52.7	47.3	0.0
1960	50.6	49.2	0.3	49.1	50.6	0.4	57.5	42.2	0.3	50.2	49.5	0.4
1962	57.2	42.6	0.3	49.7	49.7	0.6	58.9	40.7	0.3	49.8	50.3	0.0
1964	63.8	36.0	0.2	48.3	51.1	0.5	60.3	39.3	0.4	54.4	45.5	0.1
1966	58.9	38.7	2.4	46.9	52.6	0.5	53.9	45.2	0.8	48.4	51.6	0.0
1968	54.0	41.5	4.5	50.5	49.0	0.5	55.9	43.4	0.7	47.7	52.2	0.1
1970				54.0	45.5	0.4	57.8	41.6	0.6	52.9	46.9	0.2

YEAR	COMPOSITE A (P+G+S+H/4)			COMPOSITE B (G+S+H/3)			COMPOSITE C (S+H/2)		
	DEM.	REP.	OTHER	DEM.	REP.	OTHER	DEM.	REP.	OTHER
1872	41.1	58.3	0.6	42.5	56.7	0.8	38.6	61.4	0.0
1874	44.1	55.6	0.4	46.7	53.3	0.0	47.0	53.0	0.0
1876	41.4	57.2	1.4	42.4	56.4	1.2	42.0	55.7	2.3
1878	41.3	58.0	0.7	43.3	56.7	0.0	45.9	54.1	0.0
1880	37.6	57.6	4.8	38.8	55.3	6.0	38.2	56.6	5.2
1882	34.8	58.7	6.5	34.2	57.8	8.0	32.0	52.0	16.1
1884	40.8	57.2	2.0	42.7	56.4	0.9	40.9	57.4	1.7
1886	41.2	54.5	4.3	42.6	53.5	3.9	37.9	58.5	3.6
1888	41.0	52.9	6.1	41.7	52.3	6.0	41.3	53.3	5.5
1890	35.3	40.6	24.2	36.3	39.2	24.6	36.9	41.7	21.4
1892	33.6	40.0	26.4	37.0	43.6	19.4	37.1	44.5	18.4
1894	25.8	48.9	25.3	21.8	51.0	27.1	25.6	52.2	22.3
1896	44.1	53.7	2.2	45.7	52.3	2.0	43.3	55.4	1.3
1898	43.9	52.5	3.6	46.7	49.5	3.8	41.2	54.8	4.0
1900	41.3	55.2	3.5	44.1	52.7	3.2	40.2	56.7	3.0
1902	32.8	61.5	5.7	35.6	58.8	5.7	34.5	60.0	5.6
1904	31.1	64.2	4.7	37.2	59.3	3.5	25.7	72.5	1.7
1906	37.5	56.4	6.1	43.3	51.3	5.4	25.7	67.8	6.5
1908	37.8	55.3	6.8	40.2	53.3	6.5	28.2	62.9	8.9
1910	31.1	54.3	14.6	30.3	61.8	7.8	25.4	67.9	6.6
1912	29.3	38.8	31.9	28.0	48.6	23.4	24.7	56.5	18.9
1914	36.4	46.6	17.0	35.5	51.3	13.2	30.5	55.9	13.5
1916	31.4	53.3	15.3	26.5	55.6	18.0	27.8	51.9	20.4
1918	19.6	57.2	23.2	15.2	56.7	28.1	12.4	62.6	25.0
1920	13.2	57.8	29.1	11.1	53.5	35.4	11.5	53.7	34.8
1922	16.4	50.4	33.2	17.5	46.9	35.6	20.4	47.7	31.8
1924	6.4	49.6	44.0	6.3	49.0	44.7	6.5	49.2	44.3
1926	9.6	52.4	38.0	4.8	51.7	43.5	4.5	49.4	46.2
1928	20.0	50.1	29.8	13.1	47.6	39.3	9.0	43.9	47.1
1930	24.7	43.8	31.5	16.1	42.8	41.1	22.4	46.0	31.7
1932	33.5	33.3	33.2	24.7	32.2	43.1	28.8	32.2	39.0
1934	33.2	30.9	35.9	23.9	30.0	46.1	27.5	26.1	46.4
1936	19.8	37.0	43.2	5.8	39.0	55.2	8.7	39.2	52.1
1938	22.6	49.0	28.4	11.3	52.2	36.5	14.0	48.3	37.7
1940	26.2	51.5	22.3	17.8	52.7	29.5	21.2	53.0	25.8
1942	23.9	52.4	23.7	14.5	54.1	31.4	17.1	55.3	27.6
1944	39.6	55.5	5.0	35.3	58.3	6.4	33.8	57.0	9.3
1946	43.8	55.0	1.2	40.1	58.9	1.0	40.3	58.9	0.8
1948	53.0	45.7	1.3	51.6	47.7	0.7	54.9	44.9	0.2
1950	46.7	52.4	1.0	45.3	53.9	0.7	48.9	50.5	0.6
1952	44.2	55.3	0.5	44.2	55.3	0.5	44.3	55.3	0.4
1954	51.8	47.6	0.6	54.1	45.3	0.7	54.7	44.5	0.8
1956	50.9	48.7	0.4	52.5	47.1	0.5	53.0	46.5	0.5
1958	52.7	46.9	0.4	54.1	45.4	0.5	52.8	47.0	0.2
1960	51.8	47.9	0.3	52.3	47.4	0.3	53.8	45.8	0.3
1962	53.9	45.8	0.3	52.8	46.9	0.3	54.3	45.5	0.2
1964	56.7	43.0	0.3	54.4	45.3	0.4	57.4	42.4	0.3
1966	52.0	47.0	0.9	49.8	49.8	0.5	51.2	48.4	0.4
1968	52.0	46.5	1.5	51.3	48.2	0.4	51.8	47.8	0.4
1970				54.9	44.7	0.4	55.3	44.3	0.4

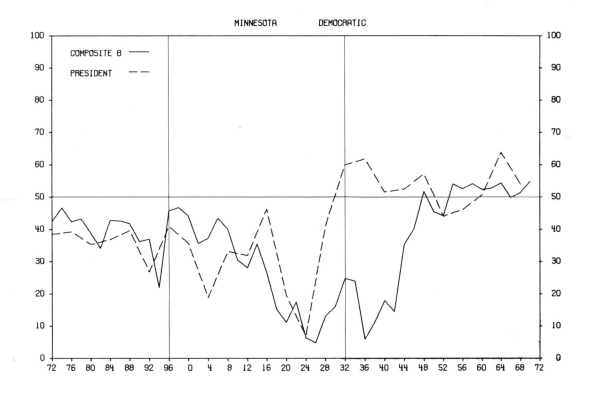

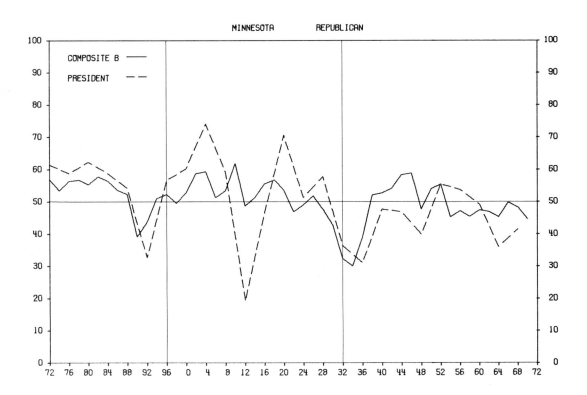

175

MISSISSIPPI

YEAR	PRESIDENT			GOVERNOR			SENATE CLASS I			SENATE CLASS II		
	DEM.	REP.	OTHER	DEM.	REP.	OTHER	DEM.	REP.	OTHER	DEM.	REP.	OTHER
1872	36.5	63.5	0.0									
1874				0.0	58.1	41.9						
1876	68.1	31.9	0.0									
1878				98.8	1.2	0.0						
1880	64.7	29.8	5.5									
1882				59.6	40.4	0.0						
1884	64.3	35.7	0.0									
1886				100.0	0.0	0.0						
1888	73.8	26.0	0.2									
1890				100.0	0.0	0.0						
1892	76.2	2.7	21.1									
1894												
1896	91.0	6.9	2.0	72.1	0.0	27.9						
1898												
1900	87.6	9.7	2.8	87.4	0.0	12.6						
1902												
1904	91.1	5.6	3.3	100.0	0.0	0.0						
1906												
1908	90.1	6.5	3.4	100.0	0.0	0.0						
1910												
1912	88.9	2.4	8.7	95.2	0.0	4.8						
1914												
1916	93.3	4.9	1.7	92.6	0.0	7.4	100.0	0.0	0.0			
1918										95.0	0.0	5.0
1920	84.0	14.0	2.0	96.9	0.0	3.1						
1922							93.2	1.9	4.9			
1924	89.4	7.5	3.1	100.0	0.0	0.0				100.0	0.0	0.0
1926												
1928	82.2	17.3	0.5	100.0	0.0	0.0	100.0	0.0	0.0			
1930										100.0	0.0	0.0
1932	96.0	3.5	0.5	100.0	0.0	0.0						
1934							100.0	0.0	0.0			
1936	97.0	2.8	0.2	100.0	0.0	0.0				100.0	0.0	0.0
1938												
1940	95.7	1.6	2.7	100.0	0.0	0.0	100.0	0.0	0.0			
1942										100.0	0.0	0.0
1944	97.8	2.2	0.0	100.0	0.0	0.0						
1946							100.0	0.0	0.0			
1948	10.1	2.6	87.3	97.5	2.5	0.0	0.0	0.0	100.0	100.0	0.0	0.0
1950												
1952	60.4	39.6	0.0	100.0	0.0	0.0	100.0	0.0	0.0			
1954										95.6	4.4	0.0
1956	58.2	24.5	17.3	100.0	0.0	0.0						
1958							100.0	0.0	0.0			
1960	36.3	24.7	39.0	100.0	0.0	0.0						
1962										91.8	8.2	0.0
1964	12.9	87.1	0.0	61.9	38.1	0.0	100.0	0.0	0.0			
1966										65.5	26.8	7.8
1968	23.0	13.5	63.5	70.3	29.7	0.0						
1970							88.4	0.0	11.6			

YEAR	PRESIDENT			GOVERNOR			SENATE			HOUSE OF REPRESENTATIVES		
	DEM.	REP.	OTHER	DEM.	REP.	OTHER	DEM.	REP.	OTHER	DEM.	REP.	OTHER
1872	36.5	63.5	0.0	0.0	62.4	37.6				31.9	62.8	5.4
1874	52.3	47.7	0.0	0.0	58.1	41.9				46.4	47.9	5.7
1876	68.1	31.9	0.0	49.4	29.7	20.9				61.0	32.9	6.1
1878	66.4	30.8	2.8	98.8	1.2	0.0				71.1	3.9	25.0
1880	64.7	29.8	5.5	79.2	20.8	0.0				66.9	21.4	11.7
1882	64.5	32.7	2.8	59.6	40.4	0.0				60.5	25.9	13.6
1884	64.3	35.7	0.0	79.8	20.2	0.0				67.9	31.8	0.3
1886	69.1	30.8	0.1	100.0	0.0	0.0				76.1	23.5	0.4
1888	73.8	26.0	0.2	100.0	0.0	0.0				76.9	23.1	0.0
1890	75.0	14.3	10.7	100.0	0.0	0.0				78.4	21.6	0.0
1892	76.2	2.7	21.1	86.0	0.0	14.0				74.3	1.1	24.7
1894	83.6	4.8	11.6	86.0	0.0	14.0				68.5	0.4	31.1
1896	91.0	6.9	2.0	72.1	0.0	27.9				75.5	5.6	18.9
1898	89.3	8.3	2.4	79.7	0.0	20.3				82.0	2.9	15.1
1900	87.6	9.7	2.8	87.4	0.0	12.6				92.8	5.0	2.2
1902	89.3	7.6	3.1	93.7	0.0	6.3				100.0	0.0	0.0
1904	91.1	5.6	3.3	100.0	0.0	0.0				99.0	0.2	0.8
1906	90.6	6.1	3.4	100.0	0.0	0.0				99.2	0.0	0.9
1908	90.1	6.5	3.4	100.0	0.0	0.0				99.4	0.6	0.0
1910	89.5	4.5	6.0	97.6	0.0	2.4				99.9	0.0	0.1
1912	88.9	2.4	8.7	95.2	0.0	4.8				99.4	0.0	0.6
1914	91.1	3.7	5.2	93.9	0.0	6.1				97.0	0.0	3.0
1916	93.3	4.9	1.7	92.6	0.0	7.4	100.0	0.0	0.0	100.0	0.0	0.0
1918	88.7	9.5	1.9	94.8	0.0	5.2	95.0	0.0	5.0	97.8	0.0	2.2
1920	84.0	14.0	2.0	96.9	0.0	3.1	94.1	0.9	4.9	94.8	2.3	3.0
1922	86.7	10.7	2.5	98.5	0.0	1.5	93.2	1.9	4.9	97.6	2.4	0.1
1924	89.4	7.5	3.1	100.0	0.0	0.0	100.0	0.0	0.0	99.4	0.6	0.0
1926	85.8	12.4	1.8	100.0	0.0	0.0	100.0	0.0	0.0	100.0	0.0	0.0
1928	82.2	17.3	0.5	100.0	0.0	0.0	100.0	0.0	0.0	100.0	0.0	0.0
1930	89.1	10.4	0.5	100.0	0.0	0.0	100.0	0.0	0.0	100.0	0.0	0.0
1932	96.0	3.5	0.5	100.0	0.0	0.0	100.0	0.0	0.0	96.4	3.5	0.1
1934	96.5	3.2	0.3	100.0	0.0	0.0	100.0	0.0	0.0	100.0	0.0	0.0
1936	97.0	2.8	0.2	100.0	0.0	0.0	100.0	0.0	0.0	100.0	0.0	0.0
1938	96.4	2.2	1.5	100.0	0.0	0.0	100.0	0.0	0.0	100.0	0.0	0.0
1940	95.7	1.6	2.7	100.0	0.0	0.0	100.0	0.0	0.0	100.0	0.0	0.0
1942	96.8	1.9	1.4	100.0	0.0	0.0	100.0	0.0	0.0	100.0	0.0	0.0
1944	97.8	2.2	0.0	100.0	0.0	0.0	100.0	0.0	0.0	96.7	3.4	0.0
1946	54.0	2.4	43.7	98.8	1.2	0.0	100.0	0.0	0.0	100.0	0.0	0.0
1948	10.1	2.6	87.3	97.5	2.5	0.0	43.9	0.0	56.1	99.8	0.2	0.0
1950	35.3	21.1	43.7	98.8	1.2	0.0	71.9	0.0	28.1	94.2	3.3	2.5
1952	60.4	39.6	0.0	100.0	0.0	0.0	100.0	0.0	0.0	97.5	2.5	0.0
1954	59.3	32.0	8.7	100.0	0.0	0.0	95.6	4.4	0.0	100.0	0.0	0.0
1956	58.2	24.5	17.3	100.0	0.0	0.0	97.8	2.2	0.0	100.0	0.0	0.0
1958	47.3	24.6	28.2	100.0	0.0	0.0	100.0	0.0	0.0	100.0	0.0	0.0
1960	36.3	24.7	39.0	100.0	0.0	0.0	91.8	8.2	0.0	98.1	2.0	0.0
1962	24.6	55.9	19.5	81.0	19.0	0.0	95.9	4.1	0.0	97.2	0.0	2.8
1964	12.9	87.1	0.0	61.9	38.1	0.0	100.0	0.0	0.0	90.2	9.8	0.0
1966	17.9	50.3	31.7	66.1	33.9	0.0	65.5	26.8	7.8	73.9	16.1	10.1
1968	23.0	13.5	63.5	70.3	29.7	0.0	76.9	13.4	9.7	92.5	7.5	0.0
1970							88.4	0.0	11.6	86.2	9.2	4.6

YEAR	COMPOSITE A (P+G+S+H/4)			COMPOSITE B (G+S+H/3)			COMPOSITE C (S+H/2)		
	DEM.	REP.	OTHER	DEM.	REP.	OTHER	DEM.	REP.	OTHER
1872	22.8	62.9	14.3	15.9	62.6	21.5	31.9	62.8	5.4
1874	32.9	51.2	15.9	23.2	53.0	23.8	46.4	47.9	5.7
1876	59.5	31.5	9.0	55.2	31.3	13.5	61.0	32.9	6.1
1878	78.8	12.0	9.2	85.0	2.6	12.5	71.1	3.9	25.0
1880	70.3	24.0	5.7	73.1	21.1	5.9	66.9	21.4	11.7
1882	61.6	33.0	5.5	60.1	33.1	6.8	60.5	25.9	13.6
1884	70.7	29.2	0.1	73.9	26.0	0.1	67.9	31.8	0.3
1886	81.7	18.1	0.2	88.0	11.8	0.2	76.1	23.5	0.4
1888	83.6	16.4	0.1	88.5	11.5	0.0	76.9	23.1	0.0
1890	84.5	12.0	3.6	89.2	10.8	0.0	78.4	21.6	0.0
1892	78.8	1.2	19.9	80.2	0.5	19.3	74.3	1.1	24.7
1894	79.4	1.7	18.9	77.3	0.2	22.5	68.5	0.4	31.1
1896	79.5	4.2	16.3	73.8	2.8	23.4	75.5	5.6	18.9
1898	83.7	3.7	12.6	80.9	1.4	17.7	82.0	2.9	15.1
1900	89.3	4.9	5.9	90.1	2.5	7.4	92.8	5.0	2.2
1902	94.3	2.5	3.1	96.9	0.0	3.2	100.0	0.0	0.0
1904	96.7	1.9	1.4	99.5	0.1	0.4	99.0	0.2	0.8
1906	96.6	2.0	1.4	99.6	0.0	0.4	99.2	0.0	0.9
1908	96.5	2.4	1.1	99.7	0.3	0.0	99.4	0.6	0.0
1910	95.7	1.5	2.8	98.8	0.0	1.3	99.9	0.0	0.1
1912	94.5	0.8	4.7	97.3	0.0	2.7	99.4	0.0	0.6
1914	94.0	1.2	4.8	95.4	0.0	4.6	97.0	0.0	3.0
1916	96.5	1.2	2.3	97.5	0.0	2.5	100.0	0.0	0.0
1918	94.1	2.4	3.6	95.9	0.0	4.1	96.4	0.0	3.6
1920	92.5	4.3	3.2	95.3	1.1	3.7	94.5	1.6	4.0
1922	94.0	3.8	2.3	96.4	1.4	2.2	95.4	2.1	2.5
1924	97.2	2.0	0.8	99.8	0.2	0.0	99.7	0.3	0.0
1926	96.5	3.1	0.5	100.0	0.0	0.0	100.0	0.0	0.0
1928	95.5	4.3	0.1	100.0	0.0	0.0	100.0	0.0	0.0
1930	97.3	2.6	0.1	100.0	0.0	0.0	100.0	0.0	0.0
1932	98.1	1.8	0.1	98.8	1.2	0.0	98.2	1.8	0.0
1934	99.1	0.8	0.1	100.0	0.0	0.0	100.0	0.0	0.0
1936	99.3	0.7	0.1	100.0	0.0	0.0	100.0	0.0	0.0
1938	99.1	0.5	0.4	100.0	0.0	0.0	100.0	0.0	0.0
1940	98.9	0.4	0.7	100.0	0.0	0.0	100.0	0.0	0.0
1942	99.2	0.5	0.3	100.0	0.0	0.0	100.0	0.0	0.0
1944	98.6	1.4	0.0	98.9	1.1	0.0	98.3	1.7	0.0
1946	88.2	0.9	10.9	99.6	0.4	0.0	100.0	0.0	0.0
1948	62.8	1.3	35.9	80.4	0.9	18.7	71.9	0.1	28.1
1950	75.1	6.4	18.6	88.3	1.5	10.2	83.1	1.6	15.3
1952	89.5	10.5	0.0	99.2	0.8	0.0	98.8	1.3	0.0
1954	88.7	9.1	2.2	98.5	1.5	0.0	97.8	2.2	0.0
1956	89.0	6.7	4.3	99.3	0.7	0.0	98.9	1.1	0.0
1958	86.8	6.1	7.0	100.0	0.0	0.0	100.0	0.0	0.0
1960	81.6	8.7	9.8	96.6	3.4	0.0	94.9	5.1	0.0
1962	74.7	19.8	5.6	91.4	7.7	0.9	96.6	2.1	1.4
1964	66.3	33.7	0.0	84.1	16.0	0.0	95.1	4.9	0.0
1966	55.8	31.8	12.4	68.5	25.6	5.9	69.7	21.4	8.9
1968	65.7	16.0	18.3	79.9	16.9	3.2	84.7	10.5	4.8
1970							87.3	4.6	8.1

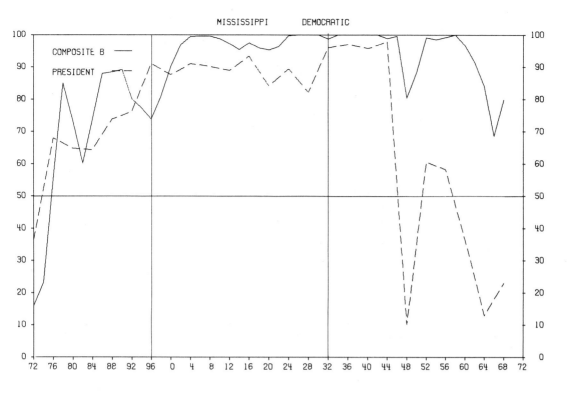

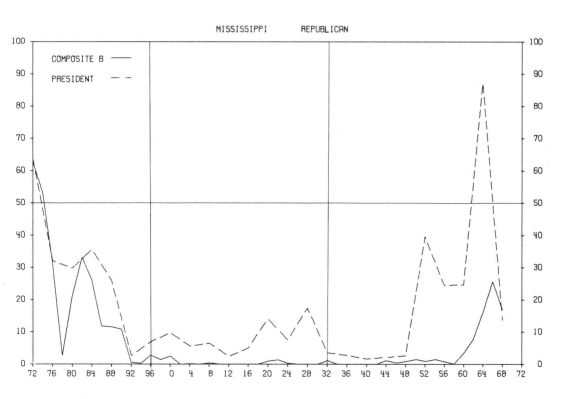

179

MISSOURI

YEAR	PRESIDENT			GOVERNOR			SENATE CLASS I			SENATE CLASS III		
	DEM.	REP.	OTHER	DEM.	REP.	OTHER	DEM.	REP.	OTHER	DEM.	REP.	OTHER
1872	55.5	43.7	0.9	56.3	43.7	0.0						
1874				57.2	42.8	0.0						
1876	57.6	41.4	1.0	57.0	42.2	0.8						
1878												
1880	52.5	38.7	8.8	52.2	38.6	9.1						
1882												
1884	53.5	46.0	0.5	50.0	47.5	2.4						
1886												
1888	50.2	45.3	4.4	49.4	46.8	3.8						
1890												
1892	49.6	42.0	8.4	49.0	43.5	7.5						
1894												
1896	54.0	45.2	0.8	52.9	46.3	0.8						
1898												
1900	51.5	45.9	2.6	51.2	46.5	2.4						
1902												
1904	46.0	49.9	4.1	50.7	46.1	3.2						
1906												
1908	48.4	48.5	3.1	47.5	49.7	2.8						
1910												
1912	47.3	29.7	22.9	48.2	31.2	20.6						
1914										50.4	41.6	8.0
1916	50.6	46.9	2.5	48.6	48.4	3.0	50.6	47.4	2.0			
1918										46.3	52.4	1.3
1920	43.1	54.6	2.3	43.6	54.3	2.1				44.5	53.7	1.9
1922							51.4	47.8	0.8			
1924	43.8	49.6	6.6	48.9	49.4	1.7						
1926										51.6	47.9	0.5
1928	44.2	55.6	0.3	48.2	51.6	0.2	47.9	51.9	0.2			
1930												
1932	63.7	35.1	1.2	60.2	39.1	0.7				63.2	35.9	1.0
1934							59.5	39.7	0.7			
1936	60.8	38.2	1.1	57.1	42.5	0.4						
1938										60.7	39.1	0.2
1940	52.3	47.5	0.2	49.9	50.1	0.1	51.2	48.7	0.1			
1942												
1944	51.4	48.4	0.2	50.9	49.0	0.1				49.9	50.0	0.1
1946							47.1	52.7	0.2			
1948	58.1	41.5	0.4	57.0	42.8	0.3						
1950										53.6	46.4	0.1
1952	49.1	50.7	0.1	52.5	47.4	0.1	54.0	45.9	0.1			
1954												
1956	50.1	49.9	0.0	52.1	47.9	0.0				56.4	43.6	0.0
1958							66.5	33.5	0.0			
1960	50.3	49.7	0.0	58.0	42.0	0.0				53.2	46.8	0.0
1962										54.6	45.4	0.0
1964	64.0	36.0	0.0	62.1	37.9	0.0	66.6	33.4	0.0			
1966												
1968	43.7	44.9	11.4	60.7	39.3	0.0				51.0	49.0	0.0
1970							51.0	48.1	0.8			

MISSOURI

YEAR	PRESIDENT			GOVERNOR			SENATE			HOUSE OF REPRESENTATIVES		
	DEM.	REP.	OTHER	DEM.	REP.	OTHER	DEM.	REP.	OTHER	DEM.	REP.	OTHER
1872	55.5	43.7	0.9	56.3	43.7	0.0				56.9	43.1	0.0
1874	56.6	42.5	0.9	57.2	42.8	0.0				67.7	21.8	10.6
1876	57.6	41.4	1.0	57.0	42.2	0.9				59.6	38.0	2.4
1878	55.1	40.0	4.9	54.6	40.4	5.0				54.9	17.5	27.6
1880	52.5	38.7	8.8	52.2	38.6	9.1				56.7	35.7	7.6
1882	53.0	42.4	4.7	51.1	43.1	5.8				54.3	28.6	17.2
1884	53.5	46.0	0.5	50.1	47.5	2.4				53.7	45.5	0.8
1886	51.9	45.7	2.5	49.7	47.2	3.1				52.1	41.2	6.7
1888	50.2	45.3	4.4	49.4	46.8	3.8				50.5	45.6	3.9
1890	49.9	43.7	6.4	49.2	45.2	5.7				54.8	39.8	5.4
1892	49.6	42.0	8.4	49.0	43.5	7.5				50.1	42.7	7.2
1894	51.8	43.6	4.6	50.9	44.9	4.2				44.2	46.5	9.4
1896	54.0	45.2	0.8	52.9	46.4	0.8				51.0	45.8	3.2
1898	52.7	45.6	1.7	52.0	46.4	1.6				51.7	46.4	1.9
1900	51.5	45.9	2.6	51.2	46.5	2.4				52.6	46.6	0.9
1902	48.8	47.9	3.3	50.9	46.3	2.8				53.8	45.2	1.0
1904	46.0	49.9	4.1	50.7	46.1	3.2				48.2	50.2	1.6
1906	47.2	49.2	3.6	49.1	47.9	3.0				49.8	48.9	1.4
1908	48.4	48.5	3.1	47.5	49.7	2.8				49.1	48.9	2.1
1910	47.9	39.1	13.0	47.9	40.4	11.7				48.9	47.5	3.6
1912	47.4	29.8	22.9	48.2	31.2	20.7				49.2	32.6	18.2
1914	49.0	38.4	12.7	48.4	39.8	11.8	50.4	41.6	8.0	53.1	40.1	6.8
1916	50.6	46.9	2.5	48.7	48.4	3.0	50.6	47.4	2.0	50.9	47.3	1.8
1918	46.9	50.8	2.4	46.1	51.3	2.6	46.3	52.4	1.3	52.2	46.5	1.2
1920	43.2	54.6	2.3	43.6	54.3	2.1	44.5	53.7	1.9	44.2	54.1	1.7
1922	43.5	52.1	4.4	46.3	51.8	1.9	51.4	47.8	0.8	50.6	48.8	0.6
1924	43.8	49.6	6.6	48.9	49.4	1.7	51.5	47.9	0.7	48.6	50.5	1.0
1926	44.0	52.6	3.5	48.6	50.5	0.9	51.6	47.9	0.5	50.6	49.3	0.1
1928	44.2	55.6	0.3	48.2	51.6	0.2	47.9	51.9	0.2	47.9	52.1	0.0
1930	53.9	45.3	0.8	54.2	45.4	0.5	55.5	43.9	0.6	50.4	49.5	0.1
1932	63.7	35.1	1.2	60.2	39.1	0.7	63.2	35.9	1.0	62.4	36.9	0.7
1934	62.2	36.6	1.2	58.6	40.8	0.6	59.5	39.7	0.7	60.4	39.0	0.5
1936	60.8	38.2	1.1	57.1	42.5	0.4	60.1	39.4	0.5	60.4	39.5	0.1
1938	56.5	42.8	0.7	53.5	46.3	0.3	60.7	39.2	0.2	59.3	40.6	0.1
1940	52.3	47.5	0.2	49.9	50.1	0.1	51.2	48.7	0.1	52.4	47.6	0.0
1942	51.8	48.0	0.2	50.4	49.5	0.1	50.5	49.4	0.1	48.4	51.6	0.0
1944	51.4	48.4	0.2	50.9	49.0	0.1	49.9	50.0	0.1	52.5	47.5	0.0
1946	54.7	45.0	0.3	54.0	45.9	0.2	47.1	52.7	0.2	47.8	52.2	0.0
1948	58.1	41.5	0.4	57.0	42.8	0.3	50.3	49.5	0.1	58.6	41.1	0.2
1950	53.6	46.1	0.3	54.8	45.1	0.2	53.6	46.4	0.1	55.8	44.2	0.1
1952	49.1	50.7	0.2	52.6	47.4	0.1	54.0	45.9	0.1	52.2	47.8	0.0
1954	49.6	50.3	0.1	52.3	47.7	0.0	55.2	44.8	0.0	56.2	43.8	0.0
1956	50.1	49.9	0.0	52.1	47.9	0.0	56.4	43.6	0.0	59.7	40.3	0.0
1958	50.2	49.8	0.0	55.1	45.0	0.0	66.5	33.6	0.0	63.2	36.9	0.0
1960	50.3	49.7	0.0	58.0	42.0	0.0	53.2	46.8	0.0	57.7	42.3	0.0
1962	57.2	42.9	0.0	60.1	40.0	0.0	54.6	45.4	0.0	56.4	43.6	0.0
1964	64.1	36.0	0.0	62.1	37.9	0.0	66.6	33.5	0.0	62.5	37.5	0.0
1966	53.9	40.4	5.7	61.4	38.6	0.0	58.8	41.2	0.0	53.7	46.3	0.0
1968	43.7	44.9	11.4	60.7	39.3	0.0	51.0	49.0	0.0	55.8	44.2	0.1
1970							51.0	48.2	0.8	57.8	41.2	1.0

181

YEAR	COMPOSITE A (P+G+S+H/4)			COMPOSITE B (G+S+H/3)			COMPOSITE C (S+H/2)		
	DEM.	REP.	OTHER	DEM.	REP.	OTHER	DEM.	REP.	OTHER
1872	56.2	43.5	0.3	56.6	43.4	0.0	56.9	43.1	0.0
1874	60.5	35.7	3.8	62.4	32.3	5.3	67.7	21.8	10.6
1876	58.1	40.5	1.4	58.3	40.1	1.6	59.6	38.0	2.4
1878	54.9	32.6	12.5	54.8	29.0	16.3	54.9	17.5	27.6
1880	53.8	37.7	8.5	54.5	37.2	8.4	56.7	35.7	7.6
1882	52.8	38.0	9.2	52.7	35.8	11.5	54.3	28.6	17.2
1884	52.4	46.3	1.2	51.9	46.5	1.6	53.7	45.5	0.8
1886	51.2	44.7	4.1	50.9	44.2	4.9	52.1	41.2	6.7
1888	50.1	45.9	4.1	50.0	46.2	3.9	50.5	45.6	3.9
1890	51.3	42.9	5.8	52.0	42.5	5.5	54.8	39.8	5.4
1892	49.5	42.8	7.7	49.5	43.1	7.4	50.1	42.7	7.2
1894	49.0	45.0	6.1	47.5	45.7	6.8	44.2	46.5	9.4
1896	52.6	45.8	1.6	52.0	46.1	2.0	51.0	45.8	3.2
1898	52.1	46.1	1.7	51.9	46.4	1.7	51.7	46.4	1.9
1900	51.7	46.3	2.0	51.9	46.5	1.6	52.6	46.6	0.9
1902	51.2	46.5	2.4	52.4	45.7	1.9	53.8	45.2	1.0
1904	48.3	48.7	3.0	49.5	48.1	2.4	48.2	50.2	1.6
1906	48.7	48.7	2.6	49.4	48.4	2.2	49.8	48.9	1.4
1908	48.3	49.0	2.6	48.3	49.3	2.4	49.1	48.9	2.1
1910	48.2	42.4	9.4	48.4	44.0	7.6	48.9	47.5	3.6
1912	48.3	31.2	20.6	48.7	31.9	19.4	49.2	32.6	18.2
1914	50.2	40.0	9.8	50.6	40.5	8.9	51.7	40.8	7.4
1916	50.2	47.5	2.3	50.0	47.7	2.3	50.7	47.4	1.9
1918	47.9	50.3	1.9	48.2	50.1	1.7	49.3	49.5	1.3
1920	43.9	54.1	2.0	44.1	54.0	1.9	44.3	53.9	1.8
1922	47.9	50.1	2.0	49.4	49.5	1.1	51.0	48.3	0.7
1924	48.2	49.3	2.5	49.7	49.2	1.1	50.0	49.2	0.8
1926	48.7	50.1	1.2	50.2	49.3	0.5	51.1	48.6	0.3
1928	47.0	52.8	0.2	48.0	51.9	0.1	47.9	52.0	0.1
1930	53.5	46.0	0.5	53.4	46.3	0.4	53.0	46.7	0.3
1932	62.4	36.7	0.9	61.9	37.3	0.8	62.8	36.4	0.8
1934	60.2	39.0	0.8	59.5	39.9	0.6	60.0	39.4	0.6
1936	59.6	39.9	0.5	59.2	40.5	0.3	60.2	39.5	0.3
1938	57.5	42.2	0.3	57.8	42.0	0.2	60.0	39.9	0.1
1940	51.4	48.5	0.1	51.1	48.8	0.1	51.8	48.2	0.1
1942	50.3	49.6	0.1	49.8	50.1	0.1	49.5	50.5	0.1
1944	51.2	48.7	0.1	51.1	48.8	0.1	51.2	48.8	0.1
1946	50.9	48.9	0.2	49.6	50.3	0.1	47.4	52.5	0.1
1948	56.0	43.7	0.3	55.3	44.5	0.2	54.5	45.3	0.2
1950	54.4	45.4	0.1	54.7	45.2	0.1	54.7	45.3	0.1
1952	52.0	48.0	0.1	52.9	47.0	0.1	53.1	46.9	0.0
1954	53.3	46.6	0.0	54.6	45.4	0.0	55.7	44.3	0.0
1956	54.6	45.4	0.0	56.1	43.9	0.0	58.1	41.9	0.0
1958	58.7	41.3	0.0	61.6	38.5	0.0	64.8	35.2	0.0
1960	54.8	45.2	0.0	56.3	43.7	0.0	55.4	44.6	0.0
1962	57.0	43.0	0.0	57.0	43.0	0.0	55.5	44.5	0.0
1964	63.8	36.2	0.0	63.7	36.3	0.0	64.5	35.5	0.0
1966	56.9	41.6	1.4	58.0	42.1	0.0	56.2	43.8	0.0
1968	52.8	44.3	2.9	55.8	44.2	0.0	53.4	46.6	0.0
1970							54.4	44.7	0.9

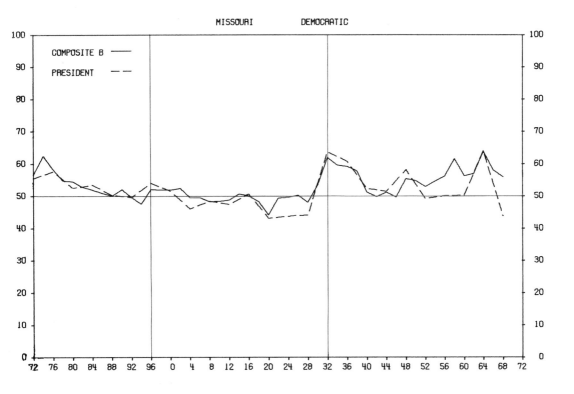

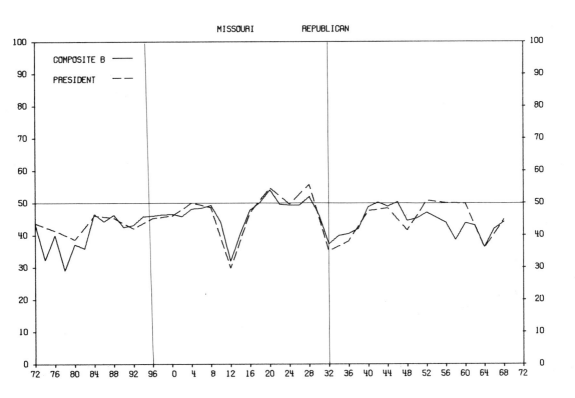

183

YEAR	PRESIDENT			GOVERNOR			SENATE CLASS I			SENATE CLASS II		
	DEM.	REP.	OTHER	DEM.	REP.	OTHER	DEM.	REP.	OTHER	DEM.	REP.	OTHER
1872												
1874												
1876												
1878												
1880												
1882												
1884												
1886												
1888												
1890				51.0	49.0	0.0						
1892	39.8	42.4	17.8	40.0	41.2	18.9						
1894												
1896	79.9	19.7	0.4	71.0	29.0	0.0						
1898												
1900	58.4	39.8	1.8	49.2	35.6	15.2						
1902												
1904	34.3	53.5	12.2	53.8	41.0	5.2						
1906												
1908	42.6	46.9	10.5	47.3	45.2	7.5						
1910												
1912	35.0	23.1	41.8	31.7	28.7	39.6						
1914												
1916	56.8	37.6	5.6	49.4	44.1	6.5	51.1	43.4	5.5			
1918										41.1	35.8	23.1
1920	32.1	61.0	6.8	40.3	59.7	0.0						
1922							55.4	43.6	1.0			
1924	19.4	42.5	38.1	51.0	42.6	6.3				52.8	42.4	4.8
1926												
1928	40.5	58.4	1.2	58.6	41.0	0.4	53.2	46.8	0.0			
1930										60.3	37.9	1.8
1932	58.8	36.0	5.2	48.5	46.7	4.8						
1934							70.1	28.7	1.1	59.6	39.5	0.9
1936	69.3	27.6	3.1	51.0	48.1	0.9				55.0	27.1	17.9
1938												
1940	58.8	40.2	1.0	48.6	50.7	0.7	73.4	26.6	0.0			
1942										49.1	48.4	2.6
1944	54.3	44.9	0.8	43.2	56.4	0.5						
1946							45.4	53.5	1.1			
1948	53.1	43.1	3.8	55.7	43.9	0.4				56.6	42.7	0.6
1950												
1952	40.1	59.4	0.5	49.0	51.0	0.0	50.7	48.6	0.7			
1954										50.4	49.6	0.0
1956	42.9	57.1	0.0	48.6	51.4	0.0						
1958							76.2	23.8	0.0			
1960	48.6	51.1	0.3	44.9	55.1	0.0				50.7	49.3	0.0
1962												
1964	58.9	40.6	0.5	48.7	51.3	0.0	64.5	35.5	0.0			
1966										53.2	46.8	0.0
1968	41.6	50.6	7.8	54.1	41.9	4.0						
1970							60.5	39.5	0.0			

184

MONTANA

YEAR	PRESIDENT			GOVERNOR			SENATE			HOUSE OF REPRESENTATIVES		
	DEM.	REP.	OTHER	DEM.	REP.	OTHER	DEM.	REP.	OTHER	DEM.	REP.	OTHER
1872												
1874												
1876												
1878												
1880												
1882												
1884												
1886												
1888												
1890				51.0	49.0	0.0				48.7	50.5	0.8
1892	39.8	42.4	17.8	40.0	41.2	18.9				41.0	41.4	17.6
1894	59.9	31.1	9.1	55.5	35.1	9.4				21.1	47.0	32.0
1896	79.9	19.7	0.4	71.0	29.0	0.0				78.1	21.9	0.0
1898	69.2	29.8	1.1	60.1	32.3	7.6				46.9	29.8	23.3
1900	58.4	39.8	1.8	49.3	35.6	15.2				45.8	37.8	16.4
1902	46.4	46.6	7.0	51.5	38.3	10.2				36.7	46.2	17.1
1904	34.3	53.5	12.2	53.8	41.0	5.2				42.0	51.7	6.3
1906	38.5	50.2	11.3	50.6	43.1	6.4				40.8	50.5	8.7
1908	42.6	46.9	10.5	47.3	45.2	7.5				43.2	48.9	7.9
1910	38.8	35.0	26.1	39.5	36.9	23.5				42.7	49.4	7.9
1912	35.1	23.1	41.8	31.7	28.7	39.6				34.6	29.6	35.9
1914	45.9	30.4	23.7	40.5	36.4	23.1	46.1	35.1	18.8	45.4	32.9	21.7
1916	56.8	37.6	5.6	49.4	44.1	6.5	51.1	43.4	5.5	49.0	45.5	5.5
1918	44.5	49.3	6.2	44.8	51.9	3.3	41.1	35.8	23.1	46.6	45.6	7.8
1920	32.1	61.0	6.8	40.3	59.7	0.0	48.2	39.7	12.1	38.2	61.8	0.0
1922	25.8	51.8	22.5	45.7	51.2	3.2	55.4	43.6	1.0	50.6	48.9	0.6
1924	19.4	42.5	38.1	51.0	42.6	6.4	52.8	42.4	4.8	45.9	49.9	4.3
1926	29.9	50.4	19.7	54.9	41.8	3.4	53.0	44.6	2.4	49.4	48.6	2.0
1928	40.5	58.4	1.2	58.7	41.0	0.4	53.2	46.8	0.0	42.7	56.9	0.5
1930	49.6	47.2	3.2	53.6	43.8	2.6	60.3	37.9	1.8	49.7	48.6	1.7
1932	58.8	36.0	5.2	48.5	46.7	4.8	62.7	35.9	1.4	55.2	41.8	3.1
1934	64.0	31.8	4.1	49.7	47.4	2.9	65.0	34.0	1.0	69.0	30.1	0.9
1936	69.3	27.6	3.1	51.0	48.1	0.9	55.0	27.1	17.9	64.3	35.4	0.4
1938	64.0	33.9	2.1	49.8	49.4	0.8	64.2	26.8	9.0	50.2	49.8	0.0
1940	58.8	40.2	1.1	48.6	50.7	0.7	73.4	26.6	0.0	54.8	44.7	0.5
1942	56.5	42.6	0.9	45.9	53.5	0.6	49.1	48.4	2.6	55.0	43.5	1.5
1944	54.3	44.9	0.8	43.2	56.4	0.5	47.2	50.9	1.9	59.9	39.3	0.8
1946	53.7	44.0	2.3	49.5	50.1	0.4	45.4	53.5	1.2	50.5	49.1	0.4
1948	53.1	43.2	3.8	55.7	43.9	0.4	56.7	42.7	0.6	57.3	42.4	0.2
1950	46.6	51.3	2.2	52.4	47.4	0.2	53.7	45.7	0.7	51.4	47.5	1.1
1952	40.1	59.4	0.5	49.0	51.0	0.0	50.8	48.6	0.7	43.3	56.4	0.4
1954	41.5	58.3	0.3	48.8	51.2	0.0	50.4	49.6	0.0	52.1	47.9	0.0
1956	42.9	57.1	0.0	48.6	51.4	0.0	63.3	36.7	0.0	55.6	44.4	0.0
1958	45.7	54.1	0.2	46.8	53.2	0.0	76.2	23.8	0.0	64.7	35.3	0.0
1960	48.6	51.1	0.3	44.9	55.1	0.0	50.7	49.3	0.0	50.9	49.1	0.0
1962	53.8	45.8	0.4	46.8	53.2	0.0	57.6	42.4	0.0	48.1	52.0	0.0
1964	59.0	40.6	0.5	48.7	51.3	0.0	64.5	35.5	0.0	49.3	50.5	0.2
1966	50.3	45.6	4.2	51.4	46.6	2.0	53.2	46.8	0.0	45.5	54.6	0.0
1968	41.6	50.6	7.8	54.1	41.9	4.0	56.9	43.2	0.0	43.5	56.5	0.0
1970							60.5	39.5	0.0	56.6	43.4	0.0

185

YEAR	COMPOSITE A (P+G+S+H/4)			COMPOSITE B (G+S+H/3)			COMPOSITE C (S+H/2)		
	DEM.	REP.	OTHER	DEM.	REP.	OTHER	DEM.	REP.	OTHER
1872									
1874									
1876									
1878									
1880									
1882									
1884									
1886									
1888									
1890				49.9	49.8	0.4	48.7	50.5	0.8
1892	40.3	41.7	18.1	40.5	41.3	18.2	41.0	41.4	17.6
1894	45.5	37.7	16.8	38.3	41.0	20.7	21.1	47.0	32.0
1896	76.4	23.5	0.1	74.6	25.4	0.0	78.1	21.9	0.0
1898	58.7	30.6	10.7	53.5	31.0	15.5	46.9	29.8	23.3
1900	51.2	37.7	11.1	47.5	36.7	15.8	45.8	37.8	16.4
1902	44.9	43.7	11.4	44.1	42.2	13.7	36.7	46.2	17.1
1904	43.4	48.7	7.9	47.9	46.4	5.8	42.0	51.7	6.3
1906	43.3	47.9	8.8	45.7	46.8	7.5	40.8	50.5	8.7
1908	44.4	47.0	8.6	45.3	47.0	7.7	43.2	48.9	7.9
1910	40.4	40.5	19.2	41.1	43.2	15.7	42.7	49.4	7.9
1912	33.8	27.1	39.1	33.1	29.1	37.7	34.6	29.6	35.9
1914	44.5	33.7	21.8	44.0	34.8	21.2	45.8	34.0	20.3
1916	51.6	42.6	5.8	49.8	44.3	5.9	50.0	44.4	5.5
1918	44.2	45.7	10.1	44.2	44.4	11.4	43.8	40.7	15.5
1920	39.7	55.6	4.7	42.2	53.8	4.0	43.2	50.8	6.0
1922	44.3	48.9	6.8	50.5	47.9	1.6	53.0	46.2	0.8
1924	42.3	44.3	13.4	49.9	45.0	5.2	49.3	46.1	4.6
1926	46.8	46.3	6.9	52.4	45.0	2.6	51.2	46.6	2.2
1928	48.8	50.8	0.5	51.5	48.2	0.3	47.9	51.8	0.2
1930	53.3	44.4	2.3	54.5	43.5	2.0	55.0	43.3	1.7
1932	56.3	40.1	3.6	55.5	41.5	3.1	58.9	38.9	2.2
1934	61.9	35.8	2.2	61.2	37.2	1.6	67.0	32.1	1.0
1936	59.9	34.5	5.6	56.7	36.9	6.4	59.6	31.2	9.1
1938	57.1	40.0	3.0	54.7	42.0	3.3	57.2	38.3	4.5
1940	58.9	40.5	0.6	59.0	40.6	0.4	64.1	35.6	0.3
1942	51.6	47.0	1.4	50.0	48.4	1.6	52.0	45.9	2.1
1944	51.2	47.9	1.0	50.1	48.9	1.0	53.6	45.1	1.3
1946	49.8	49.2	1.1	48.4	50.9	0.7	47.9	51.3	0.8
1948	55.7	43.1	1.3	56.6	43.0	0.4	57.0	42.6	0.4
1950	51.0	48.0	1.0	52.5	46.8	0.7	52.6	46.6	0.9
1952	45.8	53.8	0.4	47.7	52.0	0.4	47.0	52.5	0.5
1954	48.2	51.7	0.1	50.5	49.6	0.0	51.3	48.7	0.0
1956	52.6	47.4	0.0	55.9	44.1	0.0	59.5	40.5	0.0
1958	58.3	41.6	0.0	62.6	37.5	0.0	70.4	29.6	0.0
1960	48.8	51.1	0.1	48.9	51.2	0.0	50.8	49.2	0.0
1962	51.6	48.3	0.1	50.8	49.2	0.0	52.8	47.2	0.0
1964	55.4	44.5	0.2	54.2	45.8	0.1	56.9	43.0	0.1
1966	50.1	48.4	1.5	50.0	49.3	0.7	49.3	50.7	0.0
1968	49.0	48.0	3.0	51.5	47.2	1.3	50.2	49.8	0.0
1970							58.6	41.4	0.0

186

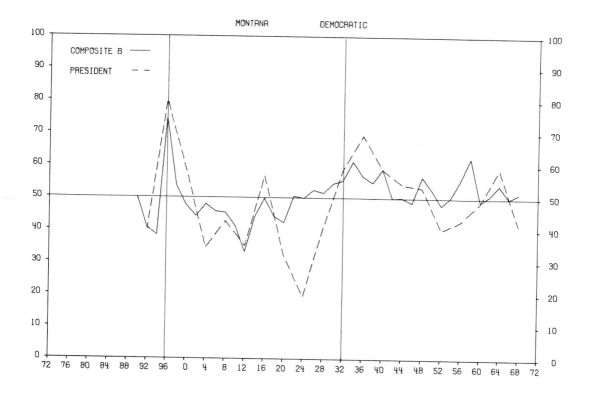

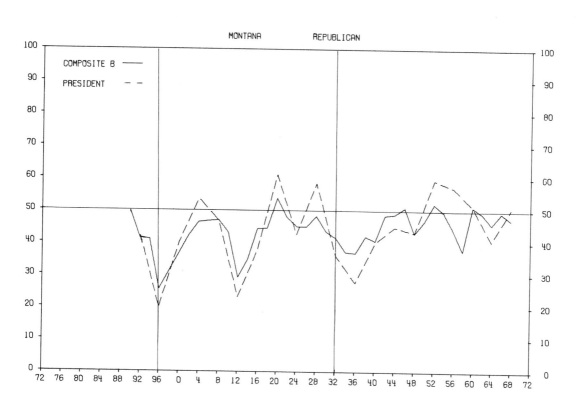

187

YEAR	PRESIDENT			GOVERNOR			SENATE CLASS I			SENATE CLASS II		
	DEM.	REP.	OTHER	DEM.	REP.	OTHER	DEM.	REP.	OTHER	DEM.	REP.	OTHER
1872	29.3	70.7	0.0	40.4	59.6	0.0						
1874				24.9	59.9	15.3						
1876	35.2	64.8	0.0	33.0	61.2	5.9						
1878				25.8	56.0	18.2						
1880	32.7	62.9	4.4	32.2	63.2	4.5						
1882				32.1	48.8	19.1						
1884	40.5	57.3	2.2	43.2	54.5	2.3						
1886				37.9	55.2	7.0						
1888	39.8	53.5	6.7	42.1	51.3	6.6						
1890				33.3	32.2	34.5						
1892	12.5	43.6	44.0	22.4	39.7	37.9						
1894				47.9	46.4	5.7						
1896	51.5	46.2	2.3	55.1	43.5	1.4						
1898				50.2	48.8	1.0						
1900	47.2	50.5	2.3	48.5	48.9	2.6						
1902				46.9	49.7	3.4						
1904	23.4	61.4	15.2	45.6	49.7	4.7						
1906				44.5	51.3	4.2						
1908	49.1	47.6	3.3	49.9	47.3	2.8						
1910				45.4	51.9	2.6						
1912	43.7	21.7	34.6	49.3	45.3	5.4						
1914				50.4	42.4	7.2						
1916	55.3	41.0	3.7	49.3	46.9	3.8	50.0	45.9	4.1			
1918				44.0	54.5	1.5				45.5	54.5	0.0
1920	31.3	64.7	4.1	34.5	40.4	25.1						
1922				54.6	42.0	3.4	38.2	56.8	4.9			
1924	29.6	47.2	23.1	41.0	51.1	7.9				37.6	62.4	0.0
1926				49.0	49.8	1.2						
1928	36.2	63.2	0.6	42.6	57.0	0.4	38.7	61.3	0.0			
1930				50.7	49.3	0.0				39.7	56.8	3.4
1932	63.0	35.3	1.7	52.5	46.3	1.2						
1934				50.8	47.7	1.4	55.9	43.2	1.0			
1936	57.1	40.7	2.1	55.9	43.1	1.0				18.4	37.8	43.8
1938				44.0	40.6	15.3						
1940	42.8	57.2	0.0	39.1	60.9	0.0	41.5	57.0	1.5			
1942				25.2	74.8	0.0				22.0	49.0	29.0
1944	41.4	58.6	0.0	23.9	76.1	0.0						
1946				34.5	65.5	0.0	29.2	70.8	0.0			
1948	45.8	54.2	0.0	39.9	60.1	0.0				43.3	56.7	0.0
1950				45.1	54.9	0.0						
1952	30.8	69.2	0.0	38.6	61.4	0.0	27.8	69.1	3.1	36.4	63.6	0.0
1954				39.7	60.3	0.0	39.1	60.9	0.0	40.6	59.4	0.0
1956	34.5	65.5	0.0	40.2	54.3	5.6						
1958				50.2	49.8	0.0	44.4	55.6	0.0			
1960	37.9	62.1	0.0	52.0	48.0	0.0				41.1	58.9	0.0
1962				52.2	47.8	0.0						
1964	52.6	47.4	0.0	60.0	40.0	0.0	38.6	61.4	0.0			
1966				38.5	61.5	0.0				38.8	61.2	0.0
1968	31.8	59.8	8.4									
1970				53.8	43.8	2.4	47.4	52.5	0.1			

NEBRASKA

YEAR	PRESIDENT			GOVERNOR			SENATE			HOUSE OF REPRESENTATIVES		
	DEM.	REP.	OTHER	DEM.	REP.	OTHER	DEM.	REP.	OTHER	DEM.	REP.	OTHER
1872	29.3	70.7	0.0	40.4	59.6	0.0				37.8	62.2	0.0
1874	32.3	67.7	0.0	24.9	59.9	15.3				23.3	62.7	14.1
1876	35.2	64.8	0.0	33.0	61.2	5.9				33.2	59.7	7.1
1878	33.9	63.9	2.2	25.8	56.1	18.2				43.3	56.4	0.3
1880	32.7	62.9	4.4	32.3	63.2	4.5				28.1	62.5	9.5
1882	36.6	60.1	3.3	32.1	48.8	19.1				29.2	46.9	23.9
1884	40.5	57.3	2.2	43.2	54.5	2.3				45.4	52.6	2.1
1886	40.1	55.4	4.5	37.9	55.2	7.0				44.6	48.8	6.6
1888	39.8	53.5	6.7	42.1	51.3	6.6				40.6	52.6	6.9
1890	26.1	48.5	25.4	33.3	32.2	34.5				42.8	34.3	22.9
1892	12.5	43.6	44.0	22.4	39.7	37.9				33.4	42.2	24.4
1894	32.0	44.9	23.1	48.0	46.4	5.7				32.3	49.4	18.3
1896	51.5	46.2	2.3	55.1	43.5	1.4				51.8	46.2	2.0
1898	49.4	48.3	2.3	50.2	48.8	1.0				50.4	49.6	0.0
1900	47.2	50.5	2.3	48.5	48.9	2.6				48.4	49.7	2.0
1902	35.3	55.9	8.7	46.9	49.7	3.4				46.3	51.0	2.8
1904	23.4	61.4	15.2	45.6	49.7	4.7				40.1	55.3	4.6
1906	36.3	54.5	9.2	44.5	51.3	4.3				45.0	52.7	2.2
1908	49.1	47.6	3.3	49.9	47.3	2.8				49.6	48.8	1.6
1910	46.4	34.7	18.9	45.5	51.9	2.7				48.4	49.1	2.5
1912	43.7	21.7	34.6	49.3	45.3	5.4				45.6	47.5	6.9
1914	49.5	31.4	19.2	50.4	42.4	7.2				48.1	47.4	4.5
1916	55.3	41.0	3.7	49.3	47.0	3.8	50.0	45.9	4.1	47.5	49.5	3.1
1918	43.3	52.8	3.9	44.0	54.5	1.5	45.5	54.5	0.0	43.6	56.0	0.5
1920	31.3	64.7	4.1	34.5	40.4	25.1	41.9	55.7	2.5	32.3	61.6	6.0
1922	30.4	56.0	13.6	54.6	42.0	3.4	38.2	56.8	4.9	46.2	47.7	6.2
1924	29.6	47.2	23.1	41.0	51.1	7.9	37.6	62.4	0.0	45.9	50.1	4.0
1926	32.9	55.2	11.9	49.0	49.8	1.2	38.2	61.9	0.0	49.6	48.3	2.1
1928	36.2	63.2	0.6	42.6	57.0	0.4	38.7	61.3	0.0	44.6	55.4	0.0
1930	49.6	49.2	1.2	50.8	49.3	0.0	39.7	56.8	3.4	52.1	47.9	0.0
1932	63.0	35.3	1.7	52.5	46.3	1.2	47.8	50.0	2.2	54.2	38.3	7.5
1934	60.1	38.0	1.9	50.8	47.7	1.4	55.9	43.2	1.0	51.8	46.5	1.8
1936	57.1	40.7	2.1	55.9	43.1	1.0	18.4	37.8	43.8	50.8	46.1	3.1
1938	50.0	49.0	1.1	44.0	40.6	15.4	29.9	47.4	22.7	45.7	51.9	2.4
1940	42.8	57.2	0.0	39.1	60.9	0.0	41.5	57.0	1.5	40.3	55.7	4.0
1942	42.1	57.9	0.0	25.2	74.8	0.0	22.0	49.0	29.0	34.2	63.8	2.0
1944	41.4	58.6	0.0	23.9	76.1	0.0	25.6	59.9	14.5	32.2	65.3	2.5
1946	43.6	56.4	0.0	34.5	65.5	0.0	29.2	70.8	0.0	31.9	66.9	1.2
1948	45.9	54.2	0.0	39.9	60.1	0.0	43.3	56.7	0.0	41.7	58.3	0.0
1950	38.4	61.7	0.0	45.1	54.9	0.0	37.7	61.5	0.8	37.7	62.3	0.0
1952	30.9	69.2	0.0	38.6	61.4	0.0	32.1	66.4	1.5	31.8	68.2	0.0
1954	32.7	67.3	0.0	39.7	60.3	0.0	40.1	59.9	0.0	38.4	61.6	0.0
1956	34.5	65.5	0.0	40.2	54.3	5.6	42.2	57.8	0.0	40.3	59.2	0.4
1958	36.2	63.8	0.0	50.2	49.8	0.0	44.4	55.6	0.0	47.0	53.0	0.0
1960	37.9	62.1	0.0	52.0	48.0	0.0	41.1	58.9	0.0	43.5	56.5	0.0
1962	45.3	54.7	0.0	52.2	47.8	0.0	39.9	60.2	0.0	37.0	61.1	2.0
1964	52.6	47.4	0.0	60.0	40.0	0.0	38.6	61.4	0.0	48.6	51.4	0.0
1966	42.2	53.6	4.2	38.5	61.5	0.0	38.8	61.2	0.0	37.9	62.1	0.0
1968	31.8	59.8	8.4	46.2	52.7	1.2	43.1	56.8	0.0	39.9	59.2	0.9
1970				53.8	43.8	2.4	47.4	52.5	0.1	36.7	54.1	9.2

189

NEBRASKA

YEAR	COMPOSITE A (P+G+S+H/4)			COMPOSITE B (G+S+H/3)			COMPOSITE C (S+H/2)		
	DEM.	REP.	OTHER	DEM.	REP.	OTHER	DEM.	REP.	OTHER
1872	35.9	64.2	0.0	39.1	60.9	0.0	37.8	62.2	0.0
1874	26.8	63.4	9.8	24.1	61.3	14.7	23.3	62.7	14.1
1876	33.8	61.9	4.3	33.1	60.4	6.5	33.2	59.7	7.1
1878	34.3	58.8	6.9	34.5	56.2	9.2	43.3	56.4	0.3
1880	31.0	62.9	6.1	30.2	62.9	7.0	28.1	62.5	9.5
1882	32.6	52.0	15.4	30.6	47.9	21.5	29.2	46.9	23.9
1884	43.0	54.8	2.2	44.3	53.5	2.2	45.4	52.6	2.1
1886	40.9	53.1	6.0	41.2	52.0	6.8	44.6	48.8	6.6
1888	40.8	52.4	6.8	41.3	51.9	6.8	40.6	52.6	6.9
1890	34.1	38.3	27.6	38.1	33.3	28.7	42.8	34.3	22.9
1892	22.7	41.8	35.4	27.9	41.0	31.2	33.4	42.2	24.4
1894	37.4	46.9	15.7	40.1	47.9	12.0	32.3	49.4	18.3
1896	52.8	45.3	1.9	53.4	44.9	1.7	51.8	46.2	2.0
1898	50.0	48.9	1.1	50.3	49.2	0.5	50.4	49.6	0.0
1900	48.0	49.7	2.3	48.4	49.3	2.3	48.4	49.7	2.0
1902	42.8	52.2	5.0	46.6	50.3	3.1	46.3	51.0	2.8
1904	36.4	55.4	8.2	42.9	52.5	4.7	40.1	55.3	4.6
1906	41.9	52.8	5.2	44.8	52.0	3.2	45.0	52.7	2.2
1908	49.6	47.9	2.6	49.8	48.0	2.2	49.6	48.8	1.6
1910	46.8	45.2	8.0	46.9	50.5	2.6	48.4	49.1	2.5
1912	46.2	38.2	15.6	47.4	46.4	6.2	45.6	47.5	6.9
1914	49.3	40.4	10.3	49.2	44.9	5.9	48.1	47.4	4.5
1916	50.5	45.8	3.7	48.9	47.4	3.7	48.7	47.7	3.6
1918	44.1	54.5	1.5	44.4	55.0	0.7	44.5	55.2	0.2
1920	35.0	55.6	9.4	36.2	52.6	11.2	37.1	58.7	4.3
1922	42.4	50.6	7.0	46.3	48.8	4.8	42.2	52.3	5.5
1924	38.5	52.7	8.8	41.5	54.5	4.0	41.7	56.3	2.0
1926	42.4	53.8	3.8	45.6	53.3	1.1	43.9	55.1	1.0
1928	40.5	59.2	0.3	42.0	57.9	0.1	41.7	58.4	0.0
1930	48.0	50.8	1.2	47.5	51.3	1.1	45.9	52.4	1.7
1932	54.4	42.5	3.2	51.5	44.9	3.6	51.0	44.1	4.9
1934	54.6	43.8	1.5	52.8	45.8	1.4	53.8	44.8	1.4
1936	45.6	41.9	12.5	41.7	42.3	16.0	34.6	41.9	23.5
1938	42.4	47.2	10.4	39.9	46.7	13.5	37.8	49.7	12.6
1940	40.9	57.7	1.4	40.3	57.8	1.9	40.9	56.3	2.8
1942	30.9	61.4	7.8	27.1	62.5	10.3	28.1	56.4	15.5
1944	30.8	65.0	4.2	27.2	67.1	5.7	28.9	62.6	8.5
1946	34.8	64.9	0.3	31.9	67.7	0.4	30.6	68.8	0.6
1948	42.7	57.3	0.0	41.6	58.4	0.0	42.5	57.5	0.0
1950	39.7	60.1	0.2	40.2	59.6	0.3	37.7	61.9	0.4
1952	33.3	66.3	0.4	34.1	65.4	0.5	31.9	67.3	0.8
1954	37.7	62.3	0.0	39.4	60.6	0.0	39.3	60.7	0.0
1956	39.3	59.2	1.5	40.9	57.1	2.0	41.3	58.5	0.2
1958	44.5	55.6	0.0	47.2	52.8	0.0	45.7	54.3	0.0
1960	43.6	56.4	0.0	45.5	54.5	0.0	42.3	57.7	0.0
1962	43.6	55.9	0.5	43.0	56.3	0.7	38.4	60.6	1.0
1964	50.0	50.0	0.0	49.1	50.9	0.0	43.6	56.4	0.0
1966	39.4	59.6	1.1	38.4	61.6	0.0	38.4	61.6	0.0
1968	40.3	57.1	2.6	43.1	56.2	0.7	41.5	58.0	0.5
1970				46.0	50.1	3.9	42.1	53.3	4.6

190

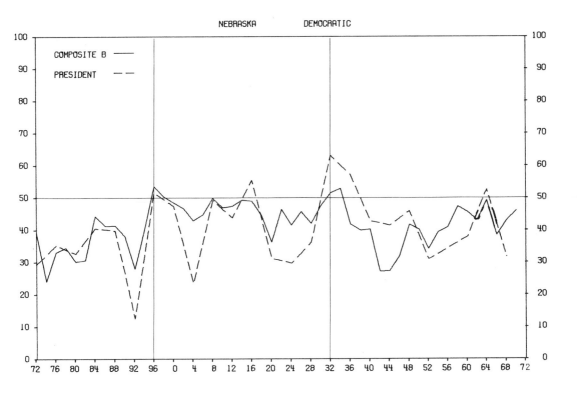

NEBRASKA   DEMOCRATIC

COMPOSITE B ———
PRESIDENT   — — —

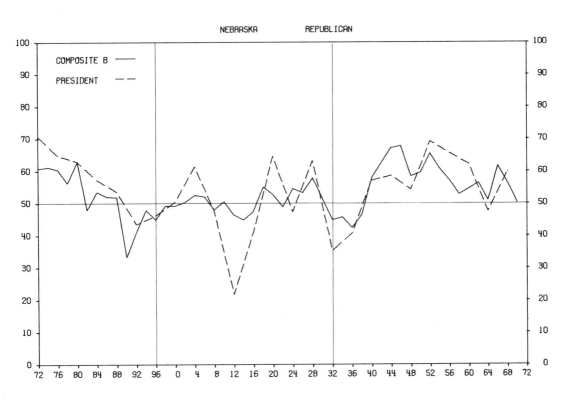

NEBRASKA   REPUBLICAN

COMPOSITE B ———
PRESIDENT   — — —

191

YEAR	PRESIDENT			GOVERNOR			SENATE CLASS I			SENATE CLASS III		
	DEM.	REP.	OTHER	DEM.	REP.	OTHER	DEM.	REP.	OTHER	DEM.	REP.	OTHER
1872	42.6	57.4	0.0									
1874				57.1	42.9	0.0						
1876	47.3	52.7	0.0									
1878				48.6	51.4	0.0						
1880	52.4	47.6	0.0									
1882				54.3	45.7	0.0						
1884	43.6	56.2	0.2									
1886				47.6	52.4	0.0						
1888	42.2	57.5	0.3									
1890				46.7	53.3	0.0						
1892	6.5	26.0	67.5									
1894				56.3	36.9	6.8						
1896	81.2	18.8	0.0									
1898				20.6	35.5	44.0						
1900	62.2	37.8	0.0									
1902				57.8	42.2	0.0						
1904	32.9	56.7	10.5									
1906				58.5	36.0	5.5						
1908	45.7	43.9	10.4									
1910				42.7	50.6	6.8						
1912	39.7	15.9	44.4									
1914				44.7	39.6	15.7				37.5	37.3	25.3
1916	53.4	36.4	10.2				38.8	32.3	28.9			
1918				52.1	47.9	0.0				47.7	31.5	20.8
1920	36.2	56.9	6.9							37.9	42.1	20.0
1922				53.9	46.1	0.0	62.8	37.2	0.0			
1924	21.9	41.8	36.3									
1926				47.0	53.0	0.0				42.5	55.8	1.7
1928	43.5	56.5	0.0				59.3	40.7	0.0			
1930				46.8	53.2	0.0						
1932	69.5	30.5	0.0							52.1	47.9	0.0
1934				53.9	34.5	11.5	64.5	33.4	2.1			
1936	72.8	27.2	0.0									
1938				61.9	38.1	0.0				59.0	41.0	0.0
1940	60.1	39.9	0.0				60.5	39.5	0.0			
1942				60.3	39.7	0.0	58.7	41.3	0.0			
1944	54.6	45.4	0.0							58.4	41.6	0.0
1946				57.4	42.6	0.0	44.8	55.2	0.0			
1948	50.4	47.3	2.4									
1950				42.4	57.6	0.0				58.0	42.0	0.0
1952	38.6	61.4	0.0				48.3	51.7	0.0			
1954				46.9	53.1	0.0				58.1	41.9	0.0
1956	42.0	58.0	0.0							52.6	47.4	0.0
1958				59.9	40.1	0.0	57.7	42.3	0.0			
1960	51.2	48.8	0.0									
1962				66.8	33.2	0.0				65.3	34.7	0.0
1964	58.6	41.4	0.0				50.0	50.0	0.0			
1966				47.8	52.2	0.0						
1968	39.3	47.5	13.2							54.8	45.2	0.0
1970				48.9	44.5	6.6	57.6	41.2	1.2			

NEVADA

YEAR	PRESIDENT			GOVERNOR			SENATE			HOUSE OF REPRESENTATIVES		
	DEM.	REP.	OTHER	DEM.	REP.	OTHER	DEM.	REP.	OTHER	DEM.	REP.	OTHER
1872	42.6	57.4	0.0	55.5	44.5	0.0				52.3	0.0	47.7
1874	44.9	55.1	0.0	57.1	42.9	0.0				47.9	52.1	0.0
1876	47.3	52.7	0.0	52.9	47.1	0.0				47.7	52.3	0.0
1878	49.8	50.2	0.0	48.6	51.4	0.0				48.2	51.8	0.0
1880	52.4	47.6	0.0	51.5	48.5	0.0				53.4	46.6	0.0
1882	48.0	51.9	0.1	54.3	45.7	0.0				54.4	45.6	0.0
1884	43.6	56.2	0.2	51.0	49.1	0.0				46.9	53.1	0.0
1886	42.9	56.8	0.3	47.6	52.4	0.0				45.8	54.2	0.0
1888	42.2	57.5	0.3	47.2	52.8	0.0				45.1	54.9	0.0
1890	24.3	41.7	33.9	46.7	53.3	0.0				46.3	53.4	0.3
1892	6.5	26.0	67.5	51.5	45.1	3.4				3.5	23.2	73.3
1894	43.8	22.4	33.8	56.3	36.9	6.8				46.5	26.9	26.7
1896	81.2	18.8	0.0	38.5	36.2	25.4				66.3	13.6	20.1
1898	71.7	28.3	0.0	20.6	35.5	44.0				65.0	0.0	35.1
1900	62.3	37.8	0.0	39.2	38.8	22.0				58.8	41.2	0.0
1902	47.6	47.2	5.2	57.8	42.2	0.0				53.6	46.5	0.0
1904	32.9	56.7	10.5	58.2	39.1	2.8				48.5	46.5	5.0
1906	39.3	50.3	10.4	58.5	36.0	5.5				51.4	39.8	8.8
1908	45.7	43.9	10.4	50.6	43.3	6.1				47.3	31.7	21.0
1910	42.7	29.9	27.4	42.7	50.6	6.8				38.1	49.9	12.0
1912	39.7	15.9	44.4	43.7	45.1	11.2				37.0	37.3	25.7
1914	46.5	26.2	27.3	44.7	39.6	15.7	37.5	37.3	25.3	37.8	42.0	20.2
1916	53.4	36.4	10.2	48.4	43.8	7.9	38.8	32.3	28.9	40.5	43.6	15.9
1918	44.8	46.7	8.6	52.1	47.9	0.0	47.7	31.5	20.8	51.3	43.2	5.6
1920	36.2	56.9	6.9	53.0	47.0	0.0	37.9	42.1	20.0	34.1	48.9	17.0
1922	29.1	49.3	21.6	53.9	46.1	0.0	62.8	37.2	0.0	57.0	43.0	0.0
1924	22.0	41.8	36.3	50.4	49.6	0.0	52.7	46.5	0.9	49.6	50.4	0.0
1926	32.7	49.2	18.1	47.0	53.0	0.0	42.5	55.8	1.7	42.3	57.7	0.0
1928	43.5	56.5	0.0	46.9	53.1	0.0	59.3	40.7	0.0	41.4	58.6	0.0
1930	56.5	43.5	0.0	46.8	53.3	0.0	55.7	44.3	0.0	45.6	54.4	0.0
1932	69.5	30.5	0.0	50.3	43.9	5.8	52.1	47.9	0.0	60.8	39.2	0.0
1934	71.2	28.9	0.0	53.9	34.5	11.5	64.5	33.4	2.1	71.2	28.8	0.0
1936	72.8	27.2	0.0	57.9	36.3	5.8	61.7	37.2	1.1	58.4	26.9	14.7
1938	66.4	33.6	0.0	61.9	38.1	0.0	59.0	41.0	0.0	66.4	33.6	0.0
1940	60.1	39.9	0.0	61.1	38.9	0.0	60.5	39.5	0.0	64.5	35.5	0.0
1942	57.4	42.7	0.0	60.3	39.8	0.0	58.7	41.3	0.0	53.6	46.4	0.0
1944	54.6	45.4	0.0	58.8	41.2	0.0	58.4	41.6	0.0	63.1	36.9	0.0
1946	52.5	46.3	1.2	57.4	42.6	0.0	44.8	55.2	0.0	41.2	58.8	0.0
1948	50.4	47.3	2.4	49.9	50.1	0.0	51.4	48.6	0.0	50.7	49.4	0.0
1950	44.5	54.4	1.2	42.4	57.6	0.0	58.0	42.0	0.0	52.8	47.2	0.0
1952	38.6	61.5	0.0	44.6	55.4	0.0	48.3	51.7	0.0	49.5	50.5	0.0
1954	40.3	59.7	0.0	46.9	53.1	0.0	58.1	41.9	0.0	45.5	54.5	0.0
1956	42.0	58.0	0.0	53.4	46.6	0.0	52.6	47.4	0.0	54.2	45.8	0.0
1958	46.6	53.4	0.0	59.9	40.1	0.0	57.7	42.3	0.0	66.9	33.1	0.0
1960	51.2	48.8	0.0	63.4	36.6	0.0	61.5	38.5	0.0	57.5	42.5	0.0
1962	54.9	45.1	0.0	66.8	33.2	0.0	65.3	34.7	0.0	71.7	28.4	0.0
1964	58.6	41.4	0.0	57.3	42.7	0.0	50.0	50.0	0.0	63.3	36.7	0.0
1966	48.9	44.4	6.6	47.8	52.2	0.0	52.4	47.6	0.0	67.6	32.4	0.0
1968	39.3	47.5	13.3	48.0	48.0	4.1	54.8	45.2	0.0	72.1	27.9	0.0
1970				48.1	43.8	8.1	57.7	41.2	1.2	82.5	17.5	0.0

NEVADA

YEAR	COMPOSITE A (P+G+S+H/4)			COMPOSITE B (G+S+H/3)			COMPOSITE C (S+H/2)		
	DEM.	REP.	OTHER	DEM.	REP.	OTHER	DEM.	REP.	OTHER
1872	50.2	34.0	15.9	53.9	22.2	23.8	52.3	0.0	47.7
1874	50.0	50.0	0.0	52.5	47.5	0.0	47.9	52.1	0.0
1876	49.3	50.7	0.0	50.3	49.7	0.0	47.7	52.3	0.0
1878	48.9	51.1	0.0	48.4	51.6	0.0	48.2	51.8	0.0
1880	52.4	47.6	0.0	52.4	47.6	0.0	53.4	46.6	0.0
1882	52.3	47.7	0.0	54.4	45.6	0.0	54.4	45.6	0.0
1884	47.2	52.8	0.1	48.9	51.1	0.0	46.9	53.1	0.0
1886	45.5	54.5	0.1	46.7	53.3	0.0	45.8	54.2	0.0
1888	44.8	55.1	0.1	46.1	53.9	0.0	45.1	54.9	0.0
1890	39.1	49.5	11.4	46.5	53.3	0.1	46.3	53.4	0.3
1892	20.5	31.4	48.1	27.5	34.1	38.4	3.5	23.2	73.3
1894	48.9	28.7	22.4	51.4	31.9	16.7	46.5	26.9	26.7
1896	62.0	22.9	15.2	52.4	24.9	22.7	66.3	13.6	20.1
1898	52.4	21.3	26.4	42.8	17.7	39.5	65.0	0.0	35.1
1900	53.4	39.3	7.3	49.0	40.0	11.0	58.8	41.2	0.0
1902	53.0	45.3	1.8	55.7	44.3	0.0	53.6	46.5	0.0
1904	46.5	47.4	6.1	53.3	42.8	3.9	48.5	46.5	5.0
1906	49.8	42.0	8.2	55.0	37.9	7.1	51.4	39.8	8.8
1908	47.9	39.7	12.5	48.9	37.5	13.6	47.3	31.7	21.0
1910	41.2	43.5	15.4	40.4	50.3	9.4	38.1	49.9	12.0
1912	40.1	32.8	27.1	40.3	41.2	18.5	37.0	37.3	25.7
1914	41.6	36.3	22.1	40.0	39.6	20.4	37.6	39.6	22.8
1916	45.3	39.0	15.7	42.6	39.9	17.5	39.7	38.0	22.4
1918	49.0	42.3	8.7	50.4	40.9	8.8	49.5	37.3	13.2
1920	40.3	48.8	10.9	41.7	46.0	12.3	36.0	45.5	18.5
1922	50.7	43.9	5.4	57.9	42.1	0.0	59.9	40.1	0.0
1924	43.7	47.1	9.3	50.9	48.8	0.3	51.1	48.5	0.4
1926	41.1	53.9	5.0	43.9	55.5	0.6	42.4	56.7	0.9
1928	47.8	52.3	0.0	49.2	50.8	0.0	50.3	49.7	0.0
1930	51.1	48.9	0.0	49.4	50.7	0.0	50.7	49.4	0.0
1932	58.2	40.4	1.4	54.4	43.7	1.9	56.4	43.6	0.0
1934	65.2	31.4	3.4	63.2	32.2	4.6	67.9	31.1	1.1
1936	62.7	31.9	5.4	59.3	33.5	7.2	60.1	32.1	7.9
1938	63.4	36.6	0.0	62.4	37.6	0.0	62.7	37.3	0.0
1940	61.5	38.5	0.0	62.0	38.0	0.0	62.5	37.5	0.0
1942	57.5	42.5	0.0	57.5	42.5	0.0	56.1	43.9	0.0
1944	58.7	41.3	0.0	60.1	39.9	0.0	60.7	39.3	0.0
1946	49.0	50.7	0.3	47.8	52.2	0.0	43.0	57.0	0.0
1948	50.6	48.8	0.6	50.7	49.4	0.0	51.0	49.0	0.0
1950	49.4	50.3	0.3	51.1	49.0	0.0	55.4	44.6	0.0
1952	45.3	54.7	0.0	47.5	52.5	0.0	48.9	51.1	0.0
1954	47.7	52.3	0.0	50.2	49.8	0.0	51.8	48.2	0.0
1956	50.6	49.4	0.0	53.4	46.6	0.0	53.4	46.6	0.0
1958	57.8	42.2	0.0	61.5	38.5	0.0	62.3	37.7	0.0
1960	58.4	41.6	0.0	60.8	39.2	0.0	59.5	40.5	0.0
1962	64.7	35.3	0.0	67.9	32.1	0.0	68.5	31.5	0.0
1964	57.3	42.7	0.0	56.9	43.1	0.0	56.7	43.3	0.0
1966	54.2	44.1	1.7	56.0	44.0	0.0	60.0	40.0	0.0
1968	53.5	42.1	4.3	58.3	40.4	1.4	63.5	36.6	0.0
1970				62.7	34.2	3.1	70.1	29.4	0.6

194

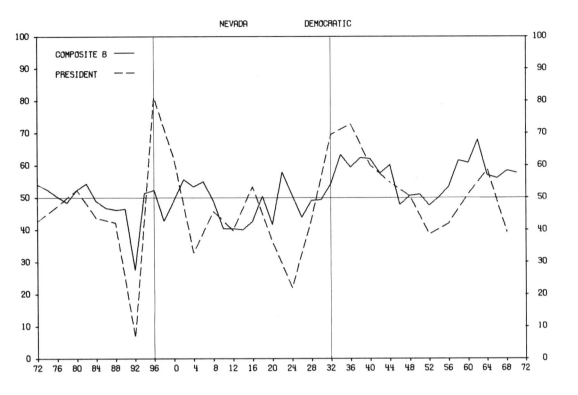

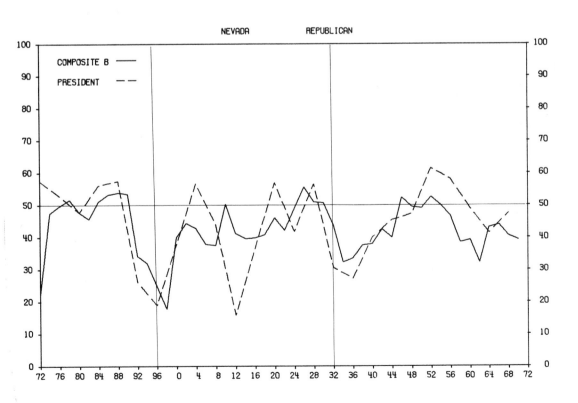

YEAR	PRESIDENT			GOVERNOR			SENATE CLASS II			SENATE CLASS III		
	DEM.	REP.	OTHER	DEM.	REP.	OTHER	DEM.	REP.	OTHER	DEM.	REP.	OTHER
1872	45.6	53.9	0.5	47.9	50.8	1.3						
1874				48.4	48.8	2.8						
1876	48.1	51.8	0.1	48.4	50.8	0.8						
1878				45.6	51.1	3.3						
1880	47.2	51.9	0.8	47.4	51.6	1.1						
1882				48.4	50.4	1.2						
1884	46.3	51.1	2.5	46.9	50.3	2.7						
1886				48.2	48.9	2.9						
1888	47.8	50.4	1.8	48.8	49.4	1.8						
1890				49.1	49.3	1.6						
1892	47.1	51.1	1.8	47.7	50.2	2.2						
1894				40.9	56.0	3.1						
1896	25.4	68.7	5.9	36.0	61.4	2.6						
1898				43.2	54.2	2.5						
1900	38.4	59.3	2.2	38.5	59.4	2.1						
1902				42.7	53.2	4.1						
1904	37.8	60.1	2.1	40.0	57.8	2.1						
1906				46.2	49.8	4.0						
1908	37.6	59.3	3.1	46.7	50.4	2.9						
1910				44.8	53.4	1.8						
1912	39.5	37.4	23.1	41.1	39.0	19.9						
1914				40.0	55.2	4.8				44.6	51.7	3.7
1916	49.1	49.1	1.8	45.1	53.2	1.8						
1918				45.9	54.1	0.0	46.4	53.6	0.0	49.2	50.8	0.0
1920	39.4	59.8	0.8	39.7	59.6	0.7				41.6	57.7	0.6
1922				53.3	46.7	0.0						
1924	34.7	59.8	5.5	46.1	53.9	0.0	40.2	59.8	0.0			
1926				40.3	59.7	0.0				37.7	62.3	0.0
1928	41.0	58.7	0.3	42.3	57.5	0.2						
1930				41.8	58.0	0.2	41.9	57.9	0.2			
1932	49.0	50.4	0.6	45.4	54.2	0.4				50.3	49.3	0.4
1934				49.2	50.5	0.3						
1936	49.7	48.0	2.3	42.6	56.6	0.8	47.7	51.9	0.5			
1938				42.8	57.1	0.1				45.8	54.2	0.0
1940	53.2	46.8	0.0	49.3	50.7	0.0						
1942				47.8	52.2	0.0	45.4	54.6	0.0			
1944	52.1	47.9	0.0	46.9	53.1	0.0				49.1	50.9	0.0
1946				36.9	63.1	0.0						
1948	46.7	52.4	0.9	47.3	52.2	0.5	41.2	58.1	0.7			
1950				43.0	57.0	0.0				38.0	55.7	6.3
1952	39.1	60.9	0.0	36.9	63.1	0.0						
1954				44.9	55.1	0.0	39.8	60.2	0.0	39.8	60.2	0.0
1956	33.8	66.1	0.0	45.3	54.7	0.0				35.9	64.1	0.0
1958				48.3	51.7	0.0						
1960	46.6	53.4	0.0	44.5	55.5	0.0	39.7	60.3	0.0			
1962				58.9	41.1	0.0	52.3	47.7	0.0	40.3	59.7	0.0
1964	63.6	36.4	0.0	66.8	33.2	0.0						
1966				53.9	46.1	0.0	54.0	45.9	0.1			
1968	43.9	52.1	4.0	47.4	52.5	0.0				40.7	59.3	0.0
1970				44.1	46.0	9.9						

YEAR	PRESIDENT			GOVERNOR			SENATE			HOUSE OF REPRESENTATIVES		
	DEM.	REP.	OTHER	DEM.	REP.	OTHER	DEM.	REP.	OTHER	DEM.	REP.	OTHER
1872	45.6	53.9	0.5	47.9	50.8	1.3				50.4	48.5	1.2
1874	46.8	52.9	0.3	48.4	48.8	2.8				49.1	49.1	1.8
1876	48.1	51.8	0.1	48.4	50.8	0.8				49.7	49.4	0.9
1878	47.7	51.9	0.5	45.6	51.1	3.3				45.2	50.7	4.1
1880	47.2	51.9	0.8	47.4	51.6	1.1				47.4	51.7	0.9
1882	46.8	51.5	1.7	48.4	50.4	1.2				45.9	53.2	0.9
1884	46.3	51.1	2.5	46.9	50.3	2.8				46.1	51.6	2.3
1886	47.1	50.8	2.2	48.2	48.9	2.9				48.0	49.2	2.9
1888	47.8	50.4	1.8	48.8	49.5	1.8				48.4	49.9	1.7
1890	47.5	50.8	1.8	49.2	49.3	1.6				50.2	48.4	1.4
1892	47.1	51.1	1.8	47.7	50.2	2.2				48.4	49.6	2.1
1894	36.3	59.9	3.9	40.9	56.0	3.1				41.0	56.3	2.7
1896	25.4	68.7	5.9	36.0	61.4	2.6				33.8	63.6	2.6
1898	31.9	64.0	4.1	43.2	54.2	2.5				44.0	53.8	2.2
1900	38.4	59.3	2.3	38.5	59.4	2.1				38.7	59.3	2.0
1902	38.1	59.7	2.2	42.8	53.2	4.1				39.2	58.0	2.8
1904	37.8	60.1	2.1	40.1	57.8	2.1				38.2	59.8	2.0
1906	37.7	59.7	2.6	46.2	49.8	4.0				39.6	57.9	2.5
1908	37.6	59.3	3.1	46.7	50.4	2.9				39.3	58.1	2.7
1910	38.5	48.4	13.1	44.8	53.4	1.8				45.8	52.7	1.5
1912	39.5	37.4	23.1	41.1	39.0	19.9				49.5	42.9	7.6
1914	44.3	43.3	12.5	40.0	55.2	4.8	44.6	51.7	3.7	43.4	52.3	4.2
1916	49.1	49.1	1.8	45.1	53.2	1.8	46.2	51.9	1.9	46.7	51.6	1.7
1918	44.3	54.5	1.3	45.9	54.1	0.0	47.8	52.2	0.0	45.8	54.3	0.0
1920	39.4	59.8	0.8	39.7	59.6	0.7	41.6	57.7	0.6	39.3	60.4	0.4
1922	37.1	59.8	3.1	53.3	46.7	0.0	40.9	58.7	0.3	51.0	49.0	0.0
1924	34.7	59.8	5.5	46.1	53.9	0.0	40.2	59.8	0.0	41.8	58.3	0.0
1926	37.9	59.2	2.9	40.3	59.7	0.0	37.7	62.3	0.0	37.8	62.2	0.0
1928	41.0	58.7	0.3	42.3	57.5	0.2	39.8	60.1	0.1	41.2	58.8	0.1
1930	45.0	54.5	0.5	41.8	58.0	0.2	41.9	57.9	0.2	42.2	57.9	0.0
1932	49.0	50.4	0.6	45.4	54.2	0.4	50.4	49.3	0.4	49.1	50.7	0.3
1934	49.4	49.2	1.4	49.2	50.6	0.3	49.0	50.6	0.4	50.3	49.4	0.2
1936	49.7	48.0	2.3	42.6	56.6	0.8	47.7	51.9	0.5	47.5	51.8	0.7
1938	51.5	47.4	1.2	42.8	57.1	0.1	45.8	54.2	0.0	43.7	56.4	0.0
1940	53.2	46.8	0.0	49.3	50.7	0.0	45.6	54.4	0.0	48.0	52.0	0.0
1942	52.7	47.3	0.0	47.8	52.2	0.0	45.4	54.6	0.0	45.0	55.1	0.0
1944	52.1	47.9	0.0	46.9	53.1	0.0	49.1	50.9	0.0	47.4	52.6	0.0
1946	49.4	50.1	0.5	36.9	63.1	0.0	45.1	54.5	0.4	38.0	62.0	0.0
1948	46.7	52.4	0.9	47.3	52.2	0.5	41.2	58.1	0.7	42.9	56.4	0.7
1950	42.9	56.7	0.5	43.0	57.0	0.0	38.0	55.7	6.3	39.3	60.7	0.0
1952	39.1	60.9	0.0	36.9	63.2	0.0	38.9	58.0	3.1	36.9	63.1	0.0
1954	36.5	63.5	0.0	44.9	55.1	0.0	39.8	60.2	0.0	45.3	54.7	0.0
1956	33.8	66.1	0.0	45.3	54.7	0.0	35.9	64.1	0.0	38.7	61.4	0.0
1958	40.2	59.8	0.0	48.4	51.7	0.0	37.8	62.2	0.0	41.2	58.4	0.4
1960	46.6	53.4	0.0	44.5	55.5	0.0	39.7	60.4	0.0	41.8	58.3	0.0
1962	55.1	44.9	0.0	58.9	41.1	0.0	46.3	53.7	0.0	45.0	55.1	0.0
1964	63.6	36.4	0.0	66.8	33.2	0.0	50.2	49.8	0.0	50.7	49.3	0.0
1966	53.8	44.2	2.0	53.9	46.1	0.0	54.0	45.9	0.1	39.2	60.8	0.1
1968	43.9	52.1	4.0	47.4	52.5	0.0	40.7	59.3	0.0	33.2	66.8	0.0
1970				44.1	46.0	9.9				31.5	68.5	0.0

YEAR	COMPOSITE A (P+G+S+H/4)			COMPOSITE B (G+S+H/3)			COMPOSITE C (S+H/2)		
	DEM.	REP.	OTHER	DEM.	REP.	OTHER	DEM.	REP.	OTHER
1872	48.0	51.1	1.0	49.2	49.6	1.2	50.4	48.5	1.2
1874	48.1	50.3	1.6	48.8	49.0	2.3	49.1	49.1	1.8
1876	48.7	50.7	0.6	49.1	50.1	0.8	49.7	49.4	0.9
1878	46.2	51.2	2.6	45.4	50.9	3.7	45.2	50.7	4.1
1880	47.3	51.7	0.9	47.4	51.6	1.0	47.4	51.7	0.9
1882	47.0	51.7	1.3	47.1	51.8	1.1	45.9	53.2	0.9
1884	46.5	51.0	2.5	46.5	51.0	2.5	46.1	51.6	2.3
1886	47.8	49.6	2.6	48.1	49.0	2.9	48.0	49.2	2.9
1888	48.3	49.9	1.8	48.6	49.7	1.7	48.4	49.9	1.7
1890	48.9	49.5	1.6	49.7	48.8	1.5	50.2	48.4	1.4
1892	47.7	50.3	2.0	48.0	49.9	2.1	48.4	49.6	2.1
1894	39.4	57.4	3.2	41.0	56.1	2.9	41.0	56.3	2.7
1896	31.7	64.6	3.7	34.9	62.5	2.6	33.8	63.6	2.6
1898	39.7	57.3	2.9	43.6	54.0	2.4	44.0	53.8	2.2
1900	38.5	59.3	2.1	38.6	59.3	2.1	38.7	59.3	2.0
1902	40.0	57.0	3.0	41.0	55.6	3.4	39.2	58.0	2.8
1904	38.7	59.2	2.1	39.2	58.8	2.0	38.2	59.8	2.0
1906	41.2	55.8	3.1	42.9	53.9	3.3	39.6	57.9	2.5
1908	41.2	55.9	2.9	43.0	54.2	2.8	39.3	58.1	2.7
1910	43.1	51.5	5.5	45.3	53.0	1.6	45.8	52.7	1.5
1912	43.3	39.8	16.9	45.3	41.0	13.8	49.5	42.9	7.6
1914	43.1	50.6	6.3	42.7	53.1	4.2	44.0	52.0	4.0
1916	46.8	51.4	1.8	46.0	52.2	1.8	46.5	51.8	1.8
1918	45.9	53.8	0.3	46.5	53.5	0.0	46.8	53.2	0.0
1920	40.0	59.4	0.6	40.2	59.2	0.6	40.5	59.0	0.5
1922	45.6	53.6	0.9	48.4	51.5	0.1	46.0	53.9	0.2
1924	40.7	57.9	1.4	42.7	57.3	0.0	41.0	59.0	0.0
1926	38.4	60.9	0.7	38.6	61.4	0.0	37.7	62.3	0.0
1928	41.1	58.8	0.2	41.1	58.8	0.1	40.5	59.4	0.1
1930	42.7	57.1	0.2	42.0	57.9	0.2	42.0	57.9	0.1
1932	48.5	51.1	0.4	48.3	51.4	0.4	49.7	50.0	0.3
1934	49.5	49.9	0.6	49.5	50.2	0.3	49.7	50.0	0.3
1936	46.9	52.1	1.1	45.9	53.4	0.7	47.6	51.8	0.6
1938	45.9	53.8	0.3	44.1	55.9	0.0	44.7	55.3	0.0
1940	49.0	51.0	0.0	47.6	52.4	0.0	46.8	53.2	0.0
1942	47.7	52.3	0.0	46.1	53.9	0.0	45.2	54.8	0.0
1944	48.9	51.1	0.0	47.8	52.2	0.0	48.3	51.8	0.0
1946	42.3	57.5	0.2	40.0	59.9	0.1	41.6	58.3	0.2
1948	44.5	54.8	0.7	43.8	55.6	0.6	42.0	57.3	0.7
1950	40.8	57.5	1.7	40.1	57.8	2.1	38.7	58.2	3.1
1952	37.9	61.3	0.8	37.6	61.4	1.1	37.9	60.5	1.6
1954	41.6	58.4	0.0	43.3	56.7	0.0	42.6	57.5	0.0
1956	38.4	61.6	0.0	40.0	60.1	0.0	37.3	62.7	0.0
1958	41.9	58.0	0.1	42.4	57.4	0.2	39.5	60.3	0.2
1960	43.1	56.9	0.0	42.0	58.0	0.0	40.7	59.3	0.0
1962	51.3	48.7	0.0	50.1	50.0	0.0	45.6	54.4	0.0
1964	57.8	42.2	0.0	55.9	44.1	0.0	50.4	49.6	0.0
1966	50.2	49.3	0.5	49.0	50.9	0.1	46.6	53.3	0.1
1968	41.3	57.7	1.0	40.5	59.5	0.0	37.0	63.0	0.0
1970				37.8	57.3	5.0	31.5	68.5	0.0

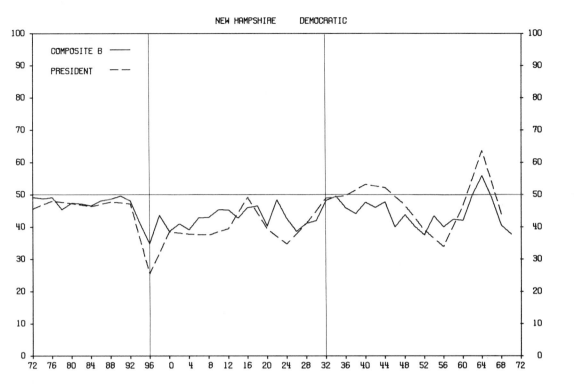

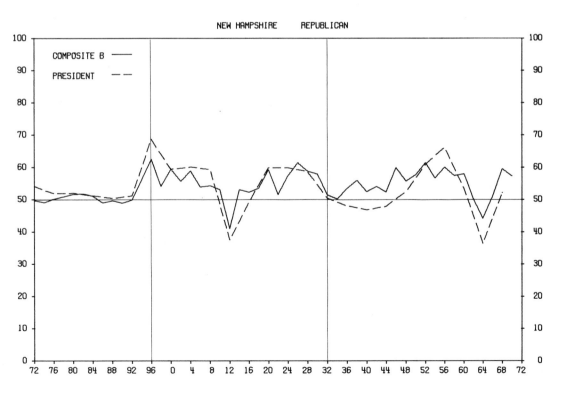

NEW JERSEY

YEAR	PRESIDENT			GOVERNOR			SENATE CLASS I			SENATE CLASS II		
	DEM.	REP.	OTHER	DEM.	REP.	OTHER	DEM.	REP.	OTHER	DEM.	REP.	OTHER
1872	45.5	54.5	0.0	51.9	48.1	0.0						
1874				53.6	46.4	0.0						
1876	52.7	47.0	0.3									
1878				51.6	44.9	3.4						
1880	49.8	49.0	1.1	49.5	49.3	1.2						
1882												
1884	49.0	47.3	3.7	49.9	46.7	3.4						
1886				47.4	44.0	8.6						
1888	49.9	47.5	2.6									
1890				51.4	46.1	2.6						
1892	50.7	46.2	3.1	49.7	47.4	3.0						
1894												
1896	36.0	59.7	4.3	43.6	52.3	4.1						
1898				47.3	48.9	3.8						
1900	41.1	55.3	3.6									
1902				46.1	50.9	3.0						
1904	38.1	56.7	5.2	41.6	53.5	4.9						
1906												
1908	39.1	56.8	4.1	47.3	49.3	3.5						
1910				53.9	42.6	3.5						
1912	41.2	20.5	38.3									
1914				46.1	37.4	16.5						
1916	42.7	54.4	2.9	39.8	55.4	4.7	38.9	56.0	5.1			
1918							44.6	49.2	6.2	43.2	50.3	6.4
1920	28.4	67.7	3.9	49.2	45.9	4.9						
1922				52.2	46.8	1.0	54.9	44.0	1.1			
1924	27.4	62.2	10.4							33.7	61.8	4.5
1926				51.9	47.6	0.5						
1928	39.8	59.8	0.4	44.7	54.9	0.4	41.8	57.9	0.3			
1930										38.8	58.8	2.4
1932	49.5	47.6	2.9	57.8	39.7	2.4				48.5	49.6	1.9
1934				49.0	49.9	1.1	57.9	40.8	1.2			
1936	59.6	39.5	0.9							54.9	44.3	0.8
1938				50.8	47.8	1.4	45.7	53.0	1.3			
1940	51.5	47.9	0.7	51.4	48.0	0.6	44.1	55.1	0.8			
1942										45.8	53.1	1.1
1944	50.3	49.0	0.7	44.1	55.2	0.7	48.8	50.4	0.7			
1946				41.4	57.1	1.5	40.1	58.5	1.4			
1948	45.9	50.3	3.7							47.3	50.0	2.7
1950				47.1	51.5	1.3						
1952	42.0	56.8	1.2				43.6	55.5	0.9			
1954				53.2	44.7	2.2				48.5	48.7	2.9
1956	34.2	64.7	1.1									
1958				54.6	44.5	1.0	51.4	46.9	1.7			
1960	50.0	49.2	0.9							43.2	55.7	1.1
1962				50.4	48.7	0.9						
1964	65.6	33.9	0.5				61.9	37.3	0.8			
1966				57.4	41.1	1.5				37.0	60.0	3.0
1968	44.0	46.1	9.9									
1970				39.2	60.8	0.0	54.0	42.2	3.8			

200

NEW JERSEY

YEAR	PRESIDENT			GOVERNOR			SENATE			HOUSE OF REPRESENTATIVES		
	DEM.	REP.	OTHER	DEM.	REP.	OTHER	DEM.	REP.	OTHER	DEM.	REP.	OTHER
1872	45.5	54.5	0.0	51.9	48.1	0.0				44.7	55.3	0.0
1874	49.1	50.8	0.2	53.7	46.4	0.0				52.7	47.4	0.0
1876	52.7	47.0	0.3	52.7	45.6	1.7				52.8	41.5	5.7
1878	51.3	48.0	0.7	51.7	44.9	3.4				40.8	46.2	13.0
1880	49.8	49.0	1.1	49.5	49.3	1.2				49.8	49.0	1.2
1882	49.4	48.2	2.4	49.7	48.0	2.3				48.5	47.5	4.0
1884	49.0	47.3	3.7	49.9	46.7	3.4				49.1	48.0	3.0
1886	49.4	47.4	3.1	47.4	44.0	8.6				42.6	45.6	11.8
1888	49.9	47.5	2.6	49.4	45.0	5.6				47.5	48.1	4.3
1890	50.3	46.9	2.8	51.4	46.1	2.6				51.0	45.6	3.4
1892	50.7	46.2	3.1	49.7	47.4	3.0				49.8	47.2	3.0
1894	43.4	53.0	3.7	46.7	49.8	3.5				38.9	55.3	5.8
1896	36.0	59.7	4.3	43.6	52.3	4.1				36.1	59.7	4.1
1898	38.6	57.5	4.0	47.3	48.9	3.8				46.6	49.7	3.7
1900	41.1	55.3	3.6	46.7	49.9	3.4				41.4	55.2	3.4
1902	39.6	56.0	4.4	46.1	50.9	3.0				45.5	50.9	3.6
1904	38.1	56.7	5.2	41.6	53.5	4.9				40.2	54.8	5.0
1906	38.6	56.8	4.7	44.4	51.4	4.2				47.2	48.1	4.8
1908	39.1	56.8	4.1	47.3	49.3	3.5				44.7	52.3	3.0
1910	40.1	38.7	21.2	53.9	42.6	3.5				52.5	43.6	3.9
1912	41.2	20.5	38.3	50.0	40.0	10.0				47.3	31.4	21.3
1914	41.9	37.5	20.6	46.1	37.4	16.5				44.4	46.1	9.5
1916	42.7	54.4	2.9	39.8	55.4	4.7	38.9	56.0	5.1	42.5	51.3	6.2
1918	35.6	61.0	3.4	44.5	50.7	4.8	43.9	49.8	6.3	45.5	49.6	4.9
1920	28.4	67.7	3.9	49.2	45.9	4.9	49.4	46.9	3.7	35.3	61.8	2.9
1922	27.9	64.9	7.2	52.2	46.8	1.0	54.9	44.1	1.1	44.6	49.6	5.8
1924	27.4	62.2	10.4	52.0	47.2	0.7	33.7	61.8	4.5	36.4	61.7	2.0
1926	33.6	61.0	5.4	51.9	47.6	0.5	37.8	59.9	2.4	42.9	56.6	0.5
1928	39.8	59.8	0.4	44.7	54.9	0.4	41.8	57.9	0.3	39.3	60.6	0.1
1930	44.6	53.7	1.7	51.3	47.3	1.4	38.8	58.8	2.4	42.9	56.4	0.7
1932	49.5	47.6	2.9	57.8	39.7	2.4	48.5	49.6	1.9	48.3	50.0	1.7
1934	54.5	43.6	1.9	49.0	49.9	1.1	57.9	40.9	1.3	50.9	48.1	1.1
1936	59.6	39.6	0.9	49.9	48.8	1.3	54.9	44.3	0.8	53.4	45.4	1.2
1938	55.5	43.7	0.8	50.8	47.8	1.4	45.7	53.0	1.4	47.0	51.9	1.1
1940	51.5	47.9	0.7	51.4	48.0	0.6	44.1	55.1	0.8	46.7	52.6	0.7
1942	50.9	48.4	0.7	47.7	51.6	0.7	45.8	53.1	1.1	45.4	53.9	0.7
1944	50.3	49.0	0.7	44.1	55.2	0.7	48.8	50.4	0.7	46.3	53.1	0.6
1946	48.1	49.6	2.2	41.4	57.1	1.5	40.1	58.5	1.4	40.1	59.0	0.9
1948	45.9	50.3	3.7	44.3	54.3	1.4	47.3	50.0	2.7	47.4	50.5	2.1
1950	44.0	53.6	2.5	47.1	51.5	1.3	45.5	52.8	1.8	43.9	54.7	1.4
1952	42.0	56.8	1.2	50.2	48.1	1.7	43.6	55.5	0.9	42.2	56.9	0.9
1954	38.1	60.7	1.1	53.2	44.7	2.2	48.5	48.7	2.9	48.2	50.7	1.2
1956	34.2	64.7	1.1	53.9	44.6	1.6	49.9	47.8	2.3	40.7	58.3	1.0
1958	42.1	56.9	1.0	54.6	44.5	1.0	51.4	46.9	1.7	49.2	49.5	1.2
1960	50.0	49.2	0.9	52.5	46.6	0.9	43.2	55.7	1.1	48.0	51.2	0.8
1962	57.8	41.5	0.7	50.4	48.7	0.9	52.6	46.5	0.9	50.1	49.2	0.7
1964	65.6	33.9	0.5	53.9	44.9	1.2	61.9	37.3	0.8	54.5	45.1	0.4
1966	54.8	40.0	5.2	57.4	41.1	1.5	37.0	60.0	3.0	48.7	49.8	1.5
1968	44.0	46.1	9.9	48.3	50.9	0.8	45.5	51.1	3.4	47.2	51.1	1.7
1970				39.2	60.8	0.0	54.0	42.2	3.8	52.3	46.9	0.9

201

YEAR	COMPOSITE A (P+G+S+H/4)			COMPOSITE B (G+S+H/3)			COMPOSITE C (S+H/2)		
	DEM.	REP.	OTHER	DEM.	REP.	OTHER	DEM.	REP.	OTHER
1872	47.4	52.7	0.0	48.3	51.7	0.0	44.7	55.3	0.0
1874	51.8	48.2	0.1	53.2	46.9	0.0	52.7	47.4	0.0
1876	52.7	44.7	2.6	52.7	43.6	3.7	52.8	41.5	5.7
1878	47.9	46.4	5.7	46.2	45.6	8.2	40.8	46.2	13.0
1880	49.7	49.1	1.2	49.7	49.1	1.2	49.8	49.0	1.2
1882	49.2	47.9	2.9	49.1	47.7	3.1	48.5	47.5	4.0
1884	49.3	47.3	3.4	49.5	47.3	3.2	49.1	48.0	3.0
1886	46.5	45.7	7.8	45.0	44.8	10.2	42.6	45.6	11.8
1888	48.9	46.9	4.2	48.5	46.6	5.0	47.5	48.1	4.3
1890	50.9	46.2	2.9	51.2	45.9	3.0	51.0	45.6	3.4
1892	50.0	47.0	3.0	49.7	47.3	3.0	49.8	47.2	3.0
1894	43.0	52.7	4.3	42.8	52.6	4.6	38.9	55.3	5.8
1896	38.6	57.2	4.2	39.9	56.0	4.1	36.1	59.7	4.1
1898	44.1	52.0	3.8	46.9	49.3	3.8	46.6	49.7	3.7
1900	43.1	53.5	3.5	44.1	52.5	3.4	41.4	55.2	3.4
1902	43.8	52.6	3.7	45.8	50.9	3.3	45.5	50.9	3.6
1904	40.0	55.0	5.0	40.9	54.2	5.0	40.2	54.8	5.0
1906	43.4	52.1	4.5	45.8	49.7	4.5	47.2	48.1	4.8
1908	43.7	52.8	3.5	46.0	50.8	3.2	44.7	52.3	3.0
1910	48.8	41.6	9.5	53.2	43.1	3.7	52.5	43.6	3.9
1912	46.2	30.7	23.2	48.7	35.7	15.6	47.3	31.4	21.3
1914	44.2	40.3	15.5	45.3	41.8	13.0	44.4	46.1	9.5
1916	41.0	54.3	4.8	40.4	54.3	5.4	40.7	53.7	5.7
1918	42.4	52.8	4.9	44.7	50.0	5.3	44.7	49.7	5.6
1920	40.6	55.6	3.9	44.6	51.6	3.8	42.3	54.4	3.3
1922	44.9	51.4	3.8	50.5	46.8	2.6	49.7	46.8	3.5
1924	37.4	58.2	4.4	40.7	56.9	2.4	35.0	61.8	3.2
1926	41.5	56.3	2.2	44.2	54.7	1.1	40.4	58.2	1.4
1928	41.4	58.3	0.3	42.0	57.8	0.2	40.6	59.3	0.2
1930	44.4	54.1	1.5	44.3	54.2	1.5	40.9	57.6	1.5
1932	51.0	46.7	2.2	51.5	46.5	2.0	48.4	49.8	1.8
1934	53.1	45.6	1.3	52.6	46.3	1.1	54.4	44.5	1.2
1936	54.4	44.5	1.0	52.7	46.2	1.1	54.1	44.9	1.0
1938	49.8	49.1	1.2	47.8	50.9	1.3	46.3	52.4	1.2
1940	48.4	50.9	0.7	47.4	51.9	0.7	45.4	53.8	0.7
1942	47.5	51.8	0.8	46.3	52.9	0.8	45.6	53.5	0.9
1944	47.4	51.9	0.7	46.4	52.9	0.7	47.6	51.8	0.7
1946	42.4	56.1	1.5	40.5	58.2	1.3	40.1	58.8	1.2
1948	46.2	51.3	2.5	46.3	51.6	2.1	47.4	50.2	2.4
1950	45.1	53.1	1.8	45.5	53.0	1.5	44.7	53.7	1.6
1952	44.5	54.3	1.2	45.3	53.5	1.2	42.9	56.2	0.9
1954	47.0	51.2	1.8	49.9	48.0	2.1	48.3	49.7	2.0
1956	44.7	53.8	1.5	48.2	50.2	1.6	45.3	53.0	1.6
1958	49.3	49.5	1.2	51.7	47.0	1.3	50.3	48.2	1.5
1960	48.4	50.7	0.9	47.9	51.2	1.0	45.6	53.5	1.0
1962	52.7	46.5	0.8	51.0	48.2	0.9	51.3	47.9	0.8
1964	59.0	40.3	0.7	56.8	42.5	0.8	58.2	41.2	0.6
1966	49.5	47.7	2.8	47.7	50.3	2.0	42.8	54.9	2.3
1968	46.3	49.8	4.0	47.0	51.0	2.0	46.4	51.1	2.5
1970				48.5	49.9	1.6	53.2	44.5	2.3

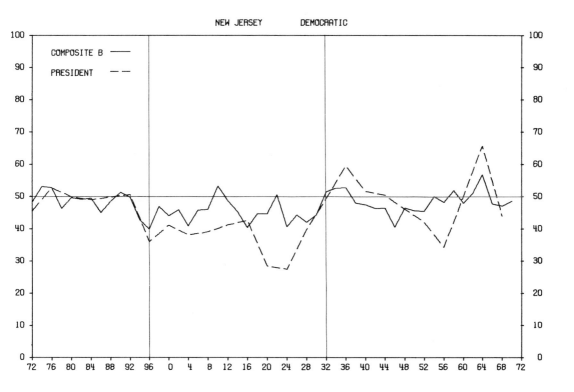

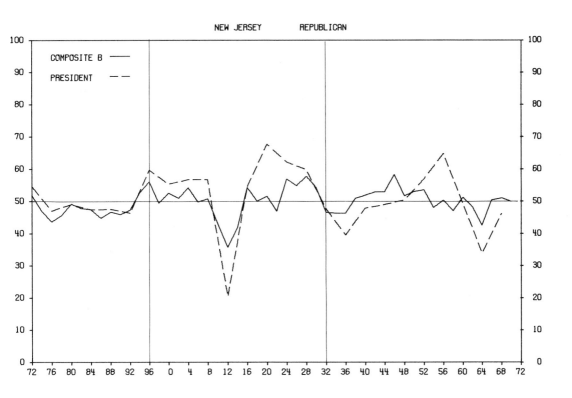

203

YEAR	PRESIDENT			GOVERNOR			SENATE CLASS I			SENATE CLASS II		
	DEM.	REP.	OTHER	DEM.	REP.	OTHER	DEM.	REP.	OTHER	DEM.	REP.	OTHER
1872												
1874												
1876												
1878												
1880												
1882												
1884												
1886												
1888												
1890												
1892												
1894												
1896												
1898												
1900												
1902												
1904												
1906												
1908												
1910												
1912	41.9	35.2	23.0	51.8	46.7	1.5						
1914												
1916	50.4	46.5	3.1	49.4	47.4	3.2	51.1	45.8	3.0			
1918				47.7	50.5	1.8				47.5	51.4	1.1
1920	44.3	54.7	1.0	47.8	51.3	0.9						
1922				54.6	44.7	0.8	55.2	44.1	0.7	43.7	51.3	5.0
1924	43.0	48.5	8.5	48.8	48.6	2.5				49.9	47.4	2.7
1926				48.1	51.6	0.3						
1928	40.8	59.0	0.1	44.3	55.6	0.1	43.3	56.7	0.0			
1930				53.2	46.6	0.2				58.6	41.2	0.2
1932	62.8	35.7	1.5	54.8	44.2	1.0						
1934				51.9	47.6	0.5	49.4	50.2	0.5	54.5	45.0	0.5
1936	62.7	36.5	0.8	57.2	42.7	0.0	55.7	44.2	0.0	61.7	38.3	0.0
1938				52.2	47.6	0.2						
1940	56.6	43.3	0.1	55.6	44.4	0.0	55.9	44.1	0.0			
1942				54.5	45.5	0.0				59.2	40.8	0.0
1944	53.5	46.4	0.1	51.8	48.2	0.0						
1946				52.8	47.2	0.0	51.5	48.5	0.0			
1948	56.3	43.0	0.7	54.7	45.3	0.0				57.2	42.4	0.4
1950				46.3	53.7	0.0						
1952	44.2	55.4	0.3	46.2	53.8	0.0	51.1	48.9	0.0			
1954				57.0	43.0	0.0				57.3	42.7	0.0
1956	41.8	57.8	0.4	47.8	52.2	0.0						
1958				50.5	49.5	0.0	62.7	37.3	0.0			
1960	50.2	49.4	0.4	49.7	50.3	0.0				63.4	36.6	0.0
1962				53.0	47.0	0.0						
1964	59.0	40.4	0.5	60.2	39.8	0.0	54.7	45.3	0.0			
1966				48.3	51.7	0.0				53.1	46.9	0.0
1968	39.7	51.8	8.4	49.5	50.5	0.0						
1970				51.3	46.4	2.4	52.3	46.6	1.2			

YEAR	PRESIDENT			GOVERNOR			SENATE			HOUSE OF REPRESENTATIVES		
	DEM.	REP.	OTHER	DEM.	REP.	OTHER	DEM.	REP.	OTHER	DEM.	REP.	OTHER
1872												
1874												
1876												
1878												
1880												
1882												
1884												
1886												
1888												
1890												
1892												
1894												
1896												
1898												
1900												
1902												
1904												
1906												
1908												
1910												
1912	41.9	35.2	23.0	51.8	46.7	1.5				47.5	45.4	7.2
1914	46.1	40.8	13.0	50.6	47.1	2.3				42.7	51.3	6.0
1916	50.4	46.5	3.1	49.4	47.4	3.2	51.1	45.8	3.0	49.0	48.0	3.1
1918	47.3	50.6	2.1	47.7	50.5	1.8	47.5	51.4	1.1	48.1	50.7	1.2
1920	44.3	54.7	1.0	47.8	51.3	1.0	49.1	49.2	1.8	46.9	51.9	1.2
1922	43.7	51.6	4.8	54.6	44.7	0.8	50.6	47.0	2.4	54.0	45.3	0.8
1924	43.0	48.5	8.5	48.8	48.6	2.5	49.9	47.4	2.7	51.2	47.8	1.0
1926	41.9	53.8	4.3	48.2	51.6	0.3	46.6	52.1	1.4	51.4	48.3	0.3
1928	40.8	59.0	0.1	44.3	55.6	0.1	43.3	56.7	0.0	47.8	52.2	0.0
1930	51.8	47.4	0.8	53.2	46.6	0.2	58.6	41.2	0.2	57.5	42.3	0.3
1932	62.8	35.7	1.5	54.8	44.2	1.0	55.3	44.4	0.4	63.5	35.2	1.3
1934	62.7	36.1	1.2	51.9	47.6	0.5	51.9	47.6	0.5	51.8	47.7	0.5
1936	62.7	36.5	0.8	57.2	42.8	0.0	58.7	41.2	0.0	63.1	36.8	0.0
1938	59.6	39.9	0.5	52.2	47.6	0.2	57.3	42.7	0.0	58.4	41.4	0.2
1940	56.6	43.3	0.1	55.6	44.4	0.0	56.0	44.1	0.0	58.8	41.2	0.0
1942	55.0	44.8	0.1	54.6	45.5	0.0	59.2	40.8	0.0	58.0	42.0	0.0
1944	53.5	46.4	0.1	51.8	48.2	0.0	55.3	44.7	0.0	55.5	44.5	0.0
1946	54.9	44.7	0.4	52.8	47.2	0.0	51.5	48.5	0.0	52.4	47.6	0.0
1948	56.3	43.0	0.7	54.7	45.3	0.0	57.2	42.4	0.4	58.6	41.2	0.2
1950	50.3	49.2	0.5	46.3	53.7	0.0	54.2	45.6	0.2	57.3	42.7	0.0
1952	44.2	55.5	0.3	46.2	53.8	0.0	51.1	48.9	0.0	52.1	47.9	0.0
1954	43.0	56.6	0.4	57.0	43.0	0.0	57.3	42.7	0.0	59.0	41.0	0.0
1956	41.8	57.8	0.4	47.8	52.2	0.0	60.0	40.0	0.0	53.2	46.8	0.0
1958	46.0	53.6	0.4	50.5	49.5	0.0	62.7	37.3	0.0	62.6	37.4	0.0
1960	50.2	49.4	0.4	49.7	50.3	0.0	63.4	36.6	0.0	58.3	41.4	0.3
1962	54.6	44.9	0.5	53.0	47.0	0.0	59.1	40.9	0.0	58.4	41.6	0.0
1964	59.0	40.4	0.5	60.2	39.8	0.0	54.7	45.3	0.0	56.6	43.4	0.0
1966	49.4	46.1	4.5	48.3	51.7	0.0	53.1	46.9	0.0	53.2	46.8	0.0
1968	39.8	51.9	8.4	49.5	50.5	0.0	52.7	46.7	0.6	47.8	51.8	0.5
1970				51.3	46.4	2.4	52.3	46.6	1.2	45.3	53.4	1.4

YEAR	COMPOSITE A (P+G+S+H/4)			COMPOSITE B (G+S+H/3)			COMPOSITE C (S+H/2)		
	DEM.	REP.	OTHER	DEM.	REP.	OTHER	DEM.	REP.	OTHER
1872									
1874									
1876									
1878									
1880									
1882									
1884									
1886									
1888									
1890									
1892									
1894									
1896									
1898									
1900									
1902									
1904									
1906									
1908									
1910									
1912	47.0	42.4	10.5	49.6	46.1	4.3	47.5	45.4	7.2
1914	46.5	46.4	7.1	46.6	49.2	4.2	42.7	51.3	6.0
1916	50.0	46.9	3.1	49.8	47.1	3.1	50.0	46.9	3.1
1918	47.7	50.8	1.6	47.8	50.9	1.4	47.8	51.1	1.2
1920	47.0	51.8	1.2	47.9	50.8	1.3	48.0	50.5	1.5
1922	50.7	47.1	2.2	53.1	45.6	1.3	52.3	46.1	1.6
1924	48.2	48.1	3.7	50.0	48.0	2.1	50.5	47.6	1.9
1926	47.0	51.4	1.6	48.7	50.7	0.6	49.0	50.2	0.8
1928	44.1	55.9	0.1	45.1	54.8	0.0	45.6	54.4	0.0
1930	55.3	44.4	0.4	56.4	43.3	0.2	58.1	41.7	0.2
1932	59.1	39.9	1.0	57.9	41.3	0.9	59.4	39.8	0.8
1934	54.6	44.8	0.7	51.9	47.6	0.5	51.9	47.6	0.5
1936	60.4	39.3	0.2	59.7	40.3	0.0	60.9	39.0	0.0
1938	56.9	42.9	0.2	56.0	43.9	0.1	57.9	42.0	0.1
1940	56.7	43.3	0.0	56.8	43.2	0.0	57.4	42.7	0.0
1942	56.7	43.3	0.0	57.2	42.8	0.0	58.6	41.4	0.0
1944	54.0	45.9	0.0	54.2	45.8	0.0	55.4	44.6	0.0
1946	52.9	47.0	0.1	52.3	47.8	0.0	52.0	48.0	0.0
1948	56.7	43.0	0.3	56.8	43.0	0.2	57.9	41.8	0.3
1950	52.0	47.8	0.2	52.6	47.4	0.1	55.7	44.2	0.1
1952	48.4	51.5	0.1	49.8	50.2	0.0	51.6	48.4	0.0
1954	54.1	45.8	0.1	57.8	42.2	0.0	58.2	41.8	0.0
1956	50.7	49.2	0.1	53.6	46.4	0.0	56.6	43.4	0.0
1958	55.4	44.5	0.1	58.6	41.4	0.0	62.7	37.3	0.0
1960	55.4	44.4	0.2	57.1	42.8	0.1	60.9	39.0	0.1
1962	56.3	43.6	0.1	56.8	43.2	0.0	58.7	41.3	0.0
1964	57.7	42.2	0.1	57.2	42.8	0.0	55.7	44.3	0.0
1966	51.0	47.9	1.1	51.5	48.5	0.0	53.2	46.8	0.0
1968	47.4	50.2	2.4	50.0	49.7	0.4	50.2	49.2	0.5
1970				49.6	48.8	1.6	48.8	50.0	1.3

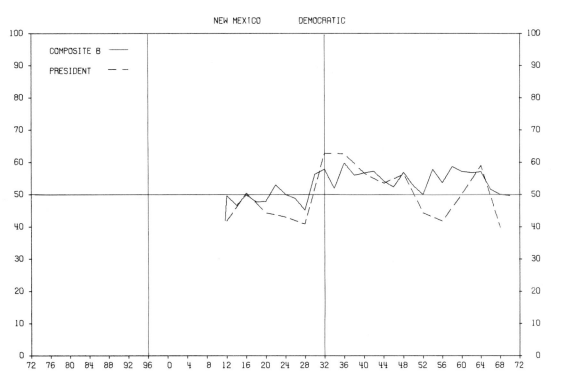

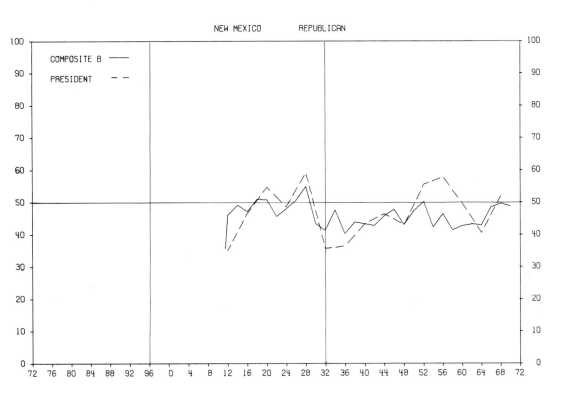

207

YEAR	PRESIDENT			GOVERNOR			SENATE CLASS I			SENATE CLASS III		
	DEM.	REP.	OTHER	DEM.	REP.	OTHER	DEM.	REP.	OTHER	DEM.	REP.	OTHER
1872	46.8	53.2	0.0	46.8	53.2	0.0						
1874				52.4	46.0	1.6						
1876	51.4	48.2	0.4	51.3	48.3	0.5						
1878												
1880	48.4	50.3	1.3	41.9	46.7	11.4						
1882				58.5	37.3	4.2						
1884	48.2	48.2	3.6									
1886				48.9	47.8	3.2						
1888	48.2	49.3	2.5	49.4	48.0	2.6						
1890												
1892	49.0	45.6	5.4	50.1	46.0	3.9						
1894				40.8	53.1	6.1						
1896	38.7	57.6	3.7	40.1	55.3	4.6						
1898				47.7	49.0	3.3						
1900	43.8	53.1	3.1	44.8	52.0	3.2						
1902				47.4	48.1	4.5						
1904	42.3	53.1	4.6	45.3	50.3	4.4						
1906				45.4	50.5	4.1						
1908	40.7	53.1	6.2	44.8	49.1	6.1						
1910				48.0	43.3	8.7						
1912	41.3	28.7	30.0	41.4	28.3	30.2						
1914				28.6	47.7	23.7				42.0	47.0	10.9
1916	44.5	50.9	4.6	42.5	51.7	5.7	39.2	54.3	6.5			
1918				47.4	44.8	7.8						
1920	27.0	64.6	8.5	44.0	46.6	9.4				32.9	52.4	14.7
1922				55.2	40.0	4.8	52.6	41.0	6.4			
1924	29.1	55.8	15.1	50.0	46.6	3.4						
1926				52.3	43.8	3.9				46.5	42.4	11.1
1928	47.4	49.8	2.8	49.0	48.4	2.7	49.1	47.9	3.0			
1930				56.1	33.1	10.8						
1932	54.1	41.3	4.6	56.7	38.6	4.7				55.8	38.6	5.7
1934				57.8	36.6	5.6	55.3	36.9	7.8			
1936	53.9	39.0	7.1	48.7	44.1	7.2						
1938				50.4	49.0	0.6	53.6	45.4	1.0	54.5	44.9	0.6
1940	51.6	48.0	0.4				53.3	46.7	0.1			
1942				36.4	52.1	11.5						
1944	52.3	47.3	0.4							53.1	46.7	0.2
1946				43.1	56.9	0.0	47.4	52.6	0.0			
1948	45.0	46.0	9.0									
1950				42.3	53.1	4.6				51.1	46.6	2.2
1952	43.6	55.5	1.0				36.1	55.2	8.7			
1954				49.6	49.4	1.0						
1956	38.8	61.2	0.0							46.7	53.3	0.0
1958				39.7	54.7	5.5	48.4	50.7	0.9			
1960	52.5	47.3	0.2									
1962				44.0	53.1	3.0				40.1	57.4	2.5
1964	68.6	31.3	0.1				53.5	43.4	3.1			
1966				38.1	44.6	17.3						
1968	49.8	44.3	5.9							32.7	49.7	17.6
1970				40.4	52.6	7.0	36.8	24.3	38.9			

208

NEW YORK (CANDIDATE)

YEAR	PRESIDENT			GOVERNOR			SENATE			HOUSE OF REPRESENTATIVES		
	DEM.	REP.	OTHER	DEM.	REP.	OTHER	DEM.	REP.	OTHER	DEM.	REP.	OTHER
1872	46.8	53.2	0.0	46.8	53.2	0.0				46.7	52.1	1.2
1874	49.1	50.7	0.2	52.4	46.1	1.6				52.1	43.0	4.9
1876	51.4	48.2	0.4	51.3	48.3	0.5				49.9	47.4	2.7
1878	49.9	49.3	0.8	46.6	47.5	5.9				37.6	50.3	12.1
1880	48.4	50.3	1.3	41.9	46.7	11.4				46.3	50.7	3.1
1882	48.3	49.2	2.4	58.5	37.3	4.2				52.1	44.0	3.9
1884	48.3	48.2	3.6	53.7	42.6	3.7				47.2	45.9	6.9
1886	48.2	48.7	3.1	48.9	47.9	3.2				46.2	47.3	6.5
1888	48.2	49.3	2.5	49.4	48.0	2.6				45.7	49.8	4.6
1890	48.6	47.4	4.0	49.8	47.0	3.2				51.3	43.9	4.9
1892	49.0	45.6	5.4	50.1	46.0	3.9				48.7	46.5	4.8
1894	43.9	51.6	4.6	40.8	53.1	6.1				39.6	54.5	5.9
1896	38.7	57.6	3.7	40.1	55.3	4.6				36.1	59.7	4.2
1898	41.3	55.3	3.4	47.7	49.0	3.3				47.0	49.8	3.2
1900	43.8	53.1	3.1	44.8	52.0	3.2				43.9	53.5	2.6
1902	43.1	53.1	3.8	47.4	48.1	4.5				47.7	48.5	3.9
1904	42.3	53.1	4.6	45.3	50.3	4.4				42.2	53.7	4.1
1906	41.5	53.1	5.4	45.4	50.5	4.1				43.2	48.3	8.5
1908	40.7	53.1	6.2	44.8	49.1	6.1				43.4	50.7	5.9
1910	41.0	40.9	18.1	48.0	43.3	8.7				48.8	45.3	5.9
1912	41.3	28.7	30.1	41.5	28.3	30.2				41.6	31.2	27.3
1914	42.9	39.8	17.3	28.6	47.7	23.7	42.0	47.0	10.9	40.9	45.9	13.2
1916	44.5	50.9	4.6	42.5	51.8	5.7	39.2	54.3	6.5	41.1	51.1	7.9
1918	35.7	57.7	6.5	47.4	44.8	7.8	36.1	53.3	10.6	39.4	51.7	8.9
1920	27.0	64.6	8.5	44.0	46.6	9.4	32.9	52.4	14.7	34.3	55.0	10.7
1922	28.0	60.2	11.8	55.2	40.0	4.8	52.6	41.0	6.4	46.7	46.2	7.1
1924	29.1	55.8	15.1	50.0	46.6	3.4	49.5	41.7	8.8	43.4	51.8	4.8
1926	38.3	52.8	8.9	52.3	43.8	3.9	46.5	42.4	11.1	47.8	49.2	3.0
1928	47.4	49.8	2.8	49.0	48.4	2.7	49.1	47.9	3.0	47.2	49.2	3.6
1930	50.8	45.6	3.7	56.1	33.1	10.8	52.4	43.2	4.4	50.7	43.1	6.2
1932	54.1	41.3	4.6	56.7	38.6	4.7	55.8	38.6	5.7	54.0	40.3	5.7
1934	54.0	40.2	5.9	57.8	36.6	5.6	55.3	36.9	7.8	54.3	39.6	6.1
1936	53.9	39.0	7.1	48.7	44.1	7.2	54.7	41.0	4.3	56.8	39.4	3.8
1938	52.8	43.5	3.7	50.4	49.0	0.6	54.1	45.2	0.8	50.9	45.8	3.3
1940	51.6	48.0	0.4	43.4	50.6	6.1	53.3	46.7	0.1	51.5	46.6	2.0
1942	52.0	47.7	0.4	36.4	52.1	11.5	53.2	46.7	0.2	48.3	49.9	1.9
1944	52.3	47.3	0.4	39.7	54.5	5.8	53.1	46.7	0.3	49.1	48.9	2.0
1946	48.7	46.7	4.7	43.1	56.9	0.0	47.4	52.6	0.0	41.6	53.5	4.9
1948	45.0	46.0	9.0	42.7	55.0	2.3	49.3	49.6	1.1	49.7	42.9	7.4
1950	44.3	50.7	5.0	42.3	53.1	4.6	51.2	46.6	2.2	46.9	46.9	6.2
1952	43.6	55.5	1.0	46.0	51.3	2.8	36.1	55.2	8.7	44.7	52.3	3.1
1954	41.2	58.3	0.5	49.6	49.4	1.0	41.4	54.3	4.3	48.4	49.8	1.9
1956	38.8	61.2	0.0	44.7	52.1	3.3	46.7	53.3	0.0	44.6	54.4	1.0
1958	45.7	54.2	0.1	39.7	54.7	5.5	48.4	50.8	0.9	50.0	48.7	1.3
1960	52.5	47.3	0.2	41.9	53.9	4.2	44.3	54.1	1.7	51.7	46.5	1.8
1962	60.6	39.3	0.2	44.0	53.1	3.0	40.1	57.4	2.5	50.0	48.3	1.7
1964	68.6	31.3	0.1	41.0	48.9	10.1	53.5	43.4	3.1	58.1	40.2	1.7
1966	59.2	37.8	3.0	38.1	44.6	17.3	43.1	46.5	10.4	50.1	45.0	4.9
1968	49.8	44.3	5.9	39.3	48.6	12.2	32.7	49.7	17.6	48.8	46.1	5.1
1970				40.4	52.6	7.1	36.8	24.3	38.9	50.0	44.9	5.1

NEW YORK (CANDIDATE)

YEAR	COMPOSITE A (P+G+S+H/4)			COMPOSITE B (G+S+H/3)			COMPOSITE C (S+H/2)		
	DEM.	REP.	OTHER	DEM.	REP.	OTHER	DEM.	REP.	OTHER
1872	46.8	52.8	0.4	46.7	52.7	0.6	46.7	52.1	1.2
1874	51.2	46.6	2.2	52.2	44.6	3.2	52.1	43.0	4.9
1876	50.9	48.0	1.2	50.6	47.8	1.6	49.9	47.4	2.7
1878	44.7	49.0	6.3	42.1	48.9	9.0	37.6	50.3	12.1
1880	45.5	49.2	5.3	44.1	48.7	7.2	46.3	50.7	3.1
1882	53.0	43.5	3.5	55.3	40.7	4.1	52.1	44.0	3.9
1884	49.7	45.6	4.8	50.4	44.3	5.3	47.2	45.9	6.9
1886	47.8	47.9	4.3	47.6	47.6	4.9	46.2	47.3	6.5
1888	47.8	49.0	3.2	47.6	48.9	3.6	45.7	49.8	4.6
1890	49.9	46.1	4.0	50.5	45.4	4.0	51.3	43.9	4.9
1892	49.3	46.0	4.7	49.4	46.3	4.3	48.7	46.5	4.8
1894	41.4	53.1	5.5	40.2	53.8	6.0	39.6	54.5	5.9
1896	38.3	57.5	4.2	38.1	57.5	4.4	36.1	59.7	4.2
1898	45.3	51.4	3.3	47.4	49.4	3.3	47.0	49.8	3.2
1900	44.2	52.9	3.0	44.3	52.7	2.9	43.9	53.5	2.6
1902	46.1	49.9	4.1	47.5	48.3	4.2	47.7	48.5	3.9
1904	43.3	52.4	4.4	43.8	52.0	4.3	42.2	53.7	4.1
1906	43.4	50.6	6.0	44.3	49.4	6.3	43.2	48.3	8.5
1908	43.0	51.0	6.1	44.1	49.9	6.0	43.4	50.7	5.9
1910	45.9	43.2	10.9	48.4	44.3	7.3	48.8	45.3	5.9
1912	41.4	29.4	29.2	41.5	29.8	28.7	41.6	31.2	27.3
1914	38.6	45.1	16.3	37.2	46.9	15.9	41.5	46.5	12.1
1916	41.8	52.0	6.2	40.9	52.4	6.7	40.1	52.7	7.2
1918	39.6	51.9	8.5	40.9	50.0	9.1	37.7	52.5	9.8
1920	34.6	54.6	10.8	37.1	51.3	11.6	33.6	53.7	12.7
1922	45.6	46.8	7.5	51.5	42.4	6.1	49.7	43.6	6.8
1924	43.0	49.0	8.0	47.6	46.7	5.7	46.5	46.8	6.8
1926	46.2	47.1	6.8	48.9	45.1	6.0	47.1	45.8	7.1
1928	48.2	48.8	3.0	48.4	48.5	3.1	48.1	48.6	3.3
1930	52.5	41.3	6.3	53.1	39.8	7.1	51.5	43.2	5.3
1932	55.1	39.7	5.2	55.5	39.2	5.4	54.9	39.4	5.7
1934	55.4	38.3	6.3	55.8	37.7	6.5	54.8	38.3	6.9
1936	53.5	40.9	5.6	53.4	41.5	5.1	55.7	40.2	4.1
1938	52.0	45.9	2.1	51.8	46.7	1.6	52.5	45.5	2.0
1940	49.9	48.0	2.1	49.4	47.9	2.7	52.4	46.6	1.0
1942	47.5	49.1	3.5	45.9	49.5	4.5	50.7	48.3	1.0
1944	48.6	49.4	2.1	47.3	50.0	2.7	51.1	47.8	1.1
1946	45.2	52.4	2.4	44.0	54.4	1.6	44.5	53.1	2.4
1948	46.7	48.4	4.9	47.2	49.2	3.6	49.5	46.3	4.2
1950	46.2	49.3	4.5	46.8	48.9	4.4	49.0	46.8	4.2
1952	42.6	53.6	3.9	42.3	52.9	4.8	40.4	53.8	5.9
1954	45.1	52.9	1.9	46.5	51.1	2.4	44.9	52.0	3.1
1956	43.7	55.2	1.1	45.3	53.2	1.4	45.7	53.8	0.5
1958	46.0	52.1	2.0	46.1	51.4	2.6	49.2	49.7	1.1
1960	47.6	50.4	2.0	45.9	51.5	2.6	48.0	50.3	1.7
1962	48.7	49.5	1.8	44.7	52.9	2.4	45.1	52.9	2.1
1964	55.3	40.9	3.8	50.9	44.2	5.0	55.8	41.8	2.4
1966	47.6	43.5	8.9	43.8	45.4	10.9	46.6	45.8	7.7
1968	42.6	47.2	10.2	40.3	48.1	11.6	40.8	47.9	11.3
1970				42.4	40.6	17.0	43.4	34.6	22.0

210

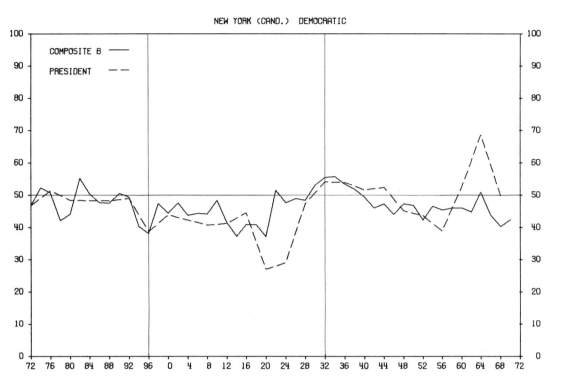

NEW YORK (CAND.) DEMOCRATIC

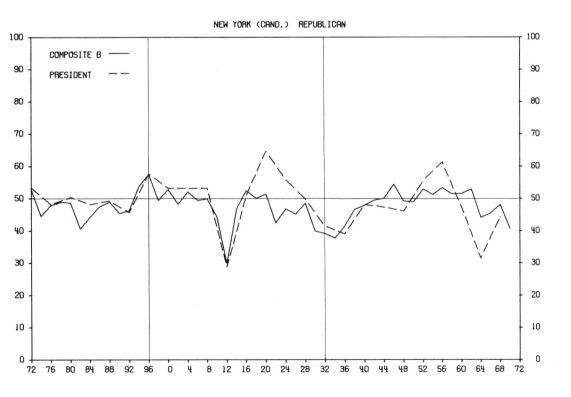

NEW YORK (CAND.) REPUBLICAN

YEAR	PRESIDENT			GOVERNOR			SENATE CLASS I			SENATE CLASS III		
	DEM.	REP.	OTHER	DEM.	REP.	OTHER	DEM.	REP.	OTHER	DEM.	REP.	OTHER
1872	46.8	53.2	0.0	46.8	53.2	0.0						
1874				52.4	46.0	1.6						
1876	51.4	48.2	0.4	51.3	48.3	0.5						
1878												
1880	48.4	50.3	1.3	41.9	46.7	11.4						
1882				58.5	37.3	4.2						
1884	48.2	48.2	3.6									
1886				48.9	47.8	3.2						
1888	48.2	49.3	2.5	49.4	48.0	2.6						
1890												
1892	49.0	45.6	5.4	50.1	46.0	3.9						
1894				40.8	53.1	6.1						
1896	38.7	57.6	3.7	40.1	55.3	4.6						
1898				47.7	49.0	3.3						
1900	43.8	53.1	3.1	44.8	52.0	3.2						
1902				47.4	48.1	4.5						
1904	42.3	53.1	4.6	45.3	50.3	4.4						
1906				45.4	50.5	4.1						
1908	40.7	53.1	6.2	44.8	49.1	6.1						
1910				48.0	43.3	8.7						
1912	41.3	28.7	30.0	41.4	28.3	30.2						
1914				28.6	47.7	23.7				42.0	47.0	10.9
1916	44.5	50.9	4.6	42.5	51.7	5.7	39.2	54.3	6.5			
1918				47.4	44.8	7.8						
1920	27.0	64.6	8.5	44.0	46.6	9.4				32.9	52.4	14.7
1922				55.2	40.0	4.8	52.6	41.0	6.4			
1924	29.1	55.8	15.1	50.0	46.6	3.4						
1926				52.3	43.8	3.9				46.5	42.4	11.1
1928	47.4	49.8	2.8	49.0	48.4	2.7	49.1	47.9	3.0			
1930				56.1	33.1	10.8						
1932	54.1	41.3	4.6	56.7	38.6	4.7				55.8	38.6	5.7
1934				57.8	36.6	5.6	55.3	36.9	7.8			
1936	53.9	39.0	7.1	48.7	44.1	7.2						
1938				41.5	48.5	10.0	45.3	45.4	9.3	45.8	44.7	9.5
1940	45.0	48.0	7.0				47.1	46.7	6.3			
1942				36.4	52.1	11.5						
1944	39.2	47.3	13.5							40.0	46.7	13.3
1946				30.9	56.9	12.2	34.7	52.6	12.7			
1948	41.4	46.0	12.6									
1950				37.3	53.1	9.6				43.9	46.6	9.5
1952	37.7	55.5	6.8				36.1	55.2	8.7			
1954				44.5	49.4	6.1						
1956	34.7	61.2	4.1							42.4	53.3	4.3
1958				39.7	54.7	5.5	43.5	50.7	5.8			
1960	47.0	47.3	5.8									
1962				39.8	53.1	7.1				37.1	57.4	5.6
1964	63.8	31.3	4.9				49.5	43.4	7.1			
1966				38.1	44.6	17.3						
1968	45.2	44.3	10.5							32.7	42.7	24.6
1970				36.0	51.8	12.2	36.8	20.0	43.3			

NEW YORK (PARTY)

YEAR	PRESIDENT			GOVERNOR			SENATE			HOUSE OF REPRESENTATIVES		
	DEM.	REP.	OTHER	DEM.	REP.	OTHER	DEM.	REP.	OTHER	DEM.	REP.	OTHER
1872	46.8	53.2	0.0	46.8	53.2	0.0				46.7	52.1	1.2
1874	49.1	50.7	0.2	52.4	46.1	1.6				52.1	43.0	4.9
1876	51.4	48.2	0.4	51.3	48.3	0.5				49.9	47.4	2.7
1878	49.9	49.3	0.8	46.6	47.5	5.9				37.6	50.3	12.1
1880	48.4	50.3	1.3	41.9	46.7	11.4				46.3	50.7	3.1
1882	48.3	49.2	2.4	58.5	37.3	4.2				52.1	44.0	3.9
1884	48.3	48.2	3.6	53.7	42.6	3.7				47.2	45.9	6.9
1886	48.2	48.7	3.1	48.9	47.9	3.2				46.2	47.3	6.5
1888	48.2	49.3	2.5	49.4	48.0	2.6				45.7	49.8	4.6
1890	48.6	47.4	4.0	49.8	47.0	3.2				51.3	43.9	4.9
1892	49.0	45.6	5.4	50.1	46.0	3.9				48.7	46.5	4.8
1894	43.9	51.6	4.6	40.8	53.1	6.1				39.6	54.5	5.9
1896	38.7	57.6	3.7	40.1	55.3	4.6				36.1	59.7	4.2
1898	41.3	55.3	3.4	47.7	49.0	3.3				47.0	49.8	3.2
1900	43.8	53.1	3.1	44.8	52.0	3.2				43.9	53.5	2.6
1902	43.1	53.1	3.8	47.4	48.1	4.5				47.7	48.5	3.9
1904	42.3	53.1	4.6	45.3	50.3	4.4				42.2	53.7	4.1
1906	41.5	53.1	5.4	45.4	50.5	4.1				43.2	48.3	8.5
1908	40.7	53.1	6.2	44.8	49.1	6.1				43.4	50.7	5.9
1910	41.0	40.9	18.1	48.0	43.3	8.7				48.8	45.3	5.9
1912	41.3	28.7	30.1	41.5	28.3	30.2				41.6	31.2	27.3
1914	42.9	39.8	17.3	28.6	47.7	23.7	42.0	47.0	10.9	40.9	45.9	13.2
1916	44.5	50.9	4.6	42.5	51.8	5.7	39.2	54.3	6.5	41.1	51.1	7.9
1918	35.7	57.7	6.5	47.4	44.8	7.8	36.1	53.3	10.6	39.4	51.7	8.9
1920	27.0	64.6	8.5	44.0	46.6	9.4	32.9	52.4	14.7	34.3	55.0	10.7
1922	28.0	60.2	11.8	55.2	40.0	4.8	52.6	41.0	6.4	46.7	46.2	7.1
1924	29.1	55.8	15.1	50.0	46.6	3.4	49.5	41.7	8.8	43.4	51.8	4.8
1926	38.3	52.8	8.9	52.3	43.8	3.9	46.5	42.4	11.1	47.8	49.2	3.0
1928	47.4	49.8	2.8	49.0	48.4	2.7	49.1	47.9	3.0	47.2	49.2	3.6
1930	50.8	45.6	3.7	56.1	33.1	10.8	52.4	43.2	4.4	50.7	43.1	6.2
1932	54.1	41.3	4.6	56.7	38.6	4.7	55.8	38.6	5.7	54.0	40.3	5.7
1934	54.0	40.2	5.9	57.8	36.6	5.6	55.3	36.9	7.8	54.3	39.6	6.1
1936	53.9	39.0	7.1	48.7	44.1	7.2	50.4	41.0	8.6	56.8	39.4	3.8
1938	49.5	43.5	7.0	41.5	48.5	10.0	45.6	45.0	9.4	45.2	44.8	10.0
1940	45.0	48.0	7.0	39.0	50.3	10.7	47.1	46.7	6.3	47.0	46.6	6.5
1942	42.1	47.7	10.2	36.4	52.1	11.5	43.6	46.7	9.8	40.3	49.6	10.2
1944	39.2	47.3	13.5	33.6	54.5	11.9	40.0	46.7	13.3	41.4	46.9	11.7
1946	40.3	46.7	13.0	30.9	56.9	12.2	34.7	52.6	12.7	34.8	53.5	11.7
1948	41.4	46.0	12.6	34.1	55.0	10.9	39.3	49.6	11.1	43.5	44.3	12.2
1950	39.6	50.7	9.7	37.3	53.1	9.6	43.9	46.6	9.5	42.8	47.2	10.0
1952	37.7	55.5	6.8	40.9	51.3	7.8	36.1	55.2	8.7	40.2	52.4	7.4
1954	36.2	58.3	5.5	44.5	49.4	6.1	39.3	54.3	6.5	44.6	50.1	5.3
1956	34.7	61.2	4.1	42.1	52.1	5.8	42.4	53.3	4.3	41.3	54.4	4.4
1958	40.8	54.2	5.0	39.7	54.7	5.5	43.5	50.8	5.8	45.7	48.9	5.4
1960	47.0	47.3	5.8	39.8	53.9	6.3	40.3	54.1	5.7	47.9	46.5	5.6
1962	55.4	39.3	5.3	39.8	53.1	7.1	37.1	57.4	5.6	47.0	48.3	4.7
1964	63.8	31.3	4.9	39.0	48.9	12.2	49.5	43.4	7.1	55.2	39.9	4.9
1966	54.5	37.8	7.7	38.1	44.6	17.3	41.1	43.1	15.9	46.2	43.1	10.8
1968	45.2	44.3	10.5	37.1	48.2	14.8	32.7	42.7	24.6	46.6	42.1	11.3
1970				36.0	51.8	12.2	36.8	20.0	43.3	43.9	41.6	14.6

213

YEAR	COMPOSITE A (P+G+S+H/4)			COMPOSITE B (G+S+H/3)			COMPOSITE C (S+H/2)		
	DEM.	REP.	OTHER	DEM.	REP.	OTHER	DEM.	REP.	OTHER
1872	46.8	52.8	0.4	46.7	52.7	0.6	46.7	52.1	1.2
1874	51.2	46.6	2.2	52.2	44.6	3.2	52.1	43.0	4.9
1876	50.9	48.0	1.2	50.6	47.8	1.6	49.9	47.4	2.7
1878	44.7	49.0	6.3	42.1	48.9	9.0	37.6	50.3	12.1
1880	45.5	49.2	5.3	44.1	48.7	7.2	46.3	50.7	3.1
1882	53.0	43.5	3.5	55.3	40.7	4.1	52.1	44.0	3.9
1884	49.7	45.6	4.8	50.4	44.3	5.3	47.2	45.9	6.9
1886	47.8	47.9	4.3	47.6	47.6	4.9	46.2	47.3	6.5
1888	47.8	49.0	3.2	47.6	48.9	3.6	45.7	49.8	4.6
1890	49.9	46.1	4.0	50.5	45.4	4.0	51.3	43.9	4.9
1892	49.3	46.0	4.7	49.4	46.3	4.3	48.7	46.5	4.8
1894	41.4	53.1	5.5	40.2	53.8	6.0	39.6	54.5	5.9
1896	38.3	57.5	4.2	38.1	57.5	4.4	36.1	59.7	4.2
1898	45.3	51.4	3.3	47.4	49.4	3.3	47.0	49.8	3.2
1900	44.2	52.9	3.0	44.3	52.7	2.9	43.9	53.5	2.6
1902	46.1	49.9	4.1	47.5	48.3	4.2	47.7	48.5	3.9
1904	43.3	52.4	4.4	43.8	52.0	4.3	42.2	53.7	4.1
1906	43.4	50.6	6.0	44.3	49.4	6.3	43.2	48.3	8.5
1908	43.0	51.0	6.1	44.1	49.9	6.0	43.4	50.7	5.9
1910	45.9	43.2	10.9	48.4	44.3	7.3	48.8	45.3	5.9
1912	41.4	29.4	29.2	41.5	29.8	28.7	41.6	31.2	27.3
1914	38.6	45.1	16.3	37.2	46.9	15.9	41.5	46.5	12.1
1916	41.8	52.0	6.2	40.9	52.4	6.7	40.1	52.7	7.2
1918	39.6	51.9	8.5	40.9	50.0	9.1	37.7	52.5	9.8
1920	34.6	54.6	10.8	37.1	51.3	11.6	33.6	53.7	12.7
1922	45.6	46.8	7.5	51.5	42.4	6.1	49.7	43.6	6.8
1924	43.0	49.0	8.0	47.6	46.7	5.7	46.5	46.8	6.8
1926	46.2	47.1	6.8	48.9	45.1	6.0	47.1	45.8	7.1
1928	48.2	48.8	3.0	48.4	48.5	3.1	48.1	48.6	3.3
1930	52.5	41.3	6.3	53.1	39.8	7.1	51.5	43.2	5.3
1932	55.1	39.7	5.2	55.5	39.2	5.4	54.9	39.4	5.7
1934	55.4	38.3	6.3	55.8	37.7	6.5	54.8	38.3	6.9
1936	52.5	40.9	6.7	52.0	41.5	6.5	53.6	40.2	6.2
1938	45.4	45.5	9.1	44.1	46.1	9.8	45.4	44.9	9.7
1940	44.5	47.9	7.6	44.3	47.9	7.8	47.0	46.6	6.4
1942	40.6	49.0	10.4	40.1	49.5	10.5	41.9	48.1	10.0
1944	38.6	48.9	12.6	38.3	49.4	12.3	40.7	46.8	12.5
1946	35.2	52.4	12.4	33.5	54.4	12.2	34.7	53.1	12.2
1948	39.6	48.7	11.7	39.0	49.6	11.4	41.4	47.0	11.7
1950	40.9	49.4	9.7	41.3	49.0	9.7	43.4	46.9	9.7
1952	38.7	53.6	7.7	39.1	52.9	8.0	38.2	53.8	8.0
1954	41.1	53.0	5.9	42.8	51.3	6.0	41.9	52.2	5.9
1956	40.1	55.2	4.7	41.9	53.2	4.8	41.8	53.8	4.3
1958	42.4	52.2	5.4	43.0	51.5	5.6	44.6	49.8	5.6
1960	43.7	50.4	5.9	42.6	51.5	5.9	44.1	50.3	5.6
1962	44.8	49.5	5.7	41.3	52.9	5.8	42.0	52.9	5.1
1964	51.8	40.9	7.3	47.9	44.1	8.1	52.3	41.7	6.0
1966	45.0	42.1	12.9	41.8	43.6	14.6	43.6	43.1	13.3
1968	40.4	44.3	15.3	38.8	44.3	16.9	39.7	42.4	17.9
1970				38.9	37.8	23.4	40.3	30.8	28.9

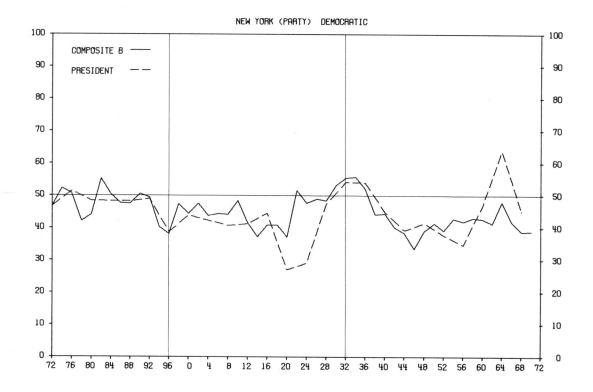

NEW YORK (PARTY) DEMOCRATIC

COMPOSITE B ———
PRESIDENT — —

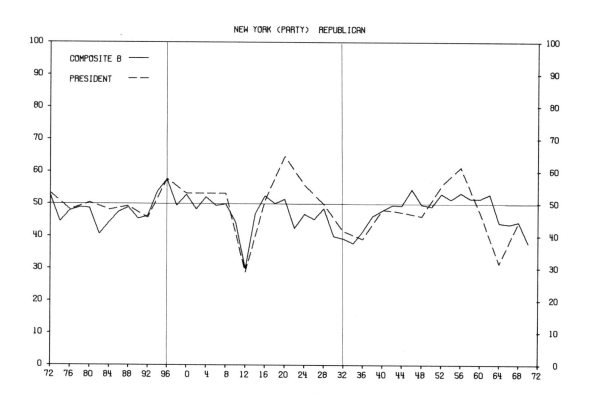

NEW YORK (PARTY) REPUBLICAN

COMPOSITE B ———
PRESIDENT — —

215

YEAR	PRESIDENT			GOVERNOR			SENATE CLASS II			SENATE CLASS III		
	DEM.	REP.	OTHER	DEM.	REP.	OTHER	DEM.	REP.	OTHER	DEM.	REP.	OTHER
1872 1874	42.5	57.4	0.2	49.5	50.5	0.0						
1876 1878	53.6	46.4	0.0	52.8	47.2	0.0						
1880 1882	51.5	48.0	0.5	51.3	48.7	0.0						
1884 1886	53.3	46.6	0.2	53.8	46.1	0.1						
1888 1890	51.8	47.2	1.0	52.0	46.9	1.1						
1892 1894	47.4	35.8	16.8	48.3	33.8	17.9						
1896 1898	52.6	46.8	0.5	43.9	46.5	9.6						
1900 1902	53.9	45.5	0.6	59.6	40.3	0.1						
1904 1906	59.7	39.7	0.6	61.7	38.1	0.2						
1908 1910	54.2	45.5	0.3	57.3	42.6	0.1						
1912 1914	59.2	11.9	28.8	61.3	17.8	20.8				58.1	41.7	0.2
1916 1918	58.1	41.7	0.2	58.1	41.7	0.2	60.5	39.5	0.0			
1920 1922	56.7	43.2	0.1	57.2	42.8	0.0				57.5	42.5	0.0
1924 1926	59.0	39.6	1.4	61.3	38.7	0.0	61.6	38.4	0.0	60.5	39.5	0.0
1928 1930	45.1	54.9	0.0	55.6	44.4	0.0	60.6	39.4	0.0			
1932 1934	69.9	29.3	0.8	70.1	29.9	0.0				68.3	31.7	0.0
1936 1938	73.4	26.6	0.0	66.7	33.3	0.0	70.8	29.2	0.0	63.8	36.2	0.0
1940 1942	74.0	26.0	0.0	75.7	24.3	0.0	65.9	34.1	0.0			
1944 1946	66.7	33.3	0.0	69.6	30.4	0.0				70.3	29.7	0.0
1948 1950	58.0	32.7	9.3	73.2	26.4	0.4	70.7 28.8 0.5 67.4 32.6 0.0			68.7	31.3	0.0
1952 1954	53.9	46.1	0.0	67.5	32.5	0.0	79.3	20.7	0.0	100.0	0.0	0.0
1956 1958	50.7	49.3	0.0	67.0	33.0	0.0	70.0	30.0	0.0	66.6	33.4	0.0
1960 1962	52.1	47.9	0.0	54.5	45.5	0.0	61.4	38.6	0.0	60.4	39.6	0.0
1964 1966	56.2	43.8	0.0	56.6	43.4	0.0	55.6	44.4	0.0			
1968 1970	29.2	39.5	31.3	52.7	47.3	0.0				60.6	39.4	0.0

NORTH CAROLINA

YEAR	PRESIDENT			GOVERNOR			SENATE			HOUSE OF REPRESENTATIVES		
	DEM.	REP.	OTHER	DEM.	REP.	OTHER	DEM.	REP.	OTHER	DEM.	REP.	OTHER
1872	42.5	57.4	0.2	49.5	50.5	0.0				49.2	50.8	0.0
1874	48.0	51.9	0.1	51.2	48.8	0.0				53.6	38.9	7.5
1876	53.6	46.4	0.0	52.8	47.2	0.0				53.8	46.3	0.0
1878	52.6	47.2	0.2	52.1	47.9	0.0				52.5	32.2	15.3
1880	51.6	48.0	0.5	51.3	48.7	0.0				52.5	43.6	3.9
1882	52.4	47.3	0.3	52.6	47.4	0.0				49.0	50.7	0.3
1884	53.3	46.6	0.2	53.8	46.1	0.1				54.2	45.8	0.0
1886	52.5	46.9	0.6	52.9	46.5	0.6				54.5	20.1	25.4
1888	51.8	47.2	1.0	52.0	46.9	1.1				52.9	46.6	0.5
1890	49.6	41.5	8.9	50.1	40.4	9.5				56.7	42.6	0.7
1892	47.4	35.8	16.8	48.3	33.8	17.9				49.0	25.9	25.1
1894	50.0	41.3	8.7	46.1	40.2	13.8				45.7	31.6	22.7
1896	52.6	46.8	0.6	43.9	46.5	9.6				44.8	47.7	7.5
1898	53.3	46.1	0.6	51.7	43.4	4.9				51.5	37.3	11.3
1900	53.9	45.5	0.6	59.6	40.3	0.1				55.6	38.1	6.3
1902	56.8	42.6	0.6	60.7	39.2	0.1				68.8	30.1	1.2
1904	59.7	39.7	0.6	61.7	38.1	0.2				62.3	37.7	0.1
1906	57.0	42.6	0.5	59.5	40.3	0.2				61.5	38.4	0.1
1908	54.2	45.5	0.3	57.3	42.6	0.1				56.9	43.0	0.2
1910	56.7	28.7	14.6	59.3	30.2	10.5				59.8	40.0	0.2
1912	59.2	12.0	28.8	61.4	17.9	20.8				66.2	30.1	3.8
1914	58.7	26.8	14.5	59.7	29.8	10.5	58.1	41.7	0.2	60.2	39.4	0.4
1916	58.1	41.7	0.2	58.1	41.7	0.2	59.3	40.6	0.1	57.9	42.0	0.1
1918	57.4	42.5	0.1	57.7	42.2	0.1	60.5	39.5	0.0	60.9	39.2	0.0
1920	56.7	43.2	0.1	57.2	42.8	0.0	57.5	42.5	0.0	57.7	42.3	0.0
1922	57.9	41.4	0.7	59.3	40.7	0.0	59.5	40.5	0.0	62.1	37.9	0.0
1924	59.0	39.6	1.4	61.3	38.7	0.0	61.6	38.5	0.0	61.7	38.3	0.0
1926	52.0	47.3	0.7	58.5	41.5	0.0	60.5	39.5	0.0	61.3	38.7	0.0
1928	45.1	54.9	0.0	55.6	44.4	0.0	60.6	39.4	0.0	55.1	44.9	0.0
1930	57.5	42.1	0.4	62.8	37.2	0.0	60.6	39.4	0.0	62.8	37.2	0.0
1932	69.9	29.3	0.8	70.1	29.9	0.0	68.3	31.7	0.0	69.7	30.3	0.0
1934	71.7	27.9	0.4	68.4	31.6	0.0	69.5	30.5	0.0	64.9	35.1	0.0
1936	73.4	26.6	0.0	66.7	33.3	0.0	70.8	29.2	0.0	71.2	28.8	0.0
1938	73.7	26.3	0.0	71.2	28.8	0.0	63.8	36.2	0.0	66.5	33.5	0.0
1940	74.0	26.0	0.0	75.7	24.3	0.0	64.9	35.1	0.0	75.5	24.5	0.0
1942	70.4	29.6	0.0	72.7	27.4	0.0	65.9	34.1	0.0	72.7	27.3	0.0
1944	66.7	33.3	0.0	69.6	30.4	0.0	70.3	29.8	0.0	69.5	30.5	0.0
1946	62.4	33.0	4.7	71.4	28.4	0.2	70.5	29.3	0.2	61.3	38.7	0.0
1948	58.0	32.7	9.3	73.2	26.4	0.4	70.7	28.8	0.5	70.8	28.7	0.4
1950	56.0	39.4	4.7	70.3	29.5	0.2	68.0	32.0	0.0	70.0	30.0	0.0
1952	53.9	46.1	0.0	67.5	32.5	0.0	76.6	23.4	0.0	68.0	32.0	0.0
1954	52.3	47.7	0.0	67.2	32.8	0.0	85.3	14.8	0.0	64.6	35.4	0.0
1956	50.7	49.3	0.0	67.0	33.1	0.0	66.6	33.4	0.0	69.9	30.2	0.0
1958	51.4	48.6	0.0	60.7	39.3	0.0	70.0	30.0	0.0	70.8	29.2	0.0
1960	52.1	47.9	0.0	54.5	45.5	0.0	61.4	38.6	0.0	60.4	39.6	0.0
1962	54.1	45.9	0.0	55.6	44.4	0.0	60.5	39.6	0.0	58.9	41.1	0.0
1964	56.2	43.9	0.0	56.6	43.4	0.0	58.0	42.0	0.0	60.4	39.6	0.0
1966	42.7	41.7	15.6	54.7	45.4	0.0	55.6	44.4	0.0	52.9	47.1	0.0
1968	29.2	39.5	31.3	52.7	47.3	0.0	60.6	39.4	0.0	54.6	45.4	0.0
1970										55.3	44.2	0.6

217

YEAR	COMPOSITE A (P+G+S+H/4)			COMPOSITE B (G+S+H/3)			COMPOSITE C (S+H/2)		
	DEM.	REP.	OTHER	DEM.	REP.	OTHER	DEM.	REP.	OTHER
1872	47.1	52.9	0.1	49.4	50.6	0.0	49.2	50.8	0.0
1874	50.9	46.5	2.5	52.4	43.9	3.8	53.6	38.9	7.5
1876	53.4	46.6	0.0	53.3	46.7	0.0	53.8	46.3	0.0
1878	52.4	42.5	5.2	52.3	40.1	7.6	52.5	32.2	15.3
1880	51.8	46.8	1.5	51.9	46.2	1.9	52.5	43.6	3.9
1882	51.3	48.5	0.2	50.8	49.1	0.2	49.0	50.7	0.3
1884	53.8	46.2	0.1	54.0	45.9	0.1	54.2	45.8	0.0
1886	53.3	37.9	8.9	53.7	33.3	13.0	54.5	20.1	25.4
1888	52.2	46.9	0.9	52.4	46.8	0.8	52.9	46.6	0.5
1890	52.2	41.5	6.4	53.4	41.5	5.1	56.7	42.6	0.7
1892	48.3	31.8	19.9	48.7	29.8	21.5	49.0	25.9	25.1
1894	47.3	37.7	15.0	45.9	35.9	18.2	45.7	31.6	22.7
1896	47.1	47.0	5.9	44.4	47.1	8.6	44.8	47.7	7.5
1898	52.2	42.3	5.6	51.6	40.3	8.1	51.5	37.3	11.3
1900	56.4	41.3	2.3	57.6	39.2	3.2	55.6	38.1	6.3
1902	62.1	37.3	0.7	64.7	34.6	0.7	68.8	30.1	1.2
1904	61.2	38.5	0.3	62.0	37.9	0.1	62.3	37.7	0.1
1906	59.3	40.4	0.2	60.5	39.4	0.1	61.5	38.4	0.1
1908	56.1	43.7	0.2	57.1	42.8	0.2	56.9	43.0	0.2
1910	58.6	33.0	8.4	59.6	35.1	5.3	59.8	40.0	0.2
1912	62.2	20.0	17.8	63.8	24.0	12.3	66.2	30.1	3.8
1914	59.2	34.4	6.4	59.4	37.0	3.7	59.2	40.5	0.3
1916	58.4	41.5	0.2	58.5	41.4	0.1	58.6	41.3	0.1
1918	59.1	40.8	0.1	59.7	40.3	0.0	60.7	39.3	0.0
1920	57.3	42.7	0.0	57.5	42.5	0.0	57.6	42.4	0.0
1922	59.7	40.1	0.2	60.3	39.7	0.0	60.8	39.2	0.0
1924	60.9	38.8	0.4	61.5	38.5	0.0	61.6	38.4	0.0
1926	58.1	41.7	0.2	60.1	39.9	0.0	60.9	39.1	0.0
1928	54.1	45.9	0.0	57.1	42.9	0.0	57.8	42.2	0.0
1930	60.9	39.0	0.1	62.1	37.9	0.0	61.7	38.3	0.0
1932	69.5	30.3	0.2	69.3	30.7	0.0	69.0	31.0	0.0
1934	68.6	31.3	0.1	67.6	32.4	0.0	67.2	32.8	0.0
1936	70.5	29.5	0.0	69.5	30.5	0.0	71.0	29.0	0.0
1938	68.8	31.2	0.0	67.2	32.8	0.0	65.2	34.8	0.0
1940	72.5	27.5	0.0	72.0	28.0	0.0	70.2	29.8	0.0
1942	70.4	29.6	0.0	70.4	29.6	0.0	69.3	30.7	0.0
1944	69.0	31.0	0.0	69.8	30.2	0.0	69.9	30.1	0.0
1946	66.4	32.3	1.3	67.7	32.1	0.2	65.9	34.0	0.1
1948	68.2	29.2	2.7	71.6	28.0	0.4	70.8	28.8	0.4
1950	66.1	32.7	1.2	69.5	30.5	0.1	69.0	31.0	0.0
1952	66.5	33.5	0.0	70.7	29.3	0.0	72.3	27.7	0.0
1954	67.3	32.7	0.0	72.4	27.7	0.0	74.9	25.1	0.0
1956	63.5	36.5	0.0	67.8	32.2	0.0	68.2	31.8	0.0
1958	63.2	36.8	0.0	67.2	32.8	0.0	70.4	29.6	0.0
1960	57.1	42.9	0.0	58.8	41.2	0.0	60.9	39.1	0.0
1962	57.3	42.7	0.0	58.3	41.7	0.0	59.7	40.3	0.0
1964	57.8	42.2	0.0	58.3	41.7	0.0	59.2	40.8	0.0
1966	51.5	44.6	3.9	54.4	45.6	0.0	54.2	45.8	0.0
1968	49.3	42.9	7.8	56.0	44.0	0.0	57.6	42.4	0.0
1970							55.3	44.2	0.6

218

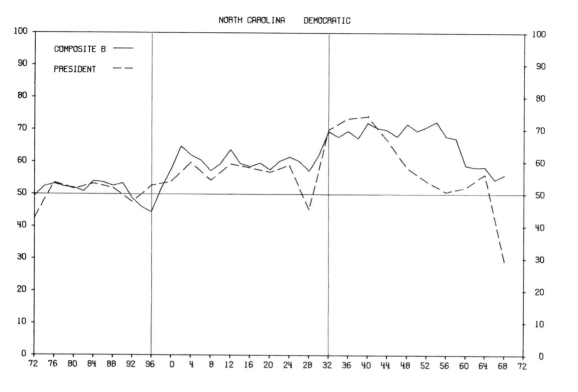

NORTH CAROLINA   DEMOCRATIC

COMPOSITE B ———
PRESIDENT   — —

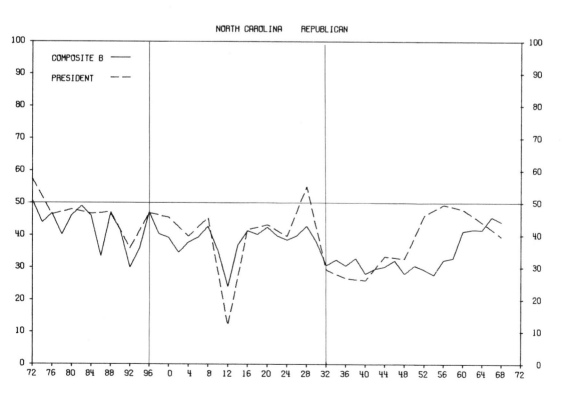

NORTH CAROLINA   REPUBLICAN

COMPOSITE B ———
PRESIDENT   — —

YEAR	PRESIDENT			GOVERNOR			SENATE CLASS I			SENATE CLASS III		
	DEM.	REP.	OTHER	DEM.	REP.	OTHER	DEM.	REP.	OTHER	DEM.	REP.	OTHER
1872												
1874												
1876												
1878												
1880												
1882												
1884												
1886												
1888												
1890				34.0	59.6	6.5						
1892	48.8	48.8	2.4	52.4	47.6	0.0						
1894				19.2	55.8	25.0						
1896	43.6	55.6	0.8	44.4	55.6	0.0						
1898				41.7	58.3	0.0						
1900	35.5	62.1	2.4	38.7	59.2	2.1						
1902				34.8	62.7	2.5						
1904	20.4	75.1	4.5	24.7	70.7	4.6						
1906				53.2	45.3	1.5						
1908	34.8	61.0	4.2	51.1	48.4	0.5						
1910				50.0	47.4	2.7						
1912	34.2	26.6	39.2	36.0	45.4	18.5						
1914				38.9	49.6	11.5				33.9	55.8	10.2
1916	47.8	46.3	5.8	18.4	79.2	2.4	38.2	53.9	7.9			
1918				40.3	59.7	0.0						
1920	18.3	77.7	4.0	49.0	51.0	0.0				40.2	59.8	0.0
1922				0.0	26.9	73.1	47.7	52.3	0.0			
1924	7.0	47.7	45.4	46.1	53.9	0.0						
1926				15.2	81.7	3.1				4.3	34.5	61.2
1928	44.5	54.8	0.7	43.2	56.5	0.4	19.3	79.6	1.0			
1930				23.2	73.6	3.2						
1932	69.6	28.0	2.4	45.0	54.7	0.3				27.4	72.3	0.2
1934				53.0	46.6	0.4	40.2	58.2	1.5			
1936	59.6	26.6	13.8	29.3	34.7	36.0						
1938				52.5	47.5	0.0				7.3	50.1	42.6
1940	44.2	55.1	0.8	63.1	36.9	0.0	26.4	38.1	35.4			
1942				57.6	42.4	0.0						
1944	45.5	53.8	0.7	28.9	52.0	19.1				45.2	33.0	21.8
1946				31.1	68.9	0.0	23.2	53.3	23.5	27.4	55.5	17.0
1948	43.4	52.2	4.4	37.5	61.3	1.2						
1950				33.7	66.3	0.0				32.4	67.6	0.0
1952	28.4	71.0	0.6	21.3	78.7	0.0	23.3	66.3	10.4			
1954				35.8	64.2	0.0						
1956	38.1	61.7	0.2	41.5	58.5	0.0				36.0	63.6	0.4
1958				46.9	53.1	0.0	41.5	57.2	1.3			
1960	44.5	55.4	0.1	49.4	44.5	6.1	49.7	49.2	1.1			
1962				50.4	49.6	0.0				39.3	60.7	0.0
1964	58.0	41.9	0.2	55.7	44.3	0.0	57.6	42.4	0.0			
1966												
1968	38.2	55.9	5.8	54.8	43.7	1.5				33.7	64.6	1.7
1970							61.3	37.8	0.9			

NORTH DAKOTA

YEAR	PRESIDENT			GOVERNOR			SENATE			HOUSE OF REPRESENTATIVES		
	DEM.	REP.	OTHER	DEM.	REP.	OTHER	DEM.	REP.	OTHER	DEM.	REP.	OTHER
1872												
1874												
1876												
1878												
1880												
1882												
1884												
1886												
1888												
1890				34.0	59.6	6.5				36.1	63.9	0.0
1892	48.8	48.8	2.4	52.4	47.6	0.0				30.5	49.0	20.6
1894	46.2	52.2	1.6	19.2	55.8	25.0				0.0	57.3	42.7
1896	43.7	55.6	0.8	44.4	55.6	0.0				45.3	54.0	0.8
1898	39.6	58.9	1.6	41.7	58.4	0.0				39.1	60.9	0.0
1900	35.5	62.1	2.4	38.7	59.2	2.1				37.0	61.0	2.0
1902	28.0	68.6	3.4	34.9	62.7	2.5				30.3	68.4	1.2
1904	20.4	75.1	4.5	24.7	70.7	4.6				23.3	72.7	4.1
1906	27.6	68.1	4.3	53.2	45.3	1.5				35.2	62.9	1.9
1908	34.8	61.0	4.2	51.1	48.4	0.5				33.7	65.7	0.7
1910	34.5	43.8	21.7	50.0	47.4	2.7				32.1	63.9	4.0
1912	34.2	26.6	39.2	36.0	45.5	18.5				30.5	58.8	10.7
1914	41.0	36.5	22.5	38.9	49.6	11.5	34.0	55.8	10.2	31.7	60.4	7.9
1916	47.8	46.3	5.8	18.4	79.2	2.4	38.2	53.9	7.9	30.1	65.4	4.5
1918	33.1	62.0	4.9	40.3	59.7	0.0	39.2	56.8	4.0	35.0	65.0	0.0
1920	18.3	77.7	4.0	49.0	51.0	0.0	40.2	59.8	0.0	11.7	57.3	31.0
1922	12.6	62.7	24.7	0.0	26.9	73.1	47.7	52.3	0.0	0.0	77.1	22.9
1924	7.0	47.7	45.4	46.1	53.9	0.0	26.0	43.4	30.6	16.5	66.6	16.8
1926	25.7	51.2	23.1	15.2	81.7	3.1	4.3	34.5	61.2	17.7	77.8	4.5
1928	44.5	54.8	0.7	43.2	56.5	0.4	19.4	79.6	1.0	25.7	74.3	0.0
1930	57.0	41.4	1.6	23.2	73.6	3.2	23.4	76.0	0.6	28.5	69.5	1.9
1932	69.6	28.0	2.4	45.0	54.8	0.3	27.5	72.3	0.2	33.9	65.7	0.3
1934	64.6	27.3	8.1	53.0	46.6	0.4	40.2	58.2	1.5	34.9	54.8	10.3
1936	59.6	26.6	13.8	29.3	34.7	36.0	23.8	54.2	22.0	42.5	55.2	2.3
1938	51.9	40.8	7.3	52.5	47.5	0.0	7.3	50.1	42.6	24.3	73.7	2.0
1940	44.2	55.1	0.8	63.1	36.9	0.0	26.5	38.1	35.4	29.4	60.3	10.3
1942	44.8	54.5	0.7	57.6	42.4	0.0	35.8	35.6	28.6	28.4	54.3	17.3
1944	45.5	53.8	0.7	28.9	52.0	19.1	45.2	33.0	21.8	29.9	56.7	13.4
1946	44.5	53.0	2.6	31.1	68.9	0.0	25.1	54.3	20.6	25.7	74.3	0.0
1948	43.4	52.2	4.4	37.5	61.3	1.2	28.8	61.0	10.3	17.8	81.7	0.6
1950	35.9	61.6	2.5	33.7	66.3	0.0	32.4	67.6	0.0	29.3	70.7	0.0
1952	28.4	71.0	0.6	21.3	78.7	0.0	23.3	66.4	10.4	12.9	87.2	0.0
1954	33.2	66.4	0.4	35.8	64.2	0.0	29.6	65.0	5.4	32.9	67.1	0.0
1956	38.1	61.7	0.2	41.5	58.5	0.0	36.0	63.6	0.4	37.7	62.3	0.0
1958	41.3	58.6	0.1	46.9	53.1	0.0	41.5	57.2	1.3	48.4	51.6	0.0
1960	44.5	55.4	0.1	49.4	44.5	6.1	49.7	49.2	1.1	46.7	53.3	0.0
1962	51.3	48.7	0.1	50.4	49.6	0.0	39.4	60.7	0.0	45.7	54.3	0.0
1964	58.0	41.9	0.2	55.7	44.3	0.0	57.6	42.4	0.0	49.8	50.0	0.3
1966	48.1	48.9	3.0	55.3	44.0	0.7	45.7	53.5	0.8	40.9	59.2	0.0
1968	38.2	55.9	5.8	54.8	43.7	1.5	33.7	64.6	1.7	39.6	58.8	1.6
1970							61.3	37.8	0.9	41.9	58.1	0.0

221

YEAR	COMPOSITE A (P+G+S+H/4)			COMPOSITE B (G+S+H/3)			COMPOSITE C (S+H/2)		
	DEM.	REP.	OTHER	DEM.	REP.	OTHER	DEM.	REP.	OTHER
1872									
1874									
1876									
1878									
1880									
1882									
1884									
1886									
1888									
1890				35.1	61.7	3.2	36.1	63.9	0.0
1892	43.9	48.5	7.7	41.4	48.3	10.3	30.5	49.0	20.6
1894	21.8	55.1	23.1	9.6	56.5	33.8	0.0	57.3	42.7
1896	44.4	55.1	0.5	44.8	54.8	0.4	45.3	54.0	0.8
1898	40.1	59.4	0.5	40.4	59.6	0.0	39.1	60.9	0.0
1900	37.1	60.8	2.1	37.9	60.1	2.0	37.0	61.0	2.0
1902	31.0	66.6	2.4	32.6	65.6	1.9	30.3	68.4	1.2
1904	22.8	72.8	4.4	24.0	71.7	4.3	23.3	72.7	4.1
1906	38.7	58.8	2.6	44.2	54.1	1.7	35.2	62.9	1.9
1908	39.8	58.4	1.8	42.4	57.1	0.6	33.7	65.7	0.7
1910	38.8	51.7	9.5	41.0	55.7	3.4	32.1	63.9	4.0
1912	33.6	43.6	22.8	33.2	52.1	14.6	30.5	58.8	10.7
1914	36.4	50.6	13.1	34.9	55.3	9.9	32.8	58.1	9.1
1916	33.7	61.2	5.2	28.9	66.2	4.9	34.2	59.6	6.2
1918	36.9	60.9	2.2	38.2	60.5	1.3	37.1	60.9	2.0
1920	29.8	61.5	8.8	33.6	56.0	10.3	26.0	58.6	15.5
1922	15.1	54.7	30.2	15.9	52.1	32.0	23.9	64.7	11.5
1924	23.9	52.9	23.2	29.5	54.7	15.8	21.3	55.0	23.7
1926	15.7	61.3	23.0	12.4	64.7	22.9	11.0	56.2	32.8
1928	33.2	66.3	0.5	29.4	70.1	0.5	22.5	77.0	0.5
1930	33.0	65.1	1.8	25.0	73.0	1.9	26.0	72.8	1.3
1932	44.0	55.2	0.8	35.5	64.3	0.3	30.7	69.0	0.3
1934	48.2	46.7	5.1	42.7	53.2	4.1	37.6	56.5	5.9
1936	38.8	42.7	18.6	31.9	48.0	20.1	33.2	54.7	12.2
1938	34.0	53.0	13.0	28.0	57.1	14.9	15.8	61.9	22.3
1940	40.8	47.6	11.6	39.7	45.1	15.2	28.0	49.2	22.9
1942	41.7	46.7	11.7	40.6	44.1	15.3	32.1	44.9	23.0
1944	37.4	48.9	13.7	34.7	47.3	18.1	37.6	44.9	17.6
1946	31.6	62.6	5.8	27.3	65.8	6.9	25.4	64.3	10.3
1948	31.9	64.0	4.1	28.0	68.0	4.0	23.3	71.3	5.4
1950	32.8	66.5	0.6	31.8	68.2	0.0	30.9	69.1	0.0
1952	21.4	75.8	2.8	19.1	77.4	3.5	18.1	76.8	5.2
1954	32.9	65.7	1.5	32.8	65.4	1.8	31.3	66.1	2.7
1956	38.3	61.5	0.1	38.4	61.5	0.1	36.9	63.0	0.2
1958	44.5	55.1	0.4	45.6	54.0	0.4	45.0	54.4	0.7
1960	47.6	50.6	1.8	48.6	49.0	2.4	48.2	51.3	0.5
1962	46.7	53.3	0.0	45.2	54.9	0.0	42.5	57.5	0.0
1964	55.3	44.6	0.1	54.4	45.5	0.1	53.7	46.2	0.1
1966	47.5	51.4	1.1	47.3	52.2	0.5	43.3	56.3	0.4
1968	41.6	55.8	2.6	42.7	55.7	1.6	36.7	61.7	1.6
1970							51.6	47.9	0.5

222

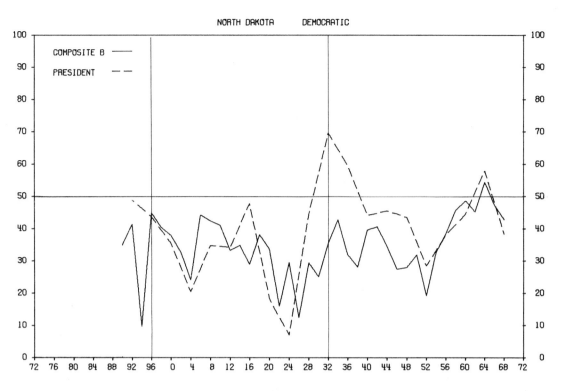

NORTH DAKOTA   DEMOCRATIC

COMPOSITE B ———
PRESIDENT   — —

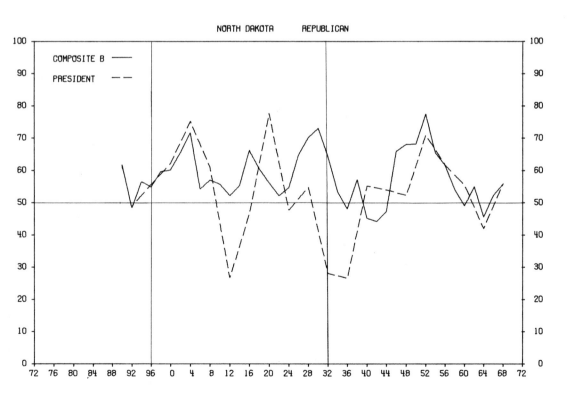

NORTH DAKOTA   REPUBLICAN

COMPOSITE B ———
PRESIDENT   — —

223

OHIO

YEAR	PRESIDENT			GOVERNOR			SENATE CLASS I			SENATE CLASS III		
	DEM.	REP.	OTHER	DEM.	REP.	OTHER	DEM.	REP.	OTHER	DEM.	REP.	OTHER
1872	46.1	53.2	0.6	47.4	51.7	0.9						
1874				47.8	47.6	4.5						
1876	49.1	50.2	0.7	49.3	50.2	0.4						
1878				48.9	44.9	6.2						
1880	47.0	51.7	1.3	47.7	50.3	2.1						
1882				46.2	50.1	3.7						
1884	46.9	51.0	2.1	50.1	48.3	1.6						
1886				46.7	49.1	4.1						
1888	47.1	49.6	3.3	44.8	47.9	7.3						
1890				48.9	47.5	3.6						
1892	47.5	47.7	4.8	45.9	48.6	5.5						
1894				42.8	52.6	4.6						
1896	46.8	51.9	1.3	39.9	51.0	9.0						
1898				47.0	50.3	2.7						
1900	45.7	52.3	2.0	40.5	45.9	13.5						
1902				44.5	52.7	2.8						
1904	34.3	59.7	5.9	41.8	54.9	3.4						
1906				50.5	46.0	3.5						
1908	44.8	51.0	4.1	49.2	47.5	3.3						
1910				51.6	40.7	7.6						
1912	41.0	26.8	32.2	42.4	26.3	31.3						
1914				43.7	46.3	9.9				39.6	49.2	11.2
1916	51.9	44.2	4.0	48.4	47.8	3.8	49.3	46.2	4.6			
1918				50.6	49.4	0.0						
1920	38.6	58.5	2.9	45.9	51.9	2.2				40.8	59.1	0.1
1922				50.5	49.4	0.0	47.7	50.9	1.4			
1924	23.7	58.3	18.0	54.0	45.0	1.0						
1926				50.5	49.0	0.5				46.6	53.2	0.2
1928	34.5	64.9	0.7	44.7	54.8	0.5	39.1	60.7	0.2	37.4	62.4	0.2
1930				52.8	47.2	0.0						
1932	49.9	47.0	3.1	52.8	44.8	2.3				52.5	45.8	1.7
1934				51.1	48.1	0.7	59.9	39.4	0.6			
1936	58.0	37.4	4.6	52.0	47.7	0.2						
1938				47.6	52.4	0.0				46.4	53.6	0.0
1940	52.2	47.8	0.0	44.5	55.5	0.0	47.6	52.4	0.0			
1942				39.5	60.5	0.0						
1944	49.8	50.2	0.0	51.8	48.2	0.0				49.7	50.3	0.0
1946				48.9	50.6	0.5	43.0	56.6	0.3			
1948	49.5	49.2	1.3	53.7	46.3	0.0						
1950				52.6	47.4	0.0				42.5	57.5	0.0
1952	43.2	56.8	0.0	55.9	44.1	0.0	45.4	54.6	0.0			
1954				54.1	45.9	0.0				49.9	50.1	0.0
1956	38.9	61.1	0.0	44.0	56.0	0.0				52.9	47.1	0.0
1958				56.9	43.1	0.0	52.5	47.5	0.0			
1960	46.7	53.3	0.0									
1962				41.1	58.9	0.0				61.6	38.4	0.0
1964	62.9	37.1	0.0				50.2	49.8	0.0			
1966				37.8	62.2	0.0						
1968	42.9	45.2	11.8							48.5	51.5	0.0
1970				54.2	43.4	2.4	47.4	49.7	2.9			

224

OHIO

YEAR	PRESIDENT			GOVERNOR			SENATE			HOUSE OF REPRESENTATIVES		
	DEM.	REP.	OTHER	DEM.	REP.	OTHER	DEM.	REP.	OTHER	DEM.	REP.	OTHER
1872	46.2	53.2	0.6	47.4	51.8	0.9				48.5	51.3	0.3
1874	47.6	51.7	0.7	47.8	47.6	4.5				51.5	46.4	2.2
1876	49.1	50.2	0.7	49.3	50.3	0.4				49.0	50.0	1.0
1878	48.0	51.0	1.0	48.9	44.9	6.2				45.5	47.4	7.1
1880	47.0	51.7	1.3	47.7	50.3	2.1				47.9	50.9	1.2
1882	47.0	51.4	1.7	46.2	50.1	3.7				50.4	47.1	2.5
1884	46.9	51.0	2.1	50.1	48.3	1.6				48.0	50.5	1.5
1886	47.0	50.3	2.7	46.8	49.1	4.1				47.0	48.5	4.5
1888	47.1	49.6	3.3	44.8	47.9	7.3				47.2	49.7	3.1
1890	47.3	48.6	4.1	48.9	47.5	3.6				47.5	49.0	3.4
1892	47.5	47.7	4.8	45.9	48.6	5.5				48.4	47.2	4.4
1894	47.2	49.8	3.1	42.8	52.6	4.6				36.3	54.1	9.5
1896	46.8	51.9	1.3	40.0	51.0	9.1				47.1	52.2	0.7
1898	46.2	52.1	1.7	47.0	50.3	2.7				46.2	52.5	1.3
1900	45.7	52.3	2.1	40.5	45.9	13.5				46.6	52.2	1.3
1902	40.0	56.0	4.0	44.5	52.7	2.8				41.7	54.3	4.0
1904	34.3	59.8	5.9	41.8	54.9	3.4				36.0	59.0	5.0
1906	39.6	55.4	5.0	50.5	46.0	3.5				42.9	52.8	4.3
1908	44.8	51.0	4.2	49.2	47.5	3.3				46.8	47.7	5.5
1910	42.9	38.9	18.2	51.6	40.8	7.7				50.3	42.6	7.1
1912	41.0	26.8	32.2	42.4	26.3	31.4				44.4	29.9	25.7
1914	46.4	35.5	18.1	43.7	46.3	10.0	39.6	49.2	11.2	45.4	45.0	9.6
1916	51.9	44.2	4.0	48.4	47.8	3.8	49.3	46.2	4.6	48.8	48.6	2.6
1918	45.2	51.3	3.5	50.6	49.4	0.0	45.0	52.6	2.4	43.4	54.7	1.9
1920	38.6	58.5	3.0	45.9	51.9	2.2	40.8	59.1	0.1	41.2	58.1	0.7
1922	31.1	58.4	10.5	50.5	49.4	0.0	47.7	50.9	1.4	45.0	53.7	1.3
1924	23.7	58.3	18.0	54.0	45.0	1.0	47.2	52.0	0.8	41.4	56.7	1.9
1926	29.1	61.6	9.3	50.5	49.0	0.5	46.6	53.2	0.2	43.6	56.2	0.2
1928	34.5	64.9	0.7	44.7	54.8	0.5	38.3	61.6	0.2	39.2	60.7	0.1
1930	42.2	56.0	1.9	52.8	47.2	0.0	45.4	53.7	0.9	48.5	50.8	0.7
1932	49.9	47.0	3.1	52.8	44.9	2.3	52.5	45.8	1.7	51.7	47.3	1.0
1934	53.9	42.2	3.8	51.1	48.1	0.7	60.0	39.4	0.6	53.4	45.8	0.7
1936	58.0	37.4	4.6	52.0	47.7	0.3	53.2	46.5	0.3	55.9	43.1	1.0
1938	55.1	42.6	2.3	47.6	52.5	0.0	46.4	53.6	0.0	47.8	52.2	0.1
1940	52.2	47.8	0.0	44.5	55.6	0.0	47.6	52.4	0.0	50.0	50.0	0.0
1942	51.0	49.0	0.0	39.5	60.5	0.0	48.7	51.3	0.0	43.7	56.1	0.2
1944	49.8	50.2	0.0	51.8	48.2	0.0	49.7	50.3	0.0	47.0	53.0	0.0
1946	49.7	49.7	0.6	48.9	50.6	0.5	43.1	56.6	0.3	41.5	58.2	0.2
1948	49.5	49.2	1.3	53.7	46.3	0.0	42.8	57.1	0.2	52.2	47.8	0.0
1950	46.4	53.0	0.6	52.6	47.4	0.0	42.5	57.5	0.0	45.8	53.2	1.1
1952	43.2	56.8	0.0	55.9	44.1	0.0	45.4	54.6	0.0	43.5	54.3	2.2
1954	41.1	58.9	0.0	54.1	45.9	0.0	49.9	50.1	0.0	44.6	53.7	1.8
1956	38.9	61.1	0.0	44.0	56.0	0.0	52.9	47.1	0.0	42.7	57.3	0.0
1958	42.8	57.2	0.0	56.9	43.1	0.0	52.5	47.5	0.0	50.8	49.2	0.0
1960	46.7	53.3	0.0	49.0	51.0	0.0	57.0	43.0	0.0	45.9	54.1	0.0
1962	54.8	45.2	0.0	41.1	58.9	0.0	61.6	38.4	0.0	41.7	58.2	0.1
1964	62.9	37.1	0.0	39.5	60.6	0.0	50.2	49.8	0.0	51.3	48.7	0.0
1966	53.0	41.1	5.9	37.8	62.2	0.0	49.3	50.7	0.0	42.8	57.2	0.0
1968	43.0	45.2	11.8	46.0	52.8	1.2	48.5	51.5	0.0	39.3	60.7	0.0
1970				54.2	43.4	2.4	47.5	49.7	2.9	43.5	56.1	0.4

225

OHIO

YEAR	COMPOSITE A (P+G+S+H/4)			COMPOSITE B (G+S+H/3)			COMPOSITE C (S+H/2)		
	DEM.	REP.	OTHER	DEM.	REP.	OTHER	DEM.	REP.	OTHER
1872	47.3	52.1	0.6	47.9	51.5	0.6	48.5	51.3	0.3
1874	49.0	48.6	2.5	49.7	47.0	3.4	51.5	46.4	2.2
1876	49.1	50.1	0.7	49.2	50.1	0.7	49.0	50.0	1.0
1878	47.5	47.8	4.8	47.2	46.1	6.6	45.5	47.4	7.1
1880	47.5	51.0	1.5	47.8	50.6	1.6	47.9	50.9	1.2
1882	47.9	49.5	2.6	48.3	48.6	3.1	50.4	47.1	2.5
1884	48.3	50.0	1.7	49.1	49.4	1.5	48.0	50.5	1.5
1886	46.9	49.3	3.8	46.9	48.8	4.3	47.0	48.5	4.5
1888	46.4	49.1	4.6	46.0	48.8	5.2	47.2	49.7	3.1
1890	47.9	48.4	3.7	48.2	48.3	3.5	47.5	49.0	3.4
1892	47.3	47.8	4.9	47.1	47.9	5.0	48.4	47.2	4.4
1894	42.1	52.2	5.7	39.6	53.4	7.1	36.3	54.1	9.5
1896	44.6	51.7	3.7	43.5	51.6	4.9	47.1	52.2	0.7
1898	46.5	51.6	1.9	46.6	51.4	2.0	46.2	52.5	1.3
1900	44.3	50.1	5.6	43.6	49.1	7.4	46.6	52.2	1.3
1902	42.1	54.3	3.6	43.1	53.5	3.4	41.7	54.3	4.0
1904	37.4	57.9	4.8	38.9	56.9	4.2	36.0	59.0	5.0
1906	44.3	51.4	4.3	46.7	49.4	3.9	42.9	52.8	4.3
1908	47.0	48.7	4.3	48.0	47.6	4.4	46.8	47.7	5.5
1910	48.3	40.8	11.0	50.9	41.7	7.4	50.3	42.6	7.1
1912	42.6	27.7	29.7	43.4	28.1	28.5	44.4	29.9	25.7
1914	43.8	44.0	12.2	42.9	46.8	10.3	42.5	47.1	10.4
1916	49.6	46.7	3.7	48.8	47.5	3.7	49.0	47.4	3.6
1918	46.1	52.0	1.9	46.3	52.3	1.4	44.2	53.7	2.1
1920	41.6	56.9	1.5	42.6	56.4	1.0	41.0	58.6	0.4
1922	43.6	53.1	3.3	47.7	51.4	0.9	46.3	52.3	1.4
1924	41.6	53.0	5.4	47.5	51.3	1.2	44.3	54.4	1.4
1926	42.5	55.0	2.6	46.9	52.8	0.3	45.1	54.7	0.2
1928	39.2	60.5	0.4	40.7	59.0	0.3	38.7	61.2	0.1
1930	47.2	51.9	0.9	48.9	50.6	0.6	46.9	52.3	0.8
1932	51.7	46.2	2.0	52.3	46.0	1.7	52.1	46.5	1.4
1934	54.6	43.9	1.5	54.8	44.5	0.7	56.7	42.6	0.7
1936	54.8	43.7	1.5	53.7	45.8	0.5	54.5	44.8	0.7
1938	49.2	50.2	0.6	47.2	52.8	0.0	47.1	52.9	0.0
1940	48.6	51.4	0.0	47.4	52.6	0.0	48.8	51.2	0.0
1942	45.7	54.2	0.1	43.9	56.0	0.1	46.2	53.7	0.1
1944	49.6	50.4	0.0	49.5	50.5	0.0	48.4	51.6	0.0
1946	45.8	53.8	0.4	44.5	55.2	0.4	42.3	57.4	0.3
1948	49.5	50.1	0.4	49.5	50.4	0.1	47.5	52.4	0.1
1950	46.8	52.8	0.4	47.0	52.7	0.4	44.1	55.4	0.5
1952	47.0	52.4	0.6	48.3	51.0	0.7	44.5	54.4	1.1
1954	47.4	52.1	0.5	49.5	49.9	0.6	47.3	51.9	0.9
1956	44.6	55.4	0.0	46.5	53.5	0.0	47.8	52.2	0.0
1958	50.8	49.3	0.0	53.4	46.6	0.0	51.6	48.4	0.0
1960	49.7	50.3	0.0	50.6	49.4	0.0	51.5	48.5	0.0
1962	49.8	50.2	0.0	48.1	51.8	0.0	51.7	48.3	0.1
1964	51.0	49.0	0.0	47.0	53.0	0.0	50.8	49.2	0.0
1966	45.7	52.8	1.5	43.3	56.7	0.0	46.1	53.9	0.0
1968	44.2	52.6	3.3	44.6	55.0	0.4	43.9	56.1	0.0
1970				48.4	49.7	1.9	45.5	52.9	1.6

226

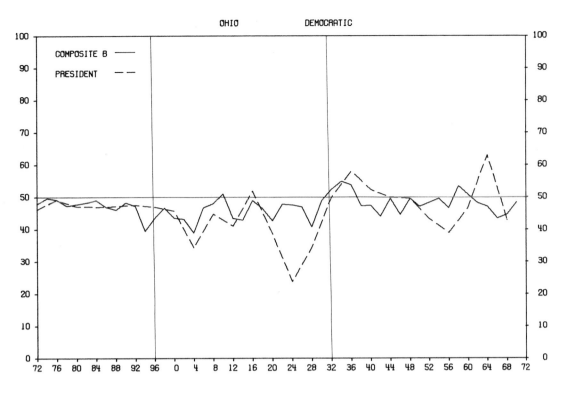

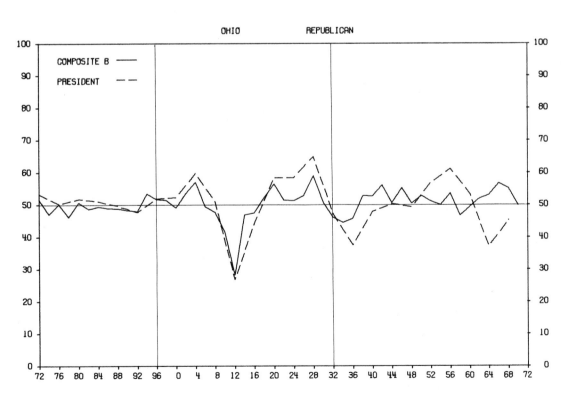

227

YEAR	PRESIDENT			GOVERNOR			SENATE CLASS II			SENATE CLASS III		
	DEM.	REP.	OTHER	DEM.	REP.	OTHER	DEM.	REP.	OTHER	DEM.	REP.	OTHER
1872												
1874												
1876												
1878												
1880												
1882												
1884												
1886												
1888												
1890												
1892												
1894												
1896												
1898												
1900												
1902												
1904												
1906												
1908	48.1	43.4	8.4	53.4	42.8	3.8						
1910				48.6	40.2	11.2						
1912	47.0	35.8	17.3				50.4	33.3	16.3			
1914				39.7	37.8	22.5				48.0	29.4	22.6
1916	50.7	33.3	16.1									
1918				53.5	42.6	3.8	55.4	40.7	3.8			
1920	44.5	50.2	5.3							44.6	50.6	4.8
1922				54.4	44.8	0.8						
1924	48.5	42.8	8.8				35.4	61.6	3.0			
1926				54.9	44.2	0.9				54.8	44.7	0.6
1928	35.4	63.7	0.8									
1930				59.0	40.8	0.2	52.3	47.5	0.2			
1932	73.3	26.7	0.0							65.6	33.7	0.7
1934				58.2	38.8	2.9						
1936	66.8	32.7	0.5				68.0	31.5	0.5			
1938				70.0	29.3	0.7				65.4	33.9	0.7
1940	57.4	42.2	0.4									
1942				51.9	47.6	0.5	44.8	54.8	0.4			
1944	55.6	44.2	0.2							55.6	44.0	0.3
1946				52.5	46.0	1.6						
1948	62.7	37.3	0.0				62.3	37.4	0.3			
1950				51.1	48.6	0.3				54.8	45.2	0.0
1952	45.4	54.6	0.0									
1954				58.7	41.3	0.0	55.8	43.7	0.5			
1956	44.9	55.1	0.0							55.3	44.7	0.0
1958				74.1	19.9	5.9						
1960	41.0	59.0	0.0				54.8	44.6	0.5			
1962				44.4	55.3	0.3				53.2	46.3	0.4
1964	55.7	44.3	0.0				51.2	48.8	0.0			
1966				43.8	55.7	0.6	53.7	46.3	0.0			
1968	32.0	47.7	20.3							46.2	51.7	2.1
1970				48.4	48.1	3.5						

228

OKLAHOMA

YEAR	PRESIDENT			GOVERNOR			SENATE			HOUSE OF REPRESENTATIVES		
	DEM.	REP.	OTHER	DEM.	REP.	OTHER	DEM.	REP.	OTHER	DEM.	REP.	OTHER
1872												
1874												
1876												
1878												
1880												
1882												
1884												
1886												
1888												
1890												
1892												
1894												
1896												
1898												
1900												
1902												
1904												
1906												
1908	48.1	43.5	8.4	53.4	42.8	3.8				54.3	40.3	5.4
1910	47.5	39.6	12.9	48.6	40.2	11.2				50.5	39.8	9.8
1912	47.0	35.8	17.3	44.1	39.0	16.9				48.6	34.9	16.5
1914	48.8	34.5	16.7	39.7	37.8	22.5	48.0	29.4	22.6	45.8	30.8	23.4
1916	50.7	33.3	16.1	46.6	40.2	13.2	51.7	35.1	13.2	49.2	34.1	16.7
1918	47.6	41.7	10.7	53.5	42.6	3.8	55.4	40.7	3.8	54.9	41.4	3.7
1920	44.5	50.2	5.3	54.0	43.7	2.3	44.6	50.6	4.8	46.9	47.9	5.2
1922	46.5	46.5	7.0	54.5	44.8	0.8	40.0	56.1	3.9	60.3	38.8	0.9
1924	48.5	42.8	8.8	54.7	44.5	0.8	35.4	61.6	3.0	56.2	40.4	3.4
1926	42.0	53.2	4.8	54.9	44.2	0.9	54.8	44.7	0.6	56.4	43.4	0.2
1928	35.4	63.7	0.8	57.0	42.5	0.5	53.5	46.1	0.4	50.0	49.6	0.4
1930	54.4	45.2	0.4	59.1	40.8	0.2	52.3	47.5	0.2	61.9	38.1	0.0
1932	73.3	26.7	0.0	58.6	39.8	1.6	65.6	33.7	0.7	71.8	27.6	0.6
1934	70.1	29.7	0.2	58.2	38.8	2.9	66.8	32.6	0.6	66.9	30.7	2.4
1936	66.8	32.7	0.5	64.1	34.1	1.8	68.0	31.6	0.5	69.5	30.1	0.4
1938	62.1	37.5	0.4	70.0	29.3	0.7	65.4	33.9	0.7	68.6	31.1	0.4
1940	57.4	42.2	0.4	61.0	38.5	0.6	55.1	44.4	0.6	66.0	33.5	0.5
1942	56.5	43.2	0.3	51.9	47.6	0.5	44.8	54.8	0.4	57.5	42.0	0.5
1944	55.6	44.2	0.2	52.2	46.8	1.0	55.7	44.0	0.3	58.6	41.2	0.2
1946	59.2	40.7	0.1	52.5	46.0	1.6	59.0	40.7	0.3	58.5	41.5	0.0
1948	62.8	37.3	0.0	51.8	47.3	0.9	62.3	37.4	0.3	67.3	32.7	0.0
1950	54.1	45.9	0.0	51.1	48.6	0.3	54.8	45.2	0.0	59.9	40.1	0.0
1952	45.4	54.6	0.0	54.9	45.0	0.1	55.3	44.4	0.3	58.5	41.1	0.4
1954	45.1	54.9	0.0	58.7	41.3	0.0	55.8	43.7	0.5	64.9	35.1	0.0
1956	44.9	55.1	0.0	66.4	30.6	3.0	55.4	44.7	0.0	59.7	40.2	0.1
1958	42.9	57.1	0.0	74.1	20.0	5.9	55.1	44.6	0.3	69.7	30.0	0.3
1960	41.0	59.0	0.0	59.3	37.6	3.1	54.8	44.6	0.6	54.9	45.1	0.0
1962	48.4	51.6	0.0	44.4	55.3	0.3	53.2	46.3	0.4	61.1	38.9	0.0
1964	55.8	44.3	0.0	44.1	55.5	0.4	51.2	48.8	0.0	63.0	37.0	0.0
1966	43.9	46.0	10.2	43.8	55.7	0.6	53.7	46.3	0.0	52.4	47.6	0.0
1968	32.0	47.7	20.3	46.1	51.9	2.0	46.2	51.7	2.1	55.0	45.1	0.0
1970				48.4	48.1	3.5				63.5	36.3	0.2

229

YEAR	COMPOSITE A (P+G+S+H/4)			COMPOSITE B (G+S+H/3)			COMPOSITE C (S+H/2)		
	DEM.	REP.	OTHER	DEM.	REP.	OTHER	DEM.	REP.	OTHER
1872									
1874									
1876									
1878									
1880									
1882									
1884									
1886									
1888									
1890									
1892									
1894									
1896									
1898									
1900									
1902									
1904									
1906									
1908	52.0	42.2	5.9	53.9	41.5	4.6	54.3	40.3	5.4
1910	48.9	39.9	11.3	49.5	40.0	10.5	50.5	39.8	9.8
1912	46.6	36.6	16.9	46.3	37.0	16.7	48.6	34.9	16.5
1914	45.6	33.1	21.3	44.5	32.7	22.9	46.9	30.1	23.0
1916	49.5	35.7	14.8	49.2	36.5	14.4	50.4	34.6	15.0
1918	52.9	41.6	5.5	54.6	41.6	3.8	55.2	41.1	3.8
1920	47.5	48.1	4.4	48.5	47.4	4.1	45.8	49.2	5.0
1922	50.3	46.5	3.2	51.6	46.6	1.9	50.2	47.5	2.4
1924	48.7	47.3	4.0	48.8	48.8	2.4	45.8	51.0	3.2
1926	52.0	46.4	1.6	55.3	44.1	0.6	55.6	44.0	0.4
1928	49.0	50.5	0.5	53.5	46.1	0.4	51.8	47.8	0.4
1930	56.9	42.9	0.2	57.7	42.1	0.1	57.1	42.8	0.1
1932	67.3	32.0	0.7	65.3	33.7	1.0	68.7	30.7	0.7
1934	65.5	33.0	1.5	64.0	34.0	2.0	66.9	31.7	1.5
1936	67.1	32.1	0.8	67.2	31.9	0.9	68.7	30.8	0.4
1938	66.5	32.9	0.5	68.0	31.4	0.6	67.0	32.5	0.5
1940	59.9	39.6	0.5	60.7	38.8	0.6	60.6	38.9	0.5
1942	52.7	46.9	0.4	51.4	48.2	0.5	51.1	48.4	0.5
1944	55.5	44.1	0.4	55.5	44.0	0.5	57.1	42.6	0.2
1946	57.3	42.2	0.5	56.7	42.7	0.6	58.7	41.1	0.2
1948	61.0	38.7	0.3	60.5	39.1	0.4	64.8	35.1	0.2
1950	55.0	45.0	0.1	55.3	44.6	0.1	57.4	42.7	0.0
1952	53.5	46.3	0.2	56.2	43.5	0.3	56.9	42.8	0.3
1954	56.1	43.7	0.1	59.8	40.0	0.2	60.4	39.4	0.3
1956	56.6	42.7	0.8	60.5	38.5	1.0	57.5	42.4	0.0
1958	60.5	37.9	1.6	66.3	31.5	2.1	62.4	37.3	0.3
1960	52.5	46.6	0.9	56.3	42.5	1.2	54.9	44.9	0.3
1962	51.8	48.0	0.2	52.9	46.8	0.2	57.2	42.6	0.2
1964	53.5	46.4	0.1	52.8	47.1	0.1	57.1	42.9	0.0
1966	48.4	48.9	2.7	50.0	49.8	0.2	53.1	46.9	0.0
1968	44.8	49.1	6.1	49.1	49.6	1.4	50.6	48.4	1.1
1970				55.9	42.2	1.9	63.5	36.3	0.2

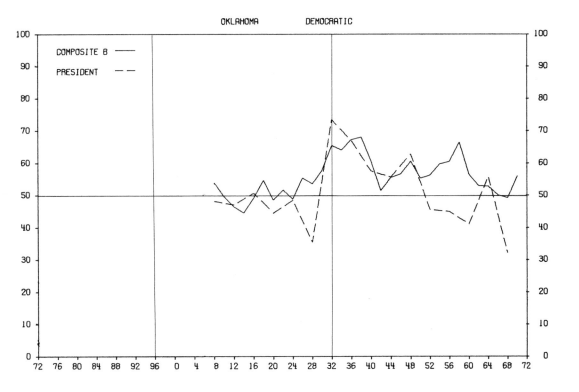

OKLAHOMA   DEMOCRATIC

COMPOSITE B ———
PRESIDENT   — —

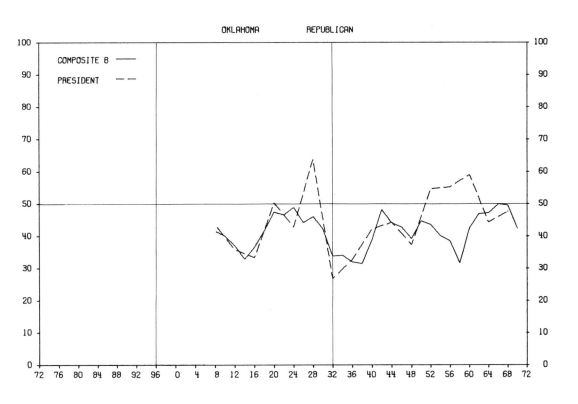

OKLAHOMA   REPUBLICAN

COMPOSITE B ———
PRESIDENT   — —

231

OREGON

YEAR	PRESIDENT			GOVERNOR			SENATE CLASS II			SENATE CLASS III		
	DEM.	REP.	OTHER	DEM.	REP.	OTHER	DEM.	REP.	OTHER	DEM.	REP.	OTHER
1872	38.5	58.8	2.7									
1874				38.2	36.1	25.7						
1876	47.4	50.9	1.7									
1878				47.9	47.7	4.4						
1880	48.9	50.5	0.7									
1882				48.2	51.7	0.0						
1884	46.7	51.0	2.4									
1886				50.9	44.1	5.0						
1888	42.8	53.8	3.4									
1890				53.5	46.5	0.0						
1892	18.2	44.7	37.2									
1894				20.5	47.2	32.3						
1896	48.0	50.0	1.9									
1898				40.8	53.2	6.0						
1900	39.4	55.5	5.1									
1902				46.2	45.9	7.9						
1904	19.3	67.3	13.4									
1906				86.5	0.0	13.5						
1908	34.2	56.5	9.3									
1910				46.6	41.4	12.0						
1912	34.3	25.3	40.4									
1914				38.1	48.8	13.1				45.5	36.0	18.5
1916	45.9	48.5	5.6									
1918				42.8	53.0	4.2	23.4	67.7	8.9			
1920	33.5	60.2	6.3									
1922				57.4	42.6	0.0				43.5	50.7	5.7
1924	24.2	51.0	24.8				24.7	66.0	9.4			
1926				41.4	53.1	5.5				36.3	39.8	23.9
1928	34.1	64.2	1.7									
1930				25.1	18.8	56.1	27.9	58.1	14.0			
1932	58.0	36.9	5.1									
1934				38.6	28.7	32.7				38.9	52.7	8.4
1936	64.4	29.6	5.9				48.3	49.7	2.0			
1938				42.6	57.4	0.0				45.5	54.5	0.0
1940	53.7	45.6	0.7									
1942				22.1	77.9	0.0	22.9	77.1	0.0			
1944	51.8	46.9	1.3				42.5	57.5	0.0	39.3	60.7	0.0
1946				30.9	69.1	0.0						
1948	46.4	49.8	3.8	44.5	53.2	2.2	40.0	60.0	0.0			
1950				33.9	66.1	0.0				23.2	74.8	2.0
1952	38.9	60.5	0.5									
1954				43.1	56.9	0.0	50.2	49.8	0.0			
1956	44.8	55.2	0.0	50.5	49.5	0.0				54.2	45.8	0.0
1958				44.7	55.3	0.0						
1960	47.3	52.6	0.1				54.8	45.2	0.0			
1962				41.6	54.2	4.2				54.2	45.8	0.0
1964	63.7	36.0	0.3									
1966				44.7	55.3	0.1	48.2	51.7	0.0			
1968	43.8	49.8	6.4							49.8	50.2	0.0
1970				44.1	55.5	0.4						

232

YEAR	PRESIDENT			GOVERNOR			SENATE			HOUSE OF REPRESENTATIVES		
	DEM.	REP.	OTHER	DEM.	REP.	OTHER	DEM.	REP.	OTHER	DEM.	REP.	OTHER
1872	38.5	58.8	2.7	44.8	42.3	12.9				48.3	51.7	0.0
1874	43.0	54.8	2.2	38.2	36.1	25.7				38.1	36.9	25.1
1876	47.4	50.9	1.7	43.1	41.9	15.0				48.1	51.9	0.0
1878	48.1	50.7	1.2	47.9	47.7	4.4				49.9	46.5	3.5
1880	48.9	50.5	0.7	48.1	49.7	2.2				47.8	51.4	0.8
1882	47.8	50.7	1.5	48.3	51.8	0.0				46.0	54.0	0.0
1884	46.7	51.0	2.4	49.6	47.9	2.5				47.9	52.1	0.0
1886	44.8	52.4	2.9	50.9	44.1	5.0				46.0	49.0	5.0
1888	42.9	53.8	3.4	52.2	45.3	2.5				42.2	54.5	3.3
1890	30.5	49.2	20.3	53.6	46.5	0.0				41.3	54.8	3.9
1892	18.2	44.7	37.2	37.0	46.8	16.1				33.2	45.7	21.1
1894	33.1	47.4	19.6	20.5	47.2	32.3				23.0	47.7	29.3
1896	48.0	50.0	2.0	30.6	50.2	19.1				16.8	35.7	47.5
1898	43.7	52.8	3.5	40.8	53.2	6.0				40.9	51.4	7.7
1900	39.4	55.5	5.1	43.5	49.6	7.0				37.3	52.2	10.5
1902	29.4	61.4	9.3	46.2	45.9	7.9				36.0	53.2	10.7
1904	19.3	67.3	13.4	66.3	23.0	10.7				31.9	54.4	13.7
1906	26.8	61.9	11.4	86.5	0.0	13.5				33.7	55.0	11.3
1908	34.2	56.5	9.3	66.5	20.7	12.8				26.0	61.2	12.8
1910	34.3	40.9	24.8	46.6	41.4	12.0				33.3	50.3	16.4
1912	34.3	25.3	40.4	42.4	45.1	12.5				27.2	45.3	27.6
1914	40.1	36.9	23.0	38.1	48.8	13.1	45.5	36.0	18.5	28.5	43.2	28.3
1916	45.9	48.5	5.6	40.5	50.9	8.7	34.4	51.9	13.7	4.4	58.9	36.7
1918	39.7	54.3	5.9	42.8	53.0	4.2	23.4	67.7	8.9	18.5	69.7	11.9
1920	33.6	60.2	6.3	50.1	47.8	2.1	43.5	50.7	5.7	6.5	71.7	21.7
1922	28.9	55.6	15.5	57.4	42.6	0.0	34.1	58.4	7.6	29.1	68.3	2.6
1924	24.2	51.0	24.8	49.4	47.9	2.7	24.7	66.0	9.4	32.6	60.0	7.4
1926	29.2	57.6	13.2	41.4	53.1	5.5	36.3	39.8	23.9	28.8	71.2	0.0
1928	34.1	64.2	1.7	33.2	36.0	30.8	32.1	48.9	18.9	19.0	67.0	14.0
1930	46.1	50.5	3.4	25.1	18.8	56.1	27.9	58.1	14.0	46.9	51.0	2.1
1932	58.0	36.9	5.1	31.8	23.8	44.4	38.9	52.7	8.4	47.1	42.4	10.5
1934	61.2	33.3	5.5	38.6	28.7	32.7	43.6	51.2	5.2	41.5	45.1	13.3
1936	64.4	29.6	5.9	40.6	43.1	16.4	48.3	49.7	2.0	47.4	46.6	6.0
1938	59.1	37.6	3.3	42.6	57.4	0.0	45.5	54.6	0.0	41.4	58.6	0.0
1940	53.7	45.6	0.7	32.4	67.6	0.0	34.2	65.8	0.0	41.1	57.0	1.9
1942	52.7	46.3	1.0	22.1	77.9	0.0	22.9	77.1	0.0	41.8	58.2	0.0
1944	51.8	46.9	1.3	26.5	73.5	0.0	40.9	59.1	0.0	38.5	61.5	0.0
1946	49.1	48.4	2.6	30.9	69.1	0.0	40.4	59.6	0.0	35.2	64.8	0.0
1948	46.4	49.8	3.8	44.5	53.2	2.2	40.0	60.0	0.0	35.8	60.4	3.8
1950	42.7	55.2	2.2	34.0	66.1	0.0	23.2	74.8	2.0	40.3	57.7	2.0
1952	38.9	60.5	0.5	38.5	61.5	0.0	36.7	62.3	1.0	38.7	61.3	0.0
1954	41.8	57.9	0.3	43.1	56.9	0.0	50.2	49.8	0.0	45.6	54.5	0.0
1956	44.8	55.3	0.0	50.5	49.5	0.0	54.2	45.8	0.0	52.9	47.1	0.0
1958	46.0	53.9	0.1	44.7	55.3	0.0	54.5	45.5	0.0	56.9	43.1	0.0
1960	47.3	52.6	0.1	43.1	54.8	2.1	54.8	45.2	0.0	51.1	48.9	0.0
1962	55.5	44.3	0.2	41.6	54.2	4.2	54.2	45.8	0.0	54.2	45.7	0.0
1964	63.7	36.0	0.3	43.2	54.7	2.1	51.2	48.8	0.0	60.1	39.8	0.1
1966	53.8	42.9	3.4	44.7	55.3	0.1	48.2	51.7	0.0	47.4	52.6	0.0
1968	43.8	49.8	6.4	44.4	55.4	0.2	49.8	50.2	0.0	47.0	53.0	0.0
1970				44.1	55.5	0.4				51.8	48.2	0.0

YEAR	COMPOSITE A (P+G+S+H/4)			COMPOSITE B (G+S+H/3)			COMPOSITE C (S+H/2)		
	DEM.	REP.	OTHER	DEM.	REP.	OTHER	DEM.	REP.	OTHER
1872	43.9	50.9	5.2	46.6	47.0	6.4	48.3	51.7	0.0
1874	39.8	42.6	17.7	38.2	36.5	25.4	38.1	36.9	25.1
1876	46.2	48.2	5.6	45.6	46.9	7.5	48.1	51.9	0.0
1878	48.7	48.3	3.0	48.9	47.1	4.0	49.9	46.5	3.5
1880	48.2	50.5	1.2	47.9	50.6	1.5	47.8	51.4	0.8
1882	47.3	52.2	0.5	47.1	52.9	0.0	46.0	54.0	0.0
1884	48.1	50.3	1.6	48.8	50.0	1.3	47.9	52.1	0.0
1886	47.2	48.5	4.3	48.4	46.6	5.0	46.0	49.0	5.0
1888	45.8	51.2	3.0	47.2	49.9	2.9	42.2	54.5	3.3
1890	41.8	50.2	8.1	47.4	50.6	2.0	41.3	54.8	3.9
1892	29.5	45.7	24.8	35.1	46.3	18.6	33.2	45.7	21.1
1894	25.5	47.4	27.0	21.8	47.5	30.8	23.0	47.7	29.3
1896	31.8	45.3	22.9	23.7	43.0	33.3	16.8	35.7	47.5
1898	41.8	52.5	5.7	40.9	52.3	6.8	40.9	51.4	7.7
1900	40.0	52.4	7.6	40.4	50.9	8.8	37.3	52.2	10.5
1902	37.2	53.5	9.3	41.1	49.6	9.3	36.0	53.2	10.7
1904	39.2	48.2	12.6	49.1	38.7	12.2	31.9	54.4	13.7
1906	49.0	39.0	12.1	60.1	27.5	12.4	33.7	55.0	11.3
1908	42.3	46.1	11.6	46.3	41.0	12.8	26.0	61.2	12.8
1910	38.1	44.2	17.7	40.0	45.8	14.2	33.3	50.3	16.4
1912	34.6	38.6	26.8	34.8	45.2	20.0	.27.2	45.3	27.6
1914	38.1	41.2	20.7	37.4	42.7	20.0	37.0	39.6	23.4
1916	31.3	52.5	16.2	26.4	53.9	19.7	19.4	55.4	25.2
1918	31.1	61.2	7.7	28.2	63.5	8.3	20.9	68.7	10.4
1920	33.4	57.6	9.0	33.4	56.8	9.9	25.0	61.2	13.7
1922	37.4	56.2	6.4	40.2	56.4	3.4	31.6	63.3	5.1
1924	32.7	56.2	11.1	35.6	57.9	6.5	28.7	63.0	8.4
1926	33.9	55.4	10.7	35.5	54.7	9.8	32.6	55.5	11.9
1928	29.6	54.0	16.4	28.1	50.6	21.3	25.6	57.9	16.5
1930	36.5	44.6	18.9	33.3	42.6	24.1	37.4	54.6	8.0
1932	43.9	39.0	17.1	39.3	39.6	21.1	43.0	47.6	9.5
1934	46.2	39.6	14.2	41.2	41.7	17.1	42.6	48.2	9.3
1936	50.2	42.3	7.6	45.4	46.5	8.1	47.9	48.2	4.0
1938	47.1	52.1	0.8	43.1	56.9	0.0	43.4	56.6	0.0
1940	40.3	59.0	0.6	35.9	63.5	0.6	37.6	61.4	0.9
1942	34.9	64.9	0.3	29.0	71.0	0.0	32.4	67.6	0.0
1944	39.4	60.3	0.3	35.3	64.7	0.0	39.7	60.3	0.0
1946	38.9	60.5	0.6	35.5	64.5	0.0	37.8	62.2	0.0
1948	41.7	55.9	2.5	40.1	57.9	2.0	37.9	60.2	1.9
1950	35.0	63.4	1.6	32.5	66.2	1.3	31.7	66.3	2.0
1952	38.2	61.4	0.4	38.0	61.7	0.3	37.7	61.8	0.5
1954	45.2	54.8	0.1	46.3	53.7	0.0	47.9	52.1	0.0
1956	50.6	49.4	0.0	52.6	47.5	0.0	53.6	46.4	0.0
1958	50.5	49.5	0.0	52.0	48.0	0.0	55.7	44.3	0.0
1960	49.1	50.3	0.6	49.7	49.6	0.7	53.0	47.0	0.0
1962	51.4	47.5	1.1	50.0	48.6	1.4	54.2	45.8	0.0
1964	54.6	44.8	0.6	51.5	47.8	0.7	55.7	44.3	0.1
1966	48.5	50.6	0.9	46.8	53.2	0.0	47.8	52.2	0.0
1968	46.2	52.1	1.7	47.1	52.9	0.1	48.4	51.6	0.0
1970				47.9	51.9	0.2	51.8	48.2	0.0

234

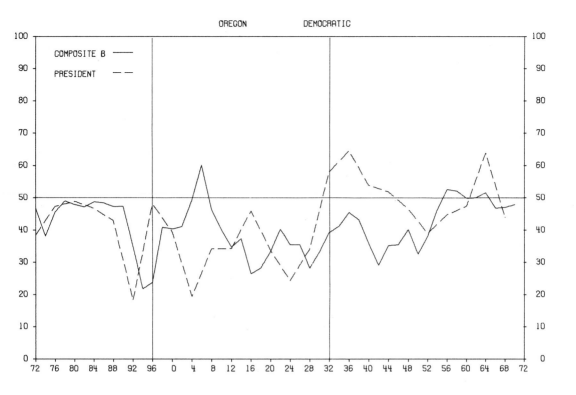

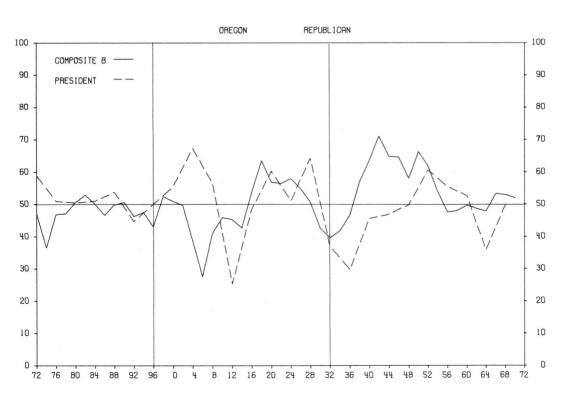

PENNSYLVANIA

YEAR	PRESIDENT			GOVERNOR			SENATE CLASS I			SENATE CLASS III		
	DEM.	REP.	OTHER	DEM.	REP.	OTHER	DEM.	REP.	OTHER	DEM.	REP.	OTHER
1872	37.8	62.2	0.0	47.3	52.5	0.2						
1874												
1876	48.2	50.6	1.1	47.9	49.9	2.2						
1878				42.3	45.5	12.2						
1880	46.6	50.8	2.6									
1882				47.8	42.4	9.8						
1884	43.9	52.5	3.6									
1886				45.1	50.3	4.6						
1888	44.8	52.7	2.5									
1890				50.0	48.2	1.7						
1892	45.1	51.4	3.5									
1894				35.0	60.3	4.7						
1896	35.3	60.9	3.8									
1898				36.9	49.0	14.1						
1900	36.2	60.7	3.1									
1902				39.9	54.2	6.0						
1904	27.1	68.0	4.9									
1906				30.0	49.9	20.2						
1908	35.4	58.8	5.8									
1910				13.0	41.3	45.7						
1912	32.5	22.4	45.1									
1914				28.2	48.0	23.8				24.0	44.1	32.0
1916	40.2	54.3	5.5				37.2	54.8	8.0			
1918				32.7	60.5	6.8						
1920	27.2	65.8	7.0							27.2	59.9	12.9
1922				39.7	56.8	3.5	29.6	56.0	14.4	32.9	57.6	9.5
1924	19.1	65.3	15.6									
1926				23.2	73.3	3.4				40.9	54.6	4.5
1928	33.9	65.2	0.9				34.0	64.4	1.6			
1930				30.5	49.2	20.2				25.6	71.5	2.9
1932	45.3	50.8	3.8							43.2	49.3	7.5
1934				50.0	47.8	2.2	50.8	46.5	2.8			
1936	56.9	40.8	2.3									
1938				45.8	53.4	0.8				44.1	54.7	1.2
1940	53.2	46.3	0.4				51.8	47.4	0.8			
1942				45.1	53.7	1.2						
1944	51.1	48.4	0.5							50.0	49.3	0.7
1946				40.7	58.5	0.8	39.8	59.3	0.9			
1948	46.9	50.9	2.2									
1950				48.3	50.7	0.9				47.7	51.3	1.0
1952	46.9	52.7	0.4				48.0	51.6	0.4			
1954				53.7	46.2	0.2						
1956	43.3	56.5	0.2							50.1	49.7	0.2
1958				50.8	48.9	0.3	48.4	51.2	0.4			
1960	51.1	48.7	0.2									
1962				44.3	55.4	0.3				51.1	48.7	0.2
1964	64.9	34.7	0.4				49.1	50.6	0.3			
1966				46.1	52.1	1.8						
1968	47.6	44.0	8.4							45.8	51.9	2.3
1970				55.2	41.7	3.1	45.4	51.4	3.2			

PENNSYLVANIA

YEAR	PRESIDENT			GOVERNOR			SENATE			HOUSE OF REPRESENTATIVES		
	DEM.	REP.	OTHER	DEM.	REP.	OTHER	DEM.	REP.	OTHER	DEM.	REP.	OTHER
1872	37.8	62.3	0.0	47.3	52.6	0.2				47.8	52.2	0.0
1874	43.0	56.4	0.6	47.6	51.2	1.2				50.5	43.7	5.7
1876	48.3	50.6	1.1	47.9	49.9	2.2				49.0	50.4	0.6
1878	47.4	50.7	1.9	42.3	45.5	12.2				40.3	45.0	14.7
1880	46.6	50.8	2.6	45.1	44.0	11.0				46.8	50.9	2.3
1882	45.2	51.7	3.1	47.8	42.4	9.8				47.8	44.8	7.5
1884	43.9	52.6	3.6	46.5	46.4	7.2				45.4	52.7	1.8
1886	44.3	52.6	3.0	45.1	50.3	4.6				45.7	49.7	4.6
1888	44.8	52.7	2.5	47.6	49.3	3.2				45.4	52.5	2.1
1890	44.9	52.1	3.0	50.0	48.2	1.8				46.6	50.7	2.7
1892	45.1	51.5	3.5	42.5	54.3	3.2				45.2	51.4	3.4
1894	40.2	56.2	3.6	35.0	60.3	4.7				34.9	60.8	4.3
1896	35.3	60.9	3.8	35.9	54.7	9.4				35.8	60.9	3.3
1898	35.8	60.8	3.4	36.9	49.0	14.1				38.2	56.3	5.6
1900	36.2	60.7	3.1	38.4	51.6	10.1				36.3	60.6	3.1
1902	31.6	64.4	4.0	39.9	54.2	6.0				33.3	61.6	5.2
1904	27.1	68.0	4.9	34.9	52.0	13.1				28.7	66.0	5.3
1906	31.3	63.4	5.3	30.0	49.9	20.2				32.2	52.8	15.0
1908	35.4	58.8	5.8	21.5	45.6	32.9				36.4	57.6	6.0
1910	34.0	40.6	25.4	13.0	41.3	45.7				24.4	51.1	24.4
1912	32.5	22.5	45.1	20.6	44.6	34.8				32.7	27.3	40.1
1914	36.4	38.4	25.3	28.2	48.0	23.8	24.0	44.1	32.0	26.6	46.9	26.5
1916	40.2	54.3	5.5	30.5	54.3	15.3	37.3	54.8	8.0	37.6	54.0	8.3
1918	33.7	60.0	6.3	32.7	60.5	6.8	32.2	57.4	10.4	31.3	62.2	6.5
1920	27.2	65.8	7.1	36.2	58.7	5.1	27.2	59.9	12.9	26.7	64.1	9.2
1922	23.1	65.6	11.3	39.7	56.8	3.5	31.3	56.8	11.9	36.2	57.2	6.6
1924	19.1	65.4	15.6	31.5	65.1	3.5	36.1	55.7	8.2	24.0	65.8	10.2
1926	26.5	65.3	8.2	23.2	73.3	3.4	40.9	54.6	4.5	24.0	70.4	5.6
1928	33.9	65.2	0.9	26.9	61.3	11.8	34.0	64.4	1.6	33.4	65.1	1.5
1930	39.6	58.0	2.4	30.6	49.2	20.2	25.6	71.5	2.9	28.1	70.4	1.5
1932	45.3	50.8	3.8	40.3	48.5	11.2	43.2	49.3	7.5	43.0	50.7	6.3
1934	51.1	45.8	3.1	50.0	47.8	2.2	50.8	46.5	2.8	49.7	46.7	3.6
1936	56.9	40.8	2.3	47.9	50.6	1.5	47.5	50.6	2.0	54.4	42.0	3.6
1938	55.1	43.6	1.4	45.8	53.4	0.8	44.1	54.7	1.2	46.4	53.0	0.5
1940	53.2	46.3	0.4	45.5	53.5	1.0	51.8	47.4	0.9	51.8	47.7	0.5
1942	52.2	47.4	0.5	45.1	53.7	1.2	50.9	48.4	0.8	45.2	54.3	0.6
1944	51.1	48.4	0.5	42.9	56.1	1.0	50.0	49.4	0.7	50.7	49.2	0.1
1946	49.0	49.6	1.3	40.7	58.5	0.8	39.8	59.3	0.9	42.0	57.7	0.3
1948	46.9	50.9	2.2	44.5	54.6	0.9	43.8	55.3	1.0	48.8	51.0	0.3
1950	46.9	51.8	1.3	48.3	50.7	1.0	47.7	51.3	1.0	47.6	52.2	0.1
1952	46.9	52.7	0.4	51.0	48.4	0.6	48.0	51.6	0.5	47.6	52.3	0.1
1954	45.1	54.6	0.3	53.7	46.2	0.2	49.0	50.6	0.3	50.6	49.4	0.0
1956	43.3	56.5	0.2	52.2	47.5	0.3	50.1	49.7	0.2	47.2	52.8	0.0
1958	47.2	52.6	0.2	50.8	48.9	0.3	48.4	51.2	0.4	51.0	49.0	0.0
1960	51.1	48.7	0.2	47.5	52.1	0.3	49.7	50.0	0.3	51.6	48.4	0.1
1962	58.0	41.7	0.3	44.3	55.4	0.3	51.1	48.7	0.2	49.1	50.9	0.0
1964	64.9	34.7	0.4	45.2	53.7	1.1	49.1	50.6	0.3	50.1	49.9	0.0
1966	56.3	39.4	4.4	46.1	52.1	1.8	47.5	51.2	1.3	47.8	52.2	0.0
1968	47.6	44.0	8.4	50.7	46.9	2.4	45.8	51.9	2.3	50.0	48.7	1.4
1970				55.2	41.7	3.1	45.4	51.4	3.2	53.8	44.6	1.6

237

PENNSYLVANIA

YEAR	COMPOSITE A (P+G+S+H/4)			COMPOSITE B (G+S+H/3)			COMPOSITE C (S+H/2)		
	DEM.	REP.	OTHER	DEM.	REP.	OTHER	DEM.	REP.	OTHER
1872	44.3	55.7	0.1	47.5	52.4	0.1	47.8	52.2	0.0
1874	47.1	50.5	2.5	49.1	47.5	3.5	50.5	43.7	5.7
1876	48.4	50.3	1.3	48.5	50.2	1.4	49.0	50.4	0.6
1878	43.4	47.1	9.6	41.3	45.3	13.4	40.3	45.0	14.7
1880	46.2	48.6	5.3	45.9	47.4	6.7	46.8	50.9	2.3
1882	46.9	46.3	6.8	47.8	43.6	8.6	47.8	44.8	7.5
1884	45.3	50.6	4.2	45.9	49.6	4.5	45.4	52.7	1.8
1886	45.0	50.9	4.1	45.4	50.0	4.6	45.7	49.7	4.6
1888	45.9	51.5	2.6	46.5	50.9	2.6	45.4	52.5	2.1
1890	47.2	50.3	2.5	48.3	49.5	2.2	46.6	50.7	2.7
1892	44.3	52.4	3.4	43.8	52.8	3.3	45.2	51.4	3.4
1894	36.7	59.1	4.2	35.0	60.6	4.5	34.9	60.8	4.3
1896	35.7	58.8	5.5	35.9	57.8	6.4	35.8	60.9	3.3
1898	36.9	55.4	7.7	37.5	52.6	9.8	38.2	56.3	5.6
1900	36.9	57.6	5.4	37.3	56.1	6.6	36.3	60.6	3.1
1902	34.9	60.0	5.1	36.6	57.9	5.6	33.3	61.6	5.2
1904	30.2	62.0	7.8	31.8	59.0	9.2	28.7	66.0	5.3
1906	31.1	55.4	13.5	31.1	51.3	17.6	32.2	52.8	15.0
1908	31.1	54.0	14.9	28.9	51.6	19.5	36.4	57.6	6.0
1910	23.8	44.4	31.9	18.7	46.2	35.1	24.4	51.1	24.4
1912	28.6	31.5	40.0	26.6	36.0	37.4	32.7	27.3	40.1
1914	28.8	44.3	26.9	26.3	46.3	27.4	25.3	45.5	29.3
1916	36.4	54.3	9.3	35.1	54.4	10.5	37.4	54.4	8.1
1918	32.5	60.0	7.5	32.1	60.1	7.9	31.8	59.8	8.4
1920	29.3	62.1	8.6	30.0	60.9	9.1	26.9	62.0	11.1
1922	32.6	59.1	8.3	35.7	56.9	7.4	33.7	57.0	9.3
1924	27.7	63.0	9.4	30.5	62.2	7.3	30.0	60.8	9.2
1926	28.7	65.9	5.4	29.4	66.1	4.5	32.5	62.5	5.0
1928	32.0	64.0	4.0	31.4	63.6	5.0	33.7	64.7	1.6
1930	31.0	62.3	6.7	28.1	63.7	8.2	26.8	71.0	2.2
1932	43.0	49.9	7.2	42.2	49.5	8.3	43.1	50.0	6.9
1934	50.4	46.7	2.9	50.2	47.0	2.8	50.3	46.6	3.2
1936	51.7	46.0	2.3	49.9	47.7	2.4	51.0	46.3	2.8
1938	47.9	51.2	1.0	45.5	53.7	0.8	45.3	53.9	0.9
1940	50.6	48.7	0.7	49.7	49.5	0.8	51.8	47.5	0.7
1942	48.4	50.9	0.8	47.1	52.1	0.8	48.0	51.3	0.7
1944	48.7	50.8	0.6	47.9	51.6	0.6	50.3	49.3	0.4
1946	42.9	56.3	0.8	40.8	58.5	0.7	40.9	58.5	0.6
1948	46.0	53.0	1.1	45.7	53.6	0.7	46.3	53.1	0.6
1950	47.6	51.5	0.8	47.9	51.4	0.7	47.7	51.8	0.6
1952	48.4	51.3	0.4	48.9	50.8	0.4	47.8	51.9	0.3
1954	49.6	50.2	0.2	51.1	48.7	0.2	49.8	50.0	0.2
1956	48.2	51.6	0.2	49.8	50.0	0.2	48.6	51.3	0.1
1958	49.3	50.4	0.2	50.1	49.7	0.3	49.7	50.1	0.2
1960	50.0	49.8	0.2	49.6	50.2	0.2	50.7	49.2	0.2
1962	50.6	49.2	0.2	48.1	51.7	0.2	50.1	49.8	0.1
1964	52.3	47.2	0.4	48.2	51.4	0.5	49.6	50.2	0.2
1966	49.4	48.7	1.9	47.1	51.9	1.0	47.6	51.7	0.7
1968	48.5	47.9	3.6	48.8	49.2	2.0	47.9	50.3	1.8
1970				51.5	45.9	2.6	49.6	48.0	2.4

238

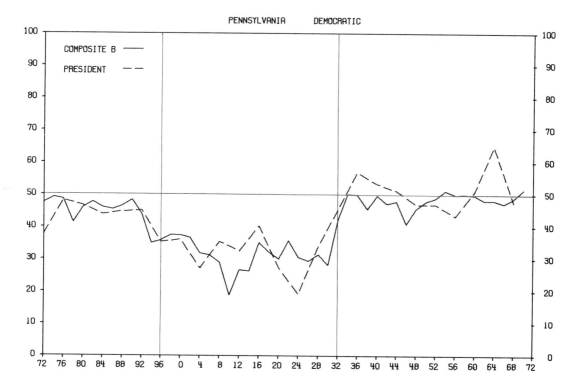

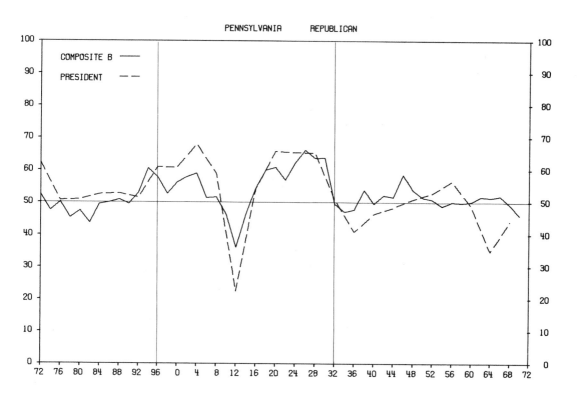

239

RHODE ISLAND

YEAR	PRESIDENT			GOVERNOR			SENATE CLASS I			SENATE CLASS II		
	DEM.	REP.	OTHER	DEM.	REP.	OTHER	DEM.	REP.	OTHER	DEM.	REP.	OTHER
1872	28.1	71.9	0.0	46.4	53.6	0.0						
1874				19.5	79.8	0.6						
1876	40.4	59.6	0.0	21.2	41.3	37.5						
1878				44.0	54.1	1.9						
1880	36.9	62.2	0.9	33.7	51.8	14.5						
1882				31.7	65.9	2.4						
1884	37.8	58.1	4.1	39.9	58.6	1.5						
1886				37.7	54.5	7.7						
1888	43.0	53.9	3.1	47.7	47.9	4.4						
1890				49.1	42.1	8.8						
1892	45.7	50.7	3.5	47.6	48.4	4.0						
1894				43.8	50.0	6.2						
1896	26.4	68.3	5.3	33.1	56.6	10.2						
1898				31.8	57.9	10.3						
1900	35.0	59.7	5.2	34.9	55.3	9.8						
1902				47.8	46.6	5.6						
1904	36.2	60.6	3.2	48.5	48.1	3.4						
1906				47.1	50.5	2.4						
1908	34.2	60.8	5.1	46.3	49.9	3.7						
1910				43.5	53.2	3.3						
1912	39.0	35.6	25.4	42.4	48.3	9.3						
1914				41.2	53.8	4.9						
1916	46.0	51.1	2.9	40.8	55.9	3.3	52.9	44.1	2.9			
1918				44.8	53.1	2.1				46.2	51.8	2.0
1920	32.8	64.0	3.2	33.1	64.6	2.2						
1922				51.7	47.2	1.1	52.2	43.4	4.4			
1924	36.5	59.6	3.9	41.0	58.6	0.4				42.2	57.0	0.8
1926				45.7	53.9	0.4						
1928	50.2	49.5	0.3	48.1	51.6	0.3	49.3	50.6	0.1			
1930				48.9	50.5	0.5				49.2	50.3	0.5
1932	55.1	43.3	1.6	55.2	43.5	1.3						
1934				56.6	42.4	0.9	57.1	42.8	0.0			
1936	53.0	40.3	6.7	53.7	45.8	0.5				48.6	44.4	7.0
1938				41.6	53.6	4.7						
1940	56.7	43.2	0.1	55.8	44.1	0.1	55.2	44.8	0.0			
1942				58.5	41.5	0.0				58.0	42.0	0.0
1944	58.6	41.3	0.1	60.6	39.4	0.0						
1946				54.1	45.9	0.0	55.1	44.9	0.0			
1948	57.6	41.4	1.0	61.2	38.4	0.4				59.3	40.7	0.0
1950				59.3	40.7	0.0	61.6	38.4	0.0			
1952	49.0	50.9	0.1	52.6	47.4	0.0	54.8	45.2	0.0			
1954				57.7	41.7	0.6				59.3	40.7	0.0
1956	41.7	58.3	0.0	50.1	49.9	0.0						
1958				49.1	50.9	0.0	64.5	35.5	0.0			
1960	63.6	36.4	0.0	56.6	43.4	0.0				68.9	31.1	0.0
1962				49.9	50.1	0.0						
1964	80.9	19.1	0.0	38.9	61.1	0.0	82.7	17.3	0.0			
1966				36.7	63.3	0.0				67.7	32.3	0.0
1968	64.0	31.8	4.2	51.0	49.0	0.0						
1970				50.3	49.7	0.0	67.5	31.5	1.0			

240

RHODE ISLAND

YEAR	PRESIDENT			GOVERNOR			SENATE			HOUSE OF REPRESENTATIVES		
	DEM.	REP.	OTHER	DEM.	REP.	OTHER	DEM.	REP.	OTHER	DEM.	REP.	OTHER
1872	28.1	71.9	0.0	46.4	53.6	0.0						
1874	34.2	65.8	0.0	19.5	79.8	0.6				30.0	69.8	0.2
1876	40.4	59.6	0.0	21.2	41.3	37.5				39.6	60.0	0.3
1878	38.7	60.9	0.5	44.0	54.1	1.9				31.7	62.6	5.7
1880	36.9	62.2	0.9	33.7	51.9	14.5				36.2	62.7	1.1
1882	37.3	60.2	2.5	31.7	65.9	2.4				32.6	67.3	0.2
1884	37.8	58.1	4.1	40.0	58.6	1.5				37.0	55.6	7.4
1886	40.4	56.0	3.6	37.8	54.5	7.7				43.6	47.4	9.0
1888	43.0	53.9	3.1	47.7	48.0	4.4				42.2	54.6	3.2
1890	44.4	52.3	3.3	49.1	42.1	8.8				50.3	45.5	4.1
1892	45.8	50.7	3.5	47.6	48.4	4.0				46.4	49.4	4.2
1894	36.1	59.5	4.4	43.8	50.0	6.2				35.8	58.5	5.8
1896	26.4	68.3	5.3	33.1	56.6	10.2				31.1	63.6	5.3
1898	30.7	64.0	5.3	31.8	57.9	10.3				34.2	56.5	9.3
1900	35.0	59.7	5.2	34.9	55.3	9.8				35.3	58.7	6.0
1902	35.6	60.2	4.2	47.8	46.6	5.6				47.8	48.4	3.8
1904	36.2	60.6	3.2	48.5	48.1	3.4				45.4	52.9	1.7
1906	35.2	60.7	4.2	47.1	50.5	2.4				48.0	50.4	1.6
1908	34.2	60.8	5.1	46.4	49.9	3.7				42.4	54.5	3.1
1910	36.6	48.2	15.2	43.5	53.2	3.3				46.4	51.5	2.2
1912	39.0	35.6	25.4	42.4	48.3	9.3				44.9	42.4	12.8
1914	42.5	43.3	14.2	41.3	53.8	4.9				45.3	50.2	4.6
1916	46.0	51.1	2.9	40.8	55.9	3.3	52.9	44.1	3.0	47.9	49.8	2.4
1918	39.4	57.5	3.1	44.8	53.1	2.1	46.2	51.8	2.0	43.5	54.3	2.2
1920	32.8	64.0	3.3	33.2	64.6	2.2	49.2	47.6	3.2	35.3	63.3	1.5
1922	34.6	61.8	3.6	51.7	47.2	1.1	52.2	43.4	4.5	52.6	47.4	0.0
1924	36.5	59.6	3.9	41.0	58.6	0.4	42.2	57.0	0.8	40.8	59.2	0.0
1926	43.3	54.6	2.1	45.7	53.9	0.5	45.8	53.8	0.5	41.9	58.1	0.0
1928	50.2	49.6	0.3	48.1	51.6	0.3	49.3	50.6	0.1	48.7	51.3	0.0
1930	52.6	46.4	1.0	48.9	50.5	0.5	49.2	50.3	0.5	48.3	51.7	0.0
1932	55.1	43.3	1.6	55.2	43.5	1.3	53.2	46.6	0.3	55.1	44.6	0.2
1934	54.0	41.8	4.2	56.6	42.4	0.9	57.1	42.9	0.0	57.4	42.6	0.0
1936	53.0	40.3	6.7	53.7	45.9	0.5	48.6	44.4	7.0	49.1	43.9	7.0
1938	54.9	41.7	3.4	41.6	53.7	4.7	51.9	44.6	3.5	46.3	53.6	0.1
1940	56.7	43.2	0.1	55.8	44.1	0.1	55.2	44.8	0.0	55.6	44.4	0.0
1942	57.7	42.2	0.1	58.5	41.5	0.0	58.0	42.0	0.0	58.2	41.8	0.0
1944	58.6	41.3	0.1	60.7	39.4	0.0	56.5	43.5	0.0	59.8	40.2	0.0
1946	58.1	41.4	0.6	54.1	45.9	0.0	55.1	44.9	0.0	54.6	45.1	0.3
1948	57.6	41.4	1.0	61.2	38.4	0.4	59.3	40.7	0.0	60.8	39.2	0.0
1950	53.3	46.2	0.5	59.3	40.7	0.0	61.6	38.4	0.0	61.9	38.1	0.0
1952	49.1	50.9	0.1	52.6	47.4	0.0	54.8	45.2	0.1	54.1	45.9	0.0
1954	45.4	54.6	0.0	57.7	41.7	0.6	59.3	40.7	0.0	59.9	40.1	0.0
1956	41.7	58.3	0.0	50.1	49.9	0.0	61.9	38.1	0.0	53.9	46.2	0.0
1958	52.7	47.3	0.0	49.1	50.9	0.0	64.5	35.5	0.0	63.1	36.9	0.1
1960	63.6	36.4	0.0	56.6	43.4	0.0	68.9	31.1	0.0	68.5	31.5	0.0
1962	72.3	27.8	0.0	49.9	50.1	0.0	75.8	24.2	0.0	65.1	34.9	0.0
1964	80.9	19.1	0.0	38.9	61.2	0.0	82.7	17.3	0.0	74.6	25.4	0.0
1966	72.5	25.5	2.1	36.7	63.3	0.0	67.7	32.3	0.0	61.2	38.7	0.2
1968	64.0	31.8	4.2	51.0	49.0	0.0	67.6	31.9	0.5	60.9	38.6	0.5
1970				50.3	49.7	0.0	67.5	31.5	1.0	64.4	35.6	0.0

241

YEAR	COMPOSITE A (P+G+S+H/4)			COMPOSITE B (G+S+H/3)			COMPOSITE C (S+H/2)		
	DEM.	REP.	OTHER	DEM.	REP.	OTHER	DEM.	REP.	OTHER
1872	37.2	62.8	0.0	46.4	53.6	0.0			
1874	27.9	71.8	0.3	24.7	74.8	0.4	30.0	69.8	0.2
1876	33.8	53.6	12.6	30.4	50.7	18.9	39.6	60.0	0.3
1878	38.1	59.2	2.7	37.8	58.4	3.8	31.7	62.6	5.7
1880	35.6	58.9	5.5	34.9	57.3	7.8	36.2	62.7	1.1
1882	33.9	64.4	1.7	32.1	66.6	1.3	32.6	67.3	0.2
1884	38.2	57.4	4.4	38.5	57.1	4.5	37.0	55.6	7.4
1886	40.6	52.6	6.8	40.7	51.0	8.4	43.6	47.4	9.0
1888	44.3	52.1	3.6	45.0	51.3	3.8	42.2	54.6	3.2
1890	47.9	46.6	5.4	49.7	43.8	6.5	50.3	45.5	4.1
1892	46.6	49.5	3.9	47.0	48.9	4.1	46.4	49.4	4.2
1894	38.5	56.0	5.5	39.8	54.2	6.0	35.8	58.5	5.8
1896	30.2	62.9	6.9	32.1	60.1	7.7	31.1	63.6	5.3
1898	32.2	59.5	8.3	33.0	57.2	9.8	34.2	56.5	9.3
1900	35.1	57.9	7.0	35.1	57.0	7.9	35.3	58.7	6.0
1902	43.7	51.8	4.5	47.8	47.5	4.7	47.8	48.4	3.8
1904	43.3	53.9	2.8	46.9	50.5	2.6	45.4	52.9	1.7
1906	43.4	53.8	2.7	47.6	50.4	2.0	48.0	50.4	1.6
1908	41.0	55.1	4.0	44.4	52.2	3.4	42.4	54.5	3.1
1910	42.2	51.0	6.9	44.9	52.4	2.7	46.4	51.5	2.2
1912	42.1	42.1	15.8	43.7	45.3	11.0	44.9	42.4	12.8
1914	43.0	49.1	7.9	43.3	52.0	4.8	45.3	50.2	4.6
1916	46.9	50.2	2.9	47.2	49.9	2.9	50.4	46.9	2.7
1918	43.5	54.2	2.3	44.9	53.1	2.1	44.9	53.0	2.1
1920	37.6	59.9	2.5	39.2	58.5	2.3	42.2	55.4	2.3
1922	47.8	49.9	2.3	52.2	46.0	1.9	52.4	45.4	2.2
1924	40.1	58.6	1.3	41.3	58.3	0.4	41.5	58.1	0.4
1926	44.2	55.1	0.8	44.4	55.3	0.3	43.8	56.0	0.2
1928	49.1	50.7	0.2	48.7	51.1	0.1	49.0	50.9	0.1
1930	49.8	49.7	0.5	48.8	50.8	0.4	48.7	51.0	0.3
1932	54.6	44.5	0.9	54.5	44.9	0.6	54.1	45.6	0.3
1934	56.3	42.4	1.3	57.0	42.6	0.3	57.2	42.7	0.0
1936	51.1	43.6	5.3	50.5	44.7	4.8	48.9	44.2	7.0
1938	48.7	48.4	2.9	46.6	50.6	2.8	49.1	49.1	1.8
1940	55.8	44.1	0.0	55.5	44.4	0.0	55.4	44.6	0.0
1942	58.1	41.9	0.0	58.2	41.8	0.0	58.1	41.9	0.0
1944	58.9	41.1	0.0	59.0	41.0	0.0	58.2	41.8	0.0
1946	55.5	44.3	0.2	54.6	45.3	0.1	54.8	45.0	0.2
1948	59.7	40.0	0.4	60.4	39.5	0.1	60.0	40.0	0.0
1950	59.1	40.8	0.1	61.0	39.0	0.0	61.8	38.2	0.0
1952	52.6	47.3	0.0	53.8	46.1	0.0	54.5	45.5	0.0
1954	55.6	44.3	0.2	59.0	40.9	0.2	59.6	40.4	0.0
1956	51.9	48.1	0.0	55.3	44.7	0.0	57.9	42.1	0.0
1958	57.3	42.6	0.0	58.9	41.1	0.0	63.8	36.2	0.0
1960	64.4	35.6	0.0	64.7	35.3	0.0	68.7	31.3	0.0
1962	65.8	34.2	0.0	63.6	36.4	0.0	70.5	29.5	0.0
1964	69.3	30.7	0.0	65.4	34.6	0.0	78.7	21.3	0.0
1966	59.5	39.9	0.6	55.2	44.8	0.1	64.4	35.5	0.1
1968	60.9	37.8	1.3	59.8	39.8	0.3	64.2	35.3	0.5
1970				60.8	38.9	0.3	66.0	33.5	0.5

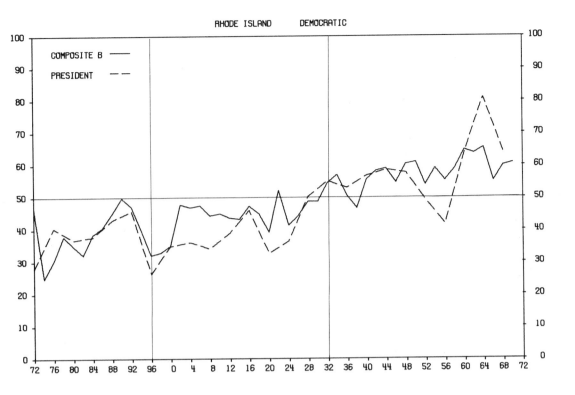

RHODE ISLAND   DEMOCRATIC

COMPOSITE B ──────
PRESIDENT ── ──

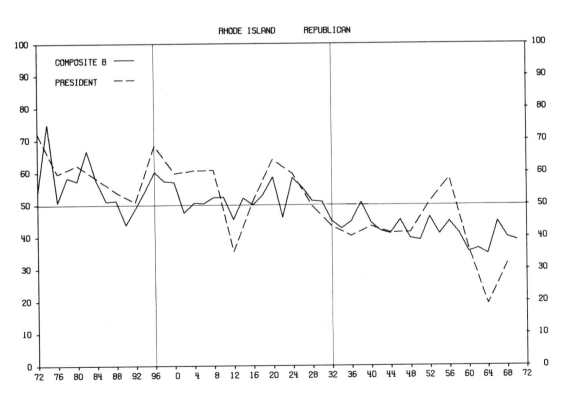

RHODE ISLAND   REPUBLICAN

COMPOSITE B ──────
PRESIDENT ── ──

243

SOUTH CAROLINA

YEAR	PRESIDENT			GOVERNOR			SENATE CLASS II			SENATE CLASS III		
	DEM.	REP.	OTHER	DEM.	REP.	OTHER	DEM.	REP.	OTHER	DEM.	REP.	OTHER
1872	23.8	75.7	0.5	34.2	65.4	0.3						
1874				0.0	53.9	46.1						
1876	49.8	50.2	0.0	49.7	50.3	0.0						
1878				99.8	0.0	0.2						
1880	65.5	34.1	0.4	96.4	0.0	3.6						
1882				79.5	0.0	20.5						
1884	75.3	23.4	1.3	100.0	0.0	0.0						
1886				100.0	0.0	0.0						
1888	82.3	17.2	0.5	100.0	0.0	0.0						
1890				79.8	0.0	20.2						
1892	77.6	18.9	3.5	99.9	0.0	0.1						
1894				69.6	0.0	30.4						
1896	85.3	13.5	1.2	89.1	10.8	0.1						
1898				100.0	0.0	0.0						
1900	93.0	7.0	0.0	100.0	0.0	0.0						
1902				100.0	0.0	0.0						
1904	95.4	4.6	0.0	100.0	0.0	0.0						
1906				99.9	0.0	0.1						
1908	93.8	5.9	0.2	100.0	0.0	0.0						
1910				99.8	0.0	0.2						
1912	95.9	1.1	3.0	99.5	0.0	0.5						
1914				99.8	0.0	0.2				99.8	0.0	0.2
1916	96.7	2.4	0.9	97.9	0.0	2.1						
1918				100.0	0.0	0.0	100.0	0.0	0.0			
1920	96.1	3.4	0.6	100.0	0.0	0.0				100.0	0.0	0.0
1922				100.0	0.0	0.0						
1924	96.6	2.2	1.2	100.0	0.0	0.0	100.0	0.0	0.0			
1926				100.0	0.0	0.0				100.0	0.0	0.0
1928	91.4	4.6	4.0									
1930				100.0	0.0	0.0	100.0	0.0	0.0			
1932	98.0	1.9	0.1							98.1	1.9	0.0
1934				100.0	0.0	0.0						
1936	98.6	1.4	0.0				98.6	1.4	0.0			
1938				99.4	0.6	0.0				98.9	1.1	0.0
1940	95.6	1.7	2.6									
1942				100.0	0.0	0.0	100.0	0.0	0.0			
1944	87.6	4.4	8.0							92.9	3.2	3.9
1946				100.0	0.0	0.0						
1948	24.1	3.8	72.1				96.4	3.6	0.0			
1950				100.0	0.0	0.0				99.9	0.0	0.1
1952	50.7	2.9	46.4									
1954				100.0	0.0	0.0	36.8	0.0	63.2			
1956	45.4	25.2	29.5				100.0	0.0	0.0	82.2	17.8	0.0
1958				100.0	0.0	0.0						
1960	51.2	48.8	0.0				100.0	0.0	0.0			
1962				100.0	0.0	0.0				57.2	42.8	0.0
1964	41.1	58.9	0.0							51.3	48.7	0.0
1966				58.2	41.8	0.0	37.8	62.2	0.0			
1968	29.6	38.1	32.3							61.9	38.1	0.0
1970				51.7	45.6	2.7						

YEAR	PRESIDENT			GOVERNOR			SENATE			HOUSE OF REPRESENTATIVES		
	DEM.	REP.	OTHER	DEM.	REP.	OTHER	DEM.	REP.	OTHER	DEM.	REP.	OTHER
1872	23.8	75.7	0.5	34.2	65.4	0.3				24.2	74.8	1.0
1874	36.8	63.0	0.2	0.0	53.9	46.1				40.8	56.0	3.3
1876	49.8	50.2	0.0	49.7	50.3	0.0				50.1	49.9	0.0
1878	57.6	42.2	0.2	99.8	0.0	0.2				72.1	27.8	0.1
1880	65.5	34.1	0.4	96.4	0.0	3.6				65.6	34.1	0.2
1882	70.4	28.8	0.8	79.5	0.0	20.5				50.5	35.6	13.9
1884	75.3	23.4	1.3	100.0	0.0	0.0				77.2	22.8	0.0
1886	78.8	20.3	0.9	100.0	0.0	0.0				84.5	15.3	0.2
1888	82.3	17.2	0.6	100.0	0.0	0.0				86.3	13.1	0.6
1890	79.9	18.1	2.0	79.8	0.0	20.2				79.9	17.8	2.3
1892	77.6	18.9	3.5	99.9	0.0	0.1				82.9	16.7	0.4
1894	81.4	16.2	2.4	69.6	0.0	30.4				74.6	22.5	3.0
1896	85.3	13.5	1.2	89.1	10.8	0.1				87.4	12.3	0.3
1898	89.2	10.2	0.6	100.0	0.0	0.0				91.1	8.8	0.1
1900	93.1	7.0	0.0	100.0	0.0	0.0				93.7	6.3	0.0
1902	94.2	5.8	0.0	100.0	0.0	0.0				97.7	2.3	0.0
1904	95.4	4.6	0.0	100.0	0.0	0.0				95.6	4.3	0.0
1906	94.6	5.3	0.1	99.9	0.0	0.1				98.5	1.5	0.1
1908	93.8	5.9	0.2	100.0	0.0	0.0				97.4	2.6	0.0
1910	94.9	3.5	1.6	99.8	0.0	0.2				98.7	1.2	0.1
1912	95.9	1.1	3.0	99.5	0.0	0.5				99.5	0.4	0.1
1914	96.3	1.7	1.9	99.8	0.0	0.2	99.8	0.0	0.2	99.0	0.8	0.2
1916	96.7	2.4	0.9	97.9	0.0	2.1	99.9	0.0	0.1	98.1	1.9	0.0
1918	96.4	2.9	0.7	100.0	0.0	0.0	100.0	0.0	0.0	99.3	0.7	0.0
1920	96.1	3.4	0.6	100.0	0.0	0.0	100.0	0.0	0.0	98.0	2.0	0.0
1922	96.3	2.8	0.9	100.0	0.0	0.0	100.0	0.0	0.0	98.1	1.9	0.0
1924	96.6	2.2	1.2	100.0	0.0	0.0	100.0	0.0	0.0	99.5	0.5	0.0
1926	94.0	3.4	2.6	100.0	0.0	0.0	100.0	0.0	0.0	100.0	0.0	0.0
1928	91.4	4.7	4.0	100.0	0.0	0.0	100.0	0.0	0.0	100.0	0.0	0.0
1930	94.7	3.3	2.0	100.0	0.0	0.0	100.0	0.0	0.0	100.0	0.0	0.0
1932	98.0	1.9	0.1	100.0	0.0	0.0	98.1	1.9	0.0	98.1	1.9	0.0
1934	98.3	1.7	0.0	100.0	0.0	0.0	98.4	1.7	0.0	98.9	1.1	0.0
1936	98.6	1.4	0.0	99.7	0.3	0.0	98.6	1.4	0.0	98.6	1.4	0.0
1938	97.1	1.6	1.3	99.4	0.6	0.0	98.9	1.1	0.0	99.2	0.7	0.2
1940	95.6	1.7	2.6	99.7	0.3	0.0	99.4	0.6	0.0	98.4	1.6	0.0
1942	91.6	3.1	5.3	100.0	0.0	0.0	100.0	0.0	0.0	100.0	0.0	0.0
1944	87.6	4.4	8.0	100.0	0.0	0.0	92.9	3.2	3.9	96.5	3.5	0.0
1946	55.9	4.1	40.0	100.0	0.0	0.0	94.7	3.4	2.0	98.9	0.9	0.2
1948	24.1	3.8	72.1	100.0	0.0	0.0	96.5	3.6	0.0	95.1	4.9	0.0
1950	37.4	3.3	59.2	100.0	0.0	0.0	99.9	0.0	0.1	100.0	0.0	0.0
1952	50.7	2.9	46.4	100.0	0.0	0.0	68.3	0.0	31.7	98.0	2.0	0.0
1954	48.0	14.0	37.9	100.0	0.0	0.0	36.8	0.0	63.2	98.7	1.3	0.0
1956	45.4	25.2	29.5	100.0	0.0	0.0	90.5	9.5	0.0	95.3	4.7	0.1
1958	48.3	37.0	14.7	100.0	0.0	0.0	95.2	4.7	0.0	100.0	0.0	0.0
1960	51.2	48.8	0.0	100.0	0.0	0.0	100.0	0.0	0.0	100.0	0.0	0.0
1962	46.2	53.8	0.0	100.0	0.0	0.0	57.2	42.8	0.0	86.0	14.0	0.0
1964	41.1	58.9	0.0	79.1	20.9	0.0	50.9	49.1	0.0	88.5	11.0	0.6
1966	35.4	48.5	16.2	58.2	41.8	0.0	44.6	55.4	0.0	70.6	29.3	0.1
1968	29.6	38.1	32.3	54.9	43.7	1.4	61.9	38.1	0.0	66.3	32.5	1.2
1970				51.7	45.6	2.7				72.5	27.1	0.5

YEAR	COMPOSITE A (P+G+S+H/4)			COMPOSITE B (G+S+H/3)			COMPOSITE C (S+H/2)		
	DEM.	REP.	OTHER	DEM.	REP.	OTHER	DEM.	REP.	OTHER
1872	27.4	72.0	0.6	29.2	70.1	0.7	24.2	74.8	1.0
1874	25.8	57.6	16.5	20.4	54.9	24.7	40.8	56.0	3.3
1876	49.9	50.1	0.0	49.9	50.1	0.0	50.1	49.9	0.0
1878	76.5	23.3	0.2	86.0	13.9	0.1	72.1	27.8	0.1
1880	75.9	22.8	1.4	81.0	17.1	1.9	65.6	34.1	0.2
1882	66.8	21.4	11.8	65.0	17.8	17.2	50.5	35.6	13.9
1884	84.1	15.4	0.4	88.6	11.4	0.0	77.2	22.8	0.0
1886	87.8	11.9	0.4	92.2	7.6	0.1	84.5	15.3	0.2
1888	89.5	10.1	0.4	93.1	6.6	0.3	86.3	13.1	0.6
1890	79.9	11.9	8.2	79.9	8.9	11.2	79.9	17.8	2.3
1892	86.8	11.9	1.3	91.4	8.3	0.3	82.9	16.7	0.4
1894	75.2	12.9	11.9	72.1	11.3	16.7	74.6	22.5	3.0
1896	87.3	12.2	0.5	88.2	11.6	0.2	87.4	12.3	0.3
1898	93.4	6.4	0.2	95.6	4.4	0.0	91.1	8.8	0.1
1900	95.6	4.4	0.0	96.8	3.2	0.0	93.7	6.3	0.0
1902	97.3	2.7	0.0	98.8	1.2	0.0	97.7	2.3	0.0
1904	97.0	3.0	0.0	97.8	2.2	0.0	95.6	4.3	0.0
1906	97.7	2.3	0.1	99.2	0.7	0.1	98.5	1.5	0.1
1908	97.1	2.8	0.1	98.7	1.3	0.0	97.4	2.6	0.0
1910	97.8	1.6	0.6	99.3	0.6	0.2	98.7	1.2	0.1
1912	98.3	0.5	1.2	99.5	0.2	0.3	99.5	0.4	0.1
1914	98.7	0.6	0.7	99.5	0.3	0.2	99.4	0.4	0.2
1916	98.2	1.1	0.8	98.6	0.6	0.7	99.0	1.0	0.1
1918	98.9	0.9	0.2	99.8	0.2	0.0	99.7	0.4	0.0
1920	98.5	1.4	0.2	99.3	0.7	0.0	99.0	1.0	0.0
1922	98.6	1.2	0.2	99.4	0.7	0.0	99.0	1.0	0.0
1924	99.0	0.7	0.3	99.8	0.2	0.0	99.7	0.3	0.0
1926	98.5	0.9	0.7	100.0	0.0	0.0	100.0	0.0	0.0
1928	97.9	1.2	1.0	100.0	0.0	0.0	100.0	0.0	0.0
1930	98.7	0.8	0.5	100.0	0.0	0.0	100.0	0.0	0.0
1932	98.6	1.4	0.0	98.8	1.2	0.0	98.1	1.9	0.0
1934	98.9	1.1	0.0	99.1	0.9	0.0	98.6	1.4	0.0
1936	98.9	1.1	0.0	99.0	1.0	0.0	98.6	1.4	0.0
1938	98.7	1.0	0.4	99.2	0.8	0.1	99.0	0.9	0.1
1940	98.3	1.0	0.7	99.2	0.8	0.0	98.9	1.1	0.0
1942	97.9	0.8	1.3	100.0	0.0	0.0	100.0	0.0	0.0
1944	94.3	2.8	3.0	96.5	2.2	1.3	94.7	3.3	2.0
1946	87.4	2.1	10.5	97.9	1.4	0.7	96.8	2.1	1.1
1948	78.9	3.1	18.0	97.2	2.8	0.0	95.8	4.2	0.0
1950	84.3	0.8	14.8	100.0	0.0	0.0	99.9	0.0	0.1
1952	79.3	1.2	19.5	88.8	0.7	10.6	83.2	1.0	15.9
1954	70.9	3.8	25.3	78.5	0.4	21.1	67.7	0.6	31.6
1956	82.8	9.8	7.4	95.3	4.7	0.0	92.9	7.1	0.0
1958	85.9	10.4	3.7	98.4	1.6	0.0	97.6	2.4	0.0
1960	87.8	12.2	0.0	100.0	0.0	0.0	100.0	0.0	0.0
1962	72.3	27.7	0.0	81.0	19.0	0.0	71.6	28.4	0.0
1964	64.9	35.0	0.1	72.8	27.0	0.2	69.7	30.0	0.3
1966	52.2	43.8	4.1	57.8	42.2	0.0	57.6	42.4	0.1
1968	53.2	38.1	8.7	61.0	38.1	0.9	64.1	35.3	0.6
1970				62.1	36.3	1.6	72.5	27.1	0.5

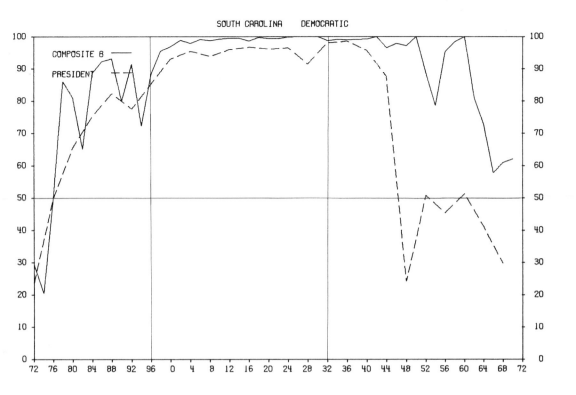

SOUTH CAROLINA   DEMOCRATIC

COMPOSITE B

PRESIDENT

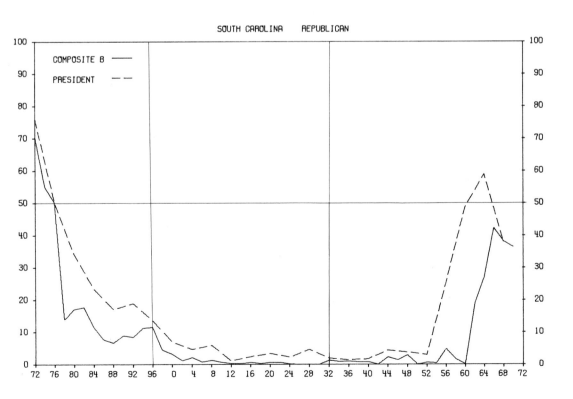

SOUTH CAROLINA   REPUBLICAN

COMPOSITE B

PRESIDENT

SOUTH DAKOTA

YEAR	PRESIDENT			GOVERNOR			SENATE CLASS II			SENATE CLASS III		
	DEM.	REP.	OTHER	DEM.	REP.	OTHER	DEM.	REP.	OTHER	DEM.	REP.	OTHER
1872												
1874												
1876												
1878												
1880												
1882												
1884												
1886												
1888												
1890				27.2	56.9	15.8						
1892	12.7	49.5	37.8	21.1	47.2	31.7						
1894				11.3	52.0	36.8						
1896	49.7	49.5	0.8	49.8	49.4	0.9						
1898				49.6	49.2	1.2						
1900	41.1	56.7	2.1	42.0	56.3	1.7						
1902				28.7	64.7	6.5						
1904	21.7	71.1	7.2	24.7	68.3	7.1						
1906				26.7	65.3	8.0						
1908	35.1	58.8	6.1	39.4	55.3	5.3						
1910				35.9	58.4	5.8						
1912	42.1	50.6	7.4	45.7	48.5	5.8						
1914				35.2	50.1	14.7				48.1	44.6	7.2
1916	45.9	49.8	4.3	39.3	56.6	4.0						
1918				18.6	53.2	28.2	38.9	55.1	6.0			
1920	19.8	60.7	19.5	17.3	56.3	26.3				20.0	50.1	29.9
1922				28.7	45.0	26.2						
1924	13.4	49.7	36.9	22.9	53.9	23.2	31.2	44.1	24.7			
1926				47.4	40.3	12.3				33.3	59.5	7.2
1928	39.2	60.2	0.6	52.5	46.9	0.6						
1930				46.2	53.0	0.8	51.6	48.4	0.0			
1932	63.6	34.4	2.0	55.6	42.4	2.0				44.6	53.8	1.6
1934				58.6	40.7	0.7						
1936	54.0	42.5	3.5	48.4	51.6	0.0	48.8	46.7	4.4			
1938				46.0	54.0	0.0				44.8	55.2	0.0
1940	42.6	57.4	0.0	44.9	55.1	0.0						
1942				38.5	61.5	0.0	41.3	58.7	0.0			
1944	41.7	58.3	0.0	34.5	65.5	0.0				36.1	63.9	0.0
1946				32.8	67.2	0.0						
1948	47.0	51.8	1.1	38.9	61.1	0.0	40.7	59.3	0.0			
1950				39.1	60.9	0.0				36.1	63.9	0.0
1952	30.7	69.3	0.0	29.8	70.2	0.0						
1954				43.3	56.7	0.0	42.7	57.3	0.0			
1956	41.6	58.4	0.0	45.6	54.4	0.0				49.2	50.8	0.0
1958				51.4	48.6	0.0						
1960	41.8	58.2	0.0	49.3	50.7	0.0	47.6	52.4	0.0			
1962				43.9	56.1	0.0				50.1	49.9	0.0
1964	55.6	44.4	0.0	48.3	51.7	0.0						
1966				42.3	57.7	0.0	33.7	66.3	0.0			
1968	42.0	53.3	4.8	42.3	57.7	0.0				56.8	43.2	0.0
1970				54.8	45.2	0.0						

248

SOUTH DAKOTA

YEAR	PRESIDENT			GOVERNOR			SENATE			HOUSE OF REPRESENTATIVES		
	DEM.	REP.	OTHER	DEM.	REP.	OTHER	DEM.	REP.	OTHER	DEM.	REP.	OTHER
1872												
1874												
1876												
1878												
1880												
1882												
1884												
1886												
1888												
1890				27.2	56.9	15.8				26.1	57.8	16.1
1892	12.7	49.5	37.8	21.1	47.2	31.7				11.3	50.8	37.9
1894	31.2	49.5	19.3	11.3	52.0	36.8				10.5	52.8	36.7
1896	49.7	49.5	0.8	49.8	49.4	0.9				24.9	49.3	25.8
1898	45.4	53.1	1.5	49.6	49.2	1.2				22.8	53.1	24.1
1900	41.1	56.8	2.1	42.0	56.3	1.7				21.2	56.1	22.7
1902	31.4	63.9	4.7	28.7	64.7	6.5				28.2	65.1	6.7
1904	21.7	71.1	7.2	24.7	68.3	7.1				22.7	70.0	7.3
1906	28.4	65.0	6.7	26.7	65.3	8.0				27.0	65.2	7.8
1908	35.1	58.8	6.1	39.4	55.3	5.3				34.3	59.9	5.8
1910	38.6	54.7	6.7	35.9	58.4	5.8				31.8	63.3	4.9
1912	42.1	50.6	7.4	45.7	48.5	5.8				38.7	55.4	5.9
1914	44.0	50.2	5.8	35.2	50.1	14.7	48.1	44.7	7.3	39.2	54.6	6.2
1916	45.9	49.8	4.3	39.3	56.6	4.0	43.5	49.9	6.6	41.8	54.8	3.4
1918	32.9	55.2	11.9	18.6	53.2	28.2	39.0	55.1	6.0	39.1	55.9	5.0
1920	19.8	60.7	19.5	17.3	56.3	26.3	20.0	50.1	29.9	21.9	56.8	21.4
1922	16.6	55.2	28.2	28.7	45.0	26.2	25.6	47.1	27.3	19.6	54.6	25.8
1924	13.4	49.7	36.9	22.9	53.9	23.2	31.2	44.1	24.7	19.4	57.3	23.3
1926	26.3	55.0	18.8	47.4	40.3	12.3	33.3	59.5	7.2	40.3	58.1	1.6
1928	39.2	60.2	0.6	52.5	46.9	0.6	42.5	53.9	3.6	42.0	57.3	0.7
1930	51.4	47.3	1.3	46.2	53.0	0.8	51.6	48.4	0.0	32.8	62.6	4.7
1932	63.6	34.4	2.0	55.6	42.4	2.0	44.6	53.8	1.6	53.7	44.3	2.0
1934	58.8	38.5	2.7	58.6	40.7	0.8	46.7	50.3	3.0	57.1	42.1	0.8
1936	54.0	42.5	3.5	48.4	51.6	0.0	48.8	46.8	4.4	50.1	50.0	0.0
1938	48.3	50.0	1.7	46.1	54.0	0.0	44.8	55.2	0.0	44.2	55.8	0.0
1940	42.6	57.4	0.0	44.9	55.1	0.0	43.0	57.0	0.0	38.9	61.1	0.0
1942	42.1	57.9	0.0	38.5	61.5	0.0	41.3	58.7	0.0	37.3	62.8	0.0
1944	41.7	58.3	0.0	34.5	65.5	0.0	36.1	63.9	0.0	34.9	65.1	0.0
1946	44.4	55.1	0.6	32.8	67.2	0.0	38.4	61.6	0.0	35.7	64.3	0.0
1948	47.0	51.8	1.1	38.9	61.1	0.0	40.7	59.3	0.0	43.6	56.4	0.0
1950	38.9	60.6	0.6	39.1	60.9	0.0	36.1	63.9	0.0	39.3	60.7	0.0
1952	30.7	69.3	0.0	29.9	70.2	0.0	39.4	60.6	0.0	31.4	68.6	0.0
1954	36.2	63.8	0.0	43.3	56.7	0.0	42.7	57.3	0.0	40.6	59.4	0.0
1956	41.6	58.4	0.0	45.6	54.4	0.0	49.2	50.8	0.0	50.5	49.5	0.0
1958	41.7	58.3	0.0	51.4	48.6	0.0	48.4	51.6	0.0	51.4	48.6	0.0
1960	41.8	58.2	0.0	49.3	50.7	0.0	47.6	52.4	0.0	44.0	56.0	0.0
1962	48.7	51.3	0.0	43.9	56.1	0.0	50.1	49.9	0.0	40.2	59.8	0.0
1964	55.6	44.4	0.0	48.3	51.7	0.0	41.9	58.1	0.0	42.8	57.2	0.0
1966	48.8	48.8	2.4	42.3	57.7	0.0	33.7	66.3	0.0	36.2	63.8	0.0
1968	42.0	53.3	4.8	42.4	57.7	0.0	56.8	43.2	0.0	41.4	58.6	0.0
1970				54.9	45.2	0.0				54.3	45.7	0.0

249

SOUTH DAKOTA

YEAR	COMPOSITE A (P+G+S+H/4)			COMPOSITE B (G+S+H/3)			COMPOSITE C (S+H/2)		
	DEM.	REP.	OTHER	DEM.	REP.	OTHER	DEM.	REP.	OTHER
1872									
1874									
1876									
1878									
1880									
1882									
1884									
1886									
1888									
1890				26.7	57.4	16.0	26.1	57.8	16.1
1892	15.0	49.2	35.8	16.2	49.0	34.8	11.3	50.8	37.9
1894	17.7	51.4	30.9	10.9	52.4	36.7	10.5	52.8	36.7
1896	41.5	49.4	9.2	37.3	49.4	13.3	24.9	49.3	25.8
1898	39.3	51.8	8.9	36.2	51.2	12.6	22.8	53.1	24.1
1900	34.8	56.4	8.8	31.6	56.2	12.2	21.2	56.1	22.7
1902	29.5	64.6	6.0	28.5	64.9	6.6	28.2	65.1	6.7
1904	23.0	69.8	7.2	23.7	69.1	7.2	22.7	70.0	7.3
1906	27.4	65.2	7.5	26.9	65.3	7.9	27.0	65.2	7.8
1908	36.3	58.0	5.7	36.9	57.6	5.5	34.3	59.9	5.8
1910	35.4	58.8	5.8	33.9	60.8	5.3	31.8	63.3	4.9
1912	42.1	51.5	6.4	42.2	52.0	5.9	38.7	55.4	5.9
1914	41.6	49.9	8.5	40.8	49.8	9.4	43.6	49.6	6.7
1916	42.6	52.8	4.6	41.5	53.8	4.7	42.7	52.3	5.0
1918	32.4	54.9	12.8	32.2	54.7	13.1	39.0	55.5	5.5
1920	19.8	56.0	24.3	19.7	54.4	25.9	20.9	53.4	25.6
1922	22.6	50.5	26.9	24.6	48.9	26.5	22.6	50.9	26.6
1924	21.7	51.3	27.1	24.5	51.8	23.8	25.3	50.7	24.0
1926	36.8	53.2	10.0	40.3	52.7	7.0	36.8	58.8	4.4
1928	44.0	54.6	1.4	45.6	52.7	1.6	42.2	55.6	2.2
1930	45.5	52.8	1.7	43.5	54.6	1.8	42.2	55.5	2.3
1932	54.4	43.7	1.9	51.3	46.9	1.8	49.2	49.1	1.8
1934	55.3	42.9	1.8	54.1	44.4	1.5	51.9	46.2	1.9
1936	50.3	47.7	2.0	49.1	49.4	1.5	49.4	48.4	2.2
1938	45.8	53.7	0.4	45.0	55.0	0.0	44.5	55.5	0.0
1940	42.3	57.7	0.0	42.3	57.7	0.0	41.0	59.0	0.0
1942	39.8	60.2	0.0	39.0	61.0	0.0	39.3	60.8	0.0
1944	36.8	63.2	0.0	35.2	64.8	0.0	35.5	64.5	0.0
1946	37.8	62.0	0.1	35.6	64.4	0.0	37.0	63.0	0.0
1948	42.6	57.2	0.3	41.1	58.9	0.0	42.1	57.9	0.0
1950	38.4	61.5	0.1	38.2	61.8	0.0	37.7	62.3	0.0
1952	32.9	67.2	0.0	33.6	66.5	0.0	35.4	64.6	0.0
1954	40.7	59.3	0.0	42.2	57.8	0.0	41.7	58.3	0.0
1956	46.7	53.3	0.0	48.5	51.6	0.0	49.9	50.1	0.0
1958	48.2	51.8	0.0	50.4	49.6	0.0	49.9	50.1	0.0
1960	45.7	54.4	0.0	46.9	53.1	0.0	45.8	54.2	0.0
1962	45.7	54.3	0.0	44.8	55.3	0.0	45.2	54.8	0.0
1964	47.2	52.8	0.0	44.4	55.6	0.0	42.4	57.6	0.0
1966	40.2	59.2	0.6	37.4	62.6	0.0	34.9	65.1	0.0
1968	45.6	53.2	1.2	46.8	53.2	0.0	49.1	50.9	0.0
1970				54.6	45.4	0.0	54.3	45.7	0.0

250

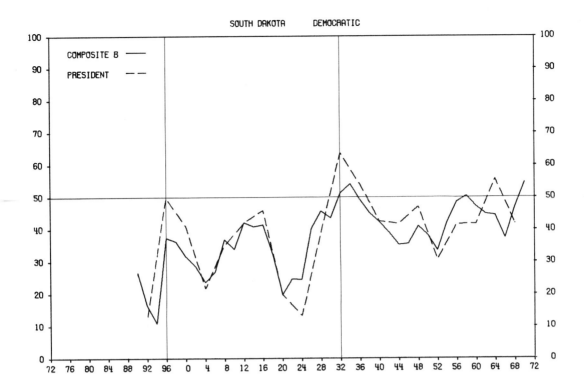

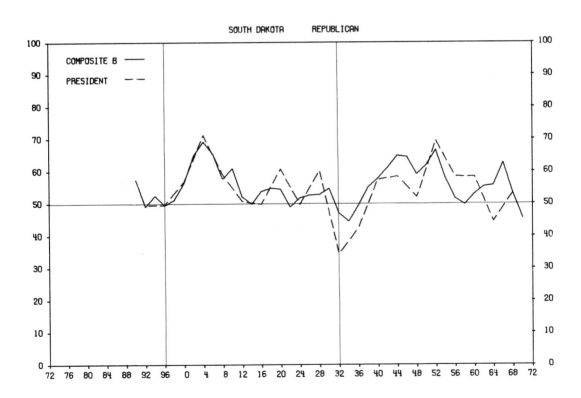

YEAR	PRESIDENT			GOVERNOR			SENATE CLASS I			SENATE CLASS II		
	DEM.	REP.	OTHER	DEM.	REP.	OTHER	DEM.	REP.	OTHER	DEM.	REP.	OTHER
1872	52.2	47.8	0.0	53.7	46.3	0.0						
1874				64.9	35.1	0.0						
1876	59.8	40.2	0.0	58.7	5.2	36.0						
1878				60.3	29.2	10.5						
1880	53.3	44.3	2.5	32.4	42.6	25.1						
1882				52.9	41.0	6.1						
1884	51.5	47.7	0.8	51.3	48.7	0.0						
1886				53.5	46.5	0.0						
1888	52.3	45.8	2.0	51.8	45.9	2.3						
1890				56.6	37.9	5.5						
1892	51.4	37.8	10.8	47.9	38.1	14.0						
1894				44.9	45.2	9.9						
1896	50.7	46.3	3.0	48.7	46.6	4.6						
1898				57.9	39.8	2.3						
1900	53.0	45.0	2.0	53.9	44.3	1.8						
1902				61.8	36.8	1.4						
1904	54.2	43.4	2.4	55.7	43.8	0.5						
1906				54.4	45.1	0.4						
1908	52.7	45.9	1.4	53.7	45.7	0.6						
1910				47.4	51.9	0.7						
1912	52.8	24.0	23.2	46.9	50.2	2.9						
1914				53.5	45.8	0.7						
1916	56.3	42.7	1.0	55.0	44.2	0.8	54.4	44.8	0.8			
1918				62.4	37.6	0.0				62.2	37.8	0.0
1920	48.3	51.2	0.5	44.6	54.9	0.5						
1922				57.9	42.1	0.0	68.0	32.0	0.0			
1924	52.9	43.5	3.6	57.2	42.8	0.0				57.3	42.6	0.1
1926				64.7	35.2	0.1						
1928	44.4	55.4	0.2	61.1	38.9	0.0	59.3	40.7	0.0			
1930				63.8	35.6	0.5				72.8	26.4	0.8
1932	66.5	32.5	1.0	42.8	29.8	27.5						
1934				61.8	38.2	0.0	63.4	35.8	0.8	80.1	0.0	19.9
1936	68.8	30.7	0.4	80.4	18.7	0.9				76.4	18.8	4.8
1938				71.7	28.3	0.0				70.5	26.2	3.3
1940	67.3	32.4	0.4	72.1	27.9	0.0	70.8	29.2	0.0			
1942				70.2	29.8	0.0				68.9	21.5	9.6
1944	60.4	39.2	0.3	62.5	36.0	1.5						
1946				65.3	31.9	2.7	66.6	26.2	7.2			
1948	49.1	36.9	14.0	66.9	33.1	0.0				65.3	33.4	1.2
1950				78.1	21.9	0.0						
1952	49.7	50.0	0.3	79.4	20.6	0.0	74.2	20.9	4.9			
1954				87.2	0.5	12.3				70.0	30.0	0.0
1956	48.6	49.2	2.2									
1958				57.5	8.3	34.2	79.0	19.0	2.0			
1960	45.8	52.9	1.3							71.7	28.2	0.0
1962				50.8	16.1	33.1						
1964	55.5	44.5	0.0				53.6	46.4	0.0	52.1	47.4	0.4
1966				81.2	0.0	18.8				44.3	55.7	0.0
1968	28.1	37.8	34.0									
1970				46.0	52.0	2.1	47.4	51.3	1.3			

252

TENNESSEE

YEAR	PRESIDENT			GOVERNOR			SENATE			HOUSE OF REPRESENTATIVES		
	DEM.	REP.	OTHER	DEM.	REP.	OTHER	DEM.	REP.	OTHER	DEM.	REP.	OTHER
1872	52.2	47.8	0.0	53.7	46.3	0.0				40.0	44.9	15.1
1874	56.0	44.0	0.0	64.9	35.1	0.0				66.3	32.9	0.9
1876	59.8	40.2	0.0	58.8	5.2	36.0				60.0	39.1	0.9
1878	56.5	42.2	1.2	60.3	29.2	10.5				62.1	23.5	14.4
1880	53.3	44.3	2.5	32.4	42.6	25.1				50.3	44.4	5.3
1882	52.4	46.0	1.6	52.9	41.0	6.1				51.2	36.0	12.8
1884	51.5	47.7	0.8	51.3	48.7	0.0				52.6	46.4	0.9
1886	51.9	46.8	1.4	53.5	46.5	0.0				54.0	46.0	0.0
1888	52.3	45.8	2.0	51.8	45.9	2.3				53.2	45.7	1.1
1890	51.8	41.8	6.4	56.6	37.9	5.5				53.3	35.9	10.8
1892	51.4	37.8	10.8	47.9	38.1	14.0				51.5	38.2	10.3
1894	51.0	42.1	6.9	44.9	45.2	9.9				47.8	38.6	13.6
1896	50.7	46.3	3.0	48.8	46.6	4.6				49.7	36.8	13.5
1898	51.9	45.6	2.5	57.9	39.8	2.3				60.3	38.4	1.3
1900	53.0	45.0	2.0	53.9	44.3	1.8				54.0	41.2	4.8
1902	53.6	44.2	2.2	61.8	36.8	1.4				64.8	35.1	0.1
1904	54.2	43.4	2.4	55.7	43.8	0.5				56.2	43.5	0.3
1906	53.5	44.6	1.9	54.4	45.2	0.4				55.7	40.2	4.1
1908	52.7	45.9	1.4	53.7	45.7	0.6				54.3	45.1	0.6
1910	52.8	34.9	12.3	47.5	51.9	0.7				63.0	32.1	4.9
1912	52.8	24.0	23.2	46.9	50.2	2.9				61.3	32.8	5.8
1914	54.6	33.4	12.1	53.6	45.8	0.7				69.5	22.3	8.2
1916	56.3	42.7	1.0	55.0	44.2	0.8	54.4	44.8	0.8	57.8	40.0	2.2
1918	52.3	47.0	0.8	62.4	37.6	0.0	62.2	37.8	0.0	77.0	22.9	0.2
1920	48.3	51.2	0.5	44.6	54.9	0.5	65.1	34.9	0.0	48.0	50.1	1.9
1922	50.6	47.3	2.1	57.9	42.1	0.0	68.0	32.0	0.0	64.7	34.7	0.6
1924	52.9	43.5	3.6	57.2	42.8	0.0	57.3	42.6	0.1	64.2	33.4	2.5
1926	48.7	49.5	1.9	64.7	35.2	0.1	58.3	41.6	0.1	70.0	30.0	0.0
1928	44.4	55.5	0.2	61.1	39.0	0.0	59.3	40.7	0.0	60.5	39.5	0.0
1930	55.4	44.0	0.6	63.8	35.6	0.5	72.8	26.4	0.8	64.1	18.4	17.5
1932	66.5	32.5	1.0	42.8	29.8	27.5	71.8	23.1	5.1	64.0	26.0	10.0
1934	67.7	31.6	0.7	61.8	38.2	0.0	70.9	19.8	9.4	70.6	25.2	4.2
1936	68.9	30.8	0.4	80.4	18.7	0.9	76.4	18.8	4.8	71.8	27.0	1.3
1938	68.1	31.6	0.4	71.7	28.3	0.0	70.5	26.2	3.3	64.5	24.3	11.3
1940	67.3	32.4	0.4	72.1	27.9	0.0	70.8	29.2	0.0	67.7	25.2	7.1
1942	63.9	35.8	0.4	70.2	29.9	0.0	68.9	21.5	9.6	65.4	33.5	1.1
1944	60.5	39.2	0.3	62.5	36.0	1.5	67.7	23.8	8.4	65.4	33.0	1.6
1946	54.8	38.1	7.2	65.3	31.9	2.7	66.6	26.2	7.2	65.4	30.4	4.3
1948	49.1	36.9	14.0	66.9	33.1	0.0	65.3	33.5	1.2	58.2	34.4	7.4
1950	49.4	43.4	7.1	78.1	21.9	0.0	69.8	27.2	3.1	63.0	27.4	9.6
1952	49.7	50.0	0.3	79.4	20.6	0.0	74.2	20.9	4.9	68.5	29.1	2.4
1954	49.2	49.6	1.3	87.2	0.5	12.3	70.0	30.0	0.0	59.4	40.6	0.0
1956	48.6	49.2	2.2	72.4	4.4	23.2	74.5	24.5	1.0	58.9	41.0	0.1
1958	47.2	51.1	1.8	57.5	8.3	34.2	79.0	19.0	2.0	74.5	25.0	0.5
1960	45.8	52.9	1.3	54.2	12.2	33.6	71.8	28.3	0.0	68.5	31.5	0.0
1962	50.6	48.7	0.7	50.9	16.1	33.1	62.3	37.6	0.1	57.0	35.1	8.0
1964	55.5	44.5	0.0	66.0	8.1	25.9	52.9	46.9	0.2	56.2	42.6	1.2
1966	41.8	41.2	17.0	81.2	0.0	18.8	44.3	55.7	0.0	47.8	47.9	4.3
1968	28.1	37.9	34.0	63.6	26.0	10.5	45.8	53.5	0.7	47.9	50.1	1.9
1970				46.0	52.0	2.1	47.4	51.3	1.3	58.6	40.8	0.6

253

TENNESSEE

YEAR	COMPOSITE A (P+G+S+H/4)			COMPOSITE B (G+S+H/3)			COMPOSITE C (S+H/2)		
	DEM.	REP.	OTHER	DEM.	REP.	OTHER	DEM.	REP.	OTHER
1872	48.6	46.3	5.1	46.9	45.6	7.6	40.0	44.9	15.1
1874	62.4	37.4	0.3	65.6	34.0	0.4	66.3	32.9	0.9
1876	59.5	28.2	12.3	59.4	22.2	18.4	60.0	39.1	0.9
1878	59.6	31.7	8.7	61.2	26.4	12.5	62.1	23.5	14.4
1880	45.3	43.7	11.0	41.3	43.5	15.2	50.3	44.4	5.3
1882	52.2	41.0	6.8	52.1	38.5	9.4	51.2	36.0	12.8
1884	51.8	47.6	0.6	52.0	47.6	0.5	52.6	46.4	0.9
1886	53.1	46.4	0.5	53.7	46.3	0.0	54.0	46.0	0.0
1888	52.4	45.8	1.8	52.5	45.8	1.7	53.2	45.7	1.1
1890	53.9	38.5	7.6	55.0	36.9	8.1	53.3	35.9	10.8
1892	50.3	38.1	11.7	49.7	38.2	12.1	51.5	38.2	10.3
1894	47.9	42.0	10.2	46.3	41.9	11.8	47.8	38.6	13.6
1896	49.7	43.3	7.0	49.2	41.7	9.1	49.7	36.8	13.5
1898	56.7	41.3	2.0	59.1	39.1	1.8	60.3	38.4	1.3
1900	53.6	43.5	2.9	53.9	42.8	3.3	54.0	41.2	4.8
1902	60.1	38.7	1.2	63.3	36.0	0.7	64.8	35.1	0.1
1904	55.4	43.6	1.0	56.0	43.7	0.4	56.2	43.5	0.3
1906	54.5	43.3	2.2	55.1	42.7	2.3	55.7	40.2	4.1
1908	53.6	45.6	0.9	54.0	45.4	0.6	54.3	45.1	0.6
1910	54.4	39.6	6.0	55.2	42.0	2.8	63.0	32.1	4.9
1912	53.7	35.7	10.7	54.1	41.5	4.4	61.3	32.8	5.8
1914	59.2	33.8	7.0	61.5	34.1	4.4	69.5	22.3	8.2
1916	55.9	42.9	1.2	55.8	43.0	1.3	56.1	42.4	1.5
1918	63.5	36.3	0.2	67.2	32.8	0.1	69.6	30.4	0.1
1920	51.5	47.8	0.7	52.6	46.6	0.8	56.6	42.5	0.9
1922	60.3	39.0	0.7	63.5	36.3	0.2	66.4	33.3	0.3
1924	57.9	40.6	1.6	59.6	39.6	0.9	60.7	38.0	1.3
1926	60.4	39.1	0.5	64.3	35.6	0.1	64.2	35.8	0.0
1928	56.3	43.6	0.1	60.3	39.7	0.0	59.9	40.1	0.0
1930	64.0	31.1	4.9	66.9	26.8	6.3	68.4	22.4	9.2
1932	61.3	27.9	10.9	59.5	26.3	14.2	67.9	24.6	7.5
1934	67.7	28.7	3.6	67.8	27.7	4.5	70.7	22.5	6.8
1936	74.4	23.8	1.9	76.2	21.5	2.3	74.1	22.9	3.0
1938	68.7	27.6	3.8	68.9	26.2	4.9	67.5	25.2	7.3
1940	69.5	28.7	1.9	70.2	27.4	2.4	69.2	27.2	3.6
1942	67.1	30.2	2.8	68.1	28.3	3.6	67.1	27.5	5.4
1944	64.0	33.0	3.0	65.2	31.0	3.8	66.6	28.4	5.0
1946	63.0	31.6	5.4	65.8	29.5	4.7	66.0	28.3	5.7
1948	59.9	34.5	5.7	63.5	33.6	2.9	61.8	33.9	4.3
1950	65.1	30.0	5.0	70.3	25.5	4.2	66.4	27.3	6.4
1952	67.9	30.1	1.9	74.0	23.5	2.5	71.3	25.0	3.7
1954	66.4	30.2	3.4	72.2	23.7	4.1	64.7	35.3	0.0
1956	63.6	29.8	6.6	68.6	23.3	8.1	66.7	32.7	0.6
1958	64.6	25.9	9.6	70.3	17.4	12.2	76.7	22.0	1.3
1960	60.1	31.2	8.7	64.8	24.0	11.2	70.1	29.9	0.0
1962	55.2	34.4	10.5	56.7	29.6	13.7	59.6	36.3	4.1
1964	57.6	35.5	6.8	58.4	32.5	9.1	54.5	44.8	0.7
1966	53.8	36.2	10.1	57.8	34.5	7.7	46.0	51.8	2.2
1968	46.4	41.9	11.8	52.5	43.2	4.4	46.9	51.8	1.3
1970				50.7	48.0	1.3	53.0	46.0	1.0

254

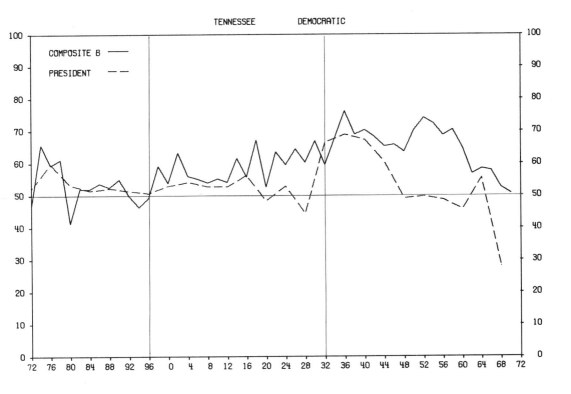

TENNESSEE   DEMOCRATIC

COMPOSITE B ———
PRESIDENT ———

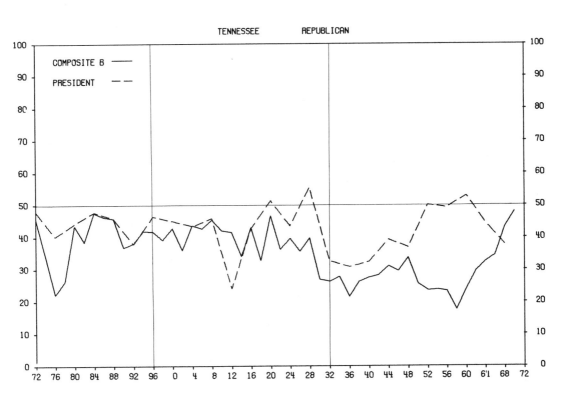

TENNESSEE   REPUBLICAN

COMPOSITE B ———
PRESIDENT ———

TEXAS

YEAR	PRESIDENT			GOVERNOR			SENATE CLASS I			SENATE CLASS II		
	DEM.	REP.	OTHER	DEM.	REP.	OTHER	DEM.	REP.	OTHER	DEM.	REP.	OTHER
1872	58.5	41.4	0.1									
1874				66.0	34.0	0.0						
1876	70.2	29.7	0.0	75.0	25.0	0.0						
1878				67.1	9.7	23.2						
1880	66.8	21.5	11.7	62.9	24.4	12.8						
1882				58.0	41.9	0.1						
1884	69.5	28.4	2.1	63.2	29.4	7.4						
1886				73.0	21.1	5.9						
1888	65.5	25.0	9.5	70.8	0.0	29.2						
1890				76.7	22.5	0.8						
1892	57.7	17.3	25.0	43.7	30.6	25.6						
1894				48.9	12.9	38.3						
1896	53.9	30.3	15.8	55.3	0.0	44.7						
1898				71.2	0.0	28.8						
1900	63.1	30.9	5.9	67.6	25.1	7.3						
1902				74.9	18.3	6.8						
1904	71.5	22.0	6.5	73.6	20.3	6.2						
1906				81.2	12.9	5.9						
1908	74.0	22.4	3.6	72.9	24.2	2.9						
1910				79.8	12.0	8.2						
1912	72.7	9.4	17.9	77.8	7.6	14.6						
1914				82.0	5.3	12.8						
1916	77.0	17.4	5.6	80.5	13.3	6.2	81.3	13.1	5.6			
1918				84.0	15.1	0.9				86.7	12.4	0.9
1920	59.4	23.5	17.1	60.2	18.6	21.2						
1922				81.9	18.1	0.0	66.6	33.4	0.0			
1924	73.7	19.8	6.5	58.9	41.1	0.0				85.4	14.6	0.0
1926				87.5	12.2	0.3						
1928	48.1	51.7	0.1	82.4	17.4	0.1	81.2	18.7	0.1			
1930				80.0	19.7	0.3				86.9	12.7	0.4
1932	88.2	11.2	0.6	61.6	38.1	0.3						
1934				96.4	3.1	0.5	96.7	2.8	0.5			
1936	86.9	12.5	0.6	92.9	7.0	0.2				92.6	7.1	0.3
1938				96.8	3.0	0.1						
1940	80.9	19.0	0.2	94.7	5.3	0.0	94.3	5.7	0.0			
1942				96.8	3.2	0.0				98.3	1.5	0.3
1944	71.4	16.7	11.9	90.9	9.1	0.0						
1946				91.2	8.8	0.0	88.5	11.5	0.0			
1948	65.4	24.6	10.0	84.7	14.7	0.6				66.2	32.9	0.8
1950				90.2	9.8	0.0						
1952	46.7	53.1	0.2	74.7	25.3	0.0	75.2	24.8	0.0			
1954				89.4	10.4	0.2				84.7	14.8	0.5
1956	44.0	55.3	0.7	78.4	14.8	6.8						
1958				88.1	11.9	0.0	72.0	23.2	4.7			
1960	50.5	48.5	1.0	72.8	27.2	0.0				58.0	41.1	0.9
1962				54.0	45.6	0.5				49.4	50.6	0.0
1964	63.3	36.5	0.2	73.8	26.0	0.2	56.2	43.6	0.2			
1966				72.8	25.8	1.4				43.1	56.4	0.5
1968	41.1	39.9	19.0	57.0	43.0	0.0						
1970				53.6	46.4	0.0	53.5	46.4	0.1			

YEAR	PRESIDENT			GOVERNOR			SENATE			HOUSE OF REPRESENTATIVES		
	DEM.	REP.	OTHER	DEM.	REP.	OTHER	DEM.	REP.	OTHER	DEM.	REP.	OTHER
1872	58.5	41.4	0.1	57.6	42.1	0.3				59.5	27.2	13.4
1874	64.4	35.6	0.1	66.0	34.0	0.0				79.6	9.0	11.4
1876	70.2	29.7	0.0	75.0	25.0	0.0				71.3	28.5	0.2
1878	68.5	25.6	5.9	67.1	9.7	23.3				68.7	8.8	22.5
1880	66.8	21.5	11.7	62.9	24.4	12.8				70.7	0.0	29.3
1882	68.1	25.0	6.9	58.0	41.9	0.1				62.3	11.6	26.2
1884	69.5	28.4	2.1	63.2	29.4	7.4				82.1	17.2	0.7
1886	67.5	26.7	5.8	73.0	21.1	5.9				70.9	8.5	20.6
1888	65.5	25.0	9.5	70.8	0.0	29.2				70.2	22.4	7.4
1890	61.6	21.1	17.3	76.7	22.5	0.8				80.5	18.5	1.1
1892	57.7	17.3	25.0	43.7	30.7	25.6				57.7	17.3	25.1
1894	55.8	23.8	20.4	48.9	12.9	38.3				50.4	7.1	42.5
1896	53.9	30.3	15.8	55.3	0.0	44.7				53.7	23.4	22.9
1898	58.5	30.6	10.9	71.2	0.0	28.8				63.0	14.6	22.4
1900	63.1	30.9	5.9	67.6	25.1	7.3				74.6	20.1	5.3
1902	67.3	26.4	6.2	74.9	18.3	6.8				82.6	16.8	0.6
1904	71.5	22.0	6.5	73.6	20.3	6.2				82.0	17.0	1.1
1906	72.8	22.2	5.1	81.2	12.9	5.9				86.9	11.8	1.2
1908	74.0	22.4	3.6	72.9	24.2	2.9				82.2	15.9	1.9
1910	73.4	15.9	10.7	79.8	12.0	8.3				87.9	8.3	3.8
1912	72.7	9.4	17.9	77.8	7.6	14.6				83.2	5.8	11.0
1914	74.9	13.4	11.7	82.0	5.3	12.8				84.8	4.7	10.5
1916	77.0	17.4	5.6	80.5	13.3	6.2	81.3	13.1	5.6	82.5	12.2	5.3
1918	68.2	20.5	11.3	84.0	15.1	0.9	86.7	12.4	0.9	96.3	3.7	0.0
1920	59.4	23.5	17.1	60.2	18.7	21.2	76.7	22.9	0.5	76.6	15.8	7.6
1922	66.5	21.7	11.8	81.9	18.1	0.0	66.6	33.4	0.0	85.0	15.0	0.0
1924	73.7	19.8	6.5	58.9	41.1	0.0	85.4	14.6	0.0	86.8	13.2	0.0
1926	60.9	35.8	3.3	87.5	12.2	0.3	83.3	16.6	0.1	87.3	12.7	0.0
1928	48.1	51.7	0.1	82.4	17.4	0.1	81.2	18.7	0.1	87.5	12.5	0.0
1930	68.2	31.5	0.4	80.0	19.7	0.3	86.9	12.7	0.4	84.6	15.4	0.0
1932	88.2	11.2	0.6	61.6	38.1	0.4	91.8	7.8	0.4	93.3	6.5	0.2
1934	87.6	11.9	0.6	96.4	3.1	0.5	96.7	2.8	0.5	98.6	1.1	0.3
1936	86.9	12.5	0.6	92.9	7.0	0.2	92.6	7.1	0.3	93.4	6.4	0.3
1938	83.9	15.7	0.4	96.8	3.1	0.1	93.4	6.4	0.2	99.1	0.9	0.0
1940	80.9	19.0	0.2	94.7	5.3	0.0	94.3	5.7	0.0	96.8	3.2	0.0
1942	76.1	17.8	6.1	96.8	3.2	0.0	98.3	1.5	0.3	98.8	1.0	0.2
1944	71.4	16.7	12.0	90.9	9.1	0.0	93.4	6.5	0.1	94.0	5.9	0.1
1946	68.4	20.6	11.0	91.2	8.8	0.0	88.5	11.5	0.0	95.1	4.9	0.0
1948	65.4	24.6	10.0	84.7	14.7	0.6	66.2	32.9	0.8	93.6	6.2	0.1
1950	56.1	38.9	5.1	90.2	9.8	0.0	70.7	28.9	0.4	90.5	9.5	0.0
1952	46.7	53.1	0.2	74.7	25.3	0.0	75.2	24.8	0.0	86.8	13.2	0.0
1954	45.3	54.2	0.5	89.4	10.4	0.2	84.7	14.8	0.5	87.5	12.5	0.0
1956	44.0	55.3	0.8	78.4	14.8	6.8	78.4	19.0	2.6	91.7	8.2	0.1
1958	47.3	51.9	0.9	88.1	11.9	0.0	72.0	23.2	4.7	87.6	11.9	0.5
1960	50.5	48.5	1.0	72.8	27.2	0.0	58.0	41.1	0.9	82.4	13.7	3.9
1962	56.9	42.5	0.6	54.0	45.6	0.5	49.4	50.6	0.0	61.7	38.3	0.0
1964	63.3	36.5	0.2	73.8	26.0	0.2	56.2	43.6	0.2	67.8	32.0	0.2
1966	52.2	38.2	9.6	72.8	25.8	1.4	43.1	56.4	0.5	82.4	16.4	1.2
1968	41.1	39.9	19.0	57.0	43.0	0.0	48.3	51.4	0.3	76.4	23.5	0.1
1970				53.6	46.4	0.0	53.5	46.4	0.1	73.0	26.0	1.0

YEAR	COMPOSITE A (P+G+S+H/4)			COMPOSITE B (G+S+H/3)			COMPOSITE C (S+H/2)		
	DEM.	REP.	OTHER	DEM.	REP.	OTHER	DEM.	REP.	OTHER
1872	58.5	36.9	4.6	58.5	34.7	6.8	59.5	27.2	13.4
1874	70.0	26.2	3.8	72.8	21.5	5.7	79.6	9.0	11.4
1876	72.2	27.7	0.1	73.1	26.8	0.1	71.3	28.5	0.2
1878	68.1	14.7	17.2	67.9	9.2	22.9	68.7	8.8	22.5
1880	66.8	15.3	17.9	66.8	12.2	21.0	70.7	0.0	29.3
1882	62.8	26.1	11.1	60.1	26.7	13.2	62.3	11.6	26.2
1884	71.6	25.0	3.4	72.7	23.3	4.1	82.1	17.2	0.7
1886	70.4	18.8	10.8	71.9	14.8	13.3	70.9	8.5	20.6
1888	68.8	15.8	15.4	70.5	11.2	18.3	70.2	22.4	7.4
1890	72.9	20.7	6.4	78.6	20.5	0.9	80.5	18.5	1.1
1892	53.0	21.7	25.2	50.7	24.0	25.3	57.7	17.3	25.1
1894	51.7	14.6	33.7	49.6	10.0	40.4	50.4	7.1	42.5
1896	54.3	17.9	27.8	54.5	11.7	33.8	53.7	23.4	22.9
1898	64.2	15.1	20.7	67.1	7.3	25.6	63.0	14.6	22.4
1900	68.4	25.4	6.2	71.1	22.6	6.3	74.6	20.1	5.3
1902	75.0	20.5	4.6	78.8	17.5	3.7	82.6	16.8	0.6
1904	75.7	19.7	4.6	77.8	18.6	3.6	82.0	17.0	1.1
1906	80.3	15.7	4.1	84.1	12.4	3.6	86.9	11.8	1.2
1908	76.4	20.8	2.8	77.6	20.1	2.4	82.2	15.9	1.9
1910	80.4	12.1	7.6	83.8	10.2	6.0	87.9	8.3	3.8
1912	77.9	7.6	14.5	80.5	6.7	12.8	83.2	5.8	11.0
1914	80.5	7.8	11.7	83.4	5.0	11.7	84.8	4.7	10.5
1916	80.3	14.0	5.7	81.4	12.9	5.7	81.9	12.6	5.5
1918	83.8	12.9	3.3	89.0	10.4	0.6	91.5	8.1	0.5
1920	68.2	20.2	11.6	71.1	19.1	9.7	76.6	19.4	4.0
1922	75.0	22.0	3.0	77.9	22.2	0.0	75.8	24.2	0.0
1924	76.2	22.2	1.6	77.0	23.0	0.0	86.1	13.9	0.0
1926	79.8	19.3	0.9	86.0	13.8	0.1	85.3	14.7	0.0
1928	74.8	25.1	0.1	83.7	16.2	0.1	84.4	15.6	0.1
1930	79.9	19.8	0.3	83.8	15.9	0.2	85.8	14.1	0.2
1932	83.7	15.9	0.4	82.2	17.5	0.3	92.6	7.1	0.3
1934	94.8	4.7	0.5	97.2	2.4	0.4	97.6	2.0	0.4
1936	91.4	8.2	0.3	92.9	6.8	0.3	93.0	6.7	0.3
1938	93.3	6.5	0.2	96.4	3.5	0.1	96.3	3.7	0.1
1940	91.7	8.3	0.1	95.3	4.7	0.0	95.5	4.4	0.0
1942	92.5	5.9	1.6	98.0	1.9	0.2	98.5	1.2	0.3
1944	87.4	9.5	3.0	92.8	7.2	0.1	93.7	6.2	0.1
1946	85.8	11.4	2.7	91.6	8.4	0.0	91.8	8.2	0.0
1948	77.5	19.6	2.9	81.5	18.0	0.5	79.9	19.6	0.5
1950	76.9	21.8	1.4	83.8	16.1	0.2	80.6	19.2	0.2
1952	70.9	29.1	0.1	78.9	21.1	0.0	81.0	19.0	0.0
1954	76.7	23.0	0.3	87.2	12.6	0.2	86.1	13.6	0.3
1956	73.1	24.3	2.6	82.8	14.0	3.2	85.0	13.6	1.4
1958	73.7	24.7	1.5	82.6	15.7	1.8	79.8	17.6	2.6
1960	65.9	32.7	1.4	71.1	27.4	1.6	70.2	27.4	2.4
1962	55.5	44.2	0.3	55.0	44.8	0.2	55.6	44.4	0.0
1964	65.3	34.5	0.2	65.9	33.9	0.2	62.0	37.8	0.2
1966	62.6	34.2	3.2	66.1	32.9	1.0	62.8	36.4	0.8
1968	55.7	39.4	4.9	60.6	39.3	0.1	62.4	37.5	0.2
1970				60.0	39.6	0.4	63.3	36.2	0.5

258

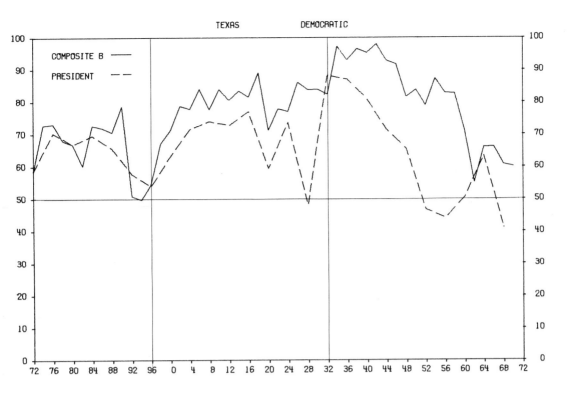

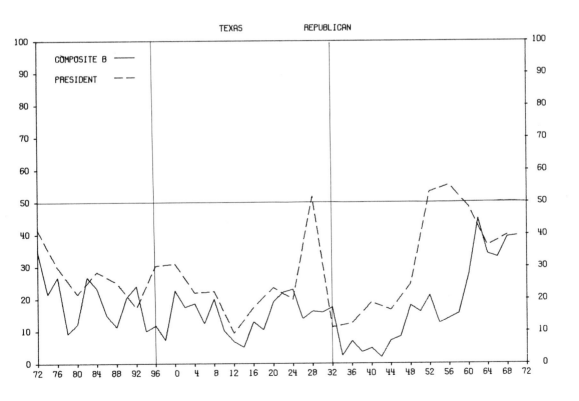

UTAH

YEAR	PRESIDENT			GOVERNOR			SENATE CLASS I			SENATE CLASS III		
	DEM.	REP.	OTHER	DEM.	REP.	OTHER	DEM.	REP.	OTHER	DEM.	REP.	OTHER
1872 1874												
1876 1878												
1880 1882												
1884 1886												
1888 1890												
1892 1894												
1896 1898	82.7	17.3	0.0	44.7	50.3	5.0						
1900 1902	48.3	50.6	1.1	48.3	51.7	0.0						
1904 1906	32.9	61.4	5.7	37.4	50.0	12.6						
1908 1910	39.2	56.2	4.6	38.8	47.4	13.8						
1912 1914	32.6	37.4	30.0	32.4	38.2	29.4				46.3	49.1	4.6
1916 1918	58.8	37.8	3.4	55.0	41.8	3.2	56.8	39.9	3.3			
1920 1922	38.8	55.9	5.2	38.2	58.2	3.6	48.6	48.2	3.2	38.6	56.6	4.8
1924 1926	29.9	49.3	20.8	53.0	47.0	0.0				37.6	61.5	0.9
1928 1930	45.9	53.5	0.6	58.5	41.1	0.4	55.5	43.9	0.6			
1932 1934	56.6	41.0	2.4	56.4	41.8	1.9	53.1	45.4	1.5	56.7	41.7	1.6
1936 1938	69.3	29.8	0.9	50.9	37.2	11.8				55.8	44.2	0.0
1940 1942	62.2	37.6	0.2	52.1	47.7	0.2	62.8	37.2	0.0			
1944 1946	60.5	39.4	0.1	50.2	49.8	0.0	48.8	51.2	0.0	59.9	40.1	0.0
1948 1950	54.0	45.0	1.0	45.0	55.0	0.0				45.8	53.9	0.3
1952 1954	41.1	58.9	0.0	44.9	55.1	0.0	45.7	54.3	0.0			
1956 1958	35.4	64.6	0.0	33.4	38.2	28.4	38.7	34.8	26.4	46.0	54.0	0.0
1960 1962	45.2	54.8	0.0	47.3	52.7	0.0				47.6	52.4	0.0
1964 1966	54.7	45.3	0.0	57.0	43.0	0.0	57.3	42.7	0.0			
1968 1970	37.1	56.5	6.4	68.7	31.3	0.0	56.2	42.5	1.4	45.8	53.7	0.5

UTAH

YEAR	PRESIDENT			GOVERNOR			SENATE			HOUSE OF REPRESENTATIVES		
	DEM.	REP.	OTHER	DEM.	REP.	OTHER	DEM.	REP.	OTHER	DEM.	REP.	OTHER
1872												
1874												
1876												
1878												
1880												
1882												
1884												
1886												
1888												
1890												
1892												
1894												
1896	82.7	17.3	0.0	44.7	50.3	5.0				61.2	35.9	2.9
1898	65.5	33.9	0.6	46.5	51.0	2.5				54.6	45.4	0.0
1900	48.3	50.6	1.1	48.3	51.7	0.0				49.9	50.1	0.0
1902	40.6	56.0	3.4	42.8	50.8	6.3				45.0	51.5	3.5
1904	32.9	61.5	5.7	37.4	50.0	12.6				36.8	51.8	11.4
1906	36.0	58.8	5.1	38.1	48.7	13.2				33.0	50.1	17.0
1908	39.2	56.2	4.6	38.8	47.5	13.8				32.3	51.6	16.1
1910	35.9	46.8	17.3	35.6	42.8	21.6				32.0	49.5	18.5
1912	32.6	37.4	30.0	32.4	38.2	29.4				33.3	38.4	28.4
1914	45.7	37.6	16.7	43.7	40.0	16.3	46.3	49.1	4.6	46.7	48.3	5.0
1916	58.8	37.8	3.4	55.0	41.8	3.2	56.8	39.9	3.3	56.1	40.6	3.3
1918	48.8	46.9	4.3	46.6	50.0	3.4	47.7	48.3	4.0	56.7	42.1	1.2
1920	38.8	55.9	5.2	38.3	58.2	3.6	38.6	56.6	4.8	38.9	56.1	5.0
1922	34.4	52.6	13.0	45.6	52.6	1.8	48.6	48.2	3.2	45.1	51.7	3.3
1924	29.9	49.3	20.8	53.0	47.0	0.0	43.1	54.8	2.1	44.3	55.8	0.0
1926	37.9	51.4	10.7	55.7	44.1	0.2	37.6	61.5	0.9	38.3	60.8	0.9
1928	45.9	53.5	0.6	58.5	41.1	0.4	55.5	43.9	0.6	44.3	55.2	0.5
1930	51.2	47.3	1.5	57.5	41.4	1.1	56.1	42.8	1.1	40.6	52.3	7.1
1932	56.6	41.0	2.4	56.4	41.8	1.9	56.7	41.7	1.6	53.6	44.6	1.8
1934	63.0	35.4	1.7	53.7	39.5	6.8	53.1	45.4	1.5	63.3	35.5	1.2
1936	69.3	29.8	0.9	51.0	37.2	11.8	54.4	44.8	0.8	69.5	30.3	0.2
1938	65.8	33.7	0.5	51.5	42.5	6.0	55.8	44.2	0.0	61.0	39.0	0.0
1940	62.2	37.6	0.2	52.1	47.7	0.2	62.9	37.2	0.0	60.2	39.8	0.0
1942	61.3	38.5	0.2	51.1	48.7	0.1	61.4	38.6	0.0	53.1	46.9	0.0
1944	60.5	39.4	0.1	50.2	49.8	0.0	59.9	40.1	0.0	60.4	39.6	0.0
1946	57.2	42.2	0.6	47.6	52.4	0.0	48.8	51.2	0.0	48.6	51.5	0.0
1948	54.0	45.0	1.0	45.0	55.0	0.0	47.3	52.6	0.2	58.1	41.9	0.0
1950	47.5	52.0	0.5	45.0	55.0	0.0	45.8	53.9	0.3	52.5	47.5	0.0
1952	41.1	58.9	0.0	44.9	55.1	0.0	45.7	54.3	0.0	44.4	55.6	0.0
1954	38.3	61.7	0.0	39.2	46.6	14.2	45.9	54.1	0.0	44.3	55.7	0.0
1956	35.4	64.6	0.0	33.4	38.2	28.4	46.0	54.0	0.0	41.2	58.9	0.0
1958	40.3	59.7	0.0	40.4	45.4	14.2	38.7	34.8	26.4	49.2	50.8	0.0
1960	45.2	54.8	0.0	47.3	52.7	0.0	43.2	43.6	13.2	50.5	49.5	0.0
1962	49.9	50.1	0.0	52.2	47.8	0.0	47.6	52.4	0.0	47.2	52.8	0.0
1964	54.7	45.3	0.0	57.0	43.0	0.0	57.3	42.7	0.0	52.9	47.1	0.0
1966	45.9	50.9	3.2	62.9	37.2	0.0	51.6	48.2	0.2	36.2	63.8	0.0
1968	37.1	56.5	6.4	68.7	31.3	0.0	45.8	53.7	0.5	47.0	53.0	0.0
1970							56.2	42.5	1.4	48.9	50.1	1.0

261

YEAR	COMPOSITE A (P+G+S+H/4)			COMPOSITE B (G+S+H/3)			COMPOSITE C (S+H/2)		
	DEM.	REP.	OTHER	DEM.	REP.	OTHER	DEM.	REP.	OTHER
1872									
1874									
1876									
1878									
1880									
1882									
1884									
1886									
1888									
1890									
1892									
1894									
1896	62.9	34.5	2.6	53.0	43.1	4.0	61.2	35.9	2.9
1898	55.6	43.4	1.0	50.6	48.2	1.2	54.6	45.4	0.0
1900	48.8	50.8	0.4	49.1	50.9	0.0	49.9	50.1	0.0
1902	42.8	52.8	4.4	43.9	51.2	4.9	45.0	51.5	3.5
1904	35.7	54.4	9.9	37.1	50.9	12.0	36.8	51.8	11.4
1906	35.7	52.6	11.8	35.5	49.4	15.1	33.0	50.1	17.0
1908	36.8	51.8	11.5	35.5	49.5	14.9	32.3	51.6	16.1
1910	34.5	46.4	19.1	33.8	46.2	20.0	32.0	49.5	18.5
1912	32.8	38.0	29.3	32.8	38.3	28.9	33.3	38.4	28.4
1914	45.6	43.8	10.7	45.6	45.8	8.6	46.5	48.7	4.8
1916	56.7	40.0	3.3	56.0	40.8	3.3	56.5	40.3	3.3
1918	49.9	46.8	3.3	50.3	46.8	2.9	52.2	45.2	2.6
1920	38.7	56.7	4.7	38.6	57.0	4.5	38.8	56.4	4.9
1922	43.4	51.3	5.3	46.5	50.8	2.8	46.9	49.9	3.2
1924	42.6	51.7	5.7	46.8	52.5	0.7	43.7	55.3	1.0
1926	42.4	54.5	3.2	43.9	55.5	0.7	37.9	61.2	0.9
1928	51.1	48.4	0.5	52.8	46.7	0.5	49.9	49.6	0.5
1930	51.3	46.0	2.7	51.4	45.5	3.1	48.3	47.6	4.1
1932	55.8	42.3	1.9	55.6	42.7	1.8	55.1	43.2	1.7
1934	58.3	39.0	2.8	56.7	40.1	3.2	58.2	40.5	1.3
1936	61.1	35.5	3.4	58.3	37.4	4.3	62.0	37.5	0.5
1938	58.5	39.8	1.6	56.1	41.9	2.0	58.4	41.6	0.0
1940	59.4	40.6	0.1	58.4	41.5	0.1	61.6	38.5	0.0
1942	56.7	43.2	0.1	55.2	44.8	0.0	57.2	42.8	0.0
1944	57.8	42.2	0.0	56.8	43.2	0.0	60.2	39.8	0.0
1946	50.5	49.3	0.1	48.3	51.7	0.0	48.7	51.3	0.0
1948	51.1	48.6	0.3	50.1	49.8	0.1	52.7	47.2	0.1
1950	47.7	52.1	0.2	47.8	52.1	0.1	49.2	50.7	0.2
1952	44.0	56.0	0.0	45.0	55.0	0.0	45.1	55.0	0.0
1954	41.9	54.5	3.6	43.1	52.1	4.7	45.1	54.9	0.0
1956	39.0	53.9	7.1	40.2	50.3	9.5	43.6	56.4	0.0
1958	42.2	47.7	10.2	42.8	43.7	13.5	44.0	42.8	13.2
1960	46.6	50.1	3.3	47.0	48.6	4.4	46.9	46.5	6.6
1962	49.2	50.8	0.0	49.0	51.0	0.0	47.4	52.6	0.0
1964	55.5	44.5	0.0	55.7	44.3	0.0	55.1	44.9	0.0
1966	49.1	50.0	0.9	50.2	49.7	0.1	43.9	56.0	0.1
1968	49.7	48.6	1.7	53.9	46.0	0.2	46.4	53.4	0.2
1970							52.6	46.3	1.2

262

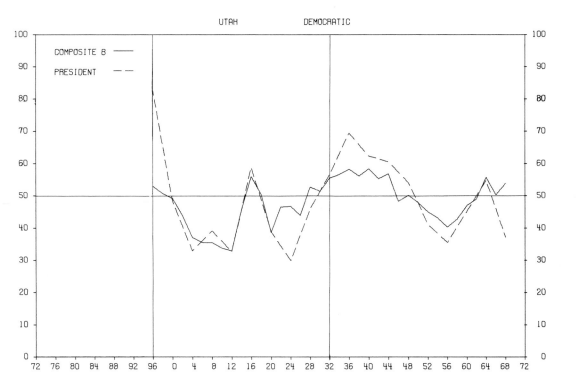

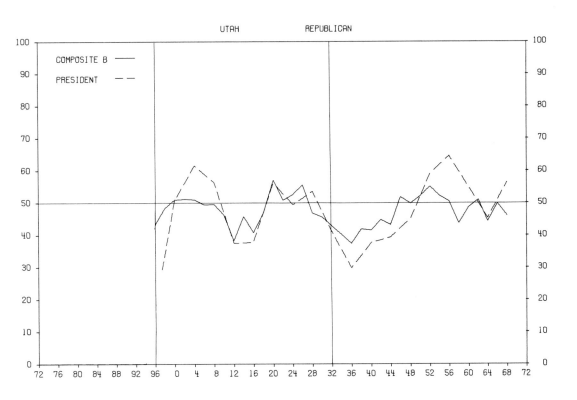

263

YEAR	PRESIDENT			GOVERNOR			SENATE CLASS I			SENATE CLASS III		
	DEM.	REP.	OTHER	DEM.	REP.	OTHER	DEM.	REP.	OTHER	DEM.	REP.	OTHER
1872	20.8	79.2	0.0	28.4	71.6	0.0						
1874				28.3	71.7	0.0						
1876	31.4	68.4	0.2	31.9	68.0	0.1						
1878				29.8	64.3	5.9						
1880	28.1	70.0	1.9	30.1	67.7	2.3						
1882				27.9	69.1	3.0						
1884	29.2	66.5	4.3	31.4	67.3	1.4						
1886				30.1	66.0	3.9						
1888	26.4	71.2	2.4	28.1	69.9	2.0						
1890				35.8	62.1	2.2						
1892	29.3	68.1	2.6	32.2	65.2	2.6						
1894				24.4	73.6	2.1						
1896	15.9	80.1	4.0	21.2	76.4	2.3						
1898				27.0	71.0	2.0						
1900	22.9	75.7	1.4	25.5	72.2	2.3						
1902				10.5	45.6	43.9						
1904	18.8	78.0	3.2	24.9	72.2	2.9						
1906				38.2	60.1	1.8						
1908	21.8	75.1	3.1	24.8	70.8	4.4						
1910				31.7	64.2	4.1						
1912	24.4	37.1	38.5	30.8	40.5	28.7						
1914				26.1	59.5	14.4				42.7	56.0	1.3
1916	35.2	62.4	2.4	25.9	71.1	3.0	23.4	74.2	2.3			
1918				29.6	67.2	3.2						
1920	23.3	75.8	0.9	21.8	76.6	1.6				21.9	78.0	0.0
1922				25.0	72.0	3.1	32.1	67.9	0.1			
1924	15.7	78.2	6.1	19.2	79.2	1.6				33.8	66.2	0.0
1926				36.0	60.9	3.1				26.5	70.7	2.8
1928	32.9	66.9	0.3	26.0	73.5	0.5	28.4	71.5	0.0			
1930				28.9	71.0	0.1						
1932	41.1	57.7	1.3	37.2	61.7	1.1				44.8	55.1	0.0
1934				42.1	57.3	0.6	48.4	51.0	0.6			
1936	43.2	56.4	0.4	38.8	60.9	0.3						
1938				33.2	66.8	0.0				34.3	65.7	0.0
1940	44.9	54.8	0.3	36.0	64.0	0.0	33.6	66.4	0.0	38.4	61.6	0.1
1942				22.1	77.9	0.0						
1944	43.0	57.0	0.0	34.1	65.9	0.0				34.2	65.8	0.0
1946				19.6	80.3	0.1	25.4	74.6	0.0			
1948	36.9	61.5	1.5	27.9	71.9	0.2						
1950				25.5	74.5	0.0				22.0	78.0	0.0
1952	28.2	71.5	0.3	39.8	51.9	8.3	27.7	72.3	0.0			
1954				47.7	52.3	0.0						
1956	27.8	72.2	0.0	42.5	57.5	0.0				33.6	66.4	0.0
1958				49.7	50.3	0.0	47.8	52.2	0.0			
1960	41.3	58.6	0.0	43.6	56.4	0.0						
1962				46.3	49.4	4.3				33.1	66.9	0.0
1964	66.3	33.7	0.0	64.9	34.4	0.7	46.5	50.7	2.8			
1966				57.7	42.3	0.0						
1968	43.5	52.8	3.7	44.5	55.5	0.0				39.7	60.2	0.1
1970				43.0	57.0	0.0	40.2	58.9	0.9			

YEAR	PRESIDENT			GOVERNOR			SENATE			HOUSE OF REPRESENTATIVES		
	DEM.	REP.	OTHER	DEM.	REP.	OTHER	DEM.	REP.	OTHER	DEM.	REP.	OTHER
1872	20.9	79.2	0.0	28.4	71.6	0.0				19.7	74.3	6.0
1874	26.1	73.8	0.1	28.3	71.7	0.0				36.0	57.8	6.2
1876	31.4	68.4	0.2	31.9	68.0	0.1				31.0	68.5	0.4
1878	29.8	69.2	1.0	29.8	64.3	5.9				24.0	58.9	17.1
1880	28.1	70.0	1.9	30.1	67.7	2.3				29.9	66.7	3.3
1882	28.7	68.3	3.1	27.9	69.1	3.0				26.2	70.6	3.2
1884	29.2	66.5	4.3	31.4	67.3	1.4				27.7	71.5	0.9
1886	27.8	68.9	3.3	30.1	66.0	3.9				28.5	70.8	0.7
1888	26.5	71.2	2.4	28.1	69.9	2.0				28.4	70.5	1.2
1890	27.9	69.7	2.5	35.8	62.1	2.2				33.2	66.7	0.1
1892	29.3	68.1	2.7	32.2	65.2	2.6				31.5	66.3	2.3
1894	22.6	74.1	3.3	24.4	73.6	2.1				24.5	75.3	0.1
1896	16.0	80.1	4.0	21.3	76.4	2.4				20.8	78.4	0.9
1898	19.4	77.9	2.7	27.0	71.0	2.0				26.8	73.0	0.1
1900	22.9	75.7	1.4	25.5	72.2	2.3				26.1	71.9	2.1
1902	20.9	76.9	2.3	10.5	45.6	43.9				19.4	76.0	4.6
1904	18.8	78.0	3.2	24.9	72.2	2.9				24.6	72.5	2.9
1906	20.3	76.5	3.1	38.2	60.1	1.8				28.8	69.5	1.7
1908	21.8	75.1	3.1	24.8	70.8	4.4				24.3	73.4	2.3
1910	23.1	56.1	20.8	31.7	64.2	4.1				27.6	70.9	1.6
1912	24.4	37.1	38.5	30.9	40.5	28.7				35.7	58.9	5.4
1914	29.8	49.8	20.4	26.1	59.5	14.4	42.7	56.0	1.3	22.3	59.3	18.4
1916	35.2	62.4	2.4	26.0	71.1	3.0	23.4	74.2	2.3	25.6	70.9	3.6
1918	29.3	69.1	1.6	29.7	67.2	3.2	22.7	76.1	1.2	24.8	73.7	1.6
1920	23.3	75.8	0.9	21.8	76.6	1.6	21.9	78.0	0.1	23.3	75.6	1.1
1922	19.5	77.0	3.5	25.0	72.0	3.1	32.1	67.9	0.1	35.5	60.6	3.9
1924	15.7	78.2	6.1	19.2	79.3	1.6	33.8	66.2	0.0	20.5	76.5	3.1
1926	24.3	72.6	3.2	36.0	60.9	3.1	26.5	70.7	2.8	23.9	76.1	0.0
1928	32.9	66.9	0.3	26.0	73.5	0.5	28.5	71.6	0.0	28.2	70.5	1.3
1930	37.0	62.3	0.8	28.9	71.0	0.1	36.7	63.3	0.0	32.6	67.4	0.0
1932	41.1	57.7	1.3	37.2	61.7	1.1	44.9	55.1	0.0	35.6	64.4	0.0
1934	42.2	57.0	0.8	42.1	57.3	0.6	48.4	51.0	0.6	42.4	56.9	0.7
1936	43.2	56.4	0.4	38.8	60.9	0.3	41.4	58.4	0.3	40.1	59.2	0.7
1938	44.1	55.6	0.3	33.3	66.8	0.0	34.3	65.7	0.0	36.0	64.0	0.0
1940	44.9	54.8	0.3	36.0	64.0	0.0	36.0	64.0	0.0	36.2	63.8	0.0
1942	43.9	55.9	0.2	22.1	77.9	0.0	35.1	64.9	0.0	29.8	70.2	0.0
1944	43.0	57.0	0.0	34.1	65.9	0.0	34.2	65.8	0.0	37.6	62.4	0.0
1946	39.9	59.3	0.8	19.6	80.3	0.1	25.4	74.6	0.0	35.7	64.3	0.0
1948	36.9	61.5	1.5	28.0	71.9	0.2	23.7	76.3	0.0	39.2	60.7	0.1
1950	32.6	66.5	0.9	25.5	74.5	0.0	22.0	78.0	0.0	25.6	73.4	1.0
1952	28.2	71.5	0.3	39.8	51.9	8.3	27.7	72.3	0.0	28.2	71.8	0.0
1954	28.0	71.8	0.2	47.7	52.3	0.0	30.6	69.4	0.0	38.6	61.4	0.0
1956	27.8	72.2	0.0	42.5	57.5	0.0	33.6	66.4	0.0	32.9	67.1	0.0
1958	34.6	65.4	0.0	49.7	50.3	0.0	47.8	52.2	0.0	51.5	48.5	0.0
1960	41.4	58.7	0.0	43.6	56.4	0.0	40.5	59.5	0.0	42.8	57.2	0.0
1962	53.8	46.2	0.0	46.3	49.4	4.3	33.1	66.9	0.0	43.3	56.7	0.0
1964	66.3	33.7	0.0	64.9	34.4	0.7	46.5	50.7	2.8	43.6	53.0	3.4
1966	54.9	43.2	1.9	57.7	42.3	0.0	43.1	55.4	1.5	34.4	65.6	0.0
1968	43.5	52.8	3.7	44.5	55.5	0.0	39.7	60.2	0.1	39.3	60.6	0.1
1970				43.0	57.0	0.0	40.2	58.9	0.9	29.1	68.0	2.8

YEAR	COMPOSITE A (P+G+S+H/4)			COMPOSITE B (G+S+H/3)			COMPOSITE C (S+H/2)		
	DEM.	REP.	OTHER	DEM.	REP.	OTHER	DEM.	REP.	OTHER
1872	23.0	75.0	2.0	24.1	73.0	3.0	19.7	74.3	6.0
1874	30.2	67.8	2.1	32.2	64.7	3.1	36.0	57.8	6.2
1876	31.5	68.3	0.2	31.5	68.3	0.3	31.0	68.5	0.4
1878	27.8	64.2	8.0	26.9	61.6	11.5	24.0	58.9	17.1
1880	29.4	68.1	2.5	30.0	67.2	2.8	29.9	66.7	3.3
1882	27.6	69.3	3.1	27.0	69.9	3.1	26.2	70.6	3.2
1884	29.4	68.4	2.2	29.5	69.4	1.1	27.7	71.5	0.9
1886	28.8	68.6	2.6	29.3	68.4	2.3	28.5	70.8	0.7
1888	27.6	70.5	1.8	28.2	70.2	1.6	28.4	70.5	1.2
1890	32.3	66.1	1.6	34.5	64.4	1.1	33.2	66.7	0.1
1892	31.0	66.5	2.5	31.8	65.8	2.4	31.5	66.3	2.3
1894	23.8	74.3	1.8	24.5	74.4	1.1	24.5	75.3	0.1
1896	19.3	78.3	2.4	21.0	77.4	1.6	20.8	78.4	0.9
1898	24.4	74.0	1.6	26.9	72.0	1.1	26.8	73.0	0.1
1900	24.8	73.3	1.9	25.8	72.0	2.2	26.1	71.9	2.1
1902	16.9	66.1	17.0	15.0	60.8	24.3	19.4	76.0	4.6
1904	22.8	74.2	3.0	24.7	72.4	2.9	24.6	72.5	2.9
1906	29.1	68.7	2.2	33.5	64.8	1.7	28.8	69.5	1.7
1908	23.6	73.1	3.3	24.6	72.1	3.4	24.3	73.4	2.3
1910	27.5	63.7	8.8	29.6	67.5	2.8	27.6	70.9	1.6
1912	30.3	45.5	24.2	33.3	49.7	17.1	35.7	58.9	5.4
1914	30.2	56.2	13.6	30.4	58.3	11.4	32.5	57.7	9.9
1916	27.5	69.7	2.8	25.0	72.1	3.0	24.5	72.5	3.0
1918	26.6	71.5	1.9	25.7	72.3	2.0	23.7	74.9	1.4
1920	22.6	76.5	0.9	22.3	76.8	0.9	22.6	76.8	0.6
1922	28.0	69.4	2.6	30.9	66.8	2.3	33.8	64.2	2.0
1924	22.3	75.0	2.7	24.5	74.0	1.6	27.1	71.3	1.5
1926	27.7	70.1	2.3	28.8	69.2	2.0	25.2	73.4	1.4
1928	28.9	70.6	0.5	27.5	71.9	0.6	28.3	71.0	0.7
1930	33.8	66.0	0.2	32.7	67.2	0.0	34.6	65.4	0.0
1932	39.7	59.7	0.6	39.2	60.4	0.4	40.2	59.8	0.0
1934	43.8	55.6	0.7	44.3	55.1	0.6	45.4	54.0	0.7
1936	40.9	58.7	0.4	40.1	59.5	0.4	40.7	58.8	0.5
1938	36.9	63.0	0.1	34.5	65.5	0.0	35.2	64.8	0.0
1940	38.3	61.7	0.1	36.0	64.0	0.0	36.1	63.9	0.0
1942	32.7	67.2	0.1	29.0	71.0	0.0	32.4	67.5	0.0
1944	37.2	62.8	0.0	35.3	64.7	0.0	35.9	64.1	0.0
1946	30.1	69.6	0.2	26.9	73.1	0.1	30.5	69.5	0.0
1948	31.9	67.6	0.5	30.3	69.6	0.1	31.4	68.5	0.1
1950	26.4	73.1	0.5	24.4	75.3	0.4	23.8	75.7	0.5
1952	31.0	66.9	2.2	31.9	65.3	2.8	27.9	72.1	0.0
1954	36.3	63.7	0.0	39.0	61.0	0.0	34.6	65.4	0.0
1956	34.2	65.8	0.0	36.3	63.7	0.0	33.2	66.8	0.0
1958	45.9	54.1	0.0	49.7	50.3	0.0	49.7	50.3	0.0
1960	42.1	57.9	0.0	42.3	57.7	0.0	41.6	58.4	0.0
1962	44.1	54.8	1.1	40.9	57.7	1.4	38.2	61.8	0.0
1964	55.3	43.0	1.7	51.7	46.0	2.3	45.0	51.9	3.1
1966	47.5	51.6	0.8	45.1	54.4	0.5	38.7	60.5	0.7
1968	41.7	57.3	1.0	41.1	58.8	0.1	39.5	60.4	0.1
1970				37.4	61.3	1.3	34.7	63.5	1.9

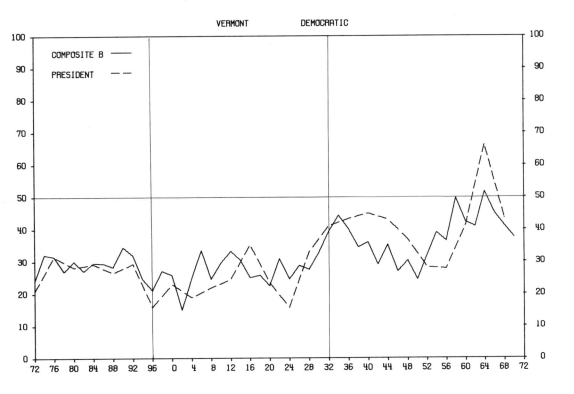

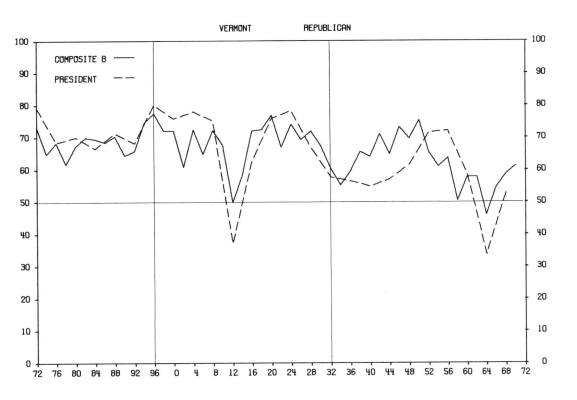

267

VIRGINIA

YEAR	PRESIDENT			GOVERNOR			SENATE CLASS I			SENATE CLASS II		
	DEM.	REP.	OTHER	DEM.	REP.	OTHER	DEM.	REP.	OTHER	DEM.	REP.	OTHER
1872	49.5	50.5	0.0									
1874				56.2	43.8	0.0						
1876	59.6	40.4	0.0									
1878				95.9	4.1	0.0						
1880	45.6	39.5	14.9									
1882				47.0	0.0	53.0						
1884	51.1	48.9	0.0									
1886				52.8	47.2	0.0						
1888	50.0	49.5	0.6									
1890				57.2	42.5	0.3						
1892	56.2	38.7	5.1									
1894				59.7	0.0	40.3						
1896	52.5	45.9	1.6									
1898				64.6	33.2	2.2						
1900	55.3	43.8	0.9									
1902				58.2	40.6	1.2						
1904	61.8	36.9	1.2									
1906				64.5	35.1	0.4						
1908	60.5	38.4	1.1									
1910				63.4	36.1	0.5						
1912	65.9	17.0	17.1									
1914				91.9	0.0	8.1						
1916	67.0	31.8	1.2				99.9	0.0	0.1			
1918				71.5	27.8	0.8				99.7	0.0	0.3
1920	61.3	37.9	0.8									
1922				66.1	31.2	2.6	71.9	26.5	1.6			
1924	62.5	32.8	4.7									
1926				74.1	25.9	0.0				73.1	2.7	24.2
1928	45.9	53.9	0.2				99.8	0.0	0.2			
1930				62.8	36.9	0.3				76.7	0.0	23.3
1932	68.5	30.1	1.5									
1934				73.7	24.2	2.0	73.5	24.0	2.5			
1936	70.2	29.4	0.4							91.7	4.7	3.6
1938				82.8	0.0	17.2						
1940	68.1	31.6	0.4				93.3	0.0	6.7			
1942				80.6	0.0	19.4				91.1	0.0	8.9
1944	62.4	37.4	0.2									
1946				66.6	0.0	33.4	64.8	30.5	4.7	68.2	29.0	2.8
1948	47.9	41.0	11.1							65.6	30.8	3.6
1950				70.4	27.4	2.1						
1952	43.4	56.3	0.3				73.4	0.0	26.6			
1954				54.8	44.3	0.9				79.9	0.0	20.1
1956	38.4	55.4	6.3									
1958				63.2	36.4	0.4	69.3	0.0	30.7			
1960	47.0	52.4	0.6							81.3	0.0	18.7
1962				63.8	36.1	0.0						
1964	53.5	46.2	0.3				63.8	19.0	17.2			
1966				47.9	37.7	14.4	53.3	37.4	9.3	58.6	33.5	7.9
1968	32.5	43.4	24.1									
1970				45.2	52.7	2.0	31.2	15.3	53.5			

268

YEAR	PRESIDENT			GOVERNOR			SENATE			HOUSE OF REPRESENTATIVES		
	DEM.	REP.	OTHER	DEM.	REP.	OTHER	DEM.	REP.	OTHER	DEM.	REP.	OTHER
1872	49.5	50.5	0.1	55.2	44.8	0.0				49.6	41.1	9.3
1874	54.5	45.5	0.0	56.2	43.8	0.0				52.7	43.1	4.2
1876	59.6	40.4	0.0	76.0	24.0	0.0				59.3	40.5	0.2
1878	52.6	40.0	7.5	95.9	4.1	0.0				57.5	21.5	20.9
1880	45.6	39.5	14.9	71.5	2.0	26.5				46.9	25.6	27.6
1882	48.3	44.2	7.5	47.0	0.0	53.0				47.2	1.9	50.9
1884	51.1	48.9	0.1	49.9	23.6	26.5				50.7	47.0	2.3
1886	50.5	49.2	0.3	52.8	47.2	0.0				45.5	45.4	9.1
1888	50.0	49.5	0.6	55.0	44.9	0.2				50.1	48.6	1.3
1890	53.1	44.1	2.8	57.2	42.5	0.3				66.8	24.6	8.6
1892	56.2	38.7	5.1	58.5	21.3	20.3				58.3	13.6	28.2
1894	54.3	42.3	3.4	59.7	0.0	40.3				52.8	41.4	5.8
1896	52.5	45.9	1.6	62.2	16.6	21.2				52.2	40.8	7.0
1898	53.9	44.9	1.2	64.6	33.2	2.2				60.5	32.3	7.2
1900	55.3	43.8	0.9	61.4	36.9	1.7				61.3	36.7	2.0
1902	58.6	40.4	1.1	58.2	40.6	1.2				67.0	27.3	5.7
1904	61.8	37.0	1.2	61.4	37.8	0.8				65.4	33.4	1.2
1906	61.2	37.7	1.2	64.5	35.1	0.4				64.2	35.5	0.3
1908	60.5	38.4	1.1	63.9	35.6	0.5				64.6	34.5	1.0
1910	63.2	27.7	9.1	63.4	36.1	0.5				67.0	31.4	1.6
1912	66.0	17.0	17.1	77.6	18.1	4.3				73.5	17.7	8.8
1914	66.5	24.4	9.1	91.9	0.0	8.1				68.9	27.7	3.4
1916	67.0	31.8	1.2	81.7	13.9	4.4	99.9	0.0	0.1	67.7	30.5	1.8
1918	64.2	34.8	1.0	71.5	27.8	0.8	99.7	0.0	0.3	79.8	20.1	0.1
1920	61.3	37.9	0.8	68.8	29.5	1.7	85.8	13.3	1.0	62.7	35.9	1.5
1922	61.9	35.3	2.8	66.2	31.2	2.6	71.9	26.5	1.6	67.9	31.8	0.3
1924	62.5	32.8	4.7	70.1	28.6	1.3	73.1	2.7	24.2	71.8	27.4	0.7
1926	54.2	43.4	2.5	74.1	25.9	0.0	86.5	1.4	12.2	68.9	30.1	1.0
1928	45.9	53.9	0.2	68.4	31.4	0.1	99.8	0.0	0.2	67.4	30.0	2.6
1930	57.2	42.0	0.8	62.8	36.9	0.3	76.7	0.0	23.3	65.7	33.4	1.0
1932	68.5	30.1	1.5	68.3	30.6	1.2	75.1	12.0	12.9	73.9	20.3	5.8
1934	69.4	29.7	0.9	73.7	24.2	2.0	73.5	24.0	2.5	73.3	22.3	4.4
1936	70.2	29.4	0.4	78.3	12.1	9.6	91.7	4.7	3.6	72.4	27.0	0.6
1938	69.2	30.5	0.4	82.8	0.0	17.2	92.5	2.3	5.2	77.4	20.7	1.9
1940	68.1	31.6	0.4	81.7	0.0	18.3	93.3	0.0	6.7	80.1	19.2	0.7
1942	65.2	34.5	0.3	80.6	0.0	19.4	91.1	0.0	8.9	85.6	12.5	1.9
1944	62.4	37.4	0.3	73.6	0.0	26.4	78.8	14.9	6.3	69.8	23.5	6.7
1946	55.1	39.2	5.7	66.6	0.0	33.4	66.5	29.7	3.8	66.2	32.2	1.7
1948	47.9	41.0	11.1	68.5	13.7	17.8	65.6	30.8	3.6	66.6	31.7	1.7
1950	45.6	48.7	5.7	70.4	27.4	2.1	69.5	15.4	15.1	73.4	24.3	2.3
1952	43.4	56.3	0.3	62.6	35.9	1.5	73.4	0.0	26.7	66.7	31.0	2.2
1954	40.9	55.9	3.3	54.8	44.3	0.9	79.9	0.0	20.1	59.7	37.5	2.8
1956	38.4	55.4	6.3	59.0	40.4	0.7	74.6	0.0	25.4	59.7	40.1	0.2
1958	42.7	53.9	3.4	63.2	36.4	0.4	69.3	0.0	30.7	73.8	20.0	6.2
1960	47.0	52.4	0.6	63.5	36.3	0.2	81.3	0.0	18.7	64.2	31.2	4.6
1962	50.3	49.3	0.4	63.8	36.1	0.0	72.5	9.5	18.0	59.9	39.9	0.3
1964	53.5	46.2	0.3	55.9	36.9	7.2	63.8	19.0	17.2	57.8	34.7	7.5
1966	43.0	44.8	12.2	47.9	37.7	14.4	56.0	35.4	8.6	57.4	39.3	3.4
1968	32.5	43.4	24.1	46.6	45.2	8.2	43.6	25.4	31.1	49.0	47.4	3.7
1970				45.2	52.8	2.0	31.2	15.3	53.5	51.4	45.8	2.9

YEAR	COMPOSITE A (P+G+S+H/4)			COMPOSITE B (G+S+H/3)			COMPOSITE C (S+H/2)		
	DEM.	REP.	OTHER	DEM.	REP.	OTHER	DEM.	REP.	OTHER
1872	51.4	45.5	3.1	52.4	43.0	4.6	49.6	41.1	9.3
1874	54.5	44.1	1.4	54.4	43.5	2.1	52.7	43.1	4.2
1876	65.0	35.0	0.1	67.7	32.2	0.1	59.3	40.5	0.2
1878	68.7	21.9	9.5	76.7	12.8	10.5	57.5	21.5	20.9
1880	54.7	22.4	23.0	59.2	13.8	27.0	46.9	25.6	27.6
1882	47.5	15.4	37.1	47.1	0.9	51.9	47.2	1.9	50.9
1884	50.6	39.8	9.6	50.3	35.3	14.4	50.7	47.0	2.3
1886	49.6	47.3	3.1	49.2	46.3	4.6	45.5	45.4	9.1
1888	51.7	47.6	0.7	52.5	46.7	0.7	50.1	48.6	1.3
1890	59.0	37.1	3.9	62.0	33.5	4.5	66.8	24.6	8.6
1892	57.6	24.5	17.9	58.4	17.4	24.2	58.3	13.6	28.2
1894	55.6	27.9	16.5	56.3	20.7	23.1	52.8	41.4	5.8
1896	55.6	34.5	9.9	57.2	28.7	14.1	52.2	40.8	7.0
1898	59.7	36.8	3.5	62.5	32.8	4.7	60.5	32.3	7.2
1900	59.3	39.1	1.5	61.4	36.8	1.8	61.3	36.7	2.0
1902	61.3	36.1	2.7	62.6	33.9	3.5	67.0	27.3	5.7
1904	62.9	36.1	1.1	63.4	35.6	1.0	65.4	33.4	1.2
1906	63.3	36.1	0.6	64.4	35.3	0.3	64.2	35.5	0.3
1908	63.0	36.2	0.8	64.2	35.1	0.7	64.6	34.5	1.0
1910	64.5	31.7	3.7	65.2	33.7	1.1	67.0	31.4	1.6
1912	72.3	17.6	10.1	75.5	17.9	6.6	73.5	17.7	8.8
1914	75.7	17.4	6.9	80.4	13.9	5.8	68.9	27.7	3.4
1916	79.1	19.1	1.9	83.1	14.8	2.1	83.8	15.3	0.9
1918	78.8	20.7	0.6	83.6	16.0	0.4	89.7	10.1	0.2
1920	69.6	29.1	1.2	72.4	26.2	1.4	74.2	24.6	1.2
1922	67.0	31.2	1.8	68.7	29.9	1.5	69.9	29.2	0.9
1924	69.4	22.9	7.7	71.7	19.6	8.7	72.5	15.1	12.5
1926	70.9	25.2	3.9	76.5	19.1	4.4	77.7	15.8	6.6
1928	70.4	28.8	0.8	78.6	20.5	1.0	83.6	15.0	1.4
1930	65.6	28.1	6.4	68.4	23.4	8.2	71.2	16.7	12.2
1932	71.4	23.3	5.3	72.4	21.0	6.6	74.5	16.2	9.4
1934	72.5	25.1	2.5	73.5	23.5	3.0	73.4	23.1	3.5
1936	78.2	18.3	3.6	80.8	14.6	4.6	82.1	15.8	2.1
1938	80.5	13.4	6.2	84.2	7.7	8.1	84.9	11.5	3.5
1940	80.8	12.7	6.5	85.0	6.4	8.6	86.7	9.6	3.7
1942	80.6	11.8	7.6	85.8	4.2	10.1	88.4	6.3	5.4
1944	71.1	18.9	9.9	74.1	12.8	13.2	74.3	19.2	6.5
1946	63.6	25.3	11.1	66.4	20.6	13.0	66.3	31.0	2.7
1948	62.2	29.3	8.5	66.9	25.4	7.7	66.1	31.3	2.6
1950	64.7	29.0	6.3	71.1	22.4	6.5	71.4	19.9	8.7
1952	61.5	30.8	7.7	67.6	22.3	10.1	70.1	15.5	14.4
1954	58.8	34.4	6.8	64.8	27.3	7.9	69.8	18.7	11.5
1956	57.9	34.0	8.1	64.4	26.8	8.7	67.1	20.1	12.8
1958	62.2	27.6	10.2	68.8	18.8	12.4	71.6	10.0	18.4
1960	64.0	30.0	6.0	69.7	22.5	7.8	72.8	15.6	11.7
1962	61.6	33.7	4.7	65.4	28.5	6.1	66.2	24.7	9.1
1964	57.7	34.2	8.0	59.1	30.2	10.6	60.8	26.9	12.3
1966	51.1	39.3	9.7	53.7	37.5	8.8	56.7	37.4	6.0
1968	42.9	40.3	16.8	46.4	39.3	14.3	46.3	36.4	17.4
1970				42.6	37.9	19.5	41.3	30.5	28.2

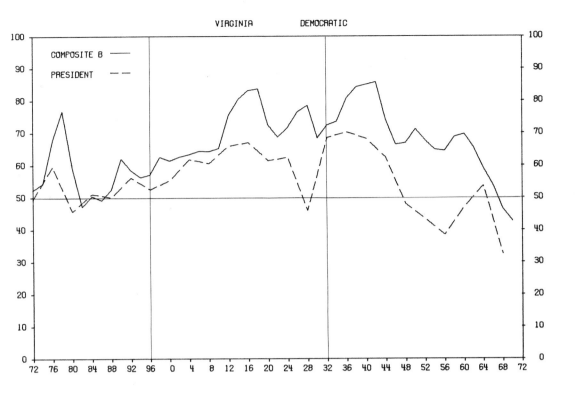

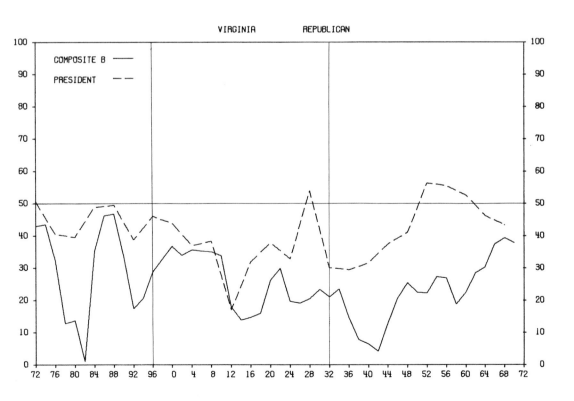

271

YEAR	PRESIDENT			GOVERNOR			SENATE CLASS I			SENATE CLASS III		
	DEM.	REP.	OTHER	DEM.	REP.	OTHER	DEM.	REP.	OTHER	DEM.	REP.	OTHER
1872												
1874												
1876												
1878												
1880												
1882												
1884												
1886												
1888												
1890				42.3	57.7	0.0						
1892	33.9	41.4	24.7	32.2	37.0	30.8						
1894												
1896	57.0	41.8	1.2	55.5	41.7	2.8						
1898												
1900	41.7	53.4	4.9	48.9	46.8	4.3						
1902												
1904	19.4	70.0	10.7	40.9	51.3	7.8						
1906												
1908	31.8	57.8	10.4	33.0	62.6	4.4						
1910												
1912	26.9	21.8	51.3	30.6	30.4	39.1						
1914										26.6	37.8	35.6
1916	48.1	43.9	8.0	48.1	44.4	7.5	37.1	55.4	7.5			
1918												
1920	21.1	56.0	22.9	16.5	52.7	30.7				17.8	56.4	25.8
1922							44.2	42.9	12.8			
1924	10.2	52.2	37.6	32.4	56.4	11.2						
1926										46.5	51.3	2.2
1928	31.4	67.1	1.6	42.7	56.2	1.1	53.4	46.4	0.1			
1930												
1932	57.5	33.9	8.6	57.3	33.8	9.0				60.6	32.7	6.7
1934							60.9	34.0	5.1			
1936	66.4	29.9	3.7	69.4	28.1	2.5						
1938										62.6	37.1	0.3
1940	58.2	40.6	1.2	49.5	50.2	0.3	54.2	45.8	0.0			
1942												
1944	56.8	42.2	0.9	51.5	48.1	0.4				55.1	44.4	0.4
1946							45.2	54.3	0.4			
1948	52.6	42.7	4.7	47.2	50.5	2.3						
1950										53.4	46.0	0.6
1952	44.7	54.3	1.0	47.4	52.6	0.0	56.2	43.5	0.2			
1954												
1956	45.4	53.9	0.6	54.6	45.0	0.4				61.1	38.9	0.0
1958							67.3	31.4	1.3			
1960	48.3	50.7	1.0	50.3	48.9	0.8						
1962										52.1	47.3	0.6
1964	62.0	37.4	0.7	43.9	55.8	0.3	72.2	27.8	0.0			
1966												
1968	47.1	45.2	7.7	44.3	54.7	1.0				64.4	35.3	0.3
1970							82.4	16.0	1.6			

272

WASHINGTON

YEAR	PRESIDENT			GOVERNOR			SENATE			HOUSE OF REPRESENTATIVES		
	DEM.	REP.	OTHER	DEM.	REP.	OTHER	DEM.	REP.	OTHER	DEM.	REP.	OTHER
1872												
1874												
1876												
1878												
1880												
1882												
1884												
1886												
1888												
1890				42.3	57.7	0.0				42.8	57.2	0.0
1892	33.9	41.5	24.7	32.2	37.0	30.8				33.3	40.9	25.8
1894	45.4	41.6	12.9	43.9	39.3	16.8				19.1	46.5	34.4
1896	57.0	41.8	1.2	55.6	41.7	2.8				28.5	42.1	29.4
1898	49.3	47.6	3.0	52.2	44.2	3.6				0.0	51.8	48.2
1900	41.7	53.4	4.9	48.9	46.8	4.3				42.8	52.5	4.7
1902	30.5	61.7	7.8	44.9	49.1	6.1				33.3	59.5	7.3
1904	19.4	70.0	10.7	40.9	51.3	7.8				25.3	66.0	8.8
1906	25.6	63.9	10.6	36.9	57.0	6.1				27.3	63.1	9.7
1908	31.8	57.8	10.4	33.0	62.6	4.4				33.6	64.3	2.2
1910	29.4	39.8	30.9	31.8	46.5	21.8				32.4	56.6	10.9
1912	26.9	21.8	51.3	30.6	30.4	39.1				24.7	30.3	45.0
1914	37.5	32.9	29.6	39.3	37.4	23.3	26.6	37.8	35.6	28.8	38.2	33.0
1916	48.1	43.9	8.0	48.1	44.4	7.5	37.1	55.4	7.6	42.6	51.4	6.0
1918	34.6	49.9	15.4	32.3	48.6	19.1	27.4	55.9	16.7	40.4	55.7	3.9
1920	21.1	56.0	22.9	16.5	52.7	30.7	17.8	56.4	25.8	16.9	58.3	24.8
1922	15.7	54.1	30.2	24.5	54.6	21.0	44.2	43.0	12.8	22.6	62.2	15.2
1924	10.2	52.3	37.6	32.4	56.4	11.2	45.4	47.1	7.5	26.0	64.4	9.7
1926	20.8	59.7	19.6	37.6	56.3	6.1	46.5	51.3	2.2	29.3	70.5	0.2
1928	31.4	67.1	1.6	42.7	56.2	1.1	53.4	46.5	0.1	31.5	68.3	0.2
1930	44.4	50.5	5.1	50.0	45.0	5.0	57.0	39.6	3.4	26.1	71.2	2.8
1932	57.5	33.9	8.6	57.3	33.8	9.0	60.6	32.7	6.7	59.2	33.7	7.1
1934	61.9	31.9	6.2	63.3	30.9	5.7	60.9	34.0	5.1	65.7	31.6	2.7
1936	66.4	29.9	3.7	69.4	28.1	2.5	61.8	35.6	2.7	65.9	33.9	0.3
1938	62.3	35.2	2.5	59.4	39.2	1.4	62.6	37.1	0.3	61.0	38.9	0.1
1940	58.2	40.6	1.2	49.5	50.2	0.3	54.2	45.8	0.0	57.8	42.1	0.0
1942	57.5	41.4	1.1	50.5	49.2	0.3	54.6	45.1	0.2	52.6	47.3	0.2
1944	56.8	42.2	0.9	51.5	48.1	0.4	55.1	44.4	0.4	53.1	46.8	0.2
1946	54.7	42.5	2.8	49.4	49.3	1.3	45.2	54.3	0.4	41.4	58.3	0.3
1948	52.6	42.7	4.7	47.2	50.5	2.3	49.3	50.2	0.5	49.2	49.1	1.7
1950	48.7	48.5	2.8	47.3	51.6	1.1	53.4	46.0	0.6	47.3	52.3	0.4
1952	44.7	54.3	1.0	47.4	52.7	0.0	56.2	43.5	0.2	46.9	53.0	0.1
1954	45.1	54.1	0.8	51.0	48.8	0.2	58.7	41.2	0.1	50.3	49.5	0.2
1956	45.4	53.9	0.7	54.6	45.0	0.4	61.1	38.9	0.0	51.8	48.2	0.0
1958	46.9	52.3	0.9	52.5	46.9	0.6	67.3	31.4	1.3	46.4	53.4	0.3
1960	48.3	50.7	1.1	50.3	48.9	0.8	59.7	39.3	1.0	42.5	57.5	0.0
1962	55.1	44.0	0.9	47.1	52.3	0.6	52.1	47.3	0.6	38.3	61.7	0.0
1964	62.0	37.4	0.7	43.9	55.8	0.4	72.2	27.8	0.0	51.2	48.8	0.0
1966	54.5	41.3	4.2	44.1	55.2	0.7	68.3	31.5	0.2	50.5	47.9	1.7
1968	47.1	45.2	7.7	44.3	54.7	1.0	64.4	35.3	0.3	51.8	47.8	0.4
1970							82.4	16.0	1.6	50.9	33.3	15.8

WASHINGTON

YEAR	COMPOSITE A (P+G+S+H/4)			COMPOSITE B (G+S+H/3)			COMPOSITE C (S+H/2)		
	DEM.	REP.	OTHER	DEM.	REP.	OTHER	DEM.	REP.	OTHER
1872									
1874									
1876									
1878									
1880									
1882									
1884									
1886									
1888									
1890				42.6	57.4	0.0	42.8	57.2	0.0
1892	33.1	39.8	27.1	32.8	39.0	28.3	33.3	40.9	25.8
1894	36.1	42.5	21.4	31.5	42.9	25.6	19.1	46.5	34.4
1896	47.0	41.9	11.1	42.0	41.9	16.1	28.5	42.1	29.4
1898	33.9	47.9	18.3	26.1	48.0	25.9	0.0	51.8	48.2
1900	44.5	50.9	4.6	45.8	49.6	4.5	42.8	52.5	4.7
1902	36.2	56.7	7.0	39.1	54.3	6.7	33.3	59.5	7.3
1904	28.5	62.4	9.1	33.1	58.7	8.3	25.3	66.0	8.8
1906	29.9	61.3	8.8	32.1	60.0	7.9	27.3	63.1	9.7
1908	32.8	61.5	5.7	33.3	63.4	3.3	33.6	64.3	2.2
1910	31.2	47.6	21.2	32.1	51.6	16.4	32.4	56.6	10.9
1912	27.4	27.5	45.1	27.7	30.3	42.0	24.7	30.3	45.0
1914	33.1	36.6	30.4	31.6	37.8	30.6	27.7	38.0	34.3
1916	44.0	48.8	7.2	42.6	50.4	7.0	39.8	53.4	6.8
1918	33.7	52.5	13.8	33.4	53.4	13.2	33.9	55.8	10.3
1920	18.1	55.9	26.1	17.1	55.8	27.1	17.4	57.3	25.3
1922	26.8	53.5	19.8	30.5	53.2	16.3	33.4	52.6	14.0
1924	28.5	55.0	16.5	34.6	56.0	9.5	35.7	55.7	8.6
1926	33.5	59.4	7.0	37.8	59.4	2.8	37.9	60.9	1.2
1928	39.8	59.5	0.7	42.6	57.0	0.5	42.5	57.4	0.2
1930	44.4	51.6	4.1	44.4	51.9	3.7	41.5	55.4	3.1
1932	58.6	33.5	7.8	59.0	33.4	7.6	59.9	33.2	6.9
1934	63.0	32.1	4.9	63.3	32.2	4.5	63.3	32.8	3.9
1936	65.8	31.9	2.3	65.7	32.5	1.8	63.8	34.7	1.5
1938	61.3	37.6	1.1	61.0	38.4	0.6	61.8	38.0	0.2
1940	54.9	44.7	0.4	53.8	46.1	0.1	56.0	44.0	0.0
1942	53.8	45.8	0.5	52.6	47.2	0.2	53.6	46.2	0.2
1944	54.1	45.4	0.5	53.2	46.4	0.3	54.1	45.6	0.3
1946	47.7	51.1	1.2	45.3	54.0	0.7	43.3	56.3	0.4
1948	49.6	48.1	2.3	48.6	49.9	1.5	49.3	49.6	1.1
1950	49.2	49.6	1.3	49.3	50.0	0.7	50.3	49.1	0.5
1952	48.8	50.9	0.3	50.2	49.7	0.1	51.6	48.3	0.2
1954	51.3	48.4	0.3	53.3	46.5	0.2	54.5	45.3	0.2
1956	53.2	46.5	0.3	55.8	44.1	0.1	56.4	43.6	0.0
1958	53.3	46.0	0.8	55.4	43.9	0.7	56.8	42.4	0.8
1960	50.2	49.1	0.7	50.9	48.6	0.6	51.1	48.4	0.5
1962	48.2	51.3	0.5	45.9	53.8	0.4	45.2	54.5	0.3
1964	57.3	42.4	0.3	55.8	44.1	0.1	61.7	38.3	0.0
1966	54.4	44.0	1.7	54.3	44.9	0.8	59.4	39.7	0.9
1968	51.9	45.8	2.3	53.5	45.9	0.6	58.1	41.6	0.3
1970							66.7	24.7	8.7

274

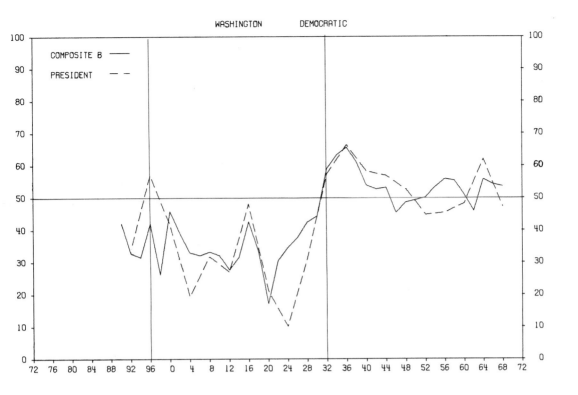

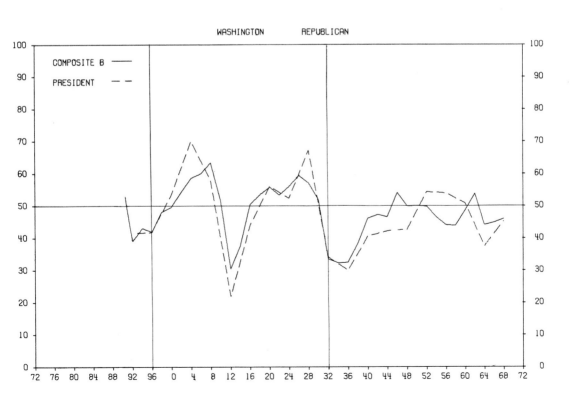

275

WEST VIRGINIA

YEAR	PRESIDENT			GOVERNOR			SENATE CLASS I			SENATE CLASS II		
	DEM.	REP.	OTHER	DEM.	REP.	OTHER	DEM.	REP.	OTHER	DEM.	REP.	OTHER
1872	47.3	51.7	1.0	48.4	0.0	51.6						
1874												
1876	56.7	42.1	1.1	56.2	43.5	0.3						
1878												
1880	50.9	41.1	8.0	51.3	37.7	11.0						
1882												
1884	50.9	47.7	1.3	51.9	48.1	0.0						
1886												
1888	49.3	49.0	1.6	50.0	50.0	0.0						
1890												
1892	49.4	46.9	3.7	49.4	47.1	3.5						
1894												
1896	46.8	52.2	0.9	46.4	52.4	1.2						
1898												
1900	44.8	54.3	1.0	45.4	53.8	0.8						
1902												
1904	42.0	55.3	2.7	47.0	50.8	2.2						
1906												
1908	43.2	53.4	3.4	46.1	50.7	3.2						
1910												
1912	42.1	21.1	36.8	44.5	47.7	7.8						
1914												
1916	48.5	49.4	2.1	49.5	48.6	1.9	48.2	50.1	1.7			
1918										45.4	53.5	1.1
1920	43.3	55.3	1.4	36.3	47.3	16.4						
1922							51.1	47.6	1.3			
1924	44.1	49.5	6.5	45.8	53.0	1.3						
1926										47.7	50.9	1.4
1928	41.0	58.4	0.5	46.1	53.7	0.2	49.2	50.7	0.1			
1930										61.9	37.9	0.2
1932	54.5	44.5	1.1	53.8	45.8	0.4						
1934							55.1	44.4	0.5			
1936	60.6	39.2	0.2	59.2	40.8	0.0						
1938										59.1	40.9	0.0
1940	57.1	42.9	0.0	56.4	43.6	0.0	56.3	43.7	0.0			
1942										46.1	53.9	0.0
1944	54.9	45.1	0.0	54.4	45.6	0.0						
1946							50.3	49.7	0.0			
1948	57.3	42.2	0.4	57.1	42.9	0.0						
1950										57.0	43.0	0.0
1952	51.9	48.1	0.0	51.5	48.5	0.0	53.6	46.4	0.0			
1954										54.8	45.2	0.0
1956	45.9	54.1	0.0	46.1	53.9	0.0	46.3	53.7	0.0			
1958							59.2	40.8	0.0	59.3	40.7	0.0
1960	52.7	47.3	0.0	54.0	46.0	0.0						
1962										55.3	44.7	0.0
1964	67.9	32.1	0.0	54.9	45.1	0.0	67.7	32.3	0.0			
1966										59.5	40.5	0.0
1968	49.6	40.8	9.6	49.1	50.9	0.0						
1970				51.5	42.4	6.1	77.6	22.4	0.0			

276

WEST VIRGINIA

YEAR	PRESIDENT			GOVERNOR			SENATE			HOUSE OF REPRESENTATIVES		
	DEM.	REP.	OTHER	DEM.	REP.	OTHER	DEM.	REP.	OTHER	DEM.	REP.	OTHER
1872	47.3	51.7	1.0	48.5	0.0	51.6				79.4	19.8	0.8
1874	52.0	46.9	1.1	52.3	21.7	25.9				56.7	42.6	0.7
1876	56.8	42.2	1.1	56.2	43.5	0.3				56.7	43.3	0.0
1878	53.9	41.6	4.6	53.8	40.6	5.7				53.0	38.2	8.8
1880	51.0	41.1	8.0	51.3	37.7	11.0				51.3	44.0	4.7
1882	50.9	44.4	4.7	51.6	42.9	5.5				49.4	45.0	5.6
1884	50.9	47.8	1.3	52.0	48.1	0.0				51.4	48.6	0.0
1886	50.1	48.4	1.5	51.0	49.0	0.0				49.8	49.1	1.2
1888	49.4	49.0	1.6	50.0	50.0	0.0				50.0	49.2	0.8
1890	49.4	48.0	2.7	49.7	48.6	1.8				52.8	46.5	0.7
1892	49.4	46.9	3.7	49.4	47.1	3.6				50.4	47.3	2.4
1894	48.1	49.6	2.3	47.9	49.7	2.4				44.8	52.7	2.6
1896	46.8	52.2	0.9	46.4	52.4	1.2				47.4	52.5	0.1
1898	45.8	53.3	1.0	45.9	53.1	1.0				49.0	50.5	0.6
1900	44.8	54.3	1.0	45.4	53.8	0.8				45.6	53.7	0.7
1902	43.4	54.8	1.9	46.2	52.3	1.5				46.3	52.0	1.8
1904	42.0	55.3	2.7	47.0	50.8	2.2				45.7	52.0	2.4
1906	42.6	54.3	3.1	46.6	50.7	2.7				42.2	53.8	4.0
1908	43.2	53.4	3.4	46.1	50.7	3.2				44.1	52.7	3.2
1910	42.6	37.3	20.1	45.3	49.2	5.5				49.2	45.2	5.7
1912	42.1	21.1	36.8	44.5	47.7	7.8				44.5	48.6	6.9
1914	45.3	35.3	19.5	47.0	48.2	4.8				44.2	46.3	9.5
1916	48.5	49.4	2.1	49.5	48.6	1.9	48.2	50.1	1.7	49.8	50.3	0.0
1918	45.9	52.4	1.8	42.9	48.0	9.1	45.4	53.5	1.1	46.7	52.4	0.9
1920	43.3	55.3	1.4	36.3	47.3	16.4	48.3	50.6	1.2	45.3	54.7	0.0
1922	43.7	52.4	3.9	41.0	50.1	8.8	51.2	47.6	1.3	51.0	48.5	0.5
1924	44.1	49.5	6.5	45.8	53.0	1.3	47.7	50.9	1.4	48.2	51.3	0.6
1926	42.6	53.9	3.5	45.9	53.4	0.7	48.5	50.8	0.8	48.3	51.7	0.0
1928	41.0	58.4	0.5	46.1	53.7	0.2	49.2	50.7	0.1	45.7	54.3	0.0
1930	47.8	51.5	0.8	49.9	49.8	0.3	61.9	37.9	0.2	50.6	49.5	0.0
1932	54.5	44.5	1.1	53.8	45.8	0.4	58.5	41.1	0.4	53.4	46.4	0.2
1934	57.5	41.8	0.7	56.5	43.3	0.2	55.1	44.4	0.5	55.7	43.9	0.5
1936	60.6	39.2	0.2	59.2	40.8	0.0	59.1	40.9	0.0	60.0	40.0	0.0
1938	58.8	41.1	0.1	57.8	42.2	0.0	57.7	42.3	0.0	55.1	44.9	0.0
1940	57.1	42.9	0.0	56.4	43.6	0.0	56.3	43.7	0.0	57.5	42.5	0.0
1942	56.0	44.0	0.0	55.4	44.6	0.0	46.1	53.9	0.0	49.7	50.4	0.0
1944	54.9	45.1	0.0	54.4	45.6	0.0	48.2	51.8	0.0	54.2	45.8	0.0
1946	56.1	43.7	0.2	55.8	44.2	0.0	50.3	49.7	0.0	50.1	49.9	0.0
1948	57.3	42.2	0.4	57.1	42.9	0.0	57.0	43.0	0.0	58.3	41.7	0.0
1950	54.6	45.2	0.2	54.3	45.7	0.0	55.3	44.7	0.0	56.6	43.4	0.0
1952	51.9	48.1	0.0	51.5	48.5	0.0	53.6	46.4	0.0	53.9	46.1	0.0
1954	48.9	51.1	0.0	48.8	51.2	0.0	54.8	45.2	0.0	57.5	42.5	0.0
1956	45.9	54.1	0.0	46.1	53.9	0.0	46.3	53.7	0.0	53.1	46.9	0.0
1958	49.3	50.7	0.0	50.1	49.9	0.0	59.3	40.7	0.0	61.9	38.1	0.0
1960	52.7	47.3	0.0	54.0	46.0	0.0	55.3	44.7	0.0	57.1	42.9	0.0
1962	60.3	39.7	0.0	54.5	45.6	0.0	61.5	38.5	0.0	56.0	44.0	0.0
1964	67.9	32.1	0.0	54.9	45.1	0.0	67.7	32.3	0.0	58.4	41.6	0.0
1966	58.8	36.4	4.8	52.0	48.0	0.0	59.5	40.5	0.0	53.0	47.0	0.0
1968	49.6	40.8	9.6	49.1	50.9	0.0	68.6	31.4	0.0	61.0	39.0	0.0
1970							77.6	22.4	0.0	65.3	34.7	0.0

277

WEST VIRGINIA

YEAR	COMPOSITE A (P+G+S+H/4)			COMPOSITE B (G+S+H/3)			COMPOSITE C (S+H/2)		
	DEM.	REP.	OTHER	DEM.	REP.	OTHER	DEM.	REP.	OTHER
1872	58.4	23.8	17.8	63.9	9.9	26.2	79.4	19.8	0.8
1874	53.7	37.1	9.2	54.5	32.2	13.3	56.7	42.6	0.7
1876	56.5	43.0	0.5	56.4	43.4	0.2	56.7	43.3	0.0
1878	53.5	40.1	6.3	53.4	39.4	7.2	53.0	38.2	8.8
1880	51.2	40.9	7.9	51.3	40.9	7.8	51.3	44.0	4.7
1882	50.6	44.1	5.3	50.5	44.0	5.6	49.4	45.0	5.6
1884	51.4	48.1	0.4	51.7	48.3	0.0	51.4	48.6	0.0
1886	50.3	48.8	0.9	50.4	49.1	0.6	49.8	49.1	1.2
1888	49.8	49.4	0.8	50.0	49.6	0.4	50.0	49.2	0.8
1890	50.6	47.7	1.7	51.2	47.6	1.2	52.8	46.5	0.7
1892	49.7	47.1	3.2	49.9	47.2	3.0	50.4	47.3	2.4
1894	46.9	50.7	2.4	46.3	51.2	2.5	44.8	52.7	2.6
1896	46.9	52.4	0.8	46.9	52.4	0.7	47.4	52.5	0.1
1898	46.9	52.3	0.8	47.4	51.8	0.8	49.0	50.5	0.6
1900	45.3	53.9	0.8	45.5	53.7	0.8	45.6	53.7	0.7
1902	45.3	53.0	1.7	46.2	52.1	1.6	46.3	52.0	1.8
1904	44.9	52.7	2.4	46.3	51.4	2.3	45.7	52.0	2.4
1906	43.8	53.0	3.3	44.4	52.3	3.4	42.2	53.8	4.0
1908	44.5	52.3	3.3	45.1	51.7	3.2	44.1	52.7	3.2
1910	45.7	43.9	10.4	47.2	47.2	5.6	49.2	45.2	5.7
1912	43.7	39.2	17.2	44.5	48.2	7.4	44.5	48.6	6.9
1914	45.5	43.3	11.3	45.6	47.3	7.1	44.2	46.3	9.5
1916	49.0	49.6	1.4	49.2	49.7	1.2	49.0	50.2	0.9
1918	45.2	51.6	3.2	45.0	51.3	3.7	46.1	53.0	1.0
1920	43.3	52.0	4.7	43.3	50.9	5.9	46.8	52.7	0.6
1922	46.7	49.7	3.6	47.7	48.8	3.5	51.1	48.1	0.9
1924	46.4	51.2	2.4	47.2	51.7	1.1	48.0	51.1	1.0
1926	46.3	52.5	1.3	47.6	52.0	0.5	48.4	51.3	0.4
1928	45.5	54.3	0.2	47.0	52.9	0.1	47.4	52.5	0.1
1930	52.5	47.1	0.3	54.1	45.7	0.2	56.2	43.7	0.1
1932	55.0	44.4	0.5	55.2	44.4	0.3	56.0	43.8	0.3
1934	56.2	43.4	0.5	55.8	43.9	0.4	55.4	44.1	0.5
1936	59.7	40.2	0.1	59.4	40.6	0.0	59.6	40.4	0.0
1938	57.4	42.6	0.0	56.9	43.1	0.0	56.4	43.6	0.0
1940	56.8	43.2	0.0	56.7	43.3	0.0	56.9	43.1	0.0
1942	51.8	48.2	0.0	50.4	49.6	0.0	47.9	52.1	0.0
1944	53.0	47.1	0.0	52.3	47.7	0.0	51.2	48.8	0.0
1946	53.1	46.9	0.1	52.1	47.9	0.0	50.2	49.8	0.0
1948	57.4	42.5	0.1	57.5	42.5	0.0	57.7	42.3	0.0
1950	55.2	44.7	0.1	55.4	44.6	0.0	55.9	44.1	0.0
1952	52.7	47.3	0.0	53.0	47.0	0.0	53.8	46.3	0.0
1954	52.5	47.5	0.0	53.7	46.3	0.0	56.2	43.9	0.0
1956	47.9	52.1	0.0	48.5	51.5	0.0	49.7	50.3	0.0
1958	55.1	44.9	0.0	57.1	42.9	0.0	60.6	39.4	0.0
1960	54.8	45.2	0.0	55.5	44.5	0.0	56.2	43.8	0.0
1962	58.1	41.9	0.0	57.3	42.7	0.0	58.8	41.3	0.0
1964	62.2	37.8	0.0	60.3	39.7	0.0	63.1	37.0	0.0
1966	55.8	43.0	1.2	54.9	45.2	0.0	56.3	43.7	0.0
1968	57.1	40.5	2.4	59.6	40.4	0.0	64.8	35.2	0.0
1970							71.5	28.5	0.0

278

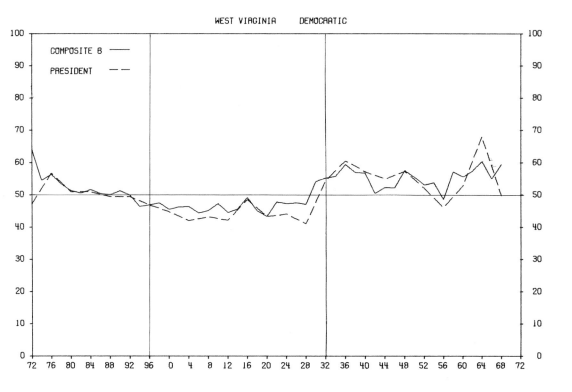

WEST VIRGINIA   DEMOCRATIC

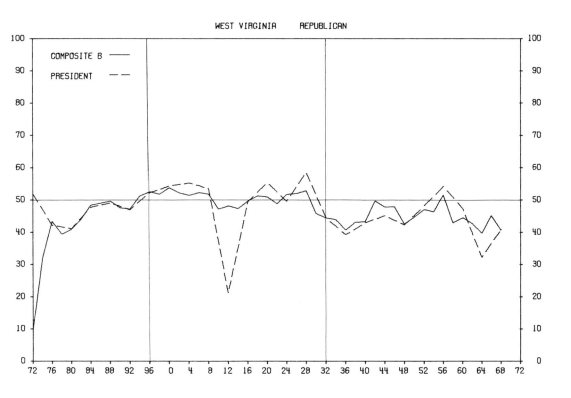

WEST VIRGINIA   REPUBLICAN

WISCONSIN

YEAR	PRESIDENT			GOVERNOR			SENATE CLASS I			SENATE CLASS III		
	DEM.	REP.	OTHER	DEM.	REP.	OTHER	DEM.	REP.	OTHER	DEM.	REP.	OTHER
1872	44.9	54.6	0.4	46.8	53.2	0.0						
1874				55.2	44.8	0.0						
1876	48.2	50.6	1.2	49.8	50.2	0.0						
1878				40.2	44.9	14.9						
1880	42.9	54.0	3.0	39.7	53.2	7.1						
1882				40.6	47.6	11.8						
1884	45.8	50.4	3.8	45.0	51.0	4.0						
1886				40.0	46.5	13.5						
1888	43.8	49.8	6.4	43.8	49.5	6.6						
1890				51.9	42.7	5.4						
1892	47.7	46.1	6.2	47.9	45.9	6.2						
1894				37.9	52.3	9.8						
1896	37.0	59.9	3.1	38.1	59.7	2.2						
1898				41.1	52.6	6.3						
1900	36.0	60.1	4.0	36.4	59.8	3.8						
1902				39.9	52.9	7.2						
1904	28.0	63.2	8.8	39.2	50.6	10.2						
1906				32.2	57.4	10.4						
1908	36.7	54.5	8.8	36.9	54.0	9.1						
1910				34.6	50.6	14.9						
1912	41.1	32.7	26.3	42.5	45.6	11.9						
1914				36.7	43.3	20.0				43.8	43.5	12.7
1916	42.8	49.4	7.8	38.1	52.7	9.2	31.9	59.3	8.8			
1918				34.0	47.0	19.1						
1920	16.1	71.1	12.7	35.8	53.0	11.2				13.2	41.6	45.2
1922				10.6	76.4	13.0	16.6	80.6	2.8			
1924	8.1	37.1	54.8	39.9	51.8	8.4						
1926				13.1	63.5	23.4	3.1	67.5	29.4	12.2	55.0	32.8
1928	44.3	53.5	2.2	39.9	55.4	4.7	0.0	85.6	14.4			
1930				28.0	64.8	7.2						
1932	63.5	31.2	5.4	52.5	41.9	5.6				57.0	36.2	6.8
1934				37.7	18.1	44.2	24.2	22.8	52.9			
1936	63.8	30.3	5.9	21.7	29.4	48.9						
1938				8.0	55.4	36.6				24.7	47.7	27.6
1940	50.1	48.3	1.5	19.3	40.7	40.0	13.2	41.4	45.4			
1942				12.3	36.5	51.3						
1944	48.6	50.4	1.1	40.6	52.8	6.5				42.8	50.5	6.7
1946				39.1	59.8	1.1	37.4	61.3	1.3			
1948	50.7	46.3	3.0	44.1	54.1	1.8						
1950				46.2	53.2	0.6				46.2	53.3	0.5
1952	38.7	61.0	0.3	37.3	62.5	0.2	45.6	54.2	0.2			
1954				48.4	51.5	0.1						
1956	37.8	61.6	0.6	48.1	51.9	0.0				41.2	58.6	0.2
1958				53.6	46.3	0.1	56.9	41.9	1.3			
1960	48.0	51.8	0.2	51.6	48.4	0.0						
1962				50.4	49.4	0.2				52.6	47.2	0.2
1964	62.1	37.7	0.2	49.4	50.6	0.0	53.3	46.6	0.1			
1966				46.1	53.5	0.4						
1968	44.3	47.9	7.8	46.8	52.9	0.3				61.7	38.3	0.0
1970				54.2	44.9	0.9	70.8	28.5	0.7			

280

YEAR	PRESIDENT			GOVERNOR			SENATE			HOUSE OF REPRESENTATIVES		
	DEM.	REP.	OTHER	DEM.	REP.	OTHER	DEM.	REP.	OTHER	DEM.	REP.	OTHER
1872	44.9	54.6	0.4	46.8	53.2	0.0				45.6	54.4	0.0
1874	46.6	52.6	0.8	55.2	44.8	0.0				50.1	49.9	0.0
1876	48.2	50.6	1.3	49.8	50.2	0.0				49.1	50.3	0.6
1878	45.6	52.3	2.2	40.2	44.9	14.9				45.2	48.5	6.3
1880	42.9	54.0	3.1	39.7	53.2	7.1				43.8	54.2	2.0
1882	44.4	52.2	3.4	40.6	47.6	11.8				47.8	41.9	10.4
1884	45.8	50.4	3.8	45.0	51.0	4.0				46.7	50.4	2.9
1886	44.8	50.1	5.1	40.0	46.5	13.5				40.4	51.0	8.6
1888	43.8	49.8	6.4	43.8	49.5	6.7				44.3	50.8	5.0
1890	45.8	47.9	6.3	51.9	42.7	5.4				53.6	42.4	4.0
1892	47.7	46.1	6.2	47.9	45.9	6.2				47.9	46.7	5.4
1894	42.4	53.0	4.6	37.9	52.3	9.8				36.5	54.4	9.1
1896	37.0	59.9	3.1	38.1	59.7	2.2				37.8	61.1	1.2
1898	36.5	60.0	3.5	41.1	52.6	6.3				39.7	56.0	4.3
1900	36.0	60.1	4.0	36.4	59.8	3.8				37.3	59.5	3.3
1902	32.0	61.6	6.4	39.9	52.9	7.2				38.6	55.0	6.4
1904	28.0	63.2	8.8	39.2	50.6	10.2				34.4	57.4	8.2
1906	32.3	58.9	8.8	32.3	57.4	10.4				36.6	54.7	8.7
1908	36.7	54.5	8.8	36.9	54.0	9.1				38.1	54.7	7.2
1910	38.9	43.6	17.6	34.6	50.6	14.9				33.6	52.1	14.3
1912	41.1	32.7	26.3	42.5	45.6	12.0				41.3	46.6	12.1
1914	41.9	41.0	17.1	36.7	43.3	20.0	43.8	43.5	12.7	37.4	51.6	11.0
1916	42.8	49.4	7.8	38.1	52.7	9.2	31.9	59.3	8.9	32.9	57.2	9.9
1918	29.5	60.3	10.3	34.0	47.0	19.1	22.5	50.4	27.0	22.0	54.4	23.6
1920	16.2	71.1	12.7	35.8	53.0	11.2	13.2	41.6	45.2	17.3	68.7	14.0
1922	12.1	54.1	33.8	10.6	76.4	13.0	16.6	80.6	2.8	6.5	76.5	17.0
1924	8.1	37.1	54.8	39.9	51.8	8.4	12.6	70.3	17.2	21.8	70.5	7.8
1926	26.2	45.3	28.5	13.1	63.5	23.4	8.6	59.9	31.5	7.6	79.5	13.0
1928	44.3	53.5	2.2	39.9	55.4	4.7	0.0	85.6	14.4	26.2	66.7	7.1
1930	53.9	42.4	3.8	28.0	64.8	7.2	28.5	60.9	10.6	14.0	76.2	9.8
1932	63.5	31.2	5.4	52.5	41.9	5.6	57.0	36.2	6.8	47.9	44.7	7.4
1934	63.6	30.7	5.6	37.7	18.1	44.2	24.2	22.8	52.9	31.7	24.3	44.0
1936	63.8	30.3	5.9	21.7	29.4	48.9	24.5	35.3	40.3	28.8	28.1	43.2
1938	57.0	39.3	3.7	8.0	55.4	36.6	24.7	47.7	27.6	18.2	43.8	38.0
1940	50.2	48.3	1.5	19.3	40.7	40.0	13.2	41.4	45.4	17.4	45.7	37.0
1942	49.4	49.4	1.3	12.3	36.5	51.3	28.0	45.9	26.1	27.2	46.9	26.0
1944	48.6	50.4	1.1	40.6	52.8	6.5	42.8	50.5	6.7	34.6	58.4	7.0
1946	49.6	48.3	2.0	39.1	59.8	1.1	37.4	61.3	1.3	31.8	62.6	5.7
1948	50.7	46.3	3.0	44.1	54.1	1.8	41.8	57.3	0.9	42.4	55.9	1.7
1950	44.7	53.6	1.7	46.2	53.2	0.6	46.2	53.3	0.5	42.4	57.6	0.0
1952	38.7	61.0	0.3	37.3	62.5	0.2	45.6	54.2	0.2	38.4	61.6	0.0
1954	38.3	61.3	0.5	48.4	51.5	0.2	43.4	56.4	0.2	47.5	52.5	0.0
1956	37.8	61.6	0.6	48.1	51.9	0.0	41.2	58.6	0.2	45.8	54.2	0.0
1958	43.0	56.7	0.4	53.6	46.3	0.1	56.9	41.9	1.3	53.6	46.4	0.0
1960	48.1	51.8	0.2	51.6	48.4	0.0	54.7	44.5	0.8	48.9	50.9	0.2
1962	55.1	44.8	0.2	50.4	49.4	0.2	52.6	47.2	0.2	49.9	50.1	0.0
1964	62.1	37.7	0.2	49.4	50.6	0.0	53.3	46.6	0.1	52.1	47.9	0.0
1966	53.2	42.8	4.0	46.1	53.5	0.4	57.5	42.5	0.1	46.2	53.8	0.0
1968	44.3	47.9	7.9	46.8	52.9	0.3	61.7	38.3	0.0	45.2	54.6	0.2
1970				54.2	44.9	0.9	70.8	28.5	0.7	55.8	43.5	0.7

YEAR	COMPOSITE A (P+G+S+H/4)			COMPOSITE B (G+S+H/3)			COMPOSITE C (S+H/2)		
	DEM.	REP.	OTHER	DEM.	REP.	OTHER	DEM.	REP.	OTHER
1872	45.8	54.1	0.2	46.2	53.8	0.0	45.6	54.4	0.0
1874	50.6	49.1	0.3	52.7	47.3	0.0	50.1	49.9	0.0
1876	49.0	50.4	0.6	49.4	50.3	0.3	49.1	50.3	0.6
1878	43.7	48.6	7.8	42.7	46.7	10.6	45.2	48.5	6.3
1880	42.1	53.8	4.1	41.7	53.7	4.6	43.8	54.2	2.0
1882	44.3	47.2	8.5	44.2	44.7	11.1	47.8	41.9	10.4
1884	45.8	50.6	3.6	45.9	50.7	3.5	46.7	50.4	2.9
1886	41.7	49.2	9.1	40.2	48.8	11.1	40.4	51.0	8.6
1888	44.0	50.0	6.0	44.0	50.2	5.8	44.3	50.8	5.0
1890	50.4	44.4	5.2	52.7	42.6	4.7	53.6	42.4	4.0
1892	47.9	46.2	5.9	47.9	46.3	5.8	47.9	46.7	5.4
1894	38.9	53.2	7.9	37.2	53.3	9.5	36.5	54.4	9.1
1896	37.6	60.2	2.2	37.9	60.4	1.7	37.8	61.1	1.2
1898	39.1	56.2	4.7	40.4	54.3	5.3	39.7	56.0	4.3
1900	36.5	59.8	3.7	36.8	59.7	3.5	37.3	59.5	3.3
1902	36.8	56.5	6.7	39.2	54.0	6.8	38.6	55.0	6.4
1904	33.9	57.0	9.1	36.8	54.0	9.2	34.4	57.4	8.2
1906	33.7	57.0	9.3	34.4	56.1	9.5	36.6	54.7	8.7
1908	37.2	54.4	8.3	37.5	54.4	8.1	38.1	54.7	7.2
1910	35.7	48.8	15.6	34.1	51.3	14.6	33.6	52.1	14.3
1912	41.6	41.6	16.8	41.9	46.1	12.0	41.3	46.6	12.1
1914	40.0	44.8	15.2	39.3	46.1	14.6	40.6	47.5	11.9
1916	36.4	54.6	8.9	34.3	56.4	9.3	32.4	58.2	9.4
1918	27.0	53.0	20.0	26.2	50.6	23.2	22.3	52.4	25.3
1920	20.6	58.6	20.8	22.1	54.4	23.5	15.2	55.1	29.6
1922	11.5	71.9	16.7	11.2	77.8	11.0	11.5	78.6	9.9
1924	20.6	57.4	22.0	24.7	64.2	11.1	17.2	70.4	12.5
1926	13.9	62.0	24.1	9.8	67.6	22.6	8.1	69.7	22.2
1928	27.6	65.3	7.1	22.0	69.2	8.8	13.1	76.1	10.8
1930	31.1	61.1	7.9	23.5	67.3	9.2	21.2	68.6	10.2
1932	55.2	38.5	6.3	52.5	40.9	6.6	52.5	40.4	7.1
1934	39.3	24.0	36.7	31.2	21.8	47.0	28.0	23.6	48.5
1936	34.7	30.8	34.6	25.0	30.9	44.1	26.6	31.7	41.7
1938	27.0	46.5	26.5	17.0	48.9	34.1	21.5	45.7	32.8
1940	25.0	44.0	31.0	16.6	42.6	40.8	15.3	43.5	41.2
1942	29.2	44.7	26.2	22.5	43.1	34.4	27.6	46.4	26.0
1944	41.6	53.0	5.3	39.3	53.9	6.8	38.7	54.5	6.9
1946	39.5	58.0	2.6	36.1	61.2	2.7	34.6	61.9	3.5
1948	44.8	53.4	1.9	42.8	55.8	1.5	42.1	56.6	1.3
1950	44.9	54.4	0.7	44.9	54.7	0.4	44.3	55.5	0.3
1952	40.0	59.8	0.2	40.4	59.4	0.2	42.0	57.9	0.1
1954	44.4	55.4	0.2	46.4	53.5	0.1	45.5	54.5	0.1
1956	43.2	56.6	0.2	45.0	54.9	0.1	43.5	56.4	0.1
1958	51.8	47.8	0.5	54.7	44.8	0.5	55.2	44.1	0.7
1960	50.8	48.9	0.3	51.7	48.0	0.3	51.8	47.7	0.5
1962	52.0	47.9	0.2	50.9	48.9	0.2	51.2	48.7	0.1
1964	54.2	45.7	0.1	51.6	48.4	0.0	52.7	47.3	0.1
1966	50.7	48.1	1.1	49.9	49.9	0.2	51.8	48.1	0.0
1968	49.5	48.4	2.1	51.2	48.6	0.2	53.5	46.4	0.1
1970				60.3	38.9	0.8	63.3	36.0	0.7

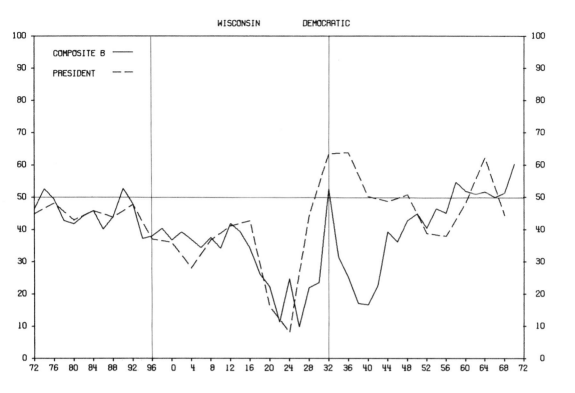

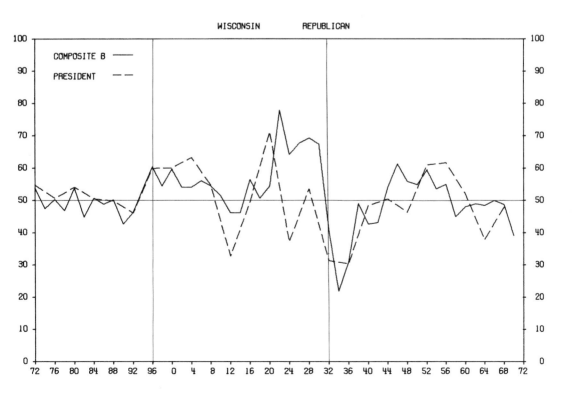

283

WYOMING

YEAR	PRESIDENT			GOVERNOR			SENATE CLASS I			SENATE CLASS II		
	DEM.	REP.	OTHER	DEM.	REP.	OTHER	DEM.	REP.	OTHER	DEM.	REP.	OTHER
1872												
1874												
1876												
1878												
1880												
1882												
1884												
1886												
1888												
1890				44.6	55.4	0.0						
1892	46.2	50.6	3.2	53.8	43.5	2.6						
1894				36.1	52.6	11.3						
1896	49.3	47.8	2.9									
1898				45.4	52.4	2.2						
1900	41.1	58.6	0.3									
1902				40.0	57.8	2.2						
1904	29.2	66.9	3.9	39.3	57.5	3.3						
1906				34.8	60.2	5.0						
1908	39.7	55.4	4.9									
1910				55.6	40.2	4.2						
1912	36.2	34.4	29.4									
1914				51.6	44.2	4.2						
1916	54.7	41.8	3.5				51.5	45.5	3.1			
1918				43.9	56.1	0.0				42.2	57.8	0.0
1920	31.9	64.2	4.0									
1922				50.6	49.4	0.0	57.3	42.7	0.0			
1924	16.1	52.4	31.5	55.1	44.9	0.0				44.8	55.2	0.0
1926				49.0	50.9	0.1						
1928	35.4	63.7	1.0				53.5	46.1	0.4			
1930				49.4	50.6	0.0				41.0	59.0	0.0
1932	56.1	40.8	3.1	50.9	47.2	1.9						
1934				57.9	41.4	0.7	56.8	43.0	0.2			
1936	60.6	37.5	2.0							53.8	45.4	0.8
1938				40.2	59.8	0.0						
1940	52.8	46.9	0.3				58.7	41.3	0.0			
1942				51.3	48.7	0.0				45.4	54.6	0.0
1944	48.8	51.2	0.0									
1946				52.9	47.1	0.0	56.2	43.8	0.0			
1948	51.6	47.3	1.1							57.1	42.9	0.0
1950				43.9	56.1	0.0						
1952	37.1	62.7	0.2				48.4	51.6	0.0			
1954				49.5	50.5	0.0				51.5	48.5	0.0
1956	39.9	60.1	0.0									
1958				48.9	46.6	4.4	50.8	49.2	0.0			
1960	45.0	55.0	0.0							43.6	56.4	0.0
1962				45.5	54.5	0.0				42.2	57.8	0.0
1964	56.6	43.4	0.0				54.0	46.0	0.0			
1966				45.7	54.3	0.0				48.2	51.8	0.0
1968	35.5	55.8	8.7									
1970				37.2	62.8	0.0	55.8	44.2	0.0			

284

WYOMING

YEAR	PRESIDENT			GOVERNOR			SENATE			HOUSE OF REPRESENTATIVES		
	DEM.	REP.	OTHER	DEM.	REP.	OTHER	DEM.	REP.	OTHER	DEM.	REP.	OTHER
1872												
1874												
1876												
1878												
1880												
1882												
1884												
1886												
1888												
1890				44.6	55.4	0.0				41.8	58.2	0.0
1892	46.2	50.6	3.2	53.8	43.5	2.7				51.3	48.6	0.1
1894	47.7	49.2	3.1	36.1	52.6	11.3				32.2	52.6	15.2
1896	49.3	47.8	2.9	40.8	52.5	6.7				49.1	47.9	3.0
1898	45.2	53.2	1.6	45.4	52.4	2.2				43.0	54.7	2.3
1900	41.1	58.6	0.3	42.7	55.1	2.2				40.8	59.2	0.0
1902	35.2	62.8	2.1	40.0	57.8	2.2				36.0	64.0	0.0
1904	29.2	66.9	3.9	39.3	57.5	3.3				32.2	64.6	3.2
1906	34.4	61.2	4.4	34.8	60.2	5.0				37.6	62.2	0.2
1908	39.7	55.4	4.9	45.2	50.2	4.6				36.3	57.1	6.6
1910	37.9	44.9	17.1	55.6	40.2	4.2				39.5	54.7	5.8
1912	36.2	34.4	29.4	53.6	42.2	4.2				35.7	46.4	17.9
1914	45.4	38.1	16.4	51.6	44.2	4.2				41.5	51.3	7.2
1916	54.7	41.8	3.5	47.8	50.2	2.1	51.5	45.5	3.1	48.0	49.0	3.0
1918	43.3	53.0	3.8	43.9	56.1	0.0	42.2	57.8	0.0	35.8	64.2	0.0
1920	31.9	64.2	4.0	47.2	52.8	0.0	49.8	50.2	0.0	26.5	61.5	12.0
1922	24.0	58.3	17.8	50.6	49.4	0.0	57.3	42.7	0.0	46.7	53.3	0.0
1924	16.1	52.4	31.5	55.1	44.9	0.0	44.8	55.2	0.0	39.9	60.1	0.0
1926	25.7	58.0	16.2	49.0	50.9	0.2	49.2	50.6	0.2	38.7	60.8	0.5
1928	35.4	63.7	1.0	49.2	50.7	0.1	53.5	46.1	0.4	47.8	51.8	0.4
1930	45.7	52.3	2.0	49.4	50.6	0.0	41.0	59.1	0.0	34.4	65.6	0.0
1932	56.1	40.8	3.1	50.9	47.2	1.9	48.9	51.0	0.1	47.7	49.7	2.6
1934	58.3	39.2	2.5	57.9	41.4	0.7	56.8	43.0	0.2	58.3	41.0	0.7
1936	60.6	37.5	2.0	49.1	50.6	0.4	53.8	45.4	0.8	57.2	42.1	0.8
1938	56.7	42.2	1.1	40.2	59.8	0.0	56.3	43.3	0.4	47.1	52.9	0.0
1940	52.8	46.9	0.3	45.8	54.3	0.0	58.7	41.3	0.0	53.4	46.5	0.2
1942	50.8	49.1	0.1	51.3	48.7	0.0	45.4	54.6	0.0	49.3	50.7	0.0
1944	48.8	51.2	0.0	52.1	47.9	0.0	50.8	49.2	0.0	44.3	55.7	0.0
1946	50.2	49.3	0.6	52.9	47.1	0.0	56.2	43.8	0.0	44.0	56.0	0.0
1948	51.6	47.3	1.1	48.4	51.6	0.0	57.1	42.9	0.0	48.5	51.5	0.0
1950	44.4	55.0	0.7	43.9	56.2	0.0	52.7	47.3	0.0	45.5	54.5	0.0
1952	37.1	62.7	0.2	46.7	53.3	0.0	48.4	51.6	0.0	39.9	60.1	0.0
1954	38.5	61.4	0.1	49.5	50.5	0.0	51.6	48.5	0.0	43.8	56.2	0.0
1956	39.9	60.1	0.0	49.2	48.6	2.2	51.2	48.8	0.0	41.8	58.2	0.0
1958	42.5	57.6	0.0	48.9	46.6	4.4	50.8	49.2	0.0	46.4	53.6	0.0
1960	45.0	55.0	0.0	47.2	50.6	2.2	43.6	56.4	0.0	47.7	52.3	0.0
1962	50.8	49.2	0.0	45.5	54.5	0.0	42.2	57.8	0.0	38.6	61.4	0.0
1964	56.6	43.4	0.0	45.6	54.4	0.0	54.0	46.0	0.0	50.8	49.2	0.0
1966	46.0	49.6	4.4	45.7	54.3	0.0	48.2	51.8	0.0	47.7	52.3	0.0
1968	35.5	55.8	8.7	41.5	58.5	0.0	52.0	48.0	0.0	37.3	62.7	0.0
1970				37.2	62.8	0.0	55.8	44.2	0.0	50.3	49.7	0.0

YEAR	COMPOSITE A (P+G+S+H/4)			COMPOSITE B (G+S+H/3)			COMPOSITE C (S+H/2)		
	DEM.	REP.	OTHER	DEM.	REP.	OTHER	DEM.	REP.	OTHER
1872									
1874									
1876									
1878									
1880									
1882									
1884									
1886									
1888									
1890				43.2	56.8	0.0	41.8	58.2	0.0
1892	50.5	47.6	2.0	52.6	46.1	1.4	51.3	48.6	0.1
1894	38.7	51.5	9.8	34.1	52.6	13.2	32.2	52.6	15.2
1896	46.4	49.4	4.2	44.9	50.2	4.9	49.1	47.9	3.0
1898	44.5	53.5	2.0	44.2	53.6	2.2	43.0	54.7	2.3
1900	41.5	57.7	0.8	41.7	57.2	1.1	40.8	59.2	0.0
1902	37.1	61.5	1.4	38.0	60.9	1.1	36.0	64.0	0.0
1904	33.6	63.0	3.5	35.7	61.0	3.2	32.2	64.6	3.2
1906	35.6	61.2	3.2	36.2	61.2	2.6	37.6	62.2	0.2
1908	40.4	54.2	5.4	40.8	53.6	5.6	36.3	57.1	6.6
1910	44.3	46.6	9.1	47.5	47.4	5.0	39.5	54.7	5.8
1912	41.9	41.0	17.1	44.7	44.3	11.0	35.7	46.4	17.9
1914	46.2	44.6	9.3	46.5	47.8	5.7	41.5	51.3	7.2
1916	50.5	46.6	2.9	49.1	48.2	2.7	49.7	47.3	3.0
1918	41.3	57.8	0.9	40.7	59.4	0.0	39.0	61.0	0.0
1920	38.8	57.2	4.0	41.2	54.8	4.0	38.1	55.9	6.0
1922	44.6	50.9	4.4	51.5	48.5	0.0	52.0	48.0	0.0
1924	39.0	53.1	7.9	46.6	53.4	0.0	42.4	57.7	0.0
1926	40.6	55.1	4.3	45.6	54.1	0.3	43.9	55.7	0.3
1928	46.5	53.1	0.5	50.2	49.5	0.3	50.7	48.9	0.4
1930	42.6	56.9	0.5	41.6	58.4	0.0	37.7	62.3	0.0
1932	50.9	47.2	1.9	49.2	49.3	1.5	48.3	50.4	1.3
1934	57.8	41.1	1.0	57.7	41.8	0.5	57.5	42.0	0.4
1936	55.2	43.9	1.0	53.4	46.0	0.6	55.5	43.7	0.8
1938	50.1	49.6	0.4	47.9	52.0	0.1	51.7	48.1	0.2
1940	52.7	47.2	0.1	52.6	47.3	0.1	56.0	43.9	0.1
1942	49.2	50.8	0.0	48.7	51.3	0.0	47.3	52.7	0.0
1944	49.0	51.0	0.0	49.1	50.9	0.0	47.6	52.5	0.0
1946	50.8	49.1	0.1	51.0	49.0	0.0	50.1	49.9	0.0
1948	51.4	48.3	0.3	51.3	48.7	0.0	52.8	47.2	0.0
1950	46.6	53.2	0.2	47.4	52.6	0.0	49.1	50.9	0.0
1952	43.0	56.9	0.1	45.0	55.0	0.0	44.1	55.9	0.0
1954	45.8	54.1	0.0	48.3	51.7	0.0	47.7	52.3	0.0
1956	45.5	53.9	0.6	47.4	51.9	0.7	46.5	53.5	0.0
1958	47.2	51.7	1.1	48.7	49.8	1.5	48.6	51.4	0.0
1960	45.9	53.6	0.6	46.2	53.1	0.7	45.7	54.3	0.0
1962	44.3	55.7	0.0	42.1	57.9	0.0	40.4	59.6	0.0
1964	51.7	48.3	0.0	50.1	49.9	0.0	52.4	47.6	0.0
1966	46.9	52.0	1.1	47.2	52.8	0.0	48.0	52.1	0.0
1968	41.6	56.3	2.2	43.6	56.4	0.0	44.6	55.4	0.0
1970				47.8	52.3	0.0	53.0	47.0	0.0

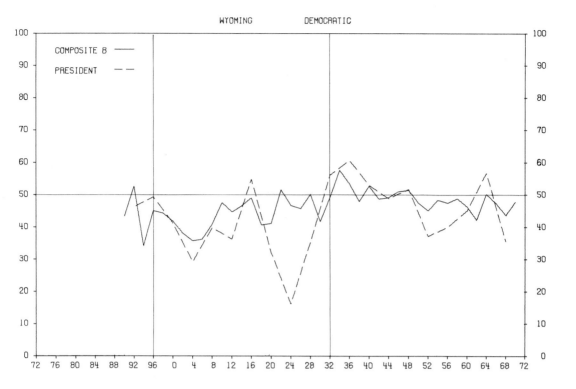

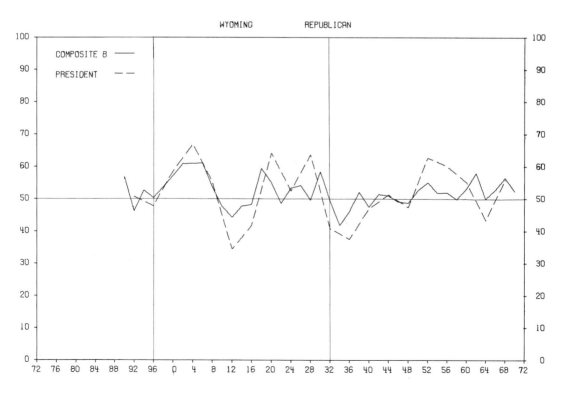

287

YEAR	PRESIDENT			GOVERNOR			SENATE			HOUSE OF REPRESENTATIVES		
	DEM.	REP.	OTHER	DEM.	REP.	OTHER	DEM.	REP.	OTHER	DEM.	REP.	OTHER
1872	39.8	60.1	0.1	45.3	52.7	2.0				45.4	54.1	0.5
1874	44.0	55.7	0.4	48.4	49.7	1.9				49.9	46.9	3.2
1876	48.2	51.2	0.6	48.0	49.2	2.8				48.5	50.2	1.3
1878	47.2	51.5	1.3	41.6	47.0	11.4				39.3	46.8	13.9
1880	46.2	51.9	2.0	42.2	47.6	10.2				46.1	51.9	2.0
1882	46.3	50.6	3.1	51.1	44.1	4.8				47.4	47.1	5.5
1884	45.8	50.0	4.3	48.8	46.8	4.4				45.4	50.2	4.4
1886	46.0	50.6	3.4	46.9	48.8	4.2				46.3	47.6	6.1
1888	46.3	51.2	2.5	47.9	49.0	3.1				45.8	51.1	3.1
1890	46.8	50.0	3.2	49.3	47.7	3.0				49.2	47.3	3.5
1892	47.2	48.9	3.9	47.5	49.1	3.4				47.1	48.9	4.0
1894	40.9	55.0	4.1	39.8	55.3	4.9				37.7	57.0	5.3
1896	34.7	61.0	4.3	37.0	56.4	6.6				35.6	60.8	3.6
1898	37.3	59.0	3.7	41.3	51.8	6.9				42.4	53.6	3.9
1900	39.9	56.9	3.1	41.3	53.2	5.6				40.2	56.8	3.0
1902	38.2	58.0	3.8	43.0	51.2	5.7				41.3	53.5	5.2
1904	36.4	59.2	4.4	42.1	51.4	6.6				37.7	58.0	4.3
1906	37.2	57.8	4.9	40.2	50.7	9.1				40.0	51.8	8.3
1908	38.0	56.5	5.5	37.1	49.0	14.0				40.4	54.5	5.0
1910	38.1	41.6	20.3	38.6	44.4	17.0				42.0	47.9	10.1
1912	38.2	26.6	35.2	37.0	38.4	24.6				40.7	33.5	25.7
1914	41.2	39.2	19.6	34.9	45.7	19.4	35.8	46.1	18.1	38.2	47.0	14.7
1916	44.1	51.8	4.0	39.9	52.7	7.4	40.8	53.7	5.5	41.1	52.5	6.4
1918	36.8	58.3	4.9	42.0	52.1	5.9	38.9	53.3	7.8	38.9	55.5	5.6
1920	29.4	64.8	5.8	39.6	54.3	6.1	36.7	53.6	9.8	32.8	60.3	6.9
1922	28.1	62.4	9.5	47.6	49.0	3.4	45.3	48.4	6.3	43.4	51.8	4.8
1924	26.8	60.1	13.1	42.7	54.8	2.5	43.4	50.9	5.7	36.6	58.6	4.7
1926	34.5	58.3	7.2	41.6	55.9	2.5	44.2	50.5	5.2	40.0	57.5	2.5
1928	42.1	56.6	1.3	41.8	54.0	4.2	43.6	54.8	1.6	41.4	56.9	1.7
1930	46.3	51.3	2.4	46.4	44.3	9.3	43.8	53.6	2.7	42.8	54.6	2.7
1932	50.6	45.9	3.5	51.0	43.8	5.2	51.7	43.8	4.5	49.9	46.1	4.1
1934	52.9	43.2	3.9	52.6	43.4	4.0	54.5	41.6	3.9	52.4	44.2	3.4
1936	55.3	40.5	4.3	49.2	46.8	4.0	51.1	45.1	3.8	54.0	42.7	3.3
1938	54.0	43.6	2.3	48.1	49.7	2.2	49.7	48.0	2.3	48.4	49.5	2.2
1940	52.8	46.8	0.4	46.8	50.6	2.6	52.3	47.0	0.6	50.9	48.2	0.9
1942	52.3	47.3	0.4	43.0	52.3	4.7	50.6	48.9	0.6	46.8	52.1	1.1
1944	51.9	47.7	0.4	44.3	53.3	2.4	49.4	50.1	0.4	49.2	50.0	0.8
1946	49.7	47.8	2.5	43.4	56.0	0.7	43.6	55.8	0.6	42.9	55.1	2.0
1948	47.5	47.9	4.5	46.4	52.3	1.3	46.9	52.0	1.1	49.5	47.6	3.0
1950	46.0	51.4	2.6	46.7	51.2	2.1	48.7	49.8	1.5	47.5	50.0	2.5
1952	44.5	54.9	0.7	47.9	50.3	1.8	43.6	53.1	3.2	45.6	53.2	1.2
1954	42.0	57.6	0.4	50.6	48.7	0.7	46.2	51.9	2.0	50.1	49.1	0.8
1956	39.5	60.3	0.2	49.9	48.7	1.4	49.3	50.2	0.5	45.8	53.8	0.5
1958	46.1	53.7	0.2	49.2	48.6	2.1	52.7	46.6	0.6	52.7	46.7	0.6
1960	52.6	47.1	0.2	47.6	50.7	1.7	47.1	52.1	0.8	52.9	46.4	0.7
1962	60.3	39.5	0.2	47.6	51.2	1.2	49.3	49.4	1.3	51.4	47.8	0.7
1964	67.9	31.8	0.2	46.9	49.0	4.2	57.9	40.9	1.3	57.7	41.6	0.7
1966	58.7	37.4	3.8	44.5	48.4	7.1	45.4	50.0	4.7	51.0	47.0	2.0
1968	49.6	43.0	7.4	45.5	49.3	5.2	43.0	49.2	7.8	49.8	47.7	2.5
1970				46.4	50.0	3.6	46.7	37.4	15.9	52.4	45.0	2.6

YEAR	COMPOSITE A (P+G+S+H/4)			COMPOSITE B (G+S+H/3)			COMPOSITE C (S+H/2)		
	DEM.	REP.	OTHER	DEM.	REP.	OTHER	DEM.	REP.	OTHER
1872	43.5	55.6	0.9	45.4	53.4	1.3	45.4	54.1	0.5
1874	47.4	50.7	1.8	49.1	48.3	2.6	49.9	46.9	3.2
1876	48.2	50.2	1.6	48.3	49.7	2.0	48.5	50.2	1.3
1878	42.7	48.5	8.9	40.4	46.9	12.6	39.3	46.8	13.9
1880	44.8	50.5	4.7	44.1	49.8	6.1	46.1	51.9	2.0
1882	48.3	47.3	4.5	49.3	45.6	5.2	47.4	47.1	5.5
1884	46.7	49.0	4.4	47.1	48.5	4.4	45.4	50.2	4.4
1886	46.4	49.0	4.6	46.6	48.2	5.2	46.3	47.6	6.1
1888	46.7	50.4	2.9	46.8	50.1	3.1	45.8	51.1	3.1
1890	48.4	48.3	3.2	49.3	47.5	3.2	49.2	47.3	3.5
1892	47.3	48.9	3.8	47.3	49.0	3.7	47.1	48.9	4.0
1894	39.5	55.8	4.8	38.7	56.2	5.1	37.7	57.0	5.3
1896	35.7	59.4	4.8	36.3	58.6	5.1	35.6	60.8	3.6
1898	40.3	54.8	4.8	41.9	52.7	5.4	42.4	53.6	3.9
1900	40.5	55.6	3.9	40.7	55.0	4.3	40.2	56.8	3.0
1902	40.8	54.3	4.9	42.1	52.4	5.5	41.3	53.5	5.2
1904	38.7	56.2	5.1	39.9	54.7	5.4	37.7	58.0	4.3
1906	39.1	53.4	7.4	40.1	51.2	8.7	40.0	51.8	8.3
1908	38.5	53.3	8.2	38.8	51.7	9.5	40.4	54.5	5.0
1910	39.6	44.6	15.8	40.3	46.2	13.5	42.0	47.9	10.1
1912	38.6	32.9	28.5	38.9	36.0	25.1	40.7	33.5	25.7
1914	37.5	44.5	18.0	36.3	46.3	17.4	37.0	46.6	16.4
1916	41.5	52.7	5.8	40.6	52.9	6.4	41.0	53.1	5.9
1918	39.1	54.8	6.1	39.9	53.6	6.4	38.9	54.4	6.7
1920	34.6	58.2	7.1	36.4	56.0	7.6	34.7	56.9	8.3
1922	41.1	52.9	6.0	45.4	49.7	4.8	44.4	50.1	5.5
1924	37.4	56.1	6.5	40.9	54.8	4.3	40.0	54.8	5.2
1926	40.1	55.6	4.4	41.9	54.6	3.4	42.1	54.0	3.9
1928	42.2	55.6	2.2	42.3	55.3	2.5	42.5	55.9	1.6
1930	44.8	50.9	4.3	44.3	50.8	4.9	43.3	54.1	2.7
1932	50.8	44.9	4.3	50.8	44.6	4.6	50.8	44.9	4.3
1934	53.1	43.1	3.8	53.2	43.1	3.8	53.4	42.9	3.7
1936	52.4	43.8	3.8	51.4	44.9	3.7	52.5	43.9	3.6
1938	50.0	47.7	2.3	48.7	49.1	2.2	49.0	48.7	2.2
1940	50.7	48.1	1.2	50.0	48.6	1.4	51.6	47.6	0.8
1942	48.2	50.1	1.7	46.8	51.1	2.1	48.7	50.5	0.8
1944	48.7	50.3	1.0	47.7	51.1	1.2	49.3	50.0	0.6
1946	44.9	53.7	1.4	43.3	55.6	1.1	43.2	55.5	1.3
1948	47.6	49.9	2.5	47.6	50.6	1.8	48.2	49.8	2.0
1950	47.2	50.6	2.2	47.6	50.4	2.0	48.1	49.9	2.0
1952	45.4	52.9	1.7	45.7	52.2	2.1	44.6	53.2	2.2
1954	47.2	51.8	1.0	49.0	49.9	1.2	48.2	50.5	1.4
1956	46.1	53.2	0.6	48.3	50.9	0.8	47.6	52.0	0.5
1958	50.2	48.9	0.9	51.6	47.3	1.1	52.7	46.7	0.6
1960	50.1	49.1	0.9	49.2	49.7	1.1	50.0	49.3	0.7
1962	52.2	47.0	0.9	49.5	49.5	1.1	50.4	48.6	1.0
1964	57.6	40.8	1.6	54.1	43.8	2.0	57.8	41.2	1.0
1966	49.9	45.7	4.4	47.0	48.5	4.6	48.2	48.5	3.3
1968	47.0	47.3	5.7	46.1	48.7	5.2	46.4	48.4	5.2
1970				48.5	44.1	7.4	49.5	41.2	9.3

MIDDLE WEST

YEAR	PRESIDENT			GOVERNOR			SENATE			HOUSE OF REPRESENTATIVES		
	DEM.	REP.	OTHER	DEM.	REP.	OTHER	DEM.	REP.	OTHER	DEM.	REP.	OTHER
1872	44.0	55.1	0.9	46.2	53.5	0.3				43.9	53.7	2.3
1874	45.7	52.8	1.5	48.9	49.5	1.7				49.6	45.5	4.8
1876	47.3	50.6	2.1	48.6	50.3	1.1				47.8	49.4	2.8
1878	45.6	50.8	3.7	43.9	47.1	8.9				41.8	43.6	14.6
1880	43.8	51.0	5.2	43.7	49.8	6.6				44.8	50.2	5.0
1882	44.2	51.2	4.6	44.7	49.3	6.0				46.2	45.4	8.5
1884	45.5	50.7	3.8	47.1	49.7	3.2				47.7	50.2	2.1
1886	45.4	50.3	4.3	46.6	49.2	4.3				45.0	48.8	6.2
1888	45.3	49.9	4.7	45.4	49.2	5.4				45.7	50.2	4.1
1890	44.3	46.6	6.5	45.8	45.4	8.7				46.6	45.2	8.2
1892	44.3	45.6	10.1	42.5	46.1	11.4				45.6	46.3	8.1
1894	44.6	49.1	6.3	41.4	50.4	8.3				35.1	52.5	12.4
1896	44.9	52.5	2.5	44.6	51.6	3.8				45.0	52.8	2.2
1898	43.4	53.1	3.5	46.2	51.1	2.7				45.0	52.6	2.4
1900	41.9	53.6	4.4	44.5	51.2	4.4				44.4	53.3	2.3
1902	36.7	57.4	5.9	42.0	53.5	4.5				43.1	53.3	3.6
1904	31.6	61.0	7.4	40.2	54.0	5.8				35.7	59.0	5.2
1906	36.5	57.2	6.3	44.3	50.4	5.3				39.6	55.3	5.1
1908	41.3	53.5	5.2	46.3	49.1	4.7				42.4	53.0	4.6
1910	40.0	39.5	20.5	44.1	44.5	11.5				43.5	50.4	6.1
1912	38.6	25.7	35.8	41.1	33.4	25.5				40.3	37.1	22.6
1914	42.8	37.1	20.2	42.8	42.1	15.1	40.3	43.5	16.2	41.3	45.9	12.8
1916	46.9	48.5	4.6	41.2	53.5	5.3	41.9	49.5	8.6	42.3	52.3	5.4
1918	38.4	56.5	5.1	39.9	53.1	6.9	38.8	54.0	7.2	38.9	56.7	4.4
1920	29.8	64.6	5.6	36.4	55.7	7.9	34.0	56.6	9.4	29.7	63.8	6.5
1922	26.4	60.1	13.5	37.2	55.1	7.6	38.3	56.0	5.7	37.7	57.4	5.0
1924	23.0	55.6	21.3	39.0	54.4	6.7	35.9	57.5	6.6	33.2	61.4	5.3
1926	30.7	58.2	11.1	37.7	56.9	5.4	35.2	54.8	10.1	35.0	61.1	3.8
1928	38.4	60.8	0.8	40.5	57.1	2.4	34.1	59.7	6.2	36.5	60.8	2.7
1930	47.6	50.5	1.8	42.7	50.2	7.1	45.5	50.2	4.3	40.2	56.0	3.8
1932	56.3	40.9	2.8	51.5	41.9	6.7	49.6	45.3	5.1	50.9	44.7	4.4
1934	57.2	39.6	3.2	49.2	43.4	7.4	50.1	41.1	8.8	49.9	43.3	6.8
1936	58.0	38.4	3.6	46.7	44.0	9.3	46.5	43.1	10.4	49.9	42.8	7.3
1938	53.9	44.1	2.0	43.0	50.8	6.2	44.4	48.7	6.8	44.3	50.6	5.1
1940	49.8	49.8	0.5	43.5	51.0	5.6	43.1	51.0	5.9	44.0	51.3	4.7
1942	49.5	50.0	0.5	39.6	53.5	6.9	42.3	51.3	6.4	41.1	55.0	3.9
1944	49.1	50.4	0.5	45.3	53.5	1.1	45.2	51.7	3.0	45.4	53.6	1.0
1946	49.7	49.2	1.1	46.1	53.2	0.7	43.3	55.7	1.0	40.8	58.4	0.8
1948	50.4	48.0	1.7	51.2	48.0	0.8	48.7	50.6	0.7	49.6	49.9	0.5
1950	46.1	52.8	1.0	48.7	50.8	0.4	46.1	53.5	0.4	45.5	54.2	0.4
1952	41.8	57.8	0.4	47.2	52.5	0.3	46.5	53.0	0.5	43.2	56.3	0.5
1954	41.5	58.2	0.3	50.0	49.8	0.2	49.5	50.1	0.4	48.0	51.6	0.4
1956	41.1	58.7	0.2	48.9	50.7	0.4	48.5	51.2	0.3	47.2	52.8	0.1
1958	44.3	55.5	0.2	53.6	46.1	0.2	52.8	46.8	0.4	53.2	46.7	0.1
1960	47.5	52.4	0.2	51.3	48.4	0.3	53.1	46.6	0.3	49.2	50.7	0.1
1962	54.5	45.3	0.2	49.8	50.0	0.2	53.0	46.8	0.1	47.9	52.0	0.1
1964	61.4	38.4	0.1	49.9	49.8	0.2	53.0	46.7	0.3	53.9	46.1	0.0
1966	52.5	42.6	4.8	46.8	53.0	0.3	48.1	51.4	0.5	45.8	54.1	0.0
1968	43.6	46.9	9.5	48.1	51.4	0.5	50.6	49.1	0.3	45.6	54.3	0.1
1970				52.2	46.3	1.5	56.6	42.4	1.0	50.0	49.5	0.6

MIDDLE WEST

YEAR	COMPOSITE A (P+G+S+H/4)			COMPOSITE B (G+S+H/3)			COMPOSITE C (S+H/2)		
	DEM.	REP.	OTHER	DEM.	REP.	OTHER	DEM.	REP.	OTHER
1872	44.7	54.1	1.2	45.0	53.6	1.3	43.9	53.7	2.3
1874	48.1	49.3	2.7	49.2	47.5	3.3	49.6	45.5	4.8
1876	47.9	50.1	2.0	48.2	49.8	2.0	47.8	49.4	2.8
1878	43.7	47.2	9.1	42.8	45.4	11.8	41.8	43.6	14.6
1880	44.1	50.3	5.6	44.2	50.0	5.8	44.8	50.2	5.0
1882	45.0	48.6	6.4	45.4	47.4	7.2	46.2	45.4	8.5
1884	46.8	50.2	3.0	47.4	49.9	2.7	47.7	50.2	2.1
1886	45.7	49.4	4.9	45.8	49.0	5.2	45.0	48.8	6.2
1888	45.5	49.8	4.7	45.6	49.7	4.7	45.7	50.2	4.1
1890	45.6	45.8	7.8	46.2	45.3	8.5	46.6	45.2	8.2
1892	44.1	46.0	9.8	44.1	46.2	9.7	45.6	46.3	8.1
1894	40.3	50.7	9.0	38.2	51.4	10.3	35.1	52.5	12.4
1896	44.8	52.3	2.9	44.8	52.2	3.0	45.0	52.8	2.2
1898	44.9	52.2	2.9	45.6	51.8	2.6	45.0	52.6	2.4
1900	43.6	52.7	3.7	44.4	52.2	3.3	44.4	53.3	2.3
1902	40.6	54.7	4.7	42.5	53.4	4.0	43.1	53.3	3.6
1904	35.8	58.0	6.1	38.0	56.5	5.5	35.7	59.0	5.2
1906	40.1	54.3	5.6	41.9	52.9	5.2	39.6	55.3	5.1
1908	43.3	51.8	4.8	44.4	51.0	4.6	42.4	53.0	4.6
1910	42.5	44.8	12.7	43.8	47.5	8.8	43.5	50.4	6.1
1912	40.0	32.0	27.9	40.7	35.2	24.0	40.3	37.1	22.6
1914	41.8	42.1	16.1	41.5	43.8	14.7	40.8	44.7	14.5
1916	43.1	50.9	6.0	41.8	51.8	6.4	42.1	50.9	7.0
1918	39.0	55.1	5.9	39.2	54.6	6.2	38.8	55.4	5.8
1920	32.5	60.2	7.4	33.4	58.7	7.9	31.9	60.2	8.0
1922	34.9	57.2	7.9	37.7	56.2	6.1	38.0	56.7	5.3
1924	32.8	57.2	10.0	36.0	57.8	6.2	34.5	59.5	6.0
1926	34.7	57.7	7.6	36.0	57.6	6.4	35.1	57.9	7.0
1928	37.4	59.6	3.0	37.0	59.2	3.8	35.3	60.3	4.4
1930	44.0	51.7	4.2	42.8	52.1	5.1	42.8	53.1	4.1
1932	52.1	43.2	4.8	50.6	43.9	5.4	50.2	45.0	4.8
1934	51.6	41.9	6.5	49.7	42.6	7.7	50.0	42.2	7.8
1936	50.3	42.0	7.6	47.7	43.3	9.0	48.2	42.9	8.8
1938	46.4	48.6	5.0	43.9	50.0	6.1	44.3	49.7	6.0
1940	45.1	50.8	4.2	43.5	51.1	5.4	43.5	51.1	5.3
1942	43.1	52.5	4.4	41.0	53.3	5.7	41.7	53.2	5.1
1944	46.3	52.3	1.4	45.3	53.0	1.7	45.3	52.7	2.0
1946	45.0	54.1	0.9	43.4	55.8	0.8	42.1	57.0	0.9
1948	50.0	49.1	0.9	49.8	49.5	0.7	49.1	50.3	0.6
1950	46.6	52.8	0.6	46.8	52.8	0.4	45.8	53.8	0.4
1952	44.7	54.9	0.4	45.6	53.9	0.4	44.8	54.7	0.5
1954	47.2	52.4	0.3	49.2	50.5	0.3	48.8	50.9	0.4
1956	46.4	53.3	0.2	48.2	51.5	0.3	47.8	52.0	0.2
1958	51.0	48.8	0.2	53.2	46.5	0.2	53.0	46.7	0.3
1960	50.3	49.5	0.2	51.2	48.6	0.2	51.2	48.7	0.2
1962	51.3	48.6	0.1	50.2	49.6	0.1	50.4	49.4	0.1
1964	54.6	45.2	0.2	52.3	47.5	0.2	53.4	46.4	0.2
1966	48.3	50.3	1.4	46.9	52.8	0.3	47.0	52.8	0.3
1968	47.0	50.4	2.6	48.1	51.6	0.3	48.1	51.7	0.2
1970				52.9	46.1	1.0	53.3	46.0	0.8

YEAR	PRESIDENT			GOVERNOR			SENATE			HOUSE OF REPRESENTATIVES		
	DEM.	REP.	OTHER	DEM.	REP.	OTHER	DEM.	REP.	OTHER	DEM.	REP.	OTHER
1872	45.9	52.1	2.1	49.5	47.7	2.8				47.8	45.0	7.3
1874	53.2	45.7	1.1	53.2	41.0	5.8				57.9	36.2	5.9
1876	60.5	39.3	0.2	61.8	32.3	5.9				60.0	37.0	3.0
1878	59.2	38.6	2.2	75.1	19.6	5.4				61.5	17.3	21.2
1880	57.9	37.8	4.3	63.2	21.3	15.5				57.9	30.3	11.8
1882	59.1	38.2	2.8	60.2	28.3	11.6				57.3	26.3	16.5
1884	59.7	39.4	0.9	70.2	26.1	3.6				62.0	35.9	2.0
1886	60.9	37.5	1.6	70.7	27.6	1.7				66.3	25.1	8.6
1888	62.1	35.6	2.3	70.0	23.4	6.6				64.2	32.5	3.3
1890	61.0	30.4	8.6	68.4	25.6	6.0				69.4	23.9	6.7
1892	59.9	24.8	15.3	57.2	19.5	23.3				61.8	20.5	17.7
1894	60.3	29.2	10.5	55.3	17.7	27.0				57.3	21.6	21.1
1896	60.7	33.5	5.8	58.4	20.9	20.8				58.4	27.7	13.9
1898	62.5	33.3	4.2	66.6	19.6	13.8				69.3	23.5	7.2
1900	64.2	33.1	2.7	68.8	24.1	7.1				69.8	27.0	3.2
1902	66.3	29.9	3.8	73.2	22.8	3.9				79.3	19.6	1.2
1904	68.1	27.0	4.9	74.7	23.8	1.5				75.2	24.0	0.8
1906	67.1	28.4	4.5	76.4	21.9	1.6				78.8	19.8	1.4
1908	65.3	30.4	4.3	72.4	25.2	2.4				74.9	23.4	1.6
1910	66.4	21.7	11.8	68.8	22.6	8.7				75.8	20.2	4.0
1912	67.3	13.4	19.4	74.3	18.5	7.2				78.4	13.9	7.7
1914	69.2	18.6	12.2	75.2	16.7	8.1	70.5	19.0	10.6	77.9	15.2	7.0
1916	71.1	23.9	5.0	73.6	19.5	6.9	71.5	18.2	3.8	75.8	20.5	3.7
1918	66.6	28.6	4.8	76.9	18.9	4.2	82.3	16.8	0.9	83.8	15.8	0.4
1920	62.2	33.2	4.6	69.9	23.6	6.5	74.9	23.6	1.5	71.6	26.2	2.2
1922	64.5	30.5	5.0	75.3	22.9	1.8	73.7	25.6	0.8	79.6	17.5	2.9
1924	66.8	27.8	5.5	74.3	25.4	0.3	76.2	21.4	2.4	78.6	20.3	1.0
1926	60.3	35.9	3.8	78.5	21.4	0.2	79.3	19.2	1.5	79.9	19.7	0.4
1928	53.9	44.1	2.0	75.5	22.9	1.6	79.5	18.8	1.7	76.1	23.6	0.2
1930	67.3	31.4	1.4	75.6	21.2	3.2	79.6	15.1	5.3	80.3	17.3	2.5
1932	80.7	18.6	0.7	73.4	22.7	3.8	84.0	14.5	1.5	83.8	14.7	1.5
1934	80.3	19.1	0.5	82.4	17.0	0.6	84.8	14.0	1.2	85.2	13.5	1.3
1936	80.0	19.6	0.4	83.8	15.1	1.1	85.6	13.4	1.0	84.4	15.3	0.3
1938	78.4	20.8	0.8	85.1	12.5	2.4	83.2	14.1	2.7	86.1	12.8	1.1
1940	76.9	22.0	1.1	85.1	12.8	2.2	84.8	13.6	1.7	86.0	13.4	0.7
1942	74.2	23.9	1.9	84.6	13.6	1.8	85.3	13.0	1.8	86.8	12.3	0.9
1944	71.4	25.9	2.7	80.6	17.0	2.4	81.5	17.0	1.5	82.5	16.8	0.8
1946	61.2	25.8	13.1	80.9	16.1	3.0	80.9	17.9	1.2	81.5	17.8	0.7
1948	50.9	25.6	23.4	80.8	17.4	1.7	72.9	22.9	4.2	82.8	16.3	0.8
1950	51.8	35.3	12.9	82.0	17.6	0.3	75.4	19.7	4.8	84.2	14.7	1.1
1952	52.4	45.1	2.5	78.2	21.6	0.2	79.8	15.2	5.1	80.3	19.3	0.4
1954	50.3	46.4	3.3	79.8	19.2	1.0	81.8	13.2	5.0	80.7	18.9	0.4
1956	48.3	47.6	4.1	78.6	18.2	3.2	81.5	15.8	2.7	77.4	22.3	0.2
1958	49.1	46.8	4.1	79.0	18.0	3.0	77.4	19.0	3.6	84.5	14.8	0.7
1960	49.9	46.0	4.1	73.2	23.8	3.0	72.6	25.6	1.8	77.7	20.8	1.5
1962	50.6	47.6	1.9	66.7	30.2	3.1	64.6	33.9	1.5	69.3	29.9	0.9
1964	51.2	48.7	0.1	64.2	32.3	3.5	64.7	33.8	1.5	66.8	32.1	1.1
1966	41.3	42.1	16.6	59.8	36.4	3.8	59.3	39.5	1.2	65.9	32.8	1.3
1968	31.3	35.5	33.1	58.0	39.0	2.9	57.9	38.3	3.8	65.1	33.5	1.4
1970				54.7	41.8	3.5	51.8	37.9	10.3	66.8	31.6	1.6

SOUTH

YEAR	COMPOSITE A (P+G+S+H/4)			COMPOSITE B (G+S+H/3)			COMPOSITE C (S+H/2)		
	DEM.	REP.	OTHER	DEM.	REP.	OTHER	DEM.	REP.	OTHER
1872	47.7	48.2	4.1	48.6	46.3	5.0	47.8	45.0	7.3
1874	54.8	40.9	4.3	55.6	38.6	5.9	57.9	36.2	5.9
1876	60.8	36.2	3.0	60.9	34.6	4.5	60.0	37.0	3.0
1878	65.3	25.1	9.6	68.3	18.4	13.3	61.5	17.3	21.2
1880	59.7	29.8	10.5	60.6	25.8	13.6	57.9	30.3	11.8
1882	58.8	30.9	10.3	58.7	27.3	14.0	57.3	26.3	16.5
1884	64.0	33.8	2.2	66.1	31.0	2.8	62.0	35.9	2.0
1886	66.0	30.1	4.0	68.5	26.3	5.1	66.3	25.1	8.6
1888	65.4	30.5	4.1	67.1	27.9	5.0	64.2	32.5	3.3
1890	66.3	26.7	7.1	68.9	24.8	6.3	69.4	23.9	6.7
1892	59.7	21.6	18.7	59.5	20.0	20.5	61.8	20.5	17.7
1894	57.6	22.8	19.5	56.3	19.6	24.0	57.3	21.6	21.1
1896	59.1	27.4	13.5	58.4	24.3	17.3	58.4	27.7	13.9
1898	66.1	25.5	8.4	67.9	21.6	10.5	69.3	23.5	7.2
1900	67.6	28.1	4.3	69.3	25.5	5.2	69.8	27.0	3.2
1902	72.9	24.1	3.0	76.2	21.2	2.5	79.3	19.6	1.2
1904	72.6	25.0	2.4	74.9	23.9	1.2	75.2	24.0	0.8
1906	74.1	23.4	2.5	77.6	20.9	1.5	78.8	19.8	1.4
1908	70.9	26.3	2.8	73.7	24.3	2.0	74.9	23.4	1.6
1910	70.3	21.5	8.2	72.3	21.4	6.3	75.8	20.2	4.0
1912	73.3	15.2	11.4	76.3	16.2	7.5	78.4	13.9	7.7
1914	73.2	17.4	9.4	74.5	16.9	8.5	74.2	17.1	8.8
1916	73.0	20.5	4.8	73.6	19.4	4.8	73.6	19.4	3.7
1918	77.4	20.0	2.6	81.0	17.2	1.8	83.0	16.3	0.6
1920	69.6	26.6	3.7	72.1	24.5	3.4	73.3	24.9	1.9
1922	73.2	24.1	2.6	76.2	22.0	1.8	76.6	21.5	1.9
1924	74.0	23.7	2.3	76.4	22.4	1.2	77.4	20.9	1.7
1926	74.5	24.0	1.4	79.2	20.1	0.7	79.6	19.5	0.9
1928	71.2	27.4	1.4	77.0	21.8	1.2	77.8	21.2	1.0
1930	75.7	21.2	3.1	78.5	17.9	3.7	79.9	16.2	3.9
1932	80.5	17.6	1.9	80.4	17.3	2.3	83.9	14.6	1.5
1934	83.2	15.9	0.9	84.1	14.9	1.0	85.0	13.8	1.2
1936	83.4	15.9	0.7	84.6	14.6	0.8	85.0	14.4	0.6
1938	83.2	15.0	1.8	84.8	13.1	2.1	84.6	13.5	1.9
1940	83.2	15.4	1.4	85.3	13.2	1.5	85.4	13.5	1.2
1942	82.7	15.7	1.6	85.6	12.9	1.5	86.1	12.6	1.3
1944	79.0	19.1	1.8	81.5	16.9	1.6	82.0	16.9	1.1
1946	76.1	19.4	4.5	81.1	17.3	1.6	81.2	17.9	1.0
1948	71.9	20.6	7.6	78.8	18.9	2.3	77.8	19.6	2.5
1950	73.4	21.8	4.8	80.6	17.4	2.1	79.8	17.2	3.0
1952	72.7	25.3	2.0	79.4	18.7	1.9	80.0	17.2	2.8
1954	73.2	24.4	2.4	80.8	17.1	2.1	81.3	16.0	2.7
1956	71.5	26.0	2.6	79.2	18.8	2.0	79.5	19.1	1.4
1958	72.5	24.6	2.8	80.3	17.3	2.4	81.0	16.9	2.1
1960	68.4	29.0	2.6	74.5	23.4	2.1	75.2	23.2	1.6
1962	62.8	35.4	1.8	66.8	31.3	1.8	66.9	31.9	1.2
1964	61.7	36.7	1.5	65.2	32.8	2.0	65.7	33.0	1.3
1966	56.6	37.7	5.7	61.7	36.2	2.1	62.6	36.1	1.3
1968	53.1	36.6	10.3	60.3	36.9	2.7	61.5	35.9	2.6
1970				57.8	37.1	5.1	59.3	34.7	6.0

YEAR	PRESIDENT			GOVERNOR			SENATE			HOUSE OF REPRESENTATIVES		
	DEM.	REP.	OTHER	DEM.	REP.	OTHER	DEM.	REP.	OTHER	DEM.	REP.	OTHER
1872	42.6	57.0	0.5	48.7	49.2	2.1				49.1	42.7	8.2
1874	45.5	54.1	0.4	48.5	39.0	12.5				46.5	46.4	7.2
1876	41.6	43.9	0.3	49.2	34.6	16.1				47.9	47.2	4.9
1878	42.0	42.9	0.8	42.3	40.7	17.0				45.0	47.4	7.6
1880	49.0	49.3	1.7	37.5	45.9	16.6				43.7	48.8	7.5
1882	47.0	50.9	2.2	53.8	43.2	3.0				52.0	46.3	1.8
1884	44.9	52.6	2.5	49.1	44.4	6.5				46.3	52.2	1.4
1886	45.0	52.1	2.9	45.4	44.5	10.1				46.8	49.0	4.2
1888	45.2	51.6	3.2	45.7	47.8	6.5				45.3	52.2	2.5
1890	26.7	32.3	10.3	46.4	51.2	2.4				44.6	52.8	2.6
1892	32.8	42.6	24.6	37.5	43.0	19.5				38.0	41.5	20.5
1894	44.5	40.8	14.7	34.7	42.1	23.2				29.2	43.9	26.9
1896	57.6	37.8	4.6	46.2	39.8	14.0				49.3	36.0	14.7
1898	51.7	44.4	3.9	47.1	46.2	6.7				41.8	43.9	14.3
1900	45.8	50.9	3.3	47.0	47.7	5.3				44.8	50.5	4.7
1902	37.4	56.1	6.5	46.4	47.5	6.1				41.3	52.3	6.4
1904	28.4	61.9	9.7	46.5	44.6	8.9				35.5	56.5	7.9
1906	32.8	57.7	9.5	44.0	41.5	14.5				35.9	55.0	9.1
1908	37.2	53.4	9.4	43.8	45.0	11.2				37.8	53.7	8.5
1910	37.3	34.7	28.0	42.4	44.6	13.0				35.6	52.8	11.6
1912	37.3	17.0	45.8	34.4	35.5	30.1				33.3	38.9	27.8
1914	44.2	29.8	26.0	31.5	37.7	30.8	36.4	34.9	28.7	35.3	42.1	22.6
1916	51.1	42.6	6.3	34.6	44.4	21.0	38.9	51.9	9.2	38.8	48.2	13.1
1918	40.4	52.0	7.6	28.2	53.1	18.6	37.4	53.3	9.3	39.0	55.1	5.9
1920	29.8	61.3	8.9	29.8	55.5	14.7	38.5	51.2	10.3	26.2	62.6	11.2
1922	23.3	57.1	19.6	40.7	52.2	7.1	38.2	53.4	8.4	32.9	61.4	5.7
1924	16.8	52.9	30.4	38.4	54.9	6.7	37.9	56.5	5.6	36.6	56.5	6.9
1926	26.2	57.9	15.9	38.8	56.2	5.0	41.2	53.8	5.0	30.8	66.6	2.6
1928	35.6	63.0	1.4	40.5	55.1	4.5	38.5	56.8	4.7	28.5	68.9	2.6
1930	47.0	50.1	2.9	41.4	51.1	7.5	43.5	48.8	7.8	32.7	65.3	2.1
1932	58.4	37.1	4.5	42.8	48.1	9.1	49.3	36.6	14.0	51.0	43.1	6.0
1934	62.2	34.4	3.4	47.0	42.6	10.3	30.2	65.8	4.1	53.8	42.6	3.5
1936	66.1	31.6	2.3	51.4	42.2	6.4	43.1	53.8	3.1	58.3	39.0	2.6
1938	61.4	37.0	1.6	51.6	46.2	2.3	56.6	42.4	1.1	51.9	44.6	3.5
1940	56.7	42.4	0.9	47.6	51.2	1.2	29.1	62.7	8.3	49.5	48.4	2.1
1942	55.9	43.4	0.7	44.6	54.7	0.7	38.5	57.1	4.3	49.5	49.0	1.6
1944	55.0	44.5	0.6	35.5	62.1	2.4	50.3	45.4	0.2	51.1	48.6	0.2
1946	52.4	45.3	2.3	25.4	70.5	4.1	42.1	46.7	9.2	46.2	53.2	0.6
1948	49.8	46.2	4.0	35.7	61.8	2.5	46.4	48.9	4.8	44.8	51.4	3.8
1950	45.7	51.9	2.4	40.5	59.3	0.2	44.2	55.5	0.3	46.8	51.1	2.0
1952	41.8	57.4	0.7	41.7	58.3	0.0	22.8	70.6	6.6	44.7	53.5	1.8
1954	42.5	56.9	0.5	46.0	53.5	0.5	48.6	50.7	0.7	50.5	49.4	0.1
1956	43.2	56.5	0.3	51.0	47.8	1.1	50.7	48.9	0.4	51.7	48.3	0.0
1958	45.8	53.8	0.4	55.2	44.1	0.7	57.0	41.8	1.2	57.1	42.8	0.1
1960	48.4	51.2	0.4	52.1	47.2	0.7	51.8	47.5	0.7	52.3	47.7	0.0
1962	54.1	45.6	0.3	50.0	48.9	1.1	48.1	51.7	0.3	50.8	49.2	0.0
1964	59.6	40.2	0.2	47.5	51.5	1.0	52.0	48.0	0.1	53.6	46.4	0.0
1966	51.6	44.4	4.0	44.2	54.8	1.0	52.1	47.5	0.4	48.0	51.7	0.2
1968	43.6	48.6	7.7	45.3	53.3	1.4	53.1	45.8	1.1	46.4	52.4	1.1
1970				46.0	52.3	1.8	56.7	41.9	1.5	49.9	46.5	3.6

YEAR	COMPOSITE A (P+G+S+H/4)			COMPOSITE B (G+S+H/3)			COMPOSITE C (S+H/2)		
	DEM.	REP.	OTHER	DEM.	REP.	OTHER	DEM.	REP.	OTHER
1872	46.8	49.6	3.6	48.9	45.9	5.2	49.1	42.7	8.2
1874	46.8	46.5	6.7	47.5	42.7	9.8	46.5	46.4	7.2
1876	46.2	41.9	7.1	48.6	40.9	10.5	47.9	47.2	4.9
1878	43.1	43.7	8.4	43.7	44.0	12.3	45.0	47.4	7.6
1880	43.4	48.0	8.6	40.6	47.3	12.1	43.7	48.8	7.5
1882	50.9	46.8	2.3	52.9	44.8	2.4	52.0	46.3	1.8
1884	46.8	49.7	3.5	47.7	48.3	4.0	46.3	52.2	1.4
1886	45.8	48.5	5.7	46.1	46.8	7.1	46.8	49.0	4.2
1888	45.4	50.5	4.1	45.5	50.0	4.5	45.3	52.2	2.5
1890	39.2	45.4	5.1	45.5	52.0	2.5	44.6	52.8	2.6
1892	36.1	42.4	21.5	37.7	42.3	20.0	38.0	41.5	20.5
1894	36.1	42.3	21.6	31.9	43.0	25.1	29.2	43.9	26.9
1896	51.1	37.9	11.1	47.8	37.9	14.3	49.3	36.0	14.7
1898	46.9	44.8	8.3	44.4	45.0	10.5	41.8	43.9	14.3
1900	45.9	49.7	4.4	45.9	49.1	5.0	44.8	50.5	4.7
1902	41.7	52.0	6.3	43.8	49.9	6.3	41.3	52.3	6.4
1904	36.8	54.4	8.8	41.0	50.6	8.4	35.5	56.5	7.9
1906	37.6	51.4	11.0	40.0	48.3	11.8	35.9	55.0	9.1
1908	39.6	50.7	9.7	40.8	49.4	9.9	37.8	53.7	8.5
1910	38.4	44.0	17.6	39.0	48.7	12.3	35.6	52.8	11.6
1912	35.0	30.5	34.5	33.8	37.2	28.9	33.3	38.9	27.8
1914	36.9	36.1	27.1	34.4	38.2	27.4	35.9	38.5	25.7
1916	40.8	46.8	12.4	37.4	48.2	14.4	38.8	50.0	11.1
1918	36.3	53.4	10.4	34.9	53.8	11.3	38.2	54.2	7.6
1920	31.1	57.6	11.3	31.5	56.4	12.1	32.4	56.9	10.8
1922	33.8	56.0	10.2	37.3	55.7	7.1	35.6	57.4	7.1
1924	32.4	55.2	12.4	37.6	56.0	6.4	37.3	56.5	6.3
1926	34.2	58.6	7.1	36.9	58.9	4.2	36.0	60.2	3.8
1928	35.8	61.0	3.3	35.8	60.3	3.9	33.5	62.9	3.6
1930	41.1	53.8	5.1	39.2	55.0	5.8	38.1	57.0	4.9
1932	50.4	41.2	8.4	47.7	42.6	9.7	50.2	39.8	10.0
1934	48.3	46.3	5.3	43.7	50.3	6.0	42.0	54.2	3.8
1936	54.7	41.7	3.6	51.0	45.0	4.0	50.7	46.4	2.8
1938	55.4	42.5	2.1	53.3	44.4	2.3	54.2	43.5	2.3
1940	45.7	51.2	3.1	42.0	54.1	3.9	39.3	55.5	5.2
1942	47.1	51.1	1.8	44.2	53.6	2.2	44.0	53.1	3.0
1944	48.0	50.2	0.8	45.6	52.1	0.9	50.7	47.0	0.2
1946	41.5	53.9	4.1	37.9	56.8	4.6	44.1	49.9	4.9
1948	44.2	52.1	3.8	42.3	54.0	3.7	45.6	50.1	4.3
1950	44.3	54.5	1.2	43.8	55.3	0.8	45.5	53.3	1.2
1952	37.8	59.9	2.3	36.4	60.8	2.8	33.8	62.0	4.2
1954	46.9	52.6	0.5	48.4	51.2	0.4	49.6	50.0	0.4
1956	49.2	50.4	0.5	51.2	48.3	0.5	51.2	48.6	0.2
1958	53.8	45.7	0.6	56.4	42.9	0.7	57.0	42.3	0.6
1960	51.2	48.4	0.4	52.1	47.5	0.5	52.0	47.6	0.3
1962	50.7	48.9	0.4	49.6	49.9	0.4	49.4	50.4	0.1
1964	53.2	46.5	0.3	51.0	48.6	0.4	52.8	47.2	0.0
1966	49.0	49.6	1.4	48.1	51.3	0.6	50.0	49.6	0.3
1968	47.1	50.0	2.8	48.3	50.5	1.2	49.8	49.1	1.1
1970				50.9	46.9	2.3	53.3	44.2	2.5

YEAR	PRESIDENT			GOVERNOR			SENATE			HOUSE OF REPRESENTATIVES		
	DEM.	REP.	OTHER	DEM.	REP.	OTHER	DEM.	REP.	OTHER	DEM.	REP.	OTHER
1872	38.1	61.2	0.7	42.6	57.0	0.4				42.4	57.2	0.3
1874	41.5	57.3	1.2	47.1	51.3	1.6				46.6	48.8	4.5
1876	44.8	53.3	1.8	46.4	51.0	2.7				45.6	52.2	2.2
1878	43.5	53.5	3.0	37.4	48.3	14.3				36.2	48.2	15.5
1880	42.2	53.6	4.2	38.8	50.3	11.0				42.5	53.3	4.3
1882	42.2	52.8	4.9	45.0	48.7	6.4				43.9	48.1	8.0
1884	42.8	51.8	5.3	45.3	49.7	5.1				44.5	52.4	3.1
1886	43.3	51.9	4.8	45.2	49.8	5.0				43.8	50.5	5.8
1888	43.7	52.1	4.2	45.0	50.3	4.7				44.4	52.1	3.6
1890	42.5	48.3	5.3	46.0	47.1	6.9				45.1	48.0	6.9
1892	44.0	48.0	8.0	42.2	48.4	9.4				44.3	48.4	7.4
1894	40.9	52.9	6.1	36.9	53.5	9.6				32.7	55.4	12.0
1896	37.8	57.9	4.3	39.2	54.8	5.9				38.5	57.2	4.3
1898	37.7	57.7	4.5	41.2	52.8	6.0				40.1	55.1	4.8
1900	37.6	57.6	4.8	41.3	53.9	4.8				39.6	57.1	3.3
1902	32.9	61.2	5.9	39.4	54.3	6.3				38.5	56.4	5.1
1904	28.3	64.7	7.0	38.3	53.4	8.3				31.9	62.1	6.0
1906	32.1	61.2	6.7	39.0	50.5	10.5				35.1	56.9	8.1
1908	36.0	57.6	6.5	37.9	49.0	13.2				37.2	57.2	5.6
1910	35.5	41.0	23.5	35.9	46.0	18.1				36.6	52.8	10.6
1912	35.0	24.2	40.9	34.2	38.8	27.1				35.6	38.2	26.1
1914	39.6	37.5	22.9	36.4	42.5	21.1	33.9	42.7	23.4	34.5	47.6	17.9
1916	44.2	50.8	5.0	35.1	54.3	10.6	37.9	53.1	9.0	37.8	54.3	7.9
1918	34.9	59.1	6.0	33.7	55.8	10.5	35.6	55.1	9.2	34.5	59.8	5.7
1920	25.6	67.5	7.0	31.9	59.0	9.1	31.7	56.2	12.1	24.3	66.7	8.9
1922	21.6	63.5	14.9	35.1	56.8	8.1	33.6	57.6	8.7	33.1	60.7	6.1
1924	17.7	59.5	22.8	33.2	59.9	7.0	32.9	59.1	8.0	27.8	64.8	7.4
1926	27.8	60.3	11.9	30.3	63.7	6.0	34.1	55.7	10.2	28.2	67.1	4.7
1928	37.9	61.1	1.0	35.2	59.5	5.3	32.9	60.7	6.3	32.1	64.8	3.0
1930	45.7	52.1	2.2	36.4	52.0	11.6	39.7	54.9	5.4	32.7	63.5	3.8
1932	53.6	42.9	3.5	45.7	45.1	9.3	46.6	44.8	8.6	47.1	47.1	5.8
1934	55.8	40.6	3.6	47.0	43.8	9.2	43.2	48.4	8.4	48.7	44.6	6.7
1936	58.1	38.3	3.6	45.4	45.1	9.5	43.1	48.1	8.8	49.4	43.3	7.3
1938	55.0	42.9	2.2	43.0	50.9	6.1	45.0	48.9	6.1	43.5	51.1	5.5
1940	51.9	47.5	0.7	44.0	51.0	4.9	39.9	53.2	6.9	44.6	51.1	4.2
1942	51.6	47.7	0.6	40.4	53.7	5.8	41.0	53.5	5.5	42.7	53.8	3.5
1944	51.3	48.2	0.6	41.0	57.3	1.7	45.9	52.0	2.1	46.8	52.5	0.7
1946	50.2	48.2	1.6	37.1	61.0	1.9	41.2	55.3	3.5	41.5	57.7	0.8
1948	49.1	48.3	2.7	44.6	54.0	1.4	46.4	51.5	2.1	46.3	52.3	1.5
1950	45.8	52.6	1.6	45.8	53.6	0.6	45.4	54.0	0.6	45.2	54.0	0.8
1952	42.6	56.9	0.5	45.1	54.2	0.7	39.0	58.4	2.6	43.9	55.5	0.7
1954	42.1	57.5	0.4	49.1	50.7	0.3	48.5	50.9	0.6	49.5	50.4	0.1
1956	41.6	58.1	0.3	51.7	48.0	0.3	49.0	50.6	0.5	48.2	51.8	0.0
1958	45.7	54.0	0.3	54.2	45.5	0.3	54.2	45.4	0.4	53.8	46.1	0.1
1960	49.8	49.9	0.3	50.8	48.7	0.5	50.9	48.8	0.3	51.2	48.8	0.1
1962	56.4	43.4	0.2	49.6	49.8	0.6	49.7	49.9	0.4	50.0	49.9	0.1
1964	62.9	36.9	0.2	48.7	50.6	0.7	53.8	45.9	0.3	54.3	45.6	0.1
1966	54.8	41.3	3.9	45.5	53.7	0.8	48.0	51.3	0.8	47.8	52.1	0.2
1968	46.7	45.7	7.6	46.5	52.5	1.0	51.1	48.1	0.9	47.0	52.2	0.8
1970				49.1	49.3	1.6	57.1	40.7	2.3	50.9	47.2	2.0

STATES PREDOMINANTLY REPUBLICAN (1896-1930)

YEAR	COMPOSITE A (P+G+S+H/4)			COMPOSITE B (G+S+H/3)			COMPOSITE C (S+H/2)		
	DEM.	REP.	OTHER	DEM.	REP.	OTHER	DEM.	REP.	OTHER
1872	41.0	58.5	0.5	42.5	57.1	0.4	42.4	57.2	0.3
1874	45.1	52.5	2.5	46.9	50.1	3.1	46.6	48.8	4.5
1876	45.6	52.2	2.2	46.0	51.6	2.4	45.6	52.2	2.2
1878	39.1	50.0	10.9	36.8	48.2	14.9	36.2	48.2	15.5
1880	41.1	52.4	6.5	40.6	51.8	7.6	42.5	53.3	4.3
1882	43.7	49.9	6.4	44.4	48.4	7.2	43.9	48.1	8.0
1884	44.2	51.3	4.5	44.9	51.0	4.1	44.5	52.4	3.1
1886	44.1	50.7	5.2	44.5	50.1	5.4	43.8	50.5	5.8
1888	44.3	51.5	4.2	44.7	51.2	4.1	44.4	52.1	3.6
1890	44.5	47.8	6.4	45.5	47.6	6.9	45.1	48.0	6.9
1892	43.5	48.3	8.2	43.2	48.4	8.4	44.3	48.4	7.4
1894	36.8	53.9	9.2	34.8	54.4	10.8	32.7	55.4	12.0
1896	38.5	56.6	4.8	38.9	56.0	5.1	38.5	57.2	4.3
1898	39.7	55.2	5.1	40.7	54.0	5.4	40.1	55.1	4.8
1900	39.5	56.2	4.3	40.5	55.5	4.0	39.6	57.1	3.3
1902	36.9	57.3	5.8	39.0	55.3	5.7	38.5	56.4	5.1
1904	32.8	60.1	7.1	35.1	57.7	7.1	31.9	62.1	6.0
1906	35.4	56.2	8.4	37.0	53.7	9.3	35.1	56.9	8.1
1908	37.0	54.6	8.4	37.5	53.1	9.4	37.2	57.2	5.6
1910	36.0	46.6	17.4	36.3	49.4	14.4	36.6	52.8	10.6
1912	34.9	33.7	31.4	34.9	38.5	26.6	35.6	38.2	26.1
1914	36.1	42.6	21.3	34.9	44.3	20.8	34.2	45.2	20.6
1916	38.8	53.1	8.1	36.9	53.9	9.2	37.8	53.7	8.5
1918	34.7	57.5	7.9	34.6	56.9	8.5	35.1	57.4	7.5
1920	28.4	62.4	9.3	29.3	60.7	10.0	28.0	61.5	10.5
1922	30.9	59.7	9.5	34.0	58.4	7.7	33.4	59.2	7.4
1924	27.9	60.8	11.3	31.3	61.3	7.5	30.3	62.0	7.7
1926	30.1	61.7	8.2	30.9	62.2	7.0	31.1	61.4	7.5
1928	34.5	61.5	3.9	33.4	61.7	4.9	32.5	62.8	4.7
1930	38.6	55.6	5.7	36.3	56.8	6.9	36.2	59.2	4.6
1932	48.2	44.9	6.8	46.5	45.6	7.9	46.9	45.9	7.2
1934	48.7	44.4	7.0	46.3	45.6	8.1	46.0	46.5	7.5
1936	49.0	43.7	7.3	46.0	45.5	8.5	46.2	45.7	8.0
1938	46.6	48.4	4.9	43.8	50.3	5.9	44.2	50.0	5.8
1940	45.1	50.7	4.2	42.9	51.8	5.4	42.3	52.2	5.6
1942	43.9	52.2	3.9	41.4	53.7	5.0	41.8	53.7	4.5
1944	46.2	52.5	1.3	44.6	53.9	1.5	46.3	52.2	1.4
1946	42.5	55.6	2.0	39.9	58.0	2.1	41.4	56.5	2.2
1948	46.6	51.5	1.9	45.7	52.6	1.6	46.3	51.9	1.8
1950	45.6	53.5	0.9	45.5	53.9	0.7	45.3	54.0	0.7
1952	42.6	56.3	1.1	42.6	56.0	1.3	41.4	56.9	1.6
1954	47.3	52.4	0.3	49.0	50.7	0.3	49.0	50.6	0.3
1956	47.6	52.1	0.3	49.6	50.1	0.3	48.6	51.2	0.2
1958	52.0	47.7	0.3	54.1	45.6	0.3	54.0	45.7	0.3
1960	50.7	49.1	0.3	50.9	48.8	0.3	51.0	48.8	0.2
1962	51.4	48.3	0.3	49.8	49.9	0.4	49.8	49.9	0.2
1964	54.9	44.8	0.3	52.3	47.4	0.4	54.0	45.8	0.2
1966	49.0	49.6	1.4	47.1	52.3	0.6	47.9	51.7	0.5
1968	47.8	49.6	2.6	48.2	50.9	0.9	49.0	50.1	0.8
1970				52.3	45.7	2.0	54.0	43.9	2.1

297

YEAR	PRESIDENT			GOVERNOR			SENATE			HOUSE OF REPRESENTATIVES		
	DEM.	REP.	OTHER	DEM.	REP.	OTHER	DEM.	REP.	OTHER	DEM.	REP.	OTHER
1872	45.0	52.8	2.2	48.3	48.5	3.2				45.4	48.8	5.8
1874	52.7	46.2	1.1	52.5	40.9	6.6				57.5	38.6	4.0
1876	60.4	39.6	0.0	62.3	31.0	6.7				60.0	37.0	3.0
1878	59.3	38.5	2.2	77.6	16.9	5.5				61.9	16.3	21.8
1880	58.2	37.5	4.3	64.3	19.3	16.4				57.9	29.3	12.8
1882	59.5	37.7	2.7	60.5	27.0	12.5				57.7	24.4	17.8
1884	60.3	38.9	0.7	71.5	24.4	4.1				62.5	35.6	1.9
1886	61.8	36.7	1.5	72.7	25.7	1.7				68.0	23.2	8.8
1888	63.2	34.4	2.3	72.5	20.6	6.9				65.5	30.9	3.6
1890	62.2	28.8	9.0	70.7	23.5	5.8				70.5	22.1	7.4
1892	61.0	23.0	16.1	58.2	16.9	24.9				62.8	18.4	18.9
1894	61.6	27.3	11.1	56.2	14.5	29.3				58.6	18.7	22.7
1896	62.1	31.7	6.2	59.9	17.5	22.6				59.8	25.2	15.0
1898	64.0	31.4	4.5	68.9	16.1	15.0				71.6	20.3	8.1
1900	65.9	31.2	2.8	71.3	21.1	7.6				72.2	24.2	3.6
1902	68.1	27.9	4.0	75.8	20.1	4.1				82.1	17.0	0.9
1904	70.1	24.8	5.1	77.2	21.3	1.5				77.9	21.4	0.8
1906	69.0	26.3	4.7	79.5	18.9	1.6				81.6	17.2	1.2
1908	67.9	27.8	4.3	76.3	21.4	2.4				78.7	19.8	1.5
1910	69.3	19.1	11.5	71.9	18.7	9.4				79.6	16.5	3.9
1912	70.6	10.4	19.0	78.5	14.3	7.2				83.1	11.6	5.3
1914	72.5	15.7	11.8	80.2	12.0	7.8	78.6	11.4	10.0	82.8	11.6	5.6
1916	74.5	21.0	4.6	78.0	15.1	6.9	74.9	14.3	3.2	80.2	16.8	2.9
1918	69.6	25.7	4.7	81.5	14.0	4.5	87.3	11.9	0.8	89.0	10.8	0.2
1920	64.7	30.4	4.9	73.4	19.2	7.4	79.6	19.0	1.4	75.5	22.4	2.0
1922	67.3	27.5	5.2	79.4	18.6	2.0	78.7	20.7	0.6	83.5	13.7	2.8
1924	70.0	24.6	5.4	77.8	22.1	0.2	82.1	15.4	2.6	82.8	16.6	0.7
1926	63.3	32.8	3.9	82.9	17.0	0.1	83.9	14.4	1.7	84.4	15.1	0.4
1928	56.6	41.1	2.3	79.5	18.6	1.9	84.1	14.0	2.0	81.3	18.4	0.3
1930	70.0	28.5	1.5	79.2	17.1	3.8	84.4	9.4	6.2	84.6	12.7	2.8
1932	83.1	16.1	0.7	76.3	19.4	4.3	87.6	10.7	1.7	86.9	11.4	1.7
1934	83.0	16.4	0.5	86.7	12.9	0.4	88.5	10.2	1.3	89.4	9.5	1.1
1936	82.9	16.8	0.4	88.0	11.0	1.0	89.4	9.6	1.0	87.9	11.9	0.3
1938	81.5	17.7	0.8	88.9	8.4	2.7	86.5	10.4	3.1	89.9	8.8	1.3
1940	80.2	18.6	1.3	89.5	8.1	2.5	89.5	8.6	1.9	89.6	9.6	0.8
1942	76.8	21.1	2.1	89.5	8.5	2.0	90.5	7.5	2.0	90.8	8.3	0.8
1944	73.8	23.2	3.0	85.4	12.0	2.6	85.5	12.8	1.7	86.4	12.8	0.8
1946	61.7	23.5	14.8	85.0	11.8	3.2	85.2	13.4	1.4	85.5	13.8	0.8
1948	49.6	23.8	26.6	84.6	13.5	1.9	75.4	19.9	4.8	85.4	13.7	0.9
1950	51.4	33.9	14.7	85.9	13.7	0.3	78.5	16.0	5.5	87.4	11.3	1.3
1952	52.8	44.5	2.7	80.5	19.2	0.2	82.8	11.5	5.6	83.1	16.5	0.4
1954	50.7	45.7	3.6	82.2	16.7	1.1	84.8	9.7	5.5	82.3	17.3	0.4
1956	48.5	47.0	4.5	80.5	16.1	3.4	85.1	11.9	3.0	79.8	19.9	0.2
1958	49.6	45.9	4.5	80.1	16.9	3.0	80.5	15.5	4.0	86.1	13.1	0.7
1960	50.6	44.9	4.5	74.3	22.5	3.2	75.5	22.6	1.9	79.8	18.5	1.7
1962	50.3	47.7	2.0	68.0	28.6	3.4	66.1	32.3	1.7	69.8	29.3	0.9
1964	50.0	49.9	0.1	65.9	30.4	3.8	66.5	31.8	1.7	66.7	32.2	1.2
1966	40.5	42.4	17.1	61.0	35.0	4.1	60.7	37.9	1.3	66.9	31.7	1.4
1968	31.0	34.9	34.1	58.9	38.0	3.1	58.8	37.2	4.0	65.9	32.5	1.5
1970				55.0	41.7	3.3	51.4	38.8	9.8	67.3	31.0	1.7

STATES PREDOMINANTLY DEMOCRATIC (1896-1930)

YEAR	COMPOSITE A (P+G+S+H/4)			COMPOSITE B (G+S+H/3)			COMPOSITE C (S+H/2)		
	DEM.	REP.	OTHER	DEM.	REP.	OTHER	DEM.	REP.	OTHER
1872	46.2	50.1	3.7	46.9	48.7	4.5	45.4	48.8	5.8
1874	54.2	41.9	3.9	55.0	39.7	5.3	57.5	38.6	4.0
1876	60.9	35.9	3.2	61.2	34.0	4.8	60.0	37.0	3.0
1878	66.3	23.9	9.8	69.7	16.6	13.6	61.9	16.3	21.8
1880	60.1	28.7	11.2	61.1	24.3	14.6	57.9	29.3	12.8
1882	59.2	29.7	11.0	59.1	25.7	15.2	57.7	24.4	17.8
1884	64.8	33.0	2.2	67.0	30.0	3.0	62.5	35.6	1.9
1886	67.5	28.5	4.0	70.4	24.4	5.2	68.0	23.2	8.8
1888	67.1	28.6	4.3	69.0	25.7	5.3	65.5	30.9	3.6
1890	67.8	24.8	7.4	70.6	22.8	6.6	70.5	22.1	7.4
1892	60.6	19.4	19.9	60.5	17.7	21.9	62.8	18.4	18.9
1894	58.8	20.2	21.1	57.4	16.6	26.0	58.6	18.7	22.7
1896	60.6	24.8	14.6	59.8	21.4	18.8	59.8	25.2	15.0
1898	68.2	22.6	9.2	70.3	18.2	11.5	71.6	20.3	8.1
1900	69.8	25.5	4.7	71.7	22.6	5.6	72.2	24.2	3.6
1902	75.3	21.7	3.0	78.9	18.5	2.5	82.1	17.0	0.9
1904	75.1	22.5	2.4	77.5	21.3	1.1	77.9	21.4	0.8
1906	76.7	20.8	2.5	80.6	18.1	1.4	81.6	17.2	1.2
1908	74.3	23.0	2.7	77.5	20.6	1.9	78.7	19.8	1.5
1910	73.6	18.1	8.3	75.8	17.6	6.6	79.6	16.5	3.9
1912	77.4	12.1	10.5	80.8	12.9	6.3	83.1	11.6	5.3
1914	78.5	12.7	8.8	80.5	11.7	7.8	80.7	11.5	7.8
1916	76.9	16.8	4.4	77.7	15.4	4.4	77.6	15.5	3.1
1918	81.9	15.6	2.6	85.9	12.2	1.8	88.2	11.3	0.5
1920	73.3	22.8	3.9	76.2	20.2	3.6	77.6	20.7	1.7
1922	77.2	20.1	2.6	80.5	17.7	1.8	81.1	17.2	1.7
1924	78.1	19.6	2.2	80.9	18.0	1.1	82.4	16.0	1.6
1926	78.6	19.8	1.5	83.8	15.5	0.7	84.2	14.8	1.0
1928	75.4	23.0	1.6	81.7	17.0	1.4	82.7	16.2	1.1
1930	79.5	16.9	3.6	82.7	13.1	4.3	84.5	11.0	4.5
1932	83.5	14.4	2.1	83.6	13.8	2.6	87.2	11.1	1.7
1934	86.9	12.3	0.8	88.2	10.9	0.9	88.9	9.9	1.2
1936	87.0	12.3	0.7	88.4	10.8	0.8	88.6	10.7	0.6
1938	86.7	11.3	2.0	88.4	9.2	2.4	88.2	9.6	2.2
1940	87.2	11.2	1.6	89.5	8.8	1.7	89.6	9.1	1.3
1942	86.9	11.3	1.7	90.3	8.1	1.6	90.7	7.9	1.4
1944	82.8	15.2	2.0	85.7	12.5	1.7	85.9	12.8	1.2
1946	79.3	15.6	5.0	85.2	13.0	1.8	85.3	13.6	1.1
1948	73.7	17.7	8.6	81.8	15.7	2.5	80.4	16.8	2.9
1950	75.8	18.7	5.4	84.0	13.7	2.4	83.0	13.7	3.4
1952	74.8	22.9	2.3	82.2	15.8	2.1	83.0	14.0	3.0
1954	75.0	22.3	2.7	83.1	14.6	2.3	83.6	13.5	2.9
1956	73.5	23.7	2.8	81.8	16.0	2.2	82.5	15.9	1.6
1958	74.1	22.9	3.1	82.2	15.2	2.6	83.3	14.3	2.3
1960	70.1	27.1	2.8	76.5	21.2	2.3	77.7	20.5	1.8
1962	63.5	34.5	2.0	68.0	30.1	2.0	67.9	30.8	1.3
1964	62.3	36.1	1.7	66.3	31.5	2.2	66.6	32.0	1.4
1966	57.3	36.7	6.0	62.9	34.9	2.3	63.8	34.8	1.4
1968	53.7	35.7	10.7	61.2	35.9	2.9	62.4	34.9	2.8
1970				57.9	37.1	5.0	59.4	34.9	5.8

299

COMPETITIVE STATES (1896-1930)

YEAR	PRESIDENT			GOVERNOR			SENATE			HOUSE OF REPRESENTATIVES		
	DEM.	REP.	OTHER	DEM.	REP.	OTHER	DEM.	REP.	OTHER	DEM.	REP.	OTHER
1872	48.0	51.5	0.5	51.2	46.8	1.9				49.9	44.8	5.4
1874	50.4	48.9	0.7	51.6	45.9	2.5				54.6	39.9	5.5
1876	52.2	45.8	0.9	51.9	46.3	1.9				52.4	45.2	2.3
1878	50.7	46.3	1.9	50.9	44.3	4.9				48.1	39.3	12.6
1880	49.6	47.3	3.0	49.0	45.3	5.7				50.2	46.7	3.2
1882	49.3	48.1	2.6	52.1	43.8	4.1				50.7	43.7	5.5
1884	49.4	48.3	2.3	51.9	45.7	2.4				49.9	47.0	3.2
1886	49.0	48.4	2.6	49.1	47.2	3.7				48.3	45.2	6.5
1888	48.7	48.5	2.9	48.5	47.4	4.1				47.9	48.7	3.3
1890	47.2	45.9	5.2	49.2	46.1	4.7				51.6	44.2	4.2
1892	46.2	44.8	9.0	47.2	45.2	7.7				48.2	44.9	7.0
1894	46.0	48.3	5.7	44.7	49.5	5.8				40.4	51.4	8.2
1896	46.1	51.5	2.4	44.4	50.2	5.4				44.9	52.0	3.1
1898	46.2	51.3	2.4	47.8	48.8	3.4				48.2	49.2	2.6
1900	46.3	51.2	2.5	46.0	49.1	4.9				46.7	51.3	1.9
1902	43.5	52.7	3.8	47.2	49.1	3.6				47.2	49.1	3.7
1904	40.6	54.2	5.2	45.9	50.2	3.9				43.0	53.3	3.7
1906	42.5	52.7	4.8	47.0	49.0	4.0				45.6	49.3	5.1
1908	44.6	50.8	4.6	47.5	48.4	4.1				46.8	49.0	4.3
1910	43.8	38.7	17.5	48.7	43.0	8.3				49.4	45.2	5.3
1912	43.0	26.9	30.1	44.7	33.5	21.8				45.5	32.0	22.4
1914	45.9	36.8	17.3	41.0	44.1	14.9	44.4	43.3	12.3	45.6	43.1	11.3
1916	48.8	46.8	4.4	46.1	49.1	4.8	45.9	48.7	5.4	46.4	48.2	5.3
1918	42.5	53.0	4.5	47.1	48.7	4.2	43.6	51.1	5.3	45.3	50.8	3.9
1920	36.1	59.2	4.7	44.1	50.1	5.8	41.3	52.6	6.2	39.7	55.5	4.8
1922	34.9	56.4	8.7	50.8	46.7	2.6	50.1	46.9	3.0	48.7	47.7	3.6
1924	33.6	53.6	12.8	50.2	47.8	2.1	46.7	49.7	3.5	45.2	52.1	2.6
1926	37.5	55.5	7.0	51.1	47.3	1.6	47.4	49.0	3.6	47.9	51.0	1.1
1928	41.5	57.4	1.2	48.6	50.3	1.0	46.6	52.4	1.1	44.9	54.0	1.1
1930	48.9	49.1	1.9	53.8	42.8	3.4	50.6	47.4	2.0	50.7	47.2	2.1
1932	56.1	41.1	2.8	55.6	41.8	2.6	56.0	41.3	2.7	55.7	41.7	2.6
1934	57.2	39.7	3.1	54.8	42.6	2.6	57.4	39.7	2.9	55.6	41.8	2.6
1936	58.3	38.3	3.5	52.9	44.3	2.8	55.1	41.4	3.4	57.7	40.4	1.9
1938	55.5	42.6	1.9	51.8	47.0	1.2	53.7	44.9	1.5	52.8	46.0	1.2
1940	52.7	47.0	0.3	48.4	49.6	1.9	52.1	47.5	0.3	52.8	46.4	0.8
1942	52.1	47.5	0.3	44.2	52.3	3.5	50.2	48.7	1.1	48.6	50.5	0.8
1944	51.5	48.2	0.3	46.4	51.7	1.9	50.5	47.6	0.7	49.9	49.3	0.8
1946	50.8	47.2	2.0	47.9	51.7	0.4	46.2	52.8	0.4	44.7	53.6	1.7
1948	50.2	46.1	3.7	49.9	49.1	1.0	49.6	49.6	0.8	53.2	44.2	2.6
1950	47.1	50.8	2.1	48.2	50.2	1.6	49.2	49.8	1.0	49.5	48.3	2.2
1952	43.8	55.6	0.6	49.0	49.9	1.1	44.3	53.0	2.7	46.1	52.6	1.4
1954	42.1	57.6	0.4	50.8	48.5	0.8	47.9	50.5	1.6	50.5	48.6	1.0
1956	40.3	59.5	0.2	48.2	49.9	1.8	49.6	50.1	0.2	47.2	52.3	0.4
1958	44.7	55.1	0.2	50.9	46.9	2.2	52.4	46.7	0.9	54.9	44.6	0.5
1960	49.2	50.6	0.2	50.0	48.5	1.5	49.5	49.7	0.8	51.9	47.5	0.6
1962	56.7	43.2	0.2	48.3	50.7	1.0	51.1	48.1	0.8	50.4	48.9	0.6
1964	64.1	35.7	0.2	47.4	49.3	3.3	55.1	43.9	1.0	57.3	42.2	0.5
1966	54.0	40.8	5.2	45.1	49.2	5.7	47.1	49.3	3.6	49.2	49.2	1.6
1968	44.0	45.8	10.2	46.5	49.1	4.4	44.3	49.5	6.2	48.2	50.1	1.8
1970				46.7	49.5	3.9	47.3	39.0	13.7	51.1	46.9	2.0

COMPETITIVE STATES (1896-1930)

YEAR	COMPOSITE A (P+G+S+H/4)			COMPOSITE B (G+S+H/3)			COMPOSITE C (S+H/2)		
	DEM.	REP.	OTHER	DEM.	REP.	OTHER	DEM.	REP.	OTHER
1872	49.7	47.7	2.6	50.5	45.8	3.6	49.9	44.8	5.4
1874	52.2	44.9	2.9	53.1	42.9	4.0	54.6	39.9	5.5
1876	52.2	45.8	1.7	52.1	45.8	2.1	52.4	45.2	2.3
1878	49.9	43.3	6.5	49.5	41.8	8.7	48.1	39.3	12.6
1880	49.6	46.4	4.0	49.6	46.0	4.4	50.2	46.7	3.2
1882	50.7	45.2	4.1	51.4	43.8	4.8	50.7	43.7	5.5
1884	50.4	47.0	2.6	50.9	46.3	2.8	49.9	47.0	3.2
1886	48.8	46.9	4.3	48.7	46.2	5.1	48.3	45.2	6.5
1888	48.4	48.2	3.4	48.2	48.1	3.7	47.9	48.7	3.3
1890	49.3	45.4	4.7	50.4	45.1	4.5	51.6	44.2	4.2
1892	47.2	45.0	7.9	47.7	45.0	7.3	48.2	44.9	7.0
1894	43.7	49.7	6.6	42.5	50.4	7.0	40.4	51.4	8.2
1896	45.1	51.2	3.6	44.6	51.1	4.3	44.9	52.0	3.1
1898	47.4	49.8	2.8	48.0	49.0	3.0	48.2	49.2	2.6
1900	46.4	50.5	3.1	46.4	50.2	3.4	46.7	51.3	1.9
1902	46.0	50.3	3.7	47.2	49.1	3.7	47.2	49.1	3.7
1904	43.2	52.6	4.2	44.4	51.8	3.8	43.0	53.3	3.7
1906	45.0	50.3	4.6	46.3	49.2	4.5	45.6	49.3	5.1
1908	46.3	49.4	4.3	47.1	48.7	4.2	46.8	49.0	4.3
1910	47.3	42.3	10.4	49.0	44.1	6.8	49.4	45.2	5.3
1912	44.4	30.8	24.8	45.1	32.8	22.1	45.5	32.0	22.4
1914	44.2	41.8	13.9	43.7	43.5	12.8	45.0	43.2	11.8
1916	46.8	48.2	5.0	46.1	48.7	5.2	46.1	48.5	5.4
1918	44.6	50.9	4.5	45.3	50.2	4.5	44.5	50.9	4.6
1920	40.3	54.3	5.4	41.7	52.7	5.6	40.5	54.0	5.5
1922	46.1	49.4	4.5	49.9	47.1	3.0	49.4	47.3	3.3
1924	43.9	50.8	5.3	47.4	49.9	2.7	46.0	50.9	3.1
1926	46.0	50.7	3.3	48.8	49.1	2.1	47.7	50.0	2.3
1928	45.4	53.5	1.1	46.7	52.3	1.1	45.7	53.2	1.1
1930	51.0	46.7	2.3	51.7	45.8	2.5	50.6	47.3	2.0
1932	55.9	41.5	2.7	55.8	41.6	2.6	55.9	41.5	2.6
1934	56.2	41.0	2.8	55.9	41.4	2.7	56.5	40.8	2.7
1936	56.0	41.1	2.9	55.2	42.0	2.7	56.4	40.9	2.7
1938	53.4	45.1	1.4	52.8	46.0	1.3	53.2	45.4	1.4
1940	51.5	47.6	0.9	51.1	47.8	1.0	52.5	46.9	0.6
1942	48.8	49.8	1.4	47.7	50.5	1.8	49.4	49.6	1.0
1944	49.6	49.2	0.9	48.9	49.5	1.1	50.2	48.4	0.7
1946	47.4	51.3	1.1	46.3	52.7	0.8	45.4	53.2	1.0
1948	50.7	47.3	2.0	50.9	47.6	1.4	51.4	46.9	1.7
1950	48.5	49.8	1.7	49.0	49.4	1.6	49.4	49.0	1.6
1952	45.8	52.8	1.4	46.5	51.8	1.7	45.2	52.8	2.1
1954	47.8	51.3	0.9	49.7	49.2	1.1	49.2	49.5	1.3
1956	46.4	53.0	0.7	48.4	50.8	0.8	48.4	51.2	0.3
1958	50.7	48.3	0.9	52.7	46.1	1.2	53.6	45.7	0.7
1960	50.1	49.1	0.8	50.5	48.6	1.0	50.7	48.6	0.7
1962	51.6	47.7	0.7	49.9	49.3	0.8	50.7	48.5	0.7
1964	56.0	42.8	1.3	53.3	45.1	1.6	56.2	43.0	0.8
1966	48.9	47.1	4.0	47.1	49.2	3.6	48.1	49.3	2.6
1968	45.7	48.6	5.6	46.3	49.6	4.1	46.2	49.8	4.0
1970				48.4	45.1	6.5	49.2	42.9	7.8

301

YEAR	PRESIDENT			GOVERNOR			SENATE			HOUSE OF REPRESENTATIVES		
	DEM.	REP.	OTHER	DEM.	REP.	OTHER	DEM.	REP.	OTHER	DEM.	REP.	OTHER
1872	43.2	55.8	1.0	47.0	51.4	1.7				45.7	50.9	3.4
1874	47.4	51.6	1.0	50.0	46.7	3.3				52.2	43.1	4.7
1876	51.5	47.2	1.0	52.5	44.1	3.5				51.7	45.8	2.5
1878	50.1	47.1	2.4	52.6	38.5	8.8				47.1	36.7	16.2
1880	49.0	47.2	3.8	49.0	40.3	10.7				49.2	44.6	6.2
1882	49.3	47.2	3.5	51.6	41.2	7.2				50.0	40.3	9.7
1884	49.8	47.2	3.0	54.5	41.6	3.8				51.2	46.0	2.8
1886	50.2	46.7	3.1	53.8	42.6	3.7				51.7	41.4	6.8
1888	50.6	46.2	3.2	53.5	41.5	5.0				51.2	45.3	3.5
1890	49.2	42.5	6.2	53.5	40.7	5.8				53.9	40.0	6.0
1892	49.0	40.6	10.3	48.0	39.4	12.7				50.3	39.6	10.1
1894	47.9	44.9	7.2	44.5	42.3	13.2				41.9	44.8	13.4
1896	46.8	49.1	4.1	46.2	43.9	9.9				46.1	47.4	6.5
1898	47.3	48.9	3.8	50.5	42.2	7.3				50.9	44.3	4.8
1900	47.8	48.7	3.5	50.5	44.0	5.5				50.3	46.8	2.9
1902	45.6	49.8	4.7	51.4	43.8	4.8				52.6	43.8	3.6
1904	43.2	50.9	5.9	50.8	44.2	5.0				47.4	48.7	3.9
1906	45.1	49.3	5.6	52.1	42.0	6.0				50.5	44.2	5.3
1908	47.0	47.7	5.3	50.9	41.9	7.2				51.0	44.9	4.1
1910	47.0	34.7	18.3	49.5	38.1	12.4				52.0	41.0	7.0
1912	46.5	21.8	31.7	48.7	30.9	20.4				50.7	29.5	19.8
1914	49.8	32.0	18.2	48.6	35.7	15.7	44.6	38.5	16.9	50.2	37.3	12.5
1916	53.2	42.1	4.7	49.5	42.9	7.6	49.7	42.1	6.3	51.2	43.1	5.8
1918	46.0	48.8	5.2	50.1	43.1	6.7	51.0	43.2	5.8	51.6	44.7	3.7
1920	38.8	55.5	5.6	46.4	46.2	7.5	46.7	45.9	7.4	42.3	52.0	5.8
1922	37.5	52.2	10.3	51.5	43.9	4.6	50.5	44.8	4.7	51.0	44.7	4.4
1924	36.1	48.9	15.0	50.1	46.3	3.6	49.8	45.2	5.1	47.4	48.6	4.0
1926	39.9	51.9	8.2	50.5	46.5	3.0	51.0	43.3	5.7	48.9	48.7	2.4
1928	43.7	54.9	1.4	50.8	46.3	2.9	50.2	46.4	3.4	48.6	49.7	1.7
1930	52.7	45.3	2.0	53.1	40.2	6.7	54.4	41.2	4.3	51.8	45.3	2.9
1932	61.5	35.9	2.6	56.5	37.8	5.7	59.7	35.5	4.8	59.7	36.7	3.7
1934	62.7	34.5	2.7	59.2	36.1	4.7	59.1	36.2	4.7	60.8	35.3	3.9
1936	64.0	33.2	2.8	58.2	36.7	5.1	58.4	36.6	5.0	61.5	34.8	3.7
1938	61.4	36.8	1.7	57.0	39.4	3.5	57.9	38.3	3.7	57.8	39.2	2.9
1940	58.9	40.4	0.7	56.4	40.4	3.3	56.1	40.6	3.3	58.2	39.6	2.2
1942	58.0	41.1	0.9	53.8	42.1	4.1	56.4	40.5	3.1	56.6	41.5	1.9
1944	56.9	42.0	1.1	53.8	44.2	2.0	57.3	40.8	1.5	57.6	41.6	0.8
1946	53.2	41.8	5.0	52.7	45.6	1.7	53.8	44.1	1.9	53.4	45.4	1.1
1948	49.6	41.5	8.9	56.3	42.3	1.4	54.7	43.1	2.3	58.3	39.9	1.7
1950	47.6	47.4	5.0	56.5	42.6	0.9	54.9	43.1	2.0	57.1	41.5	1.4
1952	45.5	53.4	1.1	55.2	44.1	0.7	51.7	44.9	3.4	54.3	44.8	0.9
1954	44.2	54.6	1.2	57.9	41.5	0.6	57.3	40.5	2.2	58.0	41.5	0.5
1956	42.9	55.8	1.3	57.7	40.8	1.6	58.2	40.8	1.0	55.7	44.1	0.2
1958	46.3	52.4	1.3	59.5	38.8	1.6	60.1	38.4	1.5	62.2	37.4	0.4
1960	49.8	48.9	1.3	56.4	42.1	1.5	56.5	42.6	0.9	58.5	40.8	0.7
1962	55.0	44.3	0.7	53.8	44.8	1.4	54.4	44.8	0.9	55.2	44.3	0.5
1964	60.2	39.7	0.2	52.6	45.1	2.3	57.4	41.7	0.9	58.4	41.1	0.5
1966	51.0	41.3	7.6	49.3	47.5	3.3	51.0	47.1	1.9	53.1	45.9	1.0
1968	41.9	43.0	15.1	49.7	47.7	2.6	50.9	45.6	3.5	52.3	46.4	1.3
1970				49.8	47.4	2.8	52.4	39.8	7.8	55.2	42.9	1.9

NATIONAL

YEAR	COMPOSITE A (P+G+S+H/4)			COMPOSITE B (G+S+H/3)			COMPOSITE C (S+H/2)		
	DEM.	REP.	OTHER	DEM.	REP.	OTHER	DEM.	REP.	OTHER
1872	45.3	52.7	2.0	46.3	51.1	2.5	45.7	50.9	3.4
1874	49.9	47.1	3.0	51.1	44.9	4.0	52.2	43.1	4.7
1876	51.9	45.7	2.3	52.1	44.9	3.0	51.7	45.8	2.5
1878	49.9	40.8	9.2	49.9	37.6	12.5	47.1	36.7	16.2
1880	49.0	44.1	6.9	49.1	42.5	8.4	49.2	44.6	6.2
1882	50.3	42.9	6.8	50.8	40.8	8.4	50.0	40.3	9.7
1884	51.8	44.9	3.2	52.9	43.8	3.3	51.2	46.0	2.8
1886	51.9	43.5	4.5	52.8	42.0	5.2	51.7	41.4	6.8
1888	51.8	44.3	3.9	52.3	43.4	4.3	51.2	45.3	3.5
1890	52.2	41.0	6.0	53.7	40.3	5.9	53.9	40.0	6.0
1892	49.1	39.9	11.0	49.1	39.5	11.4	50.3	39.6	10.1
1894	44.7	44.0	11.3	43.2	43.5	13.3	41.9	44.8	13.4
1896	46.4	46.8	6.8	46.1	45.6	8.2	46.1	47.4	6.5
1898	49.5	45.1	5.3	50.7	43.3	6.1	50.9	44.3	4.8
1900	49.5	46.5	4.0	50.4	45.4	4.2	50.3	46.8	2.9
1902	49.8	45.8	4.4	52.0	43.8	4.2	52.6	43.8	3.6
1904	47.2	47.9	4.9	49.1	46.4	4.4	47.4	48.7	3.9
1906	49.2	45.2	5.6	51.3	43.1	5.6	50.5	44.2	5.3
1908	49.7	44.8	5.5	51.0	43.4	5.7	51.0	44.9	4.1
1910	49.5	37.9	12.6	50.7	39.5	9.7	52.0	41.0	7.0
1912	48.6	27.4	23.9	49.7	30.2	20.1	50.7	29.5	19.8
1914	48.3	35.9	15.8	47.8	37.2	15.0	47.4	37.9	14.7
1916	50.9	42.6	6.1	50.1	42.7	6.6	50.4	42.6	6.1
1918	49.7	45.0	5.4	50.9	43.7	5.4	51.3	43.9	4.8
1920	43.5	49.9	6.6	45.1	48.0	6.9	44.5	48.9	6.6
1922	47.6	46.4	6.0	51.0	44.4	4.6	50.7	44.7	4.5
1924	45.8	47.3	6.9	49.1	46.7	4.2	48.6	46.9	4.6
1926	47.6	47.6	4.8	50.1	46.2	3.7	49.9	46.0	4.1
1928	48.3	49.3	2.3	49.9	47.5	2.6	49.4	48.1	2.5
1930	53.0	43.0	4.0	53.1	42.2	4.7	53.1	43.3	3.6
1932	59.3	36.5	4.2	58.6	36.6	4.7	59.7	36.1	4.2
1934	60.5	35.5	4.0	59.7	35.9	4.4	59.9	35.8	4.3
1936	60.5	35.3	4.1	59.4	36.0	4.6	59.9	35.7	4.4
1938	58.6	38.5	3.0	57.6	39.0	3.4	57.9	38.8	3.3
1940	57.4	40.2	2.4	56.9	40.2	2.9	57.2	40.1	2.8
1942	56.2	41.3	2.5	55.6	41.3	3.0	56.5	41.0	2.5
1944	56.4	42.1	1.3	56.2	42.2	1.4	57.4	41.2	1.1
1946	53.3	44.2	2.4	53.3	45.0	1.6	53.6	44.8	1.5
1948	54.7	41.7	3.6	56.4	41.8	1.8	56.5	41.5	2.0
1950	54.0	43.6	2.3	56.2	42.4	1.4	56.0	42.3	1.7
1952	51.7	46.8	1.5	53.8	44.6	1.6	53.0	44.9	2.1
1954	54.3	44.5	1.1	57.7	41.2	1.1	57.7	41.0	1.3
1956	53.6	45.4	1.0	57.2	41.9	0.9	56.9	42.5	0.6
1958	57.0	41.8	1.2	60.6	38.2	1.2	61.2	37.9	0.9
1960	55.3	43.6	1.1	57.1	41.9	1.0	57.5	41.7	0.8
1962	54.6	44.6	0.9	54.5	44.6	0.9	54.8	44.6	0.7
1964	57.1	41.9	1.0	56.1	42.6	1.2	57.9	41.4	0.7
1966	51.1	45.5	3.4	51.1	46.8	2.0	52.1	46.5	1.4
1968	48.7	45.7	5.6	50.9	46.6	2.5	51.6	46.0	2.4
1970				52.5	43.4	4.1	53.8	41.3	4.8

INDEX

Index